SOUTHERN LITERARY STUDIES

Fred Hobson, Editor

Published with the assistance
of the V. Ray Cardozier Fund

The History of Southern Women's Literature

edited by

CAROLYN PERRY *and*
MARY LOUISE WEAKS

LOUISIANA STATE UNIVERSITY PRESS
Baton Rouge

Copyright © 2002 by Louisiana State University Press
All rights reserved
Manufactured in the United States of America
First printing
11   10   09   08   07   06   05   04   03   02
5   4   3   2   1

Designer: Amanda McDonald Scallam
Typeface: Sabon, Gill Sans
Typesetter: Coghill Composition Co. Inc.
Printer and binder: Thomson-Shore, Inc.

Library of Congress Cataloging-in-Publication Data

The history of southern women's literature / edited by Carolyn
   Perry and Mary Louise Weaks.
        p.   cm.—(Southern literary studies)
   Includes bibliographical references and index.
   ISBN 0-8071-2753-1 (Hardcover : alk. paper)
      1. American literature—Southern States—History and criticism.
   2. American literature—Women authors—History and criticism.
   3. Women and literature—Southern States—History.   4. Southern
   States—In literature.   I. Perry, Carolyn.   II. Weaks, Mary
   Louise.   III. Series.

   PS261.H534   2002
   810.9'9287'0975—dc21   2001005342

A longer version of the essay "Southern Women Writers and the Beginning of the Renaissance" appeared
in *The Female Tradition in Southern Literature,* ed. Carol Manning (Urbana: University of Illinois Press,
1993). The version in this book is included with the permission of the previous publisher.

The paper in this book meets the guidelines for permanence and durability of the Committee on Production
Guidelines for Book Longevity of the Council on Library Resources. ♾

Contents

II. The Postbellum South (1865–1900)

III. Renaissance in the South (1900–1960)

IV. The Contemporary South (1960 to the Present)

Preface

Several years ago I found myself driving northward from Oxford, Mississippi, on Interstate 55 in a van packed full with tightly stuffed duffle bags, the last remnants of a rushed fast food breakfast, at least one of every novel Faulkner ever wrote, and a dozen thoroughly exhausted students. As the daffodils, green grass, and pickup trucks hauling fishing boats grew scarcer, as we passed over the state line from Missouri into Illinois, I had a sense that I had left something behind in Oxford. On one hand, I felt that my students had had at least a cursory introduction to Faulkner's world: We had pored over the Faulkner collection at the University of Mississippi library, visited Rowan Oak, and studied the architecture of the antebellum homes located off the town square. We tasted the local cuisine. Yasuko, a Japanese student enrolled in my class, ate grits for the first time. But I was returning northward to Rockford, Illinois, with a sense that I wasn't as southern as I thought I was. Had I lost my accent? I didn't sound like the other Tennesseans we met who were also touring the area. Was the Oxford, Mississippi, we toured the same place I first visited in the early 1980s during my freshman year at Emory University? Miss Pearl's general store on the road to Taylor wasn't there anymore. I knew I needed to give my own students a sense of the rural world of Faulkner's South, but every drive we made into the countryside turned up only subdivisions called "Tara," ranch-style homes with satellite dishes, and catfish houses that were now tourist traps. Sitting in the backseat of that crowded van on our ride northward, I started grappling with questions that set my head spinning. Can I still be a southerner even though I now live in northern Illinois? Was I born too late to truly know what it means to be southern? Is there still a South?

When I visit my parents at our family farm in Middle Tennessee, I feel a connection to my southern past as I walk through the rooms of the antebellum farmhouse that has been passed down through a number of generations. I feel a similar connection when we take family hikes onto the adjoining farm to visit the graves of my great-great-great-great-grandparents and the ruins of the log house they built when they first arrived in Tennessee from across the mountains in Virginia. And I feel that connection when my father tells stories about a long-dead ancestor. My Yankee husband can't understand why genealogy is so important to my family and to southerners—why my father speaks more knowingly of his great-grandfather than he does of a living relative and why we in the Weaks family are so concerned about genealogical trees.

Despite these brief moments of connection, I am, in fact, a southerner who was born into the Sun Belt—not into the South. I find myself trying to reconnect through trips to the old homeplace and through family stories, even through recipes passed down from grandmothers. But my own personal hopes for *The History of Southern Women's Literature* seem at times something like my own desire to reproduce the homemade sausage that my grandmother once cooked in her heavy iron skillet on cold winter mornings. I have a copy of her recipe that she carefully typed on the back of an old copy of an agricultural extension booklet on slaughtering hogs, but I'll never be able to truly reproduce that recipe, for I live in a world of preprocessed meats, cellophane wrappings, and Teflon.

In many ways, my work with Carolyn Perry on this book and on our anthology *Southern Women Writers: Colonial to Contemporary* (1995) has been my own personal attempt to answer some of those questions about the South that still haunt me and thus some related questions about the literature we both study. As women born in the 1960s, Carolyn and I were both schooled in the qualities traditionally used to define literature as southern: the influence of the past, including the white guilt associated with slavery and the devastation of the Confederate defeat; the importance of family, family tradition, and rural living; the clash between the ideals of the present and those of the past. Despite the commonplace use of this definition, it leaves us puzzled, for this very definition has often been used to exclude women and African American writers from the canon of southern literature, and it makes little sense of much contemporary southern literature. These "traditional" characteristics of southern literature have too often been used to segregate groups of southerners, and they do not encompass in broad enough terms the full scope of southern literature.

With *The History of Southern Women's Literature* we have attempted to suggest the consistencies and the variations, relationships and tensions among the writings of women who wrote or are writing within the framework of the South. We have identified a woman as southern if southernness has in some way become associated with her personal identity, regardless of whether she has celebrated her attachment to the South, recognized the grip the region has had on her life, or even fled its environs. In particular, we are concerned here with what it means to be southern and female. Yet in that framework, this text also strives to examine the complexities of a literature long characterized by scenes of racial conflict, social disruption, and gender bias. In bringing together those many voices, we recognize that clashes are often heard—not always melodies. Literature by southern women writers reflects a complexity perhaps unique to literatures, for while the writers of these works share commonalities, their culture can also divide them.

In many ways, this book can be used as an addendum to another book published by Louisiana State University Press over fifteen years ago, *The History of Southern Literature* (1985). Written and edited by some of the most outstanding scholars in the field, under the general leadership of Louis D. Rubin, *The History of Southern Literature* stands as a monument to the literature of the American South, but the book also leaves some prominent gaps in the history that it covers. Thus, with *The History of Southern Women's Literature,* we strive to fill those gaps—to present a full picture of a female literature of the South that only in recent years has received the attention it deserves.

In designing *The History of Southern Women's Literature,* we attempted to be as all-inclusive as possible to show the full range of writing by women of the South. As a result, and because of the constraints of page length, we were limited to passing references to some women who could easily be the subjects of entire essays. We recognize, furthermore, that the complexities of the works of writers like Eudora Welty are far from realized in an essay of only a few pages. Nevertheless, our attempt here is to give the reader an overview of the literature, to pique interest in writers and literary periods often ignored in literary criticism, and to validate the significance of this body of literature.

In each essay, readers will find birth and death dates in parentheses after the first reference to a southern woman writer whom we have not featured in an individual essay. If a woman writer is featured in an individual essay, then birth and death dates are found in these essays only. When southern women writers are mentioned in passing, without substantial discussion of their work, dates will generally not be added. In addition, publication dates for all primary and secondary texts mentioned in the book—southern and nonsouthern—are included in parentheses after the first mention of the title of the work. Although this volume may be read from cover to cover, it occurs to us that most readers will be interested in particular chapters. For that reason, we wish for each essay to stand alone and therefore to cover its topic as thoroughly as possible. Inevitably, then, some essays overlap with others, and readers will find some degree of repetition in the book as a whole. In the last few pages of the book, we have included a bibliography of secondary sources for readers interested in locating sources mentioned in the individual essays collected here.

While we understand that at times there is an uneven quality in the literature discussed here, we recognize the importance of covering a wide range of styles and genres in a history such as this. We also believe it is important to consider why certain features prevail in certain time periods (the sentimental poetry of the postbellum South, for example). This book, then, takes on the tremendous task of collecting together discussions of writers and literary works under the broad common framework of southern women's literature. The book not only presents information on individual southern women writers but also traces literary influences and movements that created one of the most complicated and compelling bodies of literature ever produced.

Many people worked tirelessly to see this book to print. At Rockford College, the following persons made significant contributions: Audrey Wilson of Howard Colman Library ordered numerous items necessary for checking factual information, and Erin Taylor, Linda Solberg, Elizabeth Edwards, Mooneen Holt, Kristi Herrald, Ashley Adams, and Elitza Alexandrova helped in preparing the manuscript. Amy Ruch spent numerous hours checking facts and proofreading, and for her meticulous work we are very grateful. Rockford College also provided funding for research and clerical assistance through a summer research grant and through the Hazel Koch fund. Westminster College supported this project through two summer research grants and through the generous assistance of the library staff. Special thanks also go to Molly Selders, Brooke Butler, Casey Kayser, and Shawn Conner for checking facts and proofreading, and to Sarah Zade and Rachelle Riggs for their help in preparing the manuscript. We would also like to thank our families for their enthusiasm for the project and their willingness to share us with our work: Brent and Andrew Baxter, and Greg, Jessica, Emily, and Erin Perry.

Most of all we would like to thank the authors of the essays included in this book, who were incredibly patient and gracious when we asked them to check and double-check facts, and who were always generous in offering their encouragement for our work on this project. Without their willingness to contribute their time and talents, their expertise and insight, this book simply would not be the rich source of information that it is—in fact, the book would not exist. We are indeed thankful that we were able to bring together so many fine critical voices in order to preserve a body of literature that is not only an occupation but also a passion for us all.

MARY LOUISE WEAKS

The History of Southern Women's Literature

Introduction

Doris Betts

I've always been haunted by the following story Robin Morgan tells in *The Word of a Woman* (1992), a news item originally reported by the Associated Press:

> In the 1980's, manuscripts were discovered in the mountains of Hunan Province in central China, written in a thousand-year-old language that had been invented by rural women of that region for their own secret use. Linguists believe that the language, called Nushi, was originally developed because women were not then allowed to acquire standard literacy so they had to create their own. By this secret means, they communicated with one another about arranged marriages, childbirth and health, the double standard of behavior applied to men and to women, the value of women's friendships; and naturally they exchanged also complaints about husbands. Because many scripts were placed (hidden?) in coffins and thus lost, when these few surviving manuscripts were discovered in the eighties, only 12 elderly women remained who could read Nushi, and only three who could write it.

If American women have rarely gone beyond Pig Latin for their coded confidences, for them, too, it has been historically harder to become literate, compared with American men, and the fact that for years many of their written words remained unread except within families provided strong early motivation for scholars rescuing both amateur and professional writing through women's history and feminist criticism. As Carolyn Kizer's poem says: women writers have been "the custodians of the world's best kept secret; / merely the private lives of half of humanity."

Some disappearance of the written record of women's lives has been circumstantial. But a deliberate need for secrecy develops when anyone's public life or social role becomes a mask layered over the personal, inner life. Certainly southern culture with its ladies/gentlemen tradition has imposed such outward roles on both sexes. Only in the South, wrote Gail Godwin in *Ms.* magazine in 1975, would a growing girl find "an image of womanhood already cut out for her." To publish diaries, letters, poems, or stories would not only be unladylike, it could even seem masculine. When Caroline Gilman's poetry—written when she was sixteen—was published without her knowledge, she felt "as alarmed as if I had been detected in men's apparel."

Not all southern women were trained to become belles and ladies. In a society with overt Jim Crow racism, certain that some women belonged *on* a pedestal while others were only meant to wash and dust it, that separation between the real self and the assigned one, with an ongoing struggle to stay hidden behind the facade of others' expectations, gaped even wider and deeper for black women. Their educational opportunities were even more limited. Maya Angelou put it this way in *I Know Why the Caged Bird Sings* (1970): "If growing up is painful for the southern black girl, being aware of her displacement is the rust on the razor that threatens the throat."

Beyond the effects of social pressures and inadequate schooling, many southern women had little time or energy left over to devote to writing down their stories or verses. Well into the twentieth century, due in part to the devastating effects of the Civil War on the South's economic and educational system, Dixie remained America's poorest and most rural region, where a majority of citizens—including tired mothers of numerous children—labored over woodstoves, cotton rows, and textile looms for long, hard, hot hours.

After decades of improvement in the lives of all American women, this entry into a new century is an especially auspicious time to publish a volume like *The History of Southern Women's Literature,* which for the first time in the following eighty-six essays traces the evolution of women's writing in the South. Today, many of the nation's foremost writers are female and southern. Their need for secrecy and protection has declined. Since the late 1960s, previous works by rediscovered women authors as well as new material by a burgeoning crowd of contemporaries have been widely taught in classrooms. One result has been revisionist regional history, i.e., in much women's writing we discover that many southerners are not eternally Civil War–obsessed; they don't all chew tobacco, hunt varmints, or make moonshine; they're neither rednecks nor aristocrats; they never owned a verandah or drank a mint julep; they don't dress like Lil' Abner or Daisy Mae; they seldom enter cars through their open windows as drawling actors do on television; and they never dated anyone remotely like Rhett Butler.

Of necessity, scholars presenting the earlier parts of this history have been forced to generalize. The table of contents indicates how little is known about particular women in the seventeenth-century Jamestown settlements, many of them probably illiterate. As the antebellum, bellum, and postbellum pages mount, however, each chapter becomes more and more specific; individuals rise out of the mass of unknown women to tell their singular experiences.

By the time this history reaches the Southern Renaissance, each broad sectional overview more rapidly presents a swelling chorus composed of individual voices, and for the last section, "The Contemporary South," the editors' hardest job must have been choosing which women writers to omit. It's as if a rising tide of amorphous creativity from the past had swelled forward and spread outward; it's also as if older and indistinct words, like the surviving bits of Nushi language from ancient China, had not vanished but been spoken anew by younger mouths to freshen universal stories for later generations.

In some cases, the influence of earlier women writers has been directly acknowledged. Alice Walker, for example, gives credit to Kate Chopin and Zora Neale Hurston. Not every writer's female forebears were literary, however. Many of us also remember (and love) grandmothers who read only the Bible, if that, or who were farm women for whom every V-mail letter to their soldier sons in World War II became an ordeal with many pencil erasures. Such women also had stories to tell, or stories to bequeath to later storytellers.

The importance of preserving foremothers' lives has long been one of Alice Walker's themes, especially strong in the African American community, but thriving among southern whites as well. Walker gave women and women writers, especially in the history-loving South, a pervasive metaphor in her well-known essay "In Search of Our Mothers' Gardens" (1983). Those women who lived and died in an earlier South, women whose words we will never be able to hear or to read, often lifted domestic skills to the level of art in their quilts, pottery, and weavings, their flower gardens, their loaded Sunday tables.

Kinswomen with writing ambitions, fulfilled or not, are also often memorialized. Gail Godwin has written of her mother laboring over her typewriter. Ellen Douglas writes about "my own and my family's small histories, which I would spend my life transforming into fiction." She mined the lives of two aunts for her first novel, *A Family's Affairs* (1962), and pacified their opposition to being known by strangers by changing her real name, Jo Haxton, to the pen name she has used ever since. It comes from her real grandmother, Ellen Henderson Ayres, a writer of children's stories and romances, "mostly," says Douglas, "not published."

Another way to seek, find, and honor their mothers' gardens has been by creating a character who is herself the type of others, inarticulate or still undiscovered. For example, in *Fair and Tender Ladies* (1988), Lee Smith uses a lifetime of letters by Ivy Rowe—a mountain girl who longed to be a writer but mistakenly thought herself incapable—and Smith lets Ivy's mind and spirit shine through her correspondence, never more movingly than in the words Rowe kept on writing to a sister she knew was dead.

As these essays take us along a chronology from pioneer women to career women, the southern writers discussed here also keep enlarging their content from restriction to freedom, from polite accounts of sanctioned outward behavior to personal revelations that recall the title of Ellen Glasgow's autobiography, *The Woman Within* (1954). As a child, Glasgow wrote in secret; as an adult woman she traveled widely and made her successful way in the world of professional writers, though she noted that in the South she always had to push against and live down "an insidious sentimental tradition." The final section of this history shows women writers pushing harder, going farther, doing more.

In her 1968 poem, "Kathe Kollwitz," which honors the German graphic artist of the title and notes especially her drawings of women and children, Muriel Ruykeyser asks and answers the frequently quoted question "What would happen if one woman told the truth about her life? / The world would split open."

What becomes clear and then clearer and at last very clear in the following pages is that women have told and keep on telling those truths, and that the literary world has not yet split open.

Instead, it has doubled in breadth and depth.

PART I

The Antebellum and Bellum South
(Beginnings to 1865)

Introduction to Part I

Mary Louise Weaks

The history of women's writing in the South ultimately finds its roots in the settlement of Europeans and Africans at Jamestown, Virginia, in the second and third decades of the seventeenth century. Although the women who arrived at Jamestown were most probably illiterate, the history of the settlement reflects the profound importance of women in establishing communities in the New World and in the initial development of myths that shaped the cultural heritage of the southern United States. As Lord Bacon, a member of His Majesty's Council for Virginia, proclaimed, "When the plantation grows to strength, then it is time to plant with women as well as with men; that the plantation may spread into generations, and not be ever pieced from without." Bacon reasoned that if the men of Jamestown married and established families, then their "minds might be faster tyed to Virginia," for with the establishment of homes came the development of cultural and religious communities in the New World. So, too, with his words was established in the South the ideal of woman as caretaker of and caregiver in the home.

Women entered the mythology of the South in the earliest descriptions of the southern land as feminine, but notably, those descriptions were authored by men rather than by women. This mythology, however, continues to influence literature by southern women writers even today. As Louise Westling notes in *Sacred Groves and Ravaged Gardens* (1985), even before

Jamestown was settled, Arthur Barlowe wrote that his ship was "allured" to Virginia's shores by "so strong a smell, as if we had bene in the midst of some delicate garden abounding with all kinds of odoriferous flowers." This image of the land as a fertile (and oftentimes erotic) female was perpetuated in John Rolfe's *A True Relation of the State of Virginia* (1616), in which Rolfe describes this new world as "the womb of the Land" and notes its potential for man's harvesting. Written to counter stories of starvation and deprivation in the New World, and influential in establishing the myth of an Edenic New World garden, Rolfe's treatise stands in sharp contrast to William Bradford's description of New England as "a hideous and desolate wilderness, full of wild beasts & wild men." As the years passed, however, the landscape of the South was increasingly described in maternal rather than in sexual terms, according to Westling. By the eighteenth century, William Gilmore Simms, speaking to a northern audience in defense of the South before the Civil War, asked his listeners, "You would not, surely, have me speak coldly in the assertion of a Mother's honour." By Simms's time, not only had the Southland become a mother, but the white male slaveholder had also placed his female counterpart on a pedestal to call attention away from the atrocities of slave society. The implications of the white woman's rise on the pedestal were thus linked inextricably with issues of race in the South.

Other myths associated with southern womanhood that developed in the antebellum years have equal significance for the history of southern women's writing. The model of the idyllic plantation populated by cavaliers, ladies, belles, mammies, and other gentle plantation folk was used not only in antebellum literature, but also in postbellum and in twentieth-century literature to draw attention away from the atrocities of slavery, to rationalize a southern slave culture, and to gain political ground for southern causes. In fact, the southern belle made her first appearance in literature as Bel Tracy in John Pendleton Kennedy's 1832 novel *Swallow Barn*—just four months after the Virginia slave revolt led by Nat Turner. The motherless daughter of a southern planter, Kennedy's Bel is of marriageable age and is described as "headlong and thoughtless, with quick impulses, that gave her the charm of agreeable expression." The belle of antebellum southern literature was clearly used for political purposes to assert the values of plantation society. She was, as Kathryn Lee Seidel explains in *The Southern Belle in the American Novel* (1985), the "ideal, uncorrupted daughter of this way of life," the "ideal South, pure and noble." In her, too, was perpetuated a future for the plantation in the love match she would make by story's end. Nevertheless, although the belle is probably the most enduring figure of southern literary history, the belle in the writings of southern women before the Civil War tended to be a model for what a southern woman should not be. As Karen Manners Smith explains in her essay for this collection, there was no place for the belle in the domestic novel because the belle did not possess the qualities of an able southern matron, the caretaker of the home. While the early examples of the mammy can also be found in antebellum southern literature, the mammy's physical stature in these writings is generally frail and her role insignificant. She is typically the complete opposite of the twentieth-century mammy, who is robust and a character to be reckoned with. In fact, the mammy appears to a much greater degree in postbellum literature to suggest the loyalty of African American women to their slave masters and to perpetuate the myth of an idyllic Old South.

Understandably, these myths of gender and race greatly influenced the development of women's literature in the South. Although the belle did not appear in the southern novel until the 1830s, the cultural mythology of the woman on the pedestal was already being perpetuated in other reading materials deemed appropriate for female readers of the colonial South. The pedestal, however, left the living, breathing woman without a voice. Public written expression by women was uncommon in the South before the nineteenth century, as it was for white women in the North and in England. Yet, as is often typical of war and its influence on literature, the tensions leading up to and the years of the Revolutionary War produced the first period of literary publication. Although there are only scattered instances of women writing for publication on the topics of manners and fashion, the first noteworthy publications by southern women were political writings in support of the colonists' boycott of tea of 1773–74. Southern women began publishing political statements in newspapers to show that, like men, women stood in support of the cause. Some males even wrote under female pseudonyms to emphasize the support of the female sex. Despite the ideal of the modest, self-effacing southern woman, when women were called to duty in support of their country, they increasingly responded with words. The first period of southern women's writing—that is, the years from settlement to the Civil War—ends, too, with a war that called white and black women to support the Confederacy and the northern army, respectively, with their men, with their labor, and again with their words.

While the number of literate white women steadily increased in the colonial years, slavery kept black women from becoming literate and from learning to write. Not coincidentally, the African slave trade was at its height during the Age of Enlightenment in Europe and in the United States. Because aristocratic and landholding whites of this age placed greater emphasis on literacy than ever before, whites judged Africans as inferior because their cultures were not literate in the same sense that European and American cultures were. Thus the political necessity of black women speaking out against slavery—arguing their humanness—was the reason for the composition and publication of the earliest writings by African American women born in the South in slavery.

For both black and white southern women, the skills of reading and writing were, understandably, tightly bound in the history of southern women's writing. While women like Eliza Lucas Pinckney refer in their journals to teaching slave children, southern laws were quickly established that forbade teaching slaves to read and to write. Historians, in particular, have traced an intentional suppression of black literacy by slave owners because of slave rebellions that were led by literate individuals. Despite those laws, some slaves were able to learn to read, as Janell Hobson and Frances Smith Foster point out in their essay for this collection, "Early African American Women Writers." According to Hobson and Foster, scholars generally agree that 5 percent of the antebellum slave population was literate. Literacy among slaves was feared among slave owners because literate slaves were sometimes able to use their abilities to forge passes for themselves or for other slaves so that they might escape to freedom in the North. Reading and writing thus became for the African American a way to gain power over slave owners. Slave women who had gained their freedom in the North often saw reading and writing as a means of ending enslavement and ultimately of supporting the abolitionist cause. Perhaps the best-known female author of a slave narrative written in support of that cause is Harriet Jacobs, who proclaims on her title page that her narrative was "written by herself." Despite her public proclamation on the written page, however, Jacobs was forced to write under an assumed name—Linda Brent—so as to protect members of her family who still remained in the South. For the antebellum black woman, then, authorship was possible only if she left the South and slavery, and even in the free North, a woman like Jacobs was forced to hide her identity as writer.

Less severely than the laws against slaves, societal restrictions of gender did, nevertheless, influence the reading and writing patterns of white women. Eliza Lucas Pinckney, for example, records in her letter book her reading of Samuel Richardson's highly popular novel *Pamela* (1793) and the works of Plutarch, Virgil, and Locke. There is even some indication that she studied law. The young Eliza Lucas also writes in a letter of a neighbor lady who believes Eliza would "read [her]self mad." Eliza's intellectual activities, according to this neighbor, would prematurely age her and leave her unmarriageable. The case was similar for women of the lower classes. Historian Cynthia Kierner tells of Lucy Gaines, a Virginia housekeeper, who is said to have desired to learn to read and write. When her lover discovered her intentions, he "declared . . . that he wou'd suffer to lose his right hand, if he ever had or ever wou'd mention it to any[one]." Scholars have become increasingly interested in examining the reading habits of colonial women and the influence that literacy had on their everyday lives. Kevin J. Hayes, in his *A Colonial Woman's Bookshelf* (1996), for instance, uses the personal writings of William Byrd of Westover to point to one particularly revealing example. When Byrd and his first wife, Lucy, argued, Byrd sometimes used his library as a way to assert his power over her: he would refuse her the use of his books. Byrd, however, took a different approach with his second wife, Maria Taylor. In fact, he seems quite taken with Taylor's intellectual abilities when he writes to her: "When indeed I learned that you also spoke Greek, the tongue of the Muses, I went completely crazy about you. In beauty you surpassed Helen, in culture of mind and ready wit Sappho: It is not meet therefore to be astonished I was smitten by such grandeur of body and soul when I admitted the poison of Love both through my eyes and my ears." Byrd never refused her a book.

Women of the South were readers long before a tradition of southern women's writing developed. A commonly accepted statistic is that one of every three colonial white women was able to sign her name, while at least three of every five white men were able to do so. Nevertheless, while literacy rates increased from the first years of settlement to the time of the American Revolution, these rates are actually difficult to gauge accurately. Literacy is typically judged by the number of people able to sign their names to documents. But this measure is not particularly accurate because people often learned to read before they learned to write, men signed documents in much greater numbers than did women, and slaves signed few, if any, documents. Noted historian Julia Cherry Spruill, in her renowned book *Women's Life and Work in the Southern Colonies* (1938), suggests that one indication of the importance placed on the education of white children is the provisions made for children in the wills of their fathers or in apprenticeship agreements. Part of the apprenticeship agreement for sister and brother Susanna and Isaac Atkins was, for example, that she be taught "to read the Bible thoroughly Sew and household work" and that he be taught "to Read write & cypher as far as the Rule of Three & the Trade of a Carpenter." A typical provision for a daughter of a more privileged family comes from the last will and testament of John Baptista Ashe, a gentleman of North Carolina: "I will that my daughter be taught to write and read & some feminine accomplishments which may render her agreeable; And that she be not kep ignorant as to what appertains to a good house wife in the management of household affairs."

During the colonial period, southern white women who did read tended to read many of the same materials as northern white women. Southern printers were scarce, most printers tended to be located in the North, and books were generally published in London and shipped to the Americas for sale. Illiteracy rates in the South also tended to be higher than in the North, so booksellers were not as eager to promote their wares there. Book ownership was also complicated by the fact that a white woman's personal items were actually the legal property of her father or husband. Nevertheless, most probably because the South tended to be more rural than the North, white families depended upon their own individual libraries for reading materials. While borrowing libraries became increasingly popular in the North, few examples are evident in the South. Many privileged young women depended upon the libraries of their fathers for their reading materials and in some cases the only education they would receive. The most commonly purchased books during the colonial period were almanacs and religious books, so we can assume these books were the ones most readily available to women. Even though privileged women were generally not given the same education as their brothers, society did recognize the importance of teaching a woman to read so that she might educate her children in the Word of God. Spruill also points out in her study of colonial women that, in keeping with English tradition, a white woman was to be at least "knowinge of the law of God" so that she might "withstonde the perilles of the sowle." The colonial lady typically had access to a copy of the Bible, a prayer book, and often a copy of a book of devotions and general instruction on religious conduct expected of members of a family, such as Richard Allestree's *The Whole Duty of Man* (1682).

Increasingly, though, books on domestic economy became popular among women. Books like E. Smith's *The Compleat Housewife; or, Accomplished Gentlewoman's Companion,* which was originally published in England but was published in a later American version in Williamsburg in 1742 and 1752, were intended, as the subtitle suggests, for the "gentlewoman." The book contains "six hundred of the most approved receipts [or recipes]," which were "all suitable to English constitutions, and English Palates." Among the "receipts" are instructions for dressing a hare and potting a swan and for making "a rich great Cake" and gooseberry wine. Also included are "three hundred family receipts of medicines," among them a cure for a cancer, a method for drawing out a thorn, and "directions for marketing." Books like Hannah Glasse's *The Art of Cookery Made Plain and Easy* (1747) were written for use by women servants responsible for the cooking in a household. In her note to the reader, Glasse states explicitly her intent in using language more appropriate to the lower classes:

> Every servant who can but read, will be capable of making a tolerable good cook, and those who have the least notion of Cookery cannot miss of being very good ones. If I have not wrote in the high polite style, I hope I shall be forgiven, for my intention is to instruct the lower sort, and therefore must treat them in their own way. For example, when I bid them lard a fowl, if I should bid them lard with large lardoons, they would not know what I meant; but when I say they must lard with little pieces of bacon, they know what I mean. So in many other things in Cookery, the great cooks have such a high way of expressing themselves, that the poor girls are at a loss to know what they mean.

Meant to lighten the load of the lady of the house by providing guidance for her workers, the book also unintentionally promoted reading among the lower classes.

As the Revolutionary War approached, books on domestic economy saw a decrease in popularity, while conduct books, often written by men, became more and more popular. Among the most popular of the conduct books was *The Ladies Calling* (1673), by the author of *The Whole Duty of Man*. For many years, the book was a sort of Bible for women in England and America on woman's conduct and responsibilities. The title page of one edition of the book, for example, declares, quoting Proverbs 31:30, that "Favour is deceitful, and beauty is vain: but a Woman that feareth the Lord, she shall be praised." Journals, too, like *The Female Spectator* and *The Ladies' Magazine,* provided similar instruction. Many of the ideals of southern womanhood—including the ideals of delicacy, piety, chastity, domesticity, motherhood—were shaped by publications such as these, which were meant for a wider reading audience, including women in England and in the North.

In the colonial period, reading materials were used as a way to guide young white women and to shape them into model ladies or homemakers. In the kitchen, receipts—passed down orally or on paper—sustained connections between the familial duties of generations of women. It is also not surprising that writing by white women in the colonial South tended to be limited to privately circulated manuscripts, such as receipts, diaries, and letters. Despite the written proclamations by women supporting the tea boycott, colonial women, in general, seem to have been at the very least uncomfortable with wider publication of their writings, whether that be because of their lack of opportunity or because of the limitations placed on them because of their gender or race. Diaries offered a written outlet that remained a semiprivate statement. Often passed down from mother to child, a diary might not be solely a record of a woman's life, but also an instructional tool for her children. Diaries also provided women writers with a means of feeling some control over their own lives as they recorded and came to terms with life situations. By using written language, women could achieve, too, some sense of mastering words.

By the nineteenth century, however, southern women increasingly faced the necessities of self-expression, monetary provision for their families, and support of social issues facing their families and region. Many women felt compelled to write. Women also found writing to be one of the few occupations open to them when they were required to support their households with income from working outside the home. Women like Anne Newport Royall (1769–1854) wrote descriptions of life in the frontier South for publication, while others recorded their lives living as captives among the Indians. Readers were eager to hear of the frontier, and the woman writer gave a unique perspective. Other women, such as Frances E. W. Harper and Louisa S. McCord, were influenced by the politics of the time to take up the pen, respectively, in support of the abolitionist cause and a "southern way of life." With increased means of publication in the South, women's magazines began publication, among them Caroline Gilman's *Southern Rose.*

Better printing methods, wider circulation of printed materials, and increased leisure time for the middle and upper classes led to increased literacy among women in the nineteenth century. So, too, did an increasing emphasis placed on women's higher education. Gilman's magazine, like others of its day, including the quite popular *Godey's,* which was published in the North, also supported higher education for women. From these efforts came support for the establishment of the first institution of higher education for women, which was founded in Macon, Georgia, in 1839, as Georgia Female College. The faculty of the school was its own—not shared with a men's college—and the intent of its founders was to provide women with a higher education comparable to that then offered for men. The South was not only a pioneer in the establishment of the first woman's college, but also, by some estimates, the number of female colleges chartered in the region during the 1850s greatly exceeded the number in the North during that same time frame.

Increased literacy and education also led to a greater number of women authors. The years from 1830 to 1860 saw tremendous growth in the number of southern women actively engaged in writing, and these years span the first significant period of literary production by southern women writers. The novel, in particular, became an increasingly popular literary form, despite criticism that reading novels was detrimental to the well-being of a young lady. During the first several decades of the nineteenth century, novels were typically imported from England, and some even from France. But by the 1830s, novel-writing among women in the South had become commonplace as the availability of paper and printing greatly increased. Many southern women—including Caroline Hentz and Maria McIntosh (1803–1878)—were eager to join the ranks of that "damned mob of scribbling women" to which Nathaniel Hawthorne referred in a letter to his editor. Anne Goodwyn Jones remarks in *Tomorrow Is Another Day* (1981) that fiction writing was one way that a woman might "circumvent the barrier between private thought and public utterance." In writing fiction, a woman might speak more forthrightly on issues in a time when it was still unacceptable for a woman to speak at public forums— even in the church—on matters concerning a woman's welfare.

Some southern women were by this time recognizing the importance of looking backward to the writings of their foremothers, while others were themselves establishing traditions. In 1839, for example, Caroline Gilman—who called for a southern literature even before William Gilmore Simms made his appeal—published a collection of letters by Eliza Wilkinson (1757–?), who tells of the British invasion of Charleston, South Carolina, during the Revolutionary War. Gilman says that Wilkinson's letters are important because they "cannot fail to excite public interest at a period, when such anxiety is abroad to gather every relic of our past history before it floats away down the stream of time." Likewise, Harriet Jacobs' slave narrative is read today because it was reclaimed by literary scholar Jean Fagan Yellin as part of a tradition of African American women's writing in the South.

By the time of the Civil War, southern women writers clearly saw themselves working within a tradition. In 1860, Julia D. Freeman published a book entitled *Women of the South Distinguished in Literature*. A series of biographical sketches, the book provides details concerning women writers of the time who "one after another, have sat down in the chair before" Freeman, "filling the air with such a gracious '*bonhomie* of presence.'" A decade later, Mary T. Tardy published a book entitled *Southland Writers* (1870), which was reprinted in 1872 as *Living Female Writers of the South* and provides biographical information on various writers, examples or excerpts of their work, and reviews. Arranged by the authors' state of origin, the book, as Tardy says in her introduction, was "intended to embody the names and works of all those ladies who have written for publication, and been recognized as 'writers' in the Southern States." She points out that "dilettantism . . . has been the bane of Southern literature" and argues that "It is incumbent upon the press of the South to try to redress this evil," to "stimulate those who write tolerably to write well if they can; and those who write well, to write better." Tardy suggests her desire to collect the female voices of the South, but she recognizes the growing need for their encouragement and their development. Tardy's collection, while not at all racially inclusive, represents one of the first stirrings of an interest in examining gender and southernness in the literature of the region. For southern women, then, the years of first settlement to the years of civil war in the South saw only the first flourishings among her writers. But these years also saw a driving urge to create and to elevate a strong tradition of women writing in the South.

Antebellum Journals and Collections of Letters

Mary D. Robertson

The earliest manifestations of southern women's self-expression are most typically found in their journals and correspondence. From the first settlements in the colony of Virginia and in subsequent colonization efforts, the roles of women were restricted by the faulty perception of female weakness and inferiority. Confined primarily to the domestic sphere, women were denied participation in the public sphere where men dominated. It follows, then, that any effort at self-expression by women in colonial America was limited to keeping journals and writing letters. For centuries, such writings of southern women were relegated to the domestic sphere and deemed of little or no historical or literary importance.

Since the 1970s, however, and because of an increasing interest among academics and general readers in women's contributions to American society, many literary scholars and historians have acknowledged that these journals and letters reflect writing that is public as well as private. Many of these journals have also been published or reprinted recently. As diarists and scribes, southern women—molded by gender, time, place, class, and race—revealed much about themselves and their world. The importance of such writing is aptly expressed by Suzanne Bunkers in "Reading and Interpreting Unpublished Diaries by Nineteenth-Century Women" (*Autobiography Studies*, 1986): "Diaries like these are not a retrospective examination and interpretation of a life already lived; they are a commentary on a life as it *was* lived, on life as *process,* not *product.*" Bunkers believes that diaries and journals might well be considered the most authentic form of autobiography. In this sense, the importance of journals and letters to history and literature is validated. Women kept journals and wrote letters for a variety of reasons. Some had a sense of history and wished to record important events of their times and their thoughts about them; others wrote with an eye to publication, to advance a political agenda or promote a cause, or as a means of recording business affairs. For many women, their journals and letters served as needed confidantes with whom they could share their most intimate thoughts and feelings.

Colonial society in America was patriarchal in nature, and women were not viewed as equals to men, but rather as helpmates of men. The stern realities of life, however, often required women to become planters and small farmers, to keep accounts, and to run businesses in addition to their domestic responsibilities. As the southern colonies prospered following the introduction of tobacco, rice, and indigo as major cash crops, large planters grew in affluence and political power. The growth of large plantations gave rise to an increased importation of slaves to meet the growing labor needs. By the eighteenth and nineteenth centuries, this class of landed gentry had developed a lifestyle similar to that of English country gentlemen. They were educated and cultured, and took pride in building mansions and amassing impressive libraries. The sons of these planters were often educated abroad or at William and Mary, Harvard, Yale, or other notable colleges. Daughters of the affluent, however, fared less well and usually obtained modest educations at home or at small private schools. Except in rare cases, the education of young southern women was limited to what was deemed appropriate for females, i.e., reading, ciphering, needlework, music, and sometimes French. Thus, it is not surprising that southern literature during this period was dominated by white males.

Many bright and talented women deplored the educational limitations and narrow roles into which their gender had cast them. Sarah Grimké, daughter of a prominent South Carolina jurist, wished to study law with her brother. Her father told her that she had "unwomanly aspirations" and forbade her to pick up a book on Latin, Greek, or law ever again. Sarah would later write: "Man has done all he could to debase and enslave woman's mind, and now he looks triumphantly on the ruin he has wrought and says she is his inferior." Many other intelligent women also made use of the libraries of their fathers or husbands to become conversant in literature, poetry, history, and philosophy.

The restrictions on women's self-expression in any literary effort during the seventeenth, eighteenth, and nineteenth centuries limited many women to writing letters and keeping journals as a means of expressing their ideas, observations, and feelings about their society and their role in it. Many collections of women's letters are found in letterbooks. Such books were kept as repositories for business correspondence and often for valued personal letters as well. Many contained memos and copies of letters sent. *The Letterbook of Eliza Lucas Pinckney (1739–1762)* was first published in 1972, and a later paperback edition, edited by Elise Pinckney, in 1997. The *Letterbook* reflects the life of a remarkable woman and limns the social, agricultural, and political history of her day.

Eliza Lucas Pinckney and her family moved to the colony of South Carolina in 1738 and settled near Charles Town. When her father was recalled to active duty, he left the management of his three rice plantations to his intelligent and capable sixteen-year-old daughter. Eliza's experiments with indigo ultimately provided South Carolina with a new cash crop. Her *Letterbook* contains memoranda and meticulously copied letters sent to her father apprising him of business affairs, political matters, and family news. In a July 1740 entry, for example, Eliza notes, "Wrote my Father a very long letter on his plantation affairs and on his change of commissions with Major Heron; On the Augustine Expedition; On the pains I had taken to bring the Indigo, Ginger, Cotton and Lucerne and Casada to perfection." In addition to business letters, she frequently wrote to family members and friends abroad and in the colonies. Such letters are often sprinkled with classical references revealing her acquaintance with the works of Virgil, Plutarch, Cicero, Locke, and others. In a letter to "Miss B," for example, Eliza says, "I have got no further than the first volume of Virgil . . . to find myself instructed in agriculture as well as entertained by his charming penn. . . . But the calm and pleasing diction of pastoral and gardening agreeably presented themselves, not unsuitably to this charming season of the year, with which I am so much delighted that had I but the fine soft language of our poet to paint it properly." Given the limited educational opportunities available to women during Eliza's time, one can only be impressed by her informative and entertaining literary style.

A vivid account of the invasion and possession of Charles Town, South Carolina, by the British during the Revolutionary War is found in a collection of letters written by Eliza Wilkinson (1757-?). *Letters of Eliza Wilkinson* (1839) was edited by Caroline Gilman. In the fashion of Eliza Lucas Pinckney, Eliza Wilkinson meticulously copied her letters into a blank quarto book. This collection is rare inasmuch as there are few such preserved records written by southern women during the Revolutionary War as compared with the many extant collections of letters and journals of the Civil War era. Wilkinson's letters written to a friend recount in narrative form the arrival of the British forces in 1779 and end with the surrender of Cornwallis at Yorktown in 1781. Her writing reveals a young woman of culture and education. The literary style is lively and eventful, especially in her description of the spirited response of the unprotected women and elderly residents faced with repeated raids upon their homes and persons by British soldiers. Forced to take responsibility for their own safety, women stepped out of their traditional roles. Wilkinson notes, "Depend upon it, never were greater politicians than the several knots of ladies, who met together. All trifling discourse . . . was thrown by, and we commenced perfect statesmen." She denied that political interests were outside of her province, asserting that women had enough sense to voice opinions outside of domestic affairs with "justice and propriety." Wilkinson's contribution to the history and literature of southern women rests in relative obscurity. Her cultured and pleasing style of writing and self-expression may have in different times gained her a degree of favorable notoriety.

Anne Newport Royall (1769–1854), reared on the western frontier of Pennsylvania, represents a woman of pioneering spirit who defied tradition to become a prolific author, writing and publishing under her own name. Anne, along with her widowed mother and family, arrived in dire straits at Sweet Springs, Virginia, in 1785. Major William Royall, a wealthy Revolutionary War veteran, hired Anne's mother to work in his home. He was taken with the brightness of young Anne and took joy in teaching her and encouraging her to read the books in his large library. Anne married the major in 1797. Following her husband's death in 1812, Anne decided to travel. When his family succeeded in breaking her husband's will in 1823, Anne's travels became her means of support. Her objective and comprehensive travel books, often sprinkled with entertaining anecdotes, enjoyed a modest success. Her publications include *Sketches of History, Life, and Manners in the United States* (1826), *The Tennessean* (1827), *The Black Book* (1828–29), *Mrs. Royall's Pennsylvania* (1829), and *Mrs. Royall's Southern Tour* (1831). She is best known for *Letters From Alabama on Various Subjects to which is added an Appendix containing Remarks on Sundry Members of the Twentieth and Twenty First Congress and other High Characters at the Seat of Government* (1830). The latter work was the first written, but last published. Written in the form of letters to a young lawyer friend, the book has an intimate style typical of most of her writing. Anne Royall's muckraking and irreverent style earned her a host of enemies and a reputation of being a "common scold." She became a pioneering newspaper woman, establishing in 1831 a weekly paper called *Paul Pry,* which gave her an opportunity to support her strongly held views on honesty in government, separation of church and state, free speech, prolabor movements and Freemasonry, gradual emancipation of slaves, and other advanced views for her day. Anne published her first issue of *The Huntress* in 1836 and continued publishing until her death in 1854 at the age of eighty-five.

Sarah Moore Grimké and Angelina Emily Grimké, daughters of highly respected members of South Carolina's plantation elite, represent southern women who also defied their society's prescriptions against women's participation in the public issues of their day. Both sisters left Charleston, Sarah in 1821 and Angelina in 1829, as a protest against slavery. They joined the antislavery movement in the Northeast, where they expressed their strongly held views on slavery and women's rights in speeches, letters, and journals. Among the important published writings and speeches of Angelina are *Slavery and the Boston Riot: A Letter to Wm. L. Garrison* (1835), *Appeal to the Christian Women of the Southern States* (1836), *Letter from Angelina Grimké Weld to the Woman's Rights Convention, Held at Syracuse, September, 1852* (1852), and "Speech before the Legislative Committee of the Massachusetts Legislature" (*The Liberator,* May 2, 1838). *An Epistle to the Clergy of the Southern States* (1836) was written by Sarah as an appeal to the southern clergy to take a stand against slavery.

Sarah's most bitter disappointment in life was having been deprived of an education because of her gender. It is thus not surprising that in addition to her antislavery stance, she also championed the cause of women's equality. Her most important work in this regard is her *Letters on the Equality of the Sexes and the Condition of Woman; Addressed to Mary Parker, President of the Boston Female Anti-Slavery Society* (1838). This work represents the first comprehensive argument on behalf of women's rights published in America. In the letters, Sarah reasons that woman like man is a free agent endowed with intellect whose duty is to God, not to father, husband, minister, or any other mortal man. Sarah's argument that woman was created as man's equal is impassioned: "All I ask our brethren is, that they will take their feet from off our necks, and permit us to stand upright on that ground which God designed us to occupy."

Another talented writer of this period who utilized writing to express her views and promote her causes was the inimitable Frances Anne Kemble (1809–1893). Kemble was born into England's most celebrated family of actors, and as a young girl she spent several years in France studying literature, poetry, music, French, and Italian. She reluctantly launched her acting career in 1829, in Shakespeare's *Romeo and Juliet.* But by 1832, she had joined her father on an American tour and enchanted audiences in Philadelphia, Baltimore, Washington, Boston, and New York. She was courted by a wealthy young Philadelphian, Pierce Butler, and before the American tour ended in 1834, Fanny and Pierce were married. Thus began a tumultuous marriage that ended in divorce in 1849. Fanny had always been more interested in writing than in acting, and in 1835 her two-volume "American" *Journal,* a record of her trip to America and her successful theatrical tour, was published in Philadelphia and abroad. This first work received mixed reviews. Her youthful vitality and enthusiasm were considered by some of her critics as indiscreet and flippant, while others considered her book impertinent but clever.

During her American tour, Fanny had met such antislavery proponents as Catharine Maria Sedgwick, Charles and Elizabeth Dwight Sedgwick, and the noted minister William Ellery Channing. She had expressed views on slavery prior to moving on December 30, 1838, to her husband's Georgia plantation near Darien. She began to keep a journal in early January to record her observations, thoughts, and feelings about plantation life. Adopting the epistolary style, she recorded her entries as letters to her friend, Elizabeth Dwight Sedgwick. Fanny was shocked and aggrieved by the wretched state of her husband's slaves and frequently complained to him of their maltreatment until he forbade her to speak to him again on the subject. This was an impossible situation for the spirited Fanny, who once wrote, "I cannot give my conscience into the keeping of another human being or submit the actions dictated by my conscience to their will." In spite of a bitter divorce in 1849 and her antislavery stance, her *Journal of a Residence on a Georgian Plantation in 1838–1839* was not published until 1863, when Fanny felt it might aid the Union's war aims. Henry James, who was Fanny's friend, claimed that her best prose was the "strong, insistent, one-sided" 1863 *Journal.* He also wrote that her *Records of a Girlhood* (1878) and *Records of a Later Life* (1882) represented "one of the most animated autobiographies in the language."

During the antebellum years, southern illiteracy reached a deplorable level, as noted in the census records of 1840 and 1850. The education of children was regarded by the southern elite as the responsibility of the individual, not of the state. During this period numerous private academies existed for the privileged, but the needs of the masses were ignored. Many of these private schools were founded in central Georgia. One of the most notable was Nathan Beman's Mt. Zion Academy in Hancock County. *Tokens of Affection, The Letters of a Planter's Daughter in the Old South* (1996) introduces us to a young woman born and educated in Mt. Zion, Georgia.

Maria Bryan (1808–1844) began corresponding with her recently married sister, Julia Bryan Cumming, on March 7, 1824. Maria wrote with regularity for almost twenty years. Her letters reflect the life of a cultured, educated young widow living on a plantation in rural Georgia. The close kinship and affection of the two sisters invoked in Maria expressions of unguarded honesty as she shared her most intimate thoughts and feelings about slaves, courtship, marriage, childbirth, family life, friendship, religion, education, politics, and travel. So personal and uninhibited were her letters that she requested Julia to burn them. Fortunately, she did not.

Maria Bryan's correspondence disabuses us of the myth of the "southern lady" regarding the notion that wives and daughters of planters led lives of idleness and unalloyed bliss. She assumed many home responsibilities, such as sewing clothes for slaves, housekeeping, tending the sick, tutoring the younger children, and grading papers for the local academy, but still she found time to satisfy her eclectic literary tastes. Like many other southern women, she resented the confining limits to her life. On July 19, 1842, Maria wrote to Julia: "How much of a slave a woman finds herself when she comes to act out of her usual routine." This collection of letters provides entertaining and substantive information about the antebellum South as viewed by an intelligent and literary young woman of privilege.

A Plantation Mistress on the Eve of the Civil War: The Diary of Keziah Goodwyn Hopkins Brevard, 1860–1861 (1992) reveals a diarist of a different stripe from those previously discussed. Keziah Brevard's brief diary covers a period of less than a year. This fifty-seven-year-old childless widow was not typical of the plantation mistress of her day. Brevard (1803–1886) had inherited a great deal of property from her father and owned more than two hundred slaves. She competently managed two plantations consisting of some 2,600 acres and lived on her Sand Hills Farm with only her house slaves for company. Brevard made journal entries daily on subjects ranging from weather, farming, domestic affairs, family, and neighborhood news to prayers, religious musings, and concerns about slavery and the impending war. Living in relative isolation, Brevard received infrequent news of the political ferment that swirled around her, and it was not until Lincoln's election that she focused her concerns on the fate of the slaveholding South and the threats to her future. "Lord we know not what is to be the result of this—but I do pray if there is to be a crisis—that we all lay down our lives sooner than free our slaves in our midst." Keziah's entries are truncated and often perfunctory. Her brief diary, however, affords an intimate view of an unusual southern woman who is facing the impending war virtually alone.

Eliza Pinckney, Eliza Wilkinson, Anne Royall, Sarah and Angelina

Grimké, Frances Anne Kemble, Maria Bryan, and Keziah Brevard exemplify but a few of the southern women whose substantive lives are being reclaimed through their journals, diaries, and letters. Neither educational limitations nor exclusion from public life prevented many southern women from leaving an important literary and historical record of their lives and times.

Captivity Narratives

Karen A. Weyler

Between the time of the earliest European settlements in the sixteenth century and the late nineteenth century, tens of thousands of whites and blacks were taken captive by the Indians of North America. Indians took captives for a variety of reasons, most often as a tactic of warfare and in retaliation for broken treaties and encroachment on their lands. Captives were sometimes held for ransom, particularly in the Northeast, or as slaves. Still other captives were intended for adoption within the tribes of their captors. The stories that the captives related upon their return to white settlements took the form of the captivity narrative, an indigenous New World genre based on interactions between Euro-Americans and their Indian captors. The first of these captivity narratives appeared in *Relation of Alvar Nuñez Cabeza de Vaca,* published in Seville in 1542. As long as captives continued to be taken, and even afterward, captivity narratives remained immensely popular among readers in North America and Europe. Although first-person narratives make up the bulk of captivity narratives written in English, the literature of captivity was never limited to the first person. Local histories, letters, newspaper accounts, sermons, and broadsides often incorporate tales of captives. And in the late eighteenth and early nineteenth centuries, captivity narratives inspired novels, plays, poetry, and fictitious atrocity stories about the white person taken into captivity by Indians. Religion, cultural values, racial attitudes, politics, and settlement patterns all influenced the content and style of captivity narratives at different times, enough so that the purposes of the captivity narrative varied widely throughout its history.

The tales of women taken captive by Indians that are best known today tend to be those drawn from seventeenth-century New England, a setting which produced narratives intensely infused with religious thought. Although Mary Rowlandson was not the first captive of Indians to tell of her experiences, her astoundingly popular narrative, *The Sovereignty and Goodness of God* (1682), served as a model for many of the narratives that would follow. Structured by her Puritan faith, Rowlandson's narrative places captivity in a theological dimension, for she describes her experiences as both a chastisement by God and a successful trial of her faith. With captivity understood in such a fashion, Puritan clergy understandably played an active role in collecting and publicizing the stories of captives.

Women were likewise taken captive in the southeastern part of British North America from the time of earliest settlement; women were, for example, captured from Martin's Hundred in the colony at Jamestown by Indians under Powhatan in 1622 and not returned until a year later. But there is a dearth of early captivity texts in English from what would later become the southern region of the United States because Florida and Louisiana were not initially settled by English-speaking peoples. As the English frontier moved westward in the eighteenth century, however, so too did the locale of the captivity narrative. Thus, most southern captivity narratives are set roughly within the boundaries of western Virginia, Kentucky, and Tennessee during the post-Revolutionary era, a time when narratives set in southern locales briefly dominate the genre. Although there is nothing distinctively southern about those works narrated by eighteenth-century settlers of the South, because they began appearing almost a century later, southern narratives are significantly more secular and sentimental in tone than the seventeenth-century New England narratives.

The Shawnee, Cherokee, and Delaware are the tribes most often described in mid-to-late eighteenth-century captivity narratives as engaging in raids on vulnerable frontier settlements in western Virginia. Attacks usually took place without warning, either at night or in the early morning, catching families unprepared. Those men who did not escape were usually killed defending their wives and families. The elderly, infants, and small children, none of whom were likely to survive a lengthy forced march into the wilderness under harsh conditions, were frequently killed in their homes, which were then pillaged and burned. Those most likely to be taken captive included children between the ages of eight and fourteen, and women; even among this group, those who could not keep up were liable to be killed on the trail.

For eighteenth-century southern women held captive, adoption was a distinct possibility. For instance, Mary Kinnan (1763–1848), Jennie Wiley (1760–1831), and Mary Moore (1776–1824) all related that their captors desired to adopt them as wives or daughters. Sometimes adoptees were specifically intended to replace lost family members; at other times, the courage or physical strength of particular captives earned them the admiration of their captors. Children and young women were frequently chosen for adoption because they were the most likely to transculturate, that is, to assimilate contentedly into Indian society through adoption and marriage. Although no southern narrative describes willing transculturation, narratives from other regions of the country do. Eunice Williams (captured in 1704 in Massachusetts), Mary Jemison (captured in 1758 in Pennsylvania), and Cynthia Ann Parker (captured in 1836 in Texas) were three of the most famous "white Indians" who transculturated. Family members and acquaintances later related their stories to audiences both horrified and fascinated by women who rejected white society in favor of their Indian families. Although there were most certainly southern female captives who transculturated, they did not record narratives. The southern narratives that do exist fervently reject the possibility of transculturation and emphasize the ardent longings of their subjects to return to their white families and friends.

To survive Indian captivity and return to white settlements required tremendous mental and physical fortitude, and the stories of those women who survived such trials enthralled readers and writers in the United States and in Europe. Given the intense interest generated by the captivity experience, even the narratives of those captives who lacked the literary sophistication necessary to record their own stories frequently found their way into print. Consequently, former captives had varying degrees of authorial control over the narratives of their experience. The narratives of both Mary Kinnan and Frances Scott (dates unknown), for instance, were probably written in collaboration with their printers or publishers, using information that Kinnan and Scott provided. Oftentimes captivity tales were recorded by someone other than the captive, frequently at some remove from the time of captivity. The story of Mary Moore, who at age ten was captured from western Virginia in 1786 and remained a captive for three years, was not recorded until 1854, thirty years after her death, when her son published *The Captives of Abb's Valley: A Legend of Frontier Life by a Son of Mary Moore*. The account of the yearlong captivity of Jennie Wiley, taken from her frontier home in western Virginia in the 1790s, was well known in her own time, circulating in newspaper reports and oral history, but it was not recorded in detail until over one hundred years later, when it appeared in several histories of Kentucky; consequently, details of her captivity differ from version to version. Stories of Indian attacks and captivity tended to be widely reported, and tales of captives often appear embedded in other kinds of narrative. For example, Jemima Boone, daughter of Daniel Boone, was for several weeks held captive by a band composed primarily of Shawnee Indians in Kentucky in 1776 until she was rescued by her father. Timothy Flint, in his *Biographical Memoir of Daniel Boone* (1833), mentions Jemima's captivity in order to illustrate the bravery of the Boone family and Daniel Boone's wilderness savvy. Indian captivity frequently found its way into the visual arts, and Jemima's captivity is famously rendered by Charles F. Wimar in his painting *The Abduction of Daniel Boone's Daughter* (1853).

Although two eighteenth-century captivity narratives by black men are extant, those of Briton Hammon and southerner John Marrant, there are no known captivity narratives recorded by black women, even though blacks, both slave and free, were frequently taken captive. To locate black women among southern captives, it is necessary to read local histories and captivity narratives by whites, for black men and women appear in captivity literature primarily in the context of stolen or lost property. In *Daring and Heroic Deeds of American Women* (1860), for example, John Frost relates a lengthy anecdote about an attack that occurred in 1788 in Tennessee. Cherokee and Creek Indians attacked the Brown family party as they moved westward, killing several family members, stealing livestock, and taking captive other family members and slaves. The white members of the Brown household later escaped or were ransomed, but two female slaves remained in captivity for nearly twenty-five years, after which time they and their children were legally reclaimed by the Brown family as compensation for the damages the family had suffered during the original Indian attack. Unfortunately, the female slaves' stories of captivity remain untold, possibly because the women were illiterate. Even more likely, though, the stories that they, as slaves, might tell of the shock of cultural adaptation and readaptation simply were not important in the eyes of the chronicler. Frost, writing in 1860, regards them merely as legal evidence—proof of Indian attack. He seems unable to conceive that these women might have stories of their own to tell. Many of the blacks held captive probably transculturated, and while some of them may have merely exchanged one form of captivity for another, for other black captives, Indian life may have offered much more freedom.

Several imperatives seem to have driven those southern women who did record the stories of their captivity. Narrating their captivities seems to have been a cathartic experience that allowed them to assert their whiteness (especially important if they were to be adopted into the tribe of their captors), as well as to defend their virtue and seek a sort of literary revenge on the Indians. All of them emphasize certain key features of captivity, especially the mental suffering brought about by the loss of and separation from husbands and children, as well as the physical hardships of enduring strange food, temperature extremes, and lengthy marches. Although few authors of captivity narratives regard Native Americans with outright sympathy, most record occasional instances of kindness or generosity on the part of their captors, especially with regard to the sharing of limited provisions.

Two of the most popular southern captivity narratives are those of Scott, taken from her home in Washington County, Virginia, in 1785 by a group of Delawares and Mingoes, and Kinnan, taken captive from her home in Randolph County, Virginia, in 1791 by Shawnees. Scott soon escaped her captors, but Kinnan was sold by the Shawnees to the Delawares and remained in captivity for over two years before she escaped from an encampment near Detroit. Conventional religious sentiments and familiar Bible verses frame both works, but overall they are much more secular in tone than narratives from seventeenth-century New England. Neither Scott nor Kinnan views her experiences as a punishment by God or a trial of faith, and both narratives lack the elaborate clerical framework that authorized many New England narratives.

Both Scott's and Kinnan's narratives open in a peaceful pastoral setting, but violence soon erupts. In *A True and Wonderful Narrative of the Surprising Captivity and Remarkable Deliverance of Mrs. Frances Scott* (1786), the third-person narrator explains that Indians attacked the Scott household as they prepared for bed; they immediately killed her husband, slashed the throats of three of her children while they lay in bed, and tomahawked her oldest daughter while her mother held her. Scott alone was taken captive, but she escaped from her captors after eleven days on the trail. Described as "almost as ignorant as a Child of the Method of steering through the Woods," Scott was soon lost, with neither food nor weapon. Threatened with either starvation or being killed by wild animals, Scott attempted suicide, but her leap from a cliff merely stunned her. All told, Scott wandered in the wilderness for nearly a month, eating sassafras leaves and cane stalks. She found her way back to civilization, she claimed, by following the path of a "beautiful Bird." The narration concludes by telling us that, although Scott survived her ordeal, she "continues in a low State of Health, and remains inconsolable for the Loss of her Family, particularly bewailing the cruel Death of her little Daughter." *A True Narrative of the Sufferings of*

Mary Kinnan (1795) is even more melodramatic in tone, evoking pathos rather than religious sentiment; it begins by asking readers, "Whilst the tear of sensibility so often flows at the unreal tale of woe, which glows under the pen of the poet and the novelist, shall our hearts refuse to be melted with sorrow at the unaffected and unvarnished tale of a female, who has surmounted difficulties and dangers, which on a review appear romantic, even to herself." Surprised one evening by an Indian attack, Kinnan initially escaped but was captured when she returned to aid her daughter, who, like Kinnan's husband, was killed and scalped in her presence. Throughout her narrative, Kinnan repeatedly emphasizes the effects of captivity on her body, which becomes not merely the site of intense physical suffering, but also the seat of sensibility: her heaving bosom and glistening eyes illustrate her civilized sensibility, which is juxtaposed against the savage cruelty of the Indian squaws, who revel in the torment of their captives.

Many narratives from the post–Revolutionary War era tend to be overtly propagandistic and therefore of questionable validity, favoring westward expansion and portraying Native American tribes as an impediment to this goal. These narratives also tend to be anti-French and anti-British, because the military forces of those countries were frequently allied with the Indians against American settlers. Thus Mary Kinnan describes her Indian captors as agents not of Satan, but of the British, whom she blames for the Indians' barbarity. Although sometimes based on actual experiences of captivity, much of the most vitriolic anti-Indian propaganda relies on fabricated atrocities. An example of this kind of propaganda is *An Affecting Narrative of the Captivity and Sufferings of Mrs. Mary Smith* (1815), composed of a pastiche of episodes from earlier narratives. Smith's is a short, exceptionally violent tale that emphasizes the tomahawking of the family's slave and the horrible torture of Smith's husband and nubile daughters. The method of torture of the daughters, who are stripped, covered with pitch, and have "upwards of six hundred" splinters driven into their flesh which are later set alight, closely echoes the torture with which John Marrant recounts being threatened by the Cherokees in his very popular work *A Narrative of the Lord's Wonderful Dealings with John Marrant, a Black* (1785) and the torture experienced by two young women in *Affecting History of the Dreadful Distresses of Frederic Manheim's Family* (1793), who amazingly have exactly the same number of splinters driven into their flesh. Inflammatory rhetoric appears throughout Smith's tale; the Indians are described as "merciless cannibals," and the plan to adopt Mrs. Smith into their tribe and marry her to an Indian is labeled prostitution. Smith pretends to submit to this plan but then escapes by knifing and tomahawking her Indian husband.

Another propagandistic southern narrative, also likely falsified, is a broadside from the Second Seminole War (1835–1841) entitled *Captivity and Sufferings of Mrs. Mason, with an Account of the Massacre of Her Youngest Child* (ca. 1836).

In the nineteenth century, as the frontier continued to move westward, captivity was no longer a threat to southerners, yet the idea of captivity continued to fascinate readers, as evidenced by contemporary retellings of captivity narratives in works such as John Frost's *Thrilling Adventures among the Indians* (1850) and *Daring and Heroic Deeds of American Women* (1860). The latter volume, in particular, emphasizes southern captivity, containing numerous narratives about women captured between 1760 and 1790 by members of the Cherokee and Shawnee tribes in western Virginia, Kentucky, and Tennessee. Frost briefly summarizes most of these narratives, deriving his information primarily from histories and newspaper reports of the settlers who sought western lands, but sometimes from the captives' own accounts as well. Frost celebrates the "cool courage" of those Amazon-like women who survived Indian attack and captivity. Unlike earlier male narrators, such as Cotton Mather, Frost betrays little anxiety about the violence these women sometimes necessarily engaged in, for he labels their feats uncommon and justifies them as arising from maternal instincts.

In the late eighteenth and nineteenth centuries, tales of Indian captivity appeared in virtually every genre of popular writing, including ballads, poems, plays, short stories, sentimental and historical fiction, dime novels, and children's literature. The captivity narrative even worked its way into humor writing when the sketch "Sal Fink, the Mississippi Screamer" appeared in the *Crockett Almanac* (1854). While hunting wildcats, Sal (supposedly the daughter of Mike Fink) is taken captive by a war party of fifty Indians who plan to roast and eat her; instead, Sal single-handedly dispatches the entire party by tying their feet together while they sleep and tossing them into their own fire. Evoking neither spiritual reflection nor pathos, "Sal Fink" suggests precisely how dramatically times had changed over the previous hundred years, for captivity by this time had become nearly devoid of its earlier religious and cultural contexts.

Gender Issues in the Old South

Mary Louise Weaks

The earliest examples of southern women attempting to achieve some degree of gender equality are instances of women using spoken rather than written voices. Their words are recorded in the court records of their day. Colonial women of the South were particularly eager to protect their families, homes, and property, but some also made efforts to receive equal treatment under the law. In Maryland, for example, a Margaret Brent—who is referred to in records of the time as "Mistresse Margarett Brent, Spinster"—petitioned the General Assembly of Maryland for the right to vote in 1648. Her request was denied despite the fact that she was a landowner who had served as a business and legal advisor to her brother and who was named executrix of the estate of Maryland's governor when he died in 1657. Historian Julia Cherry Spruill, in her book *Women's Life and Work in the Southern Colonies* (1938), points to Brent as a "remarkable" example of a colonial woman who became one of the most prominent citizens of the colony of Maryland. There are other examples, too, of colonial women who were active in public capacities but perhaps not to the same extent as Brent. Spruill, for example, also identifies another Maryland woman, Barbara Smith, who traveled to England to argue the case of her husband who was imprisoned during the Revolution of 1689. Eliza Lucas Pinckney took similar responsibility for the well-being of her family and left a written record of her efforts in her letterbook that describes her experiences at age seventeen when she was entrusted with running her family's South Carolina plantations. Literate colonial women sometimes petitioned government agencies in writing or, like Pinckney, documented the business of a family plantation in their letterbooks.

The necessity of using language and the power of words—both spoken and written—was clear to many southern women who spoke out in public to support their households. Whereas antebellum laws generally forbade a woman to own property, vote, or write a will, colonial women were typically not faced with such disenfranchisement. In sharp contrast to the antebellum South, it was generally acceptable in colonial times for women to have an active role in the running of plantations or family farms. The determination and strength of these women is apparent in their words. Women like Margaret Brent, Spruill points out, tended to make "their requests confidently and boldly." They petitioned their governments believing they had a right to do so and believing they understood the workings of politics. Women of the early South—even those of the upper class—tended to be more active than antebellum women in their participation in community affairs and in the support of their families, most likely out of necessity. Thus the seventeen-year-old Eliza Lucas was not an anomaly for her times, but rather closer to a standard. By recording her life and work in her letterbooks, Eliza claimed for herself a written style of business documentation typical of male planters.

Some of the earliest published public statements by southern women were written to show women's vital role in the colonies during the years preceding the Revolutionary War. During the tea boycott of 1773–74, for example, women were called to make public pronouncements of their support. In a time when tea was more precious than gold, the support of women was particularly important because the woman of the house was the one who typically made the marketing selections and who held the key to the home's tea caddy. Published in newspapers, women's essays and verses showed that women were not only patriotic citizens, but also supporters of the white landowning men who governed public life. In some instances, male writers even posed as women. Two particularly important examples of essays by women for women appeared on the front page of Clementina Rind's *Virginia Gazette* in September 1774. According to historian Cynthia A. Kierner, in her book *Beyond the Household: Women's Place in the Early South, 1700–1835* (1998), these essays constitute "probably the greatest concentration of women's writing to date in an American periodical and certainly the greatest in any southern colonial newspaper." One of these essays was addressed from the women of Virginia to their "countrywomen" in Pennsylvania, where merchants were leery of supporting the boycott. The Virginians called upon the women of Pennsylvania to help their men "extricate America from the evils that threaten her." Believing that women should take a public stand on such matters, the Virginians urged, "[B]e firm in withstanding luxuries of every kind; but above all, as the most pernicious of all, that you will (as we universally have done) banish *India tea* from your tables, and in its stead, substitute some of those aromatic herbs with which our fruitful soil abounds." Suggesting that by doing so, women could take a public role and influence history, the Virginia women proclaimed that "Much, very much, depends on the public virtue the ladies will exert at this critical juncture." By bonding together in support of the boycott, women of the colonies "will be so far instrumental in bringing about a redress of the evils complained of, that history may be hereafter filled with their praises, and teach posterity to venerate their virtues."

Despite these concerted public efforts, however, eighteenth-century women of the South were increasingly willing to see themselves as "shining ornaments," and they represented themselves as such in their writings. The "undaunted dames" of the early South were replaced by women who were satisfied with a lesser role in matters of public concern and who favored a weakening of the image of southern women as confident and self-sufficient. It became, in effect, unladylike to "meddle" in politics. Although women living in frontier regions of the South retained, out of necessity, those qualities of the "undaunted dames," middle- and upper-class white women of more settled regions became increasingly influenced by the myth of the southern lady. This new model of womanhood favored the delicate and pious, pure and soft-spoken. Spruill points specifically to the example of a group of women known as the Women of Wilmington, North Carolina, who petitioned the governor in 1782 "to rescind an order regarding the removal of the wives and children of Tories from the state." They explained apologetically, "It is not the province of our sex to reason deeply upon the policy of the order." According to the women, they had been prompted to set forth their "earnest supplication" in hopes of helping those who could not help themselves. Despite their desire to act, however, the Women of Wilmington perpetuated the myth of southern womanhood by suggesting their inability "to reason deeply" on a political matter.

By the nineteenth century, southern women writers who addressed themselves on the issues of gender were clearly grouped into two factions. One group believed women were deserving of equality with men, while the other celebrated the differences between the genders, especially what they believed to be the moral superiority of the female sex. While allowing for differences between the genders, this second group was, in fact, less radical than the first because in their ideology, women "stayed in their place"—the domestic realm. Nevertheless, in making public written statements about the place of woman, these writers are typically seen as "feminists" in the sense that in the act of writing, they moved beyond the traditional realm of woman. Many of these women, however, would not have supported the suffragist movement. Women who supported equality, on the other hand, found it particularly important to use their speaking voices to make public proclamations of their opinions, a decidedly unfeminine action in both the nineteenth-century South and North.

Because southern women tended to be what are called "difference" feminists rather than "equality" feminists, southern women of the antebellum period were not as active in their public pursuits of gender equality as were their northern sisters. Their efforts were not as organized as those in the North because, living in a more rural region, southern women were not as likely to have close connections with groups of women, as did northern women living in urban areas. Because of the close link between the early women's rights movement and the abolitionist movement, southern women were also unlikely to join the evolving northern women's movement of the 1840s and 1850s. Although the southern woman is typically seen in isolation from northern women, southern interest in women's issues was influenced by northern feminism, in particular, through the physical relocations of several women writers from North to South. Some of the most published women writers of the South, for example, were raised in the North and moved to the South, including Caroline Howard Gilman and Caroline Hentz. Northern publications also influenced southern women. In the *Ladies' Magazine,* for instance, editor Sarah Hale often expressed her opinions on the value of "woman's sphere." Although Hale's publication was generally limited to a northern readership, Caroline Howard Gilman published pieces in the magazine and thus likely knew of its contents. In an 1832 issue, Hale declares that "what man shall become depends upon the secret, silent, influence of woman." Although women like Hale believed in the importance of education for women, they saw this education as providing a means by which women might be better companions to their husbands rather than by which they might take part in occupations traditionally assigned to men. Hale failed to point out, however, that by taking up the pen, she, too, was taking public action.

There are, understandably, few examples of antebellum women of the South who supported "equality feminism." Speaking out—which generally meant speechmaking—was seen as unfeminine and improper by southerners and, in fact, by many people in the North. Women were to influence political affairs only through their husbands and within the privacy of their homes. Women did, however, become increasingly involved in social organizations that attempted to better the lives of women and their families, but even those outlets—especially the churches—relegated women to positions of little control. Women like Sarah and Angelina Grimké, and Frances Wright (1795–1852) were severely criticized for making public statements, and they even became the inspiration for novels like Sarah Hale's *The Lecturess* (1839), which showed what happened to a woman if she spoke out. Described by Nina Baym as "the earliest anti-feminist fiction," the novel tells the story of a woman named Marian who gives up her career as a lecturer to marry. When Marian decides she wants to return to lecturing, her marriage crumbles. Nevertheless, she takes up her career once again, but dies an early death, the typical tragic ending to a life lived outside the confines of proper society.

The Grimké sisters are, in fact, the best-known examples of antebellum southern women who attempted to change attitudes on gender and race issues. Sarah is perhaps best known for her *Letters on the Equality of the Sexes and the Condition of Woman, Addressed to Mary S. Parker, President of the Boston Female Anti-Slavery Society* (1838). Historian Anne Firor Scott says in *The Southern Lady: From Pedestal to Politics* (1970) that given "the definition of woman's role in the South, it is understandable that a southern woman should have written the earliest systematic expression in America of the whole set of ideas constituting the ideology of 'woman's rights.'" In her letters, especially Letter 8, Grimké outlines her argument for equality of the sexes, explaining that God created men and women equal: "they are both moral and accountable beings, and whatever is *right* for man to do, is *right* for woman." Using the Bible as a source for evidence to support her argument, Grimké explains that "There is neither Jew nor Greek, there is neither bond nor free, there is neither *male* nor *female;* for ye are all one in Christ Jesus." Pointing out that, in her opinion, the Bible has long been misread because male interpreters of Greek and Hebrew versions of the Bible have in some cases given "false" or "perverted" interpretations, Grimké explains that scripture will continue to be misread until women are allowed to study Greek and Hebrew. In her studies of the Bible, she has found "nothing like the softness of woman, nor the sternness of man: both are equally commanded to bring forth the fruits of the spirit, love, meekness, gentleness, c." In present-day society, Grimké explains, "In most families, it is considered a matter of far more consequence to call a girl off from making a pie, or a pudding, than to interrupt her whilst engaged in her studies." Little value is placed on educating women to the level that they become "intelligent" companions to their husbands. She longs "to see the time" when husbands "encourage their wives to devote some portion of their time to mental cultivation, even at the expense of having to dine sometimes on baked potatoes, or bread and butter."

Like her older sister, Angelina is known, too, for her public statements on women's issues and for the abolitionist cause. Finding they could no longer live in the South, both sisters had left South Carolina for good by 1829 and moved to the North. They began there a series of lecture tours that would bring them criticism even in the northern states. In particular, the fact that the sisters spoke before "mixed audiences"—that is, groups of men and women—drew heavy criticism. Even in the North, the Grimké sisters were viewed as a curiosity. But people turned out in large numbers to hear them lecture. In 1838, Angelina became the first woman to speak before a legislative body in the United States, a committee of the Massachusetts legislature. (Sarah was originally to have given the speech, but illness prevented her from doing so.) Describing her own anticipation leading up to the speech, Angelina later wrote, "I never was so near fainting under the tremendous pressure of feeling. My heart almost died within me. The novelty of the scene, the weight of responsibility, the ceaseless exercise of mind thro' which I had passed for more than a week—all together sunk me to the earth. I well nigh despaired." Lydia Maria Child wrote later of the speech that "For a moment a sense of the immediate responsibility resting on [Angelina] seemed almost to overwhelm her. She trembled and grew pale. But this passed quickly, and she went on to speak gloriously strong in utter forgetfulness of herself." Angelina was able to begin the words of her speech, first proclaiming, "I stand before you as a southerner, exiled from the land of my birth by the sound of the lash and the piteous cry of the slave." The reaction in the press was harsh. Angelina was called "Devil-ina," and one reporter for the *Olive Branch,* who believed he was listening to Sarah, wrote that "It is rather doubtful whether any of the South Carolina lords of creation will ever seek the heart and hand of their great orator in marriage." (Actually, Angelina never married, but Sarah did.) Historians have noted that the Grimké sisters had a tremendous influence on the early figures of the women's rights movement who were associated with the Seneca Falls Convention of 1848, such as Susan B. Anthony and Elizabeth Cady Stanton.

One even earlier attempt by a woman to draw attention to the gender inequities of southern society was by Frances Wright, who was born in Scotland in 1795. Wright's interest, in particular, was with the African American woman in slavery. Orphaned at an early age, she and her sister struck up an acquaintance with the Marquis de Lafayette, who Wright hoped would adopt them both. Wright and her sister moved in with the elderly, widowed Lafayette and lived with him for two months. She then followed him to the United States in 1824, where they visited with such dignitaries as Thomas Jefferson, James Madison, James Monroe, and Andrew Jackson. By making these acquaintances and traveling on her own in the South, Wright became increasingly interested in the issue of slavery. She was concerned, she said, with the detrimental effects it had on a country she believed offered the greatest potential for the human being to "awake to the full knowledge and exercise of his powers."

With part of her inheritance, in 1825 Wright bought 320 acres outside of Memphis, Tennessee, on what was then the border of Indian territory, and established a community she called Nashoba. Later expanded to an area of two thousand acres, Nashoba was, as Wright wrote in a piece for the journal *Genius of Universal Emancipation,* to be her "pioneer experiment—to prove that gradual emancipation would work." There, slaves, who either had been bought or were owned by enlightened planters, might work to pay back their purchase price and to learn a trade. After five years, they would be freed and colonized in what she described as "some foreign place such as Texas, California, or Haiti." Wright was influenced not only by Jeffersonian idealism and Lafayette's attempts at gradual emancipation at his French Guiana plantation, but also by Robert Owen's New Harmony community in Indiana. Writing in the New Harmony *Gazette* in 1828, Wright, describing her Nashoba experiment, explained that at Nashoba, "The marriage law existing without the pale of the Institution, is of no force within that pale. No woman can forfeit her individual rights or independent existence, and no man assert over her any sights or power whatsoever, beyond what he may exercise over her free and voluntary affections." Despite her hopes for these gender freedoms for women and racial freedoms for slaves, the commune faced serious problems. Few slaves actually made their way to Nashoba, which was run much like a slave plantation—children were even separated from their parents; commune living at Nashoba was viewed by many outsiders as morally unacceptable, and the bitter weather of the area created unbearable living conditions. Wright finally decided the best way to change society was through lecture tours, and she left Nashoba to an overseer in summer 1828.

Other women writers, chiefly those who supported "difference" feminism, were among those publishing the fiction of the time, generally of the sentimental variety. Writing was probably one of the first occupations open to women because it allowed women to remain in their homes, but it also gave them a voice on matters of gender. A more acceptable route than speechmaking, fiction and poetry writing for women in the South became a means for women to create an undercurrent that—while it tended to celebrate the qualities of woman that made her different from man—frequently addressed the difficulties faced by women within society because of their gender.

Perhaps two of the clearest statements of "difference" feminism can be found in the writings of Maria McIntosh (1803–1878), a popular novelist of the 1840s and 1850s, and the noted essayist Louisa McCord. The author of an extensive list of novels that were both serialized and published in book form, McIntosh also published a book called *Woman in America: Her Work and Her Reward* in 1850. In the book, she writes generally of women in the United States, but also examines the lives of women in the various regions of the country. "*Different* office and *different* powers," according to McIntosh, are assigned to men and women. "Each seems to us equally important to the fulfillment of God's designs in the formation, the preservation, and the perfection of human society." McIntosh says she leaves the question of "equality and inequality" to others. She believes that woman, by "exercising her influence, not by public associations, and debates, and petitions, but in the manifestation of all feminine grace, and all womanly delicacy," will "prove herself indeed, what one of old named her, the connecting link between man and the angelic world." In a chapter on the South, McIntosh says that because of slavery, Africans have been civilized and brought to Christianity, and the white woman has played a principal role in their salvation. The white woman's role in slave culture, according to McIntosh, is "to interpose the shield of her charity between the weak and the strong, to watch beside the sick, to soothe the sorrowing, to teach the ignorant, to soften by her influence the haughty master, and to elevate the debased slave. . . . She is a missionary to whose own door God has brought the Pagans to be instructed." Likewise, Louisa McCord writes in her 1852 essay entitled "Enfranchisement of Woman" published in *Southern Quarterly* that "Woman will reach the greatest height . . . she is capable . . . not by becoming *man,* but by becoming more than ever *woman.*"

Fictional representations of women written during the 1840s and 1850s also greatly reflected this ideal of womanhood that raised women above men. Nina Baym points out in her book *Woman's Fiction* (1993) that, especially for writers like Maria McIntosh and E.D.E.N. Southworth (1819–1899), representations of women reflected the difficulties of the writers' lives as women. Georgia-born Maria McIntosh, for example, after running her family estate in Georgia for twelve years, moved to New York to live with her half brother. She decided to invest in New York bank stock and lost all of her money in the Panic of 1837. According to Baym, McIntosh would again and again rewrite this story in her fiction. Through authorship, McIntosh was able to find a means of support that brought her security in a world where women were taught dependence. McIntosh confronted the dangers of this dependence in novels beginning with her 1843 *Woman an Enigma,* which was published anonymously. While she addressed the issue in her women's novels, according to Baym, McIntosh also "mourned the loss of an imagined world where women were protected and cared for all their lives and hence did not have to develop combative qualities." Believing that women would always be held back from reaching the same level of independence as men, in her novels McIntosh considered the limits of a woman's independence and the obstacles to it. Baym concludes that while McIntosh's novels of the 1840s and early 1850s "imply an aggressive and expansionist view of woman's potential, asserting that women underestimate and undervalue themselves," as she grew older, McIntosh suggested in her fiction that "women have become overreachers and need to remember their limitations."

Increasingly, too, southern women fiction writers portrayed women as active and strong-willed. Novelist E.D.E.N. Southworth, whose fiction, like McIntosh's, was shaped by the difficulties of her own life, wrote that the act of writing itself gave her great courage and strength. "Let me pass over in silence the stormy and disastrous days of my wretched girlhood and womanhood," she wrote, "days that stamped upon my brow of youth the furrows of fifty years—let me come at once to the time when I found myself broken in spirit, health, and purse—a widow in fate but not in fact, with my babes looking up to me for a support I could not give them. It was in these darkest days of my *woman's* life, that my *author's* life commenced." Southworth's heroines face their difficulties with as much courage. Her writing style, too, was itself in some ways a means of asserting her own independence. Described by Baym as "shamelessly decorative," Southworth's prose style is far more embellished than was acceptable for proper women of her time, who were to be self-effacing. Sarah Hale even criticized Southworth's writing for passing "beyond the limits prescribed by correct taste or good judgment." In Southworth's fiction, women often find themselves controlled by men, whether those men be fathers or marriage partners. Her novel *The Discarded Daughter* (serialized in 1851 and 1852, published in 1852), for example, points to the unfairness of property laws that leave women powerless. Not a supporter of women's rights per se, Southworth believed that women could find strength in "woman's sphere"—in separat-

ing themselves from men and in educating men of the values of true womanhood.

This model of true womanhood stood in sharp contrast to the literary
figure that has most influenced the role of woman in the South, that is, the
belle. Despite the fact that the belle has been a figure long reckoned with by
southern women writers, in the antebellum period her creators were principally male. As Kathryn Lee Seidel suggests in *The Southern Belle in the
American Novel* (1985), the plantation novel's elevation of woman onto a
pedestal was a reaction to the first stirrings of a women's rights movement
in the United States. Seidel also notes that women writers of the antebellum
period were faced with arguments like those written by Thomas R. Dew in
his "On the Characteristic Differences between the Sexes and on the Position and Influence of Woman in Society" (1835). In this essay, Dew says
that woman's "inferior strength and sedentary habits confine her within the
domestic circle." Because woman must rely on man for her protection, according to Dew, she must cultivate "those qualities which delight and fascinate—which are calculated to win over to her side the proud lord of
creation, and to make him a humble supplicant at her shrine. Grace, modesty, and loveliness are the charms which constitute her power." In effect,
then, she must assume the role of belle in order to find a husband. The belle
figure in literature was even birthed by John Pendleton Kennedy in his *Swallow Barn* (1832), just months following Nat Turner's rebellion, as part of
an attempt to portray the southern plantation as a model community. According to Seidel, Caroline Lee Hentz created women characters who "combined the virtues [Sarah] Hale extols with the beauty and liveliness of John
Pendleton Kennedy's belle." Like Hentz, other southern women writers
such as Southworth and McIntosh created women characters who faced
challenges and generally rose above them, showing they possessed intellectual capabilities and stamina Dew could not have imagined possible for
women.

As sectional divisions increased between North and South, and during
the years of civil war, southern women writers also made prominent use of
the values of "woman's sphere" in literary examinations of slavery and of
sectional disunion. Black women such as Harriet Jacobs and Frances E. W.
Harper used the cultural ideals of the domestic and of motherhood to persuade their audiences that within slavery, these ideals were impossible. Harper's 1854 poem "The Slave Mother," for example, reclaims the role of
mother for the slave woman. Although "cruel hands / May rudely tear" her
child from her arms, "She is a mother, and her heart / Is breaking in despair." She loves her child as much as her white readers love their children.

Female supporters of the Confederacy not only idealized the feminine, but also recognized and commented upon the flaws and dangers of masculinity. In her *Macaria* (1863), Augusta Jane Evans Wilson, who opposed women's suffrage, represented the North as "the worst of the masculine character, its avaricious, materialistic, soulless side. The South has the humanistic, unselfish and honorable values of the women it has put on a pedestal and the religion they cherish." She claimed that "The suffering of the South" was "like all female suffering." Likewise, Mary Chesnut writes in her journal that "Like the patriarchs of old our men live all in one house with their wives and their concubines. . . . Thank God for my countrywomen—alas for the men! No worse than men everywhere, but the lower their mistresses, the more degraded they must be."

Some white women also recognized the relationship between issues of gender and issues of race. Early on, for example, the Grimké sisters' efforts on behalf of the abolitionist movement were clearly tied to their perspectives as southern women. When they spoke out on issues of race, their voices were quieted in the South and viewed as novelties in the North because of their gender. By the time of the Civil War, Mary Chesnut, although by no means an abolitionist, was equating marriage and slavery. After describing in her diary seeing an African American woman sold into bondage, Chesnut writes, "You know how women sell themselves and are sold in marriage, from queens downward, eh? You know what the Bible says about slavery— and marriage. Poor women. Poor slaves."

By the end of the Civil War, gender roles in the South had become increasingly complicated. Although some southern women were interested in supporting the causes of the women's movement in the North, that movement had long been associated with abolitionism. Nevertheless, in the postwar South, woman's right to vote was increasingly linked to the race issue. If women were given the right to vote, many whites reasoned, then white southerners could have greater control in a system where black males had that right. As women—both black and white—assumed new roles in their families and in their communities during the Civil War, and as men felt the strong pull of the domestic world as they reentered their families, the war and the years of Reconstruction that followed became, in effect, a period of what has been called a gender crisis in the South, and that crisis would greatly shape the literature that was to come.

Eliza Lucas Pinckney

Linda Garner

According to Elise Pinckney, a direct descendant of Eliza Lucas Pinckney and editor of the 1997 paperback edition of her letterbook, "The total of the surviving manuscripts of Eliza Lucas Pinckney constitutes the largest corpus of personal writings of any woman in colonial America." That fact alone would earn Pinckney a significant place in southern literary history, but her writing is also invaluable in understanding eighteenth-century customs and pervasive philosophies and themes, such as rationalism applied to religious beliefs, virtue as a product of reason, marriage as a means of enhancing one's financial status, filial duty, and the value of industry over indolence. Furthermore, she anticipates the entrenched noblesse oblige that defined the planter culture of the early nineteenth-century South.

The daughter of George Lucas, a lieutenant colonel in the British Army, Eliza was born on December 28, 1722, in Antigua, and was provided a classical education in London during the 1730s. At the age of fifteen she, along with her mother and younger sister Polly, was sent to live on the family's six-hundred-acre plantation Wappoo, near Charleston, South Carolina. There Eliza supervised the slaves and the overseers of Wappoo and two other plantations, while military duty prevented her father from joining them. Anticipating that war between England and her European neighbors might produce a dearth of imports into England, George Lucas sent indigo seeds to the industrious Eliza, asking that she experiment with the plant's growth. Several years of work yielded a competitive crop in 1744, and she shared the seeds with other planters. Before the American Revolution, blue dye cakes created from indigo plants were instrumental in establishing the credit in London banks that sustained the Carolina economy. At the age of seventeen, Eliza began writing letters to family and friends. She collected copies of them and had them hardbound with dry parchment covers into a handwritten letterbook containing drafts, finished copies, and memoranda. Written between 1739 and 1762, these letters reveal, as Elise Pinckney notes, Eliza Pinckney's "carefulness and ability as well as her sense of self-importance for what she was undertaking."

In 1744, Eliza married Charles Pinckney, a forty-five-year-old widower who held many prominent positions in Carolina's colonial government. A member of the Royal Council, Charles also served as justice of the peace for Berkeley County, as speaker of the Commons House of Assembly, and as Carolina's chief justice. When Charles was replaced as chief justice in 1752, he moved the family, including children Charles Cotesworth, Harriott, and Thomas, to England, where he served as the Carolina governor and the Royal Council's representative to the Board of Trade. Charles and Eliza, along with Harriott, returned to Carolina in 1758, leaving the boys behind, in order to sell property in the colony Charles considered vulnerable, its protection weakened by Britain's diminishing power. Although the separation was difficult for Eliza, the boys were safer in England, and the family planned to be reunited shortly. Tragically, her husband contracted malaria one month after their arrival and died. Eliza thus faced the dual challenges of maintaining the Pinckney properties and financial security and ensuring her sons' salvation in what she believed was a morally corrupt London. She would not see Charles Cotesworth again until 1768 and Thomas until 1775.

Despite the miles between mother and sons, Pinckney succeeded in inculcating a strong allegiance to community and God in her children. Both sons, as Federalists, became prominent in creating and ratifying the Constitution, and both followed in their mother's footsteps, experimenting with agriculture and promoting scientific methods among farmers. The country's free use of the Mississippi River and a favorable southwest boundary were stipulations of a treaty with Spain named after Thomas Pinckney.

During the Revolutionary War, Eliza Pinckney survived the destruction of her plantations, desertions of slaves, and the illnesses and imprisonment of her children, only to be felled by cancer in Philadelphia on May 26, 1793. The fact that President George Washington asked to serve as one of her pallbearers attests to her stature as a pivotal figure of the Colonial and Federalist periods. Her obituary in the Charleston *City Gazette* eulogizes the depth of her understanding of her times and the strength of her religious faith: "Her understanding, aided by an uncommon strength of memory, had been so highly cultivated and improved by travel and extensive reading, and was so furnished, as well with scientific, as practical knowledge, that her talent for conversation was unrivalled. . . . Her religion was rational, liberal, and pure. The source of it was seated in the judgment and the heart, and from thence issued a life, regular, placid and uniform."

Pinckney's most lasting and instructive legacy is the letterbook, which captures eighteenth-century colonial culture, manners, historical events, and views. It consistently calls attention to her grateful use of her classical education in interactions with family and friends and portrays a hardworking, practical woman who, like Benjamin Franklin, commends to others the wise use of time and the importance of rising early. Devising a tight daily schedule at age 20, she read and supervised the servants' work before breakfast, devoted an hour afterward to music and another hour to a subject, such as French or shorthand, which she had "learned least," believing that "for want of practice it should be quite lost." Grateful for a priceless education and motivated by noblesse oblige, she spent her afternoons teaching Polly and two slave girls to read so the slave girls might in turn teach other slave children. In a 1744 letter to her father before her marriage, one not included in the letterbook, she asserts that she values the training her father paid for more than any fortune he could bestow upon her, for it will provide happiness to both her and those whose lives she touches. This commitment to enriching the lives of others pervades her gestures and concerns, large and small, from the sharing of indigo seeds with the community to later instructions to her sons' caretakers in England, advising them to remind her boys to acknowledge their servants' service during the holidays.

The subjects of the letters written between 1739 and 1746 range from her personal definition of appropriate public and private behavior and accounts of daily activities to commentary on local political and economic issues and on diverse writers, thinkers, and prominent men. True to Enlightenment thinking, she inextricably ties virtue and faith to reason and emphasizes other prevalent eighteenth-century values such as patience, humility, filial duty, and a cheerful acceptance of God's will leading to an assurance of immortality. At age eighteen she declares she knows that her father, opposing the practice of arranging marriages for financial gain, will not sacrifice her to wealth. In Eliza's letters, the daily endeavors of improving the indigo and of assiduously observing nature in her immediate surroundings are intermingled with pondering local issues: new legislation's impact on the economy and her father's business, tyrannies of the government in Georgia, and notions of insurrection introduced to slaves. She refers to George Whitefield, the famous Anglican revivalist, and to a comet foretold by Sir Isaac Newton. When contemplating her own identity, she probably, as Elise Pinckney explains, rereads John Locke's "Essay Concerning Human Understanding" (1690). She enjoys Virgil's pastoral and gardening passages, and faults Samuel Richardson's Pamela for a lack of modesty, recognizing Richardson's satire on female vanity and alluding to Don Quixote (1687).

The letters from England, dated 1753–1757, concentrate on her active social life and reluctance to return quickly to Carolina, despite Charles' desires. Eliza's decision to follow Charles dutifully and lovingly to Carolina rather than to remain in England to care for their two sons is further complicated by her enjoyment of the London theaters and museums and her more cosmopolitan friends.

The last letters postdate Charles' death in July 1758 and are naturally more effusive, as she details her intense and abiding grief for a husband she adored and admired. Letters to her sons reflect earlier ones to her brothers, underscoring reason-based virtue, piety, and filial duty. In the letter reporting Charles' death, she asserts his faith, religious sincerity, resignation to God's will, and hope for eternal salvation as traits to be emulated, establishing a motif threaded throughout her correspondence with them. Elsewhere, she chastises herself for excessive grief and then defends herself because she is mourning an exemplary Christian husband who blessed her life abundantly. Wearied by the varied demands of managing the Pinckney estate and settling debts, she nevertheless vows her gratitude for these diversions, revealing that she superintended a smallpox hospital during a 1760 outbreak. Nationalistically, she applauds and criticizes the ongoing efforts of Carolina's governor and the British military to squelch Cherokee raids on the Carolina frontier, expressing outrage over atrocities committed by the Indians but little over those inflicted upon them.

Pinckney's contributions to the colonial milieu are evident in the first noteworthy scholarship on her writings, an 1896 biography by her great-granddaughter Harriott Horry Ravenel, who greatly admired her ancestress as an embodiment of colonial culture. Published as part of Scribner's Women of Colonial and Revolutionary Times Series and largely based on Eliza Pinckney's letters and those of family and friends, it is considered by Elise Pinckney "the most significant early publication" about this dynamic colonial woman. Three notable twentieth-century publications provide an even more personal and penetrating portrayal, preserving Pinckney's views, interests, insights, and values in her own words. In 1936 the South Carolina branch of the National Society of the Colonial Dames of America salvaged and disseminated a 1756 recipe book in which Pinckney shares household advice. The most comprehensive and poignant portrait of Pinckney, though, emerges from the 1972 edition of the letterbook, edited by Marvin Zahniser, and the subsequent 1997 paperback edition, edited by Elise Pinckney. The introductory commentary in the 1997 edition illuminates Eliza's motivations and substantive contributions to agricultural progress, the success of the Carolina colony, and the establishment of the United States.

With the resurgence of feminism in the 1960s and 1970s, interest in Eliza Pinckney revived, as it did in two other female colonial writers whose themes and beliefs somewhat parallel Pinckney's: Anne Bradstreet and Phillis Wheatley. All three women received classical educations that informed their world views and writings, and all wrote from an essentially orthodox Christian perspective. Whereas Pinckney incorporates insights into the influence of rational thought on religious belief, she mirrors Bradstreet in memorializing a loving marriage and instilling an unwavering virtue and faith into the lives of her children.

In one of the final paragraphs of the letterbook, Pinckney seems acutely distressed by the "sacrilidgious Enemies to posterity" who cut down an old oak planted by Charles. Throughout the letters she depicts herself as a worshiper and observer of nature, one who, nonetheless, scientifically manages nature to achieve agricultural and economic progress. National and international in outlook, she was equally intent on fulfilling her religious obligations as a devoted wife and mother in order to perpetuate through her family—for posterity—the blessings concomitant to a virtuous life dedicated to noblesse oblige. It is her success in these single-mindedly interwoven public and private endeavors that has ensured Pinckney's prominence as an integral advancer of South Carolinian and American culture in the eighteenth and early nineteenth centuries.

The Novel

Karen Manners Smith

In the forty years preceding the Civil War, advances in printing technology and the unprecedented national growth of literacy produced an American reading public hungry for fiction and a publishing industry—authors, editors, publishers, and booksellers—eager to satisfy the new demand. In the South, only a few male authors, notably William Gilmore Simms, John Pendleton Kennedy, William Alexander Caruthers, and John Esten Cooke, were ready at this stage to abandon the traditional southern posture of genteel amateurism, but a number of women writers embraced the opportunity for professional authorship. It was a welcome alternative to teaching, the only other "respectable" profession open to an educated southern woman who needed to earn a living.

Most sources list about a dozen significant antebellum female novelists. Senior among these was Caroline Howard Gilman, who was born in Massachusetts and moved to South Carolina with her Unitarian minister husband in 1819, becoming fully committed to the South and the southern way of life. Gilman began her career as the editor of a series of popular periodicals before turning her attention to novels in the mid-1830s. Caroline Lee Hentz, another transplanted New Englander, married a French immigrant professor and followed him to a series of academic postings in the South. She taught young women alongside her husband, but after 1848 she earned much of the family living by writing novels. A passionate southern convert, she is perhaps best remembered for the heroine she created in *Linda; or, the Young Pilot of the Belle Creole* (1850) and its sequel, *Robert Graham* (1855), as well as the strongly propagandistic *The Planter's Northern Bride* (1854). Maria McIntosh (1803–1878), the daughter of prominent Georgia planters, ran the family plantation for a number of years after her parents died, but eventually moved to New York to join relatives. Never married, she turned to novel writing as a way to support herself and to keep her memories of the South alive. Eliza Ann Dupuy (1814–1880), a spinster and governess who lived in Mississippi before the Civil War, made her reputation between the 1840s and the 1870s with more than two dozen Gothic thrillers, many of them serialized in the New York *Ledger*. Catherine Anne Ware Warfield (1816–1877), like Dupuy a resident of Natchez, is known for fiction published after the Civil War, but her first, most famous, and most sensational novel, *The Household of Bouverie*, appeared in 1860. Mary Virginia Terhune (1830–1922), though born in Virginia, lived most of her adult life in the North. Her antebellum southern fiction earned her a national reputation, which she later parleyed into a lucrative career as the author of dozens of cookbooks and domestic advice manuals. Augusta Jane Evans Wilson (1835–1909), who made her home in Mobile, Alabama, became a best-selling author in 1859 with her second novel, *Beulah*, but is perhaps best remembered as a fiery southern propagandist of the Civil War era and the author of the postwar *St. Elmo* (1867), one of the five most successful novels in all of nineteenth-century American literature.

E.D.E.N. Southworth (1819–1899), whose book sales made her the most consistently popular author in nineteenth-century America, can be included in a list of antebellum southern novelists, though she was a resident of Washington, D.C., and not entirely sympathetic with southern social institutions. Almost all of Southworth's books have southern settings, but her ninth novel, *Mark Sutherland* (published in 1855 and also known as *India; or, The Pearl of Pearl Island*), opens with a slave owner freeing his slaves. Southworth would support the Union during the Civil War.

There are several other noteworthy, though less prolific southern women novelists of the period. Anna Cora Mowatt Ritchie (1819–1870), a northern actress and writer who married a Richmond, Virginia, newspaper publisher, produced several novels about the theater in addition to her most famous work, a satirical play entitled *Fashion* (1845). Sue Petigru King Bowen (1824–1875), a South Carolina socialite, published her only works—three novels and a pair of novellas set in the Deep South—during a brief period between 1854 and 1859. Sarah Anne Ellis Dorsey (1829–1879), lifelong supporter of Jefferson Davis and author of two popular Civil

War–era novels, was the niece of Catherine Warfield and a pupil of Eliza Dupuy. Caroline Gilman Jervey (1823–1877), Caroline Howard Gilman's daughter, became a novelist and poet and cowrote two books with her mother.

All of these southern writers, like their northern counterparts, were better educated than most middle- and upper-class women of their day, though the southerners were likely to be educated at home by parents and tutors. Several of them attended small schools and private female academies or "seminaries" in adolescence, but self-teaching, voracious reading, and access to family libraries may have accounted more for their intellectual growth than did formal schooling. Augusta Evans Wilson, who probably had the least formal education of any antebellum southern woman novelist, displayed the most erudition in her published work.

Southern women chose writing careers for a variety of reasons. Some started writing because they urgently needed the money: McIntosh had lost all her inheritance in the Panic of 1837; Hentz supported an improvident, invalid husband; Dupuy earned only a governess's wages in Natchez. E.D.E.N. Southworth was separated from her husband, poor, in ill health and nursing a desperately sick child when she began the career that would first rescue her from poverty and later make her a very rich woman. Other writers, such as Gilman and Warfield, economically secure through marriage or other means, wrote for the love of it. Still others, Terhune and Evans, for example, had ambitions for greatness beyond the strict professionalism of most women writers of their day. Throughout the period, several of these authors used novels as a way to promote understanding between the North and the South. Closer to the war, prosouthern and proslavery propaganda infused their writings. Whatever their motivation for writing, southern women novelists fully shared in the success of the American woman's novel before the Civil War, and many of them continued to produce popular fiction through the end of the century. Wilson was thought to have earned over $100,000 in royalties during her lifetime; it was estimated that Southworth made about $6,000 a year between 1857 and her death in 1899, $4,000 of it from her serialized books alone; Dupuy also made substantial sums, about $2,600 per serialized story; and Terhune's books earned her enough money to build a country estate and make a number of trips to Europe.

Women authors who wrote southern fiction were dependent on northern publishers for the large press runs and widespread distribution that made their books best sellers. This was true even in the case of writers such as Terhune and Wilson, whose early first editions had been published by small southern presses. Similarly, a number of southern women writers reached their largest audiences, North and South, by serializing their novels in the pages of the era's mass circulation periodicals—*Godey's Lady's Book, Graham's, Peterson's, Galaxy,* and the *Saturday Evening Post*—all of them published in northern cities. E.D.E.N. Southworth's first major novel, *Retribution,* was serialized in 1849 in the *National Era,* the Washington-based periodical that was to serialize Harriet Beecher Stowe's *Uncle Tom's Cabin* in 1851. In addition to ensuring widespread readership, the periodicals paid well. Both Southworth and Dupuy made much of their incomes between 1850 and 1880 through serialization in a single periodical, Robert Bonner's New York *Ledger.* Positive relationships with northern publishers persisted for southern women writers through the increasing sectional tensions of the 1850s and the actual disruption of communication during the war itself. In 1864, New York publisher J. C. Derby intervened in the attempted piracy of Wilson's pro-Confederate novel *Macaria,* subsequently arranging for all the royalties from the wartime northern edition to be held in trust for her until after the hostilities were over. Not only was the relationship with southern women writers lucrative for publishers, but northern readers remained loyal to their favorite southern novelists and continued to consume stories of southern life throughout the period.

Southern women's books were reviewed in newspapers all over the country and in all the most prestigious literary magazines. Even allowing for the mid-century tendency for critics to "puff" or promote certain authors—often colluding with publishers in this undertaking—it is nevertheless a fact that lengthy reviews of southern women's novels appeared on the same pages as reviews of books by male American authors and British literary giants such as Tennyson and Thackeray. Later generations of literary scholars would dismiss antebellum southern women's novels as subliterary, sentimental potboilers. (In fact nearly all antebellum southern fiction—with the exception of the works of Edgar Allan Poe and, possibly, William Gilmore Simms—would be excluded from the canon of American literature.) More recently, feminist literary scholars have rediscovered these early southern women's novels, finding a number of them stylistically and psychologically complex, and all of them rich in information about antebellum southern culture and gender roles.

The novels of all antebellum women writers, northern and southern, reflect the influence of British models, notably the romances of Walter Scott and the moral tales of Maria Edgeworth and Fanny Burney. American women writers, like their readers, were also attracted to the nature imagery of Keats and Wordsworth. They adored Dickens' comic characters and fell in love with Byron's troubled heroes. In fact, the Byronic hero is a close cousin of the high-strung, hotheaded, young aristocratic male in southern women's fiction of this period. The novelists' homage to the Romantic poets, and to Scott and Dickens, appears in extensive descriptions of scenery and lengthy dialect exchanges between minor characters. In southern novels, comic dialect interludes most often feature slave characters, although Gilman and Southworth and others also found comic material in low-status whites and German, Scottish, and Irish immigrants. Humor and descriptive passages in this literature seldom advance the plot, but they help to elaborate the southern *mise en scène*. (Novelists' self-indulgent scene-setting frequently irritated periodical publishers, most notably Southworth's publisher at the *Saturday Evening Post,* who wanted her serialized novels to have much shorter episodes.)

Charlotte Brontë was a particular favorite of the southern novelists; both the example of female heroism and the scenes of Gothic horror in *Jane Eyre* (1847) were strong influences on women's fiction of the 1850s and 1860s. Southern women writers were apparently fascinated by the idea of the madwoman in the attic, although in the case of Warfield's *Household of Bouverie* (1860) and Terhune's *True as Steel* (a novel written in 1872 but set in the antebellum South), the murderous, pyromaniac lunatic is a man. In addition to Brontë, other sources for southern women writers, especially Southworth, Warfield, and Dupuy, include the sensationalism of Samuel Richardson and the Gothic tales of Ann Radcliffe, though the American women novelists always embedded Gothic elements and violent sexual passions in stories whose overall framework was irreproachably moral and fully acceptable to nineteenth-century middle-class readers. Even in Dupuy's novels, for example, which abound in murder, kidnapping, necrophilia, and uncontrollable male sexual passions, the young heroines function as lodestars of morality, ultimately forgiving their tormentors and converting villains into kindhearted Christians and model husbands. While rarely resorting to the supernatural (ghost sightings always turn out to have rational explanations), a certain percentage of this literature relies on colorful elements of romance and melodrama similar to those found in the fiction of Cooper and Bulwer-Lytton: pirates, shipwrecks, duels, missing heiresses, wild rides, stormy nights, creepy castles, and sneering landlords.

Whether the individual author's preferred mode is the comic, the romantic, the Gothic, the psychological, or some combination of these, all of the antebellum southern women writers in this discussion are recognized alongside their northern counterparts as "domestic" novelists. And within the genre of domestic fiction as a whole, there are a number of key elements that are always present and transcend sectional particularities. First of all, domestic fiction is an exploration of the nature of woman and woman's role. Most of it contains a critique of marriage, or is at least critical of the male abuse of power in marriage. It is also consistently critical of weak, dishonest, vain, silly, or materialistic women, always contrasting such women with the novel's heroine(s). In setting, pace, and incident, the scenes are familial or social; illness, death, inheritance, pride, temperament, past injustices, and persistent—often irrational—misunderstandings fuel the conflicts that drive the plot.

Much domestic fiction is written in the tradition of the male *Bildungsroman*—the story of development—and some novels show a considerable degree of psychological complexity. The heroine is young, frequently an orphan, though in southern fiction she tends to have at least one living relative, often a father. A twist of fate—the collapse of her family through death or financial disaster (Southworth's 1859 *Hidden Hand* and Terhune's 1854 *Alone*) or the machinations of a malevolent rival or interloper (Dupuy's 1857 *The Planter's Daughter*)—casts her upon her own resources, at least temporarily, so that she may learn to grow in strength, honor, and wisdom. Once fully self-dependent and mature, the heroine ends up with the comforts and love and security denied her at the beginning; when she finally marries, her choice is a man who is truly worthy of her—either a reckless, arrogant youth she has transformed or a somewhat older man who has been destined for her throughout the book's long series of trials and misunderstandings. In Terhune's *The Hidden Path* (1855), for example, which has dual heroines, both types of union are celebrated. Isabelle, a successful writer, finally wins the love of Frank, whose vanity and gallantry had led him into a short-lived engagement with a silly young woman; and Bella, an impoverished orphan who becomes a schoolteacher, marries Maurice, a sober intellectual who has been waiting patiently for her to realize she loves him. In another example, the delicate but determined heroine of Southworth's *Changed Brides* (1869) and its sequel, *The Bride's Fate* (1869), seduced after a sham wedding ceremony, waits years in lonely exile for her ridiculously immature husband to appreciate her loyalty and conduct her through a legal marriage.

Southern domestic fiction differs in several important ways from its northern counterpart. Most significantly, the heroine in this fiction does not seek to transcend or escape the limitations of woman's role, as some northern heroines do in pursuing education, professional careers, or—rarely—permanent spinsterhood. Though she may become educated or work to support herself or to put God-given artistic or literary talents to use, the southern heroine always embraces marriage, motherhood, and domestic responsibility as her appropriate destiny. Wilson's intellectual heroine in *Beulah* (1859) learns this lesson. Deciding after years of resistance that she has been ignoring the imperatives of her heart and her womanhood, Beulah Benton gives up teaching and writing to marry the aristocratic Guy Hartwell and take up her position as a wife, mother, and leader of local society.

For the most part, southern women's fiction before the Civil War does not discuss or confront issues raised by the women's rights movement. Politics, for most of these writers, must have seemed impossibly distant, northern, and irrelevant to the traditional roles they promoted for women of their own section. A notable exception is Terhune's *Moss-Side* (1857), which explores the movement but, in keeping with the southern position, condemns it as an intellectual seducer of women and a threat to marriage and the family.

Southern domestic fiction glorifies the traditional woman's role because that role is seen as central to the preservation of the southern family and the extended community, which frequently includes dependent slaves and white neighbors of all classes. The heroine of southern women's fiction asserts her moral and intellectual independence within the overall context of submission to the patriarchal social system. Her failure to assume her role in the southern hierarchy threatens the system with collapse. The heroine in this literature learns that it is her responsibility, even when she is misunderstood—or temporarily banished—to hold fast to what she knows to be true because she is the conscience, the moral arbiter, of that system. Thus Hentz's eponymous heroine in *Eoline* (1852), originally fleeing her plantation home to avoid an arranged marriage, finds herself teaching at a girls' school and absorbing lessons in womanly responsibility from the other teachers. Eventually she learns to control her temper, comes to terms with the young man whom she discovers she loves, and assumes her rightful place as mistress of her husband's plantation and moral exemplar to the neighbors. Similarly, Southworth's Catherine Kavanaugh, in *The Curse of Clifton* (1852), a poor mountain girl who has married a wealthy Virginian, is left on her own by her rash and arrogant husband. She has learned to cope with the slaves and the crops of two plantations by the time her husband repudiates his false friends, recognizes his wife's true worth, and shoulders his own responsibility in southern society.

Not uncommonly in these antebellum novels, men who abuse patriarchal authority or neglect the responsibilities of southern manhood are punished. At the very least, their moral compasses have to be reset by the love and persistence of southern women. A greedy planter, the heroine's father in

Hentz's *Linda; or, the Young Pilot of the Belle Creole,* is burned to death in the explosion of a riverboat. Donald Montrose, in McIntosh's *The Lofty and the Lowly; or, Good in All and None All-Good* (1853), succumbs to the classic weaknesses of southern aristocrats: drinking, gambling, and idleness. He nearly destroys the plantation that is his inheritance and is forced to sell off slaves that have been in his family for generations. In the end he must meekly take business advice from a northerner and lessons in humane plantation management from his sister, a female cousin, and the woman he will eventually marry. In almost all of these novels, whether it is the young man or the young woman learning life's lessons, the goal is conformity to the southern social system and the affirmation of southern gender roles.

Heroines in antebellum southern novels are not usually southern belles, though they may be beautiful and sought after, and they are certainly not southern ladies. The authors of the southern domestic novel firmly reject the ideal of the southern lady. Her fragility and inactivity, her adherence to the purely ornamental, her parasitical dependence, and the superficiality of her occupations and accomplishments are seen as totally inimical to the southern woman's true calling. The southern lady is frequently satirized in southern domestic fiction; sometimes she is pitied, and sometimes she is the villain. Unless her experiences or her conscience transforms her from a southern lady into a southern woman, she does not succeed.

In many of Southworth's novels, passive, weak-willed women suffer and die. Gilman's novel *Recollections of a Southern Matron* (1838) contrasts the physically robust and morally purposeful heroine, Cornelia Wilton, with her cousin, Anna Allston, a southern lady of the languishing, dependent, and ornamental type, who eventually wastes away when the husband upon whom she has placed all her reliance dies in an accident. In the same book Gilman pillories a typical southern belle, the selfish and undisciplined flirt, Miss Lawton. For Gilman, the belle is a "body without a soul, and sometimes a dress without a body." Sue Petigru King Bowen's paired novellas, *Sylvia's World; and Crimes Which the Law Does Not Reach* (1859), also contrast stable and virtuous young women with frivolous coquettes, or belles. The beautiful young widow, Georgia Clifton, in Southworth's *The Curse of Clifton,* is the novel's villain. She wastes her late husband's fortune on fashionable dress and riotous city living, sends a vulnerable young woman to her death of starvation, and nearly destroys the marriage of the book's hero and heroine. A further aspect of her villainy is her illicit sexual passion for her stepson. Waging a literary war on the belle and the lady, southern women novelists insisted that their section could not afford to cultivate feminine ideals that included weakness, venality, or self-indulgence.

The promotion of a strong model of southern womanhood is only one aspect of the defense of southern culture undertaken by women novelists in the years before the Civil War. Faced after 1835 with a growing abolitionist movement and increasing tensions between the North and the South, McIntosh, Gilman, and Hentz, in particular, used novels to promote sectional understanding. In doing so they incidentally created southern local color fiction and some early versions of the plantation novel. The origin of the plantation novel is usually attributed to male authors—James H. Heath, William Gilmore Simms, and John Pendleton Kennedy—writing in the 1820s and 1830s. However, the setting and subject matter of novels by McIntosh, Gilman, and Hentz from the 1830s through the 1850s do not differ substantially from those of the male authors, except in the gender of the central character. In every other respect they share the characteristics of the genre.

Conscious of their role as sectional propagandists, southern women writers packed their books with descriptions of the southern climate and landscape, painting scenes of gracious living and warm hospitality on the plantation and depicting slavery as a benign institution, a far better program for the laboring classes than the miserable wage slavery of free white factory workers in the North. Slaves themselves appear mostly as stock characters: the beloved old nurse, or mammy, the irascible but talented cook, the comical male house servant or coachman (this last character sometimes resembles Shakespeare's wise fools). The South in these books is represented as a rural utopia, a collection of plantation neighborhoods headed by benevolent patriarchs, contrasted with the cold, materialistic urban North, where the loving bonds of the human community have been exchanged for individual progress and gain. McIntosh's *The Lofty and the Lowly* (1853) and her *Two Pictures; or, What We Think of Ourselves and What the World Thinks of Us* (1863), Gilman's *Recollections of a Southern Matron* (1838), Hentz's *Marcus Warland; or, The Long Moss Spring* (1852) and *The Planter's Northern Bride* (1854), along with Terhune's *Moss-Side* (1857), probably represent the most significant fictional elaborations of southern culture in defense of itself.

In these novels a favorite plot device for fostering understanding is the intersectional visit followed by the intersectional romance. And when romances blossom across the Mason-Dixon Line, it is always the northerner—male or female—who becomes converted to an appreciation of southern culture, even if the hero and heroine, finally married after all their difficulties, sometimes end up living in the North. McIntosh's *The Lofty and the Lowly* features a great deal of travel between Massachusetts and Georgia, and at least two intersectional unions. In Terhune's *Moss-Side,* the heroine's northern suitor becomes persuaded of the beneficence of slavery during a Christmas visit to a modest plantation, where he sees happy slaves enjoying a holiday under the generous supervision of the white family. In Hentz's *The Planter's Northern Bride,* both the heroine and her abolitionist father become converted to the southern cause after living on the hero's plantation. Marriages and visits symbolize the authors' hope that the North and the South will become reconciled to each other instead of drifting farther apart. Toward the end of the period, especially after the publication of *Uncle Tom's Cabin* (1851), the defense of southern life in southern women's novels becomes more intense and more propagandistic; characters in McIntosh and Hentz, for example, seem to abandon conversation for debates and orations on the comparative merits of slavery and abolition.

With the coming of the Civil War, some women novelists, such as Dupuy and Bowen, suspended their writing; others, like Southworth and Warfield, wrote as if the war were not happening. Hentz had died in 1856 and Ritchie was living in Europe. Gilman simply reissued two of her earlier novels, but McIntosh published *Two Pictures* (1863), which discusses sectional tensions without dealing with the war itself, and Sarah Ann Dorsey wrote *Lucia Dare* (1867), a novel about the experiences of an English heiress who finds herself in Texas in the middle of the Civil War. Perhaps the most powerful southern novel to appear during the war was Wilson's *Macaria,* a fierce piece of pro-Confederate propaganda that celebrated southern heroism and, unlike almost all previous examples of domestic fiction, did not hesitate to discuss politics or wade into the blood and gore of the battlefield. Martial and political though it is, *Macaria* is nevertheless a domestic novel because it features the stories of paired heroines, Electra and Irene, who happen to be in love with the same man. When Russell Aubrey dies in battle, the two heroines dedicate themselves to permanent spinsterhood and service to the women of the South, for which Wilson is still predicting, at the time of publication, a new existence as a separate nation. In eschewing the conventional marriage plot of southern domestic fiction, Wilson subverts the genre, but she reflects the realities of the war-torn South, foretelling the fate of many young women who will never marry and whose future lives will be filled with work heretofore unfamiliar to genteel southern women.

When Terhune wrote *Sunnybank* (1866), she had the benefit of knowing the war's outcome, but she did not share Wilson's fierce southern partisanship. In fact, the novel, set on a Virginia plantation during the war, and structured in epistolary style with paired heroines, is a remarkably successful attempt to use the narrative materials of the war without taking sides.

Terhune, living in New Jersey, was by this time a committed Unionist, though she never abandoned her love for her native state and her large southern family. During the war she had produced at least one novel, *Helen Gardener's Wedding Day; or, Colonel Floyd's Wards* (1863), which was critical of some southern institutions, including slavery and kin marriage. In the postwar years, Terhune and other antebellum southern novelists—Southworth, Evans, and Dupuy among them—would continue to produce works of fiction with southern settings. Their sales figures in the late nineteenth century benefited from the national spirit of reconciliation and a growing interest in a new, largely male-authored, popular plantation literature that celebrated the antebellum South as a golden age and place in American history.

Women's Magazines

Cindy A. Stiles

Writing in 1832 in one of the early issues of her magazine *Rose Bud,* founder and editor Caroline Gilman commented that in the decade of the 1830s it was apparent that for women the "needle is giving way to the pen." This observation aptly characterizes the expanding role women played in magazine publishing in the period 1825–1860, with southern women enjoying no small share of recognition in that arena. Whereas at the beginning of the century merely a dozen periodicals existed nationally, by 1825 there were almost one hundred. This figure multiplied immensely over the next quarter century, until by 1850 the United States could boast close to six hundred periodicals, with the South contributing approximately one hundred of them. This exponential growth in periodicals during the first half of the nineteenth century can be explained by the fact that the growth of the cylinder press combined with a rapidly expanding literate population created an unprecedented demand for reading material. The South had a more specific reason for founding journals and magazines in this period: through regional periodicals southerners hoped to overturn both British and northern condemnation of the southern states. As the South felt increasingly polarized from its northern neighbors as antislavery agitation intensified, magazines and journals became important forums for sectional pride and defense.

Nevertheless, during the period 1825–1860 a large number of southern periodicals dealt very little or very discreetly with sectional concerns in their pages. Among these were some twenty magazines begun primarily for the enjoyment and instruction of an expanding number of female readers. The editors of these periodicals—half of them women themselves—sought to prepare their readers to be educators of their children and moral guardians of their homes and husbands. A common misperception of nineteenth-century women's magazines holds that their pages were filled almost exclusively with vapid romances and frivolous entertainment. In fact, fiction composed only about 25 percent of the total content and in general was morally instructive and written with the intent of uplifting and guiding the lives of women readers. The majority of these women's magazines sought to prepare women to meet both the domestic and community obligations imposed upon them; magazines devoted purely to entertainment would serve no salutary purpose. If the education of women was a popular theme in these magazines, it was also a safe one, as it was widely understood by both writers and readers alike that women were to be educated for the private rather than for the public sphere.

Southern women's magazines could in no overt way be termed "reform" periodicals akin to those springing up in the North in this same period. In response to the advent of women's rights conventions in the North, for example, the editor of the *Southern Lady's Companion* in Nashville, Tennessee, chided participants for doing the work of men while neglecting the duties "belonging to the sphere in which they were placed by the Providence of God." Southern women, he affirmed, were rightfully content to leave "the rough conflicts with the outside world" to the stronger sex. But if the editors of women's magazines did not intend to change the social order, they nevertheless initiated a gentle revolution by adding legions of women readers to the population. Some of those readers found a voice through their contributions to the pages of these magazines, and a select few who became editors enjoyed one of the first careers available to women.

Like their counterparts in other areas of the country, women's magazines in the South wished to offer their readers smatterings from published material in literature, science, and the arts, without the more costly engravings and embellishments featured in their larger northern competitors such as *Godey's* and *Peterson's*. The *Southern Ladies' Book,* begun in Macon, Georgia, in January 1840, spoke for its genre in asking why its readers should not offer their viewpoints on matters that "appertained in any degree to the welfare and improvement of their sex." The fiction in the women's magazines was virtually always didactic in nature and thus fulfilled its mission to be morally instructive to its readers. Book reviews and editorials stressed virtue and piety as the cardinal virtues, as did the vast amount of sentimental poetry which, together with biography, made up a large percentage of the content. Because the relatively fledgling United States still looked to England for much of its literature, women's magazines contained reprints from the four major British reviews as well as foreign news items. There was some variety among these numerous magazines; while some leaned more heavily toward serious reading material, others contained lighter fare such as fashion, marriage announcements, and entertaining prose and verse.

Perhaps the biggest challenge the editors of these magazines faced was finding enough contributions to fill the pages of their publications. Publishers often sought to enlist the editorial skills of a well-known woman writer in an effort both to boost subscriptions and to attract contributions, and frequently editors were forced to write much of the material themselves. But even with a notable woman's name on the masthead, submissions were often so meager that the bulk of a magazine's contents was frequently pirated from other publications, most of them British. The lack of an international copyright law encouraged such a practice by enabling editors to borrow freely from overseas publications. Even those contributions that were original were largely imitative; with the United States having yet to develop a native literature of its own, English periodicals provided the acceptable standard.

It was also incumbent upon editors to be savvy about balancing the demands of their female readers with the mores and values of their conservative southern society. Although the women's magazines enjoyed a diverse readership, they were bought primarily by the upper and middle classes. The majority of antebellum southern women, burdened by domestic responsibility, had neither the time nor the income for reading. Thus, editors had to be sensitive to the attitudes of the merchant class that largely composed their audience. One particular challenge was posed by an increasing skepticism about fiction on the part of educators and clergy of the period. To some degree the women's magazines, generally accepted as morally upstanding, were exempt from attack. However, the boom in paperback publishing prior to the war intensified reactions against fiction. In response, editors sought to placate adversaries while at the same time continuing to meet the demands of their readership. One way they did so, and successfully, was to append to fictional titles a qualifying label, such as "Founded in Fact" or "A Tale from Truth." Together with the pat moral endings these fictional stories invariably contained, such labels appeased the detractors of fiction while still satisfying subscribers.

Editors did not always abide by societal constraints, though, and the resulting effects could be detrimental. Mary Chase Barney, editor of the *National Magazine, or Lady's Emporium* of Baltimore, begun in 1830, thought it necessary to give women readers a knowledge of, if not a voice in, political affairs. Her efforts were rebuked by readers who neglected to contribute to the magazine and by critics who questioned the appropriateness of an article on tariffs while there was a noticeable lack of romantic fiction. In disgust Barney asked, "Shall it be said with a sneer that a female has no right to meddle in politics? Has she no motive for desiring to understand the principles of a science in which the interest and happiness of her children are concerned? Away with such Turkish doctrines." Barney attempted to revive her flagging publication by introducing travel and biographical material as well as literary commentary. But her refusal to include romantic fiction and her unpopular efforts to engage women in the political life of the region doomed the magazine to extinction, and it folded within the year. By the 1850s, women's magazines in the South, like other periodicals in the region, found themselves drawn into the deepening political debate. But until then editors were wise to follow the example of Sarah Josepha Hale of *Godey's Lady's Book* of Philadelphia, who candidly addressed moral and social issues while deftly avoiding the political.

The early bankruptcy of many of these magazines was invariably, if indirectly, due to the growing political conflict. Early attempts by southerners like William Gilmore Simms to establish a tradition of letters in the South were thwarted once political sentiment became the focus of the region's literature. Those individuals who attempted to found periodicals in the South were often frustrated by a persistent preference of local readers for both British periodicals and, ironically, northern periodicals that were often hostile to southern institutions. Despite active campaigns to boycott them, the sale of northern periodicals continued to be great. While southern booksellers met these demands by their readers, their counterparts in the North refused to carry works by southern writers, especially as the political climate worsened. Increasingly, too, contributors were forced to send their work to periodicals in the North because those at home could not afford to pay them. And finally, southern magazines were hurt by a smaller reading public than in the North, by the difficulty of distributing magazines to readers in predominantly rural areas, and by the relative paucity of publishing houses in the South.

Nevertheless, the women's magazines that were begun both nationally and in the South during the antebellum period left an important legacy. Beyond the cultural value of southern magazines in this period, women's involvement with periodicals—as readers, writers, and editors—had significant sociological implications. Through the women's magazines, female readers were able to share in the cultural life of the nation, and as contributors and editors, women found not only an outlet for the expression of their ideas, but also one of the first socially sanctioned employment opportunities. Although many of these publications enjoyed only a short life, they added thousands of women readers to a perpetually expanding audience.

Caroline Howard Gilman

Cindy A. Stiles

Caroline Howard Gilman's first literary effort was in the form of a poem, "Jephthah's Rash Vow," written when she was sixteen and published in 1810 without her knowledge. In her autobiography, Gilman confesses that "when I learned that my verses had been surreptitiously printed in a newspaper, I wept bitterly, and was as alarmed as if I had been detected in men's apparel." Gilman's early fears of exposure in print were to undergo a profound change over the next two decades. Indeed, seventeen years after her embarrassment at being published, this change was evident when Gilman asked her sister to keep a letter private because it was "too womanish, and wifelike, and motherish." Five years later, at age thirty-eight, Gilman distinguished herself as the first professional woman in South Carolina as well as the first female editor of a southern periodical in the nineteenth century.

The youngest daughter of five children, Caroline Howard was born in Boston on October 8, 1794, to Anna Lillie and Samuel Howard. After losing her father at age three and her mother seven years later, Caroline went to live with an older sister in Watertown, Massachusetts, paying winter visits to her brothers Charles and Samuel, who had established themselves as merchants in Savannah, Georgia. Although Gilman described her formal education as "exceedingly irregular, a perpetual passing from school to school," she developed an avid interest in literature, music, and foreign languages, learning to play the guitar at age fifteen by listening to a schoolmate's lessons and writing a pseudonymous epistolary novel. When she was sixteen, Caroline met her future husband, Samuel, at a party in Cambridge. A year later, in 1811, Samuel Gilman graduated from Harvard, and after several interim jobs, in 1819 he accepted a position as minister of the Second Independent Church of Charleston, South Carolina, which at that time had just adopted Unitarianism. After his ordination, Samuel and Caroline married, and the couple moved to Charleston.

Gilman spent her first eleven years in Charleston adjusting to her new home and giving birth to seven children, three of whom died in infancy. During this period, she wrote only a few scattered poems before undertaking in 1832 her most significant project, the editorship of the *Rose* magazines. The periodical began as a weekly children's magazine titled the *Rose Bud,* which in 1833 became the *Southern Rose Bud,* adding more adult material without relinquishing the juvenile segments. With the third volume the magazine became a bimonthly, doubling its pages and becoming increasingly more adult in content, and with the fourth, in 1835 the periodical became fully a magazine for adults, newly titled the *Southern Rose.* Under that name it enjoyed a successful run of four more volumes until its expiration in 1839.

The *Southern Rose* included, in addition to original fiction and poetry, translations of French and German writings, travel accounts, reviews of literature and music, and critiques of the American copies of the four major British reviews of the day. Although a great many of the contributions to the magazine came from Gilman herself, the *Southern Rose* was also an early forum for the work of prominent writers of the nineteenth century, among them Nathaniel Hawthorne, Harriet Beecher Stowe, and Charleston's own William Gilmore Simms. Even before Simms, Gilman called for a distinctly southern literature, and the pages of the *Rose* showcase those efforts. Her attempts to promote regional writers and subjects were in large part a response to regional antipathies developing between North and South. As sectional tensions began to escalate in the 1830s, Charleston became a closed city marked by an entrenched conservatism. Such a climate was inhospitable to the development of an imaginative literature like that germinating in the North as the seeds of the American Renaissance.

Despite this impediment, Gilman successfully established her *Rose* magazines, though not without a calculating finesse. The contents of the periodical illustrate that Gilman had to walk a veritable tightrope between fervent defense of the ways of her adopted southern home, which was stubbornly resistant to progress, and a gentle defiance of such inertia through the promotion of intellectual, cultural, and material progress. If the paradoxes evident in the pages of the *Rose* reflect those in the culture, they also mirror tensions within Gilman herself, as she sought to reconcile within herself her role as wife of a Unitarian minister with her needs as an intellectual and professional woman. Most prominent are Gilman's conflicting responses to race and gender issues as she sought to meet the approval of the status quo in Charleston at the same time that she often, if subtly, opposed it.

As early as the first volume of the *Rose Bud,* Gilman laments the lack of recognition afforded talented and intelligent women. Under a column of local Charleston news, Gilman mentions the publication of a "Catalogue of Youthful Genius and Learning" in which, she dryly notes, "Our little girls will be surprised to learn that there are only nine of their sex in the whole seventy." One of Gilman's intentions in founding the magazine was to promote women's education through numerous references to the opening of female academies, to literature written by and about women, and to accomplishments by women in the arts and sciences. In describing one school for girls in Georgia, Gilman gloats, "Then comes a list of Text Books used at the school. . . . Read it, . . . ye haughty specimens of the masculine gender, and tremble at the prospect that your dominion over the realms of science and literature is to be shared by the 'weaker members.'" However, in characteristic retreat from such a brazen assertion, Gilman appeases those same male readers when she tells them that better-educated wives will "adorn and dignify your homes, . . . appreciate your own advancement in intellectual excellence," and "give to your children those happy lights and impulses which will secure the best interests of coming generations." Perhaps because Gilman could not explicitly acknowledge her feminist impulses, she often created fictionalized characters to serve as mouthpieces for her own viewpoints. One humorous anecdote appearing in the *Southern Rose* reads: "A lady meeting a girl who had lately left her service, inquired, 'Well, Mary, where do you live now?' 'Thank ye, ma'am, replied the girl; I don't live now; I am married.'"

Gilman had to tread even more carefully in her treatment of slavery than she did in her handling of women's issues. In most of her depictions of slavery, black slave and white master are yoked together in a relationship of benevolent reciprocity. Gilman is careful to reveal in her stories and sketches the mutual responsibility slave and master feel toward each other and the contentment with plantation life of both. It is apparent in these sketches that Gilman felt compelled to defend southern ways, as she does in a review of Maria Sedgwick's novel, *The Linwoods* (1836). Her fictional young reviewers, Medora and Lisa, praise the work but decry its antislavery sentiments. Medora exclaims, "It is not true that African slaves pine for 'free breath;'

they are the most careless, light-hearted creatures in the world. . . . Let them come and stay with us awhile. We will show them happy black faces enough, particularly on plantations, to modify their views." As early as the second volume of the *Rose Bud*, a series of letters, ostensibly from a northern visitor, reveal Gilman's shrewd editorial decision to defend her region while avoiding any charge of polemics in her magazine. The visitor comments that her young son is made uncomfortable by the sight of the military guard in Charleston, whose nightly installation provides a watch against slave insurrection. Nevertheless, he "is convinced, as every one must be, who is not determinedly obtuse, that the system here is kindly and wisely ordered, and that unusual happiness prevails among the class of individuals, who seem to labor under restrictions."

Although Gilman keenly understood the oppression of women by antebellum southern society, rarely does that understanding extend to empathy for the similar oppression of black slaves. A noteworthy exception is a tale entitled "Old Stephen" (1838), which appears in the final volume of the *Southern Rose*. Stephen, a slave, takes to beating his wife after a night of drinking. His wife retaliates, both verbally and physically, and extracts a promise from Stephen that he will never dare beat her again. Stephen displays his feelings of emasculation by riding into town in his wife's clothing, whereupon he is further humiliated by his master and his fellow slaves. Having disgraced himself completely, Stephen takes his own life in an act of self-assertion praised by Gilman, who calls Old Stephen "a spirit more unbending and unconquerable than Napoleon himself." Although Gilman lauds Stephen, an equally intriguing facet of the story is the corresponding defiance of Old Stephen's wife against spousal abuse. Thus in linking race and gender abuse in a tale in which both woman and slave strike out against their oppressors, Gilman displays a rare understanding of the matrix of southern race relations in which gender and race are inextricably linked. Unfortunately, if Gilman perceived the mutual oppression of women and slaves in her society, she customarily felt restrained by that same society from expressing it.

Between the start of the *Rose Bud* in 1832 and the publication of a collaborative book of poetry with her daughter Caroline in 1874, Gilman edited a second periodical for eight years and published a total of sixteen books, many of which were serialized in the pages of the *Rose* magazines. Her three novels, in particular, are important registers of the lives of antebellum women and Gilman's complex response to them. Clarissa Gray Packard, heroine of *Recollections of a New England Housekeeper* (1834), soon after her marriage finds herself resentful of her husband Edward's constant preoccupation with business and civic affairs, while she must manage a string of impudent, drunken, and generally inefficient servants. Gilman's own ambiguity about women's domestic trials is suggested by Clarissa's conflicting attitudes toward woman's sphere: she describes housekeeping as "the fang-like chains of custom," yet she also evinces resignation to male authority. Clarissa advises young housewives like herself, "Oh, young and lovely bride, watch well the first moments when your will conflicts with his to whom God and society have given the control. Reverence his wishes even when you do not his opinions."

In *Recollections of a Southern Matron* (1837), Cornelia Wilton is very much Clarissa Packard's southern counterpart. Like Clarissa, Cornelia experiences a growing sense of frustration and despair upon realizing that the role of plantation mistress is rife with loneliness and adversity. As her northern counterpart had done, Cornelia realizes that in order to fulfill her duties as wife and mother she must relinquish much of her independence and assertiveness. Nevertheless, it is not without a suggestion of resentment that she cautions her readers that "to repress a harsh answer, to confess a fault, and to stop (right or wrong) in the midst of self-defence, in gentle submission, sometimes requires a struggle like life and death. . . . [A woman's] first study must be self-control, almost to hypocrisy."

Gilman's third novel, *Love's Progress; or, Ruth Raymond* (1840), departs from the format of her two earlier novels in its use of gothic and psychological material. The title character is a strong, noble young woman whose father grows progressively madder, first driving his wife to a premature death, then becoming so possessive of Ruth that he imagines he has killed her suitor, Alfred. Fearing discovery and capture, Ruth's father kidnaps his daughter and flees from New England to Trenton Falls, New York. He is about to end both of their lives when Alfred suddenly emerges to save Ruth, though her father dies. The novel ends with this remark from Alfred that is disturbing in its implications: "I have traced the self-sacrificing progress of your heart's love, through life's varied duties, and I know that the tender daughter will be the faithful wife." Through Alfred's comment, Gilman implies the equivalence of woman's life with both father and husband, a subservience shared by the heroines of all three of Gilman's novels and quite possibly by the author herself. In fact, in writing *Love's Progress*, Gilman conceded that through the novel she had hoped to record the story of her own life, but in its completion it represented only a fragment.

Also notable among Gilman's publications is *The Letters of Eliza Wilkinson* (1839), an account of the Revolutionary War told through the perspective of its outspoken young heroine. Gilman's collected letters, too, provide a chronicle of seventy historically significant years in the nation's history. After her husband Samuel's death in 1858, Gilman remained in Charleston until 1862, when her house on Orange Street was struck by a shell, prompting her to move to her daughter's home in Greenville, South Carolina, for the remainder of the war. While in Greenville, Gilman took an active part in the war effort, becoming director of the Greenville Ladies Association in Aid of the Volunteers of the Confederate Army. When the war was over, Gilman returned to Charleston and lived there until 1873, at which time she moved to her daughter's home in Washington, D.C. She died there on September 15, 1888, shortly before her ninety-fifth birthday.

As one of the most popular and prolific women of the antebellum South, Caroline Gilman was a gentle reformer who defended southern culture at the same time that she sought to improve its values and direction. She was also an early feminist in the sense that as a woman active in both the public and private spheres she helped blur the boundaries between the two and thus served as a model for legions of her female contemporaries. By introducing hundreds of women to the reading public, Gilman involved them in the social, intellectual, and political life of their city, region, and nation. If to a great degree the inflexible conservatism of southern patriarchal culture curtailed Gilman's vision on the issue of slavery, in the area of women's rights she provided a valuable model of achievement, giving her female readers the knowledge of and the desire for something better.

The Grimké Sisters

Ellen H. Todras

In the entire 245-year history of slavery in America, only two southern women had the will and conviction to speak out against this most peculiar institution. The Grimké sisters, Sarah (1792–1873) and Angelina (1805–1879), were born into the southern aristocracy at a time when slavery was expanding throughout the South as a result of the cotton gin and its economic implications for plantations. From their pedigree, no one would have expected social activism to be a central factor in the Grimké sisters' lives. Their father, Charles Faucheraud Grimké, had served as a colonel in the Revolutionary War, was a judge on the Supreme Court of South Carolina, and owned a number of successful plantations. Their mother, Mary Smith Grimké, was a direct descendant of Thomas Smith, one of the original eight proprietors of Carolina. She counted colonial and state governors among her ancestors. Her father, one of the richest men in the state, was known as "Banker Smith of Broad Street."

The Grimkés had fourteen children, eleven of whom survived infancy and early childhood. Sarah was the sixth of these children, and Angelina the youngest. Sarah was twelve years older than Angelina. Even as a young girl, Sarah exhibited a disgust for slavery. For example, against the rules of her household and the laws of South Carolina, little Sarah taught her waiting maid to read, until the pair was discovered and severely reprimanded.

Sarah loved learning and eagerly joined in her brother Thomas' studies.

When he began to learn Latin, however, Sarah's parents objected to her participation, and no amount of begging dissuaded them. Subjects such as Latin were for boys only. That was the end of Sarah's formal education. Nevertheless, Judge Grimké was said to have been proud of his daughter's intelligence, claiming that if she had been born a boy, she would have made the best jurist in the United States. Sarah, on the other hand, bitterly regretted her lack of education throughout her life.

When Sarah was twelve, Thomas went to Yale College to continue his studies. Sarah was devastated by the departure of this favorite brother. When, shortly thereafter, the baby Angelina was born, Sarah pleaded with her parents to let her be Angelina's godmother. Her parents agreed, thinking it might do Sarah some good to have this new responsibility. Thus began the historic relationship between the two sisters. Angelina followed Sarah everywhere and even called her "Mother," indicating the role Sarah played in her upbringing. Sarah, a great intellect, encouraged Angelina to think for herself.

As Angelina grew up, Sarah realized that she could not protect her "precious Nina" against the horror of slavery. When Angelina was twelve, for example, she attended a day school for the daughters of the finest families of Charleston. Yet one day Angelina fainted there because of the wretched condition of a young slave boy who had been beaten for disobedience. Eventually the sisters would find ways to act upon their responses to the slave system.

Both Sarah and Angelina were influenced by the Second Great Awakening, a religious revival movement that stressed the individual's free will and ability to improve society. At age twenty-four, Sarah experienced a religious conversion that promised to give her life new meaning. Instead of dancing, reading novels, and attending pleasant social gatherings, she began to attend prayer meetings, read religious books, and pay charitable visits to the poor.

In 1818, Judge Grimké took ill with an undiagnosed disease. The following year, his Charleston doctors recommended a physician in Philadelphia, and the judge took Sarah with him to see this man. During their time in Philadelphia, Sarah made the acquaintance of several Quakers. She found herself attracted to their simple dress and plain ways. Although her father died in August, Sarah remained in Philadelphia for several more months, learning about this new faith. After her return to Charleston, she continued to read Quaker books. In 1821 Sarah, age twenty-seven, became a Quaker and moved back to Philadelphia.

Angelina at this time was sixteen, involved with the hectic Charleston social scene. But over the next few years she too experienced a conversion, first to the Presbyterian faith, and then, after a long visit from Sarah, a more radical conversion to Quakerism. The year 1827 found Angelina at odds with her family, sickened by their material focus and by their unquestioning acceptance of slavery, which to Angelina was so contradictory to the dictates of Christianity. In vain she tried to convince her family to give up their slaves. Finally, in despair, Angelina too moved to Philadelphia in 1829.

The sisters lived with a fellow Quaker woman, enjoying the freedom of being without the constrictions placed upon southern women and without the constant reminder of slavery. Quaker women were considered the spiritual equals of men and thus were allowed to be ministers. Although Sarah had experienced difficulty in being accepted as a speaker in Quaker meetings, she continued to study for this calling. Angelina considered the ministry as well and thought about teaching. Eventually, however, the restrictions of Quaker life frustrated the more assertive and volatile Angelina.

At the same time that Angelina was chafing under the Quaker life-style, the abolition movement was gaining strength and numbers in the Northeast. By 1833 the sisters were discussing abolition between themselves and in their letters to others. Many of their fellow Quakers admonished them for this interest. Although Quakers were generally against slavery, they frowned upon abolition, because it was so radical in nature and because it drew people away from contemplation of God. Sarah adhered to the Quaker ways, but Angelina grew more and more impatient with them. In May 1835 Angelina confided in her diary for the first time in five months: "I have become deeply interested in the subject of abolition. I had long regarded this cause as utterly hopeless, but since I have examined anti-slavery principles, I find them so full of the power of truth, that I am confident that not many years will roll by before the horrible traffic in human beings will be destroyed in this land of Gospel privileges."

Angelina became an avid reader of William Lloyd Garrison's newspaper the *Liberator*. In the summer of 1835 Angelina stepped beyond her Quaker boundaries, and the boundaries of respectable women of the time, to write a letter to Garrison, thanking him and other abolitionists for not backing down under the pressure of widespread criticism of the abolition movement. "The ground upon which you stand," she wrote, "is holy ground: never— never surrender it." And then she identified herself with the cause of abolition: "If persecution is the means which God has ordained for the accomplishment of this great end, EMANCIPATION, then . . . I feel as if I could say, LET IT COME; for it is my deep, solemn, deliberate conviction, that *this is a cause worth dying for*." Angelina never dreamed Garrison would publish the letter, but he did. The Quakers ordered Angelina to retract the letter, but she refused. Sarah and the rest of the family were distressed at the disgrace she had brought upon the family, but Angelina maintained, "I could not blame the publication of the letter, nor would I have recalled it if I could."

By 1836, Angelina felt a great need to contribute to the abolitionist movement. In the space of a few short weeks, she wrote the pamphlet "Appeal to the Christian Women of the South," in which she exhorted her southern sisters to act against slavery. With characteristic logic she argued, "Are you willing to enslave *your* children? You start back with horror and indignation at such a question. But why, if slavery is *no wrong* to those upon whom it is imposed?" She sent the manuscript to the American Anti-Slavery Society, which published it immediately. In the North the pamphlet became a mainstay of abolition literature, but in the South it led to her being banned in Charleston.

The American Anti-Slavery Society also invited Angelina to speak to women's groups in New York about her experience with slavery. At first, Sarah was undecided as to whether to accompany Angelina. However, the rudeness of a respected Quaker elder toward her while she was speaking at a meeting was the final straw, convincing her that for her too it was time to abandon their Quaker life.

The next three years mark a period of intense activism in the sisters' lives. They arrived in New York City in October 1836 and immediately joined in a three-week training session that the American Anti-Slavery Society had organized for forty of its most trusted agents (i.e., speakers). Angelina and Sarah were the only women present but were consistently treated as equals. Here the sisters received training in arguments to present in speeches about abolition, techniques in turning a hostile crowd, and so on. At first Sarah was there only as Angelina's companion, but she soon decided that she too would speak about her experiences.

The sisters were originally going to speak in women's parlors. Their lecture aroused so much interest that it was clear that no parlor could hold the attendees. And so they arranged to speak in a church—a public place. This marked one of the first times that women addressed people publicly in the United States. These first meetings were for women only, since for a woman to address men publicly was yet a further scandal. The first speaking engagement, on December 16, 1836, was a complete success, with both sisters speaking about their experiences to avid listeners.

The sisters continued to speak out against slavery in New York through the spring of 1837. At this time they also helped establish the first national abolitionist organization for women. The sisters were the first to point out the prejudice within the very ranks of women interested in abolition, for at the New York women's meeting groups, no black women were present. In May 1837, at the first convention of the American Female Anti-Slavery Society, seventy-one delegates attended, with Angelina and Sarah representing the state of South Carolina. In her biography *The Grimké Sisters from South Carolina* (1967), historian Gerda Lerner counts as their most significant contribution at this convention "their insistence that race prejudice must be fought in the North as well as in the South."

In May 1837 the sisters moved to Boston to begin a speaking tour through New England. Over the next six months, according to Lerner, they spoke to an estimated forty thousand people, many of whom became converts to the cause of abolition. As the tour progressed both sisters gained enormous confidence in their abilities to present arguments to the public. Angelina was the better speaker, but Sarah's written work was original and highly respected. The sisters' speaking had unanticipated repercussions as well. The audiences they addressed became mixed (both men and women listening) over time, and although this seemed perfectly logical to the sisters, it was an abomination to many others throughout the country.

The issue of women speaking out against slavery became known as "the woman question." One critic of the Grimkés, Catherine Beecher, wrote a book called *Essay on Slavery and Abolition with reference to the Duty of American Females* (1837). This book was addressed specifically to Angelina. In it Beecher defended colonizationists, who believed in freeing the slaves gradually and sending them back to Africa. She also defended the concepts that women should be subordinate to men and that women had no business in any public sphere of the antislavery movement. At about the same time as this book was released, an association of Congregational ministers issued a pastoral letter condemning women as public reformers and refusing to let abolitionists speak in Congregational churches. Both Sarah and Angelina addressed these denouncements in writing.

Angelina took on Catherine Beecher in a series of thirteen letters, originally published in the *Liberator* and in 1838 published as the book *Letters to Catherine E. Beecher in Reply to an Essay on Slavery and Abolitionism Addressed to A. E. Grimké*. In condemning gradual approaches to emancipation, Angelina wrote, "I have seen too much of slavery to be a gradualist." And in defending woman as man's equal in every respect, she wrote: "I affirm, that woman was never given to man. She was created, like him, in the image of God, and crowned with glory and honor; created only a little lower than the angels,—not, as is almost universally assumed, a little lower than man."

Sarah addressed her letters to fellow abolitionist Mary Parker. They were published first in the New England *Spectator,* then in the *Liberator,* and finally in 1838 as the single volume *Letters on the Equality of the Sexes.* She wrote a total of fifteen letters, addressing such issues as education, the pitfalls of marriage, and the biblical foundation of the sexes' equality. Early in the letters, she wrote: "I ask no favors for my sex. I surrender not our claim to equality. All I ask of our brethren is, that they will take their feet from off our necks, and permit us to stand upright on that ground which God designed us to occupy." The letters were a seminal writing in feminist theory and have become a classic in that field.

In February 1838, Angelina Grimké broke yet another barrier when she addressed the Massachusetts state legislature on the issue of slavery. Two months later she delivered a series of six speeches at the famous Odeon theater in Boston, to sold-out houses and great acclaim.

Over the previous few months, Angelina had become engaged to Theodore Weld, a great and highly respected abolitionist. Shortly after the Odeon lectures, Sarah and Angelina left Boston to attend the national antislavery conventions in Philadelphia. There they met up with Theodore, and he and Angelina were wed on May 14, 1838. It had been decided that Sarah would live with them. They moved to a house in Fort Lee, New Jersey, where the sisters learned to houseclean and cook, and Theodore crossed the Hudson River to work at the national office of the American Anti-Slavery Society.

They also began work on one of the most powerful antislavery books ever written, *American Slavery As It Is: Testimony of a Thousand Witnesses* (1839). Theodore compiled the accounts with the help of Sarah and Angelina, and of course with their personal accounts of what they had witnessed in their early lives.

After this period, Angelina bore three children and retreated from the public scene. She continued to work for abolition, but in a more private capacity. Sarah continued to write for the cause of women's rights, although many of these works ("The Education of Women," "The Condition of Women," "Essay on the Laws Respecting Women," "Marriage," and "Sisters of Charity") were not published until the late twentieth century. Both sisters were vitally interested in the budding women's rights movement and attended several annual conventions after 1848.

Angelina spoke in public again in 1863, on behalf of the women's effort for the Union Army during the Civil War. After the war, the sisters came across an article mentioning two young southern black men named "Grimkie" studying at a college in Pennsylvania. Of course they wondered if there were any connection between themselves and these men. Angelina wrote to them, and she and Sarah found to their amazement that these young men were their nephews, sons of their brother Henry and one of his slaves. The sisters and Weld immediately embraced the brothers as the long-lost relatives that they were and virtually adopted them into the family.

In 1870, when Angelina was sixty-five years old and Sarah was seventy-eight, they organized a march of women to vote in the local election in their hometown of Hyde Park, Massachusetts. Even though voting was illegal for women, and even though there was a blizzard that night, the sisters led a group of women to the polls, where they cast their votes in a separate ballot box that would ultimately be discarded. This demonstration marked the first time that any women in Massachusetts went to the polls.

Sarah died in 1873, and Angelina in 1879. Both sisters made significant contributions to the reform movements of their day, Angelina more to the abolition movement, and Sarah to the women's rights movement. Both are remembered as examples of living one's beliefs and putting principles into action.

Louisa S. McCord

Richard C. Lounsbury

The place of Louisa S. McCord (1810–1879) in southern literature has not been settled—it has scarcely been investigated. Indeed, by whom ought her contribution to be assessed? Economists have stressed her writings on political economy; intellectual historians have preferred to focus upon her uniqueness as an intellectual woman in the South; to political and social historians, she has offered testimony—testimony seldom well received, for she defended slavery and woman's traditional role—of southern women and of the class of slave-owning planters to which she belonged. Because she published only one book of poetry, *My Dreams* (1848), some fugitive poems in newspapers, and one play, *Caius Gracchus* (1851), she has seemed to supply but little material to literary historians for whom literature has meant primarily fiction, poetry, and drama. It is a regrettable, and unhistorical, narrowness, and especially regrettable toward an author who preferred to compose in many genres.

McCord wrote poetry, tragedy, political essays. Her letters are vigorous and astute. Late in life she ventured a memoir of her father: lawyer, politician, and president of the Bank of the United States, Langdon Cheves. A particular situation might call forth from her a multiple response. She wrote essays on woman's role and a long poem in blank verse, "Woman's Progress." Against British abolitionists embracing Harriet Beecher Stowe's *Uncle Tom's Cabin* (1851), she wrote essays in southern periodicals, but against their chief aristocratic patron she adopted the form of an open letter: her "Letter to the Duchess of Sutherland from a Lady of South Carolina" (1853) emulated Edmund Burke's *Letter to a Noble Lord* (1796) with an irony and wit not unworthy of its model. Perceiving her southern world to be embattled, she had resolved to stand up for it. But her resolution had come also from deeper sources. Although her mother's early death in 1836 had left her, in her twenties, in charge of a numerous household, and being later married with three children of her own and deriving most of her livelihood from her management of Lang Syne, her plantation near Columbia, nevertheless she was troubled, as she wrote in 1848, by her "effortless life," which was, "to a restless mind, a weary fate to be doomed to; and as no other door is open to me, I may as well push on at this." By "this," she meant her literary ambition, the fuel of her writings until failing eyesight and civil war diverted, and for the most part crushed, her hopes as a writer.

Her first published works, both appearing in 1848, *My Dreams* and a translation of the French economist Frédéric Bastiat's *Sophismes économiques,* demonstrated concisely the incongruity, at least in the eyes of the public, that would characterize McCord's writings. Women did not write on political economy. True, it was only a translation, but the next year McCord was contributing her own essays on that subject to the *Southern Quarterly Review.* If *My Dreams* looked to be more customary—it was a collection of poems, mostly in lyric meters, and women wrote such with regularity—they were strange poems. Caroline May's anthology, *The American Female Poets* (1848), which included two poems from *My Dreams,* praised McCord's talents and her mind "by nature strong" but regretted that her "vivid imagination and warm feeling" had not been "well disciplined by good taste and correct judgment." Perhaps it was the plethora of meters, not only among but within poems, that was troublesome. Although McCord remains carefully detached in her poetry, avoiding any autobiographical reference, the poems dwell much on loneliness, often as the price that must be paid for striving to rise above something—McCord never states what—that clings from below. There are hints in the poems that a reader can use, however uncertainly, to locate their author, for instance, McCord's restlessness in "The Fire-fly":

> What though thou, like me, must find—
> Born to Earth, doomed to regretting—
> Vainly that the restless mind
> Seeks to soar, its birth forgetting?

But in general *My Dreams* has proved rebarbative. It is a journeyman's book of illustrative examples, to show, or test, what the poet can do. She writes, for example, in "To My Father":

> Doubting and trembling still, I cast my lines,
> Then, here, before the world; and it must judge
> 'Twixt me, and my own struggling thoughts, which rise,
> Now in Hope's wild commotion, and now sink
> Back, back, upon myself and nothingness.

Unexpectedly—for classical tragedy is a genre traditionally excluding the person of the author—McCord's *Caius Gracchus* has seemed to supply what the more intimate genre of lyric poetry denied, a portrait of the tragedian. Its models were irreproachable, the first and most important of them being Shakespeare, whom McCord called "that great master of the human mind." But its heroes were less so. In an 1848 letter replying modestly to criticism of an early draft, McCord nevertheless protested: "I must stand up though for the Gracchi. They are among my *bona fide* heroes. Plutarch from whom I have pilfered largely, gives them I think a high position;—and does not [German historian Barthold Georg] Niebuhr (I ask, for truly I am lamentably difficient in information and have forgotten what little I have known about it) consider them as having nobly acted in a good cause?" In 133 B.C. Tiberius Gracchus had been murdered by enemies who opposed his land and other reforms. His brother Gaius, whose story McCord skillfully telescopes in her play, after two years of success restoring and augmenting his brother's reforms, was killed in 121 B.C. with thousands of his supporters.

But while she admired the Gracchi, it was to develop the roles of their mother, Cornelia, and Gaius' wife, Licinia, that McCord went to Shakespeare's *Coriolanus,* where the hero's conversations with his mother and wife about his proper duty echo in the similar confrontations in *Caius Gracchus.* There was, too, John Dryden's *Cleomenes* (1692). Cleomenes was a Spartan king whom the Greek biographer Plutarch had chosen to pair with Gaius Gracchus in his parallel lives of Greek and Roman statesmen, and in Dryden's play the hero's mother and wife debate with him their duty even in the face of death. But much as these precedents had to offer, McCord expanded the roles of the wife and, more, Cornelia the mother in order to address at length and in dramatic terms the contemporary dispute over woman's place in society—to such a degree that McCord's friend Mary Chesnut retitled the play when introducing McCord in her diaries as "she who wrote *The Mother of the Gracchi.*" Not only that, but Cornelia was taken to be the author's self-portrait. Appearance and manner confirmed. The American sculptor Hiram Powers, for whom, at his studio in Florence, McCord sat in 1859 during a tour of Europe, carved his bust of her in austere Roman republican dress. She was also remembered by a former tutor of her children as possessing a mind "Roman in its cast, and heroic in its energy, . . . in person Mrs. McCord might personate Cornelia herself."

De Bow's Review interpreted the whole play to be an illustration of the South's predicament, which in turn had nourished McCord's splendid dramatic verse. "In the agitated state of public feeling which has prevailed in South Carolina for some years past, exist important requisites for the nourishment and development of the poetic faculty in its greatest vigor. The idea of external oppression, exciting personal feeling, and turning the mind to the contemplation of examples of heroic resistance, has, in past times, produced the noblest specimens of eloquence, and plumed the wings of poesy to her most sustained flights." This eloquence McCord poured also into her prose. From 1849 to 1856 she contributed at least fourteen lengthy articles to the *Southern Quarterly Review, De Bow's Review,* and the *Southern Literary Messenger.* The articles have been cited often by political and social historians, not always with a due sense of the complexity of their arguments in form and purpose—a failing largely owing to the fact that McCord's prose writings have been analyzed only rarely as literature. The want of criticism is unfortunate. Albeit she might adopt a position common among her fellow southerners, the kinds of arguments chosen, the style and disposition they take, the variety of tone and of generic influences make her essays unique. Paradoxes ought to warn. Praising slavery as both a civilizing force of Western civilization and the protection of the slaves, she also informed a visitor from Rhode Island that "she would prefer to have $25,000 in good bank stock rather than $100,000 in negroes and plantations." Was it an easy and comfortable defender of woman's traditional role who wrote that "the positions of women and children are in truth as essentially states of bondage as any other"? Finally, although the polemical occasion for an article might demand the appearance of certainty, beside her essays there lies always the counterpoint of *Caius Gracchus.* In the essays her native state is blessed for its principles "among the most conservative in all the country"; woman is "the conservative power in the world"; but *Caius Gracchus* shows her Roman heroine, the preeminent model of heroic Roman motherhood, Cornelia, able to conserve nothing: her persuasion comes too late or is ignored, and like a Greek chorus she is the moral voice of the tragedy while being unable ever to determine or to arrest that tragedy's course.

In 1855, the year of her husband's death, Louisa McCord's eyesight began to deteriorate alarmingly, exacerbated by the painful descent into senility of her revered father, for whom she cared at her house in Columbia. Of Langdon Cheves's fourteen children, Louisa had probably been the closest to him emotionally, certainly in intellect: he bequeathed to her his library. It was he who, recognizing her abilities and interests, had insisted that she be instructed in subjects regularly taught only to boys, mathematics in particular, thus laying the foundations of her devotion to political economy. In the dedicatory poem to *My Dreams,* she had honored his "hope-inspiring praise" that sustained her literary ambitions, and in 1876 she wrote in a letter that "my feelings towards my Father have through life been almost those of worship, rather than simply of affection." His death in June 1857 freed her, however, to accept medical advice to visit specialists in Paris, who brought a remission to her worsening eyesight. After a tour with her children of Britain, France, Italy, the Germanic states, and Switzerland, she returned to the United States a few days after John Brown's raid on Harpers Ferry.

She welcomed the secession of South Carolina. "Our spirited little State has declared its independence," she wrote to Hiram Powers in Florence. "A bloodless revolution (an unheard of event in history) can scarcely be expected; and yet some of us hope that such may be." Civil war, when it came, exalted her reputation within South Carolina for her indefatigable efforts on its behalf, especially in the hospitals of Columbia. Civil war also killed her son, plundered her property, and (she saw clearly) obliterated her world. Although she began her memoir of her father in 1876 at a nephew's request, otherwise she wrote little. "Our War came,—and sorrow upon sorrow piled until I scarcely felt the whole world worth writing about." Reconstruction in South Carolina she regarded with ever increasing disgust and dismay, until after 1870 she chose five years of exile in Canada. Finally retiring to Charleston, her birthplace, she sought through a funeral monument to prop her father's tottering name, though hoping little of the result "as the man is now 21 years in his grave and in such a country as ours now is, that is enough to stamp into oblivion every thing worth remembering." Her elder daughter had predeceased her in 1872. She bore her own dying, which at the end was an agony, bravely. Even when prosperous, she had been intimate with suffering for a long time. In 1852 her essay "Enfranchisement of Woman" had preached to woman the acceptance of duty however harsh, with an austerity come of experience. "If she suffers, what is this but the fate of every higher grade of humanity, which rises in suffering as it rises in dignity? for is not all intellect suffering?"

Caroline Lee Hentz

Miriam J. Shillingsburg

Caroline Lee (Whiting) Hentz was an educator of young women and, beginning in 1850, a prolific author of domestic romances. Born in Lancaster, Massachusetts, on June 1, 1800, she was a direct descendent of Rev. Samuel Whiting, who had arrived in Massachusetts in 1636. The youngest in a family of eight children, Caroline was the daughter of Colonel John Whiting, who had fought in the Revolutionary War, and his wife Orpah. Three of her brothers became officers and served in the War of 1812, and it was probably with great enthusiasm that Caroline read their letters and listened to their tales of patriotic adventure.

Young Caroline was popular with her companions, playing games, taking woodland walks, and studying nature. By the time she was twelve, Caroline had begun writing poems, stories, and plays, including a fairy tale and a tragedy. On September 30, 1824, she married Nicholas Marcellus Hentz, a political refugee from Metz, son of a member of the French National Convention. Hentz was an accomplished painter of miniatures, the author of a novel, and a scientist who contributed to the literature of entomology. At the time of their marriage, he was an instructor at the Round Hill School in Northampton, Massachusetts.

In 1826 Professor Hentz took the chair of Modern Languages at the University of North Carolina at Chapel Hill, but he left abruptly for Covington, Kentucky, in 1830 to found a girls' school. There, in 1831, Caroline Hentz wrote the prize-winning tragedy *De Lara; or, The Moorish Bride* for Boston actor William Pelby, who offered a prize of $500. Unable to pay it, Pelby returned the copyright to Hentz. The play, published in 1842, was performed at the Arch Street Theatre in Philadelphia and the Tremont in Boston. While in Covington, Caroline also wrote *Constance of Werdenberg*, which was performed at the Park Theatre in New York in 1832, and *Lamorah; or, the Western Wild*, which played in Cincinnati in 1832 and at Caldwell's in New Orleans on January 1, 1833.

In 1832 the Hentzes opened a girls' school in Cincinnati; there Caroline joined the Semi-Colon Club, in which she probably met Harriet Beecher Stowe, whose *Uncle Tom's Cabin* (1851) she would answer in *The Planter's Northern Bride* (1854). It was in Cincinnati that Nicholas Hentz revealed an irrational jealousy, a trait that appears in several of Caroline Hentz's Byronic heroes. According to their son, Dr. Charles A. Hentz, Colonel King of the Semi-Colon Club sent an improper note to the dignified and accomplished Mrs. Hentz. Instead of returning the note unread, she attempted to answer it. Her suspicious husband—having pretended to go fishing—found her writing. A scene followed and a duel was threatened. Mr. Hentz quickly closed the school, and the couple removed to Florence, Alabama, where they opened another school.

In Florence, most of Caroline's time and energy was devoted to caring for the couple's four children and the family's home, teaching, and managing the boarding school. Consequently, her writing languished. Occasionally she wrote poetry, and she kept a diary that seems to have been a source for the letters, deathbed confessions, and other lamentations that are hallmarks of her novels.

After nine years in Florence, the family established another academy in 1843 in Tuscaloosa, a thriving cultural and intellectual center, where Caroline wrote *Aunt Patty's Scrap Bag* (1846). Time for writing had to be "snatched from the watches of the night," one of her friends noted, as she conducted her "throng of devoted school-girls, commanding the respect, [and] . . . the affectionate esteem" of all who knew her. In 1845 the family opened a school in Tuskegee, then merely a village. For the next three years, she published nothing, perhaps because she was preoccupied with family concerns: her children were entering adulthood, and one daughter married.

In 1848 the Hentzes opened a school in Columbus, Georgia, where Caroline's literary career began in earnest. Professor Hentz became an invalid in 1849, and though Caroline herself was not well, it was necessary for her to support the family. Caroline published *The Mob Cap; and Other Tales* in 1850, and although at first she relied on the female school for financial support, after the spring of 1851, she found writing best sellers more to her liking and set aside mornings for her writing.

Two of their children settled in Marianna, Florida, and the Hentzes joined them there in 1852. During her husband's illness, Caroline wrote at his bedside, dividing her attention among his care, the demands of the literary public, and the occasional visitors who would disturb her routine. Her friends, however, were careful not to interrupt her at her writing. In 1853 she visited her native New England, then returned to Florida to continue to write a succession of best-selling books. After nursing her husband and supporting the family financially for half a decade, Caroline Lee Whiting Hentz died of pneumonia on February 11, 1856, the same day her last novel, *Ernest Linwood,* was published. Professor Hentz died a few months later, and they are buried under one stone in the Episcopal Cemetery in Marianna. Over the course of their marriage, they had lived in five southern states.

At first glance, Hentz's novels seem mere melodramatic entanglements typical of the nineteenth-century domestic fiction especially loathed by Nathaniel Hawthorne. Nevertheless, they have deep autobiographical roots. For example, the jealous hero of *Linda; or, The Young Pilot of Belle Creole* (1850) and of its sequel, *Robert Graham* (1855), vows revenge on Linda's other suitors and occasionally falls unconscious during his melodramatic fits of rage. Charles Hentz recalled that his attractive mother inevitably drew attention and thus "excited my poor, dear father's jealous temperament to frenzy."

The stories also have their genesis in historical events outside the family. The tale of *Linda,* for instance, was told to Hentz by the captain of an Alabama River steamer. He had witnessed the *Belle Creole* being blown to pieces, and he had seen Linda escape into the woods. Encouraged by the captain to write the tale, Hentz composed it at her desk, which always held "a vase of flowers," and she read the chapters aloud to the great appreciation of the family.

Besides the rather sensational plots of kidnappings, assaults, and murders, shipwrecks, melancholy deaths, abolitionist near-riots, drownings, and runaway slaves, Hentz invests her fiction with strong religious and moral sentiments. Robert Graham, for example, becomes converted to religion, marries the widowed Linda, and takes her to India as a missionary. This theme also has personal roots, as may be seen from a passage in her Florence diary: "How inextricable are the paths of sin! . . . Would to God I could lay hand on mine & say I had never stooped to deceit. . . . My spirit is gloomy & the night cloud is on my soul."

Despite the trite use of undelivered or misplaced letters, unrequited love, sudden discoveries (often of long-lost kinsmen), and other melodramatic devices, Hentz's works were widely read, probably because they are consistently well-written examples of popular domestic literature of the period. During a three-year period, 100,000 copies of her books were sold, and for 20 years after her death they were kept in print.

Eoline; or, Magnolia Vale (1852) is a remarkable early feminist tract that posits the theme of the powerful versus the powerless. Attempting to escape an arranged engagement, Eoline defies her father and becomes a music teacher. After numerous complications of honor, duty, will, pride, and love, she discovers the merits of her father's choice of suitor and marries him. They live happily ever after. The theme of the novel is readily manifest in the symbol of male-female and father-child domination, but it is only through the arts that Eoline can find a respectable expression of "self." The story of a rather unconventional young woman has a conventional ending.

For the modern reader, Hentz's *The Planter's Northern Bride* (1854) is probably her most important work because of its compelling style as well as its commentary on the times. Though it is in many ways typical of southern answers to *Uncle Tom's Cabin,* Hentz's New England background provided an interesting perspective on the South she had grown to love deeply. Troubled by the widening breach between the North and the South, she dwelt, as the reviewers noted, upon "the wisdom of loving the whole country." Her eye for detail, enhanced by her own transplantation to the South and her interest in her husband's study of insects, makes this novel, and others, remarkable for its local color.

Her last novel, *Ernest Linwood* (1856), which sold twenty thousand copies in the first edition, is notable for the author's attempt to study the new field of irrational psychology. The hero suffers from a passionate temper, which, his mother tells him, may be "fatal to the peace of those who love him—fatal to his own happiness; suspicion haunts him like a dark shadow,—jealousy, like a serpent, lies coiled in his heart." His mother believes his jealousy to be congenital, for his father had acted similarly. The novel is also clearly autobiographical. Professor Hentz believed his jealous temper stemmed from "the fearful agitation" of his pregnant mother during the Reign of Terror and his own excessive snuff-taking. Linwood is prostrated by his rage after he has wounded his wife, Gabriella, and her supposed lover. Gabriella grows to regret her choice of the furious Linwood as husband. Interestingly, after Caroline Hentz's death the book carried the subtitle "The Inner Life of the Author."

Caroline Lee Hentz's last volumes carried bittersweet titles, such as

Courtship and Marriage; or, Joys and Sorrows of American Life (1856) and *Love after Marriage; and Other Stories of the Heart* (1857). Hentz is important for her attempt to treat sympathetically certain irrational psychological conditions, unhappy marriages, and repressed feminism, and for her efforts to be objective and conciliatory in the fictional war leading up to secession.

Early African American Women Writers

Janell Hobson and Frances Smith Foster

From New Orleans, Louisiana, came one of antebellum America's most controversial and intriguing African American writers, Adah Isaacs Menken (1835–1868). Mary Shadd Cary (1823–1893), the first African American woman known to edit a newspaper, was born in Wilmington, Delaware. In the earliest extant short story by an African American woman, Baltimore-born Frances Ellen Watkins Harper has an African American woman writer as the protagonist. Harper's protagonist in "The Two Offers" (1859), Janette, is a respected and effective professional, but more importantly, she has a higher and better object in all her writings than the mere acquisition of gold, or acquirement of fame. Janette feels she has a high and holy mission on the battlefield of existence. It is entirely possible that persistent literary archeology will uncover other southern African American women who published earlier, who edited sooner, or who were even more controversial, but it is very unlikely that any newly discovered writers will have had mere gold or fame as the primary reason for their writings. African American women of the American South became writers against odds so overwhelming that theirs had to be "higher and holier" missions.

The greatest challenge was becoming literate. The overwhelming majority of African Americans in the South were slaves, and laws forbidding slaves from learning to read and write were widespread. The minuscule southern communities of free African Americans had little time or money to spend on education. Yet, despite all this, African American women and men in the South not only learned to read, but wrote and published in virtually every genre that any other early southern writer did. Laws against slaves learning to read and write made it exceedingly difficult, but these laws were sometimes broken. Free African Americans were generally poor, and their efforts to establish schools were often met with hostility and violence. But individuals and groups, slave and free, white and black, surreptitiously taught others. As a slave girl, Susie King Taylor (1848–1912) attended a school taught by a free black woman in Savannah, Georgia. Taylor's autobiography, *Reminiscences of My Life in Camp* (1902), focuses on her experiences as a Civil War nurse and as a teacher in South Carolina and Georgia from 1862 to 1868. Harriet Jacobs, Louisa Jacobs, Frances Harper, Lucy Laney, Arabella Jones, Emma Brown, and Mary Peake all taught in the South before, during, or immediately after the Civil War. Some, like Taylor, Harper, and Harriet Jacobs, became published writers. African American schools produced literature as well as literacy, as the many manuscripts and published plays, poems, stories, and essays composed by African American teachers and students clearly reveal. Examples include *Christmas Bells, A One-Act Play for Children* (n.d.) by Raleigh, North Carolina, native Anna Julia Cooper and *Christmas Eve Story* (1880) by Fanny Jackson Coppin (1837–1913), a former slave born in Washington, D.C. Though there seem to be few, if any, extant texts from southern schools prior to 1865, it is logical to assume that these and other antebellum teachers and students also wrote more than exams and ritualistic compositions.

Statistics on the percentage of literate slaves in the antebellum South vary, but most scholars agree that at least 5 percent of the slave population was literate in English. It is possible, then, that some slave women found ways to record their poems, stories, songs, and meditations. However, slave women's writings that survive today are generally autobiographical narratives and personal letters. Extant letters from slave women to their husbands, parents, children, and friends are from all parts of the South, from Texas and Missouri to Virginia and Maryland. One such slave writer was Elizabeth Ramsey (dates unknown), who kept correspondence with her daughter, Louisa Picquet (ca. 1827–?), in order to facilitate the negotiation of her slave price, as well as to keep track of family members. Writing from Wharton, Texas, Ramsey gave Picquet, who was free and living in the North, advice on how to purchase freedom for her mother and her brother. Ramsey's letters were brief and pragmatic, but she was aware of the importance of tone and diction. In her March 8, 1859, letter Elizabeth Ramsey advises her daughter thus: "You must write very kind to Col Horton. . . . I think you can change his Price by writing Kindly to him. I think you can soften his heart." By 1860, Picquet managed to purchase her mother's freedom but was unable to persuade Col. Horton to sell her brother.

One of the most interesting and tragic series of letters is from Harriet Newby (dates unknown) of Brentville, Virginia, to her husband, Dangerfield, who had gone to the North to raise money to purchase her and their six children. In her letter of August 16, 1859, Harriet wrote:

> Dear Husband you [know] not the trouble I see; the last two years has been like a trouble dream. It is said Master is in want of money. If so, I know not what time he may sell me, and then all my bright hopes of the futer are blasted, for their has been one bright hope to cheer me in all my troubles, that is to be with you. If I thought I shoul never see you this earth would have no charms for me. Do all you can for me, witch I have no doubt you will.

Perhaps it was such stirring words as these that made Dangerfield switch his priorities from earning money to more direct action: later that year he was killed as he fought with John Brown and others at Harpers Ferry. When Harriet's letters were found on his body, she was sold into the Deep South. Not only do Newby's letters demonstrate the biblical linguistic affinities in African American vernacular and invoke African American folk poetry in written communication, but they also reveal her devotion and love for her husband, expressions often belied by nineteenth-century whites who perpetuated stereotypes of black women as immoral and faithless. Newby's faithful and loving letters to her husband show that some slave families resisted slavery's systematic separation. Her harsh punishment demonstrates also that African American women writers were recognized as insubordinate and dangerous.

A genre of slave letters that is particularly interesting is that between slave women and their owners or former owners. Many of these women, such as Isabella T. Soustan, Lucy Lee, and Rebecca Sales, we know only through the page or two that was preserved. Some women, such as Lucy Skipwith (dates unknown), left fairly extensive letters that offer fascinating glimpses of the complex relations among masters, overseers, and slaves in both house and field work. Skipwith's letters reveal her fondness for her master, John Hartwell Cocke, a religious Virginian who planned to free his slaves and send them to Liberia once they became "civilized." In addition, her letters indicate her boldness, self-assertion, and willingness to exploit the privileges that being in charge of Cocke's Alabama plantation furnished her.

The famous fugitive slave from Macon, Georgia, Ellen Craft (ca. 1826–ca. 1897), collaborated with her husband, William, to publish the book *Running a Thousand Miles for Freedom; or, the Escape of William and Ellen Craft from Slavery* (1860). Ellen Craft developed her separate literary identity through her correspondence with editors of the abolitionist press. Ellen Craft's letters, published in newspapers such as the *Liberator* and *Anti-Slavery Advocate,* illustrate her intention to write for a public audience and thereby influence the public with her own perspectives on political issues.

While still a child, Fanny Jackson Coppin was purchased by an aunt who lived in the North. Coppin distinguished herself as a public speaker and class poet while a student at Oberlin College, and after her graduation in 1865, Coppin's literary accomplishments flourished. She wrote articles for the *Christian Recorder,* and in 1913 Coppin published her autobiography, *Reminiscences of School Life, and Hints on Teaching.* However, it is her letters written before 1865 that detail her desire and diligence for education, mark her beginnings as a writer, and make Coppin a worthy representative of the group of former slave women who left sufficient letters to constitute epistolary autobiographies.

The letters that Skipwith and others wrote record the personal desires and concerns of southern African American women. They also manifest these women's involvement in the political and economic issues of their era and their perspectives on current events. They demonstrate that southern women wrote to transcend the domestic sphere to which they were relegated. These letters indicate the authors' desire for self-agency, their resistance to the expectations placed on their race and gender, and their attempts to write themselves and others into empowerment. They also show that their authors were mindful of multiple and diverse audiences, including the addressee and others who might see their texts. Sometimes this is explicit, as Lucy Skipwith makes clear in her August 15, 1863, letter to John Hartwell Cocke, which begins: "I received your last letter & have carefully considered its contents. . . . The white people who have stayed on the plantation are always opposed to my writeing to you & always want to see my letters and that has been the reason why my letters has been short, but there is no white person here at preasent." Implicit in such correspondences are the intelligence, self-awareness and social consciousness of women who understood the importance of diction and style to negotiate autonomy and effect. As the century progressed, the number of African American women writing public letters to periodicals and organizations increased.

Letters to friends, her master, and eventually newspapers were among the earliest publications of Edenton, North Carolina's, most famous female slave, Harriet Jacobs. Because Jacobs deliberately constructed letters intended to mislead and manipulate her owner, Dr. Flint, some of these letters could be read as fiction. Before she attempted to write her book-length autobiographical narrative, Jacobs apprenticed with shorter narratives that she submitted for newspaper publication. Her writing process points to the strong relationship between letter writing and other literary genres.

But it is for her narrative *Incidents in the Life of a Slave Girl* (1861) that Jacobs is best known. With this publication, Jacobs significantly altered the slave narrative, which since the eighteenth century had been dominated by the male protagonist who follows the North Star from slave South to free North, and adopts a new name and a new life. Jacobs' text features a heroic slave who resists with wit and ingenuity but who remains with her family as long as possible. Jacobs replaces the image of victimized slave women common to narratives by men with a community of heroic and self-determined slave women, including her mother, her grandmother, her aunt, and their friends. Jacobs' narrative is important also for its incorporation of elements from the novel of seduction, for its demonstration of black women's empowerment through writing, and for its direct challenge to "women of the North" to consider that their sexual oppression is intrinsically linked to that of slave women. Jacobs intended her writing as an important connection to the broader women's writing community, including northern white writers such as Lydia Maria Child and Harriet Beecher Stowe and southern white writers such as Angelina Grimké and Mattie Griffith (d. 1906).

Published the same year as Jacobs' *Incidents,* the narrative of Louisa Picquet, a Georgia slave, is also an account of a strong woman harassed, but not broken in spirit by a lascivious master. Picquet, whose mother's letters are mentioned earlier, was literate and probably capable of writing her own life but chose to dictate her story to Hiram Mattison, a Methodist minister whose fascination with Picquet's near-white appearance continuously serves to eroticize his subject while he probes the nature of her dress, her "whippings," and the number of "mulatta" children that she and her mother produced. Though written in the first person and generally factual, *Louisa Picquet, the Octoroon* (1861) is shaped by its editor's leading and oftentimes voyeuristic questioning, and his concerns with the corruptions of slavery in the South. Though her editor seems determined to present Picquet as a concubine, or at least a sexual victim, Picquet maintains some autonomy, for the narrative reveals her struggles for self-expression and self-protection.

Similar struggles exist in other dictated slave narratives, such as *Narrative of Phebe Ann Jacobs* (ca. 1850), *The Kidnapped and the Ransomed* . . .

Personal Recollections of Peter Still and His Wife "Vina" (1856), and *Aunt Sally; or, the Cross the Way of Freedom* (1858). Although the subjects of dictated narratives relate their stories to ghostwriters and capitulate, at times, to the recorders' interpretations of their lives, they recognize a responsibility to "witness slavery." Generally, a careful reader detects their voices and their attempts at what William L. Andrews calls the self-revelation as an "I-witness."

The tradition of the dictated or heavily edited slave narrative varies a bit with *Memoir of Old Elizabeth, a Coloured Woman* (1863), a spiritual narrative of an evangelist, and with postbellum narratives such as *The Story of Mattie J. Jackson* (1866) and Elizabeth Keckley's *Behind the Scenes: Thirty Years a Slave and Four Years in the White House* (1868). Old Elizabeth's *Memoir* combines the slave narrative genre with the spiritual autobiography as her freedom struggle moves from legal bondage to the restrictions of a patriarchal African Methodist Episcopal Church that would deny her right and ability to be an evangelist. Like the spiritual narratives of other nineteenth-century African American women writers, including Maryland-born Amanda Berry Smith (1837–1915), Keckley's narrative boldly challenges limitations imposed by gender or racial bigotry, proclaiming that God loves and gives words of wisdom even to poor black women.

The postbellum narratives, such as those by Mattie Jackson (dates unknown) and Elizabeth Keckley (1818–1907), present different aims from those of the antebellum slave narratives. Rather than condemning the evils of slavery and other patriarchal systems, Jackson and Keckley prove that they have been made stronger because they have survived the "crucible" of slavery and that they are therefore prepared to exercise equal rights and full citizenship in the post–Civil War United States. More than Keckley's *Behind the Scenes*, Jackson's narrative emphasizes her desire for justice and strongly condemns the violent actions of slave owners as well as the forcible separations of family members. Perhaps this is because Keckley had worked her way into financial prosperity and friendships with national leaders, including Jefferson and Varina Davis, and Abraham and Mary Lincoln. Keckley not only reconciles with the Garlands, her former owners, toward the end of her narrative but devotes only three chapters to her "thirty years a slave." Most of *Behind the Scenes* reveals Keckley's observations of the unfolding drama of the Civil War during her "four years in the White House" and her experiences as friend and confidante of Mary Todd Lincoln. Keckley's narrative functions as a lesson of progress and as a business adventure in which those who work hard eventually meet with success, sentiments that are also expressed in an earlier narrative, *A Hairdresser's Experience in*

High Life (1859) by Eliza Potter (1820–?), who may have been from New Orleans. Slave narratives continued to be written well into the twentieth century. Many more southern women, including Lucy Delaney (1830–ca. 1890s), Kate Drumgoold (ca. 1858–?), Bethany Veney (dates unknown), and Annie L. Burton (1860–?), wrote their memories of life in slavery and their achievements as free women.

The experiences of free African Americans in the South are less well documented, but writers such as Frances Rollins (1847–1901) of Charleston, South Carolina, and Clarissa Thompson (dates unknown) of Columbia, South Carolina, offer glimpses while demonstrating adaptations of the slave narrative genre. Rollins published *Life and Public Service of Martin R. Delany* (1868), the narrative of a Virginia slave who became a major in the United States Army, a newspaper editor, and a novelist, and Thompson published a serialized novel, *Treading the Winepress* (1885–86), based upon slave testimonies. In 1862 Sarah Gibson Jones (1845–?) of Alexandria, Virginia, began writing articles for the *Colored Citizen*. Jones was but one of many southern women who contributed to newspapers in the North and later in the South. The two most successful southern-born journalists, however, were Mary Shadd Cary and Frances Ellen Watkins Harper.

Mary Ann Shadd Cary distinguished herself as a lecturer, educator, journalist, editor, and political activist. Cary was educated in the North, but her first pamphlet, entitled "Condition of Colored People" (1849), was published in her hometown of Wilmington, Delaware. When the Fugitive Slave Act was passed in 1850, Cary migrated to Canada, where she founded *The Provincial Freeman* and became the first African American woman known to edit an international periodical. During the antebellum period, Cary wrote numerous editorials and corresponded with such newspaper editors and abolitionist leaders as Frederick Douglass, William Lloyd Garrison, and Robert Hamilton. Although Cary wrote on various subjects, she emphasized in much of her writing the issue of abolitionism, as well as racial pride, education, religion, and poverty. Her literary contributions to politics and journalism indicate a growing number of literate African Americans who not only read each other's work but also recognized self-autonomy in writing. The various letters to the editor that Cary received in her newspaper, as well as Cary's own responses to such letters, illustrate the development of an active writing community among antebellum African Americans.

Frances Ellen Watkins Harper, called the "mother of black journalism," was friend, mentor, and role model for countless other southern African American women, including Victoria Earle Matthews (1861–1907) of Fort Valley, Georgia; Ida B. Wells (1862–1931) of Holly Springs, Mississippi;

and Alice Dunbar-Nelson of New Orleans, who distinguished themselves as writers in the second half of the nineteenth century. A free African American woman born and reared in the slave state of Maryland, Harper attended the William Watkins Academy, a school founded by her uncle in Baltimore. Harper participated in the Underground Railroad in Philadelphia, lectured on the abolitionist circuit, established herself within a writing community of abolitionists who corresponded on various subjects, and published poems and essays in periodicals, such as the *Liberator, Frederick Douglass' Paper,* and *Aliened American.*

Although Frances Harper wrote about numerous subjects and became a national spokesperson for other political movements, such as the Women's Christian Temperance Union and the American Women's Suffrage Association, she is best known for her abolitionist letters, essays, and poems, many of which appeared in *Poems on Miscellaneous Subjects* (1854), a book that sold over twenty thousand copies in numerous editions throughout the nineteenth century. As its title suggests, *Poems on Miscellaneous Subjects* is concerned with several topics, but her most anthologized works are about slavery and democratic freedoms. She is particularly known for her dramatizations of the plight and heroism of fugitive slaves as embodied in the Slave Mother archetype. Examples are "Eliza Harris" (1853) and "The Slave Mother: A Tale of the Ohio" (1856), the latter concerning Margaret Garner, the slave mother memorialized in the twentieth century in Toni Morrison's *Beloved* (1987). Frances E. W. Harper was a professional writer for nearly sixty-five years, wielding her pen as a weapon in battles for equal rights and self-esteem for all.

Harper and Cary were among the most prolific and prominent women writer reformers of the 1850s, but as the debate over slavery intensified, the number of African Americans who testified on behalf of their enslaved kin increased dramatically. Although most of these public speakers and writers were men, a few African American women earned their moments on center stage of the movement. Miss Paulyon, whose first name is unknown, was one such person who, seven years after her escape, lectured about her experiences under slavery and was, we are told, also the author of several poems, including "Slave's Farewell." Reflecting upon the times in which they lived, African American women writers of the South illustrate in their writings and speeches the movement of the country toward the inevitable civil war that would settle "the slavery question," if not the race question, even as many understood that slavery was not the issue at hand.

In contrast to these dedicated black women's involvement within the public sphere of writing is Adah Isaacs Menken, who published her poems in various periodicals, but who wrote without any particular identification with African American or women's literary communities. Menken also lived a vastly different life-style from that of Harper, Cary, or Miss Paulyon. She is best known for her performances in the theaters of New Orleans, New York, and Paris, among others. Born a free woman of color in New Orleans, perhaps with the name Philomene Croi Theodore, to Auguste Theodore, a mulatto registered as a "free man of color," and to Magdaleine Jean Lois Janneaux, Menken cultivated a flamboyant persona with an ambiguous racial and ethnic identity. When at the age of fifteen she married Alexander Isaacs Menken, she even identified herself as Jewish, perhaps to appease his family. Not unlike many African Americans who incorporate biblical themes from the Hebrew scriptures in their writings and identify American slavery with that of the Hebrews in Egypt, Menken shows her understanding of and identification with Jewish history in poems such as "Hear, O Israel!" This poem, like several of her poems and articles, was published in a Jewish periodical, *Israelite.*

Because of her public persona, Menken received unrelenting press coverage of her private life, which she lived in defiance of the mores of antebellum society. Breaking every tenet of the "cult of true womanhood," Menken divorced and married four times—these marriages lasting from a few days to a few months—engaged in various love affairs, and moved in very public, glamorous circles. Although she maintained such a public life, much of her private life still remains a mystery. Because of her ambiguous identities—sometimes giving the names of five different men as her father, sometimes admitting to her African American heritage, especially while she engaged in affairs with such renowned mulatto writers as Alexandre Dumas *père* and Aleksandr Pushkin—Menken remains a difficult figure to place.

On the other hand, much of Menken's personality is captured in *Infelicia,* published posthumously in 1868. Despite her biographical ambiguities, Menken's poetry is stark and candid. Her soul literally and literarily lies bare. Her free verse also indicates her advanced, experimental style with both form and content. Despite Joan R. Sherman's characterization of Menken's tone as "extremely hysterical," there are moments when her melodrama gives way to somber viewpoints and serious social criticism of the limitations imposed on women and, perhaps implicitly, on free persons of color. Her poems abound in apocalyptic images and themes of love, despair, and suicidal desperation. Menken's exploration of herself, which is oftentimes confessional and relentlessly critical of a world that restricts women's freedom, appealed to many women of her time, presumably white, thus indicating that her writing was not necessarily in isolation but in conversation with a community of such readers. In fact, *Infelicia* was so popular that twelve editions were published between 1868 and 1902. Menken's most significant contribution to the tradition of early southern African American women writers is her contrasting presentation of herself, not as heroic and praiseworthy, as in many black women's slave narratives, but as a trickster and a woman of "sass," denigrated and at times defeated, yet continually struggling. In this way, Menken serves as a foremother to twentieth-century writers such as Zora Neale Hurston and as a representative of those as yet unidentified "wild women" who surely lived and also left written legacies.

Consideration of the early African American women writers of the South offers crucial insights into the historical past of the American South and new considerations in the analysis of American literature. Undoubtedly, there are still more texts written by these women and others that have yet to be discovered—published or otherwise. There certainly are other southern African American women writers who have yet to be identified. They await the move from the shadowy margins into the revered circle of immortality.

Southern Women Writers' Responses to
Uncle Tom's Cabin

Karen Manners Smith

Harriet Beecher Stowe's grand antislavery epic, *Uncle Tom's Cabin; or, Life among the Lowly,* first appeared in 1851 as a serial in the *National Era.* Issued as a book in March 1852, it sold ten thousand copies in a matter of days. Within a year 300,000 copies had been sold in the United States and nearly a million in England. *Uncle Tom's Cabin* tells the story of the saintly Kentucky slave, Tom, a family man and his master's loyal lieutenant, who is sold South to pay his master's debts. Tom meets slaves in a variety of conditions as well as a succession of weak or noble whites before he finally succumbs to the brutality of Simon Legree, a Louisiana planter. In a parallel story, the slaves Eliza and George run away to avoid being sold, escape successfully to Canada, and later become colonists in West Africa. There are numerous complex subplots dealing with both black and white characters. The book's religious fervor, its emphasis on the redemptive power of love, and its sad portraiture of African American families torn apart by slavery had an especially powerful appeal to northern women. Abolitionists and free blacks in the North, however, greeted *Uncle Tom's Cabin* with tepid enthusiasm, displeased with Stowe's ossified race ideology and her insistence on African colonization as the solution to the problem of slavery. Other northerners—intellectuals and some clergy—objected to the book's emotional evangelicalism. Nearly everyone agreed, however, that *Uncle Tom's Cabin* was powerful propaganda, and that, since its publication, more and more northerners had begun to sympathize with the abolitionist cause.

In the South, the reaction to *Uncle Tom's Cabin* was almost universal outrage. The book's few moderate reviewers, gently suggesting that Stowe had attacked slavery, not individuals and not the South as a whole, published their articles anonymously. For nearly everyone else, the South was all about slavery; slavery was the foundation of the southern social and economic system, and it was an institution they were certain northerners knew nothing about. Stowe and the abolitionists meddled at their peril. Indeed, Stowe was viciously and personally reviled. Southern writer William Gilmore Simms referred to her as a beast; a Tennessee clergyman who had never seen her described her as a witch; other critics claimed she had lost all feminine decency and decried her supposed prurient interest in the sexual evils of slavery. The furious southern press response to Stowe continued throughout the early 1850s. Longer responses in the form of fiction appeared right up to the Civil War.

At the base of all southern defense of slavery, including attempts to refute Stowe, lay southern race theory: a convenient—and unshakable—belief in the innate racial inferiority of the Negro. Ironically, it was a belief southerners shared with most white northerners of the period, so it became the fulcrum of all their proslavery rhetoric. Without the basic rationale of racial inferiority, all further proslavery arguments were indefensible. Without this rationale, southern insistence that slavery was a benign institution in which a superior race lovingly cared for an inferior one was nothing but camouflage for human history's most exploitive economic relationship.

Southern women who read *Uncle Tom's Cabin*—and many managed to find a copy—were particularly offended by Stowe's indelicacy in referring to the sexual abuse of female slaves by their masters, especially as southern society required ladies to pretend that this pervasive custom did not exist. But southern women also had other issues with *Uncle Tom's Cabin,* and they adopted a variety of methods to defend southern culture and respond to the charges Stowe had laid down. Like southern men, they wrote review essays, open letters to newspapers, and fictional counterattacks in the form of proslavery novels; many discussed *Uncle Tom's Cabin* in their private letters and diaries. Their responses were highly political—though politics was supposed to be forbidden territory for southern women—but they were also gendered. A woman had attacked the southern way of life; these southern women felt the defense of their homeland was their responsibility.

South Carolinian Louisa S. McCord, perhaps the most respected female intellect in the South of her day, responded to *Uncle Tom's Cabin* in the *Southern Quarterly Review* (January 1853). McCord was revolted by what she called Stowe's "malignant bitterness" and "foul imagination." She was also thoroughly exasperated with Stowe. As far as she was concerned, answering abolitionists had become as tiresome as the "labour of Sisyphus." Methodically, she attacked Stowe point by point. Mostly, McCord faulted Stowe's logic and her research, quite correctly guessing that Stowe had never spent any time in the South. How could she, then, McCord wondered, know anything of master/slave relations as they actually existed? No slave owner—McCord refers here to Simon Legree—would beat a valuable slave to death when he could profitably get rid of him by selling him to a neighbor. Similarly, McCord insisted, no southern planter would sell his most loyal slave, his farm manager, for a measly debt, as Mr. Shelby sells Tom. And any true plantation mistress, any real Mrs. Shelby, would talk her husband out of his mad scheme. Still more ludicrous, for McCord, was Stowe's character Marie St. Claire, Tom's New Orleans owner: no properly raised and educated southern lady would exhibit the coarse, heartless brutality of a Marie St. Claire. McCord was certain that such a woman would be ostracized by refined society.

Not only were Stowe's ignorant assertions insulting to southerners, claimed McCord, but her ideas were also dangerous: their logical outcome would be slave insurrection and race intermarriage. McCord concluded her essay with a ringing endorsement of slavery: "We do not say it is a necessary evil. . . . We proclaim it, on the contrary, a Godlike dispensation, a providential caring for the weak, and a refuge for the portionless. . . . Slavery is [the Negro's] destiny and his refuge from extinction."

McCord became particularly incensed at the outpouring of support for Stowe in influential British periodicals. In the summer of 1853 she responded to the Duchess of Sutherland and a group of English noblewomen who had published an antislavery "Address to the Women of America." In a tone purporting to speak "in the spirit of sisterly affection," but laden with sarcasm, McCord reiterated her race theory and suggested the British tend to their own problems. She offered to sell her 160 slaves to the Duchess so the latter could demonstrate her sincerity by transporting them to England and freeing them.

Domestic novelist Maria McIntosh (1803–1878) spoke to these same British women in the pages of the New York *Observer* in 1853. She forgave them for being swayed by Stowe's skillfully written but distorted picture of the South and urged them to listen to the other side. According to McIntosh,

Stowe had failed to communicate the beneficence of the institution of slavery, its civilizing effects on the descendants of Africans, and the sense of community it engendered throughout the South. McIntosh urged her British sisters to stop interfering in the male world of politics and, like the good women of the American South, to seek only domestic solutions to the world's problems: "Let us each, in our own land and our own sphere, labor to teach the ignorant, to comfort the sorrowing, to reclaim the vicious in whatever condition we find them."

McIntosh's next foray into proslavery propaganda, *The Lofty and the Lowly* (1853), was less overtly political, but she was far from alone in choosing the domestic novel to present a positive picture of southern life. It has been estimated that between fourteen and twenty-seven book-length fictional responses to *Uncle Tom's Cabin* appeared before the Civil War, at least eight of them written by southern women. There may also have been a number of other novels of the 1850s that told proslavery tales without specific reference to Mrs. Stowe. Among the best known anti-Tom novels by male southerners were William Gilmore Simms's *Woodcraft; or, Hawks about the Dovecote: A Story of the South at the Close of the Revolution* (1854) and John W. Page's *Uncle Robin in His Cabin in Virginia, and Tom without One in Boston* (1853). Among novels by southern women, the most popular were Mary H. Eastman's *Aunt Phillis's Cabin; or, Southern Life as It Is* (1852) and the works of two well-established domestic novelists: Maria McIntosh's *The Lofty and the Lowly; or, Good in All and None All Good* (1853) and Caroline Lee Hentz's *The Planter's Northern Bride, a Novel* (1854). Hentz's earlier novel, *Marcus Warland; or, the Long, Moss Spring* (1852), was in part a rebuttal of *Uncle Tom's Cabin* as it first appeared in serial form. Other women's books included Martha Haines Butt's *Antifanaticism: A Tale of the South* (1853). Martha Butt was an adolescent girl in 1853 and may have been a pupil of Mrs. Hentz, to whom she dedicated her book. Mary E. Herndon published *Louise Elton; or, Things Seen and Heard* in 1853 and, in 1860, Mrs. Henry R. Schoolcraft wrote *The Black Gauntlet, A Tale of Plantation Life in South Carolina,* a novel filled with irrelevant poetry and quotations, which was perhaps the most aggressively racist of all the works in this genre. It is significant that all of these passionately prosouthern, proslavery women's novels were published in Philadelphia, for they were an intended corrective for northern minds whose view of southern culture had been poisoned by Harriet Beecher Stowe.

As a group, women's proslavery novels were didactic. They were filled with authorial intrusions in the plot, as well as pages and pages of biblical justification and long intellectual arguments between male characters about the pros and cons of slavery. Stowe, of course, had freely interjected her commentary in *Uncle Tom's Cabin,* but proslavery novels had a tendency to sacrifice dramatic tension for political argument. In these works, the South is depicted as an agrarian utopia, where slave owners never break apart slave families through sale and masters reason with slaves who misbehave, rather than whip them. In the North, selfishness and materialism govern the lives of the rich, while the free, white working classes—exploited wage labor-ers—suffer and die in cities that are sinks of depravity, disease, and ungodli-ness. Northerners treat Irish immigrant laborers and poor, consumptive seamstresses far worse than southerners treat their slaves. In fact, white northern servants in *The Planter's Northern Bride* actually envy the hero's enslaved manservant, Albert, because he is better dressed and more kindly treated than they are.

These books all differ from *Uncle Tom's Cabin* in that the white charac-ters and their tangled love stories occupy center stage; the slaves, with few exceptions indistinguishable from one another, are stereotypically loqua-cious, superstitious, lethargic, and susceptible to drink, but unfailingly loyal and grateful for the blessings of slavery and the kindness of their masters. One of the more fully developed black characters in this literature, Mary Eastman's (1818–1887) Aunt Phillis, functions as a female Uncle Tom. She is described by the son of her owner as a servant whose "price is above ru-bies. Her industry, her honesty, her attachment to our family, exceeds every-thing. . . . She is a slave here, but she is destined to be a saint hereafter."

Frequently the southern women's stories feature fanatical abolitionists: Hentz's *The Planter's Northern Bride* has a triumphant abolitionist mad-man who nearly succeeds in fomenting a slave rebellion, and McIntosh's *The Lofty and the Lowly* has a militant female abolitionist from Boston who attempts to liberate the heroine's already freed slave. The heroine's ab-olitionist father in *The Planter's Northern Bride* is converted to the southern cause on a visit to the hero's sunny plantation and its community of con-tented slaves. In this literature the loyal slaves scorn abolitionists. In *Aunt Phillis's Cabin,* for example, it is not the plantation owner but his tipsy old retainer, Bacchus, who enthusiastically contemplates tarring and feathering an abolitionist, should he chance to meet one. Aunt Phillis thinks running away with the abolitionists would be like stealing her master's property, an act no honest Christian slave would even consider. In these stories, slaves who are encouraged by abolitionists to escape always live to regret it, some of them begging their old masters to take them back.

This fiction consistently derides the northern women's rights movement, linking it—accurately, to be sure—to the antislavery movement and calling a plague on both houses. A group of meddlesome northern women in *Aunt Phillis's Cabin,* for example, attend meetings of the F. S. F. S. T. W. T. R. (Female Society for Setting the World to Rights). Southern novelists argued that northern women who engaged in politics had completely forgotten woman's appropriate role: the care of home and family. By contrast, the plantation mistress, the "true" woman in this literature, magnified and glorified woman's role by caring for her husband's enslaved dependents in addition to her own children. "Northern ladies," claimed Mrs. Schoolcraft in *The Black Gauntlet,* "never saw a day in their lives that could comprise all the responsibilities of a Southern planter's wife."

Alternately cajoling and admonishing their readers, McCord, Hentz, McIntosh, Eastman, and the others published the literary response to Harriet Beecher Stowe. None of them had her tremendous emotional power. In the privacy of her diary, Mary Chesnut also contended with Stowe. Chesnut dismissed what she found implausible in *Uncle Tom's Cabin,* but she was willing to admit the truth of Stowe's allegations about the sexual immorality of slave owners and the possibility that there were white women like Marie St. Claire, so corrupted and infantilized by the southern social system that they came to embody the worst excesses of slave ownership.

Southern women writers waged their campaign against Harriet Beecher Stowe in the sincere belief that they could convince readers that she was wrong. All of them agreed that the interests of the country as a whole would be best served if northerners ceased to interfere with southern institutions, *not* if southerners freed their slaves. Even as early as 1854, however, Caroline Lee Hentz suspected the propaganda war was lost: disunion and civil war would be the result of the sectional antagonism that had been exacerbated by *Uncle Tom's Cabin,* and "the American eagle [would] flap its wings in blood."

Harriet Ann Jacobs

William L. Andrews

Harriet Jacobs, daughter of Delilah, the slave of Margaret Horniblow, and Daniel Jacobs, the slave of Andrew Knox, was born in Edenton, North Carolina, in 1813 under "unusually fortunate circumstances," she wrote in her autobiography, *Incidents in the Life of a Slave Girl* (1861). Until she was six years old, Harriet was unaware that she was in fact the property of Margaret Horniblow. Before her death in 1825, Harriet's relatively kind mistress taught her slave to read and sew. In her will, Margaret Horniblow bequeathed eleven-year-old Harriet to a niece, Mary Matilda Norcom. Because Mary Norcom was only three years old when Harriet Jacobs became her slave, Mary's father, Dr. James Norcom, an Edenton physician, became Jacobs' de facto master. Under the regime of James and Maria Norcom, Jacobs was introduced to the harsh realities of slavery. Only a few weeks after her arrival in the Norcom household, Jacobs recalls in her autobiography, she overheard a hushed exchange between Dr. Norcom and a female slave whom he was preparing to sell away from Edenton. The slave complained of the master's failure "to treat me well." The master replied, "You have let your tongue run too far; damn you!" Though barely a teenager, Jacobs realized from this moment on that her master was a sexual threat to black women. She also discovered that in the South it was "a crime" for a slave mother to speak publicly of the white paternity of any of her children.

From 1825, when she entered the Norcom household, until 1842, the year she escaped from slavery, Harriet Jacobs struggled to avoid the sexual victimization that Dr. Norcom intended to be her fate. By the time she was fifteen, Jacobs was compelled to endure relentless sexual harassment from Norcom. Although she loved and admired her grandmother, Molly Horniblow, a free black woman who wanted to help Jacobs gain her freedom, the teenage slave could not bring herself to reveal to her unassailably upright grandmother the nature of Norcom's threats. Despised by the doctor's suspicious wife and increasingly isolated by her situation, Jacobs in desperation formed a clandestine liaison with Samuel Tredwell Sawyer, a white attorney with whom Jacobs had two children, Joseph and Louisa, by the time she was twenty years old. Hoping that if Norcom believed she had run away, then he would sell her children to their father, Jacobs hid herself in a crawl space above a storeroom in her grandmother's house in the summer of 1835. In that "little dismal hole" she remained for the next seven years, sewing, reading the Bible, keeping watch over her children as best she could, and writing occasional letters to Norcom designed to confuse him as to her actual whereabouts. In 1837 Sawyer was elected to the United States House of Representatives. Although he had purchased their children in accordance with their mother's wishes, Sawyer moved to Washington without emancipating either Joseph or Louisa. In 1842, Jacobs escaped to the North by boat, determined to reclaim her daughter from Sawyer, who had sent her to Brooklyn, New York, to work as a house servant.

For ten years after her escape from North Carolina, Harriet Jacobs lived the tense and uncertain life of a fugitive slave. She found Louisa in Brooklyn, secured a place for both children to live with her in Boston, and went to work as a nursemaid to the baby daughter of Mary Stace Willis, wife of the popular editor, poet, and magazine writer Nathaniel Parker Willis. Norcom made several attempts to locate her in New York, which forced Jacobs to keep on the move and to enlist the aid of antislavery activists in Rochester, New York, where she took up an eighteen-month residence in 1849. Working in a Rochester antislavery reading room and bookstore above the offices of Frederick Douglass' newspaper, the *North Star,* Jacobs met and began to confide in Amy Post, an abolitionist and pioneering feminist who gently urged the fugitive slave mother to consider making her story public. Because of the tremendous response to *Uncle Tom's Cabin* (1852), Jacobs thought of enlisting the aid of the novel's author, Harriet Beecher Stowe, in getting her own story published. But Stowe had little interest in any sort of creative partnership with Jacobs. Early in 1852, after receiving the gift of her freedom from Cornelia Grinnell Willis, the second wife of her employer, Jacobs decided to write her autobiography herself.

In 1853 Jacobs took her first steps toward authorship, sending several anonymous letters to the New York *Tribune*. In the first, "Letter from a Fugitive Slave. Slaves Sold under Peculiar Circumstances" (June 21, 1853), Jacobs broached the sexually sensitive subject matter that would become the burden of her autobiography: the sexual abuse of slave women and their mothers' attempts to protect them. By the summer of 1857, Jacobs had completed what she called in a letter to Post "a true and just account of my own life in Slavery." Jacobs admitted to Post, "There are some things that I might have made plainer I know," but, acknowledging her anxiety about telling her story to even as sympathetic and supportive a friend as Post, Jacobs continued, "I have left nothing out but what I thought the world might believe that a Slave Woman was too willing to pour out—that she might gain their sympathies." Still, Jacobs hoped her book "might do something for the Antislavery Cause" both in England and in the United States. To that end she engaged the editorial services of Lydia Maria Child, a prominent white antislavery writer, who, as she wrote in an August 30, 1860, letter to Jacobs, "exercised [her] bump of mental order" on the manuscript, before contracting with a Boston publishing house, Thayer and Eldridge. However, Thayer and Eldridge went bankrupt before Jacobs' autobiography could be published. But Jacobs persevered, and with the support of her antislavery friends saw to the publication of *Incidents in the Life of a Slave Girl* late in 1861 by a Boston printer. In 1862 a British edition of *Incidents*, entitled *The Deeper Wrong; or, Incidents in the Life of a Slave Girl*, appeared in London.

The antislavery press in the United States and Great Britain received Jacobs' autobiography favorably, but *Incidents* was quickly overshadowed by the gathering clouds of civil war in America. The book was never reprinted. It remained in obscurity until the civil rights and women's movements of the 1960s and 1970s spurred a reprint of *Incidents* in 1973. Still, scholars who commented on *Incidents* tended to question its veracity and its authorship, suggesting either that the story was too melodramatic to be taken seriously or that its editor, Child, was probably its author. Not until the extensive archival work of Jean Fagan Yellin did *Incidents* begin to take its place as a major African American slave narrative. Yellin's research has revealed that *Incidents in the Life of a Slave Girl* is the only nineteenth-century slave narrative whose genesis can be traced through a series of letters, in this case from Jacobs to various friends and advisors, including Post, and the eventual editor of *Incidents*, Child. Discovered and published in Yellin's admirable edition of *Incidents in the Life of a Slave Girl* (1987), Jacobs' correspondence with Child helps lay to rest the long-standing charge against *Incidents* that it is at worst a fiction and at best the product of Child's pen, not Jacobs'. Child's letters to Jacobs and others make clear that her role as editor was no more than she acknowledged in her introduction to *Incidents:* to ensure the orderly arrangement and directness of the narrative, without adding anything to the text or altering in any significant way Jacobs' manner of recounting her story.

Harriet Jacobs was the first woman to author a fugitive slave narrative in the United States. Yet she was never as celebrated as Ellen Craft (1826–1891), a runaway from Georgia, who had become internationally famous for the daring escape from slavery that she and her husband, William, engineered in 1848, during which Ellen impersonated a male slave owner attended by her husband in the role of faithful slave. *Running a Thousand Miles for Freedom* (1860), the thrilling narrative of the Crafts' flight from Savannah to Philadelphia, was published under both of their names but has always been attributed to William's hand. In contrast, Harriet Jacobs' autobiography was "written by herself," as the subtitle to the book proudly states. Even more astonishing than the Crafts' story, *Incidents* represents no less profoundly an African American woman's resourcefulness, courage, and dauntless quest for freedom. Yet nowhere in Jacobs' autobiography, not even on its title page, did its author disclose her own identity, as Ellen Craft willingly did. Instead, Jacobs called herself "Linda Brent" and masked the important places and persons in her narrative in the manner of a novelist, renaming Norcom "Dr. Flint" and Sawyer "Mr. Sands" in her narrative. Despite her longing to speak out frankly and fully, Jacobs dreaded writing candidly about the obscenities of slavery for fear that giving tongue to these "foul secrets" would impute to her the guilt that should have been reserved for those like Norcom who hid behind such secrets. "I had no motive for secrecy on my own account," Jacobs insists in her preface to *Incidents,* but given the harrowing and sensational story she had to tell, the onetime fugitive felt she had little alternative but to shield herself from a readership whose understanding and empathy she could not take for granted.

Jacobs' primary motive in writing *Incidents* was to address white women of the North on behalf of thousands of "Slave mothers that are still in bondage" in the South. Jacobs hoped "to kindle a flame of compassion" in her female reader's heart without searing her sensibilities with a frank account of such inflammatory subjects as seduction, rape, and miscegenation. The mother of two slave children fathered by a white man, Jacobs faced a task considerably more complicated than that of any African American woman author before her. She wanted to indict the southern patriarchy for its sexual tyranny over black women like herself. But she could not do so without confessing with "sorrow and shame" her willing participation in a miscegenetle liaison that produced two illegitimate children. Resolved, she informs her female reader, "to tell you the truth . . . let it cost me what it may," Jacobs fully acknowledges her transgressions against conventional sexual morality when she was a slave girl. At the same time, however, Jacobs articulates a bolder truth—that the morality of free white women has little ethical relevance or authority when applied to the situation of enslaved black women in the South.

"I know what I did, and I did it with deliberate calculation," Jacobs admits in an extraordinarily candid explanation of her decision to accept Sawyer as her lover. "I will not try to screen myself behind the plea of compulsion from a master; for it was not so. Neither can I plead ignorance or thoughtlessness." In such language Jacobs skirted dangerously close to the line that southern defenders of slavery had used to excuse race-mixing in the South by claiming that sexually aggressive and promiscuous slave women were the ultimate threats to the sanctity of southern families. Jacobs leaves little doubt in *Incidents* as to the southern patriarchy's responsibility for the subversion of the family, but she is equally determined not to seek moral exculpation by picturing herself, even in her girlhood, as innocent, unwary, or deceived. Jacobs refuses, in short, to adopt an image of herself as merely a sexual victim. In making this decision, she broke with one of the predominant themes of the antebellum male slave narrative. She knew that fugitive slave narrators such as Frederick Douglass and William Wells Brown had helped to popularize an image of slave women as for the most part defenseless and pathetic objects of the slaveholders' lust. Jacobs knew that in keeping with this defense of slave women, white abolitionist propaganda only rarely discussed how slave women resisted sexual exploitation. This fueled her determination to portray herself as an agent rather than as a victim, a woman motivated by a desire for freedom much stronger than a fear of sexual retribution.

"There is something akin to freedom in having a lover who has no control over you," Jacobs informs her reader, thereby invoking a sociopolitical standard as an alternative to that of conventional female virtue. Freedom, Jacobs argues, was what impelled her to take Sawyer as her lover. "I knew nothing would enrage Dr. Flint so much as to know that I favored another. . . . I thought he would revenge himself by selling me, and I was sure my friend, Mr. Sands, would buy me." Thus Jacobs discloses that her "calculation" in taking Sawyer as a lover was motivated at least as much by a desire for freedom as by a desire for a man. Such calculated use of sexuality as both an instrument of "revenge" against Norcom and as a means to freedom via Sawyer may have unsettled Jacobs' northern readers as much as her confessions of sexual transgressions. But in the end, Jacobs claims, "in looking back, calmly on the events of my life, I feel that the slave woman ought not to be judged by the same standard as others." Whatever her moral failings, Jacobs suggests in her discussion of her sexual affairs as a slave woman, the traditional ideals of the nineteenth-century "cult of true womanhood" cannot adequately address them. Thus *Incidents in the Life of a Slave Girl* does not offer the reader a way out of the moral dilemmas inherent in the slave woman's situation. But it does invalidate facile judgmentalism while providing an alternative to stereotypes of the black woman in slavery as either victim or victimizer in the sexual arena.

Writing an unprecedented mixture of confession, self-justification, and societal exposé, Jacobs turned her autobiography into a unique analysis of the myths and the realities that defined the situation of the African American woman and her relationship to nineteenth-century standards of womanhood. As a result, *Incidents in the Life of a Slave Girl* occupies a crucial place in the history of American women's literature in general and southern women's literature in particular. Before *Incidents,* southern literature had produced no significant and probing analysis of the predicament and aspirations of antebellum black women, slave or free. Published in the North, *Incidents in the Life of a Slave Girl* proved that until slavery was overthrown, only expatriate southern women writers, such as Jacobs and her contemporary, Angelina Grimké Weld, who left South Carolina to speak out against slavery in the South, could write freely about social problems in the South.

From 1862 to 1866 Jacobs devoted herself to relief efforts among former slaves who had become refugees of the war in and around Washington. With her daughter, Jacobs founded a school in Alexandria, Virginia, which was open from 1863 until 1865, when both mother and daughter returned south to Savannah, Georgia, to engage in further relief work among the freedmen and freedwomen. The spring of 1867 found Jacobs back in Edenton, actively promoting the welfare of the ex-slaves and reflecting in her correspondence on "those I loved" and "their unfaltering love and devotion toward myself and [my] children." This sense of dedication and solidarity with those who had been enslaved kept Jacobs at work in the South until racist violence ultimately drove her and Louisa back to Cambridge, Massachusetts. By the mid-1880s Jacobs had settled with Louisa in Washington, but little is known about the last decade of her life. Harriet Jacobs died in Washington on March 7, 1897.

Civil War Diaries and Memoirs

Walter Sullivan

It would be wrong to say that the diarists discussed here represent a cross section of Confederate women. In 1861, at the beginning of the Civil War, a large segment of the population, not only of the South, but of the United States, was illiterate. Of those southern women who could read and write, many had neither the time for writing nor the paper and ink with which to record their experiences. Most of those who kept diaries, although impoverished and plagued by shortages of almost everything as the war advanced, were, when hostilities commenced, members of the upper and upper middle classes. Like Mary Boykin Chesnut, the most famous Confederate woman diarist, many were daughters and wives of planters, some of whom owned several plantations. Others were married to professionals, most frequently lawyers who, like Sarah Rice Pryor's husband, were likely to be active in politics, or, like Cornelia Peak McDonald's husband, men of business as well as members of the bar.

Some of the women who kept diaries were better educated than others. Some appear to have had only the most rudimentary schooling; their grammar was deficient and their writing skills were poor. The majority of southern women received most or all of their education at home under the supervision of a parent or relative or, in more affluent households, a governess or a tutor who lived with the family. A few, like Kate Stone (1841–1907), had been sent away to finishing schools. But however and wherever

they were taught, they learned the same things, usually in the same sequence: how to read and write; the fine points of English grammar along
with literature and mathematics; Latin, music, and the arts and manners
that were considered necessary to the training of a lady. Depending on how
much education they received, after Latin, or along with it, they learned
French, and some of them also learned German. Only a few studied Greek.
As would be expected, some were better writers than others. Of those considered here, four—Eliza Andrews, Constance Cary Harrison, Sarah Morgan Dawson, and Sarah Rice Pryor—became professional writers after the
war. Mary Chesnut's work, in particular, deserves special attention because
of her interest in revising her diary for publication and because of the monumental role her diary plays in the history of southern women. Some of the
others wrote almost as well as the professionals-to-be, and the worst writers
among them were usually able to convey effectively the details of their experiences during a dangerous and turbulent time.

Brokenburn (1955), the diary of Kate Stone, begins with an account of
life on a Louisiana plantation that corroborates recent scholarship concerning the important role of women in the agrarian economy of the antebellum
South. In 1855, when she was thirty-one, Kate Stone's mother was left a
widow with eight children and an estate that was deeply in debt. By hard
work and good management, doing to a large extent what she would have
done anyway had her husband lived, Mrs. Stone retired her mortgage, educated her children, and was planning trips to Europe for herself and her
family when the war began. At Brokenburn, she was mistress of all she sur-
veyed: her house, her family, and her one hundred and fifty slaves, all of
whom had to be housed, clothed, fed, and cared for when they were sick.
Doubtless, Kate Stone's depiction of plantation life, written forty years after
the war as an introduction to her diary, is in many particulars romantic, but
her account of her mother's hard work and administrative skills is confirmed by what we know of the Old South.

Beyond her description of life on an antebellum plantation, Stone's diary
is particularly valuable for its account of the relations between white families and their former slaves once the latter were freed, and for her description of the world of Confederate refugees. When Federal troops occupied
eastern Louisiana, Stone and her family, along with most of their neighbors,
receiving abuse and fearing worse at the hands of both their ex-slaves and
the invading army, began a journey westward that was ultimately to take
them hundreds of miles. In Tyler, Texas, they established with other southern families a kind of Confederacy in exile and lived lives that they themselves thought were unbecomingly easy compared to the privations of the

civilians who remained behind enemy lines and the soldiers who were fighting the war. Stone's description of this period, which she, like several other women diarists, compared to the lives of the French nobility who played charades in the Bastille while awaiting their execution, is particularly interesting and comparable to Mary Chesnut's depiction of the heightened social life that characterized Richmond during the winter of 1864–65. Stone was a perceptive observer of her place and time, and her prose is always lucid and frequently quite graceful.

At the beginning of the war, Sarah Rice Pryor (1830–1912), whose husband was a member of Congress from Virginia, was living in Washington. One of the most interesting segments of her diary, *Reminiscences of Peace and War* (1904), describes the tensions that began to develop in Washington society during the winter of 1860–61. An active hostess, Pryor entertained and was entertained by congressmen and senators, diplomats and cabinet officers, and even the president of the United States. She records how, as the war came on, animosities among her friends grew and divisions widened. At a reception at the White House, Pryor heard President James Buchanan say softly to himself, "Not in my time. Not in my time." He was referring to the breaking apart of the nation, and he was wrong. Pryor was standing by his chair at a wedding reception when news came that South Carolina had seceded from the Union. With the announcement, a roar of voices rose in the hall, and Pryor left the president's side to discover the source of the commotion. She ordered that his carriage be brought to the door before she told him that the country he so deeply loved had been divided.

Pryor was raised by her aunt and uncle who had a plantation in the Virginia countryside as well as a house in Charlottesville. A part of her diary concerns plantation life and the role of her uncle as slave owner and planter. During the war, she lived in various parts of Virginia but mostly in Richmond, as she tried to stay as close as was feasible to her husband, who had resigned from Congress and taken a commission in the Confederate Army. In early 1865, she was in Petersburg, on the outskirts of which the Army of Northern Virginia was fighting its final battle. The city itself was under fire from Federal artillery, and Pryor's is one of the best accounts available of the bombardment as it was seen and endured by civilians—women and children and a few old men. Penniless when hostilities ended, Roger Pryor moved to New York. Soon, his law practice had prospered sufficiently for Sarah to follow him. As her husband became more affluent, she became increasingly active socially, visiting and being visited by men who had once been her country's enemies. She published four books and numerous magazine articles before her death three days before her eighty-second birthday.

Rose O'Neal Greenhow (1815–1864) was a widow with an eight-year-old daughter living in Washington at the outbreak of the war. Like Sarah Rice Pryor, she was an active hostess, and what we know of her life suggests that she was a woman of great charm. Perceiving that war was imminent, Greenhow, who had always included army officers on her guest list, learned all she could about the disposition of Union forces. She claimed to have obtained and forwarded to Confederate General Robert E. Lee the Federal plan for the first Battle of Manassas. This claim has not been fully substantiated, but there is no doubt that she was a Confederate spy. Her memoir, *My Imprisonment and the First Year of Abolition Rule at Washington* (1863), is an account of her incarceration, first in her home and later in Old Capitol Prison, while Federal authorities looked for evidence against her. She and her daughter shared not only her prison cell, but also the bad food, the dirt, the noise, and at least some of the humiliation of captivity. Her literary style is somewhat marred by the anger that infuses her writing, but her circumstantial descriptions of the challenges and discomforts of prison life ring true. Released after four months in Old Capitol, she was passed through the Confederate lines and subsequently traveled to England, where her memoir was published, and where she continued her secret work for the Confederate government and became well and favorably known among English society. Fearing arrest by Federal naval officers when the ship on which she was returning to America ran aground off the coast of North Carolina, she attempted to reach land in a lifeboat and drowned.

Belle Boyd (1843–1900), an even more famous spy than Rose Greenhow, listened through a hole in a closet floor to Federal officers planning a campaign against the Confederate Army near Winchester, Virginia, in 1862. Passing through the lines, she went onto the field during the battle and delivered her information to General Thomas J. "Stonewall" Jackson, who thanked her for her help in a note delivered after the Confederate victory. When the Confederates were forced to retreat, Federal officers discovered Boyd's espionage, and she was imprisoned in Washington for several months. After her release, she continued her activities as a spy until the war ended. Like Rose Greenhow, Belle Boyd was a partisan witness, but insofar as scholars have been able to determine, her account of her activities, written in efficient, although not brilliant prose, is true.

The same cannot be said with certainty about *The Woman in Battle: A Narrative of the Exploits and Adventures and Travels of Madame Loreta Janeta Velazquez, Otherwise Known as Lieutenant Harry T. Buford, Confederate States Army* (1879). Most scholars discount Velazquez's account of her activities on behalf of the Confederacy, and it seems extremely doubtful that she could have dressed as a man, as she claims, and participated in battle disguised as a Confederate officer. Her stories of being a courier for Confederate spies in Memphis and New Orleans cannot be substantiated, but they are in close accord with the same sorts of activities in which many Confederate women were engaged and are therefore valuable. Velazquez is a shadowy figure. There is no reason to doubt her claim that she was born in Havana in 1842, but when and where she died remain a mystery.

Although officially all Confederate nurses were men, many women did nurses' work under other designations. Phoebe Yates Pember (1823–1913) was matron of Chimborazo Hospital in Richmond from December 1862 until the end of the war, continuing her service after Federal troops had occupied the city. Pember, a native of South Carolina, was a childless widow at the commencement of hostilities. Her prose is not polished, but it is clear and clean, and in *A Southern Woman's Story* (1879) she demonstrates a good sense of dramatic structure. Much of her memoir is concerned with treating the wounded, but her book is particularly valuable as an account of daily life in a Confederate hospital where not only medicines and bandages, but also food and even beds were frequently scarce. Pember's courage is tested at the end of the war by a group of Confederate deserters whom she faces down with her pistol drawn when they attempt to rob her of the hospital whisky. Later, in defiance of Federal orders, she enters the commissary to get food and supplies for the wounded still in her charge. She is delighted to learn from hospital gossip that the Federal commander is said to be "awful afraid of her." After the war, Pember lived with her family in Georgia and traveled extensively both in this country and abroad.

Kate Cumming (1835–1909) was born in Scotland, but she was living in Mobile, Alabama, with her family when she left to serve in a Confederate hospital. Unlike Pember, who spent the war in Richmond, Cumming's Georgia hospital moved several times to escape the advancing Union Army. Her *Journal of Hospital Life in the Confederate Army of Tennessee from the Battle of Shiloh to the End of the War* (1866) is written in unadorned but clear prose that appears to be a reflection of Cumming's no nonsense personality. Her diary, much longer than Pember's memoir, gives more detail concerning various kinds of wounds, their treatment, and the suffering they caused. She does not hesitate to evaluate the skills of the doctors with whom she worked, some of whom she judges to be considerably more competent than others. She reprimands soldiers for complaining and officers for failing to care for their troops properly. Some of her best irony is spent on those, including members of her own family, who think it immodest for women to do hospital work. Why, she asks, is it permissible for Catholic nuns to treat the wounded and not permissible for her? Learning that a Confederate officer killed a Federal soldier who had surrendered, she writes, "I had earnestly prayed that, when the history of this war is written, all the dark pages may be on the side of the enemy; but alas! for poor frail humanity, such is not to be the case." Cumming's honesty enhances the value of her diary.

Sarah Morgan Dawson (1842–1909) was an extraordinarily talented writer whose charming and mischievous personality infuses every line of her work. *The Civil War Diary of Sarah Morgan* (1991), brilliantly and exhaustively edited by Charles East, begins with the death of Morgan's favorite brother in a duel and ends with news that two other brothers have died in the last days of the war. Nineteen when the war started, almost twenty when she began her diary, she chronicles the movement of her family ahead of the advancing Federal troops from Baton Rouge to other parts of Louisiana. To the consternation of her elders, Morgan delighted in danger, riding her horse on the levee where she was exposed to Yankee gunfire, sitting on the porch while shells burst around the house, wondering gleefully how long it would take her generally nervous mother to discover that it was not lightning and thunder that she saw and heard. During the first months that they were running from the Yankees, the Morgans lived comfortably with friends and relatives, and Sarah and her sister were frequently visited by soldiers on leave. Morgan speculated at length concerning the romantic attachments of others, but she seemed herself to be wary of love or even infatuation.

As the war continued and the Union Army advanced, the Morgan family's circumstances became increasingly strained, and in 1863 they returned to New Orleans to live under the protection of Sarah's half brother who was loyal to the Union. Morgan's account of her family's journey back is strikingly different from her entries describing the first, almost happy days of their flight from Baton Rouge. Food was scarce, lodgings uncomfortable, transportation doubtful. Obliged to pass first through Confederate and then through Union lines, they endured bureaucratic and military delays that seemed to Sarah, who was suffering from a back injury, almost endless. In spite of this, she recovered her ironic wit in time to write a wonderfully comic scene in which her mother, expecting worse than she gets from the Yankees, causes such a commotion that the Morgans are almost denied entry to New Orleans. Morgan's style is enhanced by her command of French, which she frequently uses to supply a word or phrase. She moved to Charleston in 1872 and married Frank Dawson, editor of the Charleston *News and Chronicle,* for which she wrote until her husband's death in 1889. Ten years later, she followed her son to Paris, where she died in 1909.

Cornelia Peake McDonald (1822–1909), one of the best writers of the Confederate women diarists, endured alternating periods of joy and suffering as Winchester, Virginia, where she lived, was captured by the Yankees, recaptured by the Confederates, and captured by the Federals once again. Several of her children—she had nine in addition to the nine her husband had fathered in a previous marriage—were still at home at the beginning of the war, and two of her sons watched one of the many battles that were fought in and around Winchester from their perch on a rail fence. Subsequently, McDonald's backyard was a battlefield, and her description of the fighting is vividly detailed. At the urging of her husband, she moved from Winchester to Lexington, Virginia, in 1863. Although this took her out of the path of the fighting, the move began a period of suffering and privation that became particularly acute after her husband was captured and imprisoned, and as was the custom, his military pay was stopped. Released from captivity because of ill health, her husband died while she was on her way to Richmond to be reunited with him. To add to her agony, she spilled scalding water on her foot and endured a long and painful convalescence from the injury.

McDonald's memories of peacetime and scenes of parting, although plainly written, evoke a sense of happier days in the past and of the apprehension with which soldiers and those who loved them were obliged to live. No one is better than she at conveying the deep sense of loss women and men felt after Lee surrendered and the ways in which old enmities were forgotten in the face of a disaster that was common to all. McDonald's tribulations were great, and she survived them, according to her own testimony, only because of her profound religious faith. In her darkest hours, when she was weak from hunger and heartbroken at the sight of the pale and pinched faces of her children, she prayed not only for relief, but also for fortitude and for grace to accept God's will, whatever it might be. After 1865, her circumstances began to improve. She spent the last years of her life in Louisville, Kentucky, where most of her family then lived. She gave art lessons and participated in many charitable endeavors. She was almost eighty-seven when she died.

The journals of Mary Jones (1808–1869) and of her daughter Mary Jones Mallard (1858–1917) of Liberty County, Georgia, are included in Robert Manson Myers' expertly edited chronicle of the Jones family, *The Children of Pride* (1972). Jones, Mallard, a friend Kate King (1839–1920), and several children were living on the Jones plantation during the destructive march of General Sherman's army through Georgia in the winter of 1864–65. Federal soldiers, who came sometimes singly but usually in groups, threatened the women, took food and livestock and whatever objects of value they could find, and destroyed much of what they could not carry with them. Pregnant when the first of Sherman's troops appeared, Mary Mallard gave birth while the house was surrounded by disorderly soldiers who demanded to be let inside even after they had been told of Mallard's confinement.

Sherman's army passed through some parts of Georgia in two or three days, but for Jones, Mallard, and King, the ordeal continued from December 14, 1864, until the last Federal soldier left their premises on January 5, 1865. Both Jones and Mallard wrote vivid descriptions of the invading soldiers—the dirt on their clothes, the way they smelled, the lice that they often left behind them. Almost as bad as the visits of the soldiers was the unrelieved anxiety that the women felt for themselves and for the children whom they trained to play close to the house and to run inside at the sound of hoofbeats. Deprived of food and all basic conveniences—soldiers took the rope from the bucket with which they drew water from the well—even when they were not engaged with the Yankees, they spent their days and nights in an agony of waiting because new enemies might arrive at any hour. The journals of Jones and Mallard are gracefully written by two very intelligent women, and they are chronicles of courage. Jones writes that at the end of "trying days" she would often inquire of Mallard and King: "Tell me, girls, did I act like a coward?"

Sherman's soldiers were not the only ones who made life difficult for civilians. Jackson, Louisiana, where the family of Celine Fremaux (1850–1935) went to escape the Federal occupation of Baton Rouge, was frequently raided by Union troops and was occasionally the battleground for Yankees and Confederate irregulars. Only fourteen when the war began, Celine Fremaux Garcia did not keep a journal but wrote *Celine: Remembering Louisiana, 1850–1871* (1987) after she was married and living comfortably in New Orleans. In recollection, she reprised a perceptive child's perspective, the terror she felt at the sight of hanged men, the pity she felt for the grieving mothers of dead soldiers, her disappointment in the closing of schools, and the disappearance of social life. She was a wonderfully circumstantial writer. She lists everything that her brother will take with him when he leaves to join the army and declares him well equipped for a Confederate soldier in 1864. She describes how a family eats after all their utensils have been stolen or destroyed. She tells how she and her siblings scavenged for cartridge boxes on the battlefield that they might use the leather to resole their shoes. She is not a polished writer, but her prose is marvelously concrete. She tells the reader what the reader wants to know and recreates another aspect of the experience of women during the Civil War.

Mary Ann Harris Gay (1829–1918) wrote *Life in Dixie during the War* (1897) for the son of her favorite brother—killed at the Battle of Franklin—in the hope that it might enhance her nephew's understanding of life in the Confederacy during the war. She and her mother, with whom she lived in Decatur, Georgia, endured the privations that were prevalent throughout the Confederacy and the added hardship of having their town occupied by Federal troops. Gay, with the aid of a young girl who had been a slave, picked up grains of corn spilled when the soldiers fed their livestock, found an abandoned Union Army horse and nursed it back to health, and scavenged clothes to take to her brother who was in bivouac south of Atlanta. Touched by the plight of a young mother and her several children, all of whom were hungry, Gay set out in a rickety wagon, pulled by the ex-Yankee horse, to take the suffering family to their relatives in Atlanta. The road she was obliged to travel was frequented by Yankee marauders and Confederate deserters, any of whom might have taken her horse and done harm to her and her passengers. This journey is the highlight of her memoir, but her entire book is a tale of adventure and deep courage. Gay's prose is marred by her predilection for flowery language, but her story is vivid in spite of this, and it creates a moving portrait of a brave and resourceful woman.

The War-Time Journal of a Georgia Girl 1864–1865 (1908) by Eliza Andrews (1840–1931) describes some of the destruction Sherman's soldiers left in their path and some of the social life that continued even as the war neared its conclusion, but it is most valuable for Andrews' account of conditions in the South after the Confederate defeat. She describes the conduct of discharged Confederate soldiers as they came through Washington, Georgia, on their way back to their homes. Most of them were well behaved, but, according to Andrews, Texas cavalrymen were inveterate horse thieves, and soldiers of all branches of the service helped loot the Confederate treasury and the warehouse filled with Confederate supplies. Many nights soldiers camped in the lot beside Andrews' house, singing the songs of the Lost Cause. Some of the southern officers who were passing through Washington had not surrendered. They hoped to go to Mexico or South America and perhaps fight again. They were penniless, and to help them along their way, Andrews, her sisters, and friends gave them buttons, pins, needles, and other common household articles, all of which had been rendered valuable by their scarcity in the South. After the war, Andrews published three novels, all of which sold well, and two textbooks on botany, a subject she taught both in secondary schools and in college. She was a skillful writer with a flair for narrative and a good eye for detail.

In *A Woman's Wartime Journal* (1927), Dolly Sumner Lunt Burge (1817–1891) gives an interesting account of her experience with some of Sherman's soldiers who passed through her plantation near Social Circle, Georgia, in 1864. Emma LeConte (1848–1932) furnishes a superb description of the burning of Columbia, South Carolina, and the ruins created thereby in *When the World Ended: The Diary of Emma LeConte* (1957). Constance Cary Harrison (1843–1920) who, like Eliza Andrews and Sarah Pryor, became a novelist after the war, displays her gift for narrative structure in *Recollections Grave and Gay* (1912). She gives a very valuable account of the last days of the Confederacy in Richmond and Petersburg, Virginia. In *Diary of a Southern Lady During the War, by a Lady of Virginia* (1867), Judith White Brokenbrough McGuire (1813–?) renders everyday life in the Confederacy and the difficulties attendant thereto in concrete terms. The sense of loss that pervades her diary is extremely effective. Other significant women's journals include *A Confederate Nurse: The Diary of Ada W. Bacot, 1860–1863* (1994) by Ada Bacot; *The Diary of Miss Emma Holmes* (1979) by Emma Holmes; *A Confederate Lady Comes of Age: The Journal of Pauline DeCaradeur Heyward* (1992) by Pauline DeCaradeur Heyward; *Two Diaries from Middle St. John's Berkeley, South Carolina. February–May, 1865* (1921) by Susan R. Jervey and Charlotte St. John Ravenel; and *How It Was: Four Years among the Rebels* (1892) by Mrs. Irby (Julia) Morgan.

Mary Chesnut

Elisabeth Muhlenfeld

Of all the Civil War diaries, the best is by Mary Boykin Chesnut. Critic Edmund Wilson in *Patriotic Gore* (1962) calls it "brilliant . . . a masterpiece." Novelist William Styron has deemed it the "great epic drama of our greatest national tragedy," and historian C. Vann Woodward avows that its "enduring value" is not the wealth of information it contains, but "the life and reality with which it endows people and events and . . . evokes the chaos and complexity of a society at war." Ironically, this most famous of Civil War diaries is not a diary nor was it written during the Civil War. First published as *A Diary From Dixie* (1905), and today known by the title of the Pulitzer Prize–winning 1981 edition by Woodward, *Mary Chesnut's Civil War,* Chesnut's is a conscious literary work, meticulously based on wartime journals but written some twenty years later. Mary Chesnut is thus both the quintessential chronicler of the Confederacy and an interesting transitional figure whose major work was written during the postbellum period.

Mary Boykin Miller was born in South Carolina in 1823. Her childhood was permeated by politics; her father had served in the United States Congress and would, before Mary's tenth birthday, also serve as governor and United States senator. At twelve she was sent to a boarding school in Charleston, where she spoke only French or German during school hours. When Governor Miller discovered that his thirteen-year-old daughter had been seen walking on the Battery in the moonlight with a young man (whom she would later marry), he removed her from gossip by taking her with the family to his cotton plantation in rural Mississippi. Mary returned to Madame Talvande's school the following year, but her formal education ended with her father's death in 1838, three weeks before her fifteenth birthday.

In 1840, she married James Chesnut, Jr., only surviving son of one of the largest slaveholding families in South Carolina, and went to live at the Chesnut estate, Mulberry, near Camden. During the next twenty years, largely because the couple was childless, Mary often felt superfluous; her mother-in-law retained vigorous control of the household at Mulberry, and Mary had few outlets for her creativity or her passionate nature. She suffered from periodic illness and occasional bouts of depression. To escape household tension, she turned to reading—religious works for penitence, the classics for intellectual stimulation, and novels for pure pleasure. Despite relatively little formal schooling, Mary was deeply and broadly educated, comfortable with French and German literature in the original, epic poetry of every era, and English writers from Chaucer to Thackeray.

Between 1840 and 1860, James Chesnut, Jr., served in the state legislature, and in 1858 he was appointed to the United States Senate. Mary loved Washington but when James resigned in 1860 to protest Lincoln's election, Mary quickly cast her lot with her state and became an ardent supporter of the South and of Jefferson Davis, whose wife, Varina, had become a friend.

Although she had never kept a diary, as war became a certainty, Chesnut began to do so. The journal she kept under lock and key was private and candid. Extant portions, published as *The Private Mary Chesnut: The Unpublished Civil War Journals* (Woodward and Muhlenfeld, eds.) in 1984, consist of hurried, sometimes cryptic notes. Mary Chesnut understood from the outset not only that she was witness to a historic upheaval of cataclysmic proportions, but also that she could provide a unique perspective. And indeed, her vantage point was remarkable. In Montgomery, Alabama, James attended the Confederate Provisional Congress. There, as throughout the war, Mary's quarters served as a salon filled with the elite and the interesting, in which she presided over witty debate about the news, rumors, and gossip of the day—all of which she recorded in her journal. The Chesnuts returned to Charleston where, from a rooftop, Mary observed the firing on Fort Sumter. Then they moved to Richmond, where she waited with Varina Davis for news of the battle at Manassas and recorded visiting the first sick and wounded of the war.

As a woman Mary felt impotent, dependent on her husband's involvement. At times, she was forced to view the war from behind the pillars of Mulberry—which she found dull and infuriating. But in 1862, James was called to Richmond as aide to Jefferson Davis, placing Mary at the heart of the action. In late 1864, James, now a general, returned to South Carolina, where Mary recorded details of inevitable defeat: in Columbia her drawing room now held generals without sufficient troops; her closet held an artificial leg sent through the blockade for a family friend. By early 1865, Mary was recording flight and exile. After returning to Camden in May, she made several more entries in her journal, but by July, she set it down.

War's aftermath was characterized by uncertainty, debt, and a host of dependent relatives and former slaves. Despite bouts of illness, Mary took over the running of the household, assisted in record keeping and oversight of farming affairs, and established a small butter-and-egg business that brought pin money into the household. Thinking that she might earn money by literary work, Chesnut undertook translation of French stories, but apparently never published any of her efforts. In the early 1870s she worked on two novels more or less simultaneously. One was largely autobiographical; "Two Years of My Life" deals with a schoolgirl at Madame Talvande's French School for Young Ladies in Charleston who is taken by her father to a raw cotton plantation in Mississippi. The other is a Civil War novel, "The Captain and the Colonel," Chesnut's first effort to use the materials of her wartime journals.

"The Captain and the Colonel" is the story of the indomitable Joanna Effingham and her three daughters, accustomed to a life of graciousness and regularity. In its early chapters the novel follows the classic pattern of a novel of manners, in which the complications of flirtations, misunderstandings and jealousies threaten to undermine advantageous marriages. Into this predictable mix comes the Civil War, and Chesnut's protagonist goes from being a force of nature to the helpless victim of natural forces over which she has no control. Chesnut makes very clear in the novel the patterns and connections between the personal and the global. Marriage and family—the traditional "happy endings" of Victorian novels—offer no solace. Indeed, Chesnut sees that at war's end, little has changed for women. They remain in bondage.

Neither of Chesnut's first two efforts at fiction nor the surviving fragment of a third are polished works, but they show Chesnut, then in her mid-fifties, developing a narrative voice and learning to write vivid dialogue. Themes such as women's rights, slavery and race relations, and the impact of history on the individual life emerge in the fiction and would later be developed effectively in her revised Civil War journal.

In 1881 Chesnut began a full-scale revision of her wartime journals—work that continued for three years until she was forced to set it aside to deal, in rapid succession, with the deaths of her mother and husband, the settling of James's debt-ridden estate, and her little dairy business. Before she was able to return to her journal, she died on November 22, 1886.

The importance of *Mary Chesnut's Civil War* lies in the way it frames for us the experience of living through the most important national crisis of our history. In Chesnut's work, the Civil War is not a series of military engagements, but a kaleidoscopic shifting of the tectonic plates of a culture, accompanied by a Greek chorus of voices of every description. Retaining scrupulously the diary form, Chesnut's work is structured by the war itself: in its early pages voices are confident, comfortable (often too complacent for Mary Chesnut's taste) or jockeying for position. In the end, desolation is pervasive; the voices drone on sadly, rehashing might-have-beens, unable to let go. Chesnut's own voice is by turns skeptical, wry, passionate, analytical, keening, and, from the first, filled with foreboding.

Mary Chesnut's Civil War sees from the woman's perspective. One recurrent image pattern is love and marriage: metaphorically, the South tries to divorce the North, but is crushed, as a woman is subjugated by a domineering husband. On a personal scale, in the midst of war's carnage, romance blooms, courtships unfold, hearts are broken, and youth dances on, oblivious to defeat. Chesnut uses to great thematic effect three men in her family: her father-in-law, James Chesnut, the "old Colonel," grand patriarch and slaveholder; her husband James, intellectual and unquestioning, but ineffectual in a time of chaotic change; and her nephew Johnny, cheerfully egocentric, apolitical, and flexible, just the kind of man needed in a new South. Throughout, women carry on as they must.

This enormous work—the final revision contains nearly 500,000 words—reveals the fine intellect of its author, perhaps most impressively in the fact that Chesnut almost never allows hindsight to color her depiction of events. But *Mary Chesnut's Civil War* is unquestionably a product of the postwar years: out of the chaos of war's immediacy, it successfully weaves images, characters, and events together to craft a coherent vision: life in drawing rooms, across dining tables, in churches, railroad cars, kitchens and hospitals throughout the South, from the beginning of what seemed a glorious war to the end of a way of life.

PART II

The Postbellum South (1865–1900)

Introduction to Part II

Mary Louise Weaks

As Union soldiers marched into Baton Rouge, Louisiana, a distressed Sarah Morgan expressed her frustration at not being able to protect her home and her city by writing in her diary, "O! if I was only a man! Then I could don the breeches and slay them with a will! If some few women were in the ranks, they could set the men an example they would not blush to follow." Other white women showed a similar fortitude during the years of civil war, seeking to replace society's expectations of them as helpless women with a courage and patriotism that they believed they, like their men, possessed. An Alabama woman, for example, is said to have broken off an engagement with her fiancé because he was slow in enlisting with the Confederate Army. She sent him a skirt, a petticoat, and a note saying he should "wear these or volunteer." The pages of southern histories are full of what have become quite well-known stories about white women's desires to join their men on the battlefield and women's influence in determining the length of the war itself. In a letter to her local newspaper, a young Georgia woman asks women readers on the home front, "Shall man tread it alone? . . . no, no a thousand times no." Then she points to ways southern women might support the Cause: "hurl the destructive novel in the fire and turn our poodles out of doors, and convert our pianos into spinning wheels." Englishman George A. Sala, who was touring the United States in 1863, wrote in *My Diary in America in the Midst of War* (1865), "I question whether either ancient or modern history can furnish an example of a conflict which was so much of a 'woman's war' as this. The bitterest, most vengeful of politicians in this ensanguined controversy are the ladies."

The Civil War created for many white women the desire and the opportunity to reshape the image and the roles of white women in the South, but stories such as these also perpetuated the assumption that all white women were valiant supporters of the Confederate cause. In reality, there is no one story of women's roles or character during the Civil War. Perhaps because of this mythologizing of the white woman's role in the Civil War and the complexities of southern society in the nineteenth century for both black and white women, historians continue to speculate on women's roles during the war and the influence that the war had on their lives. What is certain is that white women worked outside the home in greater numbers than before the war, and many ran family farms and plantations while their men were off at war. Women worked in munitions factories, as nurses, and as seamstresses. In agricultural communities, they labored in the fields. Although women of the upper classes did not generally find themselves working under difficult conditions, many women of the lower classes struggled to put food on their tables and to shelter and clothe their family members. The lives of white women were also greatly affected by the countless numbers of men disabled and killed in the war, and after the war, by the migration of a significant number of men to areas outside the South, most frequently to the West. Because of the defeat of the Confederacy during the Civil War, many white women also felt disappointed in southern men's inability to protect their homeland. Others suggested in their writings the growing complexities of southern womanhood. Sarah Morgan Dawson, for instance, writes of visiting a Confederate army camp where she fell from her buggy when the horses were startled by the sound of gunfire. She realized immediately after the fall that she had seriously hurt her spine, but she knew that she must not mention her injury to the men who helped her. She was more concerned with making sure that her feet remained covered. White women of the middle and upper classes were raised to be delicate, helpless creatures, but the realities of war resulted in emotions not attuned to such characteristics.

While the Civil War resulted in confusion and, in some cases, societal change for white women, it affected black women quite differently. In slavery, black women faced separation from their families at the whim of a slave master who could sell off husbands and children to neighboring or distant plantations. During the war, slave families were often broken apart as retreating slave masters took their adult male slaves with them and left women, children, and the elderly to fend for themselves. In some cases, black men were fighting in the Union Army, leaving their families behind on plantations. Wives and mothers of the soldiers were often treated harshly by white slave masters hoping to seek vengeance against the northern soldiers. In other cases, black men were forced to work in service of the Confederate government, often as laborers. In 1863, emancipation offered black women freedom on paper, but prejudices and social restrictions continued to control black women's lives in both the North and the South. Harriet Jacobs, in her 1863 *Incidents in the Life of a Slave Girl,* pleads that her readers not judge her as they would normally judge a white woman. Jacobs believed she should not be held up to the same standards of womanhood as white women because of the atrocities of slavery that she had been forced to endure.

While studies of military battles and strategies have long been of interest to historians and to the general public, the war has only recently been discussed as what historian LeeAnn Whites calls a "crisis in gender," a crisis that was confronted by both women and men. Whites argues in her book *The Civil War as a Crisis in Gender* (1995) that while the war forced white women to be independent, white men found themselves increasingly dependent upon women—in effect, "feminized." Confederate soldiers depended upon women to provide them with their supplies, and frequently even with the very bullets they fired from their guns. Men on the battlefront often found themselves wishing for the domestic world of home—the realm of woman. As freedmen and freedwomen reassembled families separated by slavery and by war, they reclaimed their roles as husbands, wives, and parents, thus supplanting masters and mistresses who had controlled and manipulated these roles for slaves on the plantation. While stories like Sala's have portrayed southern white women as prolonging the war, historians like Drew Gilpin Faust have said that the Confederacy did not survive any longer than it did because "so many women did not want it to. The way in which their interests in the war were publicly defined—in a very real sense denied—gave women little reason to sustain the commitment modern war required. It may well have been because of its women that the South lost the Civil War." Likewise, the effect of the war on women's lives in the postwar period has been increasingly examined. Anne Firor Scott, for example, in her book *The Southern Lady: From Pedestal to Politics* (1970), says that, in effect, with the loss of the Confederacy in the Civil War, "the patriarchy was dead." But many of its ideals continued to dominate southern culture long after the war ended. Likewise, Catherine Clinton says that even though white women during the war "shouldered burdens" not typically expected of them and suffered hardships in the postwar period, they were greatly affected by their men, who "filled their heads with talk of the Lost Cause." So emerged, then, what Anne Goodwyn Jones describes as an "oxymoronic ideal of the woman made of steel yet masked in fragility."

Slavery and the Civil War had an important influence on women's reading and writing, as women increasingly used both reading and writing as means to control their lives. Like Harriet Beecher Stowe, the "little lady who started the war," southern women writers influenced the length and the character of the war. Augusta Jane Evans Wilson's *Macaria* (1863) and Harriet Jacobs' *Incidents in the Life of a Slave Girl* (1863) were, for example, both published during the war to muster support for the South and the North, respectively. Wilson gained fame as the author of the novel *Macaria,* which was banned from northern army camps because the book was said to be too damaging to northern morale. Dedicated to those "who have delivered the South from despotism," the novel presents an idealized portrait of faithful slaves and kind masters and mistresses and celebrates southern war victories. Legend had it that one Confederate soldier was saved when he was called into battle and quickly placed the book in his breast pocket; the book stopped a bullet that would have pierced his heart. The Confederate woman had saved the soldier with her stalwart support from the home front. Like Wilson's novel, Harriet Jacobs' narrative was published in 1863. While slavery prohibited black women like Jacobs from reading and writing, slaves who escaped to the North used writing as a political tool to compose slave narratives in support of abolitionism and, like Jacobs' narrative, in support of the northern cause during the war.

Reading and writing also became increasingly a way for women to examine their inner lives. While a great number of antebellum women kept diaries, that number dramatically increased with the years of civil war. One particularly revealing study of white women's reading and writing habits during the war is a chapter in Drew Gilpin Faust's book *Mothers of Invention* (1996). Faust notes that whereas antebellum writers such as E.D.E.N. Southworth and Maria McIntosh gained personal strength by fictionalizing situations from their own difficult lives, the crises and challenges of war actually made reading and writing much more intense and cathartic experiences for women during the war. Despite the difficulties women often faced in finding reading materials, novels became even more important in the war years as instructional tools for living and as a pleasure for women in a world where there were few. Reading also allowed women to examine and to confront issues beyond their traditional realms and to imagine new possibilities for their individual lives. Faust points, for example, to Lucy Buck of Virginia, who, upon reading a new novel, wrote in her diary in March 1862:

"There seems to be so little real happiness that I would like to make for myself an imaginary life in the mimic world created by the author's pen." Buck's diary entry is particularly noteworthy because she describes the intimate relationship she has with the novel: "I like to merge my individuality into that of the imaginary characters, enter into all their joys, share their trials and forget the ugly realities of real life around me." Pointing specifically to the words "merge," "enter," and "share" in the passage, Faust describes this diary entry as "an extraordinarily self-conscious statement of the purposes of reading and their relation to woman's place in the wartime South. . . . Buck finds an escape not just from reality but from dread uselessness into active possibility and participation."

In a similar fashion, Mary Chesnut writes in her diary that during the Union attack on Richmond in spring 1862, she stayed up all one night reading a novel to relieve her anxiety. She also states elsewhere in her diary that she has "an insane idea in my brain to write a tale." She felt engaged in the workings of the Confederacy as a military wife and had a sense that she was recording a story of momentous worth. After the war, she rewrote her diary again and again in hopes of reshaping it for publication. The degree to which southern women like Chesnut wrote personal documents such as diaries and, in the postwar period, memoirs, points to the significant role these women saw the war playing in their personal lives. Walter Sullivan's essay on Civil War diaries and memoirs and his book entitled *The War the Women Lived: Female Voices from the Confederate South* (1995) attest to the numbers of women picking up the pen to write. In effect, women's involvement in the war became further verified through their written documents. In 1862, for example, Sarah Morgan described her diary as "a necessity," a "resource in these days of trouble," and "relief to me where my tongue was forced to remain quiet!" After the war, many southern women likewise found that they could provide a source of income for their families by revising their diaries for publication.

More and more women in general became "writers" during the Civil War as letter writing became their only means of communication with loved ones away at war and as women found themselves responsible for making written appeals on matters facing their loved ones. Some women wrote apologetically to military and government officials that they realized the inappropriateness of a woman writing, but that a male family member was not at home to write for them. With men preoccupied with war, women also became important contributors of sentimental poetry and articles for Confederate newspapers. While women were responsible for a good deal of the imaginative literature of the time, they were, however, most commonly writers of personal letters. Faust explains that particularly in correspondence between wives and their husbands who were away at war, a new "intimacy, new frankness, heightened self-awareness, and self-revelation" often became apparent in their letters. For instance, one woman, Julia Davidson, wrote her husband, "We little knew how dear we were to each other" before the war. Only through their letters did they both come to explore their inner lives and their relationship. In fact, in letters, women discovered a way to examine their innermost emotions and feelings that they had been raised to deny or at least not talk about.

Because of the new roles southern women assumed during the war—including their increasing roles as readers and writers, the postwar years were a time of confusion for many women. While southern white men returning from war faced the difficulties of living with war injuries, increased alcoholism, and economic depression, they wished their wives and daughters to provide stability in their home lives, and often that meant preserving the ideals of antebellum southern culture. In effect, familial and societal pressures led many southern white women to assume once again those traditional roles. Although, as Emily Wright points out in her essay for this book, the New Woman of the postbellum period did not make as strong an appearance in the South as in the North, southern women did find their roles changing. Increasingly, black and white women were employed in the work place. The growing awareness of the necessity of education for women also resulted in the establishment of more and more schools for that purpose and women's organizations such as reading groups and clubs that focused specifically on social reform and sometimes career training. While a typical measure of woman's freedom has been her capacity to work outside the home for a wage, this traditional evaluation of women's rights was complicated by southern social standards and by the issue of slavery. In the postbellum South, for example, a white woman who worked outside the home was typically pitied for not having a man to support her. A black woman who worked outside the home was forced to give up once again the rights that slaves gained with emancipation, that is, the right to remain at home as a homemaker, raising her own children. In the years from 1865 until 1900, the issue of race also created divisions among women of the South, even as women struggled with their new identities. White women generally felt a greater loyalty to their race than to their gender because they shared with white men the loss of the Confederacy and the impoverishment of the years of Reconstruction. The black woman's place was even more complex. Anna Julia Cooper, writing in the 1890s, said, for example, that "the colored woman of today occupies, one may say, a unique position in this country.

In a period of itself transitional and unsettled, her status seems one of the least ascertainable and definitive of all the forces which make for our civilization. She is confronted by both a woman question and a race problem, and is as yet an unknown or an unacknowledged factor in both."

In the postwar years, most white southern authors—whether consciously or subconsciously—preserved in their writings the ideals of the Old South and this division between the races, while northern publishers often perpetuated such views by encouraging nostalgia. White southerners also frequently used literature as a tool to control the black race. White supremacist writings of the period, for example, often portrayed the black man as a potential rapist. In her book *Gender, Race, and Region in the Writings of Grace King, Ruth McEnery Stuart, and Kate Chopin* (1989), Helen Taylor says that even in the writings of King, Stuart, and Chopin, "the tamed black figure," who is "loyal, affectionate, desexualized," is "a recurrent and almost obsessive fictional motif." The image of the belle, herself, according to Anne Goodwyn Jones, was used for "conflicting ends." On one hand, in literature, the belle might be portrayed as turning down the marriage proposal of a northern suitor to make a symbolic "last stand" for the South. On the other hand, she might be portrayed as marrying a northern suitor and persuading him to the "southern" political view. In both situations, however, the belle "plays the same role: she preserves the culture of the South, thus in effect she is the soul of the South." Once again, the ideal of white womanhood was used by conflicting means to perpetuate the ideals of southern culture.

What black and white women writers of the time do share is a common struggle for voice. Although white women before the war were making profitable incomes from their craft, they were, as Anne Goodwyn Jones explains, still writing from behind a mask. Yet in the postbellum years, those anxieties of authorship still remained, causing Mary Murfree to write as Charles Egbert Craddock, and Katherine McDowell as Sherwood Bonner. Chopin also cut off her own voice by never publishing her short story "The Storm" after her experiences with the publication of *The Awakening* (1899). As the metaphorical veil was lifted from the face of Linda Brent at the end of Jacobs' *Incidents in the Life of a Slave Girl,* so, too, was the veil rising for black and white writers of the postbellum period. More and more those voices spoke out from behind the masks of race and gender. While Anna Julia Cooper, for instance, saw herself as part of an African American literary tradition (and indeed desired to celebrate that tradition and to downplay her own part in it), she described her "little Voice" as having "been added to the already full chorus."

That "full chorus" of African American women's writing has been outlined in books like Frances Smith Foster's *Written by Herself* (1993), and
for southern women writers of African heritage, Foster's observations also
clearly outline a tradition in the South. Foster quotes from Cooper to describe this tradition: whereas the works of writers like Frances E. W. Harper
had not been "unfelt," their work had been "unproclaimed." Foster refers
to the year 1892, the publication date of Cooper's *A Voice from the South*,
as "mark[ing] the beginning of a new era in African-American women's literary tradition. It became less discreet, more visible." Cooper, herself, saw
the turn of the century as a time when woman's "sentiments must strike the
keynote and give the dominant tone." She believed "The struggle with nature is over, the struggle with ideas begins." Ultimately, according to Foster,
the African American woman writer's success, or lack thereof, is indicative
of the degree to which American democracy is to succeed.

The years following the Civil War to the turn of the century thus poised
southern women writers with hopes for a new century of progress for them
as American females. While sectional divisions were slowly dissolving, black
and white southern women still struggled with their identities as southerners, remembering a past of slavery and war that was only a generation or
two away from their own lives. For black and white women, southern society remained a place of tension and conflict, of despair at the loss of the
Confederacy for some and of the hopefulness of Emancipation for others.
Many white women saw themselves as still burdened with what Jessie Daniel Ames (1883–1972) called "the crown of chivalry" that was "pressed like
a crown of thorns on [the] heads" of white southern women. But others,
like Gertrude Mossell (1855–1948), believed that ultimately the twentieth
century would prove to be the "woman's century," especially for the African American woman. Standing on the threshold of the new century, many
writers looked backward, but others like Mossell looked forward, at the
possibilities of the future.

The New Woman of the New South

Emily Powers Wright

The image of white southern womanhood constructed before the Civil War may be understood as a hyperstated version of American "true" womanhood. The nineteenth-century "Cult of True Womanhood" enjoined women to display piety, purity, submissiveness, and domesticity, and the same virtues were expected of and attributed to southern women. However, southern womanhood shouldered the additional burden of justifying the ways of the South to itself. Although historians speculate variously as to the origins and ideological functions of the South's particular construction of femininity, they are generally agreed that it served to legitimate and perpetuate antebellum class, race, and gender hierarchies. Not only the purity, piety, submissiveness, and domesticity, but also the grace, charm, and leisure of the southern lady were held up as sign and proof of the superiority of southern civilization.

During and after the Civil War, southern women encountered new responsibilities and opportunities that held the potential of destabilizing this image. The seeds of change were sown during the Civil War, when women assumed the demanding task of managing their households and farms in the absence of men, gathered together to conduct the work of hospital and soldiers' aid societies, and went out of the home to work as nurses and in factories. The resourcefulness women displayed during the war gave them a self-confidence that found fertile field for expression after the war, when conditions conspired to provide them with increasing opportunities to participate in public life.

Women of means found themselves released from the burden of directing large plantation households and supervising the care and work of slaves, while the wives of professional and middle-class townsmen also gained freedom from domestic duties as a result of changes accompanying the rapid industrialization of the late nineteenth century, such as smaller family size, better health, and the availability of canned food and ready-made clothes. The leisure time acquired from these improvements, and from the presence of large numbers of African American women willing to work for very low wages, could be devoted to activities outside the home. For less fortunate women, postwar poverty and the loss of one-fourth of the region's males to death and westward migration conspired to drive women into the work force. The need of large numbers of women to find paid employment coincided with the effort to build a public education system throughout the South, which provided job opportunities for women. As women streamed into the work force, normal and industrial colleges and programs for women were created to prepare them for teaching and for clerical and manufacturing jobs. Finally, the increasing urbanization of the South provided the opportunity for women to gather together in church societies and women's self- and community-improvement organizations.

As a result of these changes, southern women began to form voluntary associations for the purpose of learning about and beginning to respond to the world outside the home. Women first banded together to further the foreign and home mission work of their churches. As women working in church societies gained self-confidence and pride in their achievements, they asked for more independence and greater rights within the church structure. Many of these women were inspired by Frances Willard during her tour of the South in the 1880s, and they joined the Women's Christian Temperance Union (WCTU) under state leaders such as Caroline Merrick in Louisiana, Belle Kearney in Mississippi, Julia Tutwiler in Alabama, and Rebecca Felton in Georgia. Emboldened by their experiences in church societies and the WCTU, southern women began to form clubs for self-education. Although the initial goal of the many women's clubs created around the turn of the century was self-improvement, the organizational experience women acquired in these clubs served to prepare them for political participation. As Josephine K. Henry writes in "The New Woman of the New South" (1895), the "framing of constitutions and by-laws, election of officers, discussions on ways and means and all the parliamentary usages" in which women participated in these clubs made them "the primary schools which [led] to the university of politics."

Church societies, the WCTU, and women's clubs created a constituency of self-confident women who became increasingly active in a variety of social-reform movements. From the 1870s on, women participated openly not only in the temperance movement but also in efforts to change age-of-consent, child labor, and guardianship laws, to abolish the convict lease system, and to establish library and education programs. These women saw the need for voting power to legislate the changes they sought, while increasing numbers of working women and female property owners began to chafe at the vulnerability of their voteless state. Thus, by the mid-1890s, a significant portion of southern women were ready to join the small group of activists who had participated in the suffrage movement since the Civil War. According to historian Anne Firor Scott in *The Southern Lady: From Pedestal to Politics, 1830–1930* (1970), suffrage sentiment began to appear immediately after the war, and throughout the 1860s, 1870s, and 1880s a handful of southern women actively participated in the national women's rights movement and organized local suffrage efforts as well. In 1896 five southern women were among the nineteen who testified at length before the Senate Committee on Woman Suffrage, and by that year some degree of suffrage organization had taken place in every southern state. Thus, by 1895 Henry was able to quote in her article dozens of women from every state in the South who had written to her stating their desire for the vote and their determination to win equality under the law.

The arguments employed by these women indicate the degree to which they had rejected the antebellum image of southern womanhood. Many of the women Henry quotes adopted the same strategy northern suffragists employed: drawing on the doctrine of "true woman" as primary moral agent in society, they argued that women's superior moral influence was necessary for the purification of government and public life, and that in order to exercise this influence, women must have the vote. However, it is noteworthy that many of Henry's correspondents took the bold step of demanding the right to vote for their own sakes—to protect their property, their access to education, and their rights to their own children. As an Arkansas woman wrote, "Self-protection is my inherent right. For that protection I demand the ballot." Furthermore, many of the women Henry quotes demanded the vote on the basis of natural rights, arguing that the principles of justice, liberty, and equality mandated the extension of the franchise to women. Thus it appears that by 1895 at least a minority of southern women had overthrown the image of southern woman as self-effacing moral guardian. Striking directly at the heart of that image, a Louisiana woman wrote Henry, "I want men to stop calling me a queen and treating me like an imbecile."

As Henry's title indicates and historical research confirms, postbellum developments resulted in the appearance of a southern New Woman. However, the term "New Woman" is applied not only to actual women engaged in social reform and feminist activism but also to feminist writers and fictional female characters, and in none of these three incarnations did the New Woman exert a major influence on the New South. Henry admits that even in the mid-1890s the average southern woman professed herself satisfied with her condition, and although historians have uncovered more suffrage activity on the part of southern women than had once been recognized, the momentum of the movement was slower in the South than in the North and had less impact: only four southern states voted to ratify the Nineteenth Amendment.

As for fictional representations of New Women, they do not appear in the writings of postbellum southern male authors, and only a few are found in works by southern women. As Caroline Gebhard has written in an essay included in *Haunted Bodies* (1997), male writers of postbellum plantation fiction put "southern white women . . . firmly back on the pedestal of an impossible purity." Examining a large sampling of postbellum southern fiction by both men and women, John Ruoff in his 1976 dissertation entitled "Southern Womanhood, 1865–1920: An Intellectual and Cultural Study" comes to a similar conclusion. He finds that although the postbellum construction of southern womanhood was revised to reflect the moral strength and physical courage southern women had exhibited during and after the war, there was actually little change in the image. Postbellum southern womanhood was portrayed in two main modes: a middle-class, "evangelical" mode that perpetuated antebellum notions of "true womanhood" as pure, pious, submissive, and domestic and that was most closely associated with the matron; and an upper-class, "traditional" mode that perpetuated antebellum notions of the southern lady as ornament and conservator of an aristocratic and patriarchal way of life and that was most closely associated with the belle and the old lady who remained fiercely loyal to the Lost Cause of the Confederacy.

Just as antebellum southern womanhood supported the race, class, and gender hierarchies of the Old South, so postbellum southern womanhood played an important role in Lost Cause ideology: the new strength and courage assigned to southern womanhood were directed toward defense of the southern way of life. Much postbellum literature emphasized women's particularly intransigent, "unreconstructable" attitude toward all things Yankee, often by having female characters either reject northern suitors or marry northern men and then persuade their husbands to accept their ideas. In either case, the southern woman was presented as defender and preserver of southern culture, representing the last bulwark against the encroachments of northern civilization. The imperative that southern womanhood act as conservator of a threatened way of life placed constraints on southern women, whose sectional loyalty and personal welfare required that they conform to the image upheld by their culture. This requirement explains the relative weakness of the southern suffrage movement and the relative absence of feminist sentiment from writings by southern women.

Along with teaching, writing was one of the few respectable professions for middle- and upper-class women seeking means of support after the Civil War, and many southern women took up the pen at this time, producing sentimental fiction and poetry and entering into the field of journalism as writers and editors. Indeed, in an 1891 article entitled "Southern Womanhood as Affected by the War," Wilbur Fisk Tillett wrote that one of the happiest effects of the war was the discovery that the southern woman "has very remarkable gifts for narrative description and other kinds of literature." However, he reassures the reader, the broadening sphere of women's work will not "take woman out of her true place in the home. . . . The Southern woman loves the retirement of home, and shrinks from everything that would tend to bring her into the public gaze." Tillett here encapsulates the dilemma of the postbellum southern woman: despite the fact that both opportunity and necessity conspired to place her in new positions of authority and publicity, she felt compelled to present at least a surface appearance of retiring domesticity. The works of postbellum women writers reveal the tendency of southern women to sacrifice the feminist ideology that might have arisen from changing postwar conditions to the complex task of rebuilding the South's damaged self-image in a new and changing world.

This tendency is apparent, for example, in the reversal that took place in the writings of staunchly pro-South author Augusta Jane Evans Wilson. In her prewar novel *Beulah* (1859), Wilson created a remarkably independent-minded heroine who eschews the comforts of marriage and religion in order to make her own way in the world, both financially and intellectually. At the novel's end Beulah capitulates entirely to the patriarchal structure of her society and its religion, but her earlier rejection of that structure nonetheless inscribes the possibility of protest against the antebellum model of southern womanhood. After the Civil War, however, Wilson reversed the feminist direction of her fiction and reinscribed the myth of southern womanhood with a vengeance. In *St. Elmo* (1866) she again traces her heroine's development through independent thought to religion and marriage, but she adds an explicitly antifeminist statement, having her heroine describe the suffrage movement as a "ridiculous clamor raised by a few unamiable and wretched wives, and as many embittered, disappointed old maids of New England." Here Wilson describes feminist sentiment as a northern phenomenon offensive to the "true women" of the South—despite, or perhaps because of, the fact that Wilson herself enjoyed a degree of financial and intellectual independence entirely out of keeping with the prevailing image of southern womanhood.

Similarly, Louisiana writer Grace King violated that image by supporting herself through her writing, traveling widely and frequently, and embedding implied critiques of the South's patriarchal power structure in her stories about black and white women. However, just as in her personal writings she professed a strong sense of identification with the South and emphasized whenever possible her dependence upon and deference toward males, so she buried the feminist challenge of her stories so far beneath their conventional surfaces as to make the process of excavating it a tortuous one indeed. King, Wilson, and other southern women writers of the period between 1859 and 1936 were, as Anne Goodwyn Jones explains in *Tomorrow Is Another Day: The Woman Writer in the South, 1859–1936* (1981), constrained to adopt a mask of conformity in their lives and writings. Consequently, superficial readings of their lives and works perpetuate the traditional image of southern womanhood.

This masking is also evident in autobiographical narratives written in the 1880s and 1890s. In an unpublished paper entitled "A Little Girl with Her Doll House: The Role of Daughters in Mythologizing the Old South" (1998), Lucinda MacKethan points specifically to four narratives by daughters of wealthy rice planters, two of whom had assumed governance of their families' plantations. MacKethan shows that in order to accommodate their newfound authority as writers and planters to the self-effacing image of southern womanhood, each of these women took pains to camouflage her actual agency and power by constructing herself as a dutiful and adoring daughter, thereby aligning herself with the patriarchal power of the father. Negotiating this accommodation between image and reality required that each writer portray fathers, mothers, and slaves in such a way as to reinscribe antebellum class, gender, and race hierarchies.

As these examples reveal, postbellum southern women writers colluded in perpetuating an image of southern womanhood that upheld prewar power relations, often employing complex discursive strategies in order to negotiate the contradictions between that image and the realities of their lives. Thus it is not surprising that Wilson depicted the New Woman as a Yankee harpy or that Kate Chopin mocked the southern New Woman in her short story "Miss McEnders" (1897). The protagonist of Chopin's story is a member of a local Woman's Reform Club. On her way to read a paper on the dignity of women's labor, she stops in to meet her dressmaker, Mlle Salambre, and discovers that the woman has a child out of wedlock. Horrified, she dismisses the seamstress in order to teach her a moral lesson. However, the resourceful Mlle Salambre turns the tables on Miss McEnders, teaching her a moral lesson by causing her to discover the unsavory origins of her own family's wealth. Although Chopin here endorses the dignity of women's labor by privileging the experienced self-sufficiency of Mlle Salambre over the self-righteous naïveté of Miss McEnders, she nonetheless satirizes the very kind of woman who formed the basis of the southern suffrage movement.

Chopin, like other southern writers of the postbellum period, declined to endorse the public activities of the minority of southern New Women who populated the South at the end of the century. Such an endorsement does not occur until Mary Johnston's *Hagar* (1913), in which the heroine proclaims that suffragists "want the vote to use as a lever, and so do I." However, New Womanhood was a behavioral and psychosexual phenomenon as well as a political one, and in the former terms Chopin was a New Woman writer. In her personal life she exhibited unusual independence, not only by supporting herself after the death of her husband but also by taking frequent long walks around New Orleans unescorted and by smoking cigarettes—a practice strongly associated with the New Woman. She also subscribed to the *Yellow Book,* edited by Aubrey Beardsley, which was associated with the decadent movement in British art and literature. As Elaine Showalter has shown in *Daughters of Decadence: Women Writers of the Fin de Siècle* (1993), many British writers of New Woman fiction displayed a sexual candor that caused male reviewers to view New Woman writers as "threatening daughters of decadence." Showalter includes Chopin among this group of writers for her late short story "An Egyptian Cigarette" (1900), which Sally Ledger, in *The New Woman: Fiction and Feminism at the Fin de Siècle* (1997), describes as a "feminist reformulation of decadence" because of its exotic and hallucinatory exploration of the protagonist's hidden erotic life.

Chopin's effort to represent female desire as a creative force connects her with the decadent strain of New Woman fiction, and her critique of marriage aligns her work with that of many British New Woman writers. One of the most consistent themes of New Woman fiction was a questioning, or outright rejection, of the institution of marriage, and even in her earliest stories Chopin explored the effects that marriage can have on a woman's ability to develop as an individual. In later stories her increasingly independent, strong-willed female characters chafe against the constraints of marriage, and Chopin's readers were distressed by her refusal to pass authorial judgment against her characters for their transgressions against the institution. This distress culminated in public outrage at Chopin's *The Awakening* (1899), which constitutes the apotheosis of Chopin's critique of marriage and her exploration of the creative potential of female desire. In this novel the protagonist, Edna Pontellier, experiences an erotic awakening that discloses to her her own potential as a woman, an individual, and an artist. In an effort to fulfill this potential, she moves out of her husband's house and enters into an extramarital affair. However, she is finally unable to locate or even to imagine affirmation of her new vision of herself as an autonomous being, and as a result, like many protagonists of New Woman fiction, she commits suicide. Unsatisfied by the punishment Edna inflicts on herself at the end of the novel, the public responded with outrage at *The Awakening,* and therefore Chopin never published her short story "The Storm," in which she had gone so far as to endorse guilt-free adulterous love.

The public response to *The Awakening* indicates the degree of resistance to new understandings of womanhood in the South—a resistance fueled by the monolithic literary construction of southern woman as exemplar, bulwark, and conservator of a threatened way of life, as well as the average southern woman's loyal adherence to her culture's construction of femininity. However, the realities of women's lives had changed irrevocably by the turn of the century. In the New South as in the North, women had entered not only the work force but also the professions, had gained unprecedented access to formal education, and had begun to exert significant influence on public affairs. Despite their culture's virulent ideological resistance to new versions of womanhood, the real women of the New South encountered responsibilities and opportunities that rendered the traditional image of southern womanhood anachronistic.

The Postbellum Novel

Amy Thompson McCandless

Literary critics and historical analysts have long bemoaned the sad state of southern writing in the years between 1865 and 1914. Baltimore journalist H. L. Mencken entitled his 1917 critique of southern culture "The Sahara of the Bozart" to signify the sterility that characterized the beaux arts in the postbellum South. To Mencken, southern literature was an oxymoron: "A poet is now almost as rare as an oboe-player, a drypoint etcher or a metaphysician." Similarly, historian C. Vann Woodward, in the *Origins of the New South, 1877–1913* (1951), contended that "Scarcely any generation of Southerners, save that which wrestled with the frontier, was so completely isolated from the main streams of Western culture." In his examination of the southern literary scene, Woodward found a "period of comparative barrenness" between "the short-lived revival of the [eighteen] eighties and the literary flowering of the South that was to begin in the [nineteen] twenties."

Commentators have been even more critical of women's writing in the postbellum South. J. V. Ridgely, in *Nineteenth-Century Southern Literature* (1980), describes Augusta Jane Evans Wilson's 1867 bestseller, *St. Elmo,* as "an incredible brew of melodrama, pseudo-intellectualism, and mild sex which may stand as the benchmark of the low taste of the period." Yet it was this same "barren" past that would inspire the literary flowering of the Southern Renaissance, suggesting that despite the impressions of infecundity, there was something in the postbellum southern soil that nourished the seeds of future generations of regional writers and artists.

Women novelists were not new, of course, to the postbellum South. Already by 1855 Nathaniel Hawthorne had complained about the "damned mob of scribbling women" whose work the reading public preferred to his own, more "serious" compositions. Among the most popular of these antebellum writers were southern women such as Mary Virginia Terhune (1830–1922), Augusta Jane Evans Wilson, Caroline Hentz, Maria McIntosh (1803–1878), and Caroline Howard Gilman. These writers, as discussed in Elizabeth Moss's *Domestic Novelists in the Old South* (1992), saw themselves as "Defenders of Southern Culture" against the social disruption and moral corruption of the rapidly industrializing and crassly materialistic North. Elite southern women felt that the hierarchical and communal society of the plantation provided a stability and purpose lacking in the individualistic and competitive world of bourgeois capitalism, and their novels promulgated these southern virtues to northern readers. Southern attributes inevitably triumphed in their stories of intersectional romances, enabling the northern and southern characters to live together in peace and prosperity.

The outbreak of war in 1861 meant the end of the domestic novel, which many authors had hoped would promote sectional reconciliation by explaining southern institutions to the northern reading audience. Adapting to political realities, Moss contends, southern writers such as Terhune and Wilson "transformed southern domestic fiction" initially "into an assertion of southern independence" and eventually "into a panegyric to a lost cause." Wilson's novel *Macaria; or, Altars of Sacrifice,* published in 1863, presented so positive a view of southern values that it was banned by Federal generals who feared its effects on their troops.

The Civil War had a cataclysmic effect on southern life and culture. The Confederate defeat and the subsequent abolition of slavery meant that the political, economic, and social institutions of the region had to be reconstructed to accommodate a free-labor market. The call for a "New South" based on industrialization, urbanization, and reconciliation with the North put forward by industrial boosters such as Henry Grady was paralleled by a wistful longing for the agrarian and communal values of the Old South, or what C. Vann Woodward describes as a "cult of archaism, a nostalgic vision of the past." As a consequence, southern literature, especially fiction, revived in the 1880s to fill the national demand for stories of simpler times and just plain folk. Local colorists and romance novelists dominated the American literary scene of the late nineteenth century, but as Albion W.

Tourgee noted in an article in *Forum* (1888–89), this American writing was "predominantly Southern in type and character."

The local color movement had its origin in the antebellum writings of the "Old Southwest," i.e., the frontier areas of Alabama, Georgia, Louisiana, Mississippi, and Tennessee. These sketches of frontier life were realistic, humorous, and often ribald, and they provided a vivid description of the speech and manners of the people who inhabited the outposts of civilization. The best-known of these Old Southwest writers was George Washington Harris, whose 1840s stories of Sut Lovingood were collected and published in 1867 as *Sut Lovingood, Yarns Spun by a "Nat'ral Born Durn'd Fool."* Southern writers were not unique, of course, in highlighting the peculiarities of their region in the years after 1865. Sarah Orne Jewett, a native of Maine, wrote her tales about New England; Zitkala-Sa, the Indian name of Gertrude Simmons Bonnin, wrote about her Sioux ancestors; Willa Cather, who emigrated with her family from Virginia to Nebraska as a child, wrote about the western landscape and population. But the South was probably the region most associated in the public mind with local color literature.

The postbellum local colorists included a good number of southern women as well as southern men. Charles Egbert Craddock, the pseudonym of Mary Noailles Murfree, published a collection of eight stories, *In the Tennessee Mountains,* in 1884, the first of many volumes describing the people and places of Appalachia. Murfree's collected volume was immensely popular and was reissued more than a dozen times. Eventually, she would write eight novels, two of them for children, dealing with the isolated mountain communities of her native Tennessee. In his 1967 biography of Murfree, Richard Cary quotes Murfree's own explanation for her choice of subject matter: "I struck upon the mountaineers as a topic at hap-hazard, perhaps because I was myself greatly interested by them; but I did not then appreciate how very little was known of them elsewhere. I was early familiar with their primitive customs, dialect, and peculiar views of life, for I used to spend much time in the mountains long before I knew of the existence of such a thing as 'literary material.'" Although Cary does not discount Murfree's own childhood experiences, he believes that her use of local color probably had more prosaic origins: the publishing success of Bret Harte's "The Luck of Roaring Camp" in 1868 convinced many aspiring authors that local color writing was the surest path to popularity and prosperity.

Cary, like Woodward, sees the popularity of local color fiction emanating from the ambivalence of ordinary Americans toward the rapid changes accompanying industrialization and modernity. As the country became increasingly urban and its culture consequently more uniform, artists and writers hurried to record the quaint idiosyncracies of backwoods folk and their rural lifestyle before they disappeared forever from the American scene. Murfree concentrated on mountain folk; George Washington Cable, Kate Chopin, and Grace King focused on the Creoles and Acadians of Louisiana; Joel Chandler Harris examined the African American folktales of central Georgia; Sherwood Bonner employed "Negro dialect" to portray life in rural Mississippi; Ruth McEnery Stuart (1849–1917) captured the lives of ordinary Arkansas farmers. Although Cary and Woodward find redeeming elements in the local color literature that flourished in the 1880s, both criticize the fiction of the period for its lack of realism. Cary faults the local colorists for stressing "not the basic universalities of human nature and experience but the picturesque and idiosyncratic manifestations. The general result was a superficial realism of detail glossed over by a benevolent romanticism of feeling." Woodward, too, believes that the fascination with the picturesque and unusual led writers to ignore the many economic, political, and social problems facing the southern populace at the turn of the century.

The popular fervor for local color had generally exhausted itself by the end of the century to be replaced by a growing demand for historical novels. Here, too, southerners, especially southern women, dominated the national market. Woodward dubs them the "southern romancers" and contends that they "wrote in passionate vindication of the conservative South and produced melodrama crowded with sensational crime and peopled with malevolent villains, wicked turncoats, and sterling heroes." Woodward numbers the early Ellen Glasgow and the late Mary Murfree among these "romancers."

Kate Bonner McDowell (1849–1883), better known by her pen name of Sherwood Bonner, was among the first novelists to employ the genre of the romantic novel and the literary techniques of the local colorists to move toward a more realistic portrayal of the postbellum South. In her introduction to Bonner's novel *Like unto Like* (1878), republished by the University of South Carolina Press in 1997, Jane Turner Censer notes that Bonner was the first of several southern women novelists to give a feminist twist to the novels of intersectional romance and marriage that proliferated in the years after 1865. Although both men and women produced such romances, which personified the political reunion of North and South through the marriage of northern and southern characters, southern women authors were far less likely to idealize plantation life and the Lost Cause. Indeed, what Censer finds most fascinating about Bonner's novel is its lack of stereotypical southern ladies and gentlemen. *Like unto Like* has no southern hero, and its southern heroine is anything but dependent and demure.

Another unique element of *Like unto Like* is its examination of postbellum racial developments. Bonner's treatment of black southerners is much more sophisticated and sympathetic than that of other nineteenth-century authors. The novel includes a range of black and white characters, and good and evil are not limited to any one race or class. Considering the fact that this was a time when many Americans were proclaiming Reconstruction a failure and turning their backs on the plight of freedmen and freedwomen, Bonner's descriptions of the ways in which race, class, and gender shaped regional polity were unusually perceptive.

William Frank, in his 1976 study, *Sherwood Bonner (Catherine McDowell)*, argues that it was Bonner's writing style rather than her subject matter that influenced twentieth-century American literature. Frank characterizes Bonner as an important "transitional writer" and claims that her employment of African American dialect, use of satire, and application of a "tale-within-the-tale narrative" anticipate the techniques of later realists and naturalists.

Bonner was not the only woman writer of the period to use black dialect or to confront southern racism. The African American writer and social reformer Frances Ellen Watkins Harper focused her only novel, *Iola Leroy; or, Shadows Uplifted* (1892), on the complexity of color issues in the black communities of the postbellum South. Harper was born in Baltimore in 1825, the child of free parents, and was active in the abolitionist, temperance, and women's rights movements. In his book *The Afro-American Novel and Its Tradition* (1987), Bernard W. Bell commends Harper for taking on the racist stereotypes of black womanhood and manhood that abounded in the local color literature and plantation romances of the postbellum period. Harper's novel portrays black women being as committed to family and community as their white sisters and shows African Americans in the New South being as varied and complex in personality as individuals from any ethnic group or region. Although Bell considers the plot of *Iola Leroy* rather melodramatic, he finds the book's setting and characterization more realistic, reflecting Harper's understanding of the psychological and sociological consequences of prejudice and oppression. As Frances Smith Foster writes in her introduction to the 1988 edition of the novel, Harper's work suggests the many commonalities in African American and women's writings and marks an important intermediate stage between antebellum literature and the Harlem Renaissance.

Ellen Glasgow is another southern writer often seen as a transitional figure between the romanticization of the postbellum novel and the realism of modern southern fiction. As Chopin herself once proclaimed, "What the South needs is blood and irony." In her introduction to the 1989 Penguin reissue of Glasgow's novel *Virginia,* Linda Wagner-Martin remarks that Glasgow has often been dismissed as a local colorist because of her focus on southern settings and characters. Although Wagner-Martin concedes that *Virginia* is in some ways kin to the domestic novel and to the novel of manners because of its discussion of woman's sphere, she insists that the book is also much more. It is social criticism at its best, challenging readers to examine traditional gender identities, roles, and relations and to evaluate their appropriateness for a modern, industrial society. Glasgow wrote and lived the life of the New Woman, and her fiction illustrates how difficult it was for individuals to escape the burden of southern history.

Mary Johnston (1870–1936), a friend of Ellen Glasgow, also moved from popular romance to social criticism. After publishing a number of best-selling novels that celebrated the southern way of life, including *To Have and to Hold* (1900), Johnston became an enthusiastic advocate of women's suffrage. As Marjorie Spruill Wheeler explains in her introduction to the 1998 edition of *Hagar,* Johnston's 1913 novel was not at all what readers expected from an elite southern lady. Unlike Johnston's earlier work, *Hagar* challenged its readers' conceptions of the status quo and promoted a radical change in the way society was structured—economically, politically, and sexually. In *Hagar* Johnston advocated economic autonomy for women, more flexible marital and child-care arrangements, and an elimination of class privilege. Although even favorable readers at the time found the work more polemical than fictional, Wheeler believes the novel's focus on turn-of-the-century protest movements is what makes it so fascinating to contemporary readers.

The work of Kate Chopin, as that of Glasgow and Johnston, anticipates, in many ways, the writings of modern feminists. Katherine O'Flaherty was born in St. Louis, but her mother was of French Creole ancestry, as was her husband, Oscar Chopin, whom she married in 1870. The Chopins lived in Louisiana until Oscar's death in 1883. A widow with six children, Kate returned to St. Louis and began writing *Bayou Folk,* an 1894 collection of her short fiction. Chopin's stories were much more than picturesque tales of Creole life, however. Her writing style was influenced by regional writers such as Sarah Orne Jewett, but it was also shaped by the realism of the French author Guy de Maupassant. As she herself would explain, Maupassant's stories were "life, not fiction. . . . Here was a man who had escaped from tradition and authority, who had entered into himself and looked out upon life through his own being and with his own eyes; and who, in a direct and simple way, told us what he saw." Beginning with her novel *At Fault,* published at her own expense in 1890, Chopin turned increasingly to themes of individual autonomy and societal constraints as they affected women in the last decade of the nineteenth century. Although reviewers were critical of her frank treatment of women's sexuality in her later short stories, Chopin apparently was surprised by the storm of protest that followed the publication of her novel *The Awakening* in 1899.

The main character in *The Awakening* is Edna Pontellier, a married mother of two who, in the course of the story, is awakened socially and sexually to "her position in the universe as a human being." At age twenty-eight, Edna finds herself in a loveless marriage and longs for something more. She defies her husband, takes a lover, and, ultimately, unable to achieve individual self-fulfillment, drowns herself in the sea. As Wendy Martin notes in her introduction to *New Essays on "The Awakening"* (1988), the "lush prose and sensuous imagery of *The Awakening* represent a dramatic departure from the technique and point of view found in other contemporary novels about women." From the tone of their remarks, contemporary reviewers clearly did not think this departure was a good thing. The novel was described as "unhealthily introspective and morbid" as well as "essentially vulgar," and "sad and mad and bad." Chopin's willingness to challenge the rigid social conventions of the period and to assert women's need for sexual satisfaction and economic independence was personally courageous but professionally disastrous. After the initial unfavorable reviews, the novel was largely forgotten. The literary canon was simply not ready for such forthright social commentary from a woman. Only after the civil rights and women's liberation movements of the post–World War II era would Chopin's critique of patriarchy be rediscovered and reappraised as a literary classic.

The social fiction of Kate Chopin is, according to Mary E. Papke in *Verging on the Abyss* (1990), "part of the first modern female literary discourse in America." Chopin's use of psychological realism provides a multidimensional portrait of the contemporary woman that, Papke feels, anticipates twentieth-century feminist themes and styles. Significantly, Papke does not believe Chopin should be labeled a local colorist. The South may provide the setting for her fiction, but her characters and concerns are cosmic. Indeed, her heroines defy rather than deify the Old South and its notions of womanhood and manhood.

Yet despite the claims of feminist literary critics, the writings of postbellum southern literary women have generally been dismissed as inconsequential. Louis D. Rubin, Jr., in a Mercer University Lamar Memorial Lecture, published as *The Writer in the South* (1972), sadly concluded that "literary triumphs as were registered by southern authors during the years just before and after the turn of the century were mostly in the field of historical costume romance, in the manner of Mary Johnston. This literature was all but totally deficient in serious literary portraiture; it was best-seller stuff, devoid of genuine literary achievement." Rubin, like historian C. Vann Woodward, does not find much literary flowering in the postbellum South.

This perceived deficiency in southern literature, Carol Manning argues in *The Female Tradition in Southern Literature* (1993), is not so much in the writing as it is in the way the literary canon is constructed. Manning notes that surveys of American literature by experts such as Rubin and Jay B. Hubbell have overemphasized "the nostalgic, uncritical vein" in postbellum women's writing while simultaneously tolerating "popular, sentimental, inferior fiction" by nineteenth-century men. Part of this has been the assumption of male critics that works that focus on women's issues and concerns could not possibly have the "universal appeal" of those that focus on men's.

In an essay titled "The Myth of the Myth of Southern Womanhood" in *Feminism and American Literary History* (1992), Nina Baym likewise contends that the devaluation of local colorists ignores the historical importance of southern women novelists, whose works "deconstructed the monolithic vision of the South that was presented in the plantation novels." Instead of glorifying the white planter elite, women writers described people differentiated by social background and environmental circumstances, individuals who were valiantly trying to come to terms with postbellum economic, political, and social changes.

If white women writers are slighted by the canon, black women are not even acknowledged as writers. In his foreword to a 1988 reissue of Frances E. W. Harper's *Iola Leroy,* Henry Louis Gates, Jr., notes the irony of black women's omission not only from the American but also from the African American literary canon. For it was the publication of Phillis Wheatley's book of poetry in 1773 that marked the "birth of the Afro-American literary tradition." And, Gates continues, the first black American to publish a book of essays was a woman, Ann Plato, in 1841, and the first black American to publish a novel was another woman, Harriet E. Wilson, in 1859. Yet, with the exception of a few autobiographical pieces, black women's writing is ignored until the Harlem Renaissance. Gates finds this lacuna particularly deceptive for the period from 1890 to 1910, a period that featured fiction by black women such as Anna Julia Cooper, Alice Dunbar-Nelson, Frances

Harper, Pauline Hopkins, Amelia Johnson, and Emma Dunham Kelley. There was no comparable publication record by black men in the entire postbellum era. Although Gates believes that the literary accomplishments of black women merit entitling these years "The Black Woman's Era," he sadly observes that these turn-of-the-century authors have generally been ignored by black and white critics alike.

The racial segregation that engulfed the South in the years after 1890 partly accounts for the absence of black female voices from the American literary scene. The effects of *Plessy v. Ferguson* (1896) were cultural as well as political and social. Although interracial cooperation never completely ceased, racially segregated institutions increasingly became the norm throughout the nation. Blacks and whites attended separate schools and churches, belonged to separate clubs and organizations, and wrote for separate audiences and presses. Although the advent of African American periodicals such as *The Joy* (1887), the *National Notes* (1897), the *Colored American Magazine* (1900), and the *Negro Educational Review* (1904) provided more opportunities for black authors—female as well as male—these publications circulated primarily among the black intelligentsia. Frances Harper's novel *Iola Leroy*, for example, was described as the "crowning effort of her life" by the *African Methodist Episcopal Church Review*, but church periodicals such as the *Review* were hardly national venues for literary promotion. Nor were southern women the only black authors whose work failed to attract the attention of national critics. Pauline Elizabeth Hopkins, a black dramatist and novelist from New England, published four novels in the first decade of the twentieth century that dealt with southern racial issues and celebrated African American achievements. Because they were serialized in *The Colored American*, however, their circulation was more limited than that of works published by white authors and aimed at white readers; and, it goes without saying, such works were seldom read by the white males who determined the literary canon. Thus, black women's fiction, regardless of the timeliness of its themes or the excellence of its prose, remained generally unheralded.

The consequence of this diminution of the writings of black and white southern women is, of course, an incomplete picture of the southern literary scene. As Anna Julia Cooper explained in her 1892 *A Voice from the South*, "'tis woman's strongest vindication for speaking that *the world needs to hear her voice*. It would be subversive of every human interest that the cry of one-half the human family be stifled."

Augusta Jane Evans Wilson

Amy Thompson McCandless

The fiction of Augusta Jane Evans Wilson reveals the contested nature of gender identities, roles, and relations in Victorian America. In both her antebellum and postbellum novels Wilson argues that women and men, black and white, privileged and oppressed were all better off in the communal and hierarchical world of the plantation South than in the more individualistic and egalitarian society of the industrial North. Although Wilson primarily wrote domestic literature, her life and works can best be understood within the wider context of southern history and politics.

Augusta Jane Evans Wilson was born on May 8, 1835, in Wynnton, Georgia, the eldest of eight children of Matt Ryan and Sarah Skrine Howard Evans, both descendants of prominent South Carolina families. Although the family had moved into a large plantation house, Sherwood Hall, shortly after Augusta was born, Mr. Evans' mercantile investments suffered in the depression of the late 1830s and early 1840s, and he was forced to declare bankruptcy and move his family to Texas in a covered wagon. Evans tried to recoup his fortunes in Houston, Galveston, and San Antonio before finally settling in Mobile, Alabama, in 1849. The family's frequent moves meant that Augusta had little formal education; she was taught to read by her mother and given free access to her parents' books and to the library of a wealthy aunt. The eclectic nature of her readings would later be reflected in the concerns and interests of her characters. Writing not only provided an

opportunity for her to comment upon contemporary developments and ideologies, but it also offered the possibility of pecuniary remuneration. Indeed, Augusta's concern for her family's financial difficulties seems to have
been a major reason she sought publication for her works. With the outbreak of the Civil War in 1861, she dedicated her life to the Confederate
cause, organizing a hospital at Camp Beulah (named after one of her heroines) near Mobile, corresponding with Confederate leaders such as General
P. G. T. Beauregard and Congressman J. L. M. Curry, visiting military fortifications, and writing spirited defenses of Confederate policy. On December
2, 1868, she married Colonel Lorenzo Madison Wilson, a prominent Mobile financier, and took up residence at his large country estate, Ashland,
where she lived until her husband died in 1891. Augusta subsequently
moved back to Mobile, residing with her brother, John Howard Evans, until
his death in 1908. Although the Wilsons had no children, Augusta was extremely fond of her stepchildren and step-grandchildren. She died of a heart
attack on May 9, 1909.

The Alabama Women's Hall of Fame, to which Wilson was elected in
1961, labels the "favorite hostess of the City of Mobile" as the "foremost
Southern novelist of her time" and "the finest in Alabama." Wilson wrote
nine novels: *Inez: A Tale of the Alamo* was published anonymously in 1855;
Beulah, in 1859; *Macaria; or, Altars of Sacrifice*, in 1863; *St. Elmo*, in 1866;
Vashti; or, Until Death Us Do Part, in 1869; *Infelice*, in 1875; *At the Mercy
of Tiberius*, in 1887; *A Speckled Bird*, in 1902; and *Devota*, in 1907. Although her books were unfavorably reviewed by literary critics, they were
immensely popular among the reading public. *St. Elmo*, for example, was
the third-best-selling novel of the nineteenth century (in the United States,
only Harriet Beecher Stowe's *Uncle Tom's Cabin* [1852] and Lew Wallace's
Ben-Hur [1900] sold more copies), and Carleton, its publisher, claimed that
one million people had read the book within four months of its appearance.
Diane Roberts, in her introduction to a 1992 reissue of the novel by the
University of Alabama Press, describes *St. Elmo* as "the *Gone with the Wind*
of its day." In fact, the novel was adapted for the stage by John Ritter and
for the cinema by Fox Studios. The 1923 version of the film featured the
silent-picture stars John Gilbert as St. Elmo and Bessie Love as Edna Earl.

The contemporary appeal of Wilson's work is probably best expressed
in Louise Manly's biographical essay on Wilson written for the *Library of
Southern Literature* (1907), which was edited by Edwin Anderson Alderman and Joel Chandler Harris. Manly found three characteristics in Wilson's novels that "caused them to outlive the years and the changes of
taste." The first was their didactic nature. Wilson read voraciously, and her

novels included discussions of a wide range of authors and topics, which, according to Manly, "had its charm for the scholar and its incentive to study for the young and unlearned." In addition, Manly praised Wilson's "strong and effective style" and her realism: "her characters are human, the scenes and events, the sorrows and joys are such as may be seen and felt in real life." But, most important, Manly appreciated the moral lessons her writing imparted: "Her whole thought and learning are pressed fearlessly into service to render virtue attractive and vice disgusting."

Wilson's novels often contain references to the author's own experiences. Her first book, *Inez,* is based on her childhood sojourn in Texas; its anti-Catholicism reflects the views of her father. A number of Wilson's heroines are successful writers, and, like Wilson, they find their works torn to pieces by literary critics. Like Wilson, they engage in considerable "volunteer" service. Wilson served as a nurse during the yellow fever epidemic of the 1850s and later during the Civil War; her characters similarly tend to the sick and wounded. Wilson, like her heroine Beulah, suffered a crisis of faith and confronted the skepticism of Emerson and Kant before recovering her mental equilibrium. Once married, Wilson, like her heroines, dedicated herself to home and husband. And, like Edna and Beulah in her novels, she found that her health improved when she cut back on her rigid writing schedule.

A rabid southern nationalist, Wilson found her personal and professional life affected by the growing divisions between North and South. On a trip to New York in 1859, she met and fell in love with the editor of the New York *World,* James Reed Spaulding. Although she accepted his offer of marriage the following year, his Republican Party sympathies were too deep, and she broke off the engagement late in 1860. Wilson wrote a series of articles for the Mobile *Daily Advertiser* in 1859 asserting the South's cultural and political superiority over the North, and her novel *Macaria; or, Altars of Sacrifice,* written in 1863 to raise the morale of Confederate soldiers, was so popular and persuasive that Union General George H. Thomas declared it "contraband and dangerous" and forbade his soldiers to read it. As Diane Roberts writes in her introduction to *St. Elmo,* Wilson "was ever a daughter of the Confederacy—and this is central to understanding her fiction." Wilson herself claimed that "The sole enthusiasm of my life was born, lived, and perished in the eventful four years of the Confederacy."

Although the majority of Wilson's works were published after the Civil War, many twentieth-century critics identify her work with the antebellum period. Elizabeth Moss, in her study *Domestic Novelists in the Old South* (1992), includes Wilson as one of five southern writers whose domestic fiction "systematically countered charges of southern depravity leveled by antislavery advocates, arguing that the peculiar institution was but part of a larger system of reciprocal relationships that made southern society the moral superior of the individualistic North." Moss cites examples from *Beulah* (1859) and *Macaria* (1862) to illustrate the partisan nature of southern domestic literature in the mid-nineteenth century.

Even after the war, Wilson continued to critique contemporary developments that she associated with northern industrialism and materialism. Her novel *A Speckled Bird* criticized the women's and labor movements, and *Devota* critiqued Populism. In *St. Elmo* feminists are described as "unamiable and wretched wives" and "embittered, disappointed old maids of New England."

Commentators found a lot to fault in Wilson's novels. Some criticized the stilted nature of her language; others, the sentimental nature of her characters and plots. An 1855 reviewer in the *Southern Quarterly Review* considered *Inez* absolutely lacking in literary merit: "There is not a natural character and scarcely a natural phrase in the whole volume." Charles Henry Webb published a parody of *St. Elmo* in 1868, entitled *St. Twel-mo; or, The Cuneiform Cyclopedist of Chattanooga*, that featured a heroine (Etna) who had literally consumed an unabridged dictionary. But many critics simply did not consider domestic fiction serious enough to be part of the literary canon. Jay Hubbell's *The South in American Literature* (1954) refers to the writing of nineteenth-century women as "sub-literature." Carol Manning, in her 1993 book *The Female Tradition in Southern Literature*, contends that the "prejudice against a so-called feminine style and interests of female writers" led to the neglect of "a whole genre of writing" and "significantly affected the theoretical framework critics have created for the Southern Renaissance."

Recent critics have focused on Wilson's conceptions of woman's nature and role. Louis D. Rubin, Jr., in *The History of Southern Literature* (1985), contends that Wilson "explored, albeit in unpruned prose, the ambitions and capabilities of women more honestly than most of the nineteenth-century writers could ever do." Beulah Benton and Edna Earl, the heroines of *Beulah* and *St. Elmo* respectively, are determined to support themselves through their teaching and writing. Both are orphaned at an early age and befriended and educated by local worthies. Although each young woman receives numerous offers of marriage, ambition and pride entice Beulah and Edna to leave the warmth of their adopted homes and the men who love them to seek "some lofty niche in the temple of fame."

Both women eventually become successful writers, but the intellectual strain takes its toll. Beulah loses her faith and becomes a skeptic. She refuses her guardian's offer of marriage, and "a longing desire for Fame [takes] possession of her soul. . . . She live[s], as it were, in a perpetual brain-fever, and her physical frame suffer[s] proportionately." Edna retains a strong Christian faith throughout the novel and limits her own writings to discussions of woman's proper sphere, but she, too, is physically debilitated by her literary efforts. Each comes to the realization that intellectual food is not enough for a woman; her heart must be nourished as well. Beulah finds Christ and marries her guardian, Guy Hartwell; Edna marries her guardian's son, St. Elmo Murray. Both give up their literary careers.

Despite the independent natures and advanced views of her heroines, Augusta Jane Evans Wilson was reluctant to criticize the social and gender hierarchy of the nineteenth-century South. Indeed, Beulah and Edna constantly defend the restricted roles for women that they themselves have rejected. Edna entitles one of her novels *Shining Thrones on the Hearth* and attempts to prove "by illustrious examples that the borders of the feminine realm could not be enlarged, without rendering the throne unsteady, and subverting God's law of order." She warns of "the unfortunate and deluded female malcontents, who, dethroned in their own realm, and despised by their quondam subjects, roam as pitiable, royal exiles, threatening to usurp man's kingdom; and to proud, happy mothers, guarded by Praetorian bands of children, she reiterate[s] the assurance that 'Those who rock the cradle rule the world.'" After her conversion, Beulah likewise writes on traditional subjects, hoping "to warn others of the snares in which she had so long been entangled, and to point young seekers after truth to the only sure fountain." Once married, Wilson's heroines are no longer allowed even this limited literary independence. Lest there be any doubt that she had no intention of undermining the gender roles and relations so dear to the hearts of southern patriarchs, Wilson includes a quotation from John Ruskin on the frontispiece to *St. Elmo*. It reads, "Ah! The true rule is—a true wife in her husband's house is his servant; it is in his heart that she is queen."

As Mary Kelley explains in her 1984 study of literary domestics, *Private Woman, Public Stage,* Wilson's determination to alleviate her family's financial problems led her to seek pecuniary relief in the masculine and public realm of publishing, and although she did achieve financial security through her writing, she felt guilty about her intrusion in the public domain of men and business. Wilson, like other authors of domestic fiction in Victorian America, tried to justify her own "socially errant" behavior by providing the reader with heroines who personified the superior spiritual nature of the female sex and with plots that illustrated how feminine altruism could bring moral improvement to a corrupt, materialistic, and masculine society. Her life and work "were enveloped by the perspective, the language, the metaphor, and the meaning of domesticity for women."

Once dismissed as "local color" and "sub-literature," the writing of Augusta Evans Wilson, along with that of other nineteenth-century women novelists, recaptured the interest of literary critics and historians in the late twentieth century. To the modern reader, Wilson's prose is ponderous; her characters, unnatural; and her plots, predictable. Yet the recent renaissance of her work suggests that Wilson's focus on gender identities, roles, and relations and on the ways in which these concepts are shaped by political and social developments in the wider world is still germane to southern life and literature.

Southern History in the Imagination of African American Women Writers

Elizabeth Fox-Genovese

Although antislavery and even abolitionist discourses were hardly new to the 1850s, the Compromise of 1850, especially the Fugitive Slave Law, lent them a sharpness they had previously lacked. And the outpouring of antebellum writings, fictional as well as theoretical, theological, and political, on both sides of the divide crystallized what we may call a dominant pattern of discourse. The character of the debate is familiar enough. While northern abolitionists preached the inviolability of freedom ("free soil, free labor, free men") and immorality of bondage, proslavery southerners preached the necessity for social hierarchy and the wanton cruelty of free labor. Intermingling with and enriching the abstract arguments about first principles and social systems, novelists on both sides wove a tapestry of human examples designed to show the direct consequences of the two systems for specific people.

African American writers, especially women, were latecomers to this discussion that raged about their condition. Kentucky-born William Wells Brown, who broke the path with his novel, *Clotel; or, the President's Daughter* (1853), set a precedent that many would follow by taking as his heroine a mulatto (the quintessential "high yaller") woman, who, betrayed and abandoned by the white planter who claimed to love her, ultimately dies. Brown's role in establishing the beautiful mulatto as the exemplary black heroine cast a long shadow and has received much attention from subsequent critics. What has received less attention is his adaptation of a distinct southern pastoral mode to his own purposes. To drive his point home, Brown set his novel in Virginia and attributed Clotel's parentage to none other than Thomas Jefferson, thus linking high professed political principle to the despoiling of slave women. None of Brown's female successors would follow his lead in this regard, nor even in consigning their heroines to an untimely death. But then Brown depicted Clotel as a cast-aside wife (although legally she was never married) rather than as a young girl, exposed to all the horrors of random sexual exploitation. An abolitionist who wrote primarily for northern and, especially, British readers, Brown nonetheless held up for southern readers a disquieting mirror of their own professed principles. However broad and generous Brown's sympathies with the great mass of slaves, he focused upon the ways in which the system most cruelly betrayed those whom it might have embraced—literally its own offspring as embodied in a beautiful, virtually white, articulate woman. As an author and narrator, Brown draws directly upon southern history as he interprets it. And since his narrative focuses directly upon his principal protagonists, whom he carefully inscribes in literate culture, the history he explores and criticizes belongs essentially to the realm of public discourse rather than to that of the memories of oral culture and the ghosts of scarred imaginations.

Although Brown took Clotel as his heroine, he arguably did not take her as the novel's subject. Rather than subject, Clotel is best understood as a figure—a distillation of discourses—that designates the condition of the tragic mulatto, which itself represents the inherent contradictions of southern society. For unlike those who came after, Brown locates the conception of freedom (Jefferson) and the possibility of social tranquility (the garden) within the South itself. Paradoxically, by not making Clotel the center of subjectivity, he permits her a coherence of character, a freedom from soul-wrenching conflict that black women writers' protagonists frequently lack. Brown's contemporary, Harriet Jacobs, chooses subjectivity, not Brown's objectivity, for her mulatto protagonist. Although not explicitly a novelist, Jacobs located the subjectivity of her protagonist, Linda Brent, at the center of her narrative *Incidents in the Life of a Slave Girl* (1861). Drawing heavily upon abolitionist discourses, Jacobs followed Harriet Beecher Stowe and other antislavery women writers in emphasizing the ways in which slavery as a social system negated all social order, corrupting the integrity of domestic relations, white and black. Calling slavery an "obscene cage of birds," Linda Brent insists she can testify from her "own experience and observation, that slavery is a curse to the whites as well as to the blacks. It makes the white fathers cruel and sensual; the sons violent and licentious; it contaminates the daughters, and makes the wives wretched." The heart of Jacobs' problem in representing Linda Brent's subjectivity is dramatically revealed in the use of pronouns according to which "my" pen is juxtaposed with "their" sufferings. Jacobs allows Linda Brent to express some measure of the rage and anger that consume her, notably her determination "that the master, whom I so hated and loathed . . . should not, after my long struggle with him, succeed at last in trampling his victim under his feet." Repeatedly calling her master "a tyrant," Linda Brent takes pleasure in any small way that she may "triumph" over him. Slave conditions make a mockery of conventional morality. Thus a slave woman who retains "any pride or sentiment" may well taste "something akin to freedom" in taking a lover who is not her master, even if he cannot be her lawful husband. Such moral principles, Linda Brent allows, may seem like sophistry, "but the condition of a slave confuses all principles of morality, and, in fact, renders the practice of them impossible." She knows that her mother and grandmother cleaved to moral principles, but they were spared the unmediated power of a master and, by implication, did not really experience the full weight of slavery's most destructive power.

Incidents in the Life of a Slave Girl differs from *Clotel* in that it contains virtually no references to history or even to the variations in southern society as a whole. Proceeding from the consciousness of Linda Brent, the narrative encompasses only those incidents that her mind has encountered, whether family traditions, cases of brutality, or random comments on proslavery religion. Jacobs' South seems cut almost entirely from Manichean abolitionist cloth and meshes comfortably with Orlando Patterson's conception of slavery as social death (*Slavery and Social Death*, 1982). In the measure that Jacobs pays any attention to history, she restricts it to family history, primarily to establish a pedigree of fair skin, literacy, respectability, and quasi freedom for herself. And in the end, her falling off from the standards of her forebears matters considerably less than her having been reared with them in the first place.

These tactics confirm the split implied in "my" pen, "their" sufferings, a split Brown largely avoided by divesting his heroine, Clotel, of subjectivity: Jacobs does not recognize the history of slavery in the South as Linda Brent's history—an outcome she virtually assured when she decided to ground *Incidents* in Linda's consciousness. And her abolitionist commitments no less clearly assured that she would find it almost impossible simply to ground Linda's history in the history of the South. Here and there, hints of southern black history flicker in the pages of the text, notably when she links her experience in the swamp with the folklore of black oral culture. But in general, and especially in narrative voice, she claims as much distance as possible between Linda and the history that produced her. She attempts to tell Linda's story without telling in full its history.

Harriet Jacobs' difficulty in coming to terms with history derives from her fierce rejection of the personal consequences of southern history, above all slavery, despite her focus on the personal history of a slave. This was not a story she could tell, much less a story to pass on. Yet the problems emerge sharply from her text. If slavery indeed "confuses" moral principles and makes their practice "impossible," then how may she, a former slave, claim basic moral decency? Tactically, Jacobs attempts to place the blame upon the slaveholders who, as a class, corrupt everything and everyone they touch. But if everyone, why not her? To be sure, she admits to lapses from northern standards of female virtue, but consistently presents those lapses as external rather than internal to her character. The history of slavery never seems to ground her identity. But then, neither does the history of the black community.

Since the condition of slavery was transmitted through the mother and since the absence of legal marriage among slaves left fathers peculiarly exposed, the transmission of history through women assumed special importance for the African American community. Even after emancipation and the emergence of solid marriages and families, women remained privileged custodians of the history of their people under slavery. To say as much is to slight neither the sufferings of African American men under slavery nor their centrality to African American communities. It is simply to suggest that slavery did not oppress women and men as couples or even as members of coherent families, but as isolated individuals who might or might not be able to establish human ties strong enough to withstand slavery's deadly tendency to atomization.

As a people, African American slaves did withstand the worst of the atomization, notably through their creation of communities that transcended family units and that could always absorb and support those whose immediate families had been torn from them. These communities proved reliable custodians of collective memories, including those of African practices and beliefs. To these traditions they added the Anglo-American Christianity and messages of political freedom that predominated in the South, interweaving all into a sustaining culture of their own design. The message of abolition contributed a new attention to individualism. For while the slaves had never needed anyone to tell them they wanted to be free, abolition's emphasis on individualism ran counter to older collective traditions. The tension be-tween the individual and the community informed every attempt to come to terms with the southern slave experience of African Americans. For some, like Jacobs, the balance shifted in favor of the individual who had suffered unspeakable wrongs and frequently led to the refusal to bare the wellsprings that might expose the bearer to unbearable pain. Frances Ellen Watkins Harper, writing after Reconstruction, was supremely conscious of women's responsibilities both to tell the history of slavery and to assess its implica-tions for a free present and future. She was no less conscious, during an era of vicious and institutionalized racism, of the pressing need to shift the bal-ance toward the history of the African American community rather than the isolate individual. Tellingly, she returned to Brown's figure of the tragic mulatto to carry the burden of that history, although unlike Brown, she al-lowed her mulatto heroines to triumph, pointing the way in their persons, their works, their marriages, and their offspring to a promising future for their people.

Harper attended carefully to the broad historical context of her protago-nists' dramas, grounding the events that followed emancipation in the slav-ery that came before. Harper, coming from Baltimore, harshly repudiated the slaveholding system, but showed an understanding of the South as the region in which the majority of African Americans had their roots and felt at home.

Harper's *Iola Leroy* (1892), which opens in the middle of the Civil War, plunges the reader directly into the community of slaves. Robert Johnson and Thomas Anderson, both slaves, use the reports on freshness of butter and fish to trade notes about the progress of the Union forces. In a few brief chapters, Harper evokes the main features of slavery and the diverse person-alities of Robert, Thomas, and the other slave men she introduces. From the start the reader learns that some masters and mistresses are better than oth-ers, although even Robert's indulgent mistress regards him as a "pet"; that, notwithstanding prohibitions, the slaves have a complex network of prayer meetings; that some have learned to read although most have not; that some plan to leave and join the Union forces, whereas others feel bound by loyal-ties to blacks and whites to remain where they are. Deftly, Harper brings to life a small-slaveholding region of North Carolina and the textured relations and personalities of the slaves who inhabit it.

With great skill, Harper convinces the reader that her subjects have not been flattened by the weight of slavery and have built a rich human commu-nity, and that slavery as a social system is morally and politically wrong. Judging the slaveholders harshly, she nonetheless insists forcefully that the responsibility for slavery is national. Slavery, she avers, "had cast such a glamour over the Nation, and so warped the consciences of men, that they failed to read aright the legible transcript of Divine retribution which was written on the shuddering earth, where the blood of God's poor children had been as water freely spilled."

The reader first meets Iola Leroy through the eyes of Tom, who describes her to Robert as "a mighty putty young gal," whom her owners have been selling all over the country, because "she's a reg'lar spitfire; dey can't lead nor dribe her." Tom, adoring Iola and fearing for her safety in the grip of her "reckless and selfish master, who had tried in vain to drag her down to his own level of sin and shame," moves Robert to persuade the Union commander of the local fort to secure her release and to take her as a nurse in the field hospital. The general, to whom she was taken, is astonished by her beauty and refinement: "Could it be possible that this young and beautiful girl had been a chattel, with no power to protect herself from the highest insults that lawless brutality could inflict upon innocent and defenseless womanhood?" How could he take pride in his American citizenship "when any white man, no matter how coarse, cruel, or brutal, could buy or sell her for the basest purposes?"

Only sixty pages into the novel does the reader learn how one as fair and unmarked by toil as Iola Leroy could indeed be a slave. Daughter of a fair-skinned slave woman and the wealthy Louisiana planter who loved, educated, and married her, Iola grew up with no knowledge of her mixed racial heritage. As a student at a New England boarding school, she treats her antislavery classmates to a spirited rendition of the proslavery argument. But, upon her father's untimely death, a vicious, greedy cousin, to whom he has naïvely confided the secret of his wife's birth, persuades a judge to overturn the father's will and remand the mother and their children into slavery. The youngest girl mercifully dies of brain fever; the son is kept safe in the North, where he too was in school; but Iola and her mother are turned over to slave traders.

With minor variations, Iola's story became the prototype for the gothic horror of the inherent evil of slavery. One may plausibly assume that Harper herself did not necessarily view the plight of the fair-skinned woman who had been raised in the lap of luxury as slavery's worst evil. But she assuredly knew her readers and doubtless believed that, to whites like the general, the idea that a single drop of black blood could throw a young woman like their own daughters onto the vilest of sexual market places would be infinitely more moving than the plight of a dark-skinned illiterate laborer, male or female. Harper was, after all, writing for an audience that had but recently been horrified by tales of the white slave trade.

Harper relied upon the moving appeal of the figure of the beautiful mulatto to carry her larger message, which she feared readers would find more difficult to accept. The novel makes clear that Harper's main quarrel was with the racism of the 1890s. In locating the origins of her story in slavery, she doubtless hoped to tap the wellsprings of that northern sense of moral superiority that triumphed in the war. The conflation of slavery and racism permitted her, in effect, to displace some of her outrage at bourgeois racism and say to her northern readers: This injustice, which you are so proud of yourselves for having fought against, you surely will not now tolerate in your midst.

In addition Harper, who had a genuine feel for the strengths and vulnerabilities of the community of ordinary slaves, seems purposefully to have located the dramatic abuses of slavery in Louisiana with its special aura of mystery and corruption, thus underscoring the gothic dimension of Iola's personal story. In contrast, she represents the slaves of North Carolina who befriend Iola as varied and engaging human beings who have suffered the debilitation of slavery, but have assuredly not been crippled by it.

Notwithstanding Harper's narrative dependence upon the plight of the beautiful mulatto to engage the imaginations of her readers, Harper ultimately was more concerned with the fate of her people than with the personal stories of individuals. Her politics was more national than personal: She placed her greatest faith in the responsible and creative leadership of a respectable, family-based black elite. The figure she uses to dramatize her message remains effectively, indeed strikingly, silent about her own worst experiences. Like Linda Brent, Harper's mulatto women ultimately escape the scars of the history they so passionately protest against. To engage her readers' sympathy, Harper represents her mulatto heroines as essentially white—as elite young women who by the trick of a cruel fate were doomed by a few drops of black blood to slavery. Her texts carry the thinly veiled message that their unmerited destiny could threaten countless other unsuspecting young women. Iola Leroy ultimately chooses to be black, willingly casting her fate with the African American community. But Iola's role within Harper's text precludes Harper's telling the subjective story of the former slave women whose interests Iola represents. As a figure she embodies and represents a history that her mouth may never speak.

Jacobs and Harper did not publicly admit to being haunted by the ghosts of slavery. Jacobs was too much concerned with slavery as a present evil to be much concerned with its history, although she sought to rouse the North to meet its responsibilities. Harper, who wrote after slavery's formal demise, sought to convince northern readers that slavery was the nation's history and the erasure of its legacy their responsibility. Harper, who had genuine sympathy and respect for the history that blacks had made for themselves within the confines of slavery and, especially, for freedmen and freedwomen's efforts to reconstruct their own communities in the South, painted a nuanced picture of southern history, although she also condemned southern whites. Emancipation opened the way for African American women writers to begin to move into the public world, although the advent of Jim Crow and legal segregation crippled their progress. The legacy of slavery nonetheless continued to haunt them, albeit in different ways with the passage of time. Harriet Jacobs experienced slavery with a bitter immediacy that infused her account with an ill-disguised anger. Frances Harper, who lived her entire life as a free woman, did not betray the same bitterness and anger, yet even as she turned her attention to the new problems of the 1880s and 1890s, she remained preoccupied with the abiding legacy of slavery for all African Americans.

Both Jacobs and Harper acknowledged the pervasive costs of slavery for the mass of African Americans who had largely been denied access to education and who bore a disquieting resemblance to illiterate, over-worked peasants throughout the world. But recognizing the distaste of northern whites for what Cuthbert Sumner called the "mere thought of the grinning, toothless black hag," they distanced their protagonists from slavery's most common manifestations. They could not risk the story of the slave woman who willingly slept with her master, much less the one who ran off from or murdered her own child. They could not even expose the scars on a slave woman's loins or the inevitable callouses on her hands.

The real problem is not that Iola could not speak, but that, even through the mediation of a narrative figure, Harper could not. The wounds of history were too painful, the scars too raw, and, possibly, the shame too great for public exposure in the postbellum South. So the figure of Iola was shadowed by the ghosts of countless others who had no voice of their own. With the passage of time, those ghosts began to press more insistently against the consciousness of their heirs. Stories that no one had wanted to remember and assuredly had not wanted to pass on began, hesitantly, indirectly, to be told. A tenacious bunch, the ghosts would not down. Even as African American women like Anna Julia Cooper and Ida B. Wells turned their attention and talents to public affairs, African American women writers continued to explore the ways in which the shadow of slavery weighed upon their female protagonists' sense of themselves as women.

Frances Ellen Watkins Harper

Susanne B. Dietzel

Frances Ellen Watkins Harper can easily be called one of the most prolific southern women writers of her time. Her contributions to American, African American, and southern life and letters, as well as her participation in the major social justice movements of the nineteenth century, make her one of the most prominent nineteenth-century women. Also referred to as the "Bronze Muse," Harper has been considered the most popular black poet before Paul Laurence Dunbar and the most important black woman writer during the second half of the nineteenth century. Harper was a prolific writer of poetry, fiction, and nonfiction whose work was widely circulated and never out of print during her lifetime; a committed activist who fought for the abolition of slavery and rallied for temperance, woman's rights, and suffrage; and an eloquent orator whose poetic and inspiring performances captivated audiences across the United States and abroad. Her literary and activist career of almost seventy years is marked by many accomplishments: Harper was the first black woman to be employed as a lecturer by an abolitionist society; she was the first African American woman to publish a short story, "The Two Offers" in 1859; and she was one of the few women of color to rise to a position of influence in the Women's Christian Temperance Union. Most of Harper's writings are widely available today. The most comprehensive introduction to her work can be found in Frances Smith Foster's *A Brighter Coming Day: A Frances Ellen Watkins Harper Reader* (1990).

Harper's activism and literary contributions make her one of the founders of African American feminism. Her many speeches to women's and suffrage congresses here and abroad are now considered classics in the black
feminist tradition. From her earliest publication until the end of her career,
Harper espoused and advocated the feminist theme of black women's economic independence, and she encouraged her sisters to redefine true womanhood through work on behalf of their race instead of a selfish devotion
to romance. She was one of the cofounders and early vice presidents of the
National Organization of Colored Women, which became the most prominent and powerful black women's organization in the twentieth century. Together with Frederick Douglass and Lucy Stone, Harper was one of the
founding members of the American Woman Suffrage Association, and
throughout her lifelong involvement with the suffrage cause, Harper continually had to remind her comrades of the inseparability of race and gender.
Harper's work as a writer offers cogent critiques of racism, slavery, sexism,
and the debilitating effects of alcohol and political corruption, while at the
same time it celebrates the resiliency, perseverance, moral superiority, and
political successes of African Americans and women, both black and white.
Harper's political commitment to social justice for black Americans and her
feminism are thus inseparable from her literary work, and like many of her
white and black contemporaries, she believed in the social functions of literature, which, as she explains in *Iola Leroy* (1892), worked to "awaken in
the hearts of our countrymen a stronger sense of justice and a more Christ-
like humanity."

It is only appropriate that Harper should be seen as part of the South's
literary and cultural history. Not only does her work make an important
contribution to nineteenth-century southern literature in that it gives voice
to an underrepresented population, but it also lays the foundation for an
independent black southern literature to follow. Her poetry and fiction that
fit most squarely into the southern literary tradition, including *Sketches of
Southern Life* (1872) and *Iola Leroy; or, Shadows Uplifted,* map a South
and southerners that had heretofore been both underrepresented and mis-
represented. Her work frees former slaves from literary invisibility and stereotype, and gives them the active voice and literary agency denied to them
in the writings of her white male contemporaries. Whereas the majority of
black southern characters in the works of the plantation tradition and their
nineteenth-century predecessors are ventriloquists who romanticized a by-
gone era in their former master's tongue, Harper's black characters are
agents of their own history who actively resist slavery, outsmart their masters, and plot for their emancipation. In short, Harper's characters politicize

the everyday through a knowledge based in the experience of human bondage and the desire for freedom. Like many of her black literary predecessors, contemporaries, and descendants who chose the South as the setting for their fiction and poetry, Harper is a literary revisionist who transforms both literary genre and characters in her quest to tell the story of her race and to fight for social justice.

Harper was born to a free black family in Baltimore, Maryland, in 1825. Her parents died when she was only three, and she was raised by the family of her uncle William Watkins, a prominent abolitionist and teacher. It was under his tutelage that Harper received a classical education and was taught to think politically and on behalf of her race. Encouraged to write poetry by her family and her employer, a prominent white bookseller in Baltimore, Harper published her first collection of poetry, *Forest Leaves,* in 1845. No copies of it have survived, but critics speculate that the volume foreshadows Harper's lifelong concerns and themes as a writer and social activist, such as abolition, the history of slavery and Reconstruction, religion, women's rights and self-determination, social reform, and biblical history, to which she would return in such volumes as *Moses; A Story of the Nile* (1869).

Because of rising political pressures on free blacks, Harper left the city of Baltimore in 1850 to accept a position as the first female teacher at Union Seminary in Ohio. Her work as a social activist began in earnest in 1853 when the state of Maryland passed a law that allowed any free black person to be apprehended and sold into slavery. Outraged by this decision, which prohibited her from returning to the southern city of her youth, Harper accepted a position as the first full-time female lecturer with the Maine Anti-Slavery Society in 1854. Eventually, she moved to Philadelphia, where she worked for the Underground Railroad and where she would make her home until her death in 1911. Her abolitionist speeches were widely distributed and made Harper one of the most famous women orators of her time. The recitation of her poetry was part of Harper's public persona and contributed to her success as a lecturer. *Poems on Miscellaneous Subjects* (1854) features some of her most widely anthologized poems, such as "Eliza Harris" (1853), Harper's response to Stowe's *Uncle Tom's Cabin* (1851); "The Slave Auction" (1854); and "Bury Me in a Free Land" (1858), which was published in a later edition of the book. The volume was reprinted many times during her lifetime but sank into literary oblivion after her death. Immediately after the Civil War, Harper turned her attention to temperance in her serialized novels, which she published in the *Christian Recorder,* the journal of the African Methodist Episcopal Church.

Although most of her prewar poetry focused on the theme of slavery and already featured black women prominently, it was after the Civil War that her engagement with the South and her commitment to the welfare and literary representation of black southern women began in full. On her frequent lecturing and teaching tours through the former slave states between 1866 and 1871, she visited every southern state but Arkansas and Texas, and formed a bond with the freed slave women, committing herself to their service. Harper writes in one of her letters that "Part of my lectures are given privately to women. . . . I am going to talk to them about their daughters, and about things connected to the welfare of the race. Now is the time for our women to begin to try to lift up their heads and plant the roots of progress under the hearthstone." These concerns, as they would find particular expression in *Sketches of Southern Life* and in her novel *Iola Leroy; or, Shadows Uplifted*, place her squarely into the canon of southern women writers.

Sketches of Southern Life is an interconnected series of narrative folk poems and ballads whose roots can be found in the oral tradition of southern slaves and whose legacy is continued in the poetry of Margaret Walker and Maya Angelou. The principal narrator of *Sketches* is Aunt Chloe, a former slave turned griot who, in poems such as "Aunt Chloe" and "The Deliverance," relates in simple but concise and evocative language the complex history of black and white southerners, of slaves whose children have been sold away, and of their former owners and the reversal of fortunes that has befallen them. Likewise, "Aunt Chloe's Politics" shows Chloe to be a shrewd observer of Reconstruction politics, one who is not afraid to demand her own political empowerment. Central to *Sketches* are the themes of family, literacy, political representation, and Christianity. The collection as a whole offers insight into a part of black life not widely known and often suppressed in much of southern literature: the black family as it is sustained by Christian faith and brotherly love, and empowered by literacy and political participation. The reunified black family, in *Sketches* and later in *Iola Leroy*, becomes the space where personal, spiritual, and political empowerment are practiced and enacted, and where the wounds of the past can be healed.

Harper's most well-known novel, *Iola Leroy*, stands almost at the end of her long literary career, but nevertheless should be seen as a major contribution to southern women's literature of the nineteenth century. As a story of slavery and family reunion, the Civil War and Reconstruction, and return to the South, *Iola Leroy* follows, but also rewrites, the familiar plot of nineteenth-century domestic fiction as it has been outlined by Nina Baym. In fact, black feminist critic Claudia Tate has called *Iola Leroy* and other novels by black women published at this time "allegories of political desire," texts that use the plot of domestic fiction to tell the story of the black family and its reconstitution after the Civil War, which articulate the political desires of African American women and mark their entrance into the public sphere of politics. Through the use of the mulatto character of Iola—the legitimate daughter of a slave owner and his black wife, a former slave—Harper not only illuminates the gendered experience of slavery and Reconstruction from a black feminist perspective, but also critiques what we would call today the social construction of race and racial difference. Except, of course, for their race, Iola Leroy and the other women in the novel are the exemplary heroines of domestic fiction, yet they come with a feminist twist. They are virtuous, chaste, pious, and devoted to the elevation of their race, but are also feminist role models who refuse to seek fulfillment only in marriage and family.

According to Harper, individual fulfillment is thus achieved through immersion in and service to the black community. In its focus on racial cooperation, community building, and black political and educational empowerment, *Iola Leroy* stands as a literary intervention and glimmer of hope during one of the South's darkest hours. Writing against the impending shadow of Jim Crow legislation and the legalization of black disenfranchisement during the last decade of the nineteenth century, Harper did what she had done throughout her career: affirm the humanity of African Americans and celebrate the resiliency and insurgent feminism of black women.

Southern Women Journalists

Maurine H. Beasley

Journalism provided an opportunity for a limited number of southern women to express themselves and to earn their own livings following the Civil War. The pursuit, however, was less common for women in the South than in the North. Due to the myth of the genteel southern "lady" who was protected by her male relatives, journalism was seen as a questionable occupation for women because its practitioners left the home to engage in the public sphere. Nevertheless, it was considered acceptable for women to help with family-owned newspapers, handling both editorial and business matters. It was also socially acceptable for women to write for publication, although many shielded their identities with pseudonyms and confined themselves to topics associated with the feminine realm.

Studies of southern women writers have noted that they published fiction in newspapers and periodicals during the postbellum period, but relatively little research has been done on the nonfiction articles and newspaper reports produced during this time. Historical inquiries into the careers of women journalists have centered on women in large cities, particularly Boston and New York, which were the most important centers of journalistic activity during the late nineteenth century. Still, an enterprising group of both white and African American southern women achieved notable careers in journalism prior to 1900.

Certainly southern women of the postbellum period inherited a tradition of carrying on journalistic enterprises. In the colonial era Elizabeth Timothy (d. 1757) became the first American woman to publish a weekly newspaper. Timothy published her husband's newspaper, the *South-Carolina Gazette*, in Charleston, following his death in 1738 until her son Peter was old enough to take over two years later. Widowed in 1783, Peter's wife, Ann (1727–1792), also ran the newspaper until her own death. In Williamsburg, Virginia, Clementina Rind (1740–1774) supervised the publishing of the *Virginia Gazette* to provide for herself and her five children after her husband, William, died in 1773.

The most notable antebellum woman journalist was another southern widow, Anne Royall (1769–1854), who gained notoriety as the only woman in United States history to be tried and convicted on charges of being a "common scold" after she engaged in bitter exchanges with her neighbors in Washington, D.C. To earn her livelihood after the death of her husband in 1812, Royall turned to journalism, first writing and peddling travel books and then running two newspapers in Washington from 1831 to 1854. She resorted to this occupation, which barely kept bread on her table, at the age of fifty-four when her husband's relatives managed to void his will and leave her penniless on grounds that she was an adulteress. They claimed that, as a young servant girl, Royall had cohabitated with her husband, a Revolutionary War hero, before their marriage in 1797 in Sweet Springs, Virginia.

While admired today for her independence and determination, Royall, known for her vitriolic temper and biting pen, offered little in the way of a role model to postbellum southern women journalists who sought to operate within conventional bounds of femininity that called for women to avoid public controversy. According to a pioneer study, "Women in American Journalism before 1900," an unpublished master's thesis in journalism written by Edith M. Marken at the University of Missouri in 1932, some twenty southern women journalists were active between 1850 and 1900. Few of these women were known outside their immediate localities. Drawing on an article by Helen Winslow entitled "Some Newspaper Women" (*Arena*, December 1896), Marken credits Mrs. Joseph K. Ohl, whose byline of "Maud Andrews" appeared on the women's page of the Atlanta *Constitution*, with being the best known of the southern contingent.

In a twenty-four-page issue devoted to women, the January 26, 1889, issue of the *Journalist*, a New York trade publication, lists the names of nearly one hundred white women journalists, almost all of whom were from the North, as well as profiles of ten African American women journalists. The names of about half of the women appear in a long article on the New

England Woman's Press Association that pointed out the connections between its members and reform movements like abolition, temperance, and
suffrage, all of which had originated in the North. Articles on other organizations of women journalists mentioned one group connected to the South,
the Woman's National Press Association, formed in New Orleans in 1885,
which changed its name to the Woman's International Press Association
two years later when it expanded to accept members from other countries.
Although most of its national membership was in the North and West, its
president was Eliza Nicholson, publisher of the New Orleans *Picayune.*

Nicholson (1849–1896), considered a model of southern femininity, at-
tained success due to a mixture of circumstances that often led women to
careers in journalism: talent, family ties, and economic need. Born Eliza
Jane Poitevent at her family home on the Pearl River in Mississippi, she
wrote poetry as "Pearl Rivers" for newspapers and magazines after she
graduated from the Amite (Louisiana) Female Seminary. When Alva Morris
Holbrook, owner of the *Picayune,* offered her a job as literary editor, she
ventured into the male world of the newspaper office, to the dismay of her
family. In 1872 she and Holbrook, more than forty years her senior, were
married. Left a widow with a debt-laden newspaper at the age of twenty-six
in 1876, she decided to take charge herself, becoming the first woman to
publish a daily newspaper in the Deep South. Nicholson gave employees the
option to leave the *Picayune* rather than work for a woman; a few departed
but most remained as she laid out a plan for a family-oriented newspaper
that became highly profitable.

Her efforts were supported by George Nicholson, the newspaper's business manager, to whom she was married in 1878, although she maintained
editorial control. Eliza instituted society news and features and backed civic
reforms. Supportive of other women, in 1894 she hired Elizabeth Meriwether Gilmer (1861–1951), a writer from Tennessee who desperately
needed a job because of her husband's mental illness. Gilmer, who adopted
the pseudonym "Dorothy Dix," moved into the New York journalistic
world a decade later and became a highly paid syndicated advice columnist.
Another woman who worked under Eliza Nicholson was Martha R. Field,
who, as "Catherine Cole," successfully campaigned for kindergartens and
nurses' training schools and later served as a correspondent from other cities
and England.

The 1889 women's issue of the *Journalist* refers to only one other white
southern woman journalist, Sallie B. Morgan, then living in the Pacific
Northwest, where she apparently was writing for newspapers as well as acting as a correspondent for the *Clarion Ledger* of Jackson, Mississippi. She

is described as a native of Mississippi and a granddaughter of its territorial governor, Robert William. After referring to her as a former staff member of the Nashville *World,* the one-paragraph item concludes, "Now as a Southern writer she is making the Northwest see Mississippi through her own rosy glasses, and aiding in welcoming hundreds of immigrants to that genial clime."

A disinclination of white southern women to make themselves conspicuous in public, even though they worked outside the home, may have accounted for the scarcity of their names in the special issue of the *Journalist.* For example, Marion Marzolf in her history of women journalists, *Up from the Footnote* (1977), records that Piney W. Forsythe, aided by her two printer-sisters, took over her father's newspaper, the *Advocate* of Liberty, Mississippi, in 1868, but was afraid to attend a state convention of editors "for fear they would stare at me."

In his book, *Editors I Have Known Since the Civil War* (1922), R. H. Henry of Jackson, Mississippi, comments on the "large number of women editors and managers of newspapers" in his state, "some succeeding their husbands, after they had been called hence, others assuming full responsibility of editorship while their husbands conducted other business, and in some instances, girls raised and brought up in the printing offices, never left them, even to marry." Henry names only a few of these unsung heroines, among them, "Mrs. S. C. Maer of the Columbus *Dispatch,* which she managed and edited for several years," whom he called "a fine business woman . . . [who] knew exactly what she was doing every day." Other southern states doubtlessly had equal numbers of women journalists who quietly carried out major responsibilities.

For some women, periodicals, rather than newspapers, offered more congenial avenues for the employments of their literary and editing talents. In 1887, for example, Kate Garland had charge of a women's magazine, *Woman's Work,* published in Athens, Georgia. Sara Hartman was editor and publisher from 1890 to 1895 of the *Gulf Messenger,* an illustrated monthly published in San Antonio and New Orleans. The *Southland Queen* appeared in Beeville, Texas, from 1895 to 1904. One of the few magazines published in the rural South and aimed at women, the *Southland Queen* most likely did not have a woman editor, but because the publication's editors looked for cheap literary help, its contributors were most probably women. The Baltimore magazine *New Eclectic* (later the *Southern Magazine*) published from 1868 until 1875 and featured the work of Margaret J. Preston (1820–1897). Preston also wrote on southern themes for northern magazines, like *Lippincott's.*

One woman who made a name for herself in the southern periodical field was Sophia Bledsoe Herrick (1837–1919), who left her minister husband and supported herself and her children through her journalistic abilities. For some ten years she was a major contributor to the *Southern Review,* a Baltimore publication edited by her father, Albert Taylor Bledsoe, that endeavored to offer an intellectual explanation of regional thought. Bledsoe, a Methodist minister, engaged in heated theological controversies in the pages of the *Review,* which was associated with the Methodist Church South. Herrick, however, was known for gentle essays on topics like literature and nature. She became associate editor in 1875 and editor after her father's death in 1877, maintaining the *Review* for two years until it was replaced by another church publication. Herrick later became a staff member of the *Century* in New York.

Southern African American women journalists appeared less shy about taking a stand on public issues than many of their white counterparts. The *Journalist*'s special edition on women journalists features four southern African American women, three of whom were from Kentucky, in an illustrated article, "Some Female Writers of the Negro Race," written by Lucy Wilmot Smith. One southern writer profiled was Ida B. Wells (1862–1931), a teacher in the segregated schools of Memphis, whose pseudonym was "Iola." She was also known as the "Princess of the Press," and her contributions are described as "distributed among the leading race journals." Also included is Mary V. Cook. Writing under the pseudonym "Grace Ermine," Cook was a native of Bowling Green, Kentucky, and a graduate of the segregated Kentucky State University to which she had returned as a Latin professor. Cook had formerly edited both the women's department in the *American Baptist,* a religious periodical published in Kentucky, and the educational department of another African American magazine, *Our Women and Children.* Another noted writer profiled was Mary E. Britton, who wrote under her initials, MEB, and was credited with successfully campaigning for equal facilities for African Americans on railroads in Kentucky, having published articles in the local newspapers of Lexington, her hometown, and in the Cincinnati *Commercial* (a white newspaper). Ione E. Wood, a tutor in Greek at Kentucky State University and editor of the temperance department of *Our Women and Children* magazine, is also featured in Smith's article. Three other women are listed as editors of African American newspapers in Petersburg, Virginia, and Montgomery, Alabama.

Of these journalists, the fearless Ida B. Wells, who used the name Wells-Barnett after her marriage in 1895 to Ferdinand L. Barnett, a Chicago attorney, achieved the most distinguished career. Losing her job as a teacher when she criticized the inadequacies of segregated education, she bravely wrote editorials against the crime of lynching in an African American newspaper, the Memphis *Free Speech,* of which she was a part owner. As a result of the editorials, which appeared in 1892 after three of her personal friends had been lynched, the newspaper office was destroyed and threats were made on her life. Wells moved to New York, where she continued her journalistic career and led a crusade against lynching. A suffragist and lecturer, she founded women's clubs for African Americans and antilynching societies in the United States and Great Britain. After moving to Chicago in 1893, she became the first African American employed by the *Inter Ocean,* a leading newspaper for which she wrote her own column. Her style is a vigorous prose filled with righteous indignation against injustice.

Perhaps it was Wells-Barnett who most clearly saw the possibilities open to southern women within the field of journalism. Journalism was an occupation in which women could gain recognition and make an impact on society, but it required them to negotiate between the demands of the public arena and a sectional mythology that called on women to emphasize domestic pursuits. In Wells-Barnett's case, as an African American woman, little negotiation was possible because she faced both racism and sexism. She had to leave the South in order to speak out.

Other women, such as Rebecca Felton (1835–1930), worked out a compromise between the public and private while acting as a voice for the South. Felton, the first woman to be seated in the United States Senate, was appointed as a gesture to fill an unexpired term in 1922, when she was eighty-six years old. She occupied a Senate seat from Georgia for one day before turning it over to her successor. The longtime campaign manager for her husband, who served two terms in Congress and three in the state legislature, Felton helped edit the family newspaper in Cartersville, Georgia.

Beginning in 1899, Felton wrote a column for the rural edition of the Atlanta *Journal.* While she subscribed to racism, even going so far as to favor lynching in 1897, in her columns she dispensed advice in a colloquial style to thousands of farm families who were her readers for twenty years. By using journalism to straddle the line between the public world of men and the private world of women, Felton and other women journalists helped to prepare their readers and themselves for the twentieth century.

For southern women of the postbellum period, journalism provided a bridge between the ideal of the woman as a mythical being apart from the rude world of business and commerce, and the practical reality of the woman as an adult forced to earn money to take care of herself and, quite likely, her family. In some cases women journalists followed their male relatives into the occupation, inheriting the opportunity to carry on a family tradition. In other cases women found journalism a congenial field that allowed for at least some self-expression. Although their subject matter may have been somewhat limited by convention, journalism allowed them a platform for personal growth as well as monetary reward.

Southern Women Humorists

Kathryn McKee

The phrase "women humorists" is not an oxymoron. Critical studies and literary anthologies of the last ten years, including Nancy Walker's *A Very Serious Thing: Women's Humor and American Culture* (1988) and Walker and Zita Dresner's *Redressing the Balance: American Women's Literary Humor from Colonial Times to the 1980s* (1988), convincingly establish a tradition of American women's humor and confirm what Kate Sanborn, editor of *The Wit of Women,* observed in 1886: women have long written humor, but it has been persistently barred from recognition as such because comedy has traditionally been regarded as the province of men. More recent scholars, particularly Barbara Bennett in *Comic Visions, Female Voices* (1998), have identified distinctive features of southern women's humor that both ties it to region and sounds universal resonances. Contemporary southern women novelists use humor, Bennett maintains, to solidify female-centered community, to transgress societal barriers, and to launch incisive critiques at the patriarchal structure of their homeland. But the wit and the play, the satire and the double-voiced power of humor is not the invention of twentieth-century writers. Rather, humor is also fundamental to the literature produced by a number of postbellum female authors, among them Katherine McDowell (1849–1883), who wrote as Sherwood Bonner; Mary Noailles Murfree, who wrote as Charles Egbert Craddock; Ruth McEnery

Stuart (1849–1917); and Idora McClellan Moore (1843–1929), who wrote as Betsy Hamilton.

Mark Twain's status as nineteenth-century America's premiere funnyman has often eclipsed the role humor plays in the work of his contemporaries, a significant number of whom were women. Traditionally designated as local colorists and then largely dismissed for the supposed superficiality of their work, this body of postbellum female authors contains writers who, like Mark Twain, turn to humor as a fundamental component of their writing. To call these authors "humorists" implies a centrality of humor in their writing that critics have not often accorded it. But examining the ways in which postbellum female writers employ humor reveals that its function is vital to both the structure and the theme of their writing. In fact, a number of these authors exhibit affinities with male-dominated antebellum southwestern humor and thus complicate traditional classifications of their work by genre. Judith Fetterley and Marjorie Pryse, in *American Women Regionalists 1850–1910* (1992), argue for a distinction between texts written by men and those written by women, whom they term "regionalists," during the years 1850 to 1910. They note the absence of narrative distance between storyteller and plot in regionalist texts and suggest that, unlike male writers of the period, female authors enlist the audience's sympathy for their characters by identifying with those characters themselves. Fetterley and Pryse argue convincingly for understanding the work of Alice Cary, Rose Terry Cooke, Mary Wilkins Freeman, Mary Austin, and Sarah Orne Jewett within a context of these shared impulses and approaches. Yet many southern female authors of the same time period more often reinforce rather than minimize narrative distance, thus entrenching lines of social difference rather than tearing them down. Humor is their most important tool and the force that distinguishes these postbellum southern writers from the larger body of local colorists.

Katherine McDowell was, during her brief lifetime and career, a controversial figure whose mocking humor and incipient feminism antagonized audiences. "Sherwood Bonner" was "born" when Katherine McDowell left her husband and child and moved alone to Boston, where she went seeking both an education and a literary career. Between March 1874 and December 1875, she served as a correspondent for the *Daily Memphis Avalanche*, writing letters that described her life in Boston and recounting her meetings with famous New England figures, including Wendell Phillips and Ralph Waldo Emerson. She established the witty tone of her subsequent newspaper writing in her first letter, titled in full "From the 'Hub.' A Southern Girl's

Experience of Life in New England. What a Bright, Educated, Witty, Lively, Snappy Young Woman Can Say on a Variety of Topics." The dateline of the letter is the "Moral Lighthouse," a thinly veiled jab at Oliver Wendell Holmes's proclamation of the Boston State House as "the hub of the solar system." McDowell's comic voice establishes a frame for the observations of an ostensibly conventional southern woman who instantly forms a rapport with her audience by allowing them to participate vicariously in her irreverence, resounding as it does with echoes of Mark Twain's journey to the Holy Land in *The Innocents Abroad* (1871). The sacred ground on which Bonner trespasses, however, is decidedly American and regional: "For the native Bostonian there are three paths to glory. If his name be Quincy or Adams, nothing more is expected of him. . . . Failing in the happy accident of birth, the candidate for Beacon Hill honors must write a book. This is easy. The man who can breathe Boston air and not write a book is either a fool or a phenomenon. One course remains to him should he miss fame in both these lines. He must be a reformer." In one swift move, Bonner strikes out at the hallmarks of New England culture—ancestry, literature, and reform—and she suggests that none of those elements results from anything more than fate or the general atmosphere. In 1876, Katherine Mc-Dowell took her witty newspaper persona abroad, where she encountered the landmarks of European culture, from the Sistine Chapel, which threatens visitors with "a 'crick' in the neck," to an audience with the Pope. In her travel letters published in the *Avalanche,* Bonner describes how she and her traveling companion practiced for hours for the latter occasion, bowing in front of a chair draped with a sheet and outfitted with a curling stick to act as the Pope's imaginary hand. Insightful and irreverent, Sherwood Bonner, like her contemporary Mark Twain, used humor to penetrate what she perceived as superficial performance.

Perhaps McDowell's most shocking and most comical treatment of New England personalities comes in a poem called "The Radical Club," which she published in the May 8, 1875, issue of the Boston *Times.* Subtitled "A Poem, Respectfully Dedicated to 'The Infinite' By An Atom," the work comically depicts Boston's Radical Club in rollicking verse that imitates Edgar Allan Poe's "The Raven." Hubert Horton McAlexander, in *The Prodigal Daughter: A Biography of Sherwood Bonner* (1981), describes the Radical Club as "a relic of the Transcendental Club surviving in Boston's intellectual Indian Summer." McDowell characterizes key Radical Club members in undignified ways: Elizabeth Peabody she depicts as the "kindergarten mother" who "clucked an answer to this brother, / And her curls kept bobbing quaintly from the queer head dress she wore," while Ednah Dow Cheney she calls a "magnus corpus, with a figure like a porpus." McDowell concludes in the final stanza that "their long-drawn dissertations come to— / words and nothing more, / Only words and nothing more." Although the poem was published anonymously, McDowell's authorship became well known throughout the area. Horrified by McDowell's audacity, the Radical Club changed its suddenly notorious name to the Chesnutt Street Club. In her anthology *The Wit of Women* (1886), Kate Sanborn takes McDowell to task for abusing her privilege as an invited guest at the Radical Club, but proceeds to include some of the poem's less inflammatory passages in her collection, conceding that "like so many wicked things it is captivating, and while you are shocked, you laugh." "The Radical Club" itself was enormously popular; it appeared as a pamphlet in 1876, and the Boston *Times* reprinted it in 1877.

Although McDowell's second collection of short stories, the posthumously published *Suwanee River Tales* (1884), contains largely conventional plantation fiction, *Dialect Tales* (1883) includes several humorous sketches in the vein of the *Avalanche* correspondent. "Aunt Anniky's Teeth," while unsettling to the modern reader in its reliance on racial stereotypes, does locate in the female character of its title the one-upmanship of its humor. Aunt Anniky, famous for her nursing skills, is caring for an old black man, called Uncle Ned, who is overcome in the night by an incredible thirst; he grabs a glass from his bedside table and chews up what he assumes to be ice cubes. They are, in fact, Aunt Anniky's false teeth. A controversy ensues because Uncle Ned now refuses to pay Aunt Anniky the hog he promised her if she nursed him back to health. The two bring their dispute to "Mars' Charles" who suggests that they resolve their disagreement by merging property in marriage. They reluctantly agree, and Aunt Anniky receives a new set of teeth as a wedding gift from Master Charles. Uncle Ned ultimately gets cold feet and takes himself and his hogs out of harm's way, abandoning Aunt Anniky. She accepts the turn of events cheerfully, explaining, "[I]t wuz de teef I wanted, not de man!" In fact, Anniky manages rather well all of the men in her narrative, exacting from each just what she wants with little personal inconvenience. Clearly Aunt Anniky, rather than Uncle Ned or Master Charles, has the last laugh. She contends, for instance, that Uncle Ned does owe her the pig in question because "when he got so mad [after crunching her teeth] it brought on a sweat dat *broke de fever*! It saved him!" Turning every circumstance to her own advantage, Aunt Anniky learns many of her tricks from the sly manipulators of southwestern humor, particularly from a character like George Washington Harris' Sicily Burns, who matches and sometimes excels the trickery of the genre's male figures.

Unlike her fictional African American contemporary Uncle Remus, who merely tells tales of deception, Anniky herself participates in the events of her narrative, anticipating in that respect a later figure such as Charles Chesnutt's Uncle Julius. Although she belongs racially and economically to an entirely different social class than McDowell herself, Anniky shares the author's conviction that women can use humor to deflate conventional hierarchies.

In "The Gentlemen of Sarsar," McDowell likewise questions established boundaries, this time of class, rather than of race or gender. The tale is a first-person account of a prank that begins when the narrator, the blustering, self-important Ned Merewether, travels to the backwater community of Sarsar to collect a debt on behalf of his father. Once there he finds the overtures of the assertive gentlemen of Sarsar impossible to refuse, and so he joins them in a "nigger-hunt" that becomes harmless entertainment gone awry when he accidentally kills the quarry, named Bud Kane. Merewether must compensate financially all of Bud's relations and acquaintances in order to escape Sarsar alive, and he leaves with his own debt uncollected. A short time later the ringleader of the gentlemen of Sarsar, Andy Rucker, dispatches a very healthy Bud Kane to Merewether's home with an explanation of the prank and a basketful of puppies as a peace offering. That Bonner pokes fun at Ned Merewether is obvious. He surrenders unwittingly on every occasion to the superior intellect of the backwoods Andy Rucker, whom Merewether forgives at the story's conclusion, apparently without noticing that he has still not been repaid the original debt in question. At about the same time that Mark Twain was completing *Adventures of Huckleberry Finn* (1885), McDowell was yielding power to the force of the vernacular in her work, signaling as she does her own awareness that the antebellum gentleman is ill suited for the postbellum world, largely because of his unwillingness or inability to assess the changed nature of his circumstances. Time spent outside of her native South, coupled with a series of unconventional actions that resulted in near ostracization (Katherine and Edward McDowell divorced in 1881), placed McDowell in the perfect position to create humor, both inside and outside the southern society she took as her subject.

Mary Noailles Murfree was likewise distanced from the Tennessee mountaineers who populate much of her fiction. Vacationing at Beersheba Springs in the Cumberland Mountains of Tennessee in the 1850s, the Murfrees joined other affluent southern families, and in this environment, Murfree interacted with mountaineers living in proximity to the resort. In the people she observed, particularly the women, Murfree found the subject matter that would dominate her long and prolific career as a writer. Like Katherine McDowell, Murfree took a pseudonym, writing as "Charles Egbert Craddock." In fact, Murfree rocked the literary world by revealing her true identity in 1885; most readers, and certainly her editors at the *Atlantic Monthly,* had assumed that she was male, a conclusion based in part on the rugged mountaineers who people her fiction; their traditionally masculine pastimes of hunting, fishing, and fighting; and the sometimes crude nature of their humor.

Like McDowell's, the evolution of Murfree's writing persona was gradual and linked to the confidence she steadily gained as a humorist. Few of Murfree's readers remembered, if they ever knew, that before she became Charles Egbert Craddock, Murfree wrote social satire under the pseudonym "R. Emmet Dembry," sometimes abbreviated "R. E. Dembry." Dembry's first publication was a sketch called "Flirts and Their Ways" in the May 1874 issue of *Lippincott's.* It was followed by a similar piece, "My Daughter's Admirers," in the July 1875 edition of the same periodical. Both satirized the conventional romantic exchanges that Murfree probably witnessed as a member of Nashville's postwar society. In "Flirts and Their Ways," she divides flirts into categories ("the pious flirt," "the sympathetic flirt," "the sentimental flirt," etc.) and discusses the merits of each approach, while in "My Daughter's Admirers," she has an observant father perform much the same task, grouping and analyzing his daughter's gentlemen callers. In Murfree's subsequent fiction, humor is a more subtle presence. But when it surfaces, it echoes southwestern humor, as her short stories, particularly those collected in *In the Tennessee Mountains* (1884), demonstrate.

In "Driftin' Down Lost Creek," for example, Elijah Price, who is described as "a plumb idjit," strikes Jubal Tynes on the forehead with a sledge hammer. The blow leaves "blood upon the sledge, and they said brains, too." Mrs. Ware reacts with this observation: "Cur'ous enough ter me ter find out ez Jube ever had brains." A seemingly incongruous combination of humor and violence recurs throughout Murfree's texts. Inseparable from the mountain environment, violence provides the characters with the language and the context for discussing the events of their world. Much of the discourse among them takes the form of boasts and threats—often comic—about the fear or pain one can inflict upon another. In "Electioneerin' on Big Injun Mountain," for instance, Abel Stubbs recalls Rufus Chadd's warning: "[F]oolin' with me is like makin' faces at a rattlesnake: it may be satisfying to the feelin's but't ain't safe."

Murfree's deadpan narration, like that of Mark Twain and the antebellum humorists, is vital to her humor and may account in part for the failure of some readers to appreciate this dimension of her work. But unlike writers in the antebellum tradition, Murfree never includes a narrative frame provided by an intellectually superior character who periodically interjects himself into the text, as does George, for example, the ostensible recorder of Sut Lovingood's yarns. Rather the omniscient narrative voice is Murfree's, as is the sophisticated stance that frames the story's events and causes them to appear humorous in the eyes of the reader. The intended audience for her fiction is not the people about whom she writes, but rather the members of her own class; she relies on the clash between her characters' sensibilities and those of her readership, which are reflected in her own narrative voice. In depicting mountaineer families, Murfree sometimes turns to black comedy in the spirit of George Washington Harris and in anticipation of Erskine Caldwell and William Faulkner, who likewise depict their lower-class characters in a comic but unflattering light. In a scene from "Driftin' Down Lost Creek," she notes that "the animals were [a] more emotional, alert, and intelligent element [than the humans]."

Ruth McEnery Stuart, like Murfree, was born into a well-to-do family, and she too came to write about marginalized groups of people from the perspective of a detached observer. Stuart grew up in New Orleans and then moved to her husband's cotton plantation in Arkansas following their marriage in 1879. The characters in her stories and novels range from Italian immigrants to plantation blacks to white Arkansas farmers and small-town residents. Her career as a writer, beginning in the late 1880s, was highly successful, and she moved to New York, where she became one of the South's most widely recognized literary ladies. Unlike McDowell and Murfree, Stuart kept numerous speaking engagements, reading aloud from her work and thus literally articulating the humor that is fundamental to her fiction. She, like her female contemporaries and the antebellum humorists who preceded them, often depends upon the intellectual distance between herself as storyteller and the characters she creates to formulate much of her humorous effect.

African Americans were one group of people whom Stuart saw as ready subjects for her comic sketches, and her stereotypical depictions of them rightly make modern audiences uncomfortable. Although she creates a number of memorable and powerful black female characters, for instance Rose Ann in *Napoleon Jackson* (1902), African Americans are more often the objects of the reader's laughter than they are his equals. One of Stuart's early stories, "Lamentations of Jeremiah Johnson" (1888) is representative of her sketches in this vein. "Lamentations of Jeremiah" is actually the name of the main character, his parents' tenth child and only son, although, sadly, none of his nine older sisters lives until his birth. Lamentations is regularly outfitted in their clothing, however, and, as the twelve-year-old narrator of the story, he spends much time lamenting his imperiled masculinity and generally appearing silly in a dress.

Stuart's most enduring comic character, however, is the white Arkansas farmer Deuteronomy Jones, the narrator of *Sonny* (1896) and *Sonny's Father* (1910), book-length monologues that proved to be among Stuart's best-selling works. The title character, Sonny, is the precocious, undisciplined son of Deuteronomy and Martha Jones. He is his parents' only child, born to them late in life after nearly twenty years of marriage and as his father approaches his fiftieth birthday. The reader meets the family only a few hours after Sonny's birth and follows his progression through adolescence, courtship, marriage, and, in *Sonny's Father*, fatherhood. Sonny never speaks directly, however, and what begins as an account of a mischievous young boy's antics becomes the story of his father's life. Deuteronomy's ostensible auditor is an unnamed doctor, who appears periodically to interject questions in what is otherwise a stream of pithy observations, comic moments, and exaggerated descriptions, as well as a running commentary on the social and political events of his day.

The comedy of the Sonny monologues relies on the storyteller's art of relating outrageously comic situations with little emotion. In the character of Sonny, Stuart merges the backgrounds of Mark Twain's more famous boyhood adventurers: like Tom Sawyer, Sonny recognizes no limitations on his behavior, and like Huckleberry Finn, he hails, if not from the lower class, at least from the ranks of the farming class. In the first volume of Sonny sketches, the narrator recounts a number of comic episodes created by his son's resistance to the institutions of social conformity. In "Sonny's Christening," for instance, Sonny refuses to be baptized because he equates the procedure with vaccination, which he also refuses. When Sonny develops an infection in his foot from a splinter that he will not let his mother remove, she sends for the rector to have him baptized, in case he should die. In response, Sonny crawls first under the bed and then up a tree in the butterbean arbor, forcing all of the adults out into the pouring rain to coax him down. From his treetop perch, Sonny orders everyone christened. Sonny's father explains to the rector "thet the rites o' the church didn't count for nothin' on our farm, next to the right o' the boy!" and so both the narrator and his wife are rebaptized. The narrator finally proposes that the rain descending from heaven be considered blessed, and the rector, desperate to save himself if no one else, agrees.

In *Sonny's Father*, the wayward Sonny has matured into a responsible adult, complete with wife, child, and profession, and the reader's interest shifts from him to rest exclusively on his father. This masculine persona thinly disguises Stuart's own interest in issues stemming from the Spanish-American War, from the reform activities of various groups, and from the conflict between tradition and progress that gripped the South and the nation in the opening years of a new century. Stuart even takes Deuteronomy Jones to school about feminism—literally—by placing him at a lecture delivered by a traveling female speaker. Despite some good-natured jabs at the potential mannishness of suffragettes, Sonny's father finally accepts the label of "a woman's righter" affixed to him by the doctor, observing in his typically wry manner, "I like that name, an' I'd like to be all the kinds of a righter thet it comes in my way to be, an' a wronger of no man."

Yet Stuart cannot resist poking fun at feminism itself, which, she periodically suggests, is a movement that may sometimes take itself too seriously. In 1901, Stuart published a burlesque, *Snow-Cap Sisters,* in which she plays with the notion that suffrage will rob females of their femininity. Though a dedicated supporter of women's rights, Stuart here hints that the extreme behavior of some women is partly responsible for perceptions that politically active women have broken with their gender. The character of "Miss Jo-Hanna Jim-miny Snow" is to be "distinguished by masculine suggestion in her toilet" according to Stuart's stage directions. Another character describes her as having "all sorts of mannish notions. . . . Why, like as not, ef any young man was to give her a bunch of heliotropes, she'd say: 'Much obliged to you for these here she-liotropes.'" Although she parodies both misgivings about femininity and feminists in this light-hearted passage, Stuart maintained throughout her life an interest in public affairs, and in later works she directly encouraged women to participate in their country politically. Most pointed in its exploration of feminist themes is Stuart's final novel, *The Cocoon* (1915), a comic account of one woman's trip to a rest-cure facility, likely based on the treatment Stuart herself received following her son's death. Even if the novel's comic resolution is finally unsatisfying, the narrator's confinement physically illustrates the gender-based restrictions instituted by society and the barriers erected against exploring issues related to women's mental health.

Although critics most often discuss McDowell, Murfree, and Stuart as local colorists rather than as humorists, Idora McClellan Plowman Moore has virtually disappeared from all considerations of nineteenth-century literature. Moore, who moved with her first husband to the hill country of northern Alabama in the 1870s, observed there a class of white people and a way of living that had been unknown to her as she grew up on her father's plantation near Talladega. She then began writing brief comic sketches, but turned in earnest to writing as a profession following the deaths of her husband and her father. She adopted the persona of "Betsy Hamilton," a self-identified hill country cracker, to whom audiences immediately warmed. "Betsy Hamilton" columns appeared as regular features in Atlanta's literary magazine the *Sunny South* (1881–1885) and in the Atlanta *Constitution* (1884 to approximately 1900).

Additionally, Moore toured as "Betsy Hamilton," performing her sketches in costume and imitating to near perfection, according to her reviewers, the dialect spoken by the poor white and African American characters she created. Moore could assume full credit for her success; she served as her own business manager and agent. Frequently appearing at charity benefits and lyceums and chautauquas, Betsy Hamilton played to standing-room-only crowds from Mississippi to North Carolina throughout the late 1880s and the 1890s. In 1888, the Atlanta *Evening Journal* proclaimed that Betsy Hamilton "swept the audience like a cyclone"; on July 25, 1896, a newspaper in Anniston, Alabama, reported that she drew a crowd of one thousand. There were nights when Mark Twain would have been thankful to have attracted half so many. In her stage show, Moore offered an intriguing mixture of reading and acting, leading reviewers to proclaim her the female equivalent of the character actor Joseph Jefferson. Advertisements for her shows often label her as "the only woman who has a world-wide reputation for humor."

Moore's serial feature in the *Sunny South,* cast in the form of personal letters and titled "The Backwoods—Familiar Letters from Betsy Hamilton to her Cousin Saleny," is more fully developed than either of her short story collections, *Betsy Hamilton; Southern Character Sketches* (1921) and *Southern Character Sketches* (1937). The letters are numbered and feature intriguing subtitles to distinguish them, including "Maw's been Sick, ever Sense She Dried Up the Hog Fat," "What Does Ignoramus Mean?" and "Pap's Cane-tucky Mule and George's Dutchman." Betsy introduces a panorama of recurring characters, all residents of the fictional community of Hillabee, Alabama, and she counts on the reader to join her regularly because a missed letter can mean a missed piece of information that explains otherwise perplexing behavior. Against this well-developed background, the reader witnesses the transformation of Betsy Hamilton from a young girl to a woman, wife to George Washington Higgins and mother to twin girls, Saleny Sophrony and Partheny Caledony. Finally, the reader encounters Betsy as George Washington Higgins' young widow, contemplating, as had Moore herself, how to reenter the world as a single woman. Thus Betsy completes a cycle of life and reaches the emotional extremity of Moore's own existence. Although Moore, like her contemporaries, depends on class difference to execute much of her humor, the voice of Betsy Hamilton finally transcends such distinctions to unify her female readers in shared experiences.

Humor as a community-building tool is an important element of contemporary southern women's fiction noted by Barbara Bennett; in *Comic Visions, Female Voices* she catalogs the instances in which shared humor serves to clear spaces in which women can rally around their common status in the southern social order. For postbellum women writers, humor is likewise a tool, but often one that unifies readers around class-based perceptions in the spirit of the antebellum southwestern humorists, in addition to appealing to their gender-specific experiences. Most important, consideration of postbellum women's humor expands and deepens efforts to understand the tradition of southern women's writing, its relationship to the work of male authors, and its connection to the themes traditionally associated with the region's literature.

Mary Noailles Murfree

Benjamin F. Fisher

Mary N. Murfree, often better known as "Charles Egbert Craddock" and one of the South's leading woman writers during the last quarter of the nineteenth century, wrote fiction that interestingly contrasts with much other southern literature of the period. The contrasts are chiefly two. First, Murfree's use of Tennessee mountain material differs overall from what most other southern writers were writing at the time she worked. Second, that material would naturally have minimized or excluded the racial issues that, for many students of southern literature, have provided its chief reason for being. In this second sense, Murfree's work differs from that of her contemporary George Washington Cable and from the writings of William Faulkner, whose work hers in other ways anticipates. Likewise, a generation earlier, George Washington Harris offered far more comic-fantastic renderings of Tennessee mountain life in his Sut Lovingood yarns. Although Murfree knew Harris' writings, she provided greater seriousness as part of the depth in many of her characters than Harris had in his, along with creating exquisite natural atmosphere. Despite attempts at several other types of fiction, namely historical novels and tales of the Civil War, Murfree's principal contributions to southern literature, and to American literature overall, are fictions about the Tennessee mountains and their people.

Mary Murfree was born January 24, 1850, at Grantland, her family's plantation near Nashville, Tennessee, to William Law and Fanny Priscilla

Dickinson Murfree. Her sister, Fanny Noailles Dickinson, was four years older, her brother, William Law, Jr., four years younger than she. Their father, an attorney with interests in the arts, as well as an author and editor, and their mother, an accomplished pianist, were both well read and owned a fine, large library. Their children naturally grew to love reading, and Mary in particular cherished a lifelong delight in music, from folk songs to classical works. Her early schooling in Nashville and Philadelphia, trips to the Murfrees' three Mississippi Delta plantations, and summer vacations at the Beersheba Springs resort in the Cumberland Mountains, roughly a hundred miles southeast of Murfreesboro, opened Mary's eyes to regions and customs she would later employ in her fiction. The visits to the mountains especially inspired her, although her mountain fiction eventually grew repetitious. Doubtless a reviewer's suggestion that she employ another locale led to her fiction about Mississippi Delta areas, to her essays on southern history—published chiefly in *Youth's Companion* after the turn of the century—and to the posthumously published short story "The Visitants from Yesterday" (1981), set in urban environs and paying respects to such then new conveniences as electric lighting.

Grantland was burned during the Civil War and the Mississippi lands confiscated. Thus family finances were much depleted. After residing at New Grantland, a home built in 1872, then in St. Louis (where her brother maintained a solid law practice) for nine years, again at New Grantland, where Mr. Murfree died in 1892, the Murfree ladies moved to Murfreesboro. During those years, Mary's sister, Fanny, had published a novel, *Felicia,* which was serialized in the *Atlantic Monthly* (August 1890–March 1891) and issued in hardcover by Houghton Mifflin in 1891. Though some reviewers compared the technique in this work with that of Henry James, the novel has not remained popular. Despite Fanny's success, Mary's writing in the main provided for the family's livelihood. Mary also joined the Daughters of the American Revolution, became active in that organization, and served as state regent in 1912. Both she and Fanny were energetic in establishing and helping to finance the building of St. Paul's Episcopal Church in Murfreesboro. Essentially, however, the Murfree sisters' lives were uneventful and home centered. Failing eyesight troubled Mary's later years, hampering her ability to write. In 1922, Mary was awarded an honorary doctor of letters degree by the University of the South, recognizing her outstanding contributions to American literature. She died July 31, 1922, in Murfreesboro.

Murfree's life witnessed significant change in the South, and she wrote much that recognized such change. Always observant of human behavior,

Murfree was quick to transmit her observations into her writing. Whether it be the cut of a lady's dress; the flavor of a mountaineer's food; the gestures of rural or urban, educated or uneducated characters, which reveal much about them and their situations; the varieties of humor or pathos; or the beauties of natural scenery, her depictions of such persons and events convey a dynamism despite that stilted expression that intermittently irritates readers. Although she never intrudes her own character into her fiction, as, for example, Poe has been accused of doing, she never forgets her acute awareness of human thought and action.

Murfree's circumstances shifted from those of a wealthy plantation family member, a daughter cosseted because of lameness contracted at an early age, through family traumas sustained from Civil War pillaging, on to her single-handed maintenance via authorship of her family and herself. In this same era, women authors struggled to make their status as creative writers respectable, and Murfree's fiction stands as a not inconsiderable part of that movement. Her first pseudonym, "R. Emmet Dembry," and the "Craddock" signature afterward, evince her awareness of the low esteem then typically accorded women writers. Such derogation would crumble because of Murfree's accomplishments and those of such other southern women writers as Katherine McDowell (1849–1883), Kate Chopin, Alice Dunbar-Nelson, and Ellen Glasgow. Along with several who more readily gained recognition as undisputed artists in fiction, such as Edith Wharton and Willa Cather, these southern authors were instrumental in proving that the woman writer in America ought not to be lightly dismissed.

Edd Winfield Parks's influential biography (1941) and Richard Cary's Twayne series volume (1967), the only books devoted wholly to Murfree, designate her a failed novelist of manners. Indeed her earliest publications—an essay with a self-explanatory title, "Flirts and Their Ways," and a story, "My Daughter's Admirers," respectively in *Lippincott's* for May 1874 and July 1875—recall fiction by George Meredith, William Thackeray, and Jane Austen. Both pieces manifest sprightly comedy, and the story adumbrates episodes that play off spinsterhood versus marriage, as well as other family and social pastimes such as card games, gander pullings, and quiltings that would inform many of Murfree's later mountain fictions. At this same time she was experimenting. "Alleghany Winds and Waters," a lengthy and intricate novel alternating interest from buried treasure in the mountains to riverboat scenes, was never published. *Where the Battle Was Fought,* another novel, filled with quasi-supernatural trappings, did not see print until 1884.

For *Where the Battle Was Fought,* Murfree drew on her own recollections of Civil War activities and tensions at her old home and nearby areas, although there is none of the pageantry customarily coloring battle scenes here as there is in much other historical fiction of the nineteenth century. The combination of realism with supernaturalism is deft; in this respect Murfree's ghosts stand as transitional figures between the ghosts of Poe, Augusta Evans Wilson and John Esten Cooke, and those of Faulkner and Glasgow. Murfree's characterization coalesces artistically with both the mundane and the otherworldly; the schemers and their would-be victims—the latter suffering depredations that cause them financial disasters—experience sufficient psychological torments to create understandable hallucinatory or superstitious reactions. Sensationalism blended with the homely, which combination was to recur throughout the Murfree canon, differs little from that mixture in the fiction of other well-known fiction writers of her day, e. g., Mary Elizabeth Braddon (1837–1915), E.D.E.N. Southworth (1819–1899), Wilkie Collins, Charles Reade, and, nearer home, John Esten Cooke (whose early work, he admitted, bore a Collins-Reade stamp). Unlike Cooke, Murfree did not abrogate sensationalism. She made it function plausibly among her rural characters, who were always ready to interpret some unusual occurrence or some perhaps mentally deficient character as inspired by otherworldly, at times biblical, agencies.

What initially attracted attention to the abilities of "Mr. Craddock" was "The Dancin' Party at Harrison's Cove," a story about near violence among contentious mountaineer men during a rural entertainment, published in the *Atlantic Monthly* for May 1878. This tale—its dramatic element intensified because the events are viewed from an outsider's perspective, one which evinces curiosity about mountain people and their lifestyles—marks an excellent beginning for Murfree's literary career. Along with the others that were to make up the collection entitled *In the Tennessee Mountains* (1884), "The Dancin' Party" incorporates realism and fantasy in dramatizing mountaineers' everyday occupations and their recreations. All the tales are told from a narrative perspective that conveys an onlooker's zest for new situations and persons, such that trivial details assume dimensions of poetry. Murfree's natural settings constitute another variety of the "southern garden" motif that has recently drawn considerable critical attention.

Such poetics enhance other stories from *In the Tennessee Mountains*, notably "The 'Harnt' That Walks Chilhowee," where enchanting mountain scenery, in its serenity and timelessness, affords artistic backdrop to high-pitched human tragedy that ultimately proves to have a positive, albeit not comic, resolution. The two opening paragraphs evince this method. First, June in the mountains fosters the ripening of apples and corn. The latter, "planted on so steep a declivity that the stalks seemed to have much ado to keep their footing, was crested with tassels and plumed with silk." Likewise, "in honor of June's coming, and, heard by no man's ear, the pink and white bells of azalea rang out melodies of welcome." This poetic idyll throws into relief some ensuing crisp dialect dialogue concerning the likelihood of hazards to a bountiful harvest that ensues between Simon Burney and Peter Giles, whose farm is the scene of this exchange. Nevertheless, growth and the future occupy the two men, as it becomes evident that Burney, a widower, aspires to marry Giles's daughter, Clarsie (Clarissa). The girl's merits as a gentle person who could tame a bear, were she inclined, because she is in harmony with nature, prepare her for her subsequent nurturing of supposed murderer Reuben Crabb, a one-armed dwarf, of genuinely "crabbed" disposition, who perceives Clarsie's belief in ghosts as his means to survive. Ultimately released, Reuben spends his last years in the home of Simon Burney, who treats him deferentially. The narrator emphasizes that even if he is a lowly mountaineer, Simon Burney has noble impulses, and thus character and scene coalesce felicitously. Biblical names common among these mountain people enhance Murfree's art; Simon in many respects is subsumed by Peter in matters of successful farming and the marriage of Clarsie. Reuben's name indicates fragility or instability, and that a Thomas should marry Clarsie is appropriate for a farming couple if one recollects that biblical Thomas was literal-minded but finally dependable in his loyalty.

A like transformation in character enlivens *The Prophet of the Great Smoky Mountains* (1885), Murfree's most successful novel. The initial foregrounding of the "illusory mists" in peaks of the Smokies foreshadows illusions with which "prophet" Hiram Kelsey subsequently contends and then abrogates when, disguised, he sacrifices his life for that of Sheriff Micajah Green, who had offended the Cayces, mountain bootleggers. Setting forth to drown the man whom they suppose is Green, the Cayce men only eventually realize that they have probably executed Kelsey in Green's stead well after Kelsey is dead. Fractious old Pete Cayce consequently transforms into a benevolent figure, and his daughter, Dorinda, who has been loved by both Kelsey and Rick Tyler, supposes that, like biblical personages, Kelsey was taken into heaven without the usual minuses connected with ordinary humans' deaths. The book concludes with Dorinda, "cherish[ing] the last of her illusions," i.e., her suppositions concerning the men who loom important but temporarily in her emotional life. Illusion embraces deception, and *The Prophet of the Great Smoky Mountains* deftly incorporates this bracketing. Old Mrs. Cayce deceives Sheriff Green and his posse as to fugitive Rick Tyler's whereabouts, inviting them in to a substantial dinner to delay them. The Cayces deceive others with regard to their distilling liquor. Kelsey finally perpetrates the ultimate deception, having comprehended that he is in fact no prophet but only a too human being and therefore one who has led others astray (although unintentionally). His freeing of Green and dying in his place is, for Kelsey, the ultimate reparation. In this mountain world, where biblical names and credence for signs, prophecies, and judgment abound, Kelsey acts out the "greater love hath no man" and "no man can serve two masters" precepts. The novel is, however, not without Murfree's customary heightening of tragedy by means of tart humor. Comedy in this book places Murfree in good company with many other American authors, including her contemporaries Mary Wilkins Freeman and Edith Wharton, and modern writers such as Faulkner, O'Connor, and Welty.

Many of Murfree's later works show her hewing too unimaginatively to materials she had already worked. An outstanding exception is *In the Clouds* (1886), a novel involving a crime mystery in the Smokies. What is more plausible than that the male protagonist, Reuben "Mink" Lorey, comes to an early, abrupt end? The biblical name Reuben connotes water-like instability, and the abrupt death of this unpredictable "mink" near a stream is thus artistic in terms of theme and plot. So the disappointment in love sustained by Alethea Sayles, who has in effect lost her mate and thereafter remains unmarried, surpasses mere sentimentalism. Just so, another novel, *In the "Stranger People's" Country* (1891), centers on folklore surrounding a weird pygmy graveyard in the Tennessee mountains—enterprisingly employed by criminals to keep their loot hidden in one of the graves—with subtle accompaniments of "hants," presumed witches, visions and signs. Themes of illusions permeate both these novels, making them, along with works mentioned above, forerunners of much in Glasgow, Caroline Gordon, or Anne Tyler's fiction. In two novels set in Mississippi Delta regions (featuring in part Murfree's recollections of her family's holdings in that area), *The Fair Mississippian* (1908) and *The Story of Duciehurst* (1914), Murfree tapped the rough, brutal humor characteristic of Sut Lovingood's world, along with low-life characters who adumbrate many in the fiction of Erskine Caldwell, John Steinbeck, or Flannery O'Connor.

In sum, Murfree's transitional stance from the Old to the New South should be evident. She is the legatee of Poe, George Washington Harris, and Wilson, as well as the contemporary of Joel Chandler Harris, George Washington Cable, and Chopin. In terms of transforming folklore into literature, her subtly modified gothicism, keen sense of place, and artistry in the southern garden vein are important to southern literature. Her work anticipated much that was to come.

Southern Women Poets of the Victorian Age

W. Kenneth Holditch

A fictional representation of the type of poetry most women writers of the Civil War period and after produced appears in William Faulkner's *Absalom, Absalom!* (1936), in which Miss Rosa Coldfield writes odes for Confederate soldiers killed in battle. Faulkner never vouchsafes readers an example of Miss Rosa's verse, but anyone familiar with typical Confederate poetry can easily imagine its quality. Likewise, generic praise for the deceased is humorously portrayed by Mark Twain in poetess-painter Emmeline Grangerford in *Adventures of Huckleberry Finn* (1885), though the novelist was satirizing "the Sweet Singer of Michigan" and not a southerner.

Nevertheless, there were southern female poets after the Civil War worthy of critical attention. Like their male counterparts and the poets of other regions of the country, their subject matter, language, and approach tended to be predictable. They wrote about God, nature, and love in generally romantic terms. Their moral stance was usually that prevalent in the Victorian Age both in the United States and abroad, one circumscribed for the most part by the tenets of orthodox religion. Their attitudes toward the place of women in society were likewise generally characterized by the usual Victorian concepts of the structure of society and woman's place in it. Despite conditions imposed upon them and their work by the age in which they lived, their gender, and public opinion, a number of them managed to produce notable work.

One of the best was Lizette Woodworth Reese (1856–1935) of Baltimore, who published her first poems in 1874. Reese employed traditional forms, her favorite being the sonnet, and Romantic diction and phrasing typical of the age. There is, however, a conciseness in her poetry that is reminiscent of Emily Dickinson, although Reese's work is not characterized by the quirky syntax and the telegraphic style of that author. Reese's command of technical elements of prosody is strong, with few of the strained metrical effects and rhymes apparent in many of her contemporaries. A late poem, "Babylon" (1924), exemplifies well her brevity, intensity, and forceful simplicity:

> You change. I change. Not Babylon
> Not Babylon at all,
> And its rich, quiet loveliness;
> Field, turnpike, wall.

Reese's subject matter is typically Romantic, drawn from her own life and small town environment, with a strong pastoral tone. Her themes and motifs involve love, memory, and God, but her approach is personal, though never confessional, and centers on concrete sensory experiences of her own milieu.

Reese seems to have been influenced by British poets of the seventeenth century as well. Even her most individualized verse demonstrates a control that prevents emotionalism from erupting into sentimentality. Consider her metaphorical definitions of life in the sonnet "Tears" (1877):

> A wisp of fog betwixt us and the sun;
> A call to battle, and the battle done
> Ere the last echo dies within our ears;
> A rose choked in the grass; an hour of fears. . . .

Here the poet escapes fuzzy philosophical comments on the human experience by focusing on concrete, evocative images that reify what she describes, and the originality and freshness in her approach set her apart from many of her contemporaries.

Although Reese lived until the beginning of World War II, most of her poems were written between 1890 and 1910. In her best sonnets are phrasings and statements that foreshadow the work of Edna St. Vincent Millay. She did not respond to new poetic movements but is a transitional figure between the Victorian and modern ages.

Although Margaret Junkin Preston (1820–1897) was born in Pennsylvania, her father was appointed president of Washington College in Virginia before the Civil War, and the family settled there. She became so thoroughly assimilated into southern culture that she is perhaps the most distinctive female poet of the Confederacy. She married a southerner, Major John T. L. Preston, who had been a fellow University of Virginia student with Edgar Allan Poe. Another strong tie she had to the South was the fact that her sister married Confederate General Stonewall Jackson. Even though her father had gone back to Pennsylvania and her brother was in the Union Army, after the war, Margaret Preston was a strong advocate of the Confederacy and joined a legion of southern apologists for the Lost Cause. *Beechenbrook: A Rhyme of the War* (1865), a book-length poem in rhymed couplets, is the story of the family of a Confederate soldier and is dedicated to "every Southern woman who has been widowed by the war."

Preston's work was influenced by her study of the classics, the Bible, and English Romantic and Victorian poets. An admirer of Wordsworth and Coleridge, whose graves she visited on a trip to England, she also developed an affinity for Robert Browning's poetry and wrote several dramatic monologues. Other traditional forms she favored include the sonnet and the ballad. Although much of her work is marred by exaggerated emotions that easily slip into sentimentality and by occasional clumsiness in prosody, Preston's poems, motivated by deep personal feeling, transcend these weaknesses. Her monologues display a keen perception of human nature—physical, emotional, even psychological.

"Through the Pass" (1886), commemorating the death of her friend Commodore Matthew F. Maury, a V.M.I. professor noted for his navigational charts, demonstrates the effectiveness of her use of intense personal emotions. With a felicitous blend of language, imagery, and figures of speech, she pays tribute to his life and work:

> Stars lit new pages for him; seas
> Revealed the depths their waves were screening;
> The ebbs gave up their mysteries,
> The tidal flows confessed their meaning.

She concludes with the traditional pastoral elegy request that Nature empathize with the grief she feels and honor his life:

> Do homage, sky, and air, and grass,
> All things he cherished, sweet and tender,
> As through our gorgeous mountain pass
> We bear him in the May-day splendor!

The contrast in the poem between simple objects of nature and the arcane knowledge of his profession produces an interesting tension.

Another memorial work, distinguished by an ironic title and sentiment that is clearly honest, is "Euthanasia," which commemorates a friend who died suddenly without having endured a major illness. It begins by envisioning one who says good night to the family:

> With faces the dearest in sight,
> With a kiss on the lips I love best,
> To whisper a tender "Good-night"
> And pass to my pillow of rest.

Preston then proceeds to a portrayal of the quick and unexpected death as ideal:

> Without a farewell or a tear,
> A sob or a flutter of breath,
> Unharmed by the phantom of Fear,
> To glide through the darkness of death!—

Finally she asserts, "Just so would I choose to depart. . . ."

Most of Preston's best work was done after the war, as southern literature in general improved following the end of hostilities, and she published a number of volumes, including *Silverwood: A Book of Memories* (1856), *Old Song and New* (1870), *Cartoons* (1875), *Colonial Ballads, Sonnets, and Other Verse* (1887), and *For Love's Sake* (1886).

One poet who carved for herself an interesting niche in the annals of southern literature was Frances Ellen Watkins Harper, a free woman of color reared in Maryland, a slave state, as a member of a middle-class family. Popularly termed "The Bronze Muse," she was best known as the first American black woman to publish a short story and one of the first to publish a novel, but she also wrote poetry, much of it, like her fiction and her orations, devoted to political causes such as abolition and the temperance movement. Even her polemical verse, however, is universalized to include not only the specific object of complaint but also the emotions shared by all human beings. A founder of the National Association of Colored Women, Harper was involved in other organizations devoted to the betterment of women and her race.

Titles of Harper's poems indicate not only her interests but also the influences on her work. Several, including "Ruth and Naomi" (1856) and "Moses: A Story of the Nile" (1869), a lengthy blank verse narrative, were inspired by Bible study. Some, such as "Drunkard's Child" (1854), are typical of the sentimental lyrics of the age. Most, including "The Slave Master" (ca.1884) and "Bury Me in a Free Land" (1858), focus on problems faced by American slaves. Because Harper often gave speeches and readings of her work, much of her poetry is in an oral tradition.

Harper was the best-known black female American poet of the time, the "Phillis Wheatley of her century"; the extent of her reputation is indicated by the fact that William Lloyd Garrison wrote the introduction for her first collection, *Forest Leaves and Poems on Miscellaneous Subjects* (1854). Other volumes she published include *Poems* (1871), *The Sparrow's Fall and Other Poems* (1890), and *The Martyr of Alabama and Other Poems* (1894).

Another poet better known for fiction than for verse was Olive Tilford Dargan (1869–1968), who published several proletariat novels under the pseudonym Fielding Burke. A Kentuckian by birth, she later lived in the Smoky Mountains of North Carolina and Tennessee. A romantic and a southern agrarian, Dargan often seemed to echo Thomas Jefferson as she praised tillers of the land for their closeness to God. She drew her subject matter from the rural South and its people, and her poems are rich in local color details. Dargan wrote not only lyrical poems, often in the sonnet form, but also verse dramas. Her works include *Path Flower* (1904) and a sonnet sequence, *The Cycle's Rim* (1916).

One of the most remarkable careers of any female poet in the South or, indeed, the entire United States was that of Eliza Jane Poitevent Nicholson (1849–1896), a Mississippian, who at an early age moved to New Orleans to work for the *Picayune*. She married its owner in 1872, and after his death became perhaps the first woman in the world to publish and edit a big city daily newspaper. For three decades she wrote poetry and prose under the pseudonym Pearl Rivers, while overseeing the newspaper and becoming active in a wide variety of civic causes, especially those involving animal welfare. Although she was published widely in newspapers and national periodicals, her only collection of poetry was *Lyrics* (1873).

Unschooled in prosody, Nicholson owed her considerable skills at writing verse to her extensive reading, particularly of English and American Romantics. Like them, she attributed her knowledge to nature and saw herself as one who early learned to understand and speak "the tongue of flower and bee." Though she preferred the ballad form and employed conventional metrical patterns, she sometimes experimented with a mixture of feet. Her early poetry exhibits an almost pantheistic devotion to nature, but her later poems are social commentary, such as "Only a Heart" (1873), in which the persona addresses the man who rejected her, sarcastically telling him he need have no fear, for what he has injured is

> Only a heart, a woman's heart,
> Step on it, crush it! so!
> Bravely done like a gentleman,
> Turn on your heel and go.

No human being will come to her aid, she adds, and in a line reminiscent of Emily Dickinson that must have been shocking for the time, she concludes that "God is too far to hear."

Something of the same idea is present in "Hagar" (1893), a late blank verse dramatic monologue, obviously influenced by Robert Browning. Although early male commentators dismissed the poem and a similar one entitled "Leah" (1894), "Hagar" is certainly Nicholson's best work, foreshadowing feminist ideas of decades later. In Hagar's voice, the poem begins at the moment when the patriarch Abraham has come to his concubine's tent after she has been dismissed and told to go into the desert:

> Go back! How dare you follow me beyond
> The door of my poor tent? Are you afraid
> That I have stolen something? See, my hands
> Are empty, like my heart.

Later, Hagar turns her rage on Abraham's wife, accusing her of a materialistic love of "costly linen," "Chaldean spices," "golden fillets" for her brow, "ointment" for her hair, and many cattle "lowing on the hills" and "moving on the plain," while she loves only the man himself. In a passage surprising for a time when organized religion prevailed, Pearl Rivers has her heroine reject the divinity who instructed Abraham to exile Hagar and her son Ishmael:

> And tell your God I hate him, and I hate
> The cruel craven heart that worships him
> And dare not disobey.

With such unorthodox attacks on established institutions that were esteemed in the 1890s, the poem remains one of the most remarkable of any by southern women poets before the 1920s.

A contemporary of Pearl Rivers was Mollie Evelyn Moore Davis (1844–1909), a native of Alabama who grew up on a Texas farm. In 1874 she married Thomas E. Davis, a former Confederate major, and six years later they moved to New Orleans. For two decades Davis presided over a literary salon in her home on Royal Street, where guests included Grace King, Robert Louis Stevenson, Eugene Field, and Frank Stockton. Before she was sixteen, she had published her first volume, *Minding the Gap* (1867), including many tributes to Confederate soldiers. Davis' later work shows a wider range, with lyrics on nature and character sketches, some humorous, some serious. Much of it displays the influence of the English Romantics, for example, "The Passing of the Rose," in which she comments on the mutability of the natural world in contrast to the endurance of the spiritual in terms reminiscent of William Wordsworth's "Ode: Intimations of Immortality" (1807). The opening of "Throwing the Wanga" (1896), a poem about New Orleans voodoo rituals, surely shows the influence of "The Edge of the Swamp" by William Gilmore Simms:

> The trackless swamp is quick with cries
> Of noisome things that dip and rise
> On night-grown wings; and in the deep
> Dark pools the monstrous forms that sleep
> Inert by day uplift their heads.

Some of Davis' verse is in a folk or local color tradition and exhibits, as does much of her work, the strong influence of New Orleans.

Although her form of choice was the rhymed stanza, Davis occasionally employed blank verse, as in one of her best pieces, "The Flagship Goes Down" (1908), in which she contemplates her own impending death. The basic metaphor, hardly unique, is of life as a voyage that is difficult but nevertheless,

> 'Tis worth the stress
> The strain, the grinding nerve, the wearied arm.
> It hath a glory all its own, this sail
> Across Life's tumbling sea.

Despite some archaic poetic language, the work is free of the sentimentality of most poetry of death of that day and bespeaks genuine emotions on the part of the author.

Another New Orleans poet was Mary Ashley Townsend (1836–1901), whose pseudonym was Xariffa. So popular was she that when Oscar Wilde visited New Orleans in the late 1800s, he was taken to meet her. Generally committed to traditional metrical patterns and stanza forms, she did occasionally experiment with variations in both. Her subjects are typical—nature, beauty, love, and patriotism—but there is a freshness in some of her work that sets her apart. Influences on her poetry include the Romantics, as in "What I Saw in My Sleep" (1881), which echoes works of Samuel Coleridge and Edgar Allan Poe. Often she considers the lot of women and, like

Pearl Rivers, comments ironically on what fate has dealt them. In "A Woman's Wish" (1881), the female speaker yearns to be free for an hour from worry and duty to lie amid flowers and listen to the birds. Tired of the "rigid duty" and the work her "tired hands find to do," she wishes for some of "life's free beauty." Assuming an amused response from her listener, she concludes with a simple comment on her narrow life:

> Aye, laugh, if laugh you will, at my crude speech;
>   But women sometimes die of such a greed,
>   Die for the small joys held beyond their reach,
>   And the assurance they have all they need.

Although couched in traditional terms, the genuineness of the persona's cri de coeur cannot be denied.

Several other poets are worthy of mention. Caroline Lawrence Bedinger Dandridge (1858–1914) was born in Denmark, where her father served as the first American ambassador, but grew up in Virginia. Using the pseudonym Danske Dandridge, she wrote nature poems, published in two volumes, *Joy and Other Poems* (1888) and *Rose Brake Poems* (1890). Ruth McEnery Stuart (1856–1917) of New Orleans, a local color fiction author, also wrote poetry, including some in black dialect and some lyrical versions of southern songs. Her books include *Daddy Do-Funny's Wisdom Jingles* (1913) and *Plantation Songs and Other Verse* (1916). Mary Howard Weeden (1847–1905), whose simple poems were concerned mostly with nature or the lives of former slaves, produced four volumes: *Shadows on the Wall* (1898), *Bandana Ballads* (1899), *Songs of the Old South* (1900), and *Old Voices* (1904). Best known for her autobiography, Helen Keller (1880–1968) also published a book of poetry, *The Song of the Stone Wall,* in 1910.

That southern women poets of the postbellum period such as Lizette Woodworth Reese, Margaret Junkin Preston, and Pearl Rivers were not mere regionalists in their intent and in the audience they reached is evidenced by the fact that many of their works were published by such major periodicals as *Harper's.* Though they are, unfortunately, for the most part out of print and unknown to contemporary readers, they not only lived fascinating lives but also produced works of merit and exhibited interest in experimentation that foreshadows the southern poets who followed them.

Louisiana Writers of the Postbellum South

Joan Wylie Hall

In a 1914 essay for the *Bookman,* Ruth McEnery Stuart (1849–1917) describes the sensuous allure her home state has always held for readers and writers: the misty bayous, jasmine-scented verandas, and musical mockingbirds. Despite this great natural beauty, Louisiana had scarcely begun to recover from the Civil War and Reconstruction when Stuart's popular dialect stories first appeared in 1888. The region's postbellum literature was inevitably marked by the South's fall from early prosperity, the new freedom of the African American population, the rise in immigration and rural flight to the cities, the changing status of women, the decline in the French influence, and many other signs of a society in transition. Stuart viewed New Orleans, with its balconied ruins and polyglot neighborhoods, as "a great caravansary, pictorial to a degree and pathetic in human appeal." Several Louisiana women had published fiction and poetry before the war, but Barbara Ewell suggests in *Louisiana Women Writers* (1992) that enthusiasm for George Washington Cable's "exotic stories" about antebellum Creoles gave the state a "particular cachet" during the 1870s and opened the way for writers like Stuart to participate in a regional, and sometimes personal, project of "self-definition."

Many factors help to explain the state's large number of female authors. Like Massachusetts and New York, Louisiana had a major port city that served as a magnet for different social classes and ethnic groups. Increasingly during the postwar period, women joined men in reporting on this range of urban life for newspaper audiences in Boston, New York, and New Orleans. The literacy level of middle-class New Orleanians was high. Orders of Roman Catholic nuns, many of them with Continental schooling, contributed to the many educational opportunities for girls and young women in New Orleans. For writers such as Kate Chopin who grew up in other states and came to Louisiana as adults (often as newlyweds), salons and women's clubs provided crucial sites of interaction with cultural sophisticates. Louisiana natives like Grace King, who presided over one of the most popular New Orleans salons, identified themselves with the strong French tradition of a female intelligentsia—women like Madame de Staël, as well as two subjects of essays by King: the Baronne Blaze de Bury and Madame Blanc. Northern editors who traveled South in search of new talent after the war typically stopped in New Orleans, and their publishing successes with New Englanders like Mary Wilkins Freeman encouraged them to cultivate southern female authorship.

All the major northern magazines printed stories, poems, articles, and pictures of plantations, Mardi Gras festivities, Civil War battles, and the diverse cultures in this most exotic part of the newly reunited United States, side by side with voyagers' reports from Egypt and Norway. Ewell explains that "Northerners and southerners alike found reason to foster the notion of a uniquely traditional culture: its aristocratic values and unshaken loyalties in the wake of military defeat offered a consoling alternative to the harsh realities of late-nineteenth-century America." On the long road to national reunion, Louisiana became a fantastic oasis where an armchair traveler might, according to Stuart, get temporarily lost "in the general unreality of things."

Glimpsed through a romantic haze, the saddest portrayals of "tragic mulattas," lonely orphans, and hungry Italian newcomers could, unfortunately, seem as artificial as fairy tales, and postbellum Louisiana writing has frequently been devalued as local color for its rich descriptions of landscapes, customs, and linguistic peculiarities. While little poetry and few novels, except Kate Chopin's *The Awakening* (1899), either defied the conventions or survived the era, Louisiana women did make lasting contributions in the genre of short fiction. In their best stories (many of them still in print), writers like Stuart, Chopin, Mollie Moore Davis (1852–1909), Grace King, Alice Dunbar-Nelson, and Eloise Bibb Thompson (1878–1928) turned the Gulf's chill waters, the passionate dance of the Bamboula, and other local materials to stunning use, complicating such old stereotypes as the southern belle and the contented slave. In light of recent studies in canon formation, regionalism, and female authorship, less familiar works by these and other Louisiana women also merit rediscovery by today's audiences.

The boldest of the postbellum poets was one of the earliest, the multilingual actress Adah Isaacs Menken (1835–1868), who died in Paris shortly before the publication of *Infelicia* (1868), which she dedicated to Charles Dickens. This collection of thirty-one free-verse poems was influenced by Swinburne, the Pre-Raphaelites, Poe, and Whitman; the author had defended the two American writers in articles for the New York *Sunday Mercury*. She incorporated sexual imagery and a feminist perspective in melodramatic performance pieces like "Judith" (1868), in which a Biblical heroine looks forward to the "wild passionate kisses" she will "draw up from that bleeding mouth" of Holofernes, the enemy she prepares to behead. Menken's Louisiana background is less evident in her subjects and figurative language than it is in her unusually cosmopolitan attitude (with a special interest in France) and her carnivalesque facility at assuming various poetic masks.

More representative of postbellum poetry are the *Lyrics* (1873) of Eliza Jane Poitevent Nicholson (1848–1896) and Mary Ashley Van Voorhis Townsend's Petrarchan sonnet collection, *Distaff and Spindle* (1895). Both volumes recall the emotional antebellum lyrics of Anna Peyre Shackelford Dinnies (1805–1886), who idealized marriage and wrote a book of one hundred tributes to flowers, *The Floral Year* (1847). The publication of Nicholson's first poem in 1868 in *The South*, a Louisiana periodical, was the start of a journalistic career that culminated in her ownership and successful management of the New Orleans *Picayune*. Southern newspapers were an important outlet for creative writing, and Nicholson printed her own poems and columns, along with those of other women from the state. After Nicholson's death, her protégée Elizabeth Meriwether Gilmer (1870–1951) became nationally famous for the pseudonymous advice column "Dorothy Dix Talks." Edward Ayers, in *The Promise of the New South: Life After Reconstruction* (1992), says that Gilmer "counseled Southern women in a voice that rang with a new assertiveness." Ayers cites 1890s pieces in which "Dorothy Dix" declared she would write "for my sex the truth, as I have seen it, about the relationship between men and women," an unequal relationship in which wives were "human doormats" who should recognize their enslavement and "hoist the red flag of revolt."

Quite different from the early songs of nature that Nicholson published as "Pearl Rivers" is her late blank verse "Hagar" (1893). A dramatic monologue, the poem evokes both Menken's portrayal of Old Testament female pride in "Judith" and Gilmer's bracing wisdom for the southern New

Woman. Townsend's range likewise extends beyond the sweet lyrics often associated with her romantic pseudonym, "Xariffa." The flexible blank verse of her narratives, including "The Backwoodsman's Daughter" (1870), was considered remarkable by nineteenth-century reviewers. Nevertheless, "Creed" (1870), her most famous work, relies on commonplaces in depicting the "luscious sweetness" and "immortal dew" of love, that "rich crown jewel." Much in demand for public "occasional" verse that embodied her devotion to the South, Townsend (1832–1901) was known as the "poet laureate of New Orleans." The title is well suited to the author of *Down the Bayou, The Captain's Story, and Other Poems* (1896), which Townsend prefaces with Oliver Wendell Holmes's praise for "The Captain's Story," a long and poignant poem about a Yankee Civil War hero who commits suicide on learning his mother was a slave. Townsend could also write in a satiric mode, either serious or light, depending on her target. But her satires were generally essays, and her pseudonyms for these pieces—"Michael O'Quillo" and "Crab Crossbones"—were humorously masculine.

Formal lyrics about love and nature found a livelier counterpart in the dialect poems Ruth McEnery Stuart published in *Harper's, St. Nicholas,* and other magazines at the turn of the century. Speakers in a few of these popular pieces were Irish, Creole, and Italian, but most were African American. Collected years later in Stuart's *Plantation Songs and Other Verse* (1916), such energetic pieces as "Lucindy" (1892) and "Plantation Hoe Song" (1903) render the standard English and conventional sentiments of the volume's "Other Verse" trite in comparison. Mollie Moore Davis' poetry is similarly divided between the flatness of "Counsel" (1870) and the imaginative gathering of black and white voices, along with varied rhymes and rhythms, in "Throwing the Wanga (St. John's Eve)" (1889), a long poem of love and vengeful conjuring, set in a black swamp near Lake Pontchartrain's dark blue waters.

Following national trends, postbellum Louisianians wrote many sensationalist novels, including Eliza Ann Dupuy's (1814–1880) suspenseful *All for Love; or, The Outlaw's Bride* (1873), and *Wild Work: The Story of the Red River Tragedy* (1881) by the highly paid magazine editor, essayist, and poet Mary Edwards Bryan (1838–1913). Supposedly based on a real North-South love affair, Bryan's melodrama portrays a disowned and consumptive Louisiana heroine whose Yankee lover runs true to form as a greedy carpetbagger; freedmen prove no more trustworthy than the faithless mate. In contrast, Sarah Anne Ellis Dorsey (1829–1879), benefactor of Confederate President Jefferson Davis, provided a happy ending for the well-known plantation novel *Panola, A Tale of Louisiana* (1877). Dorsey's young heroine is part Cherokee, a revelation foreshadowed by the Cherokee roses that cover miles of hedgerows on the lovely estate where she is a servant. Other unusual features besides the Native American element are a paralyzed lover, death by poison, a visiting German naturalist, and a three-million-dollar inheritance. The first chapter of *Panola* begins with a lush three-page catalog of the vicinity's natural life, from perfumed yellow jasmine, white locusts, fig trees, grapevines, and "streamers of venerable gray Spanish moss (Tillandsia)" to bees, several species of butterflies, cardinals, bluebirds, hummingbirds, turtledoves, mockingbirds, and swamp warblers of "every tint and changeful sheen of color."

The rambling plots, floral effusions, and chaste young women of novels like Bryan's, Dupuy's, and Dorsey's seem ingenuous compared with the feminist classic *The Awakening,* where Chopin's treatment of Louisiana settings is as sophisticated as her delineation of Edna Pontellier's growing independence. Anne Rowe observes in an essay included in *Literary New Orleans* (1992) that "Chopin used New Orleans not only to give color and texture to her novel but also to develop characterization and plot." Rowe demonstrates that the city serves "always as a foil to Grand Isle, as a place where ritual, social distinctions, and material success are acknowledged as important." Rejecting all such limitations on her freedom, a naked Edna swims to her death in the cold Gulf, alienating many readers who found great charm in Chopin's short story collections, *Bayou Folk* (1894) and *A Night in Acadie* (1897).

Leonidas Rutledge Whipple, a Chopin contemporary who, in fact, admired the high artistry and "deep knowledge of the woman soul" in *The Awakening,* nevertheless preferred the "wonderful precision and simplicity" of the shorter fiction. Whipple discerned in these stories the strong influence of Maupassant, Flaubert, and Gautier—not surprising at a time when the well-known Louisianian Sidonie de la Houssaye (1820–1894) wrote *Pouponne et Balthazar* (1888), *Les Quarteronnes de la Nouvelle-Orléans* (1894), and other French-language novels that are indebted to European literary traditions. Like her Continental antecedents, Chopin gracefully integrates place, character, and action when the depressed protagonist of "Désirée's Baby" (1893) commits suicide in the "deep, sluggish bayou" of L'Abri plantation; Calixta passionately surrenders to Alcée beneath a thundering torrent of rain in "The Storm" (written in 1898 but not published until 1969); and the former slave La Folle desperately crosses psychological and physical boundaries in "Beyond the Bayou" (1893).

Including the tale of La Folle's great love for P'tit Maître's young son, a surprising thirty or more of Chopin's one hundred stories were written for children, says Bernard Koloski, who in *Kate Chopin: A Study of the Short Fiction* (1996) finds shared themes of maturation, identity, freedom, home, and escape in all of her fiction. The large market for young people's literature attracted other Louisiana women writers at the end of the nineteenth century. The artist Cecilia Viets Jamison (1837–1909), for example, had published novels for adults in the 1870s with Longfellow's encouragement—sentimental books like *Something to Do: A Novel* (1871), whose working-women protagonists discourse on current political, scientific, and social issues. In 1891, however, Jamison turned to the youth audience with *Lady Jane,* a popular account of a plucky orphan's adventures among the rich and the poor of New Orleans' various ethnic and racial communities. The dainty blonde's drawn-out discovery of her true identity resembles the plot of Ruth McEnery Stuart's *The Story of Babette: A Little Creole Girl* (1894), which was "Affectionately Inscribed to the Little Girls of New Orleans by Their Friend the Author." Mardi Gras, gypsies, and a mysterious mute character who looks black but is really white are the kind of regional features for which Stuart was celebrated in a *Harper's Bazaar* cover story on December 16, 1899.

Acclaimed as "the laureate of the lowly," Stuart typically portrayed three aspects of the nineteenth-century South: small-town happenings in rural Arkansas; immigrant communities in New Orleans; and African American life on antebellum and postbellum plantations, as well as in New Orleans and New York. The collections *Sonny: A Christmas Guest* (1896) and *Sonny's Father* (1910) contain humorous stories about her two most popular characters: Deuteronomy Jones, a talkative farmer from Simpkinsville, Arkansas, and his precocious child Sonny, who grows from infancy to fatherhood in the course of the two volumes. The Joneses' neighbors, including several independent women, appear in *In Simpkinsville: Character Tales* (1897) and in other collections. Among the best pieces set in the fictitious town are "The Woman's Exchange of Simpkinsville" (1893), where aging twin sisters gain "new youth-restoring life" from a home-based business venture, and "A Note of Scarlet" (1899), one of Stuart's several stories about mid-life romance. Kate Chopin singled out an immigrant tale, the sentimental "Carlotta's Intended" (1891), for special praise, but she also admired Stuart's depictions of slaves and former slaves, characterizations that have been criticized as racist by Helen Taylor and other recent scholars. Despite the tendency to caricature that was so typical of her era, Stuart does develop strong black women protagonists in "Queen O' Sheba's Triumph" (1899) and "Thanksgiving on Crawfish Bayou" (1909), and her reviewers commented approvingly on the mixture of "humor and pathos" in her many tales about African American life.

Very little humor is evident in Grace King's "A Crippled Hope" (1893), "The Little Convent Girl" (1893), and other stories of faithful black servants and tragic quadroons, which—unlike Stuart's fiction—make minimal use of dialect. King's resentment of African Americans who welcomed emancipation is obvious in "Bayou L'Ombre, An Incident of War" (1887), when two young sisters are so shocked at their slaves' desertion that they feel as if an earthquake is destroying their secure world. Loyal to the Lost Cause, King romanticizes the Confederacy in the autobiographical *Memories of a Southern Woman of Letters* (1932), where she claims that George Washington Cable's partiality for "colored people over white" and "the quadroons over the Creoles" inspired her to write in rebuttal. A Francophile at ease in Paris salons, she identified with Louisiana's French aristocracy and clearly regretted the Creoles' fall from prominence in her story collections *Tales of a Time and Place* (1892) and *Balcony Stories* (1893).

Like King, Mollie Moore Davis wrote historical novels about the earliest French settlers, but she too excelled in shorter forms, creating an exotic blend of African American and Creole materials in her poetry and stories. Although Texas was a frequent subject for Davis—notably in *Under the Man-Fig* (1895) and *The Wire Cutters* (1899)—"A Bamboula" and "The Love-Stranche," both from *An Elephant's Track and Other Stories* (1896), epitomize Louisiana's hold on the postbellum imagination. The two interracial love tragedies have quintessential southern settings: Pine Needles, a rambling plantation house whose "waveless tarn" recalls Poe's dark pool in "The Fall of the House of Usher" (1839); and a New Orleans of orange blossoms, voodoo spells, and shuttered mansions in the French Quarter. "The Soul of Rose Dédé," in the same volume, is a Gulf Coast ghost story whose Creole dead walk in a country cemetery on Midsummer Eve and reveal their secrets. The story is a supernatural tale in a tradition revitalized by many late nineteenth-century northern and southern women writers. The New Orleans journalist Sallie Rhett Roman (1844–1921) was one of the weaker practitioners of the genre in "The Madman's Home" (1893) and several other stories published by the *Times Democrat.*

Excluded from such canon-forming works as Mildred Lewis Rutherford's *The South in History and Literature* (1906) and Alderman and Harris' multivolume *Library of Southern Literature* (1907), the African American authors Alice Dunbar-Nelson and Eloise Bibb Thompson have much in common with their white contemporaries, from the Creoles, convents, and Mardi Gras scenes in Dunbar-Nelson's *Violets and Other Tales*

(1895) and *The Goodness of St. Rocque and Other Stories* (1899) to Thompson's sentimental *Poems* (1895) and tragic stories of mixed-blood romance. Both women belonged to the Phillis Wheatley Club of New Orleans, whose president, Sylvanie F. Williams, predicted in her preface to *Violets* that its twenty-year-old author would blossom into literary maturity. One of Dunbar-Nelson's longest and most effective stories, "The Stones of the Village" (1910), describes the wrenching psychological cost when an ambitious lawyer spends his adult life passing for white. Thompson's theme is similar in "Mademoiselle 'Tasie" (1925) and "Masks" (1927). Published during the Harlem Renaissance, both tales of color prejudice within the African American community are set in nineteenth-century New Orleans. Proud of her "reddish yellow complexion" and "very crinkled red hair," the impoverished Creole 'Tasie feels superior to those "English-speaking Negroes known as Americans" and is mortified by the family gossip when, desperate for financial security and yearning for love, she accepts a marriage proposal from the black-skinned Titus Johnson. More tragic is the brunette quadroon Julie Blanchard of "Masks," who marries "the whitest octoroon that she had ever seen" so that her children can pass as white. The story ends with Julie's horrified screams on the birth of her "chocolate-colored" baby.

As Violet Harrington Bryan observes in *The Myth of New Orleans in Literature* (1993), "New Orleans's minute attention to racial differences within a group of blacks . . . was unique." Dunbar-Nelson and Thompson are rare among Louisiana women writers for exposing the plight of Creoles of color from an African American perspective. But a large portion of the state's literature in the decades after the Civil War, from sensational novels and dialect poetry to humorous stories set in antebellum slave quarters, is concerned with race, mirroring society's uneasy adjustments to Reconstruction and the backlash of Jim Crow laws. Other works, as diverse as Menken's "Judith," Gilmer's advice columns, and Chopin's *The Awakening*, suggest that the South's white women, too, were pursuing new freedoms. As Anne Goodwyn Jones points out in *Tomorrow Is Another Day* (1981), "Only in 1979 did Louisiana rewrite the classification of husband as 'head and master' of the household."

Twentieth-century Louisiana writers continue to explore issues of race and gender, often in new genres, from the film scripts of Joyce Corrington (b. 1936) to Julie Hebert's (b. 1954) plays and Emily Toth's (b. 1944) scholarly work on Kate Chopin. Extending the line of celebrated novelists and short story writers are such award winners as Shirley Ann Grau and Ellen Gilchrist. The African American presence has been greatly strengthened by the dramatist Elizabeth Brown Guillory (b. 1954), the critic and biographer Thadious Davis (b. 1944), and poets Pinkie Gordon Lane (b. 1923) and Brenda Marie Osbey (b. 1957)—literary heirs of Dunbar-Nelson and Thompson. One of the biggest contributions of postbellum writers was their artful weaving of setting and psyche. Carnival disguises, secluded courtyards, and treacherous swamp waters provided the perfect metaphors for the secret inner lives of fictional Louisianians in the second half of the nineteenth century. The vampire thrillers of Anne Rice (b. 1941) and the French Quarter detective works of Julie Smith (b. 1944) now draw on this same fund of images, creating exotic scenes and psychological intrigue for large national audiences, much as the state's female authors did over a century ago.

Kate Chopin

Barbara C. Ewell

That Kate Chopin (1850–1904) may be one of the best known, and certainly the most widely read, of nineteenth-century southern women writers masks several ironies. In the first place, Chopin was born and raised and pursued her writing career in midwestern St. Louis; secondly, the places with which she eventually became identified—New Orleans and Acadian Louisiana—are too French, Caribbean, and Catholic to be truly typical of the South; and finally, though Chopin enjoyed modest acclaim as a southern local colorist during her lifetime and after her death, when her work—particularly her novel *The Awakening* (1899)—was rediscovered in the 1970s, it was not for its southernness. Rather, it was as a woman writer that Chopin entered the American literary canon, to take a prominent place as a realist, feminist, and precursor of twentieth-century modernism. Despite such quibbles about her southern status, Kate Chopin's remarkable fiction draws together many of the critical issues facing the post-Reconstruction South, including the intersecting redefinitions of race, gender, and regional identity, as well as the fictional shapes required to embody those new perceptions.

Chopin was the only surviving daughter of a prosperous Irish immigrant, Thomas O'Flaherty, and his much younger second wife, Eliza Faris, who came from a prominent French-Creole family of St. Louis. O'Flaherty died in the Gasconnade Bridge train wreck when Katie was only five, and she grew up in a family dominated by women, including her great-grandmother Victoire Verdon Charleville, who charmed her with stories of old St. Louis and encouraged her study of French and music. At the Academy of the Sacred Heart, Katie O'Flaherty received an exceptionally good education for a girl; then at nineteen she married Oscar Chopin, the son of a French émigré who had settled in central Louisiana. After a three-month wedding journey in Europe, the young couple set up residence in New Orleans, where Oscar pursued a career as a cotton factor and Kate proceeded to bear their six children—five sons and a daughter between 1871 and 1879.

Though often constrained by her pregnancies, Kate Chopin clearly enjoyed the exciting atmosphere of the South's largest city, despite the fact that her time there also coincided with some of its most depressing economic and political history. Oscar himself became involved in the White League, which defeated the Republican city government in the Battle (more properly riots) of Liberty Place in 1874. Many of the writers who were to make Louisiana famous in the 1890s, including George Washington Cable, Grace King, Ruth Stuart (1842–1917), Lafcadio Hearn, and Mollie Moore Davis (1852–1909), also lived in the city during this time. Like them, Chopin was observing the same rich environment, even keeping track of her impressions in a now lost notebook.

The crop failures of 1878 and 1879 caused the Chopins to move to Cloutierville, a village along the Cane River, about twenty miles south of Natchitoches in central Louisiana. Kate Chopin was clearly fascinated by the local people, with their Acadian ways and lilting speech. Her residence there today houses the Bayou Folk Museum, the only one of her three remaining homes that can be visited. In 1883, Oscar died of malaria. Chopin stayed on to settle her husband's estate and evidently developed a brief relationship with Albert Sampite, a local planter. But encouraged by her mother, she returned to St. Louis in 1884. Within a year of her arrival, Eliza O'Flaherty died.

Ten years later in her diary, Kate Chopin was to write of this period as the "years of my growth—my real growth." Faced with raising six children—the oldest barely fourteen—on a modest income and bereft of other immediate family, Chopin was encouraged to take up writing by her friend and former obstetrician, Frederick Kolbenheyer. Another important influence on her career was Guy de Maupassant. Chopin, who translated several of his works, wrote that in his tales she found "life, not fiction," the impressions of one "who, in a direct and simple way, told us what he saw." That insight, together with the models of his shapely prose and plotting, became the guiding vision of her own work, albeit deeply informed by her own experiences in the South and as a woman.

Chopin's first publication (January 1889) was actually poetry, which she wrote sporadically throughout her career. Her earliest short stories, such as "Wiser than a God" (1889) and "A Point at Issue!" (1889), reflect her abiding interest in the tensions inherent in female life, including the conflict between love and work, an issue increasingly important among women at the end of the century. Chopin was clearly experimenting in these first years, trying a variety of approaches and settings. And despite some later dismissive statements about writing—appropriate to women still protecting their femininity even as they sought professional status—she was also quite serious about her career, keeping detailed accounts of her manuscripts and their publication fates. Noting that her southern stories seemed to sell most quickly, by 1891 she was only writing Louisiana stories.

Though her contemporary reputation was based on short fiction, she wrote two other novels besides *The Awakening*. Chopin published *At Fault* at her own expense in 1890. Building on many of the conventions of domestic fiction as well as the Reconstruction motif of North-South romance, the novel explores the dilemmas of a young southern widow, Thérèse Lafirme, whose forests are being harvested by an attractive St. Louis businessman named Hosmer. Inconveniently for the widow's Catholic principles, however, he is also divorced. Thérèse's attempts to reunite Hosmer with the alcoholic Fanny at the expense of everyone's deepest feelings pose the expected conflicts between love and duty, passion and reason. They also expose Chopin's intellectual interests in the psychology of human choice and the tensions between conventions and natural instinct. Chopin's broad reading in Darwinism and other contemporary philosophies consistently undergirds her fiction, contributing to its distinctly modern cast. Several subplots and lively minor characters (including the "New Woman" Melicent and several figures that reappear in her short stories, such as the Santien brothers) demonstrate Chopin's ability to manage a complex narrative; and though she resorts to melodrama to resolve the novel's thorniest problems, *At Fault* was still the first American novel to treat divorce as a morally neutral solution to dysfunctional marriages. Highly readable as an exemplar of the local color novel, it is a suggestive precursor of the moral tensions of *The Awakening*. Chopin's second novel, entitled "Young Dr. Gosse and Théo," was begun barely two weeks after she finished *At Fault*, but after repeated failures to find a publisher, she destroyed the manuscript in 1895.

It was in fact with the short story rather than the novel that Chopin first made her mark. As it was for many other regional writers, the best market for her stories was children's magazines, like *Youth's Companion* or *Harper's Young People*. Featuring mild humor and uplifting plots, the distinctiveness of stories like "A Very Fine Fiddle" (*Harper's Young People*, 1891) or "Beyond the Bayou" (*Youth's Companion*, 1893) lay in the quirkiness of Chopin's characters (with their unusual Acadian names, like Lolotte, Boulôt, Nonomme, Fifine, or Azenore); their lilting, French-inflected speech; and their unfamiliar local customs. Chopin effectively capitalized on all these elements of southern local color. Gradually, she also had success placing stories with more adult characters and themes in the prestigious *Century* and in the new *Vogue*, which published both "A Visit to Avoyelles" and "Désirée's Baby" in its January 1893 issue.

Together with King's *Balcony Stories* (1893) and Cable's *Old Creole Days* (1879), Chopin's *Bayou Folk* (1894) is one of the defining collections of Louisiana local color. Its twenty-three tales are technically sophisticated in a range of fictional types, from slight sketches, like "Boulôt and Boulotte," that reflect Chopin's ability to capture character and place with astonishing economy, to complex, multilayered tales, like "At the 'Cadian Ball" (first published in 1892), "In Sabine," "Ma'ame Pélagie," or "La Belle Zoraïde," which skillfully use frames and imagery to convey their subtly shifting perspectives. The collection also demonstrates Chopin's singular use of the familiar themes and types of southern local color. Like her contemporaries King and Stuart, Chopin exploited many southern tropes (loyal and subservient black people, noble white planters, antebellum nostalgia, North-South antagonism), but she also suggests their limits and ambivalence. In her most famous tale, for example, "Désirée's Baby" (published in 1892 and her only story that remained in print throughout the twentieth century), Chopin's treatment of "the tragic mulatta" is subtly reshaped by the superbly crafted surprise ending and its deeply ironic imagery.

The modest critical success of *Bayou Folk* evidently encouraged Chopin to venture away from southern local color toward more direct examinations of women's roles and the costs of self-assertion. While many of her new stories, such as "The Story of an Hour" (1894) or "Fedora" (1897), had less obviously southern settings, their narrative ambivalence and psychological complexity were more pronounced. Chopin's continuing experimentation with narrative form together with her probing of sublimated and misdirected passion gave her work increasing subtlety. And thus while her second collection, *A Night in Acadie* (1897), includes some of her most sophisticated southern stories, it also reflects Chopin's angular relation to the idiom of southern regionalism. Locale and custom are here more incidental to the psychological dilemmas and social conflicts of characters in such fine stories

as "Athénaïse," "Regret," "A Pair of Silk Stockings," or even "Nég Créol."
As Chopin herself insisted in an 1894 essay, local color was not an end in
itself, but only a vehicle for conveying unchanging "[h]uman impulses."
Though she resisted the overt ideological compulsions of much southern
local color, Chopin nonetheless engaged many of its central concerns, including gender and (in a more limited way) race, treating them more as matters of identity than of politics. That engagement, together with a limited
use of dialect, helps to account for the continuing relevance and readability
of her fiction.

Though Chopin never found a publisher for her third collection of stories, "A Vocation and a Voice," its contents reflect these broader concerns.
Only three of its twenty-one stories are set in the South, and many are
among her most psychologically intricate and experimental tales. There are
richly allusive sketches, such as "Two Portraits: The Wanton and the Nun"
(1932) or "An Egyptian Cigarette" (1900), as well as troubling studies of
suppressed passion, such as "Lilacs" (1896) or the haunting "Her Letters"
(1895), the provocative title story, or the curiously framed "Elizabeth
Stock's One Story" (1963). The mediating function of sexuality and nature
in the discovery of identity, the compulsions of the unconscious, and a critique of moral hypocrisy become foregrounded with the absence of southern
settings, invoking a decidedly modernist temper. One of the most striking
examples of this later work is an epilogue to the more conventionally southern tale, "At the 'Cadian Ball" (1892). Unpublished in her lifetime and not
included in "A Vocation and a Voice," "The Storm" (1969) features an exceptionally frank and positive presentation of female desire. Like *The
Awakening*, it reflects Chopin's ability to allow her southern material to
support a critical examination of larger issues while withholding narrative
judgment.

Because for many readers *The Awakening* remains the substance of
Chopin's achievement, most critical attention since the publication of her
Complete Works by Per Seyersted in 1969 has been directed exclusively at
that singular text. Even so, her nearly one hundred short stories indicate the
depth of narrative talent on which that famous novel rests. Many of the
issues that emerge with such startling intensity in *The Awakening* are anticipated in her short fiction: the conflicts of private female sensuality with the
social roles of motherhood or wifehood, the tensions between conventional
morality and personal instinct, the inadequacy of models for female selfhood, the subtle explorations of emotional ambivalence. Chopin's impres-
sionist technique, honed on the deployment of setting in her local color

tales, her economical prose, and her sure sense of plotting and dialogue are also as evident in her short fiction as in her novel.

The Awakening is nonetheless a remarkable piece of fiction. Set in New Orleans and the then fashionable summer resort of Grande Isle, the novel draws on a variety of southern tropes, including ideal womanhood, recollections of the war, and the implicit tensions between "American" business and "southern" (here "Creole") culture. But the real focus of the novel is the dilemma of its heroine, the young Edna Pontellier, whose grapplings with the forces of an awakening sexuality and stifling conventional roles lead ultimately to her fatal swim out into the Gulf. Contemporary reviewers were shocked by Chopin's deliberate failure to rebuke Edna: indeed, one of the most impressive achievements of the novel is the impenetrable ambivalence of its final chapter, its rich imagery suggesting the full range of Edna's conflict. Chopin was somewhat taken aback by the negative reaction to *The Awakening,* although an ironic retraction published a month later suggests that she, like Edna, was basically unrepentant.

Despite the disappointing reviews, Chopin continued to compose and publish short stories at her usual rate of about one a month. Unfortunately, her health soon began to fail, and, for reasons still unknown, her publisher returned "A Vocation and a Voice." The stories of Chopin's final years are generally not up to her best work, although she frequently returned to southern settings and in tales like "Charlie" (written in 1900 and first published in 1969) still posed intriguing dilemmas of female identity.

Chopin died of a brain hemorrhage on August 22, 1904, after a strenuous day at the Louisiana Purchase Exposition. For much of the next sixty years, her most important novel was forgotten, and she merited only brief mention as a southern local colorist. The publication of her *Complete Works* in 1969, however, converged with the second wave of the women's movement, and *The Awakening* soon became not only a standard of women's studies classes, but an object lesson in the effects of bias in canon formation. The recovery of Chopin's fiction provided a model and a motive for a general reexamination of scores of lost women writers, including many southerners. A relative anomaly as a narrative of the late nineteenth-century South, Chopin's novel has nonetheless changed the landscape of American fiction.

Grace King

Clara Juncker

"New Orleans has been called the most feminine of cities," notes Grace King in her introduction to S. Chatwood Burton's *Pen Sketches of New Orleans* (n.d.). She continues, "This difference from other cities is one of her charms. Her people, in imagination, love to picture her in the handsome old age of a grande dame of the old regime; sitting in her high back antique chair, dressed in flowing black satin, garnished at neck and wrist with real lace." King's description suggests not only New Orleans but also her own personality and literary production. As the Grande Dame of Louisiana letters, she wrote with plenty of feminine frills about her exotic birthplace and its Creole population, both in historical works and in fiction.

Born in 1852 into a New Orleans family that scrambled to uphold its antebellum gentility during Reconstruction, King established herself as a writer in 1885, when the Cotton Centennial Exposition brought distinguished outsiders to her city. Despite King's own misgivings, Julia Ward Howe inspired within King a notion of an active, or activist, woman's life outside the domestic sphere. Richard Watson Gilder challenged King to correct the depiction of New Orleans by George Washington Cable, whom she found overly catering to northern tastes. Charles Dudley Warner helped her publish "Monsieur Motte" (1886), her first short story, in the *New Princeton Review*. Upon receiving her check for it, King reacted to economic independence with the mixture of femininity and feminism characteristic of her work: "I went out to get some white toweling to make Branch and Will some toilet mats of; and as I walked on the street I felt very proud I can tell you, the first really well satisfied moment of my life."

Literary critics have traditionally seen King as a minor local colorist, whose stories of New Orleans Creoles sought to defend her native city from Cable's criticism of its racial arrangements. In "A New Orleans Lady of Letters" (1936), John S. Kendall describes her as intellectual, but hastens to add that she was "an exemplary daughter, a devoted sister," and, to be sure, "a very competent dressmaker." Henry P. Dart notes, in "Miss King's Historical Works" (1923), her talents as a secretary. In *A History of American Literature Since 1870* (1968), Fred Lewis Pattee finds King "at her best while depicting these whimsical, impracticable, tropic femininities," although, he concludes, "she makes them not so bewitching as does Cable." Most telling is perhaps the long silence that surrounded her writings after her death in 1932.

With *Grace King of New Orleans: A Selection of Her Writings* (1973) and *Grace King: A Southern Destiny* (1983), Robert Bush helped King find a new audience. Unlike Cable, Bush argues, King learned from French realists to use contemporary subject matter and irony. As the titles of some of his articles on King would suggest, for example, "Grace King and Mark Twain" (1972) and "Charles Gayarré and Grace King" (1974), Bush focuses on King's relationship to the male intellectual establishment. Though Bush discusses the importance of women's issues in King's life and work, critics such as Helen Taylor and Anne Goodwyn Jones have placed gender issues at the center of their scholarship on King. In "The Case of Grace King" (1982), Taylor makes a case for "the liberalizing and liberating effect which the lives, works, and friendships of other women writers were to have on [King's] own." Jones identifies a distinct, if undeveloped, feminist thrust in King's central texts.

In the 1890s, King broke into the masculine field of history with *Jean Baptiste Le Moyne, Sieur de Bienville* (1892), about the founder and the founding of New Orleans; *A History of Louisiana* (1894); *New Orleans: The Place and the People* (1895), a municipal history that King came to consider her most accomplished work; and *De Soto and His Men in the Land of Florida* (1898), which established King as a regional historian in the tradition of Charles Gayarré. In *Creole Families of New Orleans* (1921), she preserved through genealogical records the contributions of prominent citizens to New Orleans history.

While King's histories of Louisiana examine male figures, her fiction focuses on the marginal, often shattered existence of women in the South.

Monsieur Motte (1888), an extended version of the short story, for instance, portrays the affectionate relationship between a little Creole girl, Marie Modeste, and her ex-slave, Marcelite, who eventually helps restore the family plantation to its orphan owner. The novel reveals King's conservative stance on region, race, and class, but points in terms of gender to *Tales of a Time and Place* (1892) and *Balcony Stories* (1893), possibly King's most accomplished works of fiction. In these volumes of Louisiana stories, as in her first novel, King claims an intimate knowledge of womankind. In *Balcony Stories,* King authoritatively describes one female protagonist's week-long sickness but surrenders expertise as to the condition of her beloved: "A man could better describe his side of that week." Nonetheless, King judges women to be the superior interpreters, in part because "God keeps so little of the truth from us women."

The well-tuned interpretative skills of King's female characters originate in the social and spatial restrictions imposed on southern women. Her male characters are free to roam the city of New Orleans, the American continent, and most of the world, but her female protagonists are symbolically immured in suffocating prisons of gender. The three sisters of "Bayou L'Ombre" (1887), secluded on a remote plantation much in the style of the King sisters' sojourn on L'Embarrasse during four Civil War years, are "passively quiet," their appearances advertising "an unwholesome lack of vitality, an insidious anamorphosis from an unexplained dearth or constraint."

King's criticism of cloistered female lives surfaces most significantly in her descriptions of convent life. As the breeding ground for traditional feminine virtues, the convent prepares young girls for lives of inaction, for living death. "It enrages me every time I think of it," exclaims Claire of "Bonne Maman" (1886) in recalling years spent among the Ursuline sisters. "It was killing!" Since the convent prepared young women for wifehood and motherhood, King's resistance to the narrowness of female lives included reservations about the institution of marriage. In "A Drama of Three" (1892), the aging Madame Honorine endures the poverty and the tirades of married life with the General and silently concludes that in matrimony, "one can give everything, and yet be sure of nothing." To King, marriage typically "interfered" with "the soul-culture of women," as she writes in "The Chevalier Alain de Triton" (1891), a historical romance published in the *Chautauquan.*

King repeatedly casts female life in bodily images, as in *Earthlings,* a serialized novel appearing in *Lippincott's* in 1888: "Experience lies between womb and tomb, and each woman has to bear her own experience, as she bears her own children, through individual joy and suffering." The Demoiselles San Antonio of *The Pleasant Ways of St. Médard* (1916), a semiautobiographical novel about a New Orleans family's adjustment to social decline in the aftermath of the Civil War, are reduced to artifacts by their enterprising companion, who rearranges their hair, their postures, their very bodies, for maximum effect, and maximum profit, in the gender economy they inhabit.

The metaphor of voyage in King's writing, however, indicates a search for new female horizons. Suggesting a passage from one level of understanding to another, the voyages of King's female characters may end in disaster, or they may prove worth the risk, as in *La Dame de Sainte Hermine* (1924), a novel about a young, aristocratic Frenchwoman exiled to the New World who eventually becomes one of the original settlers in Bienville's Nouvelle Orléans.

King's own story ended less conspicuously. The deaths of her mother and two brothers shortly after the turn of the century dried up her creative ambition, which she lavished instead on graveyard visits, a memorial journal, and foreign travel. Her feminist aspirations also eventually came to an end. Recording in a notebook her last conversation with a literary mentor, King wrote as early as 1901, "I told him, that I was happier, since I had got rid of all my hopes—and had my future behind me—that I strive no more." Her posthumous autobiography, *Memories of a Southern Woman of Letters* (1932), hides her life as a woman and a feminist behind a veil becoming a southern lady.

In April 1923, the Louisiana Historical Society and hundreds of representative New Orleans residents gathered at the Cabildo "to render tribute to Grace King and to express in substantial shape the universal approbation of her long career devoted to the history and literature of Louisiana," as the report on the event in the *Louisiana Historical Quarterly* (July 1923) reads. The program included the presentation of the society's loving cup and flowers to the Grande Dame of Louisiana letters. "Her career," writes Robert Bush in "Grace King: The Emergence of a Southern Intellectual Woman" (1977), "was an announcement that women of the South could successfully compete with men in the intellectual world." Even King's obscurity became her strength. "I have often thought how stupid and commonplace it was to write novels about what happens to people; what does not happen to them is far more interesting and exciting," she writes in "Destiny" (1898), about women much like herself.

Anna Julia Cooper

Roberta S. Maguire

The republication of *A Voice from the South* in 1988 as part of the Schomburg Library series on nineteenth-century black women writers helped assure that Anna Julia Cooper would thereafter figure prominently in discussions about the dawning of African American feminist theory. Appearing shortly after Hazel Carby's *Reconstructing Womanhood: The Emergence of the Afro-American Woman Novelist* (1987), which offered a significant discussion of Cooper's collection of essays not then widely available, the reprinting included a formidable introduction by Mary Helen Washington. In that introduction Washington gave this crucial assessment of Cooper's volume: "It is the most precise, forceful, well-argued statement of black feminist thought to come out of the nineteenth century." In the decade to follow, numerous studies likewise evaluated Cooper's book and the significance of its "little Voice," as Cooper termed her narrative positioning, using rhetoric that revealed her characteristic mix of irony and clarity, modesty and assuredness. These late twentieth-century evaluations most often either have built on Washington's view of the text as an exceptional black feminist statement or have challenged another key point Washington makes: that by using the rhetoric commonly associated with the nineteenth century's "Cult of True Womanhood," Cooper fails to speak clearly on behalf of the majority of African American women in the 1890s, who are "sharecroppers, struggling farmers, or domestic servants, few of whom could aspire to anything beyond an elementary education."

Since Cooper's work has at once been recognized as making a crucial contribution to black feminist thought while sparking significant debate among her admirers today, it seems that Cooper's place in the history of black feminist theory is indeed assured. But perhaps it is time to consider her contributions to another developing tradition that carries from the nineteenth into the twentieth century—that of the black southern woman writer. It is a tradition in which Cooper places herself throughout *A Voice,* but she does so not without indicating some ambivalence about identifying herself by region. And her ambivalence, not surprisingly, is born of both communal and individual history.

Cooper began life in Raleigh, North Carolina, in 1858, as Annie Julia Haywood, the child of a forced union between a slave woman named Hannah Stanley Haywood and her white master, George Washington Haywood. Her birth itself therefore represented the complex—and very often brutal—conjoining of the races that has marked a good deal of southern history, which Cooper's own written description in an undated autobiographical fragment reinforces: "My mother was a slave and the finest woman I have ever known. . . . Presumably my father was her master; if so I owe him not a sou and she was always too modest and shamefaced ever to mention him."

In 1868, three years after the Civil War ended, Cooper began attending the newly opened St. Augustine's Normal and Collegiate Institute, a school established in Raleigh by the Episcopal Church for recently freed slaves, with the express purpose, as Cooper writes in *A Voice,* "to prepare teachers for colored youth, furnish candidates for the ministry, and offer collegiate training for those who should be ready for it." There Cooper excelled in her studies. But, on becoming aware that the school provided a boy, "however meager his equipment and shallow his pretensions," with financial and other support, while actively discouraging a girl from pursuing higher education by withholding such support, she also started formulating one of the key tenets of her feminist philosophy: that black women's educational ambitions must not be stifled, for to do so shortchanges not only black women but also the black race as a whole. Describing her experience at St. Augustine's in *A Voice,* Cooper declares, "We might as well expect to grow leaves from trees as hope to build up a civilization or a manhood without taking into consideration our women and the home life made by them, which must be the root and ground of the whole matter."

While anxious to open up opportunities for women even while at St. Augustine's, Cooper also realized there how entrenched the constraints were. As she recounts in *A Voice,* she told the school's principal that "the only mission opening before a girl in his school was to marry one of [the school's] candidates" for the ministry. In 1877, she did marry one of those candidates, which, as Washington points out, served ultimately and ironically to free her to pursue her own mission—expanding the educational opportunities for black women—because just two years into the marriage, her husband, George Cooper, died. Widowed, and therefore no longer subject to the social restriction that women after marriage cease engaging in such professional work outside the home as teaching, Cooper continued with her training, graduating in 1881 from St. Augustine's. Following graduation, she enrolled in Oberlin College, after convincing the administration to support her studies financially. Three years later, having taken the "Gentlemen's Course" as opposed to the "Ladies' Course" at Oberlin, Cooper was graduated with a bachelor's degree in mathematics. In the next several years, she taught at Wilberforce College in Ohio and at St. Augustine's, in addition to earning a master's degree from Oberlin. In 1887, Cooper was recruited to teach in Washington, D.C., by the District's Superintendent for Colored Schools. So began her lengthy association with the M Street High School (later Dunbar High School), an association that continued over forty years. During that time she served as the school's principal; as a teacher of mathematics, science, and Latin; and as a mentor for many individual students who would themselves go on to prestigious colleges. It was an association of controversy, which came to a head in 1905 when the District's Board of Education charged that she had failed to use a required textbook, maintain discipline in the school, discourage unqualified students, and foster loyalty and unity. The following year she was dismissed, a victim, apparent even at the time, of both sexual and racial politics. But she was asked to return to the school in 1910 by a new superintendent, and return she did, to teach Latin. During her renewed association with the school, she went on to pursue her doctorate, initially at Columbia University and later at the University of Paris when she could not fulfill Columbia's one-year residency requirement. In 1925, at the Sorbonne, she successfully defended her dissertation on France and slavery.

Anna Julia Cooper was a woman of prodigious energy, drive, and intelligence, one who practiced what she preached. She believed that women, especially black women, the group most silenced and oppressed in late nineteenth-century America, must fulfill their potential, so she set about, with a remarkable lack of institutional support, to fulfill her own. Her writings are a testament to her determination and talents, and they include numerous essays written after *A Voice* was published in 1892, as well as a memoir of her friendship with the Grimké family and a translation of the French medieval text *Le Pèlerinage de Charlemagne* that Cooper completed while working on her doctorate. Consistent with her view that black women must fulfill their potential because of their unique position as the primary shapers of the black community, she embraced the role not only of teacher, but also of mother. In 1915, at the age of fifty-seven, single (because she never remarried), and one year into her doctoral studies, she adopted five children—the grandchildren of her half brother in Raleigh, who ranged in age from six months to twelve years. She raised them in Washington, where she died in 1964 at the age of 105.

What the foregoing outline of Cooper's biography indicates, in addition to her commitment to advancing the cause of black women, is the degree to which she was necessarily shaped by the region of her birth. Cooper spent nearly the entirety of her life in the South, the first 23 years in North Carolina and over 70 of the next 82 years in Washington, one of the region's northern outposts. Just as her own history was fundamentally shaped by living most of her life in the South, she saw the aggregate of African America's history likewise. In the first essay of *A Voice*, "Womanhood a Vital Element in the Regeneration and Progress of a Race," which was initially a speech Cooper delivered to black clergymen, she argues for recognizing the black southern homemaker as the truest representative of blacks in America: "We must point to homes, average homes, homes of the rank and file of horny handed toiling men and women of the South (where the masses are) lighted and cheered by the good, the beautiful, and the true." And in the essay "What Are We Worth?" Cooper contrasts the Puritan North with the cavalier South as a prelude to her bemoaning the unfortunate influence the white South has had on the black race: "I have wished . . . that as my race had to serve a term of bondage it might have been under the discipline of the successors of Cromwell and Milton, rather than under the training and example of the luxurious cavaliers."

Cooper's reluctance to embrace the heritage of the (white) South, while she insisted on her own southernness, is everywhere evident in *A Voice from the South,* beginning with the title page. Just below the book's title is a reference to its author: "by a Black Woman of the South." Such a rhetorical move at once yokes gender, race, and region and introduces distance between region and what Cooper establishes as complementary terms—gender and race—in a way that "by a Black Southern Woman," for example, would not. Cooper maintains this insider/outsider identity with respect to region throughout the text, even in "Woman vs. the Indian," an essay responding to Anna Shaw's 1891 speech to the National Woman's Council that also contains Cooper's harshest critique of the South. In this essay, she laments the compromise that northern feminists have made with white southern women in order to gain their support for a feminist agenda, a compromise that requires adopting the white southerner's devotion to caste and color. She establishes that she can speak with authority on the topic of southern women and their shortcomings because she is an insider: "Now the Southern woman (I may be pardoned, being one myself) was never renowned for her reasoning powers." Yet she also makes clear that she is simultaneously an outsider to southern womanhood by explaining that she "has tried to understand the Southern woman's difficulties; to put herself in her place," clearly a place that Cooper, the self-described "Black Woman of the South," does not occupy.

Cooper's text, then, helps to initiate an important tradition in the work of black southern women writers, one of reclaiming and then redefining the South, of wresting the region that shaped them from those who would define it and its culture to exclude them. It is a tradition that can be traced forward through such twentieth-century writers as Zora Neale Hurston of Florida; Alice Walker of Georgia; and Alice Childress (1920–1994) of South Carolina. Perhaps Childress' 1966 play *Wedding Band,* set in South Carolina, best suggests a culmination of the process Cooper began. In a heated confrontation with her white lover, Julia Augustine says what Anna Julia Cooper, by way of her careful positioning throughout *A Voice from the South,* intimates: "[G]round I'm standin' on—it's mine."

Alice Dunbar-Nelson

Anne Razey Gowdy

When Alice Dunbar-Nelson's fourteen short stories set in or near her native New Orleans appeared in 1899 as *The Goodness of St. Rocque and Other Stories,* they constituted the first collection of short stories by an African American woman to be published by a major national press. At the time, Dunbar-Nelson also enjoyed the celebrity of being married to the noted poet Paul Laurence Dunbar. Although she did not afterward publish other original volumes during her lifetime, her contributions to African American arts, journalism, and racial politics continued for more than three decades beyond the appearance of *St. Rocque*—actually her second published book—which made her famous.

Born Alice Ruth Moore on July 19, 1875, she spent her first twenty-one years in New Orleans. Her mother, Patricia Wright, earned her way as a seamstress after emerging from slavery; of Alice's father, Joseph Moore, little is known except that he was a seagoing man, very likely white. Alice and her older sister Mary Leila were educated in the city's public schools. Subsequently, Alice earned a degree in 1892 from the two-year Straight College (now Dillard University) and began soon afterward what would become a lifelong career as a teacher. From the start she engaged in women's clubs dedicated to the arts and to civic concerns, including the Delta Sigma Theta Sorority and the Phillis Wheatley Club, founded in 1894 by her friend Sylvanie F. Williams, principal of the Girls' Department of New Orleans'

Fisk School. Alice later studied at Cornell, Columbia, the Pennsylvania School of Industrial Art, and the University of Pennsylvania. One of her scholarly publications, a two-part article, "People of Color in Louisiana," appeared in the *Journal of Negro History* (1916–17).

In 1895, while she was still teaching in New Orleans, the volume *Violets and Other Tales* marked Alice Moore's formal entry into the writing profession, although she points out in her brief introduction that a number of the selections included had previously been published "in newspapers and a magazine or two." A short preface by Sylvanie Williams recognizes that these early pieces show more promise than accomplishment; the author herself, in a 1913 letter to Arthur Schomburg, declared herself "heartily ashamed" of *Violets*. The fourteen poems include conventional lyrics that bespeak adolescent romances. Yet, taken together, the twenty-nine stories, essays, sketches, poems, and reviews demonstrate a diversity of voices and a breadth of themes that the young writer would continue to explore. Most notable are three melodramatic Creole local color stories, which capitalized on the vogue set by George Washington Cable and Grace King. These stories the author would rework for inclusion in her second and more famous book four years later: "A Carnival Jangle," "Little Miss Sophie," and "Titee," which reappears with a happier ending.

Alice and her mother moved to Massachusetts in 1896 as part of the extended household of sister Leila and her husband, James Young. By 1897, Alice was teaching immigrant boys in a Brooklyn, New York, public school. In addition, she was active in founding a mission for girls in Harlem. Characters and experiences from these urban settings provide material for a different type of local color story that she would write between 1900 and 1910, with the intention of collecting them as "The Annals of 'Steenth Street." The volume was never completed; "The Ball Dress" and "The Revenge of James Brown" appeared in periodicals (1901 and 1929 respectively), but all five stories from this period appear in Volume 3 of *The Works of Alice Dunbar-Nelson* (1988), edited by Gloria T. Hull.

Some of Alice's earliest poems that appeared in the Boston *Monthly Review* attracted the attention of the already famous poet Paul Laurence Dunbar, just a few years older than she. They corresponded for two years before they met, and after a brief courtship, they married on March 8, 1898. Dunbar's celebrity influence helped Alice to place her second book, *The Goodness of St. Rocque and Other Stories,* with Dodd, Mead in New York. Many readers not aware of her earlier book wrongly credited her writing success entirely to her husband's influence; however, notably absent from *St. Rocque* is the stereotyped black dialect that Dunbar, along with numerous white writers of the previous quarter century, had helped to popularize. Alice creates instead a group of characters who defy the overworked racial caricatures so common in post–Civil War literature.

Life in cosmopolitan, racially mixed New Orleans had given Alice Moore Dunbar much literary material. With her own ambiguous black, white, and Native American ancestry, her light skin and reddish hair, the attractive young woman had found herself at home among various elements of New Orleans' postbellum society and at times expressed a sense of cultural superiority to darker skinned African Americans. Her stories, like some of the same period by Kate Chopin, portray French-speaking Creoles and local landmarks such as Bayou St. John; Dunbar's characters are of unclear racial identity, though descriptions of some as "dark" or "dusky" suggest the legally recognized gradations between black and white. But in a broader reflection of the city's ethnic variety, others are pointedly German, Italian, Irish, or Jewish. Beneath their local color facade, the St. Rocque stories depict a class of working men and women—immigrants, minorities—often unhappy and oppressed, struggling to survive. Readers are drawn to sympathize with a poor German common-law wife who is disinherited when her abusive Italian "husband" dies ("Tony's Wife"); with a foundling brought up in a convent who explores thoughts of freedom before joining the religious order herself ("Sister Josepha"); with an old man whose harsh poverty forces him to part with his most valued possession ("M'sieu Fortier's Violin"); with a poor victim caught in the middle of a riot on the levee between striking Irish "longsho'mans" and "nigger scabs" who are unloading a cotton ship ("Mr. Baptiste"). Notably, the women characters in these stories typically suffer disappointments in love. Only the title story and "La Juanita" end with a wedding. In the first, the dark Manuela's gris-gris charm combined with a prayer to St. Rocque works better than the "blonde and petite" Claralie's novena to the same saint; in the latter tale, Grandpère Colomés rejects the suitor for his granddaughter's hand until "big and blond and brawny" Mercer, "Un Américain," wins grudging acceptance after a public act of heroism. In all of these stories, set in still recognizable parts of New Orleans, at Mandeville on the north shore of Lake Pontchartrain, and on the Mississippi Gulf Coast, details of local scene, custom, religion, and accent are faithfully represented. These regional portraits reveal underlying themes indicative of race and class differences in the socially stratified New Orleans at the turn of the century. Violet Harrington Bryan concludes in *The Myth of New Orleans in Literature* (1993) that Dunbar-Nelson introduced to mainstream audiences "coded stories of Creole life" drawn from "oral discourse in the black community."

Though the Dunbars' stormy marriage soon foundered and Alice left Paul in 1902, she welcomed a public role as his widow when he died in 1906. Despite two later marriages, she continued for the rest of her life to use Dunbar's name and with it, the black racial identity that she had not fully embraced during her earlier years in the South. Three stories that she did not publish in her lifetime are clearly drawn from the Dunbars' relationship, although their characters are white: "Mrs. Newly-Wed and Her Servants," "The Decision," and "No Sacrifice." All three were first published in the 1988 *Works of Alice Dunbar-Nelson* along with her 1900 short play, "The Author's Evening at Home," which reflects her marriage to Paul.

Continuing to teach in Wilmington, Delaware, where she moved with her own family after leaving Paul, in 1910 Alice married Arthur Callis, a fellow teacher twelve years her junior; their marriage and subsequent divorce were kept secret for many years. By 1916 she married again, this time to the journalist Robert "Bobbo" Nelson. For the remaining years of her life, she worked with Nelson on newspapers that he edited, and she wrote prolifically for African American publications on a national scale. During the late 1920s, she published columns in the Pittsburgh *Courier* and the Washington *Eagle*, which were syndicated for the Associated Negro Press.

In conjunction with her teaching, Dunbar-Nelson often directed plays, pageants, and elocution events. To celebrate the fiftieth anniversary of Lincoln's Emancipation Proclamation, in 1914 she edited the collection *Masterpieces of Negro Eloquence: The Best Speeches Delivered by the Negro from the Days of Slavery to the Present Time,* dedicating the volume "To the boys and girls of the Negro Race . . . with the hope that it may help inspire them with a belief in their own possibilities." This book focuses on the rhetoric of slavery and freedom; few women are included. Dunbar-Nelson edited another more broadly based collection, *The Dunbar Speaker and Entertainer: Containing the best prose and poetic selections by and about the Negro race, with programs arranged for special entertainments* (1920), and she dedicated this book, like the earlier collection, to the children of the black race, "that they may read and learn about their own people."

The widowed Robert had two children when Alice married him, and Alice's own mother and sister and Leila's four children also remained part of her household most of her life. Partly in an effort to provide income for this larger family, Alice worked at other jobs even as she found success as a public speaker and journalist. Although she never ceased to write stories, poems, and plays, many remained unpublished. One story that did not appear in her lifetime may reveal some of the writer's own childhood experiences; Dunbar-Nelson wanted to extend it to novel length but was discouraged by editor Bliss Perry of the *Atlantic Monthly* on the grounds that the public had become less fascinated with the theme of "the color line." "The Stones of the Village" (1988), probably begun about 1900, relates the story of the light-skinned orphan Victor Grabért, brought up in a small Louisiana town under the care of his "brown" *grand-mère*. When she insists that he learn proper English, he is ostracized by darker children who call him a "white nigger." His *grand-mère* subsequently sends him to the care of a friend in New Orleans, where he finds work, inherits wealth, is educated, and marries into white society. But to his dying moment, he is haunted by his origins, fearing that he will be exposed by other taunters like the boys of his childhood, who had thrown stones at him. This powerful tale, reminiscent of the "tragic mulatta" theme of Charles Chesnutt's "The Wife of His Youth" and of numerous similar contemporary stories, has been anthologized more than once in recent years. Near the end of her life Dunbar-Nelson confronted the theme of intraracial prejudice more directly in an essay entitled "Brass Ankles Speaks" (1988).

During the last two decades of her life, Dunbar-Nelson's efforts were largely directed toward political issues affecting African Americans. Her one-act play "Mine Eyes Have Seen" (1918), published in the *Crisis,* the NAACP journal edited by W. E. B. Du Bois, questions the duty of black Americans to serve in a war waged by a country that has not given them justice. The poem "Harlem John Henry Views the Airmada" (1932) imaginatively blends echoes of black spirituals into the African American consciousness of wars in American history. Dunbar-Nelson's diary, published decades after her death as *Give Us Each Day* (1984), details her speaking tours on behalf of women's organizations and her connections with black leaders who were seeking improved race relations in the United States. Intermittent entries in 1921 and 1926 to 1931 record these larger causes against a backdrop of her day-to-day concerns about her mother's health, her sister's family, her husband and their finances, her friends and acquaintances. This journal comprises a veritable Who's Who of national leaders in black politics and the arts during the period of the Harlem Renaissance. The diarist often critiques her own public appearances, noting "I spoke fine." Her writing of any kind she regards as "producing literature." Portions of the diary also reveal some apparent lesbian relationships during the period of her marriage to Robert Nelson, liaisons reflected in some of her poems, in particular, "You! Inez!" written in 1921.

Between 1920 and her death in 1935, Dunbar-Nelson maintained a hectic schedule of lecture tours and political activism, yet found time to write extensively for newspapers and magazines. Numerous literary selections written during this period but only recently rediscovered have given Dunbar-Nelson stronger identification as a writer of the Harlem Renaissance, including experiments with the genre of hard-boiled detective fiction in "His Great Career" and "Summer Session," both written about 1930. These two stories, as well as a number of previously unpublished pieces, were collected by Hull in the three-volume *Works* published in 1988. The first volume reproduces facsimile copies of the two early collections of Louisiana and Gulf Coast local color pieces. A second volume features the novelette "A Modern Undine," twenty-five poems, four selected newspaper columns, and six essays on black American issues. The final volume offers twenty additional short stories and four short plays. Hull's biographical and critical introduction to this collection, published as part of the Schomburg Library of Nineteenth-Century Black Writers, offers a thoroughgoing assessment of Dunbar-Nelson's life and work. In addition, Hull's introduction to the published diary and her essay on Dunbar-Nelson in *Color, Sex, and Poetry: Three Women Writers of the Harlem Renaissance* (1987) round out the personal and literary profiles of this notable woman whose career captures the sensibilities of two distinct eras. The southern girl who in 1895 first published romantic lyrics and sentimental fiction became a national professional lecturer and journalist who championed the twentieth-century causes of gender and race.

PART III

Renaissance in the South (1900–1960)

Introduction to Part III

Carolyn Perry

In 1993, Carol Manning proposed a bold idea for the study of southern literature: that the beginning of the Renaissance be extended back in time to include pivotal writers of the turn of the century, most notably Belle Kearney (1863–1939), Anna Julia Cooper, Kate Chopin, and Ellen Glasgow. As Manning explained, "the orthodox view of the Southern Renaissance—as bounded by two wars, quarterbacked by the Fugitive/Agrarians at Nashville, and inspired by the South's attempt to move forward while looking backward—is neat and convenient, but it is hardly realistic." By calling attention to the way in which critics have created southern literary history, she made a strong case for reexamining the evidence of the past and exploring alternate views of how this monumental period began.

In her essay for this collection, "Southern Women Writers and the Beginning of the Renaissance," Manning again challenges traditional views of the Renaissance that link its beginning to the way World War I changed southerners' outlook on the South. She explains that not all southern writers of this period needed the impetus of the war to begin questioning the region's inherent values. For just as the war turned the male world upside down both by threatening its homeland and offering visions of glory, so did an earlier battle—the one for gender equality beginning just after the Civil War—prove to be both traumatic and exhilarating for southern women. Indeed, some women also saw their home territory threatened as feminists, primarily based in the North, demanded opportunities for them in education and business; at the same time, the battle for women's rights afforded all women the chance to gain victory over inequality. Although the South was not quick to embrace feminism, by the 1890s a significant number of southern women had joined the suffrage movement and were active in a variety of other social reform movements. Such changes in the status of women were naturally played out in the literature just before and after the turn of the century, both to resist and to forward the cause.

The tension the suffrage movement produced was profoundly felt in the South, a region that often resisted change, and many southern women rejected it outright. Well into the twentieth century, the desire of many women for greater independence was tempered by their commitment to the grand myth of the South, which depended heavily on the perpetuation of the ideal southern woman as delicate, self-sacrificial, and committed to domesticity. Leading novelists of the late nineteenth century, in particular Augusta Jane Evans Wilson, upheld this view by condemning women who moved into the male spheres of business and politics; even though Wilson often supported female independence, her novels from *St. Elmo* (1866) to *A Speckled Bird* (1902) directly oppose gender equality. Those who spoke out in favor of suffrage, such as Belle Kearney in her autobiographical *A Slaveholder's Daughter* (1900), often took a rather conservative approach, sometimes appealing to white supremacist concerns. Although relations between black and white feminists remained problematic, as the nineteenth century closed and the twentieth century emerged more and more women writers demanded a voice of their own. Kate Chopin, for example, fought the ideal of the southern woman by challenging the stereotypes or offering her characters social and sexual freedoms, and Ellen Glasgow, a leader in the suffrage movement in Virginia, created portraits of independent women in her fiction. Likewise, Anna Julia Cooper argued for the rights of African American women in *A Voice from the South* (1892).

Perhaps because the mainstream suffrage movement offered little to the African American woman, in the late nineteenth century southern intellectuals and reformers such as Cooper and Ida B. Wells (1862–1931) launched the black women's movement. In 1895 the First National Conference of the Colored Women of America convened, and by 1896 the National Association of Colored Women (NACW) was formed. Cooper promoted a balance of power between the sexes by claiming that feminism should not place women's rights or thoughts above those of men, but she demanded that the plight of African American women be given attention. Alice Dunbar-Nelson, known primarily for her poetry, also joined the forces. Having argued for women's independence early on in such essays as "Woman" (1895), she later helped organize the Middle Atlantic Women's Suffrage Group and became active in the NACW. African American women writers were so productive in these early years that Henry Louis Gates, Jr., declared 1890–1910 "The Black Woman's Era," and this outpouring included southerners such as Cooper, Wells, and Dunbar-Nelson.

The status of women writers at the height of the Southern Renaissance has also been reexamined in recent years, for traditionally southern women have been relegated to minor status. Caroline Gordon lived and wrote in the shadow of the Fugitives and Agrarians, and Eudora Welty, though recognized for her early work, for decades was regarded as a southern lady and therefore not in the same league as Faulkner and Wolfe. Zora Neale Hurston has typically been credited for her contribution to the Harlem Renaissance, not to the southern, for in the South, "renaissances" were as segregated as buses or bathrooms. Yet the impact of the women's movement, fought so ardently in the South, added force to the work of southern women writers, many of whom were determined to revise the portrait of southern womanhood. Even while southern states were refusing to ratify the Nineteenth Amendment, Evelyn Scott was creating graphic descriptions of women's bodies and sexuality in her early novels that even northern publishers could not bear to print. And while Mississippi and Alabama continued to ignore the demands of the Nineteenth Amendment in the 1920s, Frances Newman was busy dismantling the idea of southern gentility and repression of female sexuality in her novels *The Hard-Boiled Virgin* (1926) and *Dead Lovers Are Faithful Lovers* (1928). In the 1930s and 1940s, women writers continued to assert their independence. Zora Neale Hurston's *Their Eyes Were Watching God* (1937) portrayed the triumph of a black woman who demands self-definition. Carson McCullers and Eudora Welty created vivid portraits of female "outsiders," women who could not be made to fit any stereotype of the ideal. At the same time, Lillian Smith attacked southern racism with such force in *Strange Fruit* (1944) that it shocked the South and was banned in the North. Although Welty, O'Connor, and McCullers were never excluded from studies of southern literature, only recently has the importance of writers such as Hurston or Smith been recognized. The broad scope of the work by Renaissance women clearly paved the way for the more recent wave of the women's movement of the 1970s, while also providing a wealth of material for recent scholarship.

Even if we are able to redefine the borders of the Renaissance, the scope of the era remains problematic because it has largely been defined in terms of southern men. For example, a major text for the study of southern literature, *The Literary South* (1979), only briefly scans the female tradition; at the same time, Jefferson Humphries, generally progressive in his thinking about southern literature, recently declared a solid future for southern literary culture based on the perpetuation of motifs from the past, yet he cited not one text by a woman writer in his analysis "The Discourse of Southernness" in *The Future of Southern Letters* (1996). Until the 1980s, most anthologies of southern literature had been edited by men, and most book-length studies of the literature were male authored. In fact, Louis D. Rubin, Jr., admitted in *The Literary South* that "in general the study of Southern literature has largely involved a community of scholars and gentlemen who are friends and fellow workers." Because of their natural bias, such scholars establish the male perspective as the norm, and they tend to measure texts by women against this standard. With regard to the Renaissance, this bias is seen most obviously in Richard King's *A Southern Renaissance: The Cultural Awakening of the American South, 1930–1955* (1980), which includes a discussion of only one woman, Lillian Smith; King readily explains that he excludes women writers from his study because "they were not concerned primarily with the larger cultural, racial, and political themes" on which he chose to focus, nor did they "place the region at the center of their imaginative visions." One cannot fault King for limiting his study in some way, and he admits that his is not a complete study of the Renaissance. However, in light of Lillian Hellman's or Carson McCullers' treatment of social issues, most notably of intolerance of difference in race or sexual orientation, or Eudora Welty's and Flannery O'Connor's strong sense of place, it seems that King's selection is a result of preference, not reality. At the same time, as much as they have grappled with slavery, the Civil War, and southern manhood, southern writers both female and male have been preoccupied with the image of the southern lady, which has proven to be a powerful emblem of the South. In that, as Louise Westling argues in *Sacred Groves and Ravaged Gardens* (1985), this emblem is needed to sustain the "elaborate fiction of aristocratic civilization," the status of women becomes a major cultural and political theme.

Recent scholarship has not only brought attention to women writers previously unacknowledged, but it has also redefined the way in which we view their works. This situation may be especially problematic in the study of southern literature, growing out of a region that has a more conservative history than that of other literatures. Sometimes women writers themselves have contributed to the slant criticism has taken. For example, in the prefaces to her novels, Ellen Glasgow tended to cast her work as social history of Virginia, and critics followed suit, comparing her work to that of fellow

Virginian James Branch Cabell. Recently, however, Glasgow's work is being recast in light of modernism and feminism, as it exhibits defining characteristics of each, and she is seen as a pioneer in establishing a female tradition in southern literature. On a different note, Julia Peterkin was highly regarded in the 1920s; her novel *Black April* (1927), which portrays the lives of rural African Americans, was considered a masterpiece by both black and white critics, and her *Scarlet Sister Mary* (1928) won a Pulitzer Prize. However, as Peterkin became more politically conservative and her depictions of African Americans less convincing, she was all but forgotten by critics. Today Peterkin's work is being reevaluated, however, by cultural critics, such as Susan Millar Williams, interested in the relationships among Peterkin's controversial views, her novels, and the peculiarities of southern culture. Similarly, Frances Newman's *The Hard-Boiled Virgin* (1926) made her a best-selling author even though the novel was harshly criticized for its openness about women's sexuality and for its complex style, and Newman was all but forgotten after her death in 1928. However, critics today praise her frankness in exposing southern fears of female sexuality, and they find that her style perfectly matches the subject matter: the convoluted sentences themselves express the frustration of the repressed protagonist, and the lack of dialogue emphasizes how she is denied a voice. Finally, as nonfiction prose has become an established genre within the canon, autobiographical works such as Anna Julia Cooper's *A Voice from the South* (1892) and Lillian Smith's *Killers of the Dream* (1949) are now ranked among literary masterpieces.

In discussions of the Southern Renaissance, the same themes—typically derived by southern gentlemen critics from literature by southern men— come up over and over again: the influence of the past in the present, ties to the land, race relations, and the southern mode of storytelling. As critics have sought out these themes in southern literature, the definition of what it means to be southern has become more and more firmly embedded in the literary imagination. Although both men and women writers of the South have explored these concerns in their writing, it is important to resist an approach that seeks to fit *any* writer neatly into an established tradition. Studies of the history of southern women's literature seek to expand the definition of southern literature not only by carving out a larger place for women writers, but by recognizing the broad and sometimes unconventional scope of their concerns. An assessment of women writers of the Renaissance, then, must explore the ways women writers have dealt with and broadened these typical themes.

Perhaps in reaction against a decidedly male tradition, southern women writers of the Renaissance placed particular emphasis on women taking control of telling their stories. From her earliest works, Ellen Glasgow emphasized that "official" history does not tell the whole story, and in doing so, she began the process of dismantling the power male writers, critics, and historians held. At the same time, Katharine Du Pre Lumpkin's *The Making of a Southerner* (1947) has recently gained critical attention because it reveals a southern woman's version of racial turmoil in the early years of the twentieth century. Yet no writer has taken hold of the storytelling tradition as powerfully as Eudora Welty. As *The Ponder Heart* (1954) so beautifully illustrates, a Welty protagonist may take control of the story at hand so brazenly that more emphasis is placed on the act of storytelling—and thus the construction of knowledge or history—than on the stories themselves. As she explores the role of storytelling in works by such writers as Welty, Lucinda MacKethan, in *Daughters of Time* (1990), demonstrates how southern women seized power when they moved out of the role of "daughter" to the southern gentleman and moved into the role of storyteller.

Another challenge to traditional themes comes in the way southern women writers represent the female body. The southern woman as beautiful, pious, and pure, while of great benefit to the myth of the Old South, could not be sustained as women gained status and voice. Novels like Frances Newman's *The Hard-Boiled Virgin* and Julia Peterkin's *Scarlet Sister Mary* displayed female sexuality in ways never before deemed acceptable, particularly by southern women. At the same time, Welty, O'Connor, McCullers, and Hurston explored in their fiction the relationship between the body and social or political power; by creating women who could not fit themselves to the stereotype or who appear grotesque, they proved the instability of the southern myth. In the South the issue of sexual power is particularly problematic: stories of fragile southern women victimized by black men were used throughout the early years of the Renaissance to justify female dependence on white men and the horrific treatment of black men, namely lynching. Thus Patricia Yaeger writes in an article for *Haunted Bodies: Gender and Southern Texts* (1997), "[I]n reworking the image . . . southern women writers do more than protest the burdens of ladyhood. Their grotesque heroines help bring the hard facts of southern racism and sexism into focus." The politicizing of sexuality has even led to a recasting of Scarlett O'Hara in recent criticism. Long associated with the southern land, Scarlett presents an image that both reinforces and challenges the myth. In her essay for this volume, Helen Taylor takes this characterization a step further in claiming that Scarlett, "emotionally flawed, willing to move and experiment with the times, and prepared to play dangerous games with her sexuality and loved ones, has been appropriated by post-1960s feminists as well as 1980s and 1990s 'Me Generation' career women and free spirits."

In his recent examination of the southern connection to the land, "The Vanishing Agrarians" (1996), Walter Sullivan asserts that the agrarian theme that dominated southern literature during the Renaissance continues to be explored by southern writers today; in part, this holding on to a love of the land makes them southern. In his essay, Sullivan concentrates primarily on texts by male writers, but his association of the southerner with the land also holds true for women writers. The landscape is such an integral part of Glasgow's *Barren Ground* (1925) that it often seems to play the part of a character, and Katherine Anne Porter actually claimed the land as the hero of Caroline Gordon's *Penhally* (1931) and *None Shall Look Back* (1937). In *Female Pastoral* (1991), Beth Harrison states that writers such as Flannery O'Connor or Zora Neale Hurston did not lament the loss of the rural landscape, but rather were "envisioning new worlds, different kinds of communities. The connection of women to the land and to nature somehow enabled a new vision." Harrison defines the female pastoral as including a land that represents not a patriarchal view of southern womanhood, but rather an enabling force for women—women who are active agents, perhaps even heroes, and southern communities that are egalitarian rather than patriarchal. At the same time, however, Harrison acknowledges that sometimes writers must turn away from the southern landscape to achieve selfhood for themselves and for their characters. Harriette Simpson Arnow (1908–1986), for example, reverses the pastoral plot in *The Dollmaker* (1954), suggesting that exile from the South is sometimes crucial to the development of identity. Yet whether women writers embrace the land or flee from it, the southern landscape itself serves as an impetus for the creation of their stories.

Women writers of the Renaissance who directly confront social issues have often been relegated to minor standing, but their works are now being reevaluated in light of cultural history; renewed interest in such work has broadened the scope of the canon. Two issues of particular sensitivity—the antilynching and labor movements—drew the attention of many southern women around the turn of the century. During the 1890s, the most prominent leader of the antilynching movement, Ida B. Wells, began publishing articles and tracts documenting the innocence of many victims of lynching, found in *Southern Horrors: Lynch Law in All Its Phases* (1892) and *A Red Record* (1895). Her work through the NACW and NAACP inspired other African American writers to join the cause, most notably Georgia Johnson (1880–1966) and Angelina Grimké (1880–1958)—the great-niece of white abolitionists Angelina and Sarah Grimké. Some years later, white women—in particular Jessie Daniel Ames (1883–1972) and Lillian Smith—attacked the justification of lynching in defense of white womanhood. Through her work with the Association of Southern Women for the Prevention of Lynching in the 1930s, Ames helped pass legislation that put an end to lynching, while Smith used her novels and essays to explore the psychological roots of southern racial pathology.

According to Anna Shannon Elfenbein in her essay for this volume, radical women novelists of the Renaissance were also exploring the lives of working-class women in a time when the labor movement was just beginning to take off. During the 1920s, the Young Women's Christian Association and the National Women's Trade Union League moved into the South, aiming to teach women laborers to organize and fight for their rights as workers. Such organizations made a noticeable impact in Appalachia, for as Appalachian women moved into textile factories, they readily became involved in strikes. The most famous of these, the 1929 strikes in Elizabethton, Tennessee, and Gastonia, North Carolina, inspired several novels by women. Yet, as Elfenbein explains, such novels of social protest were generally put in a subcategory of literature, and even within this sphere, women writers were marginalized: the leaders of the socialist movement tended to believe that proletarian fiction should be written by men as they staked their claim within the male tradition of American literature. In the early 1930s, a few southern women writers were being recognized for their "manly" treatment of the Gastonia strike, most notably Olive Tilford Dargan (1869–1968). In *Call Home the Heart* (1932), Dargan explores the threat traditional heterosexual desire poses to female solidarity, while at the same time, according to Elfenbein, she "courageously condemns racism and classism as forces that, like sexual desire, prevent women from uniting to end their oppression." Another novel of social protest is Grace Lumpkin's (1892?–1980) *To Make My Bread* (1932), which, Parks Lanier claims in his essay for this volume, is an "outstanding example of proletarian fiction worthy to stand with Steinbeck's *Grapes of Wrath*." However, Dargan's and Lumpkin's novels were published in the midst of the Agrarian movement, and the harsh realism depicted in these novels did not fit with the romantic rural South that the Agrarians eulogized. Even though Dargan *knew* rural North Carolina, having lived there for a quarter of a century, and wrote what she saw rather than conveying the South remembered by the politically motivated Agrarians, her work fell by the wayside while the Agrarians' manifesto, *I'll Take My Stand* (1930), remains a southern classic.

Any history of southern women's literature must challenge the orthodox view of the Renaissance, not to reject the contributions male writers made, but to give greater credit to the mothers of the Renaissance. But it is not just the beginning that requires careful scrutiny. Similar to its birth, the "death" of the Renaissance has been defined through its male writers. Many critics declare the Renaissance over before World War II, primarily because by this point, Faulkner's career was waning and Thomas Wolfe was dead. Yet if we cast an even slightly broader glance, it becomes clear that southern literature was in no danger of expiring. For example, in his *Twentieth-Century Southern Literature* (1997), J. A. Bryant, Jr., claims that "The story of Southern literature since World War II consists in part of a continuing renaissance, at least during the 1950s and early 1960s," and he cites as evidence Faulkner's Nobel Prize in 1950 as well as major works by such writers as Ransom, Tate, and Warren. Although Bryant tends to focus on male writers, certainly women writing after 1945 prove the merit of his argument: during these years Welty published *The Golden Apples* (1949), *The Ponder Heart* (1954), and *The Bride of Innisfallen* (1955); McCullers won a New York Drama Critics Circle award for her play *The Member of the Wedding* (1950); Flannery O'Connor published both *Wise Blood* (1952) and *A Good Man Is Hard to Find and Other Stories* (1955); and Ellen Glasgow won the Pulitzer Prize in 1942 for *In This Our Life* (1941), as did Harper Lee for *To Kill a Mockingbird* (1961) in 1961.

In some ways, it seems odd to declare an end to the Renaissance at all, particularly with regard to its women writers. Eudora Welty's career hardly lost steam through the 1960s and 1970s; in 1973 she won the Pulitzer Prize for *The Optimist's Daughter* (1972), and her 1984 autobiography, *One Writer's Beginnings,* was on the New York *Times* best-seller list for forty-six weeks. In addition, many writers considered part of the second renaissance, including Elizabeth Spencer, Doris Betts, Shirley Ann Grau, and Sonia Sanchez, began writing in the 1950s and 1960s. In *The Southern Writer in the Postmodern World* (1991), Fred Hobson asserts that the 1960s were years of great intellectual ferment in the South and acknowledges the tremendous literary work that grew out of the civil rights and feminist movements. Linda Tate echoes Hobson's claims in her essay for this collection, "A Second Southern Renaissance," finding that the force of this renaissance is in the convergence of women's voices. Yet whether the recent flowering is an outgrowth or continuation of the first, contemporary southern writers can now claim a strong tradition, weaving not only through the works of Ellen Glasgow, Eudora Welty, and Flannery O'Connor, but through those of Alice Dunbar-Nelson, Olive Dargan, Zora Neale Hurston, and countless other women writers whose contribution to the Southern Renaissance will not be forgotten.

Southern Women Writers and the Beginning of the Renaissance

Carol S. Manning

According to orthodox theory, the South experienced a literary renaissance between the two world wars—a renaissance that began with the Fugitives and Agrarians at Nashville, that looked more critically at the South and its values than had the defensive literature that followed the Civil War, and that produced such outstanding writers as Allen Tate, Robert Penn Warren, and William Faulkner. As for what occasioned this renaissance, Lewis P. Simpson points out that, following World War I, Western civilization in general saw an "upsurge of literary and artistic activity" as artists tried to come to terms with "the abyss" left by the war. For the South, that abyss included the loss of its rural isolation as the war forced the region to confront the modern industrial world. In a much-quoted explanation, Allen Tate finds this renaissance born of the resulting conflict the South felt between its loyalty to the past and its recognition of the inevitability of the postwar present. "With the war of 1914–1918," Tate asserts, "the South re-entered the world—but gave a backward glance as it stepped over the border: that backward glance gave us the Southern renascence, a literature conscious of the past in the present."

While this long-accepted view of the Southern Renaissance's beginning has much merit, it is based largely on the works of male writers and is best understood as an explanation of when and how a literary renaissance began for some southern men. In his 1950 essay "Agrarians in Exile," Richard M. Weaver makes the male emphasis of the view explicit when he links the Renaissance's origins to the travels abroad of many of the South's "young men" during World War I: "Following such experience, it was only natural that these voyagers should return home determined to take a fresh look at their inheritance. . . . In effect, they brought to their interpretation of the Southern past a new realism." But what about the women of the South? Does World War I mark the beginning of a literary renaissance for them as well?

On the contrary, much evidence suggests that some southerners, and southern women in particular, began to question inherited values and to move toward a new realism considerably earlier. Frequently described as artists ahead of their time, Ellen Glasgow and Kate Chopin are the best-known examples. In "Kate Chopin: Tradition and the Moment," Thomas Bonner, Jr., says that Chopin "speaks not for the past but to the present" through "'modern' characters who frequently break the bounds of tradition for the demands of the moment"; and in his introduction to *Ellen Glasgow: Centennial Essays* (1976), Louis D. Rubin, Jr., calls Glasgow "the first really modern Southern novelist, the pioneer" who, years before Faulkner, "did her best to write about Southern experience as she actually saw it, not as her neighbors thought she ought to see it." Indeed, Glasgow, according to C. Vann Woodward, anticipated virtually every theme that would inspire "the bold moderns" of the Southern Renaissance.

Yet because their works do not fall within the accepted time frame, Chopin and Glasgow generally are not identified with the Southern Renaissance. Chopin is never even considered a candidate because her works all predate World War I. Glasgow's best works, on the other hand, appeared between the two world wars, yet the fact that her literary career began before World War I disqualifies her from the Renaissance, a view made official by Thomas Daniel Young in the introductory essay to the Southern Renaissance section of *The History of Southern Literature* (1985): "Ellen Glasgow and James Branch Cabell, because their literary careers were launched before World War I, are not included in the Southern Renascence, though some of their most important work was done in the twenties, thirties, and even later."

The examples of Chopin and Glasgow—and Cabell and others—should suggest that the beginning of the Southern Renaissance needs to be reconsidered. In fact, if one looks objectively for first signs of a modern southern literature, one will discover that the Southern Renaissance did not wait for

World War I and the Fugitives and Agrarians at Nashville but dawned instead with scattered individuals, chiefly women, writing alone in the last decades of the nineteenth century.

It is frequently said that significant literary movements are most likely to develop in times of tension—that the writers are inspired by and react to the tensions of a time or place. Cultural tension is certainly crucial to established explanations of the Southern Renaissance's origins. Intense cultural tension might also account for the earlier beginning of a renaissance for southern women. Toward the end of the nineteenth century, many southern women—like American women elsewhere—grew dissatisfied with traditional values and assumptions regarding the female role and began to question the culture they had inherited. Out of their questioning would develop a modern southern literature.

With the slaves emancipated, the nation growing more urbanized and mobile, and immigration, the middle class, and reform movements on the rise, the late nineteenth century brought rapid change and tension to America. For many women, it was a time of organization, action, and awakening. "These were the years," Hazel V. Carby writes in *Reconstructing Womanhood: The Emergence of the Afro-American Woman Novelist* (1987), "of the first flowering of black women's autonomous organizations and a period of intense intellectual activity and productivity [for black women]." Elizabeth Ammons writes similarly of middle-class women of the time, black and white alike. In *Conflicting Stories: American Women Writers at the Turn into the Twentieth Century* (1991), she says such women "used various means—women's clubs, settlement house work, temperance agitation, anti-lynching crusades, and the campaign for suffrage—to assert their right to direct, active participation in the public affairs of the country." In sum, these decades saw women getting out of the home more frequently, taking a more active and personal interest in local and national affairs, finding their voices. These experiences led many to become more conscious of and less satisfied with traditional values and behaviors expected of women.

Given the pervasiveness in the South of the southern belle and southern lady as ideals of southern womanhood, questioning the status quo—even privately—could not have come easily to southern women. Yet many did feel intensely the discrepancy between the conventional female role, so exaggerated in the South, and their enlarged desires. And some did question publicly. Two unlikely but influential spokeswomen of the time were Anna Julia Cooper, born a slave near Raleigh, North Carolina, in 1858, and Belle Kearney (1863–1939), born to the southern belle/lady tradition on her parents' plantation near Vernon, Mississippi, in 1863. Their lives illustrate well the struggle of late nineteenth-century women for voice and more opportunities. In young adulthood, both women came to recognize the sexism in their societies and to protest that sexism; both became teachers and through their teaching developed confidence and a sense of mission; both came to lead influential women's organizations and to be suffragettes; and both left legacies of their time and their ideas in interesting written works. In her collection of essays *A Voice from the South* (1892), which she signs "By a Black Woman of the South," Cooper protests the limited educational opportunities available to females and campaigns for more opportunities, praises women's organizations (such as the Women's Christian Temperance Union) for helping liberate women, and criticizes the southern belle/lady mystique (which pervaded black as well as white culture) for stunting women's growth. Kearney makes these same points in her autobiography, *A Slaveholder's Daughter* (1900). For example, Kearney says that her own growth was stunted because in her youth she lacked inspiring female role models: all the women she knew and read about were conventional women who were "equally dependent and equally contented—at any rate, asked no questions."

Despite their achievements, Cooper and Kearney remained in some ways conventional southern women, "never able," as Mary Helen Washington says of Cooper in the introduction to a new edition of *A Voice from the South* (1988), "to discard totally the ethics of true womanhood." Like many women of their time, Cooper and Kearney were torn between desire for independence and the pressure of gender role expectations. Cooper, for example, prefaces her book with a stanza by George Eliot that exalts traditional feminine values: it lauds as *"Royal-hearted"* those women "Who nobly love the noblest, yet have grace / For needy, suffering lives in lowliest place; / Carrying a choicer sunlight in their smile. . . ." Yet Cooper rejects the conventional when she protests the expectation that southern women "stand on pedestals" and be decorative, and she boldly accuses southern black men of hampering black women's progress by expecting women to mold themselves to that ideal. Kearney similarly shows that she too has not escaped the influence of the southern lady ideal at the same time that she speaks out against it. She at times deliberately perpetuates the image of the southern woman as selfless and accepting: southern women have not willingly sought public life, work outside the home, or "political equality with men," she writes; rather, "all this has been thrust upon them by a changed social and economic environment" resulting from the events of the Civil War. She contradicts this view of the southern woman, however, when she says that for years girls "of the New South" had restlessly longed for "a higher, stronger life" and "the right to do and to dare," and when she says that the women of the South seized on the idea of women's suffrage in "their desperate struggle for individual freedom."

Cooper and Kearney are important figures in the cultural and intellectual history of the South, and *A Voice from the South* and *A Slaveholder's Daughter* are important documents in an emerging renaissance of southern women. These books reveal the rebirth that southern women themselves were experiencing as they struggled for freedom and voice, and they also are evidence of a parallel rebirth (or birth) of a serious southern literature. The tension between adherence to and defiance of the cult of southern womanhood reflected in these works of nonfiction motivates as well many worthy creative works—and characters in such works—written from the late decades of the nineteenth century to today.

Prime examples of such works are those of Ellen Glasgow and Kate Chopin, the so-called precursors of the post–World War I Southern Literary Renaissance, modernists and realists ahead of their time. A close reading of southern literary history reveals, however, that while Glasgow and Chopin were, indeed, modernists and realists, they were squarely of—rather than ahead of—their time: a time of questioning, awakening, and challenge for increasing numbers of southern women. Near-contemporaries of Cooper and Kearney, they too grew up influenced by the cult of true womanhood, and they too would soon strain at that bridle. Glasgow in her prefaces and essays and both Glasgow and Chopin in their fiction repeatedly examine the position of the southern woman, suggesting that the South's traditional values frequently stifle her. Many of their female characters are torn between adherence to and defiance of the role expected of them.

But Chopin and Glasgow are only the best-known of late nineteenth- and early twentieth-century southern women whose writing was motivated by this tension. In *Tomorrow Is Another Day: The Woman Writer in the South, 1859–1936* (1981), Anne Goodwyn Jones discusses seven southern women from the time span cited by her title who, she finds, turned to the writing of fiction in an effort to work through the same tension. These writers—Glasgow and Chopin, Augusta Jane Evans Wilson, Grace King, Mary Johnston (1870–1936), Frances Newman, and Margaret Mitchell (1900–1949)—"criticize the ideal of southern womanhood" in their fiction, some tentatively, some boldly. In "The Ascent of Woman, Southern Style" (1983), Miriam J. Shillingsburg presents a similar argument in her focus on three nineteenth-century novels, Caroline Lee Hentz's *Eoline* (1852), Grace King's *Monsieur Motte* (1888), and Kate Chopin's *The Awakening* (1899). In recent years, scholars have elaborated similarly on the works of these and other southern writers. Through their characters, the writers explore the tension many southern women have felt between personal desire and the demands of the southern ideal of womanhood. Decades before the Fugitives put pen to paper in Nashville, that tension inspired a flurry of writing by women scattered throughout the South and provided the basis for the development of a modern southern literature.

To locate the beginning of the Southern Renaissance, then, in a circle of male friends at Nashville following World War I is to be blind to the meritorious writing that emerged at the turn of the century as women began to examine and question women's conventional roles and place. As though gaining strength from the success of the women's suffrage movement, this nascent female tradition would grow more confident in the 1920s and afterwards, at the same time that the Southern Renaissance was expanding and gaining visibility with the arrival on the scene of the Fugitives, Faulkner, Thomas Wolfe, and others. A constant of this female tradition would be a close look at family relationships and southern conventions and how these touched on women's lives, and a central theme of this tradition—the demythologizing of the cult of southern womanhood and, by extension, of the southern hero and southern traditions—would attract many male writers as well.

In fact, in the 1920s this female renaissance influenced and blended with the post–World War I renaissance that orthodox theory has described. For while the Southern Renaissance began in the late nineteenth century with scattered women writers, it caught fire in the 1920s, thanks no doubt to multiple influences: the post–World War I tensions cited by orthodox theory, the growing confidence of women as citizens and as writers, and the opportunities to publish created by the numerous small literary magazines that cropped up across the South. One of these magazines deserves special attention here.

In 1921—a year before the birth of the *Fugitive* in Nashville—a little magazine was born in Richmond, Virginia, that, in its five-year life, fueled the simmering Southern Renaissance. Though it proudly numbered non-southerners among its contributors (including Gertrude Stein, Amy Lowell, and Joseph Hergesheimer), the *Reviewer* took as its mission to promote a non-nostalgic, modern southern literature. Toward that end it published not only such well-established southern writers of the day as Ellen Glasgow, James Branch Cabell, and Mary Johnston but also new southern voices such as DuBose Heyward, Paul Green, Allen Tate, Sara Haardt (1898–1935), Gerald Johnson, Julia Peterkin, and Frances Newman. And it achieved its mission. Though all but forgotten today, the *Reviewer* during its lifetime gained an international audience and won high praise (from the New York *Tribune,* the New York *Herald,* and the New York *Times,* from H. L. Mencken, and from others) for its promotion of a modern southern literature. Women writers deserve much of the credit for its policies and its success: three of the four founding editors were women; Emily Clark (1893–1953) was its leader, and over 40 percent of its contributors were women.

In effect, the *Reviewer* became the intellectual headquarters of the still-developing Southern Renaissance. It attracted writers from throughout the South, discovered and encouraged promising new writers, declared war on second-rate literature, criticized stale southern mores, confidently joined and elaborated the feminist critique begun by women writers from the turn of the century, and gave early expression to virtually every major theme that orthodox theory associates with the Southern Renaissance. Though the *Reviewer*'s pages do include some second-rate material, a hint of the journal's modernity and realism is evident in the following brief examples.

About a decade before the Agrarians would take up the issue, the *Reviewer* frequently treated a theme that would subsequently be viewed as central to the Southern Renaissance: the theme of a South caught between the past and the future, tradition versus progress. Ellen Glasgow addresses this theme in her essay "The Dynamic Past," published in the journal's third issue. But whereas the Agrarians look backward, lamenting the changes coming to the South, Glasgow accepts and encourages change, perceiving "the law of progress as superior to the rules of precedent." Editor Emily Clark joins the debate in her essay "A Protest against Progress," published in the February 1922 issue, but she does so in order to protest what she sees as society's infatuation with progress. Anticipating the Agrarians, yet without their nostalgia for the Old South, she criticizes modern society for defining progress in terms of size, numbers, and movement and for emphasizing material possessions over spirituality and art.

The *Reviewer* was progressive (even daring, Dorothy Scura has observed in an unpublished paper) in its treatment of racial issues. It published a shocking lynching story by Helen Dick of Memphis, a satirical essay on the Ku Klux Klan by Gerald W. Johnson of Greensboro, and revealing sketches of black life by several writers, including fourteen harshly realistic ones by Julia Peterkin. But the journal's modernity is perhaps most developed in its untimid feminist spirit, as in its frequent delicious satire of the mystique of the southern lady. For example, in her poem "The Misses Poar Drive to Church" in the April 1925 issue, Josephine Pinckney (1895–1957) of Charleston presents the post–Civil War southern lady as an anachronism. The Misses Poar keep up appearances of aristocratic gentility despite the dilapidated circumstances they have lived in since 1864. Wearing neatly darned black silk mitts, they ride to church in an oxen-driven wagon, yet as they issue from the plantation gate they exhibit the proud bearing of queens. In church, at the mention of President Grant's name, they bury their "noses' patrician hook" in great-grandfather's prayer book: "Better to pray for the Restoration / Than the overseer of a patchwork Nation!" Representing southern society through one of its major images, the southern lady, the Misses Poar are pathetic figures frozen in time. In a satirical essay titled "The Southern Lady Says Grace" in the October 1925 *Reviewer,* Sara Haardt moves the critique to contemporary time, suggesting that the female ideal promotes artifice and triviality. The southern lady, she writes, "is still, and rather proudly, a slave of the conventions" who "shrinks from the shrillness, the vulgarity, above all, the pettiness of 'taking her own stand.'" She prefers "to follow the old order," for "it saves her from thinking, and she has witnessed the utter impossibility of thinking intently and looking pretty at the same time."

It is this feminist vein that remains most characteristic of the works of women writers in the early decades of the Southern Renaissance. In *The Southern Belle in the American Novel* (1985), Kathryn Lee Seidel argues that by the 1920s writers had begun to use the southern belle "not to praise the South" as antebellum writers had done "but to criticize and at times condemn" the South for its restrictive codes of behavior for men and women. Her examples include Sara Haardt and many other lesser-known writers and works, such as Evelyn Scott, *Narcissus* (1922); Frances Newman, *The Hard-Boiled Virgin* (1926); Edith Everett Taylor Pope (1905–1961), *Not Magnolia* (1928); and Isa Glenn (1888–?), *Southern Charm* (1928). Another writer and work that could be added to the list are Emma Speed Sampson (1868–1947) and her forgotten novel *The Comings of Cousin Ann* (1923), which contrasts two women, Cousin Ann, a product of the Old South who is now an aging spinster grotesquely stuck in the role of the southern belle, and young Judith Buck, the new southern woman, who is independent, self-supporting, and full of initiative. (Sampson's novel is not modern or realistic, however, in its stereotypical portrayal of the loyal black servant.) Still another example is Edith Summers Kelley (1883–1956), whose rediscovered novel *Weeds* (1923) indirectly exposes the irrelevance of the southern belle/lady ideal. *Weeds* is a bluntly realistic novel about life on Kentucky tobacco farms, especially the life of monotony, toil, and deprivation as experienced by the women.

And the list could go on.

In sum, whereas accounts of the Southern Renaissance usually begin with the aftermath of World War I and the Fugitives and Agrarians at Nashville, an account that credits the writings of women locates that beginning years earlier. For many of these women, the tension or theme that inspired their awakenings and their writings was an internal war between gender role expectation and personal desire. And even as southern women responded to other tensions and took up other themes over the years, this early vein would continue and remain central. It characterizes the beginning of the Southern Renaissance for women, and it has magnificently influenced modern southern literature.

The Modern Novel

Lucinda H. MacKethan

In the parlance of literary criticism, the word *modern* is most often used to distinguish the early twentieth-century novel from its Victorian predecessor. The modern novel, belonging chronologically to the period from 1900 to the end of World War II, is characterized by at least some of these features: a heightened, often symbolic realism; experiments in language and form; frank attention to psychosexual behaviors, often applying Freudian principles; representations of modernity defined by the experience of World War I, mass migrations to the city, and the growing tyranny of the machine. *Modernism* as a cultural designation encompasses these features, but it also refers to a mind-set responding to the chaos that exploded all traditional systems of belief in the wake of the scientific and technological breakthroughs of Darwin, Freud, and Edison and the cataclysm of World War I. Except for his settings, usually the rural environs of his mythical Yoknapatawpha County, William Faulkner's work epitomizes definitions of both *modern* and *modernist* in its temper and technique. Thematically, his novels deal with a sense of disconnection from nature and memory, a loss of religious faith, rebellion against but also longing for the past, alienation from community and tradition. Technically, many of his novels employ a brooding first-person consciousness, often fragmented into multiple points of view, and are also marked by the interiority, complex allusiveness, and disjunction in narrative flow that distinguish much modern writing on both sides of the Atlantic. Any discussion of the modern novel in the South must take into account Faulkner's practice, yet often his domination of the form has meant that other important versions of the modern novel have been neglected.

The designation "modern novel" sometimes includes works that emphasize themes of social protest that in the 1930s marked the rise of "proletarian" literature. Often, however, this kind of novel is considered separately, reflecting the somewhat elitist suspicions voiced by modernist New Critics for any art that pushed overt political or social agendas. In the study of southern literature, the novels of writers such as Grace Lumpkin (1892?–1980), Richard Wright, Olive Tilford Dargan (1869–1968), Erskine Caldwell, Lillian Smith, and T. S. Stribling have traditionally been placed in a different category from the less topical, more technically experimental fiction of writers generally grouped together as modern novelists. *The History of Southern Literature* (1985) names proletarian and sociopolitical novels "the fiction of Social Commitment" and separates them from modern novels that merit attention for "craft."

The modern novel, in the South as well as elsewhere, has usually been defined as male property; in addition to Faulkner, Thomas Wolfe, Allen Tate, Robert Penn Warren, Jean Toomer, and Ralph Ellison lead most lists of makers of modern novels in or from the South. Katherine Anne Porter and Eudora Welty are often "add-ons" to the list. However, several other women writers of the South offer important examples of this form. Indeed one of these, Evelyn Scott, deserves consideration as the South's leading modernist novelist. Ellen Glasgow, Julia Peterkin, Elizabeth Madox Roberts, Zora Neale Hurston, and Caroline Gordon, among others, join Porter and Welty as writers who have made significant contributions to the development of the modern novel in its southern forms.

Like the fiction of other regions in the early twentieth century, the modern novel of the South takes as its starting point the twin urges of alienation from tradition and longing for order. The South's "peculiar" position in America at the new century's beginning served to exacerbate the sense of loss, the need for stability, and the chafing against the restrictions of provincial communities that most Americans felt at that time. The Civil War gave the South an experience of defeat, death, and devastation that made for an extreme contrast with the rest of the nation's confidence in progress, optimism, and economic success in the last decades of the nineteenth century. As the South began to emerge from the post-Reconstruction period, the problems connected with modern change hit with dramatic force. In particular, threats to the certainty of belonging to land and community, so important to traditional southern culture, challenged the southerner's entrance into the modern world. The most important poetic statement of the modern position on man and land, T. S. Eliot's *The Waste Land* (1922), attracted young southern writers with special force. The poem's evocation of barren land, intellectual and spiritual sterility, and strained sexuality spoke with particular urgency to the generation of southerners beginning artistic careers shortly after the end of World War I. In Nashville the Fugitives, especially Allen Tate and Robert Penn Warren, heatedly debated Eliot's aesthetic and intellectual interests throughout the 1920s. Even earlier, Evelyn Scott, a Tennessee native who had fled the South in her teens, had come under Eliot's influence, publishing poetry in the *Egoist* during the time that Eliot was editorial assistant for the journal in 1919.

The Waste Land transmitted Eliot's vision of a barren land through narratives of women's sexual experience. Faulkner in 1929 recast this vision in southern terms with remarkably similar imagery in *The Sound and the Fury*. The novel places at its visual and thematic center the obsession of the Compson brothers with the sexuality of their sister Caddy, who in her waywardness stands for their culture's loss of order and fertility. In the southern novel of the modern era, the land evokes not only the sense of place but also the sense of the lost past. The endangered, failing land finds its corollary in women characters whose bodies become a battleground for the culture's struggle for creative renewal. A roll call of the South's most important novels of the 1920s and 1930s reveals the oppositional themes of creativity and aridity, imaged through women characters' sexual and maternal possibilities, as the primary link among works by African Americans as well as whites, men as well as women. The tension organizes Jean Toomer's *Cane* (1923), Julia Peterkin's *Scarlet Sister Mary* (1928), Frances Newman's *The Hard-Boiled Virgin* (1926), Ellen Glasgow's *Barren Ground* (1925), Faulkner's *Light in August* (1932) and *Absalom, Absalom!* (1936), Allen Tate's *The Fathers* (1938), Zora Neale Hurston's *Their Eyes Were Watching God* (1937), Katherine Anne Porter's *Pale Horse, Pale Rider* (1939), Margaret Mitchell's *Gone with the Wind* (1936), Caroline Gordon's *None Shall Look Back* (1937), Elizabeth Madox Roberts' *The Time of Man* (1926), and Evelyn Scott's *The Wave* (1929), as well as her closely autobiographical first novel, *Escapade* (1923). If we extend the list through 1946, we add two more central works of the modern canon published in that year, both of which, again, link the land to women's bodies: Eudora Welty's *Delta Wedding* (1946) and Robert Penn Warren's *All the King's Men* (1946).

The modern novel in its privileged modernist designation has seemed to highlight male prerogatives of power, authority, and control—both sexual and cultural. Indeed, male southern writers often depict women as objects whose sexuality and fertility are frightening (Toomer's Fern, Faulkner's Lena Grove), whose waywardness or rape threatens social order (Faulkner's Caddy and Drusilla Hawk, Toomer's Karintha, Tate's Jane Posey, Warren's Anne Stanton), or whose barrenness reflects the land's waste (Faulkner's Joanna Burden and Rosa Coldfield). When southern women novelists take up modern positions, women characters can still embody these connotations, but they are more likely to act as agents than as objects simply reflecting the barrenness of land and culture. Beginning with Evelyn Scott, Julia Peterkin, and Ellen Glasgow in the 1920s, southern women writers created women characters who challenge their cultural roles and who suggest mythologies other than that which offers a "Fisher King" figure the prerogative of attempting to redeem his land from barrenness. Glasgow's *Barren Ground,* through the character of Dorinda, projects a different vision—a woman who takes up the quest of making the land fruitful (in her case, through dairy farming instead of plowing). Zora Neale Hurston's Janie, in *Their Eyes Were Watching God,* carries seeds in her pocket as she returns to the community that has disdained her, in overalls, to reclaim her home. Eudora Welty's character Virgie Rainey, in *The Golden Apples* (1949), rebels against the village mentality of her small southern town in order to protect her artistic vision.

Ellen Glasgow as a representative woman writer of the modern southern novel is important to consider. While acclaim during the 1920s and 1930s gave her status as one of the South's most important novelists, she was rapidly eclipsed as New Critical scholars turned their attention to Faulkner and other male writers in the 1940s. However, her major novels *Barren Ground, The Romantic Comedians* (1926), and *The Sheltered Life* (1932) are incisive and ironic representations of a changing South. The characters of Dorinda in *Barren Ground* and Eva Birdsong in *The Sheltered Life* challenge the image of the southern lady who, if she had begun to disappear in fact, still dominated southern mythology. The white woman on the pedestal as the preferred icon of the region's cultural distinctiveness was hard to dislodge; however, in these two novels Glasgow also broached the subject of women's sexuality in ways that critiqued southern culture's restrictive view of female passion.

Part of the reason that Glasgow was relegated to the position of minor novelist as the twentieth century progressed was her decision to remain technically conventional. Evelyn Scott, much younger and much less traditional in upbringing and outlook, was the South's first novelist to embrace the modernist challenge of creating new ways to imagine human character in fiction. Scott also wrote the first insightful evaluation of *The Sound and the Fury* (1929), praising its technical virtuosity and revolutionary vision. Her remarkable autobiographical early novel, *Escapade,* uses dream sequence, lush sexual imagery, heightened awareness of time, and a brutal examination of women's biological entrapment in a narrative based on her own pregnancy and her life with common-law husband Cyril Scott (Frederick Creighton Wellman). Evelyn Scott (born Elsie Dunn) had eloped with Wellman, a married man, and fled to Brazil in her teens. Both in her life and her novels she challenged conventions. Her imagistic style, in poetry and prose, is one of her most important modern strategies.

Scott's *The Wave,* one of America's most powerful modernist novels, uses the Civil War as a metaphor for the interior turmoil of male and female characters thrown into a chaotic world where the old verities and decorum have been swept away. In dozens of fragmentary yet interconnected vignettes, male and female characters face the threatening darkness of their desires in a world often depicted as arid and violent. Sexuality is a central element in many of the sketches. The physical attraction of men and women is presented as a "wave" equally as overwhelming and thus potentially as destructive as the wave of war that sweeps over the nation. Margaret Mitchell's *Gone with the Wind,* usually relegated to the category of "popular fiction," exhibits through Scarlett O'Hara some of the same modern concern for the symbolism of the female body. Scarlett is easily identifiable, by name and wardrobe, with the red clay soil of Georgia desecrated through violent war. Within the guise of the historical romance genre and the subject of civil war, Mitchell (1900–1949) exposed the contemporary South's views of "the new woman" as a tantalizing threat, a bearer of fertility but also of chaos, a link to survival but also to dissolution.

Modern novelists in the South, from the 1920s to 1950, found in the thematic divisions of the pastoral a useful strategy for organizing their chronicles of change and disorder. The pastoral seizes upon images of a simpler, rural world as a counterpoint from which to criticize a more complex, mechanistic present. The Fugitive-Agrarians of Vanderbilt defined the pastoral agenda of the South in their landmark symposium *I'll Take My Stand* in 1930. Southern women writers, excluded from this group, used the pastoral in fiction in somewhat different ways. They too associated the rural with the feminine, but often with more positive qualities of maternal nurturing and health. Elizabeth Madox Roberts' *The Time of Man* and Caroline Gordon's novels *Penhally* (1931), *Aleck Maury, Sportsman* (1934), and *None Shall Look Back* all contain versions of the agrarian agenda, but particularly stress associations of land with family and endurance. *None Shall*

Look Back is, like *Gone with the Wind* and *The Wave,* a work that uses Civil War history to explore a very modern battle of the sexes in which women take on new challenges but are still associated with maternal properties of the land.

Katherine Anne Porter and Eudora Welty, the two women writers most often included in the southern literary canon as modern novelists, combine the modernist concern for craft with pastoral tensions and an emphasis on interior landscapes of grief, longing, and desire. Porter began writing stories of her experiences in revolutionary-wartime Mexico in the 1920s. Her masterwork is the collection of interlocking stories finally gathered in *The Old Order* (1958, containing six stories from *The Leaning Tower* [1944]; three from *Flowering Judas* [1930], including "The Jilting of Granny Weatherall"; and "Old Mortality" from *Pale Horse, Pale Rider*). These stories, most written during the 1930s and 1940s, are set in the South from post-Reconstruction to the early twentieth century. The character Miranda confronts her own emerging womanhood through the experience of her relatives. In this process she grows ever more aware of the dynamics of family and the magnetism of place that tie her to the South. In several stories of *The Old Order,* the family matriarch, Grandmother Sophia Jane, evokes out of memory and rich storytelling the texture of the southern past and its intricate hold over the present.

Eudora Welty published her first novel, *Delta Wedding,* in 1946 and continued to focus on the tension between memory and change, tradition and personal growth, and "love and separateness" (as she has called these divisions) in her major fiction since that time. *Delta Wedding* in many ways resembles Virginia Woolf's *To the Lighthouse* (1926) in its depiction of the magic of ordinary life within the delicately balanced, competing needs of family. Like Woolf, Welty moves in and out of the minds of her characters, creating the effect of a complete design woven out of fragments of consciousness. The artistry of her work is perhaps best exhibited in the richly allusive short story cycle *The Golden Apples,* in which myth, history, personal and communal memory, and musical imagery all combine to create a tapestry of experience. Welty's women characters can represent both the force of tradition, such as Ellen Fairchild of *Delta Wedding* or the Renfro women of *Losing Battles* (1970), or whirlwind change, as does Bonnie Dee Peacock of *The Ponder Heart* (1953) or Faye of *The Optimist's Daughter* (1972). In still other centrally important women characters, she develops the role of the observer who transfers what she watches going on around her into a richly imagined inner life. Laurel McKelva in Welty's most recent novel, *The*

Optimist's Daughter, like Cousin Laura in *Delta Wedding* and Cassie in *The Golden Apples,* lives as much through perception as through action.

The modern novel, like modernism itself (either as literary form or cultural designation), has no definitive ending date. The novels of Carson McCullers and Flannery O'Connor, published in the 1950s and 1960s, represent some of the most distinctive, experimental fiction in the modern canon. McCullers' *Ballad of the Sad Café* (1941) and O'Connor's *Wise Blood* (1952) bring elements of the grotesque—what has sometimes been called "southern gothic"—into stories that reach beyond realism for their impact. McCullers' adaptation of the ballad form in her novel creates an eerily mesmerizing effect. O'Connor's quite different application of the grotesque in *Wise Blood* and her short fiction is designed to draw readers into a consideration of spiritual realities undergirding a shallow and perilous material world that the rapidly modernizing secular South could easily be used to represent. Elements of the absurd, the symbolic, the surreal, and the bizarre (bizarre sexuality, in particular) take the fiction of both McCullers and O'Connor well beyond the boundaries of realism that earlier southern modern novelists generally respected.

Women writers of the modern novel, from Evelyn Scott in the early 1920s through Eudora Welty in the 1970s, have made major contributions to the Southern Renaissance and have influenced many contemporary writers, both men and women. Their importance stems from their experiments with prose form, their attention to language, represented both in the word and the female body, and their compelling presentations of women's social roles and interior lives in the changing South.

Gone with the Wind and Its Influence

Helen Taylor

If historians were to look back over the twentieth century and ask which single work of art proved to be its most popular and enduring, reaching the largest global audiences and achieving most purchase within world culture, there is probably only one choice: *Gone with the Wind* by Margaret Mitchell (1900–1949). Reputed to have sold more copies than any other book (except the Bible), this novel-made-film, in all its manifestations—book, film, video, soundtrack, memorabilia, sequel, plagiarized novel, fictional reworking, biographical and critical study, not to mention countless advertisements, spoof posters, songs, heritage plates, pop-up books, theme restaurants, and colloquial expressions—has reached a vast worldwide market. The novel *Gone with the Wind* (1936), a long and loving exploration of the traumatic American Civil War and the devastation of the South, sealed in celluloid immortality through its highly successful 1939 David Selznick film version, is instantly recognized and much quoted, and it has come to be associated in the international mind with American southernness, indeed with nineteenth- and twentieth-century America itself.

The novel belongs to a long tradition of southern plantation fiction and white apologist historiography. It focuses on the South's most dramatic historic period: Secession, the Civil War, the bloody demise of plantation culture and the slave economy, and the violent chaos of Reconstruction. Although this period had been fictionalized by other southern writers, such as Grace King, Mary Johnston (1870–1936), Thomas Nelson Page, and Thomas Dixon, Margaret Mitchell was unique in focusing on such a complex sweep of history from the perspective, and through the experiences, of a young white woman—one who begins by expressing boredom at the thought of war; then lives through extreme reversals of fortune and wealth; loses parents, husbands, a child, and many friends; and finally survives to rebuild her plantation home, way of life, and self-esteem.

The story revolves around Scarlett O'Hara, daughter of Irish landowner Gerald, who has made the plantation Tara into one of Georgia's finest. She is unrequitedly in love with Ashley Wilkes, who marries his cousin Melanie. As war begins, Scarlett has to protect her family and the pregnant Melanie. Staying in Atlanta with relatives, she faces Sherman's army and (with the help of a frightened, inexperienced slave, Prissy) delivers Melanie's baby as the city goes up in flames. During Reconstruction, she pragmatically does business with the Yankees and so prospers and restores the fortunes of Tara while simultaneously protecting her close circle's involvement with the Ku Klux Klan. During the course of the narrative, she marries three times—first to spite Ashley, a second time to pay off Tara's postwar taxes, and the third time for fun. Her third husband, Rhett Butler, shares his wife's pragmatism, blockade-running during the early part of the war and only later joining the Confederate Army. He engages in lucrative deals with the Federal Army from the start of the conflict and right through Reconstruction. Enraged at his wife's love for Ashley and selfish disengagement from him and their daughter, Bonnie Blue, who dies in a riding accident, he leaves her. The book ends with Scarlett realizing how much she loves him and resolving to get him back—by returning to her beloved Tara to plan her strategy.

Margaret Mitchell wrote only one novel, though she was a prolific reporter for the Atlanta *Journal* and had composed some fictional juvenilia on southern themes that were later to coalesce into her major novel. Born into a prominent Atlanta lawyer's family, which was proud of its Confederate ancestors and long residence in Atlanta, she spent much of her childhood listening to graphic accounts of Civil War battles, the burning of the city, the use of the family house as an army hospital, and the sufferings of the family and their friends during the postbellum Reconstruction period. Attending parades commemorating Atlanta's Confederate dead, learning by heart Civil War songs and minute details of military skirmishes, battle wounds, and acts of heroism, the young Margaret was well primed to write a defensive, chauvinistic account of the South's war. As she once said on a radio broadcast, "I heard everything in the world except that the Confederates lost the war." The book's huge success both surprised her and took over her life; she spent the next thirteen years "cleaning up after *GWTW*." In 1949, crossing a street to go to a theater, she was killed by a drunken driver. She left no new manuscript, but instead thousands of letters, sent to virtually every correspondent who wrote to praise, criticize, or correct details of the novel. Referring repeatedly to herself as "Margaret Mitchell of Atlanta" or "southern author," she was acutely conscious of the sectional enthusiasm afforded the novel, and of her own role in literary history and popular legend. There is no doubt, as Richard Harwell's selection from these letters testifies (*Margaret Mitchell's "Gone with the Wind" Letters, 1936–1949*, 1976), that Mitchell saw herself as southern spokesperson and guardian of a precious southern legend. Her last years were therefore spent in protracted correspondence, mainly with strangers, defending the historical precision and literary integrity of her book.

From its first publication and film premiere, there are many—not least black and white southerners anxious for their region to be represented as modern and progressive—who have wished this work would fade away and occupy a minor role in the representational history of the American South, to be overtaken by versions of the American Civil War of greater verisimilitude and relevance for a multicultural American society. However, the publicity machine for *Gone with the Wind* has long ignored such political sensitivities, invoking its character as "timeless," "legendary," and "immortal." That this work endured, indeed thrived, for two-thirds of the twentieth century is attributed to its essential greatness and universal themes. And while there is some truth in the claim that *Gone with the Wind* appeals enormously to persons of very different nations and cultures, it is important to remember that the legend and longevity of this work have been carefully nurtured by the many groups and individuals—publishers, literary estate, film and television companies, porcelain figurine makers, and so on—who have profited handsomely from the work's "universal" success. Books, articles, and Internet sites detail a plethora of relevant publications, cultural references, artifacts, and ephemera; memorabilia collections (such as the "world's largest" of Herb Bridges) include every conceivable icon, from Scarlett pop-up book to music box, powder puff and so on. The film, re-premiered seven times in Atlanta and shown daily at the Cable News Network headquarters, is screened constantly somewhere in the world and is frequently broadcast on television; the videotape has been a huge best seller. For the fiftieth anniversary of book and film (in 1986 and 1989 respectively), the sons of David Selznick compiled a television documentary, *The Making of "Gone with the Wind"* (1988). Meanwhile, scholars have unearthed a cache of letters, photographs, and two unpublished manuscripts of Margaret Mitchell juvenilia: the novella *Lost Laysen* was published in 1996, while the other, "Lady Godiva," will surely follow into print. Darden Asbury Pyron's authoritative biography, *Southern Daughter: The Life of Margaret Mitchell* (1991), provided much-needed scholarly material and well-documented interpretation of the writer's life in context. After many failed attempts, much political controversy, and the financial largesse of a German car company, Atlanta finally boasts a Margaret Mitchell Museum.

Since the book's first appearance, *Gone with the Wind* has gone from strength to strength in commercial and popular terms, though critically its reputation has waxed and waned over the decades. It is sobering to realize that the year in which the novel was published, 1936, also witnessed publication of a novel most commentators now believe to be the South's literary masterpiece, William Faulkner's *Absalom, Absalom!* Nevertheless, the 1937 Pulitzer Prize was awarded to Margaret Mitchell, and popular taste has continued to favor her populist novel over Faulkner's modernist complexities. Since its publication, *Gone with the Wind* has become a reference point for all subsequent writers about the South, with white and black writers alike compelled to recognize, if not accept, its powerful epic celebration of the plantation legend and partisan critique of the Civil War as national, regional, race, and class tragedy.

The book both came out of and spoke to Depression concerns and anxieties. The terrible economic and political insecurities of the 1930s led to a powerful sense of family and personal vulnerability that resonates through the story of the O'Hara family in crisis. The yearned-for "Never-Never Land of Dixie," as Jack Temple Kirby called it, a golden age of an ordered plantation society in which the races, genders, and classes knew and loved their place, pervades both novel and film in ways that spoke immediately to generations facing the onset of a major world war, the rise of fascism throughout the world, and the prospect of never enjoying comfortable, adequately fed days again. To international readers and audiences of the 1930s and 1940s, this tale of war, sacrifice, suffering, and survival echoed their fears, concerns, and aspirations. The figure of pampered southern belle, Scarlett, surviving with true grit the devastation of her class position, comfortable home, and familial relationships, spoke volumes to people starved of security and luxury, thrown into wartime conditions, and forced to live on their wits and survive on few resources. The pledge "never to be hungry again" had a charge in the 1930s and 1940s that it would never quite achieve later. In postwar generations, the book and film have continued to play into nostalgic fantasies of a glorious lost, innocent Eden, but they have also satisfied that hunger for large scale epic narratives that engage whole historical sweeps within one character's trajectory—even if the postmodern world has rendered inconceivable such grand narratives and certainties. In terms of popular and critical response, the figure of Scarlett—emotionally flawed, willing to move and experiment with the times, and prepared to play dangerous games with her sexuality and loved ones—has been appropriated by post-1960s feminists as well as 1980s and 1990s "Me Generation" career women and free spirits.

Indeed, a major reason for the continuing success of this work is its huge appeal to women readers and audiences, with Scarlett O'Hara one of the twentieth century's most appealing icons. Like all great heroines, Scarlett fulfils a variety of narrative and thematic functions: romantic protagonist, epic figure, outsider and villain, conservative conformist at war with ruthless iconoclast. Her appeal to different generations of women, documented in critical studies such as Richard Harwell's *"Gone with the Wind" as Book and Film* (1983) and Helen Taylor's *Scarlett's Women: "Gone with the Wind" and Its Female Fans* (1989), is apparent from the many literary and celluloid daughters she has spawned, the number of women who have named children and dogs after her, and the fact she has one of the best-known literary household names. Unusual in holding her own through such an epic work in so many different roles—wilful daughter, mother, wife and widow, capitalist and landowner, social and sexual deviant—Scarlett offers a range of readerly and iconographic pleasures to women across the century. Even if her stock has risen since the 1940s and 1950s, when women admired the goodly Melanie and regarded Scarlett with shocked awe, she has always been the focus of fascination and debate. Publishers and producers have frequently promoted women's writing and films aimed at female audiences as "the new *Gone With the Wind*." From Kathleen Winsor's *Forever Amber* (1944) to Colleen McCullough's *The Thorn Birds* (1977) and Eugenia Price's *Savannah* (1983), as well as a host of plantation blockbusters and "bodice-rippers," the epic romance, usually featuring a deviant Scarlett-style heroine, has been a feature of women's popular writing. In 1991, French novelist Régine Desforges' *The Blue Bicycle* (1982) was the subject of a plagiarism case; the Margaret Mitchell estate claimed successfully that, in this case, literary influence had gone too far. A rash of plantation-based screen and television movies, from *Mandingo* (1975) to *Beulah Land* (1980) and *North and South* (1985), has ensured the longevity of the genre.

Since its first publication, there have been many critical voices raised against the novel and, subsequently, the film. The press of the American Left unanimously condemned the book for its reactionary and racist politics. In a 1936 issue of the *New Republic*, Malcolm Cowley voiced an opinion that has been much quoted since: calling the novel "an encyclopaedia of the plantation legend," he scorned its "every last bale of cotton and bushel of moonlight, every last measure of Southern female devotion working its lily-white fingers uncomplainingly to the lilywhite bone." During the 1960s, while it continued to be popular in print and on screen, *Gone with the Wind* was dismissed by most liberal opinion as a literary and ideological embarrassment. Writing against the grain of popular enthusiasm in 1970, Floyd C. Watkins called it "a bad novel" because it "propagandizes history, fails to grasp the depths and complexities of human evil and the significances of those who prevail." In the decades since the civil rights movement, and especially within a racially sensitive postcolonial world climate, its glorification of a lost world of slavery and socioeconomic exploitation seems anachronistic and racially provocative. Scholarship continues, however, and in the latter years of the twentieth century *Gone with the Wind* has occupied an uneasy position within the college curriculum as a major example of the American epic and popular novel documenting female experience.

The film's Jewish producer, David Selznick, was acutely aware of the problems of exacerbating racial hatred and tensions of the kind stirred by D. W. Griffith's glorification of the Ku Klux Klan's role in Reconstruction southern history, *The Birth of a Nation* (1915). Selznick downplayed the white supremacist polemic within the novel and made significant changes to the Mitchell original, such as transposing Scarlett's would-be rapist into a white man. Although these minor changes did nothing to alter the fundamental ideological thrust of the work, it is sometimes argued that Selznick's film advanced the cause of African Americans because it foregrounded black actors in a way no other Hollywood film had yet done. Furthermore, it boasted relatively significant black parts that contrasted favorably with the blackface or marginalized black characters of earlier films about the South. The conferment of the first Academy Award on a black actor, Hattie Mc-Daniel as Mammy, was praised as a considerable milestone in the history of black presence in Hollywood. Indeed, some of the biggest television and film successes involving largely black casts—most notably, the television miniseries based on Alex Haley's *Roots* (1977) and Stephen Spielberg's 1985 film of Alice Walker's *The Color Purple* (1982)—are critical responses to and political revisions of this influential work. *Roots*, the novel published in America's bicentennial year, was referred to as "the black *Gone with the Wind*," and because of its huge popular success, as well as adoption in educational curricula, it probably reshaped the general public's perception of antebellum plantation life more effectively than any other work of fiction.

The critical attacks on the authenticity of Haley's "autobiography" did not adversely affect its triumphant riposte to the Ur-text.

Roots (1976) may be the most spectacular example of a reworking of the plantation legend promulgated by Gone with the Wind, but there have also been sequels and imitations. The epic nature of southern history has invited sequels: Margaret Walker long planned a sequel to her Jubilee (1966); Alex Haley produced a sequel to Roots (1976); Kyle Onstott's "Falconhurst" and John Jakes's "North and South" series were followed by a southern trilogy from Julian Green. Margaret Mitchell herself joked about a second Gone with the Wind, "Back with the Breeze," which she said would be "a highly moral tract in which everyone, including Belle Watling, underwent a change of heart and character and reeked with sanctimonious dullness." Despite desperate pleas from publishers and readers, Mitchell always refused to write a sequel and enjoined her executors to refuse to allow such a publication by any other writer. Anne Edwards, Mitchell's first biographer, wrote a sequel entitled "Tara," but it was refused permission for publication by the estate and is now sealed in a vault, never to see the light of day. However, after the death of the writer's brother, Stephens (who abided faithfully by his sister's wishes), his sons and heirs decided to capitalize on the lucrative possibilities of such a commission and, with an eye to the book's emerging from copyright, ignored Mitchell's injunction. After long deliberation, and rumored bids from writers as disparate as lesbian American novelist Rita Mae Brown and British romance queen Barbara Cartland, they hired as near a clone of Margaret Mitchell as could be found: Alexandra Ripley, southern author of such historical sagas as On Leaving Charleston (1984) and New Orleans Legacy (1987).

Scarlett: The Sequel to Margaret Mitchell's "Gone with the Wind" (1991) ends by reuniting Scarlett and Rhett, but only after a long series of picaresque adventures involving trips to Charleston, Savannah, Atlanta, and finally—for much of the book—Ireland. Scarlett hands over the management of Tara to sister Suellen and with her considerable wealth goes off to get Rhett back, as we know she must. She finds Rhett living in Charleston with his mother and working as an upmarket camellia grower and fertilizer salesman. Following a passionate roll on the beach after a near-drowning (an encounter that fortuitously impregnates our heroine), Rhett rejects Scarlett and marries a dull schoolteacher, who later conveniently dies in childbirth. Scarlett turns her back on the South and, inspired by Irish relatives she meets in Savannah, sails to her father's birthplace, County Meath, influenced by Gerald O'Hara's memories and love of the Irish soil. There she buys a huge, decaying estate called Ballyhara and becomes known as The

O'Hara, the most significant—and benevolently tyrannical—landowner and citizen. Her extended family are all active members of the Fenian Brotherhood, and for a while she finances their activities. An Irish witch delivers her of a daughter, Cat, by cesarean section on Halloween night. The O'Hara clan's revolutionary fervor is finally condemned as pathological and murderous—especially when they try to turn on the newly reunited Scarlett and Rhett. This implausible saga has a neat, conservative happy ending, the nuclear family reconstituted with Cat, substitute for the dead daughter Bonnie Blue.

Scarlett appeared in September 1991 in eighteen languages, including Japanese and Chinese, and in forty countries simultaneously. It became the fastest selling book in publishing history, with 5.5 million copies sold worldwide in its first two months. By 1993 it had sold over twenty million copies worldwide. On October 4, 1991, the New York *Times* ran a full-page advertisement from Warner Books boasting of its success as the "record-breaker for biggest first day sales," and "the overnight national best-seller," quoting booksellers across the land on the lines of people waiting to buy, the "epidemic of Scarlett fever," the mobbing of one store from opening bell to closing time, and so on. The William Morris Agency's director of foreign rights described it bombastically as the most successful publication of all time. Whether this is so is in many ways irrelevant; what is significant is the choice of a writer with a racially and politically conservative agenda similar to Margaret Mitchell's and the constraints imposed by the Mitchell estate. Ripley's contract proscribed any interracial sex scenes, graphic sex, and homosexuality; she accepted all these, and indeed went further, avoiding the racial complexities of the Reconstruction period: "I'm sure there was also a lot of long-suppressed anger [among former slaves], but I didn't bother with that. It's not my story. . . . I'm not a sociologist. I'm a novelist." Her narrative decisions, then, included killing off Mammy early on, removing Prissy to another place, and giving the extremely docile ex-slaves minor, insignificant roles. Slave dialect is almost completely absent, as is any discussion of racial issues. In many ways, this sequel's Irish setting and racial silencings echoed the political argument of southern scholars such as Grady McWhiney (*Cracker Culture: Celtic Ways of the Old South,* 1988) who argue for a southern myth of Celtic origin and centrality, with white southerners as semiaristocratic descendants of Irish kings: a thesis that excludes or marginalizes other ethnic groups, especially African Americans.

Though a popular success, this sequel was a critical disaster. Undeterred, the estate commissioned two further sequels: one by British writer Emma Tennant, who in 1995 delivered a manuscript, "Tara," that was condemned by both estate and publisher, and—like Anne Edwards' sequel of the same name—consigned to a sealed vault. The final sequel to the book was commissioned in 1998. Best-selling author Pat Conroy was contracted by Mitchell's trustees to write a first-person novel, "The Rules of Pride: The Autobiography of Captain Rhett Butler," which Conroy described as a "companion" to the original, and in which he had plans to kill off Scarlett. Recalling his southern mother's enthusiasm for *Gone with the Wind* as "a clenched fist raised to the North, an anthem of defiance," he differed from the other sequel-writers in refusing to agree to any censorship relating to miscegenation or homosexuality. Although Conroy has withdrawn from his contract, it is perhaps significant that a male novelist was to be allowed to complete the story and draw a final line beneath the twentieth century's most celebrated heroine. Part of Margaret Mitchell's genius lay in writing an open, ambiguous ending to her novel that has appealed to a female reading and movie public ever since; no woman writer would wish to close down all future possibilities for the legendary Scarlett.

Gone with the Wind has almost certainly done its ideological work. It has sealed in popular imagination a fascinated nostalgia for the glamorous southern plantation house and an ordered hierarchical society in which slaves are "family," and there is a mystical bond between landowner and the rich soil those slaves work for him. It has spoken eloquently—albeit from an elitist perspective—of the grand themes (war, love, death, conflicts of race, class, gender, and generation) that have crossed continents and cultures. For women readers and viewers, Scarlett O'Hara has provided a rich source of imaginative play and has stood for a quality of female strength, power, and bloody-mindedness that is rare in twentieth-century fiction and film. Characters (Scarlett, Mammy, Rhett), iconic sayings ("Tomorrow is another day"), and dramatic moments (Atlanta burning and "birthin' babies") in the film as well as the novel have acquired significance for *Gone with the Wind* enthusiasts worldwide and inspired a tradition of writing and filmmaking that keeps the work alive, in both its imitations and detractions. Even when, in recent years, African American writing and film—from *The Color Purple* (1982) to *Beloved* (1987)—have embarrassed *Gone with the Wind* fans into a recognition of its historical distortions, and the southern belle and her beau are now the subject of television soap opera and satire, the original retains its popular mystique.

Gone with the Wind held its own as a world cultural icon throughout two-thirds of the twentieth century. At the 1996 Olympics, international visitors poured out of the Atlanta airport asking to see Tara; a year later a German-sponsored Margaret Mitchell Museum opened to satisfy tourist demand. Memorabilia collectors and anniversary watchers are well served by an efficient, lucrative *Gone with the Wind* industry, while across the world, television comedies, talk shows, and arts programs reference the work constantly. Its manifold international circulations and reinterpretations coincided with, and imaginatively played into, a rise in reactionary movements such as the League of the South and academic challenges to multiculturalism. *Gone with the Wind* still speaks, sometimes through echoes, especially to women readers and audiences across the globe. Its continuing power should not be underestimated.

Southern Women's Autobiography

Fred Hobson

Although autobiographical writing by southern women has its roots in the nineteenth century—in Harriet Jacobs' *Incidents in the Life of a Slave Girl* (1861) and other slave narratives, as well as works such as Susan Dabney Smedes's *Memorials of a Southern Planter* (1887) and Belle Kearney's *A Slaveholder's Daughter* (1900)—the writing of autobiography and memoir (as opposed to diaries and journals) by southern women, black and white, took a somewhat different direction in the twentieth century. Evelyn Scott and Ellen Glasgow, two writers belonging to the Southern Renaissance, were pioneers in such writing—Scott with her modernist memoir *Escapade* (1923) and her somewhat more conventional story of family and childhood, *Background in Tennessee* (1937), and Glasgow with *The Woman Within* (1954), a work that she began in the 1930s and left at her death in 1945.

Scott's *Escapade*—an episodic work with the names changed but in almost every other respect autobiographical—relates a portion of Scott's five-year adventure in Brazil, to which she had fled at age twenty with her lover, a married physician and academic more than twice her age, in an episode that caused such a scandal back in New Orleans that the two had to assume new names. An imagistic work, nearly a prose poem that shares traits stylistically with Scott's modernist novels, *Escapade*, as Dorothy Scura has written in her afterword to the novel (1995), is "almost a feminist cri de coeur": Scott becomes pregnant, experiences a painful childbirth under the care of a sadistic male physician and then a botched surgery to repair damage sustained during childbirth; she battles poverty and misery, all the while viewed with suspicion and sometimes contempt by a society that she finds even more oppressive to women than the southern one from which she had fled. In the later memoir, *Background in Tennessee,* she explores that earlier rural South—first the nineteenth-century world of her grandparents and then the world of her own youth. She recalls the routines of small town life as well as such memorable events as the Kentucky-Tennessee tobacco wars and the coming of the Spanish-American War. Race is the thread that runs through much of Scott's memoir, but not race in the manner in which it would be treated by many later white memoirists who would attack racial injustice. One finds here little acknowledgment of early racial sins; rather, Scott maintains, "How I loved Negroes! They were everywhere. . . . I enjoyed them constantly for what they contributed to a pure animal enjoyment of life!" Poor whites, on the other hand, she found "a race apart, unknown, incomprehensible."

Glasgow's *The Woman Within* was more nearly a formal autobiography than Scott's ventures into the genre. Writing near the end of her career, Glasgow speaks with surprising frankness not only of her growth as an artist but also of her disappointments as a woman. "A completely honest portrayal of an interior world," as Glasgow described her work, it was written "in great suffering of mind and body. . . . I was writing for my own release of mind and heart." She describes a childhood made "unhappy" by a tyrannical Calvinistic father, "more patriarchal than paternal," and indeed the descriptions of her parents—the harsh, controlling father, a weary, submissive mother whose spirit was the "loveliest" but whose life was the "saddest" Glasgow had ever known—anticipate the depiction of fathers and mothers in numerous other memoirs by southern women. A rebel against her father's iron hand, Glasgow took refuge in reading and freethinking, but as a young woman she found suffering everywhere she turned—in her mother's early death by typhoid, in the suicides of both her brother and brother-in-law, in a love affair that ended tragically, in her own encroaching deafness. As Pamela Matthews writes in her introduction to the book (1994), *The Woman Within* is "best understood in the context of feminist reconsiderations of turn-of-the-century women writers and of recent reconfigurations of the autobiographer as a gendered subject." Glasgow came out of a tradition of women silenced (and, for one increasingly deaf, silence was more than a metaphor); in her novels, and particularly in her truth-telling autobiography, she broke that chain of silence and insisted on being heard.

But neither Glasgow nor Scott (despite Scott's treatment in *Background in Tennessee*) examines with any honesty the subject—race—that would be at the center of southern autobiography, female and male, from the 1940s forward. Beginning with Zora Neale Hurston's *Dust Tracks on a Road* (1942) and continuing with Katharine Du Pre Lumpkin's *The Making of a Southerner* (1947) and Lillian Smith's *Killers of the Dream* (1949), southern women began to treat with insight and personal investment that subject that had dominated southern minds, white and black, for more than a century. One finds it rather remarkable, in fact, that virtually no white southern writer of autobiography or memoir had addressed race openly and honestly until that time; indeed, no white male writer was to address the subject autobiographically and with any degree of insight and deep personal contrition for at least another decade.

African American writers got there much earlier, although Hurston's *Dust Tracks* hardly conformed to the pattern established by most other black writers, male and female. Writing at a time when Richard Wright was focusing on black Americans as victims of racial oppression, Hurston chose a different course. In an essay published in 1928 she had insisted that she chose not to be "tragically colored," and in *Dust Tracks* she was faithful to that dictum. In writing of her early years in the all-black town of Eatonville, Florida, she describes a rich and full black folk culture. Indeed, Hurston dwells less than any other prominent African American writer of her time on white racial oppression, prompting certain black readers to wonder at the time, with good reason, how any child could grow up black in the Deep South during the era of Jim Crow (even in an all-black town) and be so apparently oblivious to racial injustice. Others wondered if that seeming oblivion was in fact part of a strategy. In any case, Hurston chose to focus on the excitement of Joe Clarke's store porch, where the townsmen customarily held "lying" sessions, "straining against each other in telling folks tales," as all the while young Zora gave full rein to her own fertile imagination. She contends that she did not fully realize she was "a little colored girl" until, after her mother's death when Zora was nine, she was sent to Jacksonville to live. In the remainder of *Dust Tracks* Hurston relates her version of a Horatio Alger story—the young black woman who, through hard work and good fortune, lands at Howard University, then Barnard College and Columbia University, and becomes a noted anthropologist and novelist. "I have been in Sorrow's Kitchen and licked out all the pots," Hurston concludes. But she had emerged triumphant.

If the African American woman, Hurston, treated race as only one aspect of a full and varied life, the two white women, Smith and Lumpkin (1897–1988), wrote memoirs that dealt with the subject more centrally. Indeed, as white southerners who came of age in a segregated society, both were moved in the 1940s to write what amounted to narratives of racial conversion. Smith and Lumpkin, in many respects, seem nearly parallel figures— both born in December 1897, both descended from Georgia planters and slaveholders, both belonging to families of position and privilege, dominated in each case by a strong father. Each began to rebel against southern tradition in her teens, each continued that rebellion in college, and each had her eyes fully opened during a sojourn outside the South—in Lumpkin's case at Columbia University, in Smith's case in Baltimore, then as a teacher in China. Neither ever married; each lived most of her adult life with another woman, but neither ever spoke or wrote openly about her sexual orientation. One might make the case with Smith in particular that her outspokenness on the subject of racial injustice was directly tied to her position as a lesbian in a homophobic America—more to the point, in a homophobic South in which gender roles were more clearly defined, and the cults of manhood and womanhood held even more sacred, than in the rest of the United States. She could not speak openly about her sexual orientation; thus she spoke all the more boldly—more boldly than any other white southerner of her time—about the South's racial sins. For her efforts she incurred the wrath of the South's liberal establishment—journalist Ralph McGill and other men who refused to accept Smith's uncompromising position on racial segregation.

Smith's *Killers of the Dream* was part memoir, part treatise on the South's "haunted" society, "a tortured fragment of Western culture." But she had written her book, Smith insisted, not so much to expose the South as to understand it—and to understand herself. "From the day I was born," Smith wrote, "I began to learn my lessons" on how to live Jim Crow—and she goes on to describe her own Huck Finn–like struggle between deformed conscience and sound heart. But her memoir is about gender as well as racial inequities. She paints an especially poignant picture of her mother, a prime example of that southern woman who was subdued, controlled, and finally more than a little sad: "She was a wistful creature who loved beautiful things . . . and took good care of her children. We always knew this was not her world but one she accepted under duress." Smith had determined she herself would not accept such a world: through *Killers of the Dream* and another extraordinary memoir, *The Journey* (1954), as well as her novel *Strange Fruit* (1944), she broke free.

Lumpkin's memoir is a less impassioned but no less moving story of racial transformation. By the time she wrote in the 1940s, Lumpkin had become a vigorous and outspoken advocate of racial and social justice, yet for the first half of *The Making of a Southerner* she seems to speak as one of the southern status quo: that is, she sets forth uncritically the racial position of her family when she was growing up in Georgia and South Carolina. She seems at first to laud the Old South, particularly her grandfather and her father, who were unswerving in their devotion to the Confederate Lost Cause. But all the while, she is in fact undermining the southern status quo, particularly her father, appearing to praise him while at the same time portraying events—such as his beating of the black family cook—that show him to be something other than the epitome of noblesse oblige that he considered himself. A devastating attack on southern patriarchy—made all the more effective because it is delivered in a tone of understatement—Lumpkin's memoir also describes how she, like Smith, broke free. The racial sinner, as she calls her earlier self, is transformed by her associations with African Americans in graduate school and principally through her work with the Young Women's Christian Association. In her narrative, even more than in Smith's, race, gender, and class intersect with particular intensity.

Other powerful works of autobiographical writing by southern white women—works that also qualify as racial conversion narratives—followed Smith and Lumpkin. Anne Braden's little-known *The Wall Between* (1958) describes Braden's path from a segregationist childhood, spent largely in Alabama and Mississippi, to racial iconoclasm in Kentucky in the 1950s, culminating with death threats when she and her husband help a black man buy a house in a white section of Louisville. Braden (b. 1924) describes her early years as so many other southern racial converts of her generation: "I knew that something was wrong, but for years I did not understand what it was." She speaks as well for Sarah Patton Boyle (1906–1994), whose moving memoir *The Desegregated Heart* (1962) tells the story of a privileged child of one of Virginia's first families who comes, suddenly and dramatically, to see her earlier racial cruelties and who throws herself into the battle for racial justice in Virginia in the early 1950s, paying a great price for her apostasy. Fighting segregation with an almost religious intensity, Boyle, however, never fully grasps the connections of racism with gender and class discrimination—connections that Smith and Lumpkin emphatically made.

While white women—almost always of privilege—were writing of southern childhoods and personal transformations, African American women were telling stories of growing up in a very different South. Pauli Murray's *Proud Shoes* (1956) was not so much a story of self—although she does paint a partial picture of her childhood in Durham, North Carolina—as of her family. In a work that anticipates Alex Haley's *Roots* (1976) in a number of ways, Murray (1910–1985) tells the story of two sides of her family, focusing on her maternal grandfather, born free in Delaware, who came to North Carolina during Reconstruction to teach the recently freed slaves, and her maternal grandmother, the daughter of a forced union between the white son of a privileged Chapel Hill family and the beautiful, talented family slave. In discovering the earlier lives of her grandparents, with whom Pauli Murray lives as a child, Murray discovers much about herself. She is filled with pride when she considers her grandfather, who had fought with the Union Army in the Civil War. Her grandmother's story, however, "awakened long-dormant, unresolved questions of identity and intensely conflicting emotions. It . . . resurrected the ominous shadow of slavery which still hung over the South of [Murray's] childhood." Particularly disturbing to her—and to her grandfather—is that her grandmother, the product of rape, was nonetheless proud of her white father and the prominent family of which he, and thus she, was a member.

Maya Angelou's and Anne Moody's narratives focus more directly on their own lives. In *I Know Why the Caged Bird Sings* (1970) Angelou writes of growing up in rural Arkansas, living with her grandmother, believing herself to be physically ugly and unloved. Faithful to the child's point of view in the first half of the book, the older Angelou—writing in her early forties—describes a life centered around the church and her grandmother's store. She becomes aware of the curious intersections of race and class when her proud grandmother is taunted by a group of poor white girls who can find security only in race; Angelou's grandmother responds with a quiet dignity. As is the case in a number of other African American narratives from slave days forward, reading provides the young Angelou with a window on the wider world. But that larger world intrudes brutally when, at age eight, during a stay with her mother in St. Louis, she is raped by her mother's boyfriend. During the latter part of the narrative Angelou is sent to California to live with her mother (and briefly with her father), becoming pregnant at age sixteen and giving birth to a son. As this first volume of her autobiography concludes, her odyssey is far from complete.

Moody's *Coming of Age in Mississippi* (1968) reads, in its first half, somewhat like a female version of Richard Wright's *Black Boy* (1945) as Moody faces a bleak world filled with childhood fears and uncertainties. Born poor in rural Mississippi in 1943, Moody describes a world that, in many respects, had changed little from the nineteenth-century plantation South. Telling her story in an informal, almost conversational style, she portrays herself as the loner, the rebel, defying gender stereotypes—more Frederick Douglass than Harriet Jacobs. Affected by the murder of the black teenager Emmett Till in 1955 and by other acts of racial violence, she is sensitized to the perils of being black in Mississippi during the period of racial hysteria just after *Brown v. Board of Education*. In college in the early 1960s, she becomes involved in the civil rights movement; indeed, she writes her memoir in the immediate aftermath of the most intense phase of that movement. Pondering the words of the civil rights anthem "We Shall Overcome," she concludes on a note of uncertainty: "I wonder. I really wonder."

Those memoirs by Murray, Angelou, and Moody were only the first in a remarkable series of narratives—or extended personalized essays—by African American women. Nikki Giovanni's *Gemini* (1971), Lucille Clifton's *Generations* (1976), and Mary Mebane's moving *Mary* (1981) and *Mary Wayfarer* (1983) are only some of the later works in that tradition—reflections on gender, class, and color within the African American community, as well as on race. A number of autobiographies and memoirs by white women of southern birth were also to appear in the decades to follow—certain of them (by Virginia Durr, Ellen Douglas, and others) focusing on race, others (by Shirley Abbott and Dorothy Allison, among others) on class, others (by Mab Segrest and Minnie Bruce Pratt) on sexuality, others (most prominently Eudora Welty's *One Writer's Beginnings*) more exclusively on the making of the artist, still others (by Lillian Hellman, Katherine Anne Porter, Florence King, Elizabeth Spencer, and Bobbie Ann Mason) on a number of subjects, southern and otherwise. What is clear in most of these narratives, as in those in the preceding decades, is the degree to which race, gender, and class cannot be isolated in the self-expression of southern women. On the subject of race, black women knew in their souls and bodies what no one else could know, and southern white women (in particular, Lillian Smith and Katharine Du Pre Lumpkin), long before southern white men, told the whole truth about racial oppression. Whether that was because white women, through no choice of their own, were prohibited from the centers of southern power (political, economic, educational, journalistic) and thus assumed a license to speak more freely, whether a more concrete vision—as some feminist scholars have maintained—enabled women to focus more fully on the personal and to possess a more truly tragic vision, or whether for a myriad of other reasons, the result was indisputable: women's autobiographical writing during the middle third of the twentieth century was relentlessly honest and boldly revealing not only in its portrayal of the condition of women in the South but also in its overall portrait of a land haunted, as Lillian Smith maintained, by ghosts whose names heretofore had gone unspoken.

Women Writers and the Myths of Southern Womanhood

Anne Goodwyn Jones

Modernity and modernism: these are names for the profound changes of the twentieth century both in experience and in art. Modern ways of living, and modernist ways of finding meanings through art, pulled the South from the isolation of rural poverty into the world: urban, industrial, technologically advanced, aesthetically complex. So at least goes the conventional historical narrative of the first half of the twentieth century in the South. Southern men served, or wanted to serve, in the Great War and then World War II. African Americans migrated, or wanted to migrate, to Chicago and Harlem. Mountain people came down to work in the textile mills in southern Gastonia, and farm families saw their daughters leave for jobs in southern cities like Atlanta. Arguably the first flapper was southern writer Zelda Fitzgerald (1900–1948).

In the 1930s, the Depression called attention to the South as the nation's number one economic problem, but also as a site for WPA photographers like Eudora Welty and *Fortune* magazine writers like James Agee to document and make known to the world. Women entered the academic professions, notably as social scientists at the progressive University of North Carolina in Chapel Hill. The Second World War cemented the participation of the South in the modern world, with southern Rosies, black and white, riveting in southern war factories and serving along with men overseas. Painters and writers and composers throughout the period, stung initially by H. L. Mencken's label of the South as a "Sahara of the Bozart," then drawn by the excitement of the modernist movement in Europe, traveled like William Faulkner to Paris, or New York, or Minneapolis, or Denver, and came home changed, to produce a Southern Renaissance that arguably continues unabated today.

Told like this, however, with the emphasis on (re)joining the world, the story of the South in the twentieth century is the story of southern difference eroding and a South merging and blending with larger national and international economic and cultural forces. Told like this, then, the story of the myths of southern womanhood, too, should be the story of their disappearance and replacement by homogeneous national myths of womanhood. Indeed, writers like Mencken's wife Sara Haardt (1898–1935), in her essays "The Last of the Beaux" and "The Twilight of Chivalry" (*Southern Souvenirs*, 1999), wrote as though the end of the southern gender mythology were near. But this story is not adequate. The South's confrontation with modernity, and with modernism, evoked conflict and resistance as much as it did emulation and imitation. "Modern" (and "modernism") seemed to many to mean precisely what was not southern, what was even antisouthern. Could an identifiable South survive such radical change? If not, did southerners need to retreat into the past? As for gender, could there be a modern southern woman, or was the very idea an oxymoron? For others, modernity (and modernism) seemed not only compatible with, but in some senses to have emerged from, the South: the Civil War had shaken some southern hearts and minds as profoundly as World War I was to shatter European confidence a half-century later.

Prime conservative literary examples of the sense of conflict between modernity and the South were the Fugitive-Agrarian poets and thinkers, the John Crowe Ransoms and Allen Tates who fell in love with the modernism of a T. S. Eliot but flatly rejected the modernity of industrialization and egalitarianism. On the other hand, as Michael O'Brien has argued (in an essay in *Haunted Bodies*, 1997), Mary Boykin Chesnut's very writing style marked an emergent modernist sensibility. In fact, the traditional myths of southern womanhood found ways to survive in the new era—the belle made a great flapper—yet resist some of modernity's key notions, such as women's equal rights. As late as the mid-1960s, in Virginia at Hollins College, the issue was joined over the question of jeans. Overwhelmingly, the student body voted against asserting the right to wear jeans on campus, many arguing that they came to Hollins because it was a southern school, not a Smith or Wellesley. Southern ladies didn't wear jeans.

And the myth explained why. Ladies didn't labor; they didn't dress like men, and they didn't act like men. The reception William Faulkner's character Drusilla Hawk receives as she soldiers in the Civil War and then labors after it, in jeans, clarifies the myth. The women of the community in *The Unvanquished* (1938) insist that she marry her senior officer because they cannot conceive of a relationship, a proximity, between the genders that would not involve sex. A woman, her clothing implied, was a nurturer— Granny gathers the boys under her skirts to hide them from the Yankees— and not a fighter. The genders not only differed from one another: they were mythical opposites. Men dominated, women submitted to their "lords and masters." Men thought and were educated to reason and to lead; women felt and were educated to beautify and to follow. The oppositions did not differ radically from those of Western tradition generally, but they were implanted more profoundly and enforced with more power because of slavery.

In the proslavery arguments, as several scholars have noted, one can find the early development of a specifically southern myth of womanhood. In the hierarchy that was the nature of reality to the proslaver, women, like children, slaves of both sexes, and dim-witted or lunatic men occupied a lower, inferior rank. Like children, slaves, and madmen, then, women could be trained only to the limits of their capacity. Therefore the primary lesson for them had to be obedience. The myth of the southern lady—the dominant myth of southern womanhood—parceled out specific qualities and talents by categories of class and race, but each category then had its own corollary myth. Within their specific niches, women could excel at domestic skills such as management of a household (white) or cooking (black), the fine arts (white) or raising white children (black). Sexuality was natural, even desired by black women, and unnatural (thus never officially desired) for white women. Despite women's "natural" affinities for religion, both black and white women deferred to the authority of the male preacher or priest. Ultimately, whatever else they accomplished for good or ill, the myths of southern womanhood shored up the power of the slavocracy, by making black women sexually available, by rewarding white ladies with material comforts and domestic authority, and by turning categories of women against one another, as Scarlett O'Hara turns against "white trash" Emmy Slattery and Mary Chesnut against slave women's "racial" characteristics. The power of internalized myth produced from southern women some wrenchingly painful prose.

Louise McCord, a highly educated upper-class white woman, wrote vehemently against giving women the vote during the antebellum period at the same time her more famous fellow southerners, the Grimké sisters, left home for the North and joined the feminist movement there. McCord's argument? If women do not constrain their behavior to what is proper to their sex—a mission of ideality more elevated than men's quotidian politics—they will not only fail in their duties but they will, by putting themselves on the same playing field, be vulnerable to men's violence. Never willing to critique the myth, McCord nevertheless reveals that its roots are planted in fear. Harriet Jacobs meanwhile records her own struggles as a slave woman to negotiate the distance between her grandmother's upper-class sexual morality, with its resemblances to the myth of the white lady, and Jacobs' own decision to seek asylum from her master's sexual harassment by starting a relationship with another white man.

How was the South in the twentieth century to find a course that would neither capitulate to the more disturbing implications of modernity's age of mechanical reproduction nor retreat into an evasive, idealistic, and ineffective antimodernism? How, specifically, could southern women salvage something valuable from the myths of southern womanhood while moving southern women's lives forward into the changes of the new century? Would they, like the Grimkés, have to leave the South in mind if not in fact? In a sense, it could be said that southern women writers led the way toward a successful articulation of the southern past with its future, its old myths of gender with the new. In responding to and reinventing one of the most antimodern components of southern ideology—those myths of womanhood—they would draw from its virtues as they saw them and link them with the possibilities offered to womanhood by the modern world: political, legal, sexual, emotional, and economic equality and freedom. Stitching the future to the past, cutting out the most threadbare and offensive sections of the old fabric, making it fit with the new nylon and Dacron and polyesters, the women who wrote between 1900 and 1960 found it impossible to make a seamless or even a particularly fashionable garment. Yet the effort of black and white, rich and poor southern women of the period to tailor a real future out of the complexities of a mythologized past has been one of the outstanding accomplishments of the twentieth-century South.

It should be noted that, over the decades, southern womanhood has had mythical status in other venues than the South itself. In Europe and to some extent in the American North and American popular culture, for example, southern white women as well as black have been mythologized as sultry, tempestuous beings whose passion is barely contained by a veneer of manners. Alternatively, in Spike Lee's *Crooklyn,* for example, southern black women are represented as stultifying conformists in contrast to New York's best and brightest. Wherever the truths of such myths lie, the myths have very little to do with the dominant myths of white southern womanhood within the South itself, those myths that have direct effect on southern women and southern women's writing. Melanie Wilkes fits the dominant southern myth of white womanhood perfectly, as Mammy does the southern myth of black womanhood; Scarlett O'Hara, from the outset, defies those myths at the same time she longs for their power and their meanings. By the standards of the myth, Melanie is a southern lady; Scarlett is only a woman. Yet even Scarlett's sexuality is at best confused, hardly worthy of her name.

The white myths of southern womanhood have been much slower to change in the culture at large than the material changes of the century would indicate. Even during the period from 1960 to the present, the "postmodern" period, women writers have continued demythologizing the gender assumptions that prevailed in 1900 and 1850. And they have done so as often through traditional artistic forms as through modernist or postmodernist innovation. Women writing in the South between 1900 and 1960, though they had other interests and concerns, confronted residual and emerging myths that spoke directly to them as women and as writers. Because "womanhood"—especially but not exclusively in the culturally dominant form of the "southern lady"—had been central to hegemonic southern ideology since well before the Civil War, the topic was hard to avoid. And because "womanhood" in several of its manifestations explicitly denied or prescribed what women could write as well as how they could live, women writers of necessity found those myths to be part of their writing personae and material. Hence some form of realism served their interests as demythologizers as well as or better at times than the techniques of modernism.

A moment's contemplation of the differences between the lives of women in 1960 and their lives in 1900 suggests the enormity of change that took place in a single lifetime. In 1900, a woman could not buy a bra or a sanitary pad, keep food in a refrigerator, wear trousers, or vote. Many women in the South, white and black, worked as wives and mothers on farms or in the mills, with no legal birth control and inferior property rights. Yet in the writings of southern women of the period, technological and legal innovations of the century were to have less interest than the attitudinal or ideological changes that undergirded them. This may be due in part to the relative privilege of the women who wrote: they were burdened less with problems to which technology offered solutions. Instead, they focused on changes in intangibles—attitudes, ideology, myths. And here, to judge by their work,

differences between 1900 and 1960 are less dramatic. Despite or even because of modernization, the concerns of southern women writers remained
fixed on the conflicts between female identity, autonomy, and authority, on
one hand, and on the other, resistance, especially myth-based resistance, to
them. The myths, as we will see, were multiple: what they had in common,
wittingly or not, was the dependence of women on men—for identity and
for assignation to appropriate arenas of autonomy and authority.

The myths of southern womanhood stemmed from a cultural logic that
served the interests of an unequal society. The inequality, itself uneven,
ranged variously across income and blood, family and skin color, as well as
sex, in a vestigial system of honor that centered on the white privileged man.
All the myths of southern womanhood can be traced as ancillaries or corol-
laries to the foundational narratives of white and male power. Although the
normative story was that of the white lady, there were parts in the narrative
for every southern woman. Indeed, parceling out characteristics and behaviors to specific groups of women was itself, intended or not, a major player
in diffusing women's collective power and reducing for each woman the
range of possibilities of cultural identity. The "dual mother" system, for instance, attributed warmth and physical tenderness to the black "mammy"
and beauty and ideality to the white "mother"—thus precluding beauty
from the mammy and warmth from the mother.

The white narratives of mythical southern womanhood generally focus
on a range of major characters who act out a single story, the story of physical and cultural reproduction. Although the roles of the characters differ
and, as in the case of mammy and mother, bear mutually exclusive characteristics, they can be seen to serve, along with various other purposes, the
same single end: to sustain by procreating and then raising the young in a
culture in which whiteness is preserved and male dominance is not challenged. The most familiar roles for white southern women in the myth of
southern womanhood could be named as lady, belle, Christian yeowoman
of the middle class, spinster, and trash; for blacks, mammy, mulatta, Christian yeowoman of the middle class, loudmouth, and whore. But names and
categories for the roles differ. One useful elaboration of the cultural history
of certain specific roles appears in Diane Roberts' study of southern womanhood in the works of William Faulkner, *Faulkner and Southern Womanhood* (1994). Roberts names her categories Confederate Woman, New
Belle, Mammy, Tragic Mulatta, Night Sister, and Mother. Humorist Florence King (b. 1936) comes up with her own inimitable categories in *Southern
Ladies and Gentlemen* (1993), such as the "self-rejuvenating virgin," who
maintains her mythical chastity through astonishing acts of linguistic cre-

ativity. Sociologist John Shelton Reed develops a series of white female social types in his *Southern Folk, Plain and Fancy* (1988) in a chapter called, with telling humor, "Ladies and Other Women."

How does each role sustain southern traditional inequalities? First, each role is defined by its sexual and reproductive importance. The lady's and the belle's "sexual purity"—whether through age, strength of character, distaste, or "self-rejuvenating virginity"—guarantees a legitimate family line that is pure white: here is where the white man plants his seed. The tragic mulatta and the black whore offer romantic or deromanticized sites for male sexual pleasure, forbidden him at home or, when younger, in flirtation with a belle. White mothers can instill cultural norms into their white children, while black mammies give the children the more animal satisfactions of food, comfort, and bodily tenderness, satisfactions which, as Lillian Smith observes in *Killers of the Dream* (1949), the girls will grow up to deny themselves and the boys will grow up to seek from black women. White spinsters and loudmouthed black women, because of their failure or refusal to enter the reproductive myth, are lesser women, less feminine, less desirable, less powerful—and still dependent on men for a living, whether through what Blanche DuBois (in Tennessee Williams' *A Streetcar Named Desire*) calls the kindness of strangers, or what Nancy (in Faulkner's "That Evening Sun" and *Requiem for a Nun*) sees as the business of prostitution.

Inevitably, the mythology carried explicit benefits as well as costs to women and to women writers. Those benefits offered a great deal of family and social power, as long as the woman did not stretch her domain of actual authority beyond the domestic. They offered high social status, economic comfort, and a measure of safety and security to those white women who married well and the black women who worked for them "like family." Inevitably as well, women and women writers varied in the ways in which they responded to the myths: some internalized them; some resisted in numerous ways; some were baffled and conflicted. In general, because writing required or produced some degree of consciousness, some slippage between myth and person, the writers deliberately or inadvertently offered resistance to the mythology, from Kate Chopin at the beginning of the period to Harriette Arnow (1908–1986) at the end. This would have been the case even if the myths had been benign; since in most cases they were not, southern women's writing of the period is sometimes startlingly explicit.

Thus while modernity—cities, mills, cars, radios—brought tangible opportunities for new and materially different ways of living, southern women writers' responses to modernity sought (or feared) change in less tangible arenas: structures of identity, constructions of gender, dichotomies of race.

Just as there was no inevitable link between modernization and women's increasing freedom, there was also no inevitable connection between modernist experimentation and radical ideas. Thus while European and American modernism offered writers tangible opportunities for literary experimentation and change, such as representing deep interiority or using juxtaposition as a structuring device, southern women used traditional as well as experimental form to reflect upon cultural and ideological—rather than primarily aesthetic—change. Frances Newman, for example, used her extraordinary narrative experimentation in the service of startling challenges to upper-class myths of southern women's (a)sexuality, while Caroline Gordon used traditional southern settings such as Civil War battlegrounds for stories that pushed at the edges of the myths of southern women's distaste for violence.

The question that drew all these writers' attention and concern, however they articulated them and in whatever media, remained fundamental: how would the traditional myths of southern womanhood fare in the twentieth century? To answer this question, writers explored in a number of thematic directions. Because literal reproductive identity was central to the myth in all its "roles," sexuality and maternity came in for direct questioning. Because reproduction of class and race were so clearly linked through the legitimization of marriage and the raising of legitimate children, marriage and mothering were taken up. Because legal separation of the races was essential to the myth, race came under question. And because the myth required, above all, dependence on men and fidelity and obedience to itself, women's autonomy became a subject for question. At bottom, then, where the myths of southern womanhood coalesced in constructing a divided, hierarchical, and dependent view of human relations, southern women writers imagined alternatives that broke boundaries, toppled hierarchies, and led away from dependence. The very act of writing was an act that wrested, out of subjection, new subjectivities. Sometimes the changes were too fearful to sustain.

Kate Chopin's *The Awakening* (1899) and Harriette Arnow's *The Dollmaker* (1954), framing the period in question, illustrate some of these tendencies and demonstrate the persistence of both the myth of southern womanhood and women's grappling with the problems it creates. Harriette Arnow's little-remarked novel *The Dollmaker,* set during World War II, articulates these issues clearly. The dollmaker of the title is a large, strong mountain-farming woman named Gertie Nevels, whose very body defies myths of southern women's frailty and dependence on men. In the opening scene, she overrides military men's authority in order to save her son by performing a roadside tracheotomy. Her creativity links her to the woods and a traditional agrarian lifestyle. She makes play-pretties for her most imaginative daughter out of natural objects and plans, when she is able to envision a compassionate Christ, to carve his face out of a large piece of cherry wood.

Gertie's strength, creativity, and autonomy unravel as the novel progresses. From the start, her mother's unquestioning beliefs in male and biblical superiority—also part of the agrarian myth—undercut Gertie's independent thinking by introducing uncertainty and guilt. Although Gertie finds a way to buy the farm she has always wanted to work, her husband, Clovis, is ordered to Detroit to work in the armament factories. Obeying her husband, she takes the children with her to join him there. In Detroit—which can be read as the modern South—she confronts modern life: urban ghettoes, mass transit, public school, and technological "conveniences" like her new Icy Heart refrigerator that dominates, appropriately, the small kitchen. While Clovis takes instantly to modernity—as a man, it only reinforces his authority as breadwinner and decision maker—Gertie and the children swing wildly and variously from adaptation to resistance. Slowly, Gertie builds a new sense of self to survive modernity. Whether that is a gain or a loss is left open for the reader's interpretation by the final scene, in which Gertie carves up her block of cherry wood to provide material for factory-made dolls, the income from which will support the family. If the myth of southern womanhood has at its (icy) heart female dependence on men, Gertie Nevels challenges it at every level, from physical to emotional to creative to spiritual independence. Yet her own acquiescence in the myth checks her challenge, in both the traditional and modern settings.

One arena left largely unaddressed by Arnow is that of female sexuality and desire. Kate Chopin had located eros at the heart of her own very early challenge to the myth, *The Awakening* (originally entitled "A Solitary Soul"). In 1899, Kate Chopin had linked Edna Pontellier's discovery of and responses to her creativity, her autonomy, and her identity with her discovery of—and responses to—her sexual desire. For Edna, whose desires are mostly heterosexual, Gertie's quest is complicated by dependence on men for sexual intimacy and passion. Can a woman who leaves behind marriage vows of obedience and fidelity as well as self-denying traditions of mothering, who moves to her own "pigeon house" and begins to earn her own living, nevertheless satisfy her needs for intimacy and sexuality? Edna's discoveries and the choices she makes as a mother and a wife in 1899 still shock readers a century later. The intuitions of the "beginnings of a life" that she follows lead her to death/birth in the sea, for they are impossible to materialize on land. The women who survive in Edna's South either follow the myth of the "mother-woman," finding sexual and personal satisfaction in domesticity, or follow the myth of the spinster woman/artist, whose work precludes almost all sensuality in her personal life.

Although writing from black women during the period 1900–1960 emanates largely from New York's Harlem Renaissance, their work treats myths that grew out of and still defined southern women. Zora Neale Hurston, however, was herself a true southerner and wrote of the myths of southern womanhood as they worked within the black community. The story of Janie in *Their Eyes Were Watching God* (1937) shows that the myths parallel those for white women and those that whites invented for black women. Rather than the white mythical "mammy," there is the black "lady"— sitting on a "high place" as the protagonist's grandmother wishes for Janie, safe from the low life of the hoi polloi. That "lady" is likely to be light skinned; according to a representative woman, Janie's paleness will allow her to "class off" rather than, as in white mythology of the mulatta, serve as an ideal lover for white men. Otherwise she resembles the white lady, too: as Janie learns when she is the wife of ambitious Joe Starks, she must model womanhood for the community's women in her obedience to her husband, her restrained body (Janie's hair must be kept hidden), and her silence.

At the other end of the spectrum, what white mythology saw as the (black) loudmouth and whore is transformed, in *Their Eyes,* into an ideal of a sexual woman speaking freely. Janie's taking the very black and very playful Tea Cake as a lover allows her to learn to speak and shoot, and offers her sexuality and apparent equality. Hurston's positive rendering of their move "down" to the "muck" life near Lake Okeechobee sustains her remythologizing of the black field-working class in general. But the effort to remythologize black women comes up, once again, against the tradition of male power. Tea Cake's need to demonstrate his superiority is the flaw in the new myth; Hurston ends, much like Chopin, with a retreat from relationship and a move into the romantic imagination. Demythologizing black—and white—myths of black women is more successful than inventing a new story that can connect sexuality with creativity, autonomy, and identity. Hurston's efforts, however, extend to reinventing theology and religious practice to create a myth that will make black women whole.

Similar questions thread through Elizabeth Madox Roberts' all-white *The Time of Man* (1926). The novel—written in high modernist style—tells the story of a lower-class mountain woman, Ellen Chesser, daughter of an itinerant worker and his wife. The novel begins on the road as Ellen traces her name into the air, suggesting the focus of the novel on her interiority and her identity. Like Janie, Ellen struggles with class mythologies of the lady; like Edna, she struggles with joining her sexuality and her identity; like Gertie, she contends with the links between traditional southern religion and mythical womanhood. Another modernist novel of the mountains, *Call Home the Heart* (1932) takes a mountain woman as protagonist as well but puts her into a different narrative, the narrative of modernization that Gertie Nevels undergoes. Olive Tilford Dargan's (1869–1968) protagonist, Ishma, leaves her husband to move down the hills to urban life and textile mill labor. Her involvement in unionizing and in socialist thought takes her into more radical questioning of numerous social myths than most southern women characters of the period. Indeed, she seems ready to complete a narrative that leads wholly away from southern womanhood's constraints and benefits, until—astonishingly—she is diverted by her own sudden racism and longing for the natural and spiritual powers of the mountains. In a confusing conclusion, Ishma seems to return to a world that has no racial, sexual, class, or labor-related struggles, but whose cost, if it is even seen as a cost, is a return to the role of dependent wife and mother.

Other novelists of the period engaged in similar advances and retreats. Grace Lumpkin (1892?–1980), famous as a proletarian novelist, recanted in her autobiographical "Full Circle" and returned to the Episcopalian faith of her youth. Her sister, Katharine Du Pre Lumpkin (1897–1988), however, sustained her challenge to normative southern values, particularly racial but also gender myths, as she recounts in her remarkable autobiography *The Making of a Southerner* (1947). Katharine Lumpkin left the South, became a sociologist, taught in New England, and never married. Her sister Grace's best-known novel today is *The Wedding* (1939). Probably the most famous woman writer of the period in the South was, at least in her time, Ellen Glasgow. Glasgow's career had begun in the nineteenth century; her last work, the autobiographical *The Woman Within,* was published posthumously in 1954. Much of her career focused on the various forms of what she called "evasive idealism"—another phrase for which could be "southern myths." In *Virginia* (1913), she shows the costs of following the myth as an ideal southern lady loses her power, her confidence, and her identity, as she watches her husband, a modern playwright, fall in love with a more autonomous woman. In *Life and Gabriella* (1916), on the other hand, she portrays a woman who emerges from southern mythology to live in New York and fall in love with a western man. Similarly, Mary Johnston's 1913 feminist novel *Hagar* moves her protagonist outside the South and in love with a nonsouthern man in order to permit her to leave behind the myth. Glasgow later came to other terms with the myth of southern womanhood on native turf, in *Barren Ground* (1925). Instead of allowing her protagonist to work and marry in the North, she brings her home again to the land and makes her a progressive farmer. Using modern scientific farming methods, Dorinda Oakley as a grown woman manages to make more than a living, to marry if only for companionship, and to wreak polite revenge on the one passionate love of her life, who had deserted her when they were both young and she was pregnant. It may not be a satisfactory challenge to the myth, but Glasgow's remythologizing, like Hurston's, at least allows the protagonist to survive on her own new terms in her southern home.

The 1920s saw the period's most concentrated interest in sexuality until after 1960. Zelda Fitzgerald was not only the first flapper, challenging southern myths of gentility for women, but also a writer whose stories—both literally and figuratively—were appropriated by the more famous writer who was her husband. Zelda's decline into mental illness, the product of a convergence of numerous factors, can be read in part as a form of resignation to and entry into the myth she challenged as a girl. Frances Newman, the single librarian at Georgia Tech whose novels scandalized many in the 1920s, wrote explicitly about female sexuality, breaking taboos and demythologizing privileged southern womanhood. Both her novels take place in the high society set in Richmond, Atlanta, and Charleston; in her first, *The Hard-Boiled Virgin* (1926), she questions the myth of virginity by showing its consequences on her protagonist; in *Dead Lovers Are Faithful Lovers* (1928), she questions the myth of the man as prize for the ultimate female competition by dividing her narrative into stories of the wife and the would-be mistress of the male object of desire. Evelyn Scott, who ran off with the dean of the medical school at Tulane University, similarly questions the myths of motherhood in her personal narrative, *Escapade* (1923), in which she records with pitiless honesty her reactions to childbirth, mothering, and living with a man in South America.

Katherine Anne Porter's struggles with the myth of southern womanhood were hardly limited to her fiction. As her biographer has shown, Porter—like Faulkner—perpetrated her own myth of aristocratic heritage, enjoying the role of great lady at the same time she enjoyed the autonomy of single womanhood. And as with Faulkner, Porter's fiction questions and challenges the myth more directly and piercingly than did her public persona. In stories like "Flowering Judas," Porter depicts the sexism and sexual exploitation even within the revolutionary left. In "Old Mortality" and *Pale Horse, Pale Rider* (1939) a young Miranda, like Flannery O'Connor's later rebellious girls, longs for a life of adventure, independence, and creativity—and for passionate romance. When she unravels some of the truth about her family predecessor, a still very young Miranda understands more fully the contradictions between romance and autonomy, contradictions that have no doubt contributed to her own failed marriage. Later, as a journalist during World War I, Miranda continues to try to separate truth from hype—this time masculine war hype—while she is engaged in a passionate romance with Adam, all-men. Her near-death experience, and Adam's actual death, during the flu epidemic shape her sense of gender's reality and possibilities in a profoundly cynical direction: it is all a pose, a fake, and she will sustain the fiction of gender until she is allowed to die. Arguably Miranda is the unnamed protagonist of "Holiday," a story of resuscitation. In a setting of dramatic gender dichotomies, those of a German farm family in East Texas, the protagonist recovers from her unnamed loss through a largely intuitive relationship with a servant who is so grotesquely maimed as to be at first unrecognizable as a woman and a member of the family. In the midst of death—the death of the mother—the vacationing "Miranda" and Ottilie celebrate life. This resolution defies the mythology of southern womanhood on almost every count.

Later in the period, the responses to the mythology of southern woman-hood by women writers most likely to be thought of—Flannery O'Connor and Eudora Welty—seem subdued by comparison. Perhaps, however, as Louise Westling's *Sacred Groves and Ravaged Gardens* (1985) suggests, their work is instead more subtle. One of the most powerful renderings of sexual desire in print—as experienced through the prism of privileged southern womanhood—appears in Welty's short story "At the Landing," a story in which the protagonist's beautiful, eager, and desirous misunder-standing of the meaning of sex to the wild boy she loves results in what seems to be a deliberate decision to be multiply raped. Welty shows un-flinchingly the power of the myths of southern gender to filter desire through antithetical, if not antagonistic, narratives for women and men. O'Connor's stories of female desire such as "Good Country People" portray women's sexuality in close relation to their rage: it is her angry intellectuals and her mean teenagers who, contra Welty, seek sex. In both Welty and O'Connor, however, the challenge to myths of southern womanhood is evi-dent; by showing the consequences of a beautiful dream of sex and the link between sex and rage, the challenge to the dominant myth of asexuality is taken into another stage of complication and depth. Other aspects of the myth of southern womanhood, in particular the myth of the white lady, are more obviously taken on by O'Connor and Welty. Both place their "ladies" into narratives that force them to deal with another class. In O'Connor, one thinks of Mrs. Greenleaf watching her tenant writhe in religious ecstasy, or Julian's mother assaulted by the woman she thought to "help." In Welty, the "optimist's daughter" confronts the meaning of her dead father's choice of a second wife and thus the meaning of her own attachment to class. Whether the protagonists learn or not, both writers challenge the myth that the southern lady can be a satisfactory norm.

A bit later than the period in question, but in many ways culminating its accomplishments and moving on to new territory, is Ellen Douglas' *Can't Quit You, Baby* (1988). Whereas the myths of southern womanhood had implicitly or explicitly centered on men, Douglas picks up another thread of the story: relationships between women. Earlier southern women writers had addressed this: Edna's friendships with Mme Ratignolle and Mlle Reisz have a life of their own separate from Edna's obsession with Robert; Janie's story is available only because she tells it to her best friend, who grows from hearing it. In *Can't Quit You, Baby,* the focus shifts so that, instead of her past life with her husband, or even her later lover (in New York), the white protagonist's identity is shaped most profoundly in her continuing relationship with her maid, Tweet. In the dissection of its truths, Douglas offers a new story of southern womanhood—white and black—that has more to do with honesty than it does with men.

Lesbian fiction, too, offers a new story of southern womanhood in which the man's role is diminished. Again, *The Awakening* adumbrated this possibility at the beginning of the period. Edna's sensuous attraction to Adèle Ratignolle, and Mlle Reisz's evident passion for Edna, remain on the sidelines, suggesting but not developing an erotic alternative to hetero- or asexuality, both of which complicate southern women's resistances to the traditional myths of identity. Within the period 1900 to 1960, although lesbian and "third sex" writing from Britain and continental Europe flowers, there is less to notice in the American South. Interestingly, southern lesbian writers would write some of the most interesting work of the period to follow: Mab Segrest's essays on southern literature, Minnie Bruce Pratt's poetry, and Amanda Gable's fiction come to mind. But the implications of one southern writer's first novel, which appeared just at the end of the period 1900 to 1960, leave some doubt that this challenge to the myths is any less complicated than the other erotic directions for southern women. Rita Mae Brown's *Rubyfruit Jungle* (1973), named for a character's affectionate description of women's genitals, traces the picaresque adventures of its protagonist from Pennsylvania to Florida to New York. The relationships that matter most to her, over time, are those with her beloved father and her less beloved mother. Her erotic narrative demonstrates, too, the disjunction between gender and sex. There is no guarantee that a sexual relationship between women will avoid the myths of gender. The most moving scenes of the novel record the narrator's difficult reconciliation with her mother, by means of her art, filmmaking.

In the end, then, it seems to be through relationships with other women—mothers, daughters, friends, servants, lovers—that southern women writers begin to articulate new stories about themselves in the modern period.

Re-Visioning the Southern Land

Elizabeth Jane Harrison

In southern literature, the masculine "pastoral impulse"—to feminize the landscape and objectify women characters—is particularly evident. The antebellum South envisioned itself through its literature as a kind of improved paradise or cultivated garden in order to expiate guilt over its system of slavery. This purpose contrasts sharply with the New England vision of a City on a Hill, founded to establish a religious covenant rather than historical oppression. Whatever the origin of the southern garden archetype, it has served the southern white patriarchy for the past two hundred years as an effective metaphor of ownership of land and labor.

In the early nineteenth century, the southern pastoral impulse was employed to help perpetuate the South's myth of aristocratic origins and to defend the slave system. After the Civil War, a second but closely related kind of male pastoral emerged. Late nineteenth-century pastorals written by Thomas Nelson Page and others reiterated a common theme: reconciliation between the South and North accomplished through using the white woman as an instrument of plot. Typically, the pristine plantation daughter was married to a northern soldier to symbolize the healing of the nation. The contented "darky" narrator, another salient feature of the pastoral plot, reinforced the continuance of an oppressive society in which both white women and blacks were viewed as property. The aristocratic white woman's association with pristine nature and cultural refinement—her embodiment of the southern garden—depended on a counterimage, the black or poor white woman. While the genteel lady represented purity, her dark counterpart was objectified as debased sexual desire. Yet ironically, the black or poor white woman also represented the archetypal earth mother that nurtured white and black protagonists alike.

As the nineteenth century waned, the male pastoral became more a hysterical defense of the white patriarchy than a nostalgic idealization of a genteel society. But the southern male pastoral during the Southern Renaissance began to show the influence of the rising social upheaval. Now the threat to property was internal. Movements such as women's suffrage, urbanization, and finally civil rights eroded the power of the white patriarchy. Southern literature reflected fear of these social changes in its portrayal of white and black women characters. Faulkner's *Light in August* (1932), for instance, idealizes the poor white woman Lena Grove as a kind of earth mother, denying her any real agency in the plot. Another of Faulkner's novels, *The Sound and the Fury* (1929), idealizes the black woman protagonist, Dilsey, as an ever giving but one-dimensional "mammy" figure who acts more as symbol than as character. Even black male authors like Jean Toomer in *Cane* (1923) failed to challenge the southern pastoral plot of domination or to question its earth mother archetypes.

For twentieth-century southern women writers, however, the pastoral plot proved problematic. It failed to allow for the psychological development of a woman protagonist. Moreover, the prevailing literary models from the nineteenth century—the plantation romance, local color fiction, and slave narrative—offered no possibilities for developing autonomous female characters. For black women novelists, the challenge to the male pastoral was doubly difficult. Before they could imagine an empowering relationship between women characters and the rural southern landscape, African American writers had to overcome the stigma of racial inferiority. Land for them was associated with slave labor, not with nurturance or empowerment.

Nonetheless, following Willa Cather's groundbreaking midwestern pastoral novel *O Pioneers!* (1913), southern women writers, both white and black, began to develop their own vision and version of pastoral literature. Though not always completely revising the male pastoral plot, these authors offered new possibilities for women characters and set the stage for their contemporary literary successors to continue exploring new plots and characters. This alternative female pastoral, like its corresponding male version, contains specific elements. First, landscape itself figures prominently in the text, but instead of representing southern womanhood, it is re-visioned as an enabling force for the woman protagonist. Her interaction with the land changes from passive association to active identification or cultivation. The second feature of this new pastoral is the representation of the woman protagonist as active agent, even as female hero. Often this protagonist forms significant female friendships across race or class boundaries. Third, the female pastoral reimagines southern community as egalitarian rather than as patriarchal and oppressive; no longer is the pastoral plot concerned with inscribing the patriarchal order.

One challenge to the southern male pastoral in the first half of the twentieth century is the anti–plantation romance, epitomized in *Gone with the Wind* (1936) by Margaret Mitchell (1900–1949) and in the only southern novel by Willa Cather, *Sapphira and the Slave Girl* (1940). In this version of female pastoral, the female protagonist, while developing autonomy, remains a problematic character. Despite Scarlett O'Hara's heroic qualities—notable in a woman brought up under the system of southern chivalry—Mitchell's protagonist remains a static character, her drive for power less a conscious desire to assume a new role in society than an attempt to recreate the old order she rebels from. Furthermore, Scarlett's success is based upon a callous disregard for the lives of others around her, including her sisters, her children, and most glaringly, her black slaves. Still, *Gone with the Wind* inverts plantation romance conventions. First, Scarlett, as Rhett often reminds her, is not a virtuous lady. In addition, she occupies the place of the traditional male hero in the plot. Her drive and determination arise from female as well as male role models, for instance, Grandma Fontaine and Beatrice Tarleton. And there is a nascent possibility of female friendship and community in Scarlett and Melanie's relationship. But even though Mitchell challenges assigned gender roles through Scarlett, she also continues the male pastoral imagery of the southern land as female—the South as violated virgin—and thus her protagonist's quest to protect and possess the land is ultimately undermined. The only way to become a hero in this plot is to be male. Scarlett's ambivalence about her own heroism—her conflicting needs for power and submission—has roots in the controlling motif of landscape.

In *Sapphira and the Slave Girl*, Cather breaks from her earlier celebratory pastorals that she wrote about midwestern farm life. This final novel of the author's career returns to her Virginia heritage to undermine the mythic construction of the southern garden. Unlike Mitchell, Cather shows how female character is linked to landscape only through male characters' eyes. Romance is no longer even the ostensible plot complication. Female community develops at the end of the novel when Sapphira's daughter Rachel helps a slave escape. Yet even here women characters' autonomy is undermined. Because the novel represents plantation life, it ultimately precludes a complete re-visioning of the landscape and characters' relationship to it. Sapphira, the female protagonist, is problematic for reasons similar to those that make Scarlett so. Her grasp and maintenance of power is based upon exploitation of others, particularly her slaves. Like Scarlett, she assumes the role of plantation master while her husband Henry plays the submissive "female" role of plantation mistress. Female authority depends in both novels on an inverted system—not a re-visional one. Other southern women authors during the Renaissance were also unable to imagine a plantation world without domination and oppression. Katherine Anne Porter's group of stories "The Old Order" (in *Flowering Judas*, 1930), for instance, depicts a more benign female authority in the grandmother figure, but the grandmother only assumes control as a substitute for an absent husband.

On the other hand, southern women authors who chose a different southern garden to revise, the small farm or tenant farm, were more successful with their experiments. This kind of female pastoral is best represented in the novels of Ellen Glasgow, Zora Neale Hurston, and Harriette Arnow (1908–1986). Glasgow's two rural novels, *Barren Ground* (1926) and *Vein of Iron* (1935), present women protagonists who derive both identity and strength from their tie to the soil. Dorinda Oakley in *Barren Ground,* while embittered by a broken love affair, fulfills a dream to own and run her own farm and eventually marries another man out of friendship rather than out of passion. Glasgow's female hero derives comfort and purpose out of her relationship with the land. Significantly, the landscape in the novel is featured neither as female or male, but as ungendered. Akin to Cather's female hero Alexandra in *O Pioneers!* Dorinda has a mystical rather than sexual relationship with the earth. This transformed metaphor of the southern garden enables Glasgow to abandon the romance story and contributes to the author's radical plot line: a woman character on a heroic quest to save her family's farm. Still, Dorinda's ability to form female friendships and join any kind of supportive community remains limited; part of the price she pays for autonomy is isolation. However, Ada Fincastle, the protagonist of *Vein of Iron,* is less willful and autonomous than Dorinda; she sacrifices more in order to marry her lover Ralph. Like her fictional predecessor, she chooses her own actions rather than remaining a passive character and at the end of the novel is able to participate in a stable Appalachian community whose values are more egalitarian than patriarchal.

In *Their Eyes Were Watching God* (1937), Hurston creates a female pastoral that is framed by female friendship—protagonist Janie Crawford sharing her story with her friend Pheoby. Although the novel contains a beautiful romance between Janie and Tea Cake, this story does not overshadow Janie's heroic quest for identity and fulfillment. Janie's journey from her first, abusive husband to the end of her second marriage with Joe Clark, who keeps her as a trophy wife, parallels a slave's escape from servitude to freedom, both echoing and transforming a traditional African American plot. With her third relationship Janie finally begins to develop her own identity. Tea Cake, the male protagonist, is a more naturalized figure than Janie; he acts as her enabler, affirming her beauty without objectifying it. Janie is also connected with the rural landscape and community both imagistically and through the plot line. In this way she resembles Julia Peterkin's protagonist in *Scarlet Sister Mary* (1928). Yet, unlike Peterkin's novel, Hurston's ends without a full reconciliation. Janie, while sharing her story with her friend, remains aloof from the community's judgments and prejudices. Like Glasgow, Hurston must separate her female hero from conventional society in order to maintain her autonomy.

Harriette Arnow in *The Dollmaker* (1954) creates a female hero, Gertie Nevels, who pays a different price for her quest for freedom from a traditional role. Like other pastoral protagonists, she develops her strength and identity from her tie to the land, in this case her Kentucky tenant farm. Arnow's depiction of Appalachian landscape is a transformation from earlier women authors' farm novels, such as Elizabeth Madox Roberts' *The Time of Man* (1926) and Edith Summers Kelley's *Weeds* (1923), which end in drudgery and hopelessness. Still, the rural society in which Gertie lives is patriarchal and limiting. She can only establish autonomy as a substitute father figure while her husband is away at war. Once the Nevels family leaves Kentucky in search of a better future in Detroit, Gertie loses her sustaining tie with the land but gains the possibility of creating a new, less restrictive community with the women in her housing project. Ultimately, the vision of Arnow's novel is tragic. Away from the locus of her creativity and power, Gertie gradually succumbs to the dehumanizing struggle for survival in the city. Her final act of destroying her wooden sculpture, while life-giving to her family, symbolizes a defeat for her heroic quest for identity. Perhaps of all the pastoral heroes, Dorinda Oakley and Janie Crawford are the only ones who successfully define independent roles and identities. All the female protagonists, however, are depicted as active agents in the plot, sustained by the land they belong to rather than symbolic of it.

Not all southern women authors of this period, of course, were concerned with re-visioning the southern landscape. Some, like Flannery O'Connor and Carson McCullers, developed characters with internal and individualized spiritual conflicts, while others, like Caroline Gordon, created plot lines from a male perspective. In *Strange Fruit* (1944), Lillian Smith challenges the objectification and naturalization of female characters through an indictment of southern mores, but she does not envision a positive alternative. Eudora Welty's rural landscapes and communities often sidestep questions of gender and social roles. *Delta Wedding* (1946) contains a pastoral setting, but it focuses more on familial relationships than on female autonomy. Yet in these attempts to imagine new pastoral imagery, plot and characters are significant. For subsequent authors of the modern and postmodern period, the quest for female identity is a given. New roles and communities for women have already been envisioned.

Ultimately, however, the female pastoral as defined in the first half of the twentieth century is a transitory genre. Unlike the southern Agrarians of the 1920s and 1930s, "agrarian" women authors of the period urged a radical restructuring of the society rather than a return to traditional values. Curiously, for both, pastoral is a means of displacement for class mobility occurring during periods of urbanization. But while the Agrarians and other male pastoralists like William Faulkner resisted change through nostalgic evocation of the past, their female counterparts responded to the same or similar phenomena by experimenting with gender roles and reimagining rural societies. After World War II, the rural South became less a reality and more a historical and mythical concept. The concern with landscape shifted from the farm to the towns and cities, signaling new fictional concerns and possibilities.

Women Writers of the Harlem Renaissance

Susan Morrison Hebble

When Alain Locke triumphantly and defiantly declared the "New Negro" born, he did so bringing forth a male image, a male idea. The landmark March 1925 issue of *Survey Graphic,* filled exclusively with the works of black artists and writers, boasts on its cover a portrait, intense and distinctive, of an African American man, and its contents include the contributions of twenty men and only four women. Certainly Locke invites women to join the movement when he insists that the modern Negro must shake off the stereotypes of the "'aunties,' 'uncles' and 'mammies.'" Yet he offers little in the way of specific redefinition for African American women. In her eminent analysis *Women of the Harlem Renaissance* (1995), Cheryl Wall determines that Locke's pivotal essay, "Enter the New Negro," never overtly denies women a place in the proposed new paradigm, yet his essay and the entire journal in which it is contained emit a decidedly "masculinist cast." Locke remained a central figure of the Harlem Renaissance, his masculine focus consciously or unconsciously dictating a general tone for the movement. In a 1987 study of three women writers of the Harlem Renaissance entitled *Color, Sex, and Poetry,* Gloria T. Hull asserts that Locke "behaved misogynistically and actively favored men." Hull maintains that strong "antifemale prejudice" permeated the Renaissance as "male attitudes toward women impinged upon them, [and] men's so-called personal biases were translated into something larger that had deleterious effects." Even as scholars have considered the Harlem Renaissance in subsequent decades, the focus has remained essentially male oriented; the "New Negro" has been implicitly regarded as the "New *Male* Negro." However, the movement that became known as the Harlem Renaissance was not, after all, gender specific. There were women involved. And these women were involved in large numbers and in complex and significant ways: they were writers, artists, musicians; and they were teachers, editors, collaborators, and activists in a movement that reached beyond the literary and into the political, beyond the intellectual and into the practical.

Before we get ahead of ourselves, let us consider some of the factors that made the Harlem Renaissance possible. Like their white counterparts, the faction of American writers romantically self-described as "the Lost Generation," the black intelligentsia found their lives and culture in upheaval following World War I. While the white literati deemed the future as static or decadent, the "niggerati," as Zora Neale Hurston later labeled them, relished the dynamic flux in which they found themselves and took hold of the moment for its potential for reinvention. Indeed, the African American was in a position to gain opportunity and authority as never before in America. Not only had black men participated in World War I as free Americans, but they also entered a new decade, the 1920s, with more education and more professional potential than ever before. The founding of such organizations as the National Association for the Advancement of Colored People and the National Urban League promoted the growing racial confidence and optimism needed for what Locke called a "metamorphosis" in black identity from the myth of the Old Negro to the generation of the New Negro.

But probably the most significant impetus for radical change was the migration of southern blacks to the northern cities. In his landmark text, *Voices from the Harlem Renaissance* (1976), Nathan Huggins points out that heretofore "[t]he traditional 'place' of blacks was in the South, where share-cropping and tenant-farming locked them into the peonage of the post-Reconstruction era." The Great Migration, as it came to be called, afforded the chance for more money and more opportunity, and it necessitated a redefinition of identity. Indeed, Locke insisted that with the migration came an obligation to shake off the old identity: "The migrant masses, shifting from countryside to city, hurdle several generations of experience in a leap, but more important, the same thing happens spiritually in the life-attitudes and self-expression of the Young Negro, in his poetry, his art, his education, and his new outlook." Thus the reinvention of the Negro seemed to call for a shunning of the rural, agrarian focus associated with the South and an embrace of things urban and new. Energizing this change was the fact that the migration brought together into somewhat narrowly determined neighborhoods blacks from all backgrounds. Cheryl Wall identifies this significance as more than incidental: "For the first time since the advent of slavery had ruptured the ancestral community, people of African descent could through their group expression—and the art it generated— forge a new unity." Among southern women writers, Zora Neale Hurston, Alice Dunbar-Nelson, Georgia Douglas Johnson (1880–1966), and Anne Spencer (1882–1970) proved to be the key players in the movement.

Locke and cohorts like Claude McKay and James Weldon Johnson pick up where W. E. B. Du Bois left off when he famously defined the "double consciousness" of the African American in *The Souls of Black Folks* (1903) two decades earlier. Du Bois argued that "One ever feels his twoness,—an American, a Negro; two souls, two thoughts, two unreconciled strivings; two warring ideals in one dark body, whose dogged strength alone keeps it from being torn asunder." Certainly the New Negro attempts to reconcile those "warring ideals" through art, literature, music, and politics. And this duality is essential in defining the African American man. Yet, considering the African American woman, one must realize that a sort of "triple consciousness" comes into play, for there are not two but three "warring ideals"—those of the American, the Negro, and the female. The "warring" metaphor itself takes on an altered resonance when we cast in the feminine element. Indeed, in 1919 when the Negro men of the 369th Regiment proudly marched up Fifth Avenue to Harlem, were not the women standing to the side? The women of the Harlem Renaissance were keenly aware of the precarious position of being just inside this exciting movement, while at the same time facing a host of rigid gender expectations. Essentially, the intense focus on race and racial identity suppressed even further issues of gender and sexism.

In *Color, Sex, and Poetry*, Gloria T. Hull remarks on the curious position of women, thrust forward into a new era, yet held back in the old. In her study of Alice Dunbar-Nelson, Angelina Weld Grimké (1880–1958), and Georgia Douglas Johnson, Hull points out that the women constantly faced this dichotomy. While their participation in the salon discussions of the movement were encouraged, the Renaissance patriarchy continued to frown upon women participating in less decorous ways. Hull refers to the "Harlem Renaissance fraternization" when she points out that "a great deal of this professionally vital male socializing occurred after hours in bars and over bottles" at a time when women's smoking and drinking were considered "appalling." Moreover, in terms of the migration, women were not the members of the Negro race rushing to New York City. Their duties most often required them to remain wherever their husbands, children, or parents were. In fact, few of the women writers actually migrated from South to North (most were actually from the North) and few actually lived in Harlem for any length of time.

Recently critics have recognized that Washington, considered a southern rather than northern city, may have been more of a cultural center for the female literary community than Harlem. Many of the principal intellectuals, including Grimké, Dunbar-Nelson, Hurston, Jessie Redmon Fauset, and Gwendolyn Bennett, lived in Washington for some time. And in practical terms, many of the women of the Harlem Renaissance filled roles that might be termed "traditional" for women of the 1920s and 1930s yet were important to the movement. In Harlem, Washington, and Lynchburg, Virginia, women such as Fauset, Spencer, and Johnson served as hostesses, welcoming the principal players of the Renaissance into their homes for lively forums that became essential to the propagation of the movement. By offering a comfortable venue for discussing and exploring the importance of the redefinition of black identity, and even more directly by connecting new artists with the publishers and patrons who were able to bring the New Negro to the masses, these women nurtured male and female writers of the period in spiritual and practical ways. Johnson's "Saturday Nighters" in her Washington home were possibly the most effective of these salon gatherings of the time. While these gatherings in Washington were certainly valuable, Gloria Hull insists that many women writers "were adversely affected by geographical immobility and being located away from the New York social and literary scene." In the most practical terms, women based in the South were less able to move to the cultural hub of Harlem because of their obligations to their homes and families. To their credit, these women staked a claim in the movement nonetheless.

And the women of the Harlem Renaissance were never merely polite hostesses. Several women of the Harlem Renaissance maintained positions of clearly relevant authority within the movement. Some worked as journalists (such as Dunbar-Nelson, Johnson, and Mary Church Terrell), some as critics (Gwendolyn Bennett, Marita Bonner, Jessie Fauset), some as educators and scholars (Bonner, Spencer, Clarissa Scott Delaney, Dunbar-Nelson, Hurston), some as editors (Dunbar-Nelson, Fauset), and many as activists. By and large, the most impressive contributions of these women to the Harlem Renaissance are their poems, novels, short stories, and plays. According to exhaustive research by Lorraine Elena Roses and Ruth Elizabeth Randolph (*Harlem Renaissance and Beyond,* 1996), more than one hundred black women were writing, and most of those were publishing their work during the Harlem Renaissance. And in spite of the determination to shake off the dust of the South and shift the cultural and mental focus northward, women writers such as Spencer, Johnson, Dunbar-Nelson, and Hurston maintained strong ties to the South.

Poets Anne Spencer and Georgia Douglas Johnson were regarded as among the central figures of the Renaissance, their poetry at times traditionally lyrical but also often reflecting the imagistic experimentalism of the time. In an interesting contrast to the primarily urban image evoked by the Harlem Renaissance, Anne Spencer is strongly associated with the Virginia garden that she tended almost religiously and from which she wrote most of her poetry. The garden offered an appealing agrarian retreat for active members of the Harlem Renaissance as well as a stopover for those artists traveling between the North and South. Spencer's involvement in the Renaissance began with the publication of the poem "Before the Feast of Shushan" when she was forty. Thereafter, her poems could be found in such essential Renaissance journals as *Opportunity* and *Palms*. However, much of Spencer's poetry explores nature and the female identity, two subjects most likely seen as irrelevant to the movement. Yet Spencer occasionally headed her work with the declaration "I proudly love being a Negro Woman." Such blatant feminist pride from the woman called "a sophisticated genteel lady poet" may have been merely amusing to the male literati.

While Spencer adored her Lynchburg home, finding unusual support from her husband and her family, Georgia Douglas Johnson resided in Washington because of her husband's career as a lawyer and politician. After her husband's death, Johnson became one of the best-known members of the Harlem Renaissance not only for her famous "Saturday Nighters" but for her literary output in virtually every major periodical of the movement. Johnson published over two hundred poems and wrote several plays in the 1920s and 1930s. While maintaining her dedication to the most important literary movement in black history, Johnson worked a number of jobs to support her two sons and the destitute artists that occasionally stayed in what Johnson termed her "Half-Way House." Like Spencer, Johnson worked avidly to bring about change for the African American. Both women fought for civil rights. Indeed Spencer was instrumental in establishing Lynchburg's NAACP chapter, and Johnson's energies frequently went into political, racial, and feminist concerns.

Alice Dunbar-Nelson was also a prolific writer who was encouraged to write and publish by her first husband, highly regarded black poet Paul Laurence Dunbar. Although her marriage to Dunbar lasted only six years, Dunbar-Nelson maintained a respected position in the movement. She wrote in several genres, but her short stories in particular drew on her experiences growing up in New Orleans. She often peppered her fiction with French and Creole characters and frequently used New Orleans as a setting. Even some of those stories based in the North evoke in theme or plot images of the South. One of the most anthologized of these stories, "Hope Deferred," centers on a newly married couple trying to make a life in Harlem. Unable to find a job as an engineer, the well-educated husband resorts to waiting on tables but eventually is jailed after an altercation with a white patron. The story closes with the woman suggesting that they look to the South for opportunity: "Your [jail cell] window faces the south, Louis. Look up and out of it all the while you are here, for it is there, in our own southland, that you will find the realization of your dream."

Possibly the most famous female writer to come out of the Harlem Renaissance was one for whom the South was essential to her work. Although her major work came relatively late to the scene, Zora Neale Hurston offered the voice of the black oral tradition with its folktales and songs. With the 1924 publication of the short story "Drenched in Light," Hurston introduced the voice of the Deep South to a body of literature that was becoming notable for its seemingly genteel lyricism. Possibly more than any writer of the time, Hurston attempted to place the African American identity of the South in the flux of this movement borne out of the North. Hurston produced little of literary significance until her first novel in 1934 because of her intense focus not on literature but on anthropological studies of black folk tales. *Jonah's Gourd Vine* came out as the Renaissance was in decline, but it and her subsequent works were welcomed for their presentation of an authentic but largely neglected voice resonating with tradition and history in a contemporary context.

Despite complaints that the women of the Harlem Renaissance failed to address the issues that the male literati deemed most pertinent, these women continued to write and to explore topics that concerned the contemporary African American. In her preface to *Shadowed Dreams: Women's Poetry of the Harlem Renaissance* (1989), Maureen Honey insists that upon review, the poetry of the women of the Harlem Renaissance does indeed "exhibit the qualities of 'New Negro' writing: identification with the race, a militant proud spirit, anger at racism, determination to fight oppression, rejection of white culture, and an attempt to reconstruct an invisible heritage. . . . Indeed, fully half of the poetry by women published from 1918 through 1931 . . . dealt explicitly with race issues, and nearly as many women's poems were published as those by men." One might consider, then, the imagistic poems of Angelina Weld Grimké (descendant of abolitionists Sarah and

Angelina Grimké) such as "The Black Finger" and "Tenebris," both of which evoke a sense of pride yet a sense of vulnerability. And in 1922 Georgia Douglas Johnson published *Bronze,* a collection of poetry specifically focusing on race issues. In that volume, one finds such angry poems as "Question," which addresses the fear that feeds "the whirling maggot sands / Of prejudice." Interestingly, *Bronze* is often considered the weakest of Johnson's four volumes of poetry, but it is a volume written in response to claims that her 1918 collection *The Heart of a Woman* was not race conscious enough. And Anne Spencer's "White Things" is a distinctly angry poem about racism that identifies the destructive, imperialistic, and dehumanizing effects of racism not only on blacks but on the fearful, cowardly "white things" who attempt to dominate blacks.

As they wrote poetry and fiction, the women of the Renaissance walked the fine line between the conflicting ideals of the feminine and the racial. In so doing, many of these women addressed issues neglected by men but so very relevant to black women: primarily marriage and motherhood. From a male perspective, the business of marriage and motherhood were nonissues to the movement, and sexuality was a taboo topic. As Locke calls for and defines a new identity for Uncle Tom and Sambo, he does little to suggest what might become of the "auntie," the "mammy." Arguably, the male response to the stereotype of the black female was to recast black womanhood into an idealization of noble domesticity or moral motherhood. Safe at home in this role, such a figure offers little controversy, little contemplation. She becomes a figure defined not by the white racist stereotype, but by a black male imagination. As Maureen Honey asserts, the redefinition of the mammy as a glorified mother figure is illustrated by Alain Locke's selection of a portrait of a black mother and child as frontispiece for the *New Negro,* a black literary anthology that drew from the success of *Survey Graphic.* The title of the portrait is "The Brown Madonna," and that reverential portrait is one of the few feminine images Locke has to offer. While the metaphor for new life is suitable to the movement, for Locke intends to celebrate the rebirth of the Negro, women writers were less likely to exalt the glorified image of maternity. Rather, women ventured to reclaim and celebrate the humanity and sensuality of their own beauty. Anne Spencer's "Black Man o' Mine" certainly celebrates love as physical, erotic, and intense:

> Black Man o' Mine,
> If the world were your lover,
> It could not give what I give to you,
> Or the ocean would yield and you could discover

Its ages of treasure to hold and to view;
Could it fill half the measure of my heart's portion . . .
Just for you living, just for you giving all this devotion,
Black man o' mine.

Black man o' mine,
As I hush and caress you, close to my heart
All your loving is just your needing what is true;
Then with your passing dark comes my darkest part,
For living without your love is only rue.
Black man o' mine, if the world were your lover
It could not give what I give to you.

The men of the Harlem Renaissance were reluctant to acknowledge any erotic dimension to the writing of women. Heretofore, historians and critics have assumed that female sexual expression was well left to the jazz and blues singers of the 1920s and 1930s. Indeed, recent criticism has suggested that the rejection of the "mammy" figure freed women writers to consider themselves as vibrant, multifaceted, sensual beings, in spite of the implicit determination of male writers of the movement to deny this recast image of black womanhood.

Keenly aware of the sexist undercurrent of the movement, female writers found themselves writing about the concerns and sorrows of the black woman's situation. Many fiction writers, such as the well-regarded authors Jessie Fauset and Nella Larsen, centered on women of the black middle class. Issues of marriage and motherhood, but also issues regarding the conflict between the black and white cultures, such as the fair-skinned heroine passing as white, filled these novels. The common thread of the novels of the Harlem Renaissance most certainly is that of the search for identity, the hero or heroine seeking to define himself or herself while defining the New Negro. While Fauset's *There Is Confusion* (1924), *Plum Bun* (1929), and *Comedy, American Style* (1933) gave realistic portrayals of middle-class black American women dealing with contemporary race concerns, her third novel, *The Chinaberry Tree* (1931), has a southern focus as it tells the story of a slave woman whose love for her master changes after she experiences freedom. Nella Larsen's two novels, *Quicksand* (1928) and *Passing* (1929), were also lauded for their portrayals of members of the black bourgeoisie grappling with issues of black identity in an otherwise comfortable middle-class existence. But the first of those novels calls on the main character to look to the South in order to define herself.

In *Quicksand,* the protagonist, Helga Crane, struggles to find an identity as a mulatto woman. She is in a psychological limbo because she is unfulfilled in either the black community or the white community. After wandering about, failing to find solace in Harlem or Denmark, she marries a black preacher, with whom she settles in Alabama, hoping to embrace and be embraced by some vague racial heritage. Yet Helga comes to realize that she has no place in the Deep South, little connection with the people there, and no love for the man she has married. Seeing that the marriage is a mistake, Helga finds herself unable to leave her children. Indeed, as the novel closes, Helga discovers that she is pregnant with her fifth child. Larsen certainly suggests that a loveless marriage precludes a fruitful search for identity, and at their worst, marriage and even motherhood may result in a sort of spiritual paralysis.

Zora Neale Hurston was one of the few Renaissance writers little concerned with maintaining a northern focus in her works. For Hurston, the search for personal identity for the black woman must involve the South. *Their Eyes Were Watching God* (1937) was published at the close of the Renaissance, but it is often cited as one of the most important works of the period. The protagonist, Janie, sets out on a search for identity comparable to Helga's, and like Helga, Janie finds her search leading her further South. However, whereas Larsen's antiheroine sinks more deeply into discontent, Janie's spiritual journey is positive. With each of her three marriages, the first two of which result in frustration and spiritual discontent, Janie is able to claim more of herself, and she becomes stronger and more independent as she learns who she is and what she needs from life. While the story seems to end tragically, for her true love dies at her own hand, Janie is an autonomous person at novel's end. Still, fate helps Janie along on her journey: she escapes her suffocating second marriage only because her husband dies, and she remains childless throughout the novel, a fact that affords her a certain mobility for which Helga desperately longs. Essentially, the traditional entrapments for women—marriage, motherhood, male-defined gender roles—do not arrest Janie's personal growth.

The poems of the Harlem Renaissance are less overt in their depiction of women in crisis. But from a feminist perspective one can see the poetry addressing both race and gender issues. In "Calling Dreams," Georgia Douglas Johnson announces, "The right to make my dreams come true / I ask, nay, I demand of life." While this call echoes the poetry of male writers who demand the New Negro rise to his dreams of racial pride, it also suggests that as a woman Johnson determines to rise and wake, "And stride into the morning-break!" Anne Spencer, an only child, offers a sort of warning to the black sisterhood in "Letter to My Sister." With a sense of futility and stasis, she declares, "It is dangerous for a woman to defy the gods." Her suggestion for dealing with men, then, is this:

> Lock your heart, then quietly,
> And lest they peer within,
> Light no lamp when dark comes down
> Raise no shade for sun.

As Maureen Honey points out, "[I]mages of entrapment, masking, and burial appear regularly in these poems [by women], at times explicitly in conjunction with references to men." In "The Heart of a Woman," the title poem of Georgia Douglas Johnson's first volume of poetry, Johnson alludes to the sense of confinement for women. Johnson describes the female heart as a bird thwarted in its attempt to fly. The bird

> falls back with the night,
> And enters some alien cage in its plight,
> And tries to forget it has dreamed of the stars
> While it breaks, breaks, breaks on the sheltering bars.

Alice Dunbar-Nelson's "I Sit and Sew" underscores the same sort of frustration in the speaker's description of the "uselessness" of a woman's lot. Sometimes blatantly, sometimes elliptically, the writings of many of these women address the challenges of narrowly defined gender roles.

While some writers find tragic heroism in the black woman who endures the suffering of raising children in a racist society, others argue the futility of bearing children at all. Angelina Weld Grimké was a typical Renaissance writer in that much of her work is clearly borne out of the urban Harlem experience. Yet in some of her more powerful work, she focuses on the devastation of lynchings, a practice primarily associated with the South but which haunted blacks everywhere. Her play *Rachel* (first staged 1916, published 1920) tells of a young woman so horrified by lynching and by the racist society that propagates such an act that she decides she will never bear children into such a world. In *The Closing Door* Grimké offers a similar scenario with the tragic story of a woman so distraught over her brother's lynching that she takes the life of her own son. Georgia Douglas Johnson's poem "Motherhood" crystalizes this wrenching idea that a black woman might so fear for her child that she would rather deny a child life and herself motherhood:

> Don't knock on my door, little child,
> I cannot let you in;
> You know not what a world this is
> Of cruelty and sin.
>
> . . . .
>
> You do not know the monster men
> Inhabiting the earth.
> Be still, be still, my precious child,
> I cannot give you birth.

The poem, like the stories of Larsen and Grimké, addresses racism, but from a decidedly feminine position. While the works of many of the male writers of the Harlem Renaissance are filled with anger and fury over the racist conditions of the country, their work is primarily prideful and self-righteous. It offers a call to arms and a conscious belief that the movement could cause dramatic change through the arts. For women, on the other hand, that optimism for redefining what it means to be black in America is tempered by the realities of being a black woman in America, a wife and a mother. Hence we find the affirmative from Georgia Douglas Johnson—"I rise! I wake!" she exclaims in "Calling Dreams." And we hear the stubborn joy in Anne Spencer's declaration of pride in being a Negro woman. But we also feel the ache of motherhood in *The Closing Door* and the suffering and sacrifice of black womanhood in such works as Spencer's "Lady, Lady," which addresses a black washerwoman who "had borne so long the yoke of men" and whose hands are "Bleached poor white in a sudsy tub, / Wrinkled and drawn from your rub-a-dub." Spencer's poem touches on that "triple consciousness" of black womanhood: the racism, the sexism, the thwarted search for identity in America.

As the Depression took hold of America, the Harlem Renaissance came to an unceremonious close. Many argue that the Harlem Race Riot of 1935 drew the final curtain on this grand experiment in cultural regeneration. Interestingly, the work by a female writer most often called on to represent the Harlem Renaissance had yet to be published; *Their Eyes Were Watching God* came out in 1937. Like Georgia Douglas Johnson, Anne Spencer, Alice Dunbar-Nelson, and Angelina Weld Grimké, Hurston's presence was very much part of the Harlem Renaissance although her most significant work came in the few years after the movement had dissipated. Yet the works of virtually all of these women fell into obscurity by the end of World War II. Indeed, some of the more promising women writers of the Harlem Renaissance seemed to fade away even at the height of the movement. Still, many of the women of the Harlem Renaissance maintained a steady interest in writing and working toward self-expression and an autonomous identity. While her writing waned, Dunbar-Nelson remained active in organizations devoted to improving the racial situation in America. Georgia Douglas Johnson was a prolific writer well into old age, yet the bulk of her work went unpublished. Anne Spencer, who had worked tirelessly as a champion of the Renaissance, continued her idyllic life in Virginia, working as a librarian and writing but publishing little. Zora Neale Hurston worked as a domestic maid to support herself while she continued to write and to receive rejections from publishers. Thus the women of the Harlem Renaissance faded from view until a new generation of African American women writers began to seek out those before them.

In a 1975 essay for *Ms.* magazine, Alice Walker writes of her determination to find and mark Zora Neale Hurston's weed-covered grave in Florida. Walker had stumbled onto Hurston's anthropological work while doing research for a story, and she developed affection for the woman not only because of her work but also because of her neglect. Therefore, Walker's search for Hurston's final resting place offered fitting closure to the life of one extraordinary woman, and it also triggered the exhumation, if you will, of an entire body of literature by Hurston and her contemporaries, the women of the Harlem Renaissance. Indeed, by 1976, black studies programs, now African American studies departments, had begun to emerge on college campuses throughout the United States. And while students delved into the writings of Alain Locke, Langston Hughes, Countee Cullen, and Jean Toomer, the women who contributed to the New Negro movement remained unexamined until Walker took up the search for Hurston. Nearly six decades after the close of the Harlem Renaissance, we have begun to discover and therefore to understand the extent of the dynamic influence of women on this movement. Now college campuses boast both African American programs and women's studies departments as well. The two frequently converge in the classroom. And the shelves of scholarship are filling with important and perceptive works on writers whose work would quite recently have warranted little examination. Robert Hemenway's 1977 biography of Hurston was the first comprehensive study of a woman of the Harlem Renaissance. But a decade later several groundbreaking studies asserted the importance of placing these writers beside the male writers who ventured to create a New Negro. Gloria T. Hull's *Color, Sex, and Poetry* offers a fine general analysis of the place of women in the Renaissance and thorough discussion of the lives and work of Alice Dunbar-Nelson, Angelina Weld Grimké, and Georgia Douglas Johnson. In *Shadowed Dreams*, Maureen Honey thematically anthologizes poetry of over thirty women writers of the Harlem Renaissance, and *The Sleeper Wakes* (1993), edited by Marcy Knopf, is a collection of short stories by women of the Renaissance. As part of the Women of Letters series, Cheryl A. Wall's *Women of the Harlem Renaissance* provides impressive analysis of the works of Jessie Redmon Fauset, Nella Larsen, and Zora Neale Hurston. Perhaps most significant are the works of Lorraine Elena Roses and Ruth Elizabeth Randolph, who took the challenge of finding and cataloging over one hundred women writers of the Harlem Renaissance in *Harlem Renaissance and Beyond*. The two scholars followed that text with a comprehensive anthology of poetry, fiction, and nonfiction by women writers of the Renaissance in *Harlem's Glory* (1996). Essentially, the most compelling truth to emerge from the recent scholarship on women of the Harlem Renaissance is that although their legacy lay dormant for decades, the participation of women in the Harlem Renaissance at its inception and throughout its relatively short but brilliant tenure was not only relevant but vital to this important and creative period in African American history and literature.

Appalachian Writers

Parks Lanier, Jr.

The title of the Higgs, Manning, and Miller anthology *Appalachia Inside Out* (1995) captures what has always been the essential delight of Appalachian literature, its embracing of irreconcilable antitheses. Reveling in these tensions, southern Appalachian writers have produced a body of literature that is both "inside" the southern tradition and "outside" its value system. That has been especially true of women writers ever since outsider Mary Noailles Murfree embraced the antithetical identity of Charles Egbert Craddock to write about the mountains.

Local color writing at the end of the nineteenth century had defined Appalachia, albeit stereotypically, in terms of its otherness, as being essentially "outside" mainstream America. Appalachia was, and has to a great extent remained, an "other" America. Its native writers have sought to explore the region from inside. There are also many writers who have come from outside the region. Some of these outsiders, like Olive Tilford Dargan (1869–1968), who wrote as Fielding Burke, strove to be accepted as insiders. Others have merely observed and exploited the region, accurately or inaccurately, for its literary resources, much as its coal, timber, and water have been exploited wisely or foolishly. Just as Appalachia has always had in-migration and out-migration, there is also the phenomenon of writers who leave the region and either retain or discard its identity. Some dislike the label "Appalachian" and never adopt it. Others may be advised to drop the disparaging designation as soon as they can.

It was the local color writers of the late nineteenth century who discovered Appalachia for America. Later, in the 1960s, politicians such as John Kennedy and Lyndon Johnson rediscovered the region for their own purposes. This essay looks at some of the facets of Appalachian literature from that initial discovery by such writers as Murfree up to the time of Harriette Arnow. The latter three decades of the twentieth century have seen a renaissance of Appalachian studies. Largely academic, this renaissance has been marked by the growth of Appalachian studies centers at such schools as Berea (Kentucky), Appalachian State (North Carolina), East Tennessee State, and Radford (Virginia); by the creation of the Appalachian Studies Association, the Appalachian Consortium, and the Appalachian Writers' Association; and by the establishment of such journals as *Appalachian Journal* and *Appalachian Heritage,* as well as such literary outlets as *Pine Mountain Sand and Gravel.* Women writers especially have benefited from this renaissance. Names such as Emma Bell Miles (1879–1919), Muriel Earley Sheppard (1898–1951), and Olive Tilford Dargan are reemerging as their work is studied and reprinted for a new generation of readers.

When Sidney Saylor Farr published her *Appalachian Women: An Annotated Bibliography* in 1981, it included fifty-nine pages listing fiction and drama but only three pages listing poetry. It was easy to locate the collected poems of West Virginian Louise McNeill but difficult to find the dispersed poems of Emma Bell Miles or Olive Tilford Dargan, and so they were omitted. Farr's work points to a direction in which much more work needs to be done. The most complete scholarly assessment of the contributions of women writers to southern Appalachian fiction is Dr. Cratis Williams' 1,650-page New York University doctoral dissertation, "The Southern Mountaineer in Fact and Fiction" (1961). This essay, a tribute to his pioneering work, is a summary of his most salient points, with some addenda from the past forty years.

Williams observes that when Mary Noailles Murfree published her last novel with an Appalachian setting in 1912, the taste for local color writing had waned. Novelists who followed her lead across the change of the century contributed little to the nation's understanding of southern mountain people. They continued to blur the lines between highlander and "poor white" as character types. Despite avowals here and there of firsthand observation and experience, writers left the stereotypes of Murfree and John Fox, Jr., much as they had found them. The fictive truth of mountaineers remained more fiction than truth.

As the century turned, Frances Hodgson Burnett (1849–1924) of *Little Lord Fauntleroy* (1886) and *The Secret Garden* (1909) fame published the novel *Louisiana* (copyright 1880; published 1900), set in the North Carolina mountains. At the same time, anticipating what would amount to a subgenre of Appalachian settlement-school novels, Sarah Ober (writing as Huldah Herrick) published *Ginsey Kreider* (1900). Although the early years of the twentieth century were a low point for Appalachian fiction, John Fox, Jr., produced two best sellers, *The Little Shepherd of Kingdom Come* (1903) and *The Trail of the Lonesome Pine* (1908), which assured publishers' continued interest in the Appalachian motif as a money-maker.

Exploiting the remote and unfamiliar mountain locale, Margaret Prescott Montague (1878–1955) set *The Sowing of Alderson Cree* (1907) in West Virginia. This was followed by *In Calvert's Valley* (1908), *Linda* (1912), and *Deep Channel* (1923), stories that make much of the inside/outside conflicts of Appalachian life and culture. In the latter novel, the heroine leaves but returns to the mountains, her original source of strength. Outsider Alice MacGowan (1858–?), purportedly drawing on an arduous two-month trek over the back roads and trails of Appalachia, set *Judith of the Cumberlands* (1908) in an East Tennessee unfamiliar even to Murfree's readers. Kay Baker Gaston, biographer of MacGowan's friend Tennessee writer Emma Bell Miles, has called MacGowan's credibility into question, however, suggesting "after careful study, that [Emma Bell Miles] was the primary author of *Judith* and two succeeding mountain books published under the name of Alice MacGowan." When the struggling Emma Bell Miles died in Chattanooga in 1919 at age thirty-nine, she had published several dozen poems and stories in magazines, a book of essays called *The Spirit of the Mountains* (1905), a collection of poems titled *Chords from a Dulcimore* (Abby C. Milton collected Miles's poems in *Strains from a Dulcimore* in 1930), and *Our Southern Birds,* with drawings (1919). Manuscripts of her own novels, to which she refers in her journal, notably a story entitled "Bitter Herbs," have been lost. Ironically, what Cratis Williams calls "perhaps the most rewarding piece of mountain fiction in its decade," Louise R. Sanders Murdoch's *Almetta of Gabriel's Run* (1917), reminded him of the best, but largely unfulfilled, work of Emma Bell Miles.

After Murfree and a few storytellers who made feeble attempts at romance, propaganda novels about the settlement schools that brought education and inevitable value conflicts to the mountains became popular. Examples include novels by Isla May Mullins (*The Boy from Hollow Hut,* 1911), Isabel G. and Florence L. Bush (*Goose Creek Folks,* 1912), Martha S. Gielow (*The Light on the Hill,* 1915), and Emma Payne Erskine (*A Girl of the Blue Ridge,* 1915). It was Lucy Furman (1869–1958) from the Hindman Settlement School in Knott County, Kentucky, however, who gained the most considerable reputation in this subgenre. Williams says that Furman "covered more accurately than others the stirring and the awakening of the mountaineer from his century-long sleep." Catherine Marshall's *Christy* (1967) follows in the steps of such Furman novels as *Sight to the Blind* (1914), *Mothering on Perilous* (1913), *The Quare Woman* (1923), *The Glass Window* (1925), and *The Lonesome Road* (1927) in which schools are built and the best of mountain character is made even better by education.

Williams characterizes the 1920s as "a decade of hesitation for interpretations of the highlanders" when a taste for realism dominated American fiction. It was in the 1920s that Cordia Greer-Petrie published her series of nine "Angeline" novels (1921–1928). Also in this decade, two significant novels that were neither wholly outside nor wholly inside Appalachia appeared. Edith Summers Kelley's *Weeds* (1923) is not located in Appalachian Kentucky, but its strong women characters have much in common with highland models. Similarly, Elizabeth Madox Roberts, beginning with *Time of Man* (1926), is often praised as a forerunner of Appalachian realism, though her settings are not primarily highland but simply rural.

In the late 1920s, Maristan Chapman (pen name of Mary and Stanley Chapman) turned to juvenile fiction after following Murfree's lead for such novels as *The Happy Mountain* (1928) and *Glen Hazard* (1933). The hesitancy of the 1920s continued into the 1930s with Rose Battleham's *Pleasure Piece* (1935), Kathleen Morehouse's *Rain on the Just* (1936), and marked even Sherwood Anderson's last novel, *Kit Brandon* (1936), a tale of blockade running (moonshining), set in East Tennessee. Alberta Pierson Hannum (b. 1906) contributed three novels to the western Carolina scene, *Thursday April* (1931), *The Hills Step Lightly* (1934), and *The Gods and One* (1941), with the kind of folk material and characters brought to perfection in the 1990s novels of Sharyn McCrumb (b. 1948). In 1947, Hannum turned to the famous Hatfield-McCoy feud as background for *Rosanna McCoy.*

Anne W. Armstrong's *This Day and Time* (1930) broke new ground for Appalachian fiction. Williams says, "the naturalism . . . is that of Murfree freed from the genteel restrictions of her time but with biology added." It was followed in 1932 by Grace Lumpkin's *To Make My Bread,* an outstanding example of American proletarian fiction worthy to stand with Steinbeck's *The Grapes of Wrath* (1939). Lumpkin was joined in turn by crusader Olive Tilford Dargan, an accomplished writer in poetry, drama, and fiction, who, says Williams, "although not a native mountain woman, perhaps caught more accurately the isolated Carolina mountaineer's dialect, essential character, and habits of mind than any other writer of fiction ever to interpret Carolina mountain folk." Writing as Fielding Burke, Dargan published such proletarian novels as *Call Home the Heart* (1932) and *A Stone Came Rolling* (1935). In 1925, she published *Highland Annals,* which was reworked as *From My Highest Hill: Carolina Mountain Folk* and republished in 1941 with photographs by Bayard Wootten (reissued 1998). For the reissue, Anna Shannon Elfenbein has written a comprehensive introduction to Dargan's life and work.

In 1935, the year Ellen Glasgow's *Vein of Iron* (1935) drew a harsh portrait of Virginia mountain life, Muriel Earley Sheppard published her more sympathetic picture of life near the Iron Mountains of the North Carolina–Tennessee border, *Cabins in the Laurel,* with photographs by Bayard Wootten. Its 1991 reissue reminds readers of a type of creative nonfiction exemplified by Emma Bell Miles in *The Spirit of the Mountains* (1905) and by Horace Kephart in *Our Southern Highlanders* (1913), which is perpetuated in the many *Foxfire* books from Rabun Gap, Georgia. The anecdotal portrait of a people is especially popular as an Appalachian genre, and to it Sheppard added poems of her own as if they were local ballads a Cecil Sharpe might have collected. The southern moonlight-and-magnolias tradition was redrawn, Appalachian style, in the popular nostalgia of Jean Thomas' *The Traipsin' Woman* (1933) and *The Singing Fiddler of Lost Hope Hollow* (1938), whose characters act and talk like dislocated Elizabethans the better to compete with Jesse Stuart's Kentucky mountaineers for the reader's attention.

Herschel Gower's appreciative introduction to the 1968 reprinting of Mildred Haun's collection of short stories, *The Hawk's Done Gone* (1940), reminds us of how little is known about this Tennessee writer who studied at Vanderbilt and had connections with John Crowe Ransom and Allen Tate. Her stories are a powerful compendium of mountain lore and superstition served in a vigorous narrative style. The gothic horror of "Melungeon Colored" and its exotic ethnic material (also exploited by Jesse Stuart in his 1965 novel *Daughter of the Legend*) make it an anthologist's favorite.

Writing about Haun (1911–1966) in 1968, without benefit of emerging feminist theory and criticism, Gower observed, "The form Miss Haun chose—or which she let evolve—is more like that of a long traditional tale in which disparate themes occur and technical unities are not always strictly observed. Only a few of the stories . . . are complete enough to satisfy the requirements of the well-made story like the best of Hemingway and Anderson." Contemporary feminist theory, which explains how women structure narratives and tap chthonic mysteries differently from Hemingways and Andersons, would better elucidate Haun's way of organizing her material by that special feminine quality of interiority. "Although the women are silent in front of the men," Carole Ganim says of Haun's stories, "they live their secret lives in communion with nature and with full consciousness of their peculiar participation in its life forces." In a few years, Haun's work was to be eclipsed by Jesse Stuart, the voice of W-Hollow, and James Agee of Knoxville.

Although writers of fiction were not as interested in the highlands after World War II through 1960, more than sixty novels and short story collections were published during that time that focused on the hill country. Janet Taylor Caldwell's *There Was a Time* (1947) was a popular mystery set amid the mineral-rich hills of Kentucky. Historical fiction was especially prominent, exemplified by Helen Topping Miller's *The Sound of Chariots* (1947), Florette Henri's *Kings Mountain* (1950), Janice Holt Giles's *The Kentuckians* (1953) and *The Land beyond the Mountains* (1958), and Phyllis Gordon Demarest's *The Wilderness Brigade* (1957).

Janice Holt Giles (1905–1979), who had moved to Kentucky from Texas, claimed Appalachia as her own in *The Enduring Hills* (1950) and *Miss Willie* (1951). Williams says that these are "the first of the mountain novels following World War II to picture the mixing of contemporary civilization with mountain life." No longer are yesterday's people remote from the influences of modern times. They feel very keenly the encroachments of better roads, better schools, and better access to culture beyond the hills. But, like Thoreau, the mountain people often regard such improvements as "improved means to unimproved ends." In the best of Giles's fiction, the modern American Dream is tested against an older dream once fulfilled in the hills but perhaps no longer adequate.

Also writing out of the turbulent World War II period and its aftermath of social change was Harriette Simpson Arnow (1908–1986), who began her career with *Mountain Path* (1936), followed by *Hunter's Horn* (1949), *The Dollmaker* (1954), *Seedtime on the Cumberland* (1960), *Flowering of the Cumberland* (1963), *The Weedkiller's Daughter* (1970), *The Kentucky Trace* (1974), and *Old Burnside* (1977). *Hunter's Horn* and *The Dollmaker* have generated the most scholarly interest and critical acclaim. The former tells a compelling story of a man so obsessed with fox hunting that it ruins his family's life. Facile comparisons between Arnow's Nunn Ballew and Melville's Captain Ahab, however, only hint at the complexity of Arnow's characterization and thematic development, which turns finally on the fox's actually being a vixen when all along she was assumed to be male.

Gertie Nevels, the dollmaker, is Arnow's character most readers (and some television viewers since Jane Fonda portrayed her in 1984) know best.

The Dollmaker touches on such important themes as migration for economic survival. Just as Steinbeck was able to capture the plight of thousands in his story of the Joads, Arnow is able to draw the changing social history of Appalachia with the story of Gertie and her family as they struggle to adjust to World War II America. Suggesting a story that has often been repeated, a Detroit cabbie tells Gertie, "I've met youse atta station through two world wars," but Arnow is the first to tell the story of their migrations so completely. Williams says, "Only one writer, Harriette Arnow, has attempted seriously to trace the hegira of the mountaineers themselves from their highland homes to the hillbilly ghettos of northern industrial cities where they lose their old-fashioned virtues and their rural innocence in their struggle for a social and economic foothold in a highly mechanized society."

Just as Williams concluded his mammoth study in 1961 by saying, "Arnow's novels complete the story of the Southern mountaineer," Wilma Dykeman (b. 1920) was finishing her first novel, *The Tall Woman* (1962), the definitive story of post–Civil War Appalachia. It is a novel about many facets of Reconstruction, the healing of lives in an era that, for mountain people especially, was the battleground of brother against brother. Without sentimentality or stereotyping, Dykeman writes an Appalachian story that is an American story centered on Lydia McQueen, whose roles as daughter, wife, mother, and community leader illustrate Dykeman's passionate belief in how one person can make a positive difference in family and community. As her title reminds the reader, "A tall woman casts a long shadow."

Dykeman continued the saga of Lydia McQueen's family with her second novel, *The Far Family* (1966), and then built upon her theme of stewardship for the earth in her third book, the early ecological novel *Return the Innocent Earth* (1977). Thus Dykeman now ranks with Marilou Awiakta and Denise Giardina as one of the leading "ecofeminists" writing in Appalachia today. Her nonfiction study written for the Rivers of America series, *The French Broad* (1955), was one of the first books of ecohistory, and in other histories, such as *Tennessee* (1975), *With Fire and Sword: The Battle of Kings Mountain* (1978), and *The Border States* (1968), as well as in her journalism, Dykeman eloquently illustrates how the story of Appalachia is the continuing story of America.

Dykeman's work was but the prelude to the work of many other "tall women" in the following decades—Lee Smith, Sharyn McCrumb, and Cathryn Hankla of Virginia; Denise Giardina and Jayne Anne Phillips of West Virginia; Marilou Awiakta of Tennessee; Bennie Lee Sinclair of South Carolina; George Ella Lyon of Kentucky; and Bettie Sellers of Georgia to name but a few—who continue the powerful legacy that is the Appalachian story.

Southern Women Writers and Social Issues

Anna Shannon Elfenbein

For the first sixty years of the twentieth century, an oligarchy of wealthy white males ruled the South, and the lot of the vast majority of other southerners was oppression and poverty. Such social problems as the persecution of blacks, the disempowerment of women, and the exploitation of the working class afflicted the region to an extent unheard of in other parts of the country. At the same time, elitist ideologies like racism, sexism, and classism served to rationalize the perpetuation of these conditions. In order to preserve its power and privilege, the ruling elite imposed a code of silence on those who opposed the status quo and dealt harshly with anyone who violated it.

Despite the climate of fear, many southerners who were appalled by the conditions they faced joined one or more of the social and political movements that were seeking to reform or revolutionize society. The most prominent of these were the Social Gospel movement, feminism, socialism, Communism, and the Civil Rights movement. Emboldened by their affiliation with these collective efforts or by the knowledge that large numbers of other people shared their concerns, a few courageous individuals spoke out. Among them was a small but influential group of women writers whose works proclaimed their abhorrence of social injustice and their support for radical social change. These women belonged to the moral vanguard of their day, and both their impassioned writings and their willingness to risk their reputations, their livelihoods, and sometimes even their lives for the sake of their principles left an indelible mark upon the literary and social history of the United States.

Some of these women writers explicitly promoted the agenda of one movement or another in their fiction. Others simply described the social problems of the South, thereby lending implicit support to the programs of the reformers and revolutionaries. It is the novels of the first group of writers, those who took a militant stand and urged others to do likewise, that are given primary consideration here.

The first priority of the southern women who wrote novels of social commitment was not artistry but advocacy, and for all of them the cause of women was of paramount importance. By placing female characters at the center of their works, they sought to demonstrate that the South belonged to women as well as to men. And by revealing that women were suffering because of their second-sex status, that they were resisting their oppressors, and that they were striving to better the lives of others, these writers sought to inspire their readers to join the struggle to improve social conditions. The novels they wrote confronted such issues as racial prejudice, segregation, unequal access to education, lynching, the disenfranchisement of women, the lack of access to contraception, violence against women, child abuse, incest, prostitution, unsafe and unfair working conditions, alcoholism, and homophobia. Although they analyzed social problems in different ways, these works expressed a common, unshakable faith that such problems could and would be solved.

Tragically, however, these women authors lived and worked within racially segregated sisterhoods, and despite occasional moments that augured solidarity across racial lines, racism hobbled their efforts to reform southern society. Following the United States Supreme Court's "separate but equal" decision in *Plessy v. Ferguson* (1896), white supremacists throughout the South trumped the social and political protests of women by playing the race card. It was not until after the Supreme Court's reversal of *Plessy* in *Brown v. Board of Education* (1954) that white and black women began to join forces in significant numbers. Recognizing the central place that race relations occupied in the social life of the South, virtually all of the southern women authors who wrote about social issues during the first half of the twentieth century gave at least some consideration to the issue of race in their novels. By depicting the problems of women as the problems of white and black women alike, they helped their readers to see that southern women could not improve their lives unless they first broke down the racial barriers that divided them.

One of the underpinnings of racism and sexism in the United States is essentialism, the belief that race and biological sex confer upon human beings certain essential traits. Those who held this view at the beginning of the twentieth century generally believed, for example, that white women were essentially pure, whereas black women were essentially promiscuous, and that white men were essentially rational, whereas black men were essentially bestial. From such pernicious beliefs as these, it followed that white men should be allowed to hold all of the powerful positions in southern society, and that white and black women and black men should be relegated to the inferior ones. Accordingly, white males, supported not only by essentialism but also by powerful northerners, an apathetic federal government, and lynch mobs, gained and maintained almost total control over the statehouses of the South and denied the vote to women and black men. Except insofar as they were able to influence their husbands or male relatives, white women had little opportunity to participate in the political process, and blacks had even less. Despite being excluded from electoral politics, however, certain southern women authors, white and black, seized a measure of political power by writing novels that exploded the false essentialist beliefs that supported the oppressive social system.

The most important novels of social advocacy written by southern women near the beginning of the twentieth century were *Iola Leroy* (1892) by Frances Ellen Watkins Harper and *Hagar* (1913) by Mary Johnston (1870–1936). Both were politically charged works that presented truthful accounts of the southern way of life and thereby helped to demolish essentialized and romanticized portrayals of the region. Like George Washington Cable and Charles Chesnutt, their contemporaries, Harper and Johnston boldly contradicted the revisionary fictions by means of which Plantation School authors such as Joel Chandler Harris and Thomas Nelson Page had sought to convince the nation that the pre–Civil War era was a lost golden age of chivalry. By attempting to come to terms with the institution of slavery and its legacy, these women writers anticipated those male novelists, such as William Faulkner and Robert Penn Warren, whose later novels have long been regarded as major contributions to the Southern Renaissance.

Frances Harper, who was a poet, essayist, and orator as well as a novelist, published *Iola Leroy* in 1892, when she was at the pinnacle of her career as a writer and was perhaps the best-known and most respected black woman in the United States. In that same year, two influential works of nonfiction by African-American women of the South, *Southern Horrors* by Ida B. Wells (1862–1931) and *A Voice from the South* by Anna Julia Cooper, also appeared. All three of these books condemned the vicious white backlash that was then taking place in response to the gains made by blacks during Reconstruction.

Harper's message in *Iola Leroy* was that Americans should follow the example of Jesus Christ, who had uplifted the lowly by ministering to their needs. In order to ensure that she would convey this idea, which was known as "the social gospel," to as many readers as possible, she cast her novel in the form of a historical romance of the Civil War and Reconstruction and made Iola Leroy, her protagonist, a "tragic mulatta," a formulaic character type that had already proven to be popular with the book-buying public. In addition, Harper arranged for her book to be published simultaneously in two cities, Philadelphia and Boston. These efforts were successful, and *Iola Leroy* became the first best-seller by an African-American woman.

In the standard "tragic mulatta" plot, a light-skinned woman of mixed race chooses to pass as white and then suffers degradation at the hands of white men or death from despair. *Iola Leroy* subverted this plot formula. Although she looks white and receives a marriage proposal from a white physician, Iola rejects the path marked out for her by the formula and commits herself instead to serving "'the race which needs [her] most.'" Modeling the principled behavior that Harper wanted to endorse, Iola ultimately agrees to marry a black man who shares her dedication to the social gospel and will help her to achieve her social goals.

In *Iola Leroy* Harper attacked the racist, sexist mythology of her day in a variety of ways. First, she corrected prevailing racial stereotypes by creating black characters who are intelligent, dedicated, and resourceful. Second, she described the heroism that black soldiers and slaves had displayed during the Civil War, thereby revising paternalistic accounts that portrayed whites as the liberators of abject blacks. Third, through Iola, who is taken down from her pedestal and transformed into an object of sexual exploitation when it is revealed that she has black ancestry as well as white, Harper unmasked for her readers the sham of southern "chivalry," a racist, sexist double standard that prevented black and white women from perceiving their shared oppression.

The Social Gospel movement, which is central to *Iola Leroy,* inspired some of the women activists of Harper's day to devote themselves to teaching the poor what they needed to know in order to become self-sufficient. One of the most successful of these women was Mary McLeod Bethune, who founded a school for African-American girls in Florida in 1904. Such efforts contributed to the process of social reform that Frances Harper had envisioned and endorsed.

As a southern lady, Mary Johnston was expected to leave politics to men.

What she did instead was to use the financial resources she had derived from her successful career as a writer of historical romances to promote women's rights and a socialist theory of social evolution. In 1913 Johnston published *Hagar,* a feminist romance based partly on her own life.

Hagar has been called the *Uncle Tom's Cabin* (1851) of the movement for women's suffrage. This is not to say that the two works are equally compelling. Inasmuch as *Hagar* focuses on the development of a privileged and financially independent white woman who is never at risk, it is much less moving than Harriet Beecher Stowe's famous novel, which contains a number of episodes that depict the suffering of slaves. Nevertheless, the comparison is apt in that both books embody deeply held moral convictions and urge their readers, either explicitly or implicitly, to act in accordance with them. The conviction upon which *Hagar* rests is that society is evolving toward a higher stage at which the rights of the oppressed, including the right of women to vote, will be fully recognized.

When the members of Hagar's family discover that she is a suffragist, they denounce the movement as a vulgar affront to "'the chivalry of . . . Southern men'" and demand that she renounce it. But because Hagar, like Johnston herself, is a successful writer, she is under no compulsion to comply with this demand, and rather than do so, she leaves the family home to pursue her activist agenda. Thus, one of Johnston's themes, elaborated earlier by her friend Charlotte Perkins Gilman in *Women and Economics* (1898), is that women must achieve economic independence before they can hope to vindicate their political rights. This theme is sounded again when Hagar rejects several suitors who would obstruct her pursuit of her political goals.

When Hagar finally accepts a proposal of marriage at the end of the novel, she warns her intended that she plans to "'work on through life for the fairer social order,'" and he commits himself to helping her. Like Frances Harper, Mary Johnston thus implicitly exhorted her heterosexual women readers to dedicate themselves to service and prescribed equality and shared political principles as preconditions for marriage. By endorsing this view of marriage, both authors departed from the traditional formula followed by romance writers like Augusta J. Evans Wilson, who provided their women characters with handsome cads to reform. Refusing this familiar fantasy, Johnston and Harper taught their readers that the personal is indeed political and that women's liberation has to begin at home.

Several novels by southern women contemporaries of Harper and Johnston challenged essentialist beliefs concerning the inferiority of women but did so without promoting a specific agenda. Some examples are *At Fault*

(1890) and *The Awakening* (1899) by Kate Chopin; *Horace Chase* (1894) by Constance Fenimore Woolson; *The Making of Jane* (1901) by Sarah Barnwell Elliott; *O Pioneers!* (1913) by Willa Cather; and *Virginia* (1913) by Ellen Glasgow.

During the early years of the twentieth century, a number of southern black women novelists, most notably Zora Neale Hurston, emigrated to the North, where they made a significant contribution to the Harlem Renaissance. Although the exodus of these authors was not what H. L. Mencken had in mind when he dubbed the South "the Sahara of the Bozart" in 1917, it did have the effect of leaving the southern literary scene more arid than it would otherwise have been.

Southern white women novelists were extraordinarily productive, however, during the 1920s. Eschewing the moonlight-and-magnolia myths that romance writers and Hollywood screenwriters were passing off as stories of the South, several of these authors wrote novels that depicted the region's social problems realistically but did not advocate specific solutions to them. The best of these are *Barren Ground* (1925) by Ellen Glasgow and *The Time of Man* (1926) by Elizabeth Madox Roberts. The protagonists of both novels are poor women who are seduced and abandoned by men they love and must struggle to eke out a living by working the land. Glasgow's Dorinda Oakley, an unmarried subsistence farmer, and Roberts's Ellen Chesser, a married sharecropper, react to poverty and personal betrayals in opposite ways. Dorinda becomes hard and unfeeling and because of this transformation is able to turn her farm into a productive enterprise. Ellen, on the other hand, remains soft and sensitive and is driven from her land, but she nevertheless achieves a spiritual triumph by keeping her family intact in the face of adversity. Although neither *Barren Ground* nor *The Time of Man* agitated for reform or revolution, both works advanced the cause of women by heightening their readers' awareness of rural poverty and sexual exploitation. A number of other realistic feminist novels of the decade also described the efforts of women characters to cope with various social problems. Examples are *The Narrow House* (1921), *Narcissus* (1922), and *The Golden Door* (1925) by Evelyn Scott; *The Hard-Boiled Virgin* (1926) and *Dead Lovers Are Faithful Lovers* (1928) by Frances Newman; and *Black April* (1927) and the Pulitzer Prize–winning *Scarlet Sister Mary* (1928) by Julia Peterkin.

As the decade of the 1920s, a period of relative prosperity for the industrialized North, drew to a close, the largely rural South was still recovering from the devastating economic effects of the Civil War. When the nation's economy as a whole sank into a depression of vast proportions in the 1930s, the plight of the workers in the South's few mills and factories became dire, in part because of layoffs and in part because owners were trying to squeeze more production out of those who were still employed. Believing that the problems confronted by southern workers were inherent in capitalism, a small group of southerners embraced the revolutionary agenda of the Communist Party of the United States, which sought to overthrow the capitalist oligarchy and to establish a classless society. Included in this group were three women authors, Myra Page (1897–1993), Olive Tilford Dargan (1869–1968), and Grace Lumpkin (1892?–1980), all of whom wrote social-realist novels that expressly espoused Communist ideas.

In 1929, when textile workers struck their mill in Gastonia, North Carolina, and were joined by Communist organizers from the North, who hoped to enlist them in class struggle, Page, Dargan, Lumpkin, and three authors from other regions of the country began to write strike novels. Of the six Gastonia novels they produced, *Gathering Storm* by Page, *Call Home the Heart* by Dargan, and *To Make My Bread* by Lumpkin, all of which were published in 1932, are the best. At the center of all three novels are women characters from the working class. This emphasis upon female characters violated the prescriptions of Communist editor Michael Gold, who had written that both the protagonist and the author of the "proletarian" novel would be male. But in view of the fact, frequently ignored by male historians, that the majority of the Gastonia strikers, and most of those beaten and bayoneted during the strike, were women, the decision Page, Dargan, and Lumpkin made to give central roles to women characters was appropriate. The centrality of women in these novels also reflects the radical feminism of these three authors. They not only espoused a Marxist vision of world revolution, according to which class struggle will inexorably culminate, despite temporary setbacks like the breaking of the Gastonia strike, in a utopian and egalitarian social order, but also believed that women would play a crucial role in bringing the revolution about.

The Gastonia novels by southern women also celebrated new industrial technologies as the means by which workers would someday free themselves from backbreaking labor. This optimistic view challenged that of the Vanderbilt Agrarians, who had taken their stand against the industrialization of the South and in favor of a return to the values of the region's preindustrial past. One of these values was white supremacy. The position Page, Dargan, and Lumpkin took on the race question was a remarkable departure not only from this conservative view but also from the views of the most progressive white southerners of their day. For at a time when most whites in the region were still defending segregation, these women authors, following the Communist line, depicted racism as an obstacle to worker solidarity and implicitly advocated racial integration. In acknowledging that racism was problematic, Page, Dargan, and Lumpkin avoided a mistake that would fracture the women's movement in the 1970s and 1980s. As Hazel V. Carby points out in *Reconstructing Womanhood* (1987), many white feminists in that later period tended to "den[y] the hierarchical structuring of the relations" between the races because they were eager to believe that white and black women had always been united by the "bonds of sisterhood."

Prior to becoming a novelist, Myra Page, whose real name was Dorothy Gary Markey, was a labor organizer and academic. While organizing textile workers in Norfolk, Virginia, she observed the ruthlessness of the mill owners and the appalling living conditions of the workers. Later, in her doctoral dissertation on southern cotton mills, she wrote about the tactics owners commonly used to halt and avert strikes. One such tactic was the use of black workers as "scabs," which induced white workers to believe that they were expendable and that blacks were their enemies. Page believed that white and black workers had to unite before they would be able to enjoy their economic, political, and social rights. As a Communist she also favored collectivizing the ownership of industry.

Gathering Storm was Page's first novel and is less unified as a narrative than the Gastonia novels by Dargan and Lumpkin. But its descriptions of the reproductive problems faced by women of the working class, such as unwanted pregnancy and unsafe abortion methods, are vivid and disturbing. As Sylvia Jenkins Cook writes in *From Tobacco Road to Route 66* (1976), these descriptions suggest that the hero sought by the women mill workers who populate *Gathering Storm* might have been "Margaret Sanger rather than Marx."

Page addressed the subjects of racism, sexism, and classism in parallel depictions of the plight of two women of the working class, Marge Crenshaw, who is white, and Martha Morgan, who is black. Although they have grown up in shacks that are only a short distance apart, they are separated by the "invisible gulf" created by racism. When the women look "one another full in the eye," the gulf closes for a moment, and Marge decides that she wants to know Martha better. After Martha is raped and murdered by a wealthy white man, Marge reflects upon the racist proscriptions that kept her and Martha from becoming friends. When Marge overhears a white worker say that whites should stand together to keep blacks "'in their place,'" she replies: "'[W]e white folks ain't together. There's the mill owners 'n there's us.'" As the crisis caused by the strike builds, Marge's understanding of class politics deepens. After the strike is broken, her brother, a

Communist union organizer, promises her that "'[t]he day of accountin' can't be far off.'" At the end of the novel, Marge feels that she is caught up in "the gathering storm" that will soon sweep the unjust capitalist order away.

Although the storm clouds dispersed and Page never again wrote with the conviction that the revolution was at hand, she produced two other working-class novels, *Moscow Yankee* (1935) and *With Sun in Our Blood* (1950), a fine book that was reissued as *Daughter of the Hills* in 1986.

By the time of the Gastonia strike, Olive Dargan had already had a long and varied literary career. As a young woman she had embraced both socialism and feminism, and in the 1920s she had become a fellow traveler of the Communist Party. For many years Dargan had lived in the mountains of western North Carolina, and she was therefore intimately acquainted, as Page and Lumpkin were not, with the people and culture of that region, from which many of the workers in Gastonia and other mill towns had come. When Dargan learned of the unrest in Gastonia, she went there to interview strikers.

Dargan's *Call Home the Heart,* which was published under the pseudonym Fielding Burke, is generally regarded as the outstanding literary achievement among the Gastonia novels. One of the most memorable women characters in southern fiction, the novel's protagonist, Ishma Waycaster, abandons her family and the mountains she loves for the promise of a better life in a piedmont mill town. The first half of *Call Home the Heart,* which garnered the praise of critics on the Right, is a vividly realized account of Ishma's life in the mountains, where she must struggle to raise enough food to feed her growing family and must endure the strain of one pregnancy after another. The novel's second half, which impressed critics on the Left, describes Ishma's life in town, where workers must drink bad water, live in ramshackle housing, work long hours, and accumulate debts. There Ishma hears a lengthy Communist sermon given by a northern union organizer, who summarizes for a crowd of workers the history of class oppression and characterizes Communism as the "'great mother calling us to peace and plenty.'" This speech, which carries the political lesson Dargan wanted to teach her readers, persuades Ishma to commit herself to the coming strike. Convinced that racism, which poses a threat to worker solidarity, will be easily eradicated, she proclaims, "'We're going to get together till there's not a working man left out, white, black, yellow or brown, the world over.'"

In the end Ishma proves to be incapable of living up to her own rhetoric. When a black woman embraces her, she reacts with revulsion, knocks the woman to the floor, leaves the town, and returns to the mountains she loves.

Ishma's unexamined racism thus prevents her from honoring her commitment to the strike and to the Communist ideal of universal brotherhood. Although Dargan's description of Ishma's encounter with the black woman has been criticized on the ground that it makes use of racist language, the episode's larger significance is that it demonstrates the insidious power of racism to undermine even the most idealistic efforts to organize workers into a cohesive force capable of fighting effectively for revolution or economic reforms.

A few years after the publication of *Call Home the Heart,* Dargan continued Ishma's story in a second strike novel, *A Stone Came Rolling* (1935), which is even more avowedly Marxist than its predecessor. In the sequel Ishma overcomes her racism and becomes a fully committed revolutionary, but *A Stone Came Rolling* is inferior to *Call Home the Heart* as literature because its portrayal of Ishma denies her the psychological complexity and vitality she exhibits in the earlier book. Dargan also authored a third working-class novel, *Sons of the Stranger* (1947), which describes the struggle for economic justice in a western mining town at the end of the nineteenth century.

In her youth Grace Lumpkin taught school, held a government job that exposed her to the poverty of southern farm families, and affiliated herself with left-wing political activities. Her first book, *To Make My Bread,* won the Maksim Gorky prize as the best labor novel of 1932 and was then adapted into a play entitled *Let Freedom Ring* (1936), which ran for five months in New York. Lumpkin based her protagonist, Bonnie McClure, on Ella May Wiggins, a white balladeer who had participated in the Gastonia strike amid racist rumors to the effect that she had black friends. By having Bonnie relate to blacks in a casual and open way, Lumpkin provided her white readers with a model of racial tolerance. Bonnie develops a friendship with Mary Allen, a black woman who cleans at the mill, and this relationship gives Bonnie credibility with black workers, whom she wants to organize. When reactionary whites circulate a racist handbill in an effort to break the strike, white and black workers begin to unite. After Bonnie is murdered, the grief and rage of workers on both sides of the color line further reinforce their unity. The novel's last sentence, "'This is just the beginning,'" forecasts even greater solidarity among black and white workers and the start of the revolution that Bonnie envisioned and worked to bring about.

Lumpkin continued her exploration of race relations in *A Sign for Cain* (1935). Although its protagonist is a male worker, the novel broke new ground by placing black women characters in important roles and by portraying them as strong and intelligent. Because of white racism, the black women in *A Sign for Cain* are distrustful of whites. The novel shows that ordinary courtesy and communication can dissolve racial hatred and facilitate the development of interracial trust.

Other novels of the 1930s by southern women describe the struggles of ordinary people for survival without proposing solutions to the social problems they confront. Four books of this kind won Pulitzer Prizes: *The Good Earth* (1931) by Pearl S. Buck, *Lamb in His Bosom* (1933) by Caroline Miller, *Now in November* (1934) by Josephine Johnson, and *The Yearling* (1938) by Marjorie Kinnan Rawlings. Two works in this category are deserving of special recognition because of their artistry: *Their Eyes Were Watching God* (1937) by Zora Neale Hurston and *Pale Horse, Pale Rider* (1939) by Katherine Anne Porter.

The coming of World War II and the end of the Depression muted radical voices like those of Page, Dargan, and Lumpkin, but racial problems, which loom so large in their works, continued to surface in the novels published by southern women during the 1940s. The most important and controversial treatment of the race question produced in that decade by a white southerner, female or male, was *Strange Fruit* (1944) by Lillian Smith, an early advocate of civil rights for African-Americans and one of the editors of a racially progressive journal called *South Today*. A novel of interracial love set in the segregated South, *Strange Fruit* was panned throughout the region and banned in Boston. Despite or because of this opposition, it became a best-seller and was adapted for the Broadway stage.

Smith's novel, the title of which refers metaphorically to a lynching victim hanging from a tree, describes a love affair between a black woman, Nonnie Anderson, and a white man, Tracy Deen. Nonnie's pregnancy forces Tracy to decide whether to marry her in violation of the laws against miscegenation. Unwilling to do so, he pays a black man, Henry McIntosh, to marry her instead. After learning of Nonnie's condition, her brother murders Tracy. In the erroneous belief that Henry is guilty of the crime, a mob of white men lynches him. *Strange Fruit* thus indicts the irrationality and cruelty of southern racism in general and of the practice of lynching in particular. The novel also condemns the hypocrisy of white male racists, who defend racial segregation while having surreptitious affairs with black women and who pray for salvation one day and then lynch a black man the next.

The 1940s witnessed rapid social change in the South. Several works published in that decade by southern women authors captured communities and customs that were in the process of disappearing forever. Some of the most noteworthy of these are *The Hawk's Done Gone* (1940) by Mildred

Haun, *From My Highest Hill* (1941) by Olive Dargan, *Portulaca* (1941) by Bernice Kelly Harris, *The Heart Is a Lonely Hunter* (1940) by Carson Mc-Cullers, *Mexican Village* (1945) by Josephina Niggli, and *Delta Wedding* (1946) by Eudora Welty.

During the anticommunist hysteria of the late 1940s and 1950s, overtly political fiction by writers of the Left disappeared from publishers' lists. Nevertheless, southern women authors continued to represent various social problems in their fiction. In the novels they produced during the 1950s, they dealt with many of the South's perennial issues, including racial, sexual, and class oppression, but did so in new ways. Instead of marching under the banner of social and political movements and taking up the causes of blacks, women, or working people in general, they tended to explore the psychosexual effects of racism, sexism, and classism on small groups, families, or individuals in specific circumstances. Instead of pronouncing certain social conditions to be unjust, they generally left to their readers the task of forming moral judgments. And instead of urging their readers to take action, they sought to change their attitudes. In addition, a few southern women novelists of the 1950s ventured into new territory, addressing social issues that had been off limits to earlier generations of writers.

Two novels of the 1950s by southern white women hint at the possibility of redemption for white southerners who are willing to come to grips with the legacy of racism: *The Voice at the Back Door* (1956) by Elizabeth Spencer and *To Kill a Mockingbird* (1960) by Harper Lee, which won a Pulitzer Prize. Reminiscent of the social-realist novels of the 1930s, *The Dollmaker* (1954) by Harriette Simpson Arnow (1908–1986) depicts the struggle of a mountain woman to keep her family together in a hostile urban environment. *The Hard Blue Sky* (1958) by Shirley Ann Grau, which describes a Franco-Spanish fishing village at the mouth of the Mississippi River, resembles several of the novels of the 1940s in that it documents a unique way of life threatened with extinction. One of the novels of the 1950s that broke new ground is *The Price of Salt* (1952) by Patricia Highsmith (1921–1995), writing as Claire Morgan, which tells the story of a happy love affair between two young women whose only problem is that they are pursued by the vengeful husband of one of them. Because it rejected the notion then prevalent that same-sex love is a tragic perversion and gave a voice to a silenced and persecuted minority, this novel has become a lesbian cult classic.

In *Like One of the Family* (1956) by African-American playwright and novelist Alice Childress (1920–1994), an assertive black woman who works in white households as a temporary domestic recounts episodes in which she vanquishes her racist, sexist, and classist employers. The appearance of this refreshing novel in the 1950s heralded the arrival during the next few decades of a new generation of southern women authors of African-American ancestry. Together with other female novelists of the region, these talented women, among them Maya Angelou, Alice Walker, Gayl Jones, and Gloria Naylor, have inherited the literary tradition of social commitment and have carried it forward, contributing their own unique perspectives to the ongoing discussion of the social problems of the South and the nation.

The Growing Importance of Literary Circles and Mentors

Rosemary M. Magee

Defining a tradition and finding one's place in it are critical parts of the literary enterprise. While few would argue that literary circles or mentors create writers, such relationships can sustain and direct the writing process. Certainly most artists work in isolation. Perhaps because of this necessary solitude, meaningful relationships with other writers and participation in a literary community can become critically important. The connections may be formal or informal, institutional or personal; they may occur in casual conversations or in structured seminars. Until very recently the opportunities for regular, visible connections have not been available for women writers in the ways that they have been for men. As a result, women have often sought alternative paths in the creation of these important relationships. Over the course of the twentieth century, with the flourishing of arts and letters described as the Southern Renaissance, connections between women played a distinctive role in sustaining their work and shaping southern literary traditions.

Institutions of higher education play a critical role in the development of a shared sense of culture and the establishment of a literary canon, yet women have historically been on the fringes of such activities. Until the nineteenth century, women's access to colleges and universities was severely limited. Even with increased opportunities in the twentieth century, writing women faced serious limitations. Virginia Woolf, among others, has written about her inability to gain access to a university library. As Gerda Lerner emphasizes in *The Creation of Feminist Consciousness: From the Middle Ages to Eighteen-Seventy* (1993), since the seventeenth century, male intellectual groupings were located primarily around alumni in associations, clubs, political assemblies, and salons; therefore, the fact that "women were excluded from universities between their founding in the 11th century to well into the late 19th century has significantly and adversely affected women's intellectual development and productivity." Women did not have access to "the informal networks of professionals arising out of such institutions of higher learning."

These conditions persisted into the twentieth century. Louis D. Rubin, Jr., in *The Writer in the South* (1972), demonstrates the extent to which "the literature of the southern literary renascence was a college- and university-nurtured literature." The critics and teachers of literature, more often than not, were also part of that tradition. The flourishing of arts and letters in the South during the 1920s grew in large part out of this heritage. The writers and scholars at Vanderbilt University, among them those poets who became known as the Fugitives, were clearly bound together by their shared experience as southern literary men who had a place to meet, share ideas, and discuss their work. Together they exerted enormous influence on what was taught and how it was studied at institutions all across America. Women, even educated and well-connected writers whose lives were closely intertwined with the prevailing literary currents, did not have such convenient access to one another or to an established community. Caroline Gordon, for example, was closely involved in literary conversations through her fiction, critical writing, personal relationships, even her marriage to Allen Tate; however, she was not considered a full-fledged member of the community. While Gordon received substantial encouragement from Tate, Robert Penn Warren, Maxwell Perkins, and others, the conditions of her life—running a household, raising a child, and frequently entertaining visitors—were not conducive to her work as a writer. As she indicated in a 1931 letter to Perkins, "It is certainly much harder for a woman to write than it is for a man." On another occasion she confided to Katherine Anne Porter about John Crowe Ransom, "He can't bear for women to be serious about their art."

Despite the many differences in lifestyle and literary techniques among them, southern women writers have shared a perspective on a literary world as insiders and outsiders at the same time. Unwilling to be passive recipients of an established perspective on the past or present, many writers—Ellen Glasgow, Marjorie Kinnan Rawlings (1896–1953), Carson McCullers, Margaret Walker, and others—have sought to understand and configure the tradition that has also defined them. In fact, Ellen Glasgow did much to describe the emerging sense of a literary renaissance in the South. Her central role as convener of one of the first southern writers conferences gave shape to the Renaissance and allowed this movement to gather momentum. As she offered the opening speech for the event in 1931, Glasgow admitted, "When I was asked, as the only woman on this committee, to bid you welcome to Virginia, I modestly replied that women come before men only in shipwreck." However, she overcame such reservations in this and other endeavors. In her lifetime, she wrote essays on women writers, modern fiction, and many diverse subjects. Her influence on other writers is immense, as evidenced by the relationship between Rawlings and Glasgow that evolved from a correspondence that began in 1941 and continued until Glasgow's death in 1945. They were drawn to one another through their shared literary ambitions and what Glasgow described in her first letter as a "thrilling sense of friendship and sympathy."

Two important events in the life of the novelist Elizabeth Spencer further illustrate the importance of literary circles and mentors. When in the early 1940s Spencer studied at Belhaven College in Jackson, Mississippi, the Southern Literary Festival took place there. As described in her memoir *Landscapes of the Heart* (1997), "it was the first of many such gatherings. Nowadays they have broken out everywhere." This event introduced her to the work of William Faulkner; the following year, when the festival was held at the University of Mississippi and she encountered Cleanth Brooks, she wrote, "I was hearing the New Criticism for the first time." At that same meeting, she received a prize for a story that she had submitted. A completely different sense of herself and the world around her began to emerge as a result of her participation in this and subsequent conferences. Even more important, on a deeply personal level, Spencer became involved in a writing group while still a student. When it became her responsibility to invite Eudora Welty to participate in the group's discussion, she set in motion a relationship that continued for the next fifty years.

With the invitation that Elizabeth Spencer extended to Eudora Welty to cross the street to meet with her college society, the two writers began participating in a pattern of informal relationships that has allowed southern women to find a place in the literary landscape. In later years Welty was to introduce Spencer to Katherine Anne Porter and Elizabeth Bowen, as well as to editors and other writer-friends. Both Spencer and Welty have written about the importance of the initial chance meeting, and its impact exemplifies the influence of Welty on other writers as well. Her presence in the tradition of southern literature has been solid and enduring. The image that emerges from her exchanges with Katherine Anne Porter and Elizabeth Spencer, among others, is one of friendship, mentoring, and mutual support. In her review "Eudora Welty and *A Curtain of Green*" (1961), Porter praises Welty as "the child of her time and place." Likewise, Spencer identified with Welty as a sister Mississippian, and in a 1979 introduction of the older writer revered her as someone who "leaves things the same but different . . . touched by her special alchemy." In turn, Welty admired Porter's ability to see "down to the bones" and recognized a certain childhood affinity in her bond with Spencer. Late-twentieth-century writers have continued to look to Eudora Welty and her contemporaries for inspiration, such as Alice Walker, who confronted her own complicated southern past in the works of Welty and Flannery O'Connor. By examining the life and writings of Zora Neale Hurston, Walker located her own particular southern literary heritage. At the same time, by establishing a dialogue with the past through the works of O'Connor and Hurston, and through a 1973 interview with Welty, Walker identified with them as southerners and as women while implicitly probing the place of the African American writer in the southern literary tradition. In their interviews, essays, and reviews, novelists and poets have confirmed their kinship with women from their literary past, with writers they may have discovered initially only in footnotes and in margins of journals and in the asides of college lectures.

There is perhaps in modern times no better evidence of the importance of a sense of community for a writer than that provided by the letters of Flannery O'Connor. As Sally Fitzgerald has written in her collection *The Habit of Being* (1979), for O'Connor "reading was one of the great pleasures and interests in her life. She exchanged books with friends, and commentaries in turn." In a life that otherwise might have been seriously constrained due to poor health and geographic isolation, through letters and reviews—as well as occasional visits—O'Connor was very much in conversation with friends, readers, fellow writers, reviewers, students, and teachers. Not physically able to participate fully in a literary society, marginalized somewhat by other social conditions, she made important connections with other writers, many of whom were women. Through the good graces of Sally and Robert Fitzgerald, Caroline Gordon came to read and respond in extraordinary depth to O'Connor's works. In a nine-page letter written to O'Connor in 1951, Gordon commented in general on *Wise Blood* (1952) and then gave very specific advice on matters of diction, dialogue, and point of view. She was both instructive and encouraging. O'Connor responded to this intensive critique appreciatively: "All these comments on writing and my writing have helped along my education considerably and I am certainly obliged to you." When Katherine Anne Porter, Flannery O'Connor, and Caroline Gordon joined others for a panel discussion in 1960 at Wesleyan College in Macon, Georgia, their gathering demonstrated the influence of these three writers on one another. Porter and Gordon's relationship, not always characterized by warmth and equanimity, rested on an abiding respect they had for one another. Porter reviewed Gordon's fiction favorably; Gordon likewise appreciated Porter's artistry. In *The House of Fiction: An Anthology of the Short Story with Commentary* (1950), which she edited with Allen Tate, Gordon includes Porter's story "Old Mortality" along with the works of Hawthorne, Tolstoy, Joyce, Welty, and Faulkner. The relationship Gordon and Porter each had with O'Connor was of a different nature—Gordon served as her mentor and Porter as an important source of inspiration.

The rhythm and pace of women's lives have typically been different than they are for men. As Tillie Olsen demonstrates in *Silences* (1978), there have been many periods of quiet—both within an individual's life and among the voices of women in general. The expectations of family and culture can feel limiting, with few possibilities for unstructured time, reading, and reflecting. Ursula Le Guin has described how women do not always have the luxury of a "room of one's own"; they may write on the kitchen table or on the subway or waiting for children in carpools. But, finally, in her article "The Hand That Rocks the Cradle Writes the Book" (1989), she maintains that "[e]very artist needs some kind of moral support or sense of solidarity, for there *is* a heroic aspect to the practice of art; it is lonely, risky, merciless work." Women, not always in control of where they live and not always able to play a public role in the towns and cities where they reside, have had to create alternative forms of communities. Women living and writing in the South have not typically come to their development of literary connections through a philosophical or feminist perspective but from a real sense of shared need and experience. In response to an interviewer's question about the advice she would give young writers, Margaret Walker once replied, "Well, I avoid giving advice because people don't want advice; they want sympathy. They want somebody to bolster and buttress them and say what they're doing is right." These connections that women have made through reviews, letters, and essays have the added advantage of more easily crossing class, racial, and temporal boundaries—as evidenced by the relationship established between Marjorie Kinnan Rawlings and Zora Neale Hurston and by the appreciation that Alice Walker has shown for the work of Flannery O'Connor.

The story of shared experience forms the foundation of all communities. Indeed, any sense of community emerges through conversation and dialogue. In a world that is increasingly complex and distant yet closely knit together through the immediacy of technology and transportation systems, such interaction has taken on new forms. Throughout the twentieth century southern writers have been in conversation with one another—at first largely through letters and reviews, later more frequently around universities, at conferences, and in journals. They have established a public dialogue, and through that dialogue they have created a sense of common experience. The importance of a literary community and its impact is apparent in the flourishing that occurred in North Carolina in the 1980s. Writers such as Lee Smith, Kaye Gibbons, Jill McCorkle, and others benefited from these connections—with one another, with a diverse group of women writers, and with other distinguished literary figures, such as Louis D. Rubin, Jr., and Reynolds Price. Doris Betts, for instance, has written several times on the works of Anne Tyler; Tyler has in turn reviewed the works of Betts and countless other writers. Barbara Kingsolver (b. 1955) has thoughtfully examined the work of Lee Smith, who has similarly paid tribute to Welty, O'Connor, Tyler, and others. Their reviews appear in a multitude of styles and publications, often newspapers. They represent not so much an academic or scholarly form of literary criticism as an engagement in the work of one another and an effort to share that engagement with the larger community.

The importance of place—of shared idiom, locale, and experience—lingers even as the very conception of the South undergoes revision and expansion. Thus when Josephine Humphreys, Louise Shivers (b. 1929), and other women writers gathered at Furman University in 1988 to discuss the subjects of community, place, friendship, and connection, they continued in many ways the conversation begun by others on the panel at Wesleyan College twenty-five years earlier. Once a peculiar event in the literary world, such conferences and panels that recognize the special experience and contributions of the southern woman writer have occurred with increasing frequency in Chattanooga, Tennessee; Chapel Hill, North Carolina; Charleston, South Carolina; Rome, Georgia; and numerous other places, usually on or near college campuses. In the late twentieth century, literary circles that once could only be traced through piecing together correspondence, memoirs, and reviews have developed a vigorous public presence. Mindful of their heritage and appreciative of their tradition, southern women writers have acknowledged an indebtedness to literary forebears. Vital members and creators of the southern literary world that included William Faulkner, John Crowe Ransom, Allen Tate, and Robert Penn Warren, women often stood on the periphery of that world. But that periphery became defined by a set of intertwining circles—communities not contained by time or space, often without the comforts of a shared college campus or the hospitality of the literary establishment. Those circles spiraled into the late twentieth century with the continued emergence of distinctive and distinguished fiction by southern women.

Ellen Glasgow

Merrill Maguire Skaggs

Although she was visible, glamorous, vocal, and politically active in the halls of literary power, Ellen Glasgow's literary reputation has always been as it remains—volatile. Her reputation has been periodically diminished by changing social mores, changing literary tastes, and unsympathetic biographers. Recently, however, Susan Goodman's *Ellen Glasgow: A Biography* (1998) has developed another view of Glasgow: an insightful, empathetic, and positive one. Likewise, because of works like Carol Manning's *The Female Tradition in Southern Literature* (1993) that rank her among the great southern writers of the twentieth century, Ellen Glasgow is now widely accepted as the sluice gate that opened that remarkable flood of distinguished writing known as the Southern Renaissance.

Virginian Ellen Glasgow became nationally prominent first as a public personality. Like Edith Wharton and Gertrude Stein, she first caught public attention as a novelty and a bundle of contradictions. Glasgow was often described as beautiful and witty, always seen as perfectly groomed in the latest fashions, and usually stereotyped as a southern aristocrat at home in her Richmond house at One West Main, where she had lived since her fourteenth year and in which she entertained royally. Yet she emitted a quotable flow of caustic comments on man and the universe that sounded anything but conventionally ladylike. Then she took umbrage at the violence, sex, and raw shock value in works by fellow southerners such as William Faulkner and Erskine Caldwell, and thereafter she was categorized among the "old-fashioned" or "outmoded." She directly influenced virtually all prominent southern women writers who paralleled or followed her—Willa Cather, Katherine Anne Porter, Eudora Welty, and Flannery O'Connor, to name the most obvious. Paradoxically, she seemed both passé and also the virgin queen of them all. The time has come to acknowledge her secure place in southern and American letters.

Ellen Glasgow was born (a little more than half a year before Willa Cather) to Anne Gholson and Francis Glasgow in April of 1873. Although several of the Glasgow children did not survive their early years, the family of sometimes close and often combative siblings eventually included five sisters and two brothers. Of the two boys who lived to adulthood, Arthur became wealthy and intermittently supported them all, while Frank committed suicide as a young man. Young Ellen was a delicate infant and a child afflicted by migraine headaches and depressions that kept her out of school. Moreover, her early life was profoundly affected by her mother's sudden capitulation to invalidism in Ellen's tenth year. Largely self-educated, the precocious Ellen turned to writing stories about worlds of her own invention, often preferable to the one outside the family door. She became a serious student of evolution, philosophy, history, and psychology—a self-made "intellectual."

Glasgow finished writing her first novel when she was twenty; she published anonymously a revision of that novel (*The Descendant*, 1897) by the time she was twenty-four. Concomitantly with her first ambitious writing, however, she also developed the serious ear trouble that would eventually leave her deaf. Seeking medical help as well as a New York publisher, she met and fell in love with a man she called "Gerald B" in her autobiography. Yet the relationship did not stabilize, and she learned of his death from a newspaper. She later became engaged to Red Cross colonel Henry Anderson, whose devoted attentions to Queen Marie of Rumania during World War I soured Glasgow. She never married.

Having broken into print as a young woman, Glasgow published frequently, and often to acclaim. For example, *Phases of an Inferior Planet* arrived in 1898, *The Voice of the People* in 1900, and *The Battle-Ground* in 1902. She published nineteen volumes of fiction in her lifetime, and *Beyond Defeat* was published posthumously in 1966. She also published a volume of poems (*The Freeman and Other Poems*, 1902), a short story collection (*The Shadowy Third and Other Stories*, 1923), and two volumes of nonfiction prose (*A Certain Measure*, 1943; *The Woman Within*, 1954). Beyond these separate volumes, she published numerous articles, reviews, and philosophical statements. By the time she died in 1945, she had won the Pulitzer Prize for fiction for *In This Our Life* (1941), had been awarded the coveted Howells Medal by the American Academy of Arts and Letters, and had been offered many honorary degrees. She seemed in reality what she was often called in public, a "First Lady" of American letters.

Glasgow's prose remains more problematic than her public persona. Her greatest weaknesses have appeared to be her willingness to use human figures as pawns to move rather than as people to know; her facility, or ability, to write sentences providing ground cover while lacking sharply impassioned detail; and her wry irony that entertains, but keeps readers distanced from the intimate moments of her fiction. Perhaps because she did not believe in the separate ego, she did not often produce complete egos among her created characters. She did not produce vividly felt personalities near whom readers could feel they had lived. Thus, her characters do not always engage readers for long, and they are often hard to remember.

Glasgow's balancing strengths, however, are equally clear. She developed plots, themes, images, and ideas for her fiction that have proved provocatively vivid and useful to the careful craftsmen who studied to learn from her. She exploded southern gentility and pretensions, especially as they cushioned class complacency or caste myths. She made respectable and desirable the "blood and irony" she so famously declared that her region's literature needed, even when her ironic stance towards her characters left them bloodless. She vitalized such defining southern themes as memory, exile, commitment to the land, nonconformity, the tyranny of religion, evasion, and transgression. And she cultivated her talent for polishing a well-turned aphorism until she became, by the end of her career, a new kind of commonsense philosopher.

At least four of Glasgow's novels—*Virginia* (1913), *Barren Ground* (1925), *The Sheltered Life* (1932), and *Vein of Iron* (1935)—seem destined to endure. While such others as *The Romantic Comedians* (1926) or *They Stooped to Folly* (1929) have their devoted admirers, these four seem essential to a history of southern women's writing.

Virginia will remain a fiction of literary interest because it codified the archest ironies associated with the ladies and gentlemen of the Old Dominion. It also profoundly annoyed Willa Cather, who "corrected" its details often thereafter in her own work. Cather subsequently compressed Glasgow's multivolumed and multifaceted social history of Virginia into her own Virginia novel, *Sapphira and the Slave Girl* (1940). In Glasgow's *Virginia* a dewy-eyed belle named Virginia is pampered and left unskilled by her self-sacrificing mother and fond father. Thus she is unequipped to run a household smoothly, to hold the interest of her talented but roving husband, or to evoke the respect of her self-centered children. After a lifetime of doing the right thing the approved and traditional way, Virginia is left with nothing but money and time.

Barren Ground, the most familiar of Glasgow's novels, was once advertised as proof that "realism at last crosses the Potomac." Its heroine, Dorinda Oakley, becomes by hard work and self-discipline an economically independent, self-made woman. She is eventually a power in her own right, who can marry if and when she wishes, and can finally retaliate satisfactorily against the man who once, in their youth, seduced and abandoned her. Her mastery of her own destiny was a shocking and thrilling myth line for American readers. This novel was mined for gold nuggets by successive generations of southern writers and has become one of the most "absorbed" of southern books. Its details reappear for the rest of the twentieth century.

In *The Sheltered Life,* Glasgow depicts the South's euphemisms and its miscegenation as they affect both black and white populations of the region. The intricate social cat's cradles of this novel entangle all strata of a southern urban population. Thus, all eventually suffer, loyal ladies and profligate husbands alike. If the sacrificial mother of *Virginia* owes something to Glasgow's mother, her Presbyterian father's conduct with family servants contributes something as well to *The Sheltered Life.* Indeed, Glasgow's skeptical judgments about men are sometimes traced to her father's sexual sins. This novel's heroine, Jenny Blair Archbald, learns through misadventure and grief that she cannot have it all, at least not for long.

Vein of Iron may be Glasgow's most successful work of fiction. The saga traces over four generations that vein of iron which functions, not to make life endurable, but rather to make one who has life endure it. That vein of iron runs through the Fincastle family, two of whose women hold this theme-setting conversation at the start: "And are we good as the best now, Grandmother?" one asks, and another replies, "In everything but circumstances, my child."

From the hardy grandmother who can face what she has to face, through the invalid and once beautiful mother who at least dies cheerfully when she must die young, to the ruined daughter Ada, who bears and rears an illegitimate child when deprived of her lover, with a detour through the maiden aunt Meggie, who holds their impoverished family together while she cares for both them and their neighbors, the vein of iron ensures the survival of the Fincastles. The novel asks as it traces all these family conditions, what is desirable, joy or peace? It announces early, "Life may take away happiness. But it can't take away having had it." Along the way, it suggests that "self-pity was the most primitive form of sentimentality." By the end, Glasgow makes us believe that happiness is not a condition of one's daily living, but rather the abstraction one chooses, as an act of will, to identify with one's life. At the close of their lives, Ada Fincastle says to her sometimes unfaithful, usually weak, often unlucky husband, "Ralph, we have been happy together." Glasgow implies that her thinking makes it so.

"Thinking Makes It So" indeed becomes the title of a Glasgow short story. The story reminds us that Ellen Glasgow wrote more than one form of fiction. Her *Collected Stories of Ellen Glasgow* includes a dozen tales and was published with uncommonly thorough introduction and editorial comments by Richard K. Meeker in 1963. Meeker, as did the contemporary reviewers of the seven yarns collected in *The Shadowy Third and Other Stories,* remarks on the surprising quartet of ghost stories Glasgow chose for her volume. While some of her stories mercifully leave one's head quickly, Glasgow is surprisingly good with ghosts. One might ask why.

The first trait of a satisfying Glasgow ghost is that it is real. She doesn't make us wonder, because the specter typically appears with the affidavit of a trustworthy, objective, skeptical, even hardheaded first-person narrator. Glasgow doesn't tease her readers about these ghosts; she just sends them out to do what ghosts do best: accomplish magic. Even rationalists like Glasgow or ourselves can wish for magic, justice, and enduring love sometimes. And we may permit ourselves to enjoy our wish *because* we're reading a ghost story in the first place.

In "The Shadowy Third," for example, a villainous but charming doctor has contrived to marry a rich lady for her money and to kill her daughter to eliminate heirs, and he is about to eliminate his ailing wife as well. Getting his just deserts as he plans to marry a previous paramour, however, he is sent plummeting to his death by the ghost of his recently deceased wife's daughter. The little girl ghost, whom only the narrator is now able to see, leaves her jump rope coiled on the stairs down which the doctor falls when called back to his hospital. Thus justice prevails through an act of simple and satisfying revenge.

In "The Past," a household is haunted by the jealous ghost of the husband's first wife, who terrorizes his present and finer mate. When the latter turns over the job of cleaning out an old desk to her secretary and our narrator, that sympathetic staffer discovers love letters to the first wife hidden in a secret compartment. She gives the letters to the present lady of the house, who instantly realizes that they were not written by the shared husband. Wife two decides, however, that she should "fight fairly even when one fights evil." She therefore resolves to win her husband's focused attention without hurtfully revealing his first wife's betrayal. The grateful ghost, false honor still unbesmirched, subsides and leaves them in peace. Female virtue is rewarded in a world where good magic prevails.

In considering Glasgow's fictional range, one eventually realizes that her best and most memorably created character is actually herself. That multi-faceted personality—Ellen Glasgow—emerges in her two nonfiction prose works. First is the autobiography, *The Woman Within*, which she contracted to publish in 1935, completed in 1944, and left in the hands of literary executors who published it in 1954. The second is *A Certain Measure*, which includes her prefaces and critical comments on her novels. The legend for *A Certain Measure* is the signature line Glasgow stands by: "What the South needs is blood and irony."

The Woman Within was written in fits and starts, and its parts are of unequal quality. The descriptions of childhood can be embarrassing: "I was born a novelist, though I shaped myself into an artist"; "I was born with an appreciation of the best, and an equal aversion for the second best"; "As a child I loved a storm. Some caged bird in my bosom would break free"; "As I raced on, I would chant majestic verse to the wind." If one accepts these lines as a novelist's attempt to sketch in a character, however, that character grows into very interesting adulthood.

Glasgow is more convincing as the tenacious young woman who is determined to see her own novels in print and unconventionally goes to New York to charm someone into publishing her. She does so, following the formula, "I liked human beings, but I did not love human nature." Eighteen novels and a distinguished career followed her breakthrough.

When Ellen Glasgow looked back on her professional accomplishments, she saw a completed social history of Virginia and remarked: "Such as it is, there my work stands. I cannot alter it now. . . . I have tried to take the longer view; I have put my faith in ideas; I have examined life, not from a remote angle of vision but in the flesh, and with the pulse of the living. Always I have attempted, it may be unsuccessfully, to condense the results of experience and insight into a settled philosophy. To the imaginative artist, emotions, and even ideas, may be inconsistent in relation to art, but the truths of philosophy must, in a certain measure, be confirmed by the intellect." She seems actually to know herself well.

By the end of her career Ellen Glasgow had learned to weave her novels artfully around her convictions and her opinions. She could create plausible moments in which characters not unlike herself could assert those ideas that needed to be stated explicitly. In such a moment, Ada's philosopher father John Fincastle, himself good for little but thinking, comments in *Vein of*

Iron, "I have little faith in the theory that organized killing is the best prelude to peace."

Ellen Glasgow proved in her lifetime of professional work that a woman
could earn the applause of her friends and the respect of her peers without
sacrificing her "femininity" or bowing her will. By the time of her death in
1945, many had come willingly to pay court to her, to their mutual pleasure.
The work she learned to think of as a social history of Virginia—of the rich
and poor, black and white, mountaineers and tidewater gentlefolk, free-
thinkers and believers, farmers and politicians, women and men, strong and
weak, ruthless and silly—included them all. She depicted deliberately the
variety of folk in her richly diverse state, who took their appropriate places
in her murals. She wrote with an intelligence she never stopped educating.
The range of her accomplishments is equally wide.

Julia Peterkin

Susan Millar Williams

In 1921, when she turned forty, Julia Peterkin was a South Carolina plantation mistress, a member of the United Daughters of the Confederacy, and
the author of nothing. She was, in short, the least likely candidate for subversive literary fame that anyone could have imagined. Yet by 1929 she had
reinvented herself as a truth teller. Determined to "write what is, even if it
is unpleasant," she had won a Pulitzer Prize for her novel *Scarlet Sister Mary*
and helped launch the Southern Renaissance by writing seriously about the
lives of plain black farming people. In a blaze of creative energy that seemed
to come out of nowhere, Peterkin published five distinguished books in less
than a decade: *Green Thursday* (1924), *Black April* (1927), *Scarlet Sister
Mary* (1928), *Bright Skin* (1932), and *Roll, Jordan, Roll* (1933). A master
storyteller with an ear for the language of African American folk life, she
chronicled the collapse of plantation agriculture and the human impulses
behind the great black migration northward.

Julia Alma Mood was born in Laurens, South Carolina, on October 31,
1880, to Julius and Alma Archer Mood. Though Peterkin often implied to
friends that her mother died in childbirth, Alma actually succumbed to tuberculosis over a year after her baby was born. Julius Mood took his two
older daughters, Laura and Marian, to live with him in Sumter, South Carolina, where he was practicing medicine. Baby Julia, at her dying mother's
request, was sent to live with her paternal grandfather, Henry Mood, a

Methodist minister, and his wife, Laura. Julius Mood soon remarried, and ·although he stayed in close touch with his daughter, Julia always felt that he had given her away because he did not love her. She resented her step-mother, Janie Brogdon Mood, whom she and her sisters always claimed was cruel and "practically illiterate." The loss of her mother and the "desertion" of her father would show up many years later as recurring themes in Peterkin's fiction.

Although Julia Mood graduated from Converse College when she was only sixteen, she seems to have had no literary or intellectual ambitions as a young woman, and she later admitted that her older sister had written all of her college compositions. She taught briefly in a one-room school near Fort Motte, South Carolina, where she met her future husband, W. G. Peterkin, the heir to Lang Syne plantation. They married in 1903, and it was among the five-hundred-odd black folk who lived and worked at Lang Syne that Peterkin would discover what she had to say.

For almost two decades, however, from 1903 to 1921, she lived the anachronistic life of a plantation mistress presiding over a free black work force living in much the same conditions that had prevailed during slavery. She gave birth to a son, William George Peterkin, Jr., in April 1904, after a traumatic labor attended by her father. Julius Mood concluded, while his daughter was anesthetized, that another pregnancy might kill her and, with the consent of her husband, performed surgery to remove her ovaries. Peterkin took to her bed for two years after the operation, leaving the care of her baby son to an elderly black nurse named Lavinia Berry.

Like other southern white women of her class, Peterkin had many servants, and she came to depend on black women for mothering and advice. Mary Weeks and Lavinia Berry—who would later inspire the fictional characters Scarlet Sister Mary and Maum Hannah—told Peterkin stories about life in the cabins and fields of Lang Syne. They helped her recover from the traumatic birth of her son and from the anger that threatened to paralyze her. Both black women had learned to bear anger themselves: Berry had been born into slavery and Weeks was the mother of two mixed-race children, the daughters of Peterkin's brothers-in-law.

Peterkin's literary career began with a classic mid-life crisis. Her son, Bill, went off to boarding school, and she was faced with an empty nest. She signed up for piano lessons in an attempt to "cheat the silence." Her teacher, Henry Bellamann, was a handsome and articulate man with literary ambitions. (He would himself write a best-selling novel, Kings Row [1940], many years in the future.) Peterkin began telling Bellamann tales about life at Lang Syne, and he encouraged her to write them down. The piano lessons turned into writing lessons, and Peterkin soon signed up for a correspondence course and set about learning her craft. Within a year she would be published in a national magazine. In three years she would have a book contract, in four a critically acclaimed collection of short stories, in seven a best-selling novel, and in nine another best seller and a Pulitzer Prize for fiction, the first ever awarded to a southerner.

Peterkin liked to pretend that "fame surprised her," as one adoring journalist would later put it. In fact, she courted several famous men in an attempt to launch her career, including Joel Spingarn, Carl Sandburg, and H. L. Mencken, who was raising hackles across the South by dubbing it the "Sahara of the Bozart." Peterkin sent Mencken some sample stories; he published "The Merry-Go-Round" in *Smart Set* and pushed his protégée Emily Clark to publish others in her new magazine of southern culture, the *Reviewer.* These early short stories, spare and unsparing, expose the impersonal brutality of plantation life in the early twentieth century. The characters speak Gullah, a Creole dialect of the South Carolina coast that combines an English vocabulary with elements of West African grammar. Peterkin soon became a master of both dialogue and interior monologue, mixing the two forms in ways that would lead white and middle-class readers to identify with poor black farming people.

Mencken's friend Alfred A. Knopf published *Green Thursday* in 1924, to a chorus of praise that produced few sales. A collection of linked short stories in the same vein as Ernest Hemingway's *In Our Time* (1924), *Green Thursday* follows the troubles of a farmer named Killdee, his wife, Rose, and their foster daughter Missie. "Nothing so stark, taut, and poignant has come out of the white South in fifty years," wrote Joel Spingarn, the leading white academic authority on black culture. Reviewers of both races uneasily confessed that they could not tell whether the author was white or black. White southerners were outraged by what they saw as a betrayal of the white race. The book did not find a large audience, but it was a critical success.

Peterkin fell out with H. L. Mencken over her next project, an autobiographical novel about a troubled plantation mistress in which the African American characters were bit players. Mencken advised her to take out the white people and go back to portraying plantation life from a black point of view. Stung by this criticism, which implied that her own troubles were not worth writing about, and convinced that Knopf had done a poor job of publicizing *Green Thursday,* Peterkin eventually did as Mencken suggested but took her new manuscript to the Bobbs-Merrill company, a mass-market publishing house that promised extensive advertising and promotion. *Black*

April, a novel about African American life on an isolated plantation, captured the imagination of the American public and was soon a best seller. Donald Davidson, a founding editor of the *Fugitive,* declared that *Black April* was a gold mine of "superstitions and sayings" and an invaluable record of a primitive culture unchanged by civilization. But more than that, according to Davidson, it was a literary milestone, "the first genuine novel in English of the Negro as a human being." Reviewing the book for the Chicago *Defender,* a militant black newspaper, Ernest Rice McKinney hailed it as a masterpiece. "If *Black April* is not the great American novel," he wrote, "then Mrs. Peterkin is the one to write it." Critics Laurence Stallings and Robert Nathan called it "one of the outstanding books of the year" and "one of the greatest novels ever written in this country." The *Saturday Review of Literature* declared, "Other fiction of Negro life seems false in the light of Mrs. Peterkin's achievement." The *Nation* called *Black April* "the finest work produced thus far dealing with the American Negro" and predicted that it would "do more good than a dozen sociological tracts." The New York *Times* praised Peterkin's rendering of the Gullah dialect as "a lucid, yet idiomatic, racy speech."

But it was *Scarlet Sister Mary* (1928)—the fictionalized biography of Mary Weeks and a thinly disguised autobiography that tapped into the author's secret traumas—that made Julia Peterkin famous. Mary is an orphan, a "poor little motherless," who lives with old Maum Hannah and her crippled son, Budda Ben. Like Weeks, "Si' Ma'e" is abandoned by her husband. She takes many lovers, loses her firstborn son, and eventually "finds peace" as a church member, though she refuses to give up her love charm and her gold hoop earrings. The story of an independent, sexual woman—"a devil and a good woman, too"—who is not broken by the scorn of the community, *Scarlet Sister Mary* found an eager audience at the end of the Jazz Age, especially among women who had found a measure of freedom but were still hobbled by a pervasive sexual double standard.

In 1929, the year William Faulkner's *The Sound and the Fury* and Thomas Wolfe's *Look Homeward, Angel* were published, *Scarlet Sister Mary* won the Pulitzer Prize for fiction amid controversy over whether a novel about a promiscuous black woman could be said to uphold Joseph Pulitzer's wish that the winning book represent "the wholesome best of American manhood." There were British, Spanish, Italian, Danish, and Hebrew editions of the book, and Ethel Barrymore, the "Queen of the American Theater," brought it to the stage in a disastrous blackface production that nearly destroyed both her reputation and Peterkin's.

Bright Skin, Peterkin's last novel, appeared in 1932. The story of a mulatto girl named Cricket, another poor little motherless, it is Peterkin's most sophisticated novel and her least appreciated. The old ways of life are dying in *Bright Skin*. Mechanization is sweeping labor off the plantation, and the descendants of slaves have learned to resent their poverty. Several characters in the book become radical black separatists, including an evangelical minister who preaches that whites are devils. The men who flee to Harlem become slumlords, gamblers, and pimps. Cricket escapes the drudgery of the plantation only to end up as a stripper, using a stage name, Princess Kazoola, drawn from her African ancestry. Her husband, Blue, is left behind, trapped by poverty, fear, and his own fundamental decency. *Bright Skin* is a book about what people long for and what they will settle for when real opportunity proves to be an illusion. A stunning dissection of social upheaval, the book was nevertheless scorned by leftists of the 1930s, who considered it too complicated and too sympathetic to blacks who opted to stay on the plantation. Nor did it suit those who had relished the archaic, pastoral qualities of Peterkin's earlier work.

By the time she and her friend Doris Ulmann published *Roll, Jordan, Roll* in 1933, Peterkin's revolutionary fire had died, and her reputation was waning. One of the earliest documentary volumes of the 1930s, a precursor to collaborations like James Agee and Walker Evans' *Let Us Now Praise Famous Men* (1941), *Roll, Jordan, Roll* is a hybrid of fiction and nonfiction, with old *Reviewer* sketches written from a black point of view printed alongside newer, journalistic essays in a paternalistic voice. Ulmann's photographs show black people at work, at worship, and at play, cutting and sorting asparagus, plowing with oxen, hauling cotton, fishing with cast nets, being baptized. There are portraits of several of the people who inspired Peterkin's stories, though not of Mary Weeks or Lavinia Berry. The New York *Times* lambasted Peterkin for showing "a happy land of kindly masters and contented slaves," and African American historian Sterling Brown—a great admirer of Peterkin's other books—found it full of racial stereotypes. But Walter White gave it "the enthusiastic endorsement of the National Association for the Advancement of Colored People" and ordered copies to give as Christmas gifts. Flawed and enigmatic as it is, *Roll, Jordan, Roll* contains some of the most powerful writing of Peterkin's career. The trade edition was cursed with serious production problems—bad printing on poor paper resulted in murky reproduction. But the large-format limited edition, which contains eighteen additional plates hand-pulled using copperplate photogravure, is now among the most hotly collected of all photography books.

Julia Peterkin fell silent after 1935. She grew increasingly reclusive after the suicide of her daughter-in-law in 1941, though she helped raise her motherless grandson and pursued hobbies that included gardening and raising poultry. Southern writers who emerged in the 1920s and 1930s clearly felt her influence. Zora Neale Hurston's first novel, *Jonah's Gourd Vine* (1954), for example, echoes *Black April* both in themes and in dialogue, and a collection of Eudora Welty's early photographs and short stories was rejected by a publisher as "simply following Peterkin."

Unlike most of the other writers associated with the Southern Renaissance, Peterkin never lived outside the South except for four months she spent teaching literature at Bennington College (Vermont) in 1936. She traveled abroad only once, in 1925, when she spent several weeks in France and Italy. Though she made some money from her books in the late 1920s, she and her husband got their living from agriculture, and her life was dominated by chronic financial anxiety. Neither an academic nor an intellectual, she scorned the romantic view of farming promoted by the Nashville Agrarians. But Peterkin was well aware of the ironies of her position. Compared to the lives of the people who hoed her cotton fields and washed her clothes, her existence was luxurious and secure.

At the height of her career, in 1929, Peterkin fell in love with a younger man, an aspiring novelist named Irving Fineman. For a time she seemed to teeter on the brink of leaving her husband for Fineman, who was unmarried, twelve years her junior, and Jewish. Such a move would have guaranteed social ostracism, and Peterkin resisted. But the two corresponded for over a decade, and their letters show Peterkin torn between her exciting new life and the ties of home and family, struggling to reconcile her avant-garde identity with her white-supremacist roots. By the end of her life, she had given herself over to the mores of her community. She opposed integration and was terrified by the emerging civil rights movement.

When Peterkin died of congestive heart failure in Orangeburg, South Carolina, in 1961, her works were almost entirely forgotten, described in the footnotes to literary history either as local color or lurid sensationalism. Yet Peterkin was a great storyteller, recognized both as a driving force in early twentieth-century American literature and as a woman who struggled to tell the truth in a South that tried to silence her. A brilliant, enigmatic woman whose writings drew on her own emotional traumas and family scandals, Peterkin subverted the stereotypes of her time by creating powerful, unflinching stories of rural African American life. Her contradictory life and work are fertile ground for further study.

Elizabeth Madox Roberts

George Brosi

The writing career of Elizabeth Madox Roberts fits neatly between the two world wars of the twentieth century. During this time, women writers with roots in the South were prominent in American literature. At the beginning of this era, Willa Cather was dominant, and at the end Katherine Ann Porter emerged. In the space between these two giants of American literature, no southern woman writer made a stronger lasting contribution than Roberts. During the 1920s and 1930s when Roberts was publishing, Ellen Glasgow and Evelyn Scott were her most widely read and appreciated southern female contemporaries, but despite Glasgow's Pulitzer Prize, neither produced a novel as enduring as Roberts' *The Time of Man* (1926). The spirit of Roberts' writing was close to the spirit of Willa Cather's prose, for although her settings are totally consistent with literary realism, her protagonists typically overcome life's obstacles with a spirit reminiscent of literary romanticism. Roberts' heroines ordinarily find meaning in life not so much from relationships with other people, certainly not from the kind of working-class solidarity celebrated in the proletarian writing of this era, but instead from the centering of their lives through a deep-seated appreciation of the natural world.

Elizabeth Madox Roberts was born in Perryville, Kentucky, on October 30, 1881, to Simpson and Mary Elizabeth Brent Roberts, who both had come there as teachers. Her ancestors arrived in Kentucky over the Wilderness Road, and her father was a veteran of the Confederate Army. When Roberts was three, her family moved to nearby Springfield, a county seat town located about seventy-five miles southeast of Louisville. Roberts grew up the oldest of eight siblings in a prominent professional family. In 1897 she went to live with maternal relatives so she could attend high school in Covington, Kentucky, near Cincinnati. She entered the University of Kentucky in 1900, but she became ill and was forced to withdraw before the end of her first term.

After returning home to recover her health, Elizabeth Madox Roberts began giving school lessons in the front room of her family's home and later taught public school. This teaching experience brought Roberts face-to-face with the rural people of the hills and hollows and of the crossroads communities where the Kentucky Bluegrass meets the hill country. They, along with the county seat people she knew all her life, would become the subjects of her fiction in later years.

Seeking a healthier climate, Roberts lived intermittently with a sister in Colorado. There, she published a volume of nature poetry, *In the Great Steep's Garden* (1915), through a local printing company. By this time Roberts' health improved enough for her to enroll again at the University of Kentucky. A professor there, seeing promise in her work, urged her to transfer to a more rigorous intellectual environment. Thus, in 1917, at the age of thirty-six, Roberts entered the University of Chicago. The next four years were the most stimulating of her life. She became friends with many aspiring authors who were attracted to Chicago by the presence there of such literary luminaries as Carl Sandburg, Vachel Lindsay, and Edgar Lee Masters. At Chicago she won literary prizes and was encouraged to pursue fiction writing.

When Roberts returned to Springfield with her degree in 1921, she began devoting herself in earnest to her writing, achieving considerable success the very next year with an outstanding book of verse, *Under the Tree*. These poems, intended for children and written in traditional poetic rhymes and meters, were met with rave reviews and have been widely anthologized. After the success of her first book, Roberts continued to write poetry but also began work on her first two novels.

The next book Roberts published was the novel *The Time of Man*. William H. Slavick in the "Introduction" to the University Press of Kentucky reprint (1982) maintains that "the 'poetic realism' . . . that [Roberts] developed and mastered in her first novel placed *The Time of Man* with Lawrence's often poetic prose, Joyce's closely textured fiction, and Woolf's impressionism, as one of the great innovative works that came from that generation; none integrated poetry more closely into a prose style." He goes on to call *The Time of Man* the "first major novel [of] the Southern renascence." This novel follows Ellen Chesser, the daughter and wife of farmhands, and one of the most memorable and beloved protagonists in southern fiction, from her adolescence into middle age. Nothing that Roberts ever wrote surpassed this book in either critical repute or popular appeal. It became a Book-of-the-Month Club selection and was published in England and translated into six languages. It ushered in a decade of book royalties sufficient to allow Roberts to live as she pleased.

Roberts' next book was *My Heart and My Flesh* (1927). This novel shows the breadth of Roberts' range, for it is set not in the country but in "Anneville," a town sharply reminiscent of Springfield, and its heroine, Theodosia Bell, is as rich as Ellen Chesser is poor. Yet for all the differences, this book, too, presents a female protagonist who turns to inner resources to overcome adversity.

In the fall of 1927 Elizabeth Madox Roberts built a brick house adjoining her parents' home in Springfield. Here she had a loom set up for weaving; she gardened and painted, took long walks, and carried on voluminous correspondence. Although Roberts nurtured both local and long-distance friendships and did make some public appearances, she refused more social and literary invitations than she accepted. She spent the summers in her Springfield home for the rest of her life but continued to follow a pattern established when she left Chicago and wintered in urban areas including New York, Santa Monica, and Louisville.

In their book-length critical study, *Elizabeth Madox Roberts: American Novelist* (1956), Harry Modean Campbell and Ruel E. Foster characterize her next novel, *Jingling in the Wind* (1928), as one of her two allegorical novels in contrast to her other five, which exemplify poetic realism. The female protagonist of *Jingling in the Wind,* Tulip McAfee, is courted unconventionally by Jeremy, the local rainmaker. This profession gives the author ample room to satirize many of the decade's prominent conflicts, especially those between "reason" and "religion," such as evolution and prohibition.

Roberts' fourth novel, *The Great Meadow* (1930), is generally considered her second best, after *The Time of Man.* It is a story of the migration of pioneers over the Wilderness Road to Kentucky, covering the time period from 1774 to 1781. Carl Van Doren called it the "richest and loveliest of all narratives of the settlement of Kentucky." Although this is Roberts' only historical novel, the protagonist, Diony Hall, shares much with the heroines of Roberts' contemporary novels. Her inner journey parallels the progress of her family's covered wagon. *The Great Meadow* was a great commercial as well as a literary success. It was reprinted in several editions in many languages, and Metro-Goldwyn-Mayer made it into a movie.

The next novel, *A Buried Treasure* (1931), the third and last Roberts novel to become a book club selection, proved more commercially than critically successful. It is a humorous account of the consequences that descend upon a Kentucky farm couple, Andy and Philly Blair, when a pot of gold and silver is discovered on their land.

The Haunted Mirror (1932) was Roberts' first collection of short stories. Like the poems in *Under the Tree,* these stories have appeared widely in literary anthologies. "Death at Bearwallow," for example, is included in the 1997 edition of the *Heath Anthology of American Literature.* This innovative and thought-provoking story that juxtaposes recollections of youthful exposures to death with sexual initiations demonstrates Roberts' depth and willingness to tackle controversial topics. "The Sacrifice of the Maidens," which came in second for the O. Henry Memorial Prize in short story writing for 1930, currently appears in *The Literature of the American South: A Norton Anthology* (1998).

When Roberts' next novel, *He Sent Forth a Raven,* was published in 1935, Grant Knight noted in the *Saturday Review* that it "reveals more of Elizabeth Roberts than does any other of her novels, more of her exquisite sense of reality, her bewilderment with things as they are, her lyric anger, her slight vein of madness, her faith in man's redemption." In contrast Isabel Lockwood Hawley, in her 1970 Ph.D. dissertation for the University of North Carolina, articulates a more common critical conclusion: "the increasingly complex and artificial designs [Roberts] imposed upon her materials [causes] the breakdown in organic unity and consequently in artistic merit which is evident between the first novel, *The Time of Man,* and the last."

In 1937, weakened by Hodgkin's disease, Roberts began wintering in Florida. *Black Is My Truelove's Hair* (1938), Roberts' last novel, takes place in a tiny rural community. As the novel opens, the protagonist, Dena Janes, has just returned from a brief affair with Will Langtry that has scandalized the community. Like other Roberts heroines, Janes turns to inner resources and a relationship with nature to win back her self-respect and community standing.

Roberts' last two books were a poetry collection, *Song in the Meadow* (1940), and one final collection of stories, *Not by Strange Gods* (1941). At the time of her death, she was working on a book-length narrative poem or series of poems about Daniel Boone and a novel centering on the great Louísville flood of 1937, which she lived through. Elizabeth Madox Roberts died on March 13, 1941, in Orlando, Florida, at the age of 59.

The New York *Times* obituary noted, "Ever since the publication of *The Time of Man* in 1926, Miss Roberts was recognized as one of the first-ranking novelists in America." *Time*'s obituary called Roberts "one of America's most distinguished women writers." E. A. Jonas in the obituary for the Louisville *Courier-Journal* noted, "Kentucky has produced no sweeter singer, no truer story-teller than Elizabeth Madox Roberts." In the fifty years since her death, five of Roberts' seven novels and her poetry collection, *Under the Tree,* have been reprinted. At the beginning of the twenty-first century both *The Time of Man* and *The Great Meadow* are in print and continue to attract a new audience, demonstrating the timeless appeal of Roberts' work.

Among Kentucky authors, Elizabeth Madox Roberts is clearly eclipsed in literary reputation only by Robert Penn Warren. As an Appalachian author, Roberts basically ushered in the era of literary realism following John Fox, Jr.'s, romantic novels and preceding Thomas Wolfe. In American literature, Roberts is recognized as one of the leading women writers of the 1920s and 1930s. Writing in an era dominated by such male American writers as Sinclair Lewis, John Steinbeck, F. Scott Fitzgerald, Ernest Hemingway, and William Faulkner, Roberts was clearly less concerned about the social lives and more involved in the interior lives of her characters. Even though her characters had the kind of deep community roots that some other authors of the time period portrayed, they were fundamentally alone and connected more to the land itself than to other people. Elizabeth Madox Roberts made the women of the farms and small towns of America's hinterland real to readers around the world and invested them with dignity, passion, and a love for the natural world that has inspired readers of her own and each subsequent generation.

Frances Newman

Miriam J. Shillingsburg

Unfortunately for American letters, Frances Newman was soon forgotten. Her crisp, new style, experiments with point of view and voice, biting irony, and social satire had little obvious immediate or long-term influence on southern fiction. Nevertheless, her early frankness about female concerns, such as family and deference, virginity and marriage, childbirth and menstruation, and the cult of beauty and propriety, shocked the public and made her a best-selling author. But more importantly, this groundbreaking treatment provided the appropriate transition from Mary Noailles Murfree, Grace King, and even Kate Chopin and Ellen Glasgow to Flannery O'Connor, Katherine Ann Porter, Bobbie Ann Mason, Gail Godwin, and a host of nonsouthern writers.

Frances Newman was born on September 13, 1883, the fifth child and fourth daughter in a well-heeled Atlanta family. One of her maternal ancestors founded White's Fort, Tennessee (later to be known as Knoxville), in the 1780s. In 1836 her great-grandfather Hugh Lawson White was defeated for president by Martin Van Buren. Her mother, Frances Percy Alexander, to whom she dedicated her first novel, was born in Knoxville and died in April 1922 in Atlanta. Frances' father, Judge William Truslow Newman, was born in Knoxville, joined the Tennessee cavalry at seventeen, and lost his right arm in the summer of 1864 fighting on the Confederate side in Georgia. After the war he remained in Atlanta, studied law, and passed the bar at twenty-three. After marrying at twenty-eight, he became city attorney and was appointed United States District Judge for Northern Georgia. He died in Atlanta in 1920.

Newman's niece Margaret Patterson wrote, to her aunt's apparent approval, that Frances "was an unattractive child, and she knew it." She was a "pallid girl with stringy black hair and stringy black-stockinged legs . . . [but] with remarkable intelligence, she decided that her only alternative was to cultivate her cleverness." At ten Frances began reading Shakespeare and continued to read "many and varied types of literature." She also wrote her first fiction, which, carelessly left out, was read aloud and ridiculed by a sister and her beau on a Sunday afternoon. Overhearing, Newman later wrote that she "wept for a few minutes on a bed of mint in my family's garden . . . [and] gave up literature."

Young Frances was a student at Calhoun Street School, the girls' high school; in 1900 she graduated from Washington Seminary in Atlanta, where she wrote the class poem. Subsequently, she spent a year each at Agnes Scott College and Miss McVeagh's in Washington, D.C., and she concluded her education at Mrs. Semple's in New York City. These are the same schools attended by Katherine Faraday, the heroine of Newman's first published novel.

Newman's education was continued at intervals with four European tours, mastery of seven modern and ancient languages, occasional summer school, and graduation in June 1912 from the library school at the Atlanta Carnegie Library. She was a librarian at Florida State College; at the Atlanta Public Library, which she considered the best public library in the South; and at the Georgia Institute of Technology. She became a regular contributor to various periodicals and began spending her time more and more in New York. Though she seems to have had several lovers, including perhaps the collector of her published letters, the young Hansel Baugh, Frances Newman, like two of her heroines, never married.

As head of the lending department at the Atlanta Public Library, she began a column of "Library Literary Notes" in the Sunday Atlanta *Constitution.* These essays, along with regular contributions to a Richmond publication, the *Reviewer,* attracted the attention of novelists F. Scott Fitzgerald, James Branch Cabell, and Ellen Glasgow, as well as critic H. L. Mencken. Her first novel, written at age ten, having been abandoned, Newman wrote her second in 1921; like its predecessor, it no longer exists. In 1924, she published a collection of favorite stories, *The Short Story's Mutations: From Petronius to Paul Morand,* which she translated from five different languages.

Newman planned to write "a novel about a girl in a library, and . . . call it *The Goldfish Bowl*," which would be a "lovelorn story that delighted elderly ladies . . . and would delight low-brows and high-brows, and even medium-brows." However, she discovered that she must write in her own style, regardless of the low-, high-, and medium-brows, and—rejected by a few publishing houses—*The Goldfish Bowl* was abandoned. By November 1922 Newman turned to "a novel about a girl who began by believing everything that her family and her teachers said to her, and who ended by disbelieving most of those things, but by finding that she couldn't keep herself from behaving as if she still believed them—about a girl who was born and bred to be a southern lady, and whose mind never could triumph over the ideas she was presumably born with, and the ideas she was undoubtedly taught."

This is one way to characterize *The Hard-Boiled Virgin* (1926). Within six months it had seen eight printings (about 32,000 copies), and according to Newman, "lots of people like it, lots of people are shocked, but every one seems to think it's clever . . . Atlanta is almost in convulsions over the book and it is selling here by hundreds." The book was banned in Boston, both panned and praised by reviewers, and in Atlanta it shocked the conservative ladies. Cabell called the book "the most brilliant, the most candid, the most civilized, and . . . the most profound book yet written by any American woman."

In an important essay for the *Reviewer* entitled "Atlanta" (1923), Frances Newman provides an affectionate description of her native city. She called Atlanta an "up-start" town whose vitality some believed came from "constantly arriving immigrants from the frozen north who come down to supply energy to a people exhausted by . . . the sun." To be in Atlanta's social upper crust required membership in the correct clubs and churches. In her fiction, membership in the Piedmont Driving Club is a necessity; in "Atlanta," she explains: "Even in Atlanta we have a sort of social distinction, though the elements are undoubtedly mixed in them. The Piedmont Driving Club . . . is the St. Cecilia [of Charleston] . . . but the requirements for membership are different and years of reflection will not quite reveal what they are."

Although her style, erudition, experimentation, social iconoclasm, and irreverent satire are fascinating aspects of Newman's fiction, her feminism is her boldest trait. She convincingly pictures "growing up female in the South" and gives a thorough indictment of marriage as it was borne by a southern woman of her generation. In *The Hard-Boiled Virgin* Katharine is utterly bored by the proper churches and clubs, yet that is where she should find a gentleman admirer, for the brothers, fathers, and beaus of her friends all are members. Katharine satirizes the fetish for the proper clothing for the proper occasion, though Newman herself was fond of stylish hats and purple dresses.

The burden of being proper was exacerbated by Katharine's being female; she "knew that any boy is born to a more honourable social situation than any girl," apparently due to his "inability to produce a baby rather than to his ability to produce an idea." She knew that girls could be stupid but they must be beautiful, and so Katharine tried in vain to "make her thin lips touch one of her sharp elbows" because of its rumored "efficacy in changing a girl into a boy." Katharine realized that Miss Washington's school had merely paralyzed her brain, not extracted it, as did Miss Rutherford's school.

Newman believed hard-boiled virginity—clearly a mental state rather than a physical one—was the alternative to marriage. While she was writing this novel, Newman opined in a letter, "[M]arriage is an institution created for human beings in a primitive state of society and of intelligence, but I haven't any substitute for it. Perhaps I have, in a way—that will all be in the Virgin." Katherine, having survived the horrible suspense over whether she has become pregnant, feels that she will never again want a man to admire either her hair or her voice or her writing.

Because of the popularity of *The Hard-Boiled Virgin,* Newman's other novel, *Dead Lovers Are Faithful Lovers* (1928), sold over 20,000 copies before publication. It shows Evelyn Cunningham and Isabel Ramsay utterly controlled by Charlton Cunningham, respectively husband and lover. Beautiful and proper Evelyn rises every morning of her honeymoon to comb, curl, and change, afraid that Charlton will awaken to see "her tangled hair and . . . her tumbled lace and her tumbled white ribbons." Fearing that her husband will find another woman more attractive, Evelyn accepts the hollow decorum that a proper wife must maintain, realizing "that an important man's wife [has] no existence of her own."

Twelve years later Charlton does find a more attractive woman—a librarian who is willing to break the rules and conduct an affair. Even Isabel, however, is baffled by the man who strips her of control over even her own sexuality. Because every man is entitled to a virginal wife (even a second wife), Charlton keeps "saving her from himself for himself" and never consummates the affair. When Charlton unexpectedly dies of a chill, the conclusion is the rather cynical one that the only faithful lover—licit or illicit—is a dead one.

Frances Newman's career came to an abrupt end during preparation of her fourth book, a collection of stories she translated from French, entitled *Six Moral Tales from Jules Laforgue* (1928). In the last days of her life, she suffered a mysterious eye condition that incapacitated her with roaring and vibrations in the head. After vainly consulting ten doctors in Europe and the Northeast, she died, possibly of poison, in her New York City apartment on October 22, 1928. Her mentor and friend James Branch Cabell believed that if she had lived five more years, "she would have stayed remembered, not merely as unique, but as supreme, among the women writers of America."

Katherine Anne Porter

Janis P. Stout

Katherine Anne Porter, recognized as one of the great stylists of American modernism, was a southerner both by heritage and by choice. Paradoxically enough, that fact did not begin to influence her writing until she went to live in Mexico and there observed the work of writers and artists emphasizing indigenous themes and styles, but her southernness was at least intermittently important to her throughout her life. Even so, despite the fact that she identified herself with the South, associated for many years with some of the leaders of the southern Agrarians, and set much of her most important work in the South, she actually lived in the region for a relatively small part of her long life.

It was long believed, on the basis of a personal mythology cultivated by Porter herself, that Katherine Anne Porter was born in Louisiana in 1894 of an aristocratic family—the "white pillar crowd," as she put it—and was educated in convent schools in New Orleans. In fact, she was born in a simple cabin in central Texas in the now deserted community of Indian Creek, near Brownwood, in 1890. Her given name was Callie Russell, which she would change to the more elegant Katherine Anne in 1915 at the time of her first divorce. It is true that her forebears on both sides were southern and at least on her father's side had been of the slaveholding class, though never on the scale she implied. It is also true that when the Porters migrated from Kentucky to Texas they stopped for a time in Louisiana. But that was the generation before her own. In characteristic fashion, her imagination seized on details from family lore and claimed them as her own. Her bruited convent education seems to have been based either on wish or at most on a few weeks of being parked in such a school by relatives.

Claiming a history that linked her with southern aristocracy can well be seen as a disclaimer of her actual origins. In regional terms, Texas is a bifurcated state, only the eastern third clearly southern in topography and way of life, the rest, including the area where Porter was born and where she grew up, either western or more accurately, southwestern, with an ambiguous border zone. That zone consists of a strip running northeast to southwest through the middle of the state, where both land and life patterns change and the two regions meet and mingle. Porter spent most of her childhood squarely within that border zone. When she was not quite two, her mother died, probably of tuberculosis, not long after bearing her fifth child, and Harrison Boone Porter took his children to live with his mother in the town of Kyle, slightly south of Austin toward San Marcos. Porter grew up, then, with what we might call a bordered consciousness, with respect to this south-southwestern border and the more distant Texas-Mexico border, which was present in her awareness from her father's stories of having worked "south of the border" before his marriage and by virtue of a small Mexican population in Kyle. Both of these borders would be of far-reaching importance in her work.

Porter's childhood was a painful one that left scars. Bereft of a mother, she was also in effect bereft of a father, for after his wife's death he withdrew into exaggerated grief and self-pitying moodiness, openly blaming his children for their mother's death and virtually abdicating his parental responsibilities. These devolved on their grandmother, Catherine Porter, known locally as Aunt Cat. An upright, severe woman, she provided Porter a model of female strength that would later emerge in the assertive female figures of her fiction. At Grandmother Porter's home in Kyle, the family lived in cramped quarters on little income. Porter seemed to have felt disgraced by being an object of charity when neighbors provided handed-down clothes for her and her sisters and brother. Her father was unreliable in his affections, apparently according preference to whichever of the girls struck him as prettiest at any given moment. A resulting insecurity is evident in Porter's lifelong concern with physical beauty and her troubled preoccupation with masculine attention. She was married multiple times (four, five, or six, however one judges various problems in counting) and had numerous love affairs, all of them tumultuous.

Porter's career began late. Having married at barely sixteen, she spent several years in a futile effort to fulfill the role of stay-at-home wife to a man who was physically abusive, perhaps even to the extent of causing broken bones. She divorced him after nine years, the last several of which she had spent apart from him, struggling to make an inadequate living as a singer and lyceum performer, a teacher of dancing and elocution, and a movie stand-in. After the divorce she began to work as a newspaper reporter and writer, first in Texas and then in Colorado, but that effort was interrupted by a bout with tuberculosis and near death in the flu epidemic of 1919. Only at the end of 1920, at the age of thirty, did Porter leave her job at the *Rocky Mountain News* in Denver and go to New York City to try to become a serious writer. In 1921 she spent six months in Mexico, the first of four separate stays during the next decade, immersing herself in the political intrigues of the revolutionary government of President Alvaro Obregón, writing for newspapers and magazines, and making notes for fiction she would write later. Her first mature short story, "María Concepción," was published in 1922; her first volume, *Flowering Judas,* titled after the most celebrated of her Mexican stories, was not published until 1930, and then in only a very small edition.

In 1935, the volume was expanded and republished in a commercial run, *Flowering Judas and Other Stories,* which in 1937 won an award from the Book-of-the-Month Club. *Pale Horse, Pale Rider: Three Short Novels* was published in 1939, and *The Leaning Tower and Other Stories* in 1944. In 1962 Porter's long-awaited novel, *Ship of Fools,* well over two decades in the making, was published with great ballyhoo and became her first commercial success, though most critics do not number it among her best works. Movie rights were sold for $400,000, and a successful film resulted. Porter was well established as both a writer's writer, as she had long been recognized, and a writer who had caught the popular imagination, sometimes more for her persona than for her work. She always liked to present herself as a woman of glamour and mystery, and gorgeous pictures of her taken by fashion photographer George Platt Lynes were sometimes published in popular magazines. In 1965 Porter's career reached a peak when she won the Pulitzer Prize for her *Collected Stories.*

Many of Porter's best-known and most admired works draw on her early years in Texas, but she came to that material by an indirect route. The stories of Mexico that she published in the 1920s are important not only because of their own merit—they are an important and beautifully achieved body of work—but because it was there that she developed the techniques of sharp precision and caricature that she employed and extended in later writing. Well-acquainted with a number of leading artistic and intellectual figures in postrevolutionary Mexico, she transferred their emphasis on native material to her own native material, Texas, but a Texas conceived primarily in eastward-looking terms—that is, the Texas that is part of the South rather than the Southwest. In "The Jilting of Granny Weatherall," "He" (published in the *Masses* and best understood within that politically radical context), "Old Mortality," "Noon Wine," and the "Old Order" sequence, she generated a powerful sense of place in a fiction of stylistic discipline and shaping symbolism. The last three of these, in particular, as well as "Pale Horse, Pale Rider," make elaborate use of autobiographical details and the family past.

In the remarkable, underrated "Old Order" stories, Porter developed a treatment of both memory and maturation, focusing these themes through the consciousness of her celebrated Miranda, as well as through a synthesis of great historical and cultural patterns related to her origins in Texas. The sequence emphasizes movement from past to present and links that temporal movement, in a significant parallel, with movement from the Old South to the new Southwest. It is the West and western values, it seems, that represent the future, even though Porter also, with a characteristic richness of ambiguity, fully exploits the familiar association of the West with death. Here one finds, in its most explicit expression, the bordered consciousness. Interestingly, in its Bakhtinian grotesqueness and its juxtaposition of the innocent consciousness with a cruel fallen world, the "Old Order" story "The Circus" closely resembles the circus chapter of *The Adventures of Huckleberry Finn* (1884), the work of another border southerner in whose experience the Southwest was important and who also spent most of his life in the East.

Porter spent much of her life traveling from place to place, always wishing to settle into a home of her own but never able, whether financially or emotionally, to remain in place for long. She was a genuine cosmopolitan. Besides her years in Mexico and her close acquaintance with events of historic as well as aesthetic importance there (evident in several of her best stories and culminating in "Hacienda"), she spent about five years in Europe, first in Berlin, where she observed first-hand the rise of the Nazi Party, and then primarily in Paris. The most tangible fruit of the European years was the long story (Porter disliked the term *novella*) "The Leaning Tower," a chilly and elusive work but a fine one. More generally, her incessant travels and extended periods in residence outside the United States helped her attain a wide acquaintance among literary and intellectual leaders and a breadth of cultural context for her intensely localized fiction. Troubled as she was in many ways, as her letters as well as various external details of her life attest, she was also a person of intelligence who serves as a kind of window on her time. Her extensive papers, located at the University of Maryland, are enormously useful for understanding not only Porter herself but a great many figures she knew, as well as the general social scene through which she moved.

Some of the most compelling evidence of Porter's conception of herself as a southerner and the conflicted nature of that conception is to be found in the archive at Maryland. Insisting to family and friends alike that she was southern at heart and would always remain so, she also at times lashed out at the South, and in particular at Texas, and acknowledged her reluctance to live far from New York City or Washington. Her ambivalence about her origins is compellingly seen in an unpublished, uncompleted work still lying in disordered manuscript called "The Man in the Tree," where her horror of southern racism is seen side by side with her own participation in racist attitudes. It is a troubling document to read, as are, in much the same way, some of her letters and personal jottings.

Porter's relation to her home state was troubled. She said that its cultural drought and its attitudes toward women cramped her development, and she escaped at the first opportunity. After 1918, she returned to Texas only briefly in 1922 and 1936 and for a few months' residence in Houston in 1937. In 1958 she lectured at the University of Texas and went away convinced that a library being planned there (actually, the Harry Ransom Humanities Research Center) would be named for her. Such was not the case, and she added that grievance to the one she had long nursed against the Texas literary establishment for having passed over *Pale Horse, Pale Rider* for the first Texas Institute of Letters prize, in 1939, which went to J. Frank Dobie instead. She had deeply ambivalent feelings about being closely identified with Texas and on the whole preferred to create an image of herself as a southern belle or grande dame. Certainly she fulfilled the latter role in the final decades of her life, when she published reviews and occasional pieces whenever she chose to, taught in visiting appointments at many different campuses around the country, appeared regularly on the lecture circuit wearing evening gowns and long gloves and standing in soft spotlights, and attended public events of all sorts, including the inaugural festivities for President John F. Kennedy and a moon shot at Cape Canaveral. Porter died in Silver Spring, Maryland, in 1980.

Katherine Anne Porter has been remembered chiefly as a consummate stylist and symbolist, but biographical scholarship has demonstrated her significance as a thinker and a sounding board for the complex political and social changes through which she lived.

Evelyn Scott

Mary Wheeling

During her career, Evelyn Scott wrote steadily and voluminously, publishing ten novels, four children's books, one volume of short stories, two autobiographies, and two collections of poetry, along with several dozen individual short stories, critical essays, reviews, and poems. At her death, she left two novels, two volumes of poems, and a score of short stories yet unpublished. Many of Scott's works of fiction and poetry share concerns with those of her southern contemporaries including Faulkner, especially the post–Civil War disintegration of the white aristocracy, which gave rise to changes in social mores affecting sexual behavior, race relations, spiritual beliefs, and class attitudes. At the same time, though, most of Scott's work is set outside the South. Indeed, except for several years after her birth and during her adolescence, Scott herself lived outside the South; she was not widely known as a southern writer until the publication of her eighth book, *The Wave* (1929).

Scott shared a heritage with other notable southern women writers of her day. First, she was born into an enclave of older relatives who kept alive stories of life before the Civil War; second, she was born into a generation of women who forsook their elders' Victorian moral codes for newer, freer attitudes toward family, sex, and career; and third, she was dogged by physical infirmity. Like Julia Peterkin and Ellen Glasgow, Evelyn Scott was able when necessary to exploit the gracious myth of mannered southern gentlewoman, but was at other times also able to decry loudly the damage this myth and its culture had wrought upon white females.

Named Elsie Dunn at her birth on January 17, 1893, in Clarksville, Tennessee, Evelyn Scott was raised to be a southern belle, continuing the tradition esteemed by her mother's family. Scott's father was an outsider from the Midwest, yet he condoned this upbringing. During her depressed adolescence in New Orleans, the precocious Elsie attempted courses at Sophie Newcomb College of Tulane University, but she found herself undisciplined and soon quit. At twenty and still unmarried, she longed to escape the frustrating world of her parents, whose marriage had deteriorated into silence on her father's side and neurotic concern with appearances on her mother's. A married Tulane professor twice Elsie's age invited the young woman to run away with him, so the two eloped, changing their names to "Scott" in order to appear married during their travels. Elsie decided on "Evelyn" as a first name, and the former Professor Frederick Creighton Wellman became "Cyril Kay Scott." The couple eventually settled in Brazil for five and a half years, as described in Evelyn's 1923 memoir, *Escapade*. There she gave birth to her only child, Creighton "Jig" Scott.

Brazil served as backdrop for much of Scott's poetry, which she began writing during her stay. After returning to the United States, she moved from one exotic locale to another in search of literary opportunity and economic security—first to Greenwich Village, then Cape Cod, and next, Bermuda. Two locales in France and two in Algeria were home to Scott and her companions at various periods in her life, as were three British cities, two Canadian, and three more in New York. After these came stints in New Jersey, New Mexico, and California. She lived her last ten years in a seedy communal apartment in New York City, her fame and health having faded years earlier.

Scott's early imagist poems collected in *Precipitations* (1920), her first novel, *The Narrow House* (1921), and her play *Love* (produced by the Provincetown Players in 1921) established Scott as an "experimental" or "modern" writer, admired by H. L. Mencken and William Carlos Williams. Throughout her career, however, she hesitated to ally herself with writers; notable exceptions were Lola Ridge, Kay Boyle, Theodore Dreiser, Charlotte Wilder, and exiled activist Emma Goldman.

To complement the imagist technique used in her verse, Scott employed a poetic expressionism in her novel *The Narrow House,* a story of three generations living in claustrophobic quarters. The novel's main conflict is dysfunctional American sexuality, which Scott treats frankly, pushing the accepted limits of the day. Consonant with her era's popular conception of

Freud's theories of repression and sublimation, Scott's stream-of-consciousness narrative technique reveals the roots of sexual frustration within the inner lives of her characters. *The Narrow House* and her next two novels, *Narcissus* (1922) and *The Golden Door* (1923), make up a trilogy that ends as the youngest member of the original family struggles within a love triangle. The plot situations in these and indeed in most of her other novels mirrored Scott's own personal life, in which she was, until her forties, involved in similarly complex love affairs.

A constant theme throughout Scott's career was woman's struggle to forge a discrete identity. Her best treatment of this subject, and some say her best work overall, is the 1923 memoir *Escapade*. In this boundary-breaking work, which includes poetic, imagistic prose and a fantasy drama, Scott details her life in Brazil as the lover of an egoistic jack-of-all-trades and as the suffering mother of their only child. Like her third novel, *The Golden Door,* parts of *Escapade* had to be censored, in particular graphic physical descriptions of the female body during pregnancy and breast-feeding, much to Scott's disapproval.

Several years later, her five-story collection *Ideals* (1927) appeared, as did the first installment of Scott's historical fiction trilogy. *Migrations* (1927), *The Wave* (1929), and *A Calendar of Sin* (1931) chronicle aspects of American culture from the 1840s to World War I, and since the characters were based on Scott's own midwestern and southern ancestors, she was able to present and sustain distinctly southern characters, settings, and issues. Of these lengthy books, the middle volume became Scott's most widely read and critically acclaimed work of fiction. *The Wave* follows the Civil War—from the first shots fired to the Union's victory parade—through a series of vignettes concerning over one hundred characters. Scott's technique in this novel creates a panoramic view of the war's effect on the American psyche. During the span of her historical trilogy's publication, Scott fell in love with and married British fiction writer William John Metcalfe, best known for his tales of the macabre.

The success of the 1929 novel led Scott's publishers, Cape and Smith, to ask her help in assessing a manuscript by another of their southern authors, William Faulkner. Her essay in response to his yet-unpublished *The Sound and the Fury* so delighted Cape and Smith that they asked her permission to reprint it for distribution with the novel itself, for they knew that Faulkner's stylistic complexity would certainly frustrate his readers. Thus Evelyn Scott's "On William Faulkner's *The Sound and the Fury*" became the first important work of criticism concerning a novel representative both of high modernism and the Southern Renaissance. Scott became a frequent reviewer of southern literature for the *Nation* and *Scribner's* magazine, evaluating works including Gordon's *Penhally* (1931), Wolfe's *Of Time and the River* (1935), and Mitchell's *Gone with the Wind* (1936). A year after *The Wave*, Scott's second poetry collection, *The Winter Alone* (1930), appeared to less-than-enthusiastic reviews. The verse was consistent with themes present from the beginning of her career: important among them, how women fit into the world—biologically, relationally, mythically.

Exploration of the artist's need for freedom had always intrigued Scott and provided additional thematic material for her writing. The lives of artists as they exist in relation to each other is the subject of her 1933 autobiographical novel *Eva Gay*, based on the lives of Scott and her two early loves, common-law husband Cyril Kay Scott and her concurrent lover, watercolorist Owen Merton (father of Catholic mystic Thomas Merton). Her romantic relations with these two men had long since ended, but her emotional issues with them remained unresolved. *Eva Gay* was followed quickly by her next novel, *Breathe upon These Slain* (1934), a story within a story told by a tourist renting an English seaside cottage. Still experimenting with style, Scott here stuck close to a favorite issue of how succeeding generations must revolt against the codes of their parents.

Early in 1937 Scott published her novel *Bread and a Sword*, about a writer's quest for artistic freedom and financial security. This, of course, was the quest of Scott's own life, a search made more dire by her increasing concern in the 1930s with what she perceived as communist dictation of the arts in the United States. She felt personally pressured by editors, publishers, and colleagues to produce writing that was in line with the leftist sentiments of the literary community. Although she proclaimed an affinity for many leftist views, her response to the coercion she sensed was to denounce communism publicly as a misguided philosophy, so that eventually most of her fiction and poetry became vehicles to serve her own political purposes. Never having made enough money to support herself or her family for very long, Scott finally became convinced that the fault was not entirely hers; she felt that perhaps because of some concerted effort on the part of communist publishers and editors, her work was not being given the regard it warranted. This feeling developed in the 1940s and 1950s into a full-blown paranoia, which further troubled the literary establishment she had already alienated with her complaints.

Scott again highlighted southern themes in her autobiographical work *Background in Tennessee* (1937). Race, feminism, class, and agrarianism were topics she addressed in this hybrid of Tennesseana and childhood memoir, which fellow southerners Lillian Smith and Paula Snelling hailed as subtly and tenderly wise.

The Shadow of the Hawk, Scott's final published novel, came out in small numbers to little attention in 1941. Although she had more manuscripts that she still sought to publish, by this time no one was interested in pursuing a literary relationship with such a troublesome writer. She was to continue publishing individual poems and critical essays in journals, but these small jobs were never enough to support her and her husband. In the end she relied mainly on the charity of her few friends to fund their room, board, and medical care, until her death in 1963 from the combined effects of heart disease and lung cancer.

Caroline Gordon

Nancylee Novell Jonza

In "Caroline Gordon and the Historic Image," a 1949 article for the *Sewanee Review,* Andrew Lytle published an evaluation of Caroline Gordon's fiction that, taken with Gordon's reaction to it, illuminates Gordon's achievements as a writer and the difficulties scholars and readers face when confronting her work and literary reputation. Echoing earlier comments by British novelist Ford Madox Ford, Lytle praised the "masculine" nature of Gordon's prose. "If she did not sign her name, it would be at first hard to know her sex," he wrote. Nevertheless, according to Lytle, the theme of her fiction was "what Life, the sly deceiver, does to womankind but particularly to the woman of great passion and sensibility."

Although pleased with his first assertion, Gordon insisted that Lytle misread her: she wrote about men called to be heroes; the women in her fiction were only minor characters creating chaos and disaster whenever they were given or took control of life. Furthermore, Gordon resisted attempts to consider her writing in the context of female literary history. Consciously shaping her reputation from the 1950s onward, Gordon claimed to write in the tradition of Henry James, Ford, and Gustave Flaubert. Although she depended on her friends Katherine Anne Porter and Josephine Herbst early in her career, she later declared that her husband, poet and critic Allen Tate, taught her everything she knew about writing. Yet all of Gordon's fiction is informed by her female heritage and her acute sense of the barriers women face.

Born in 1895 in Todd County, Kentucky, the middle child and only daughter of James Morris Gordon and Nancy Minor Meriwether Gordon, Caroline was named for her maternal grandmother and surrounded by strong-willed, often highly educated women in her extended family "connection." Her parents ran a well-respected classical preparatory school for boys in Clarksville, Tennessee (before J. M. Gordon pursued a career as a Disciples of Christ minister), and Gordon, like her mother, excelled at her study of Latin and Greek. She also developed her passion for southern history and storytelling from her grandmother and father. Old Miss Carrie, as her grandmother was known, revered the South and her family's history; J. M. Gordon, a mesmerizing speaker, fueled his daughter's imagination with tales of his own hunting and fishing as well as accounts of the heroes of Greek and Roman myth.

After completing a bachelor's degree in classical studies at Bethany College in West Virginia, Gordon taught high school for several years. In 1919, following in the footsteps of her great-aunt Elizabeth Meriwether Gilmer (1861–1951), known to most as Dorothy Dix, the celebrated advice columnist and crime reporter, Gordon became a journalist, first in Chattanooga, Tennessee, then in Wheeling, West Virginia. Like other members of her extended family—including Elizabeth Avery Meriwether (1824–1917) and Amélie Rives (1863–1945)—Gordon also began writing fiction.

Gordon's interest in southern literature is evident in her book reviews of the time. On February 10, 1923, in the Chattanooga *News*, Gordon published one of the first serious notices of the southern little magazine the *Fugitive*: "U. S. Best Poets Here in Tennessee." In her summary of those poets, Gordon noted the work of Allen Tate, "the most radical member of the group." Gordon did not meet Tate until 1924, and by then she had completed a major portion of her first novel. Moving to New York City, she worked for Johnson Features and wrote fiction in her spare time until she discovered she was pregnant with Tate's child in early 1925. Tate agreed to marry her—temporarily—but the couple decided to stay married after their daughter was born later that year.

Although Gordon and Tate lived a hand-to-mouth existence, Gordon completed her first novel, *Darkling I Listen*, by 1926. She destroyed it after showing it to Tate, but immediately started another. Later that year, she began working as a secretary for Ford Madox Ford. The following year, she completed her first short stories, although she would not find a publisher until 1929 when "Summer Dust: Four Episodes" appeared in the little magazine *Gyroscope*. By 1930, Gordon had other stories published in *Gyroscope* and *Scribner's* magazine. She also had an editor (Maxwell Perkins) and a publishing contract with Scribner's for her novel. Once again living in Clarksville, Tennessee, near her maternal ancestors, the Meriwethers, Gordon completed her fictionalized account of southern life, *Penhally* (1931), while Tate worked on his contributions to *I'll Take My Stand: The South and the Agrarian Tradition* (1930).

Taking its name from the ancestral home of the Llewellyn family (loosely modeled on the Meriwethers), *Penhally* begins in 1826, with Ralph Llewellyn fighting with his brother Nicholas over the elder's refusal to divide the family estate. The novel spans four generations, following the family through the Civil War and Reconstruction into the twentieth century. It is the tale of brothers, heroes, and betrayal, the family estate as much a character as the various Llewellyns who use and misuse it. In the end, the land Nicholas had struggled to keep intact is sold to a rich northern socialite. Penhally becomes a hunting club, and another set of brothers end up enemies. Although many saw *Penhally* as a tragedy, a lament and a yearning for days gone by, Gordon turns a critical eye on both her family history and that of the Old South, lacing her narrative with women's stories of pain and misunderstanding. She uses women's screams as bookends to the novel, suggesting that no matter her color or place in history, a woman's lot is desperate, her choices limited.

In her next novel, *Aleck Maury, Sportsman* (1934), Gordon created a fictionalized autobiography of her father's sporting adventures. The first-person narrative is laced with classical allusions, and Gordon later joked that she should have called the book "Portrait of the Artist as an Angler." Noble and heroic, Maury is sustained through the hard times by his life's passion. Technique is more important than the actual capture of his prey, and no sacrifice too great for his art. Yet Gordon's novel is not a one-sided celebration of the artist's life. Using her female characters as ironic counterpoint to Aleck Maury's self-absorbed and often selfish behavior, Gordon explores the conflict between living in community and creating art. Maury isolates himself so that he can hunt and fish; he learns from others yet refuses to share his knowledge. In time, Maury would need to depend on others and yet he had not prepared for the waning of his faculties. However heroic, Maury's life lacks balance.

Gordon returned to her maternal family history in *None Shall Look Back* (1937). Originally intending to retell her grandmother's life from the Civil War until the twentieth century, Gordon ultimately narrowed her focus to the experiences of one soldier, Rives Allard, who fought under Confederate General Bedford Forrest. The novel was not well received. Allard's grim, almost headlong rush to death did not engage readers' sympathies as did Margaret Mitchell's *Gone with the Wind* (1936), and Allard's wife, Lucy, while a sensitive, perceptive observer, played only a minor role in Gordon's narrative. Yet as Katherine Anne Porter observed in a letter to her friend, Gordon's "real hero is the same as it was in *Penhally*—The Land." And as Ford Madox Ford noted in his review, the effect of the book was cumulative: "[I]t is only when you have finished the reading that you realize that you have been present at a very horrid affair and one that you will not soon forget."

The Garden of Adonis (1937) follows the Allards and their relationship to the land into the twentieth century. In two parallel stories of illicit love, Gordon contends that those who lose touch with the land, a source of strength, usually wither and die. Contrasting the almost pastoral love of Idelle Sheeler and Ote Mortimer, poor white tenants, with the adulterous affair of Letty Allard, the landowner's daughter, and Jim Carter, a married man, Gordon reflected on her own experience of marriage and betrayal. The novel's uneven quality reflects its history. Gordon got the idea for the novel in early 1931 but worked on it only intermittently. By the summer of 1933, she had completed seven of a planned eleven chapters, but after her husband's adultery and their subsequent separation, Gordon abandoned the novel. She did not return to work on the manuscript until 1937, when she was pressured to finish it quickly.

In *Green Centuries* (1941), Gordon more successfully explored the issues of love, family, marriage, and betrayal in the lives of Cassy Dawson and Rion Outlaw, pioneers settling the wilds of Tennessee during the time of Daniel Boone. To demonstrate the importance of history and community, Gordon contrasted the story of Cassy and Rion with powerful images of redemption in Native American rituals. Rion, like his namesake, the mythical hunter, is a wanderer who ignores his heritage; his alienation from community destroys him. The Cherokee people—especially the matriarch Dark Lanthorn—celebrate their heritage and guide their future through story and art. Returning to ideas developed in *Aleck Maury, Sportsman,* Gordon suggests that the wanderer, like the artist, needs to find a balance between the individual and community.

In 1944, Gordon published *The Women on the Porch,* the first of three novels often dismissed as romans à clef. Inverting the myth of Orpheus and Eurydice, Gordon creates a complex narrative with several levels of interpretation. On the surface, Gordon seems to assert traditional values. Catherine Chapman returns to her maternal home after the discovery of her husband Tom's infidelity, and her impulsive action is destined to lead her further astray. Jim Chapman must come to rescue his wife from her neurotic female relatives: he is the intellectual who sees life clearly and can therefore act and protect his wife. Yet Gordon also critiques this view, suggesting that male analytical powers can be insufficient and must be balanced by the feminine, instinctual nature. Jim Chapman would have perished without Catherine's help, and in the closing scene of the novel, Jim humbly bends down to kiss his wife's bare foot, acknowledging her superiority. To further this interpretation, Gordon uses narrative patterns similar to those used by Charlotte Perkins Gilman and Kate Chopin in stories of other marriages gone awry, and she refers to Cleena, an ancient goddess who has some level of power— Gordon leaves it somewhat vague—over the land Catherine calls home.

Reflecting Gordon's own conversion to Catholicism, *The Strange Children* (1951) and *The Malefactors* (1957) continue to explore the depths and limits of women's power. Set in the same landscape as *Penhally,* a world marked by literal and figurative underground streams, *The Strange Children* examines the marriage of Stephen and Sarah Lewis—thinly disguised portraits of Gordon and Tate. *The Malefactors* tells the story of Tom Claiborne, an intellectual like Tate who must wrestle with his wife's conversion and his own lack of faith. In both books, through references to female saints and images of feminine power, Gordon defends the importance of being sensitive to the spiritual side of life as she is also demonstrating how devastating pure intellectualism can be.

Gordon also published *The Glory of Hera* (1972), a novel of the exploits of Heracles; *A Good Soldier: A Key to the Novels of Ford Madox Ford* (1963); *How to Read a Novel* (1957); numerous articles; and three collections of short fiction: *The Forest of the South* (1945), *Old Red and Other Stories* (1963), and *The Collected Stories of Caroline Gordon* (1981). With Tate, she coedited two editions of *The House of Fiction* (1950, 1960). From 1938 until 1977, Gordon also taught creative writing at numerous colleges, universities, and conferences across the country, nurturing many aspiring writers. Her most famous "students" approached her by mail in the fall of 1951. Both Walker Percy and Flannery O'Connor wanted Gordon's advice on their first novels, and Gordon readily gave it. Until her death, O'Connor regularly consulted Gordon about her fiction.

Gordon's literary output and support of younger writers is surprising given her difficult personal life. Gordon and Tate moved frequently and often faced financial crises. From the summer of 1933 until their divorce in 1945, Tate had numerous affairs. Gordon and Tate remarried in 1946, but Tate continued to be unfaithful. In 1956, they separated, although Gordon hoped for a permanent reconciliation long after their final divorce in 1959. She died in San Cristóbal de las Casas, Mexico, in 1981.

Lillian Smith

Will Brantley

Lillian Smith defined herself as an analyst of American culture and its various modes of segregation; she also regarded herself as something of a prophet in that she—like the prophet Cassandra, a figure she sometimes evoked—attempted to warn others of the dehumanization that inevitably accompanies a segregated culture. But equally important, Smith defined herself as an artist—a poet even—and one whose vision was as compelling as that of a social analyst. An early theorist of autobiography, Smith knew that she was a woman of many "selves." The diversity of her literary output is evidence of her many voices and her many attempts to confront the splits and fissures within the human psyche.

Smith was born in Jasper, Florida, in 1897. She lived there until 1915, when her father relocated his family to Rabun County in the north Georgia mountains, where he opened first a summer hotel and then a summer camp for girls. Smith studied at the local Piedmont College and the Peabody Conservatory of Music in Baltimore. In 1922 she gave up her formal training in music and accepted a teaching position at a Methodist girls' school in Huchow, China, where she lived from 1922 until 1925. There Smith had the opportunity to observe patterns of racism and segregation in another culture, which proved to be crucial to her developing social consciousness. Smith was not eager to leave China but did so in order to assume the directorship of Laurel Falls, her father's camp, where she instituted an innovative mode of education, one that emphasized creativity rather than competition, and one that prepared her student campers for the difficult decisions they would have to make as adults.

It was at Laurel Falls that Smith fell in love with Paula Snelling, an athletics instructor. The two women would remain together for the rest of Smith's life. With Snelling's encouragement, Smith in 1936 began publishing a little magazine, *Pseudopodia,* which became the *North Georgia Review* in 1937 and *South Today* in 1942. Together Snelling and Smith reviewed the works of their contemporaries and provided a forum in which the region's liberal intellectuals could exchange ideas. The magazine, which published both white and black writers, and which became the source of controversy on more than one occasion, eventually saw a circulation of ten thousand. In *From the Mountain* (1972), Helen White and Redding S. Sugg, Jr., provide a history of the magazine and a representative selection of its contents.

While coediting *South Today* and directing her camp, Smith was at work on *Strange Fruit* (1944), the book that brought her to the public's attention. *Strange Fruit* has been described variously as a thriller, a sensational best seller, a love story, and a novel about miscegenation, all of which imply something significant about the nature of Smith's first published novel. Set in the fictional town of Maxwell, Georgia, the story centers on the doomed love affair between the son of a wealthy white doctor and a young black woman. Praised by liberal critics such as Malcolm Cowley and Diana Trilling but loudly denounced in other quarters, *Strange Fruit* was banned for a period of time in Boston—a ban lifted at the urging of Smith's friend Eleanor Roosevelt. In "Personal History of *Strange Fruit*" (1945), an essay for the *Saturday Review,* Smith says that the novel evolved from her childhood memories of Jasper, Florida, with its "white mill town, colored mill town, little white church, little colored church—and one big commissary for all." *Strange Fruit* provides a rich dissection of racial ironies; Smith's 1945 stage adaptation met with less success, however, and ran on Broadway for less than two months.

Smith closed Laurel Falls in 1948 in order to complete *Killers of the Dream* (1949). She anticipated the hostile reaction that greeted the book, for she knew that she had exposed the sex secrets and "ghost relationships" of many southern men. But the book did something that Smith had not fully anticipated: it established her as a social commentator rather than as an artist. Given the originality of her approach, it is not surprising that many of Smith's early critics failed to see that *Killers of the Dream* is in fact a consummate work of literary nonfiction, one that merges the genres of confessional autobiography, historical essay, parable, and sermon in an often elliptical but always psychological approach to the destructive ideology of white supremacy. In "Why I Wrote *Killers of the Dream*," which appeared in the New York *Herald Tribune* shortly before the book's release, Smith said that she wanted to understand the "psychic fortifications" of the southern mind. "I want to know, too," she wrote, "why the Southern liberal is weak and the Southern demagogue has access to energies that carry through mammoth tasks for evil. I want to know what kind of children we grow in the South; and who put the Southern woman on her pedestal and why she crept down from it again. . . . I want to know why our region has, proportionately, not only the most churches of any region in the United States, but the most murders, the most poverty, the highest rate of illiteracy, the lowest wages and the poorest health." More than any other writer of her generation, Smith explored the "lessons" that undergird the life of a segregated culture. *Killers of the Dream* shows not only how the ideology of white supremacy takes shape, but also how it manages to sustain itself. Smith's tone ranges from indignant sarcasm to intense sorrow. In a chapter called "Southern Waste," she observes that southern culture has not traditionally sanctioned the kind of self-scrutiny that is crucial to the literary imagination. She thus mourns the "wasting away of our people's talents and skills" as perhaps "the South's greatest loss."

Smith had once planned to use the title *Give Us Tears,* but settled instead on *Killers of the Dream.* It is easy to emphasize the "killers" of the title, but the second noun is also significant, for the "dream" is the means by which to counter the harms of racism and segregation. Smith's next book, *The Journey* (1954), is a more complete exploration of the dream. The book is a sustained philosophical meditation rooted in Smith's personal past. As an epigraph, she cites a remark by Ernst Cassirer: "If I put out the light of my own personal experience I cannot see and I cannot judge the experience of others." Smith defines her goal as the search for positive images of the human being: "I wanted the faith to believe that we can fulfill our role in this evolving universe of which we have been given such awesome glimpses." If *Killers of the Dream* focuses on the mysterious prohibitions regarding race and the body, *The Journey* sets out to find the life-affirming mysteries that are not rooted in myth and ideology—the mysteries that sensitize men and women to the full complexities of their needs and obligations. Smith concludes the book with a passage that captures the essence of her own liberal, encompassing vision: "To believe in something not yet proved and to underwrite it with our lives: it is the only way we can leave the future open . . . to lay down one's power for others in need; to shake off the old ordeal and get ready for the new; to question, knowing that never can the full answer be found; to accept uncertainties quietly, even our incomplete knowledge of God: this is what man's journey is about, I think." A year before the book was published, Smith found out that she had cancer and underwent a radical mastectomy. She had the above passage read at her memorial service when the disease finally took her life in 1966.

In 1955 Smith published *Now Is the Time,* a small book that she intended as pure polemic. She hoped her "pamphlet" would prepare the South to accept the 1954 Supreme Court decision to desegregate the public schools. The book included practical advice in addition to Smith's philosophical speculations. She discovered, however, that many booksellers were refusing to stock the book and that Dell, the publisher of the paperback edition, had failed to fill orders. Smith faced an even more daunting crisis in 1955 when two white youths broke into her home and caused a fire that consumed hundreds of letters and manuscripts.

Smith's second novel, *One Hour* (1959), concerns a man who is wrongfully accused of molesting a child. Smith had been an early and public opponent of the Cold War witch-hunts, and *One Hour* is her response to the repressive McCarthy era. The novel embodies Smith's theories about mob psychology; it also explores the ways in which the lives of women, in particular, are shaped by gender norms and notions of sexual normality. Smarting from its generally negative reviews—Leslie Fiedler provided one under the title "Decency Is Not Enough"—Smith presented a defense of socially engaged literature in her expanded edition of *Killers of the Dream* (1961). Here Smith takes on the New Critics, many of whom had been the southern Agrarians of the 1930s. Smith attacks the limitations of formalist criticism as well as the conservatism of the Agrarians' social philosophy. Her remarks are not apologetic: "No writers in literary history have failed their region as completely as these did." It would take nearly two decades for critics to see the value of Smith's position, but since the late 1970s intellectual historians such as Morton Sosna, Richard King, and Fred Hobson have acknowledged the ways in which Smith disrupts a stifling conservative consensus and have made her writings a notable component in their rethinking of southern intellectual history.

Smith published two small books in the 1960s. *Memory of a Large Christmas* (1962) is a brief memoir in which Smith details some of the family rituals of her childhood. *Our Faces, Our Words* (1964) is a collection of fictional monologues by men and women in the civil rights movement, including an epilogue in which Smith speaks in her own voice. This book is Smith's final testament to her belief that nonfiction can be as fully "creative" as fiction. Since her death, two important volumes have appeared. Edited by novelist Michelle Cliff, *The Winner Names the Age* (1978) is a collection of Smith's essays and speeches, including key pieces on the nature of gender and autobiography. Edited by Margaret Rose Gladney, *How Am I to Be Heard?* (1993) is an award-winning collection of Smith's letters that charts the evolution of her thinking and her ongoing involvement with organizations such as the Southern Conference for Human Welfare and the Congress of Racial Equality.

By 1944, the year *Strange Fruit* was published, Smith had worked out her belief that segregation is "an ancient, psychological mechanism used by men the world over, whenever they want to shut themselves away from problems which they fear and do not feel they have the strength to solve." Among these problems, perhaps none is more pernicious than racism. In 1964 Smith wrote to her publisher, George Brockway, that racism "is a psychosis, yes; but we can't explain it by labeling it. . . . A racist will not only kill—he wants even more to give pain, to hurt terribly as he kills. It is this *giving pain* that we have to look at. And with this is always sex, sex, sex. We have scarcely begun to probe this illness. Let's call it what it is: evil. I'm not sure it is an illness, it may be simply evil. We can't understand the human condition without that word."

Smith believed that such evil is one of the dark, life-destroying mysteries that can be fought only when human beings embrace the search for something better—hence the visionary quality of her later writings. The evil and the good, the killers and the dream: Lillian Smith's life work is a passionate exploration of these dualities.

Zora Neale Hurston

John Lowe

Perhaps no other figure in American literary history save Herman Melville or Emily Dickinson has had such a spectacular return to prominence after decades of neglect than Zora Neale Hurston. Her image now appears on murals in chain bookstores, on coffee cups, t-shirts, and notepads. She is claimed by feminists, womanists, folklorists, anthropologists, journalists, dramatists, and humorists as a founding member of their "clubs." So why was she forgotten for so many years?

Hurston certainly wasn't born to celebrity. Although she said she was born in 1901 (or sometimes it was 1903) in the all-black town of Eatonville, Florida, where her daddy was the local Baptist preacher and sometime mayor, she actually came into the world in 1891 in Notasulga, Alabama, near Booker T. Washington's Tuskegee Institute. It was only after the family moved to Eatonville a few years later that they began to rise in the world through her father's growing reputation in the Baptist hierarchy.

Hurston grew up learning all the biblical stories but also the wonderful tales she heard listening in on the "lyin' sessions" townsmen had on the porch of Joe Clarke's store. She soon learned to invent tales herself and imagined a glorious world where she could mimic the deeds of Thor and other European gods. Her family's domestic security was shattered, however, by her mother's death in 1904. The daughter of "respectable" people and a former schoolteacher, Lucy Potts Hurston nevertheless had had a hard time raising her eight children, as John Hurston was often not home. Part of his traveling included philandering, which brought discord into the home, especially after Lucy's death when he married his current girlfriend, Mattie. She and Zora were soon fighting, and John farmed his daughter out, first to boarding school in Jacksonville, where she learned what it meant to be "colored," and later to other family members. Bored with tending children and doing domestic chores, Hurston escaped to become a lady's maid with a Gilbert and Sullivan troupe; there she learned the ways of the theater and how she could use humor to deal with domineering whites. She wound up in Baltimore, where she studied at Morgan State; thrilled by her return to reading, she wangled her way into Howard University, where she studied with some of the leading scholars of the time, such as Alain Locke. Subsequently, she received scholarship money to become the first black student at Barnard College. Soon she was under the spell of legendary founders of American anthropology, Barnard's Ruth Benedict and Columbia's Franz Boas, and working toward a doctorate.

Hurston's arrival in New York City coincided with the eruption of the fabled Harlem Renaissance. Her student magazine writing in Washington prepared her for literary competitions that journals such as *Crisis* and *Opportunity* were offering. She won second place for a story and first place for a short play; this led to her publication of a short story, "Spunk," in Locke's groundbreaking *New Negro* (1925) and instant inclusion in the Harlem literary scene. Hurston, with her dazzling wit, storytelling ability, and constant readiness to act out all the parts of her many stories, became a universal favorite with the other young writers of the day such as Countee Cullen, Wallace Thurman, and especially Langston Hughes. The latter and Hurston joined with Wallace Thurman to publish the one-issue wonder, *FIRE!!* (1926), an amazing magazine bent on thumbing its nose at more "polite" and mostly older writers such as W. E. B. Du Bois and Jessie Redmon Fauset, who to these "young Turks" seemed to care far too much about respectability and "dictee" ways.

Hurston made other contacts too; her growing friendships with white writers Fannie Hurst and Carl Van Vechten led to more support from white patrons, most significantly Charlotte Mason ("Godmother of the Primitives" as she was known to her "children"). This relation was often strained, however, since Mason, who bankrolled Hurston's folklore-gathering trips for several years, kept tight control over her protégée's publications.

Hurston at this point wanted to be an anthropologist more than a creative writer, and she used Mason's funds to gather southern and Caribbean materials for doctoral studies with Boas. Initially, Hurston informed her backwoods subjects that she was researching a scholarly article—did they know some folklore? Suspicious, they would say they did not. Discouraged, Hurston returned North to weep "salty tears" at Boas' feet, only to be sent right back into the field. She bought a jazzy dress, loaded her things into a saucy Chevy coupe, and sped off to the sawmill camps and turpentine woods with a tale about her bootlegging man, trouble with the law, and a need for a safe refuge. Once installed, she would casually prime the pump by telling a "tale" herself, and then sit back and soak up the "lie-swappin'" that would ensue.

Eventually, Hurston published her research, taking up a whole issue of the prestigious *Journal of American Folklore*. All this while, however, she continued working on her fiction, and when one of her best stories, a bittersweet tale about a tested marriage, "The Gilded Six-Bits," was published in *Story*, Lippincott wrote her asking if she had a novel they could see. She replied that she did, and then had to write one. As most writers would do in a clutch, Hurston went with material she knew well, penning the story of her parents' fated marriage in *Jonah's Gourd Vine* (1934), a lyrical but troubling saga that ends tragically with John's collision with a train. She larded the tale with rich folklore, poetic dialogue, and a provocative central paradox: John's undeniable talent in the pulpit derives from the same thing that undoes him, his powerful physical presence and appetite for life.

Getting the novel accepted meant that she could finally publish her folklore material in a new form. Reshaping the material by inserting herself as a "character" who links the tales together as we watch her gather them, she came up with *Mules and Men* (1935), still a classic of American folklore that also reads like a novel, especially the scenes dealing with the narrator's initiation as a hoodoo priestess in New Orleans.

Hurston got more grants to extend her research and was soon off to Jamaica and Haiti. These trips eventually led to a second anthropological work, *Tell My Horse* (1938). During this period, she wrote another novel, her magnificent *Their Eyes Were Watching God* (1937), in order, she said, to embalm the love she had for a man, whose demand that she end her career for him led her instead to drop him. The narrative, also set in Eatonville, as well as the Everglades, details the three marriages of Janie Mae Crawford Killicks Starks Woods. In doing so, it reveals how each marriage factors in her inner growth, and eventually, in her solitary but transcendent personhood, even though she has to kill and then bury her third husband, Tea Cake, the great love of her life. The novel's amazing poetic voice comes right out of African American folk culture but is shaped by Hurston's fully developed and very personal aesthetic. It has often been taught as a book about women's liberation, but it speaks in many registers for all readers everywhere.

Mention must also be made of Hurston's lifelong attempts to found a new Negro theater. She wrote her first short plays during the Harlem Renaissance, during which time she also constructed a three-act entertainment with music, *Mule-Bone,* with her darling Langston Hughes. He had come to Harlem from Kansas and knew little of southern African American culture until he met Zora. Eventually, he joined her for a car tour of the South, visiting Tuskegee, Eatonville, and many points in between. They paid a call on Bessie Smith, heard great gospel and blues, and soaked up plenty of stories and jokes. Their relationship foundered, however, when Hughes insisted that Louise Thompson, their typist, be included in royalties. Hurston, stung (possibly because of romantic jealousy), became enraged; over a stormy period of time, the play was on, then off, and finally the friendship was off too. *Mule-Bone,* written in 1930, only came to life in 1990, when it opened on Broadway in a lavish staging, but to rather mediocre reviews and disappointing attendance. The central element of the plot is a rather slight romantic triangle, which is mostly eclipsed by the surrounding and boisterous presentation of folk culture, children's games, and lying sessions on Joe Clarke's porch. The hilarious second act features a mock trial that also pits rival Baptist and Methodist congregations against each other. The play concludes when the male rivals, formerly friends and partner-entertainers, discover their mutual ladylove wants them to settle down to demeaning work for white folks. They happily leave her, their quarrel forgotten.

In 1944, Hurston wrote another three-act play with Dorothy Waring entitled *Polk County,* an alternately realistic and surreal comedy with music that concerns the adventures of a backwoods turpentine camp community; it was never published or produced. In 1997, a cache of unpublished plays by Hurston was found in the Library of Congress. These vary in subject and tone, but most are set in Florida and are meant to amuse. The two most significant are *The Turkey and the Law,* Hurston's own personal version of *Mule-Bone,* and a three-act *Spunk,* which extends and importantly changes the events of Hurston's famous 1925 short story.

During the 1930s, Hurston spent eighteen months working for the Federal Writers Project in Florida. She collected some amazing material and learned about other groups in the state, but she also used some of her time to write her third novel, *Moses, Man of the Mountain* (1939), a superb retelling of the events of Exodus, from a black perspective and in dialect. Although the book often verges on parody of the sacred text, it also transforms Moses into an African hoodoo man and comments cogently and powerfully on the problems and opportunities of racial leadership, religion, and the conundrums of exceptionalist definitions of group identity.

Readers are often disappointed with Hurston's autobiography, *Dust Tracks on a Road* (1942), which she did not truly want to write. It is maddeningly reticent about the most vital facts (such as date of birth, Hurston's two husbands, her involvement in the Harlem Renaissance); however, as a piece of writing it dazzles, especially now that we have the chapters expurgated by her publisher during World War II, chapters highly critical of American imperialism and racism. The book also presents an intriguing portrait of Hurston's aesthetics—how they were generated, transformed, and employed in her writing and work. Throughout, Hurston evinces a supremely confident, humor-drenched voice, but she also plumbs many of the key conundrums of human existence and offers observations in highly poetic and poignant formulations, often based in an Afrocentric aesthetic.

Hurston wandered a good bit during the 1940s and 1950s, embarking on a strange voyage to Honduras in search of buried treasure, finding teaching and clerical jobs here and there, but she never gave up her writing. Hurston's final published work was in some ways her most ambitious. *Seraph on the Suwanee* (1948) focuses on white figures and "cracker" culture, drawing on Hurston's Federal Writer's Project work and her absorbed reading of her white friend Marjorie Kinnan Rawlings' (1896–1953) Florida frontier narratives. Jim and Arvay Meserve's troubled marriage receives a Freudian presentation, against the backdrop of an accurately observed cultural milieu. The novel also shows Hurston's beloved Florida undergoing tremendous changes, as industrialization, tourism, and real estate developments pick up steam. Arvay's slow grappling with her psychological problems and her difficult marriage in many ways echoes *Their Eyes Were Watching God*, but with a different kind of treatment and conclusion. In several ways the novel reveals Hurston experimenting with tone, voice, and quite modernist concepts of the self.

In the same year that she published *Seraph on the Suwanee*, Hurston was falsely accused of sexual corruption of a minor. When the black press convicted her of charges that were ultimately dismissed by the courts, Hurston felt betrayed and briefly considered suicide. Artistically, she turned away from the material that always inspired her and began to concentrate increasingly on narratives set in the ancient past, most significantly a novel about Herod the Great. Indeed, many of her unfinished pieces from this period are set in biblical times. She found few publishers interested in these projects and tried to support herself with another series of odd jobs, including working with William Bradford Huie to report the sensational trial of Ruby Mc-Collum, a black woman accused of murdering a white lover. Hurston also found time to rail against the *Brown v. Board of Education* decision of 1954, which she felt insulted the achievements of black teachers and schools by inferring African Americans could only get a good education in white settings.

After resorting to domestic work, Hurston became ill; too proud to appeal to her family, she found refuge in the county welfare home in Fort Pierce, Florida. She died there in 1960, penniless, but certainly not alone. Three ministers presided at her funeral service and hundreds attended. After her death, her papers were thrown on a fire, but someone rescued many of the manuscripts, including the almost finished Herod novel. Two other novels, "The Golden Bench of God" and "The Lives of Barney Turk," have disappeared, as perhaps have other works. Since her death, Hurston has been claimed by a new generation of African American women writers. Alice Walker asserts no book is more important to her than *Their Eyes Were Watching God,* and she personally had a tombstone placed near Hurston's unmarked grave in Fort Pierce in 1973. The following year, Robert Hemenway published his groundbreaking biography of Hurston, and her revival began in earnest, especially after the University of Illinois Press republished *Their Eyes Were Watching God, Moses,* and *Dust Tracks on a Road.* One finds echoes of Hurston in Gloria Naylor, Toni Morrison, Sherley Anne Williams, and many other contemporary writers. Her folklore collections have regained prominence, too, and are taught as primary texts in many anthropology courses. Hurston loved the South, always considered herself a southerner, and wrote her best work out of her native Florida. Her books mirror a dynamic and varied African American culture as well as that of the larger South to which this group has contributed. Her attentiveness to social issues, historical events, and national politics are often eclipsed by the power and beauty of her characters and language, but all these elements function integrally to form one of the most compelling and memorable portraits of the American South we have.

Today, the Zora Neale Hurston Society has a journal and an annual conference in Baltimore, and Eatonville sponsors a yearly "Zora!" festival of the arts, which generates much interest in their native daughter as well as funding for community needs. Each year brings more dissertations and scholarly work forward, and a collection of her letters is currently under way. Plays have been written about Zora, and several actresses have impersonated her in one-woman shows. Hurston still has critics, however, especially those who feel she should have made racial struggle more prominent in her work, and charges of romanticism or "cuttin' the monkey for the white folks" continue. Why can't a Hurston, these critics seem to argue, write like a Wright? Even Hurston's fans often confine themselves to *Their Eyes,* a few short stories, and *Dust Tracks;* much work remains to be done on the rest of her canon, and a new biography is long overdue. Hurston's many essays and unpublished writings need consideration, too. New materials have recently come to light at the Smithsonian Institution and in the pages of Hurston's sorority journal. We may be in for even more revelations about this protean, provocative, and fascinating writer, whose sly masks sometimes hide all too well her profound, searching intellect, which she used to probe crucial issues that remain urgently central to our national culture and soul.

Lillian Hellman

Katherine Powell

In *An Unfinished Woman* (1969), Lillian Hellman recalls the advice of her childhood nurse, Sophronia: "Don't go through life making trouble for people." It was advice that Hellman seemed to disregard throughout her nearly eighty years. From her entrance into the literary world in 1934 as the author of the controversial Broadway success *The Children's Hour,* through her legendary standoff with the House Un-American Activities Committee in 1952, to her death in 1984, at which time she was embroiled in bitter litigation against author Mary McCarthy, Hellman was never far from one sort of conflict or another. Even in death, Hellman remains a troublesome figure for literary scholars and biographers alike. Despite evidence that she fabricated entire sections of her famous memoirs, aggrandizing her role in personal and national affairs while diminishing the roles of others, Hellman retains her reputation as a major playwright, screenwriter, memoirist, and uncompromising defender of political freedom.

Born June 20, 1905, in New Orleans, the daughter of Max Hellman and Julia Newhouse Hellman, Lillian Hellman spent her youth living half the year in the New Orleans boardinghouse of her paternal aunts and half in New York City among her wealthy Newhouse relatives. After brief stints at New York and Columbia universities, Hellman worked as an editor in New York until her marriage in 1925 to Arthur Kober. During the five-year marriage, Hellman worked off and on as a theater publicist and published a few short stories. In 1930 Kober was hired as a junior screenwriter, and Hellman followed him to Hollywood, where she found work as a reader for Metro-Goldwyn-Mayer. In Hollywood Hellman met crime novelist Dashiell Hammett who became her lover and literary mentor. Although she and Hammett were both unfaithful to each other during their lengthy relationship and lived apart for long periods, their connection endured for thirty years, and Hammett was without question a significant influence on Hellman's writing as well as on her politics.

The Children's Hour (1934), Hellman's first and longest-running play, tells the story of two teachers whose lives are destroyed when a disgruntled student falsely accuses them of lesbianism. The play garnered critical attention as much for its taboo subject matter as for its strongly drawn characters and carefully crafted plot. Banned in Boston, the play was snubbed by the Pulitzer committee, prompting outraged critics to form the New York Drama Critics Circle in order to give their own award. Hellman always argued that the play was not about lesbianism but about the power of a lie. Indeed, when she later wrote a film adaptation of the play called *We Three*, Hellman replaced the lesbian subplot with a conventional heterosexual love triangle. The play's central theme, an exploration of the way individual lives are shaped and often destroyed by outside forces, is one that Hellman would continue to explore in subsequent dramatic works and later in her memoirs.

Following the success of *The Children's Hour*, Hellman returned to Hollywood and became one of the founding members of the Screen Writers Guild. Although she was one of the best-paid writers in Hollywood during that period, Hellman was a vigorous advocate of a strong union for screenwriters, most of whom were underpaid and had little job security. Hellman brought her growing awareness of workers' rights to her next play, *Days to Come* (1936), which focuses on a labor-management dispute in a small town. More overtly political than most of Hellman's plays, *Days to Come* was Hellman's only commercial failure, closing after seven performances.

In *The Little Foxes* (1939), which most critics consider her best work, Hellman drew upon memories of her mother's family to create her most memorable characters, the Hubbards. Regina Hubbard Giddens and her brothers, Oscar and Ben, are unrepentant scoundrels who have prospered by exploiting the cheap labor, racial tension, and economic hardship of the post–Civil War South and who gleefully turn on each other in their struggle to acquire still more money and power. Typical of Hellman's plays, *The Little Foxes* contains many conventions of melodrama: archvillains, noble servants, righteous victims, theft, blackmail, and a dramatic death scene. However, as Hellman pointed out to her critics, contrary to conventional melodrama, evil does not get its just desserts in the play. Regina triumphs, while her well-intentioned husband, Horace, dies; the sensitive aristocratic sister-in-law Birdie is reduced to a helpless alcoholic; and Addie, the black servant who is the play's conscience, can only observe and comment, powerless to alter events. In its exploration of the historical and psychological origin and far-reaching impact of self-interest and greed, *The Little Foxes*, like its less successful prequel, *Another Part of the Forest* (1947), is not simply an examination of family politics but a critique of unchecked capitalism. Set at the turn of the century, *The Little Foxes* is as much a comment on the Depression that gripped the country in 1939 as it is an analysis of the rise of New South industrialism.

In *Watch on the Rhine* (1941), Hellman addresses American isolationism in response to growing fascist oppression in Europe. In the play, the Farelly family's genteel comfort is shattered by the return of Sarah Farelly Muller and her husband Kurt, a fighter in the antifascist underground. When Kurt is recognized by a visiting Romanian exile and forced to kill the man in self-defense, the Farellys become accomplices to the murder. Just as the play's events bring the European war home to the characters, so the play itself issued a similar wake-up call to American audiences. Debuting at a time when American feeling about World War II was sharply divided, the play gained considerable attention. Critics applauded its restrained moralism, authentic characterization, and humor and awarded it that year's Drama Critic's Circle Award.

In *The Searching Wind* (1944) Hellman blames the horrors of European fascism as much on those who observed its rise and failed to act as on the perpetrators themselves. It was a theme that she had voiced earlier and eloquently in Addie's lines in *The Little Foxes*: "Well, there are people who eat the earth and eat all the people on it like in the Bible with the locusts. Then there are people who stand around and watch them eat it. Sometimes I think it ain't right to stand and watch them eat it." In *Scoundrel Time* (1976), her memoir of the McCarthy era, Hellman would again level her harshest criticism against those who failed to speak out against anticommunist hysteria.

Critics often note Henrik Ibsen's influence on Hellman's first six plays, with their tight craftsmanship and focus on social and political concerns. Her last two original plays, *The Autumn Garden* (1951) and *Toys in the Attic* (1960), in contrast, are driven more by character than by plot and are concerned with interpersonal relationships and individual regrets. Many critics have noted shades of Anton Chekhov, whose collected letters Hellman edited in 1955, in these later works. *The Autumn Garden*, which Hellman considered her best play, presents a group of middle-aged summer boarders at Sophie Tuckerman's Gulf Coast home who one by one come to accept the disappointing paths their lives have taken and their failure to fulfill their dreams. In *Toys in the Attic* sisters Carrie and Anna Berniers, having struggled most of their lives to support their unsuccessful brother Julian, are unable to accept his sudden success and independence. As she had in *The Little Foxes* and *Another Part of the Forest*, Hellman drew upon family memories for these plays, also set in the South. The boardinghouse of *The Autumn Garden* is reminiscent of the New Orleans boardinghouse of Hellman's paternal aunts, who are also obvious models for the Berniers sisters. Hellman's father, with his numerous business failures, seems to be the prototype for Julian. Her longest-running play since *The Children's Hour, Toys in the Attic* received the Drama Critics Circle Award in 1960.

In the last two decades of her life, Hellman published her memoirs and gained a new generation of readers, many of whom were unfamiliar with her dramatic work. In *An Unfinished Woman* (1969), which won the National Book Award, and to an even greater extent in *Pentimento* (1973), Hellman perfected the portrait form. Through a string of vignettes in *An Unfinished Woman,* she renders telling portrayals of Dashiell Hammett, Dorothy Parker, and her maid Helen Jackson. Although she casts herself in an ancillary role in these pieces, she also depicts herself as an independent, principled, and loyal woman.

The most memorable and controversial of Hellman's portraits is "Julia" in *Pentimento*. In the story, Hellman's childhood friend Julia becomes part of the antifascist underground in Europe. On a trip to Moscow, Hellman is asked by Julia to smuggle $50,000 across the German border, where the two are briefly reunited. After her stay in Moscow, Hellman receives word that Julia has been killed. The story emphasizes a familiar theme for Hellman, that passivity in the face of evil constitutes complicity. Although she portrays herself as a reluctant hero compared to Julia, Hellman clearly intends the audience to recognize her heroism.

Hellman again cast herself as the hero in *Scoundrel Time* (1976), an account of her appearance before the House Un-American Activities Committee. Hellman includes in the book her letter to the committee in which she offers to answer questions about her own activities but refuses to provide information about others, stating that "to hurt innocent people whom I knew many years ago in order to save myself is, to me, inhuman and indecent and dishonorable. I cannot and will not cut my conscience to fit this year's fashion." In portraying herself as a coward who nevertheless overcomes her own fears and does the right thing, Hellman both implicitly and explicitly points an accusing finger at her fellow liberals who, in her eyes, took a less courageous stand. While the book received generally favorable reviews in the mainstream press, many of Hellman's peers were quick to attack it, pointing out that Hellman was not the first or only person to resist the committee's demand to name names. Other critics note that while Hellman is evasive about her political affiliations in *Scoundrel Time,* her own records confirm that she was indeed a member of the Communist Party, if only briefly.

The distinguishing feature of Hellman's memoirs is prose that, like her dramatic dialogue, is remarkably unsentimental and direct. This narrative voice is central to the image Hellman carefully constructed of herself as a woman of integrity and high morals. It is ironic, then, to note that considerable portions of Hellman's memoirs are either distortions of events, as noted in the responses to *Scoundrel Time,* or complete falsehoods, most notably "Julia." There is no evidence to corroborate Hellman's claim that she transported money across Germany for the antifascists. Julia herself seems to be a fictional character, based on the life of a real woman, Muriel Gardner, whose story Hellman knew about from mutual acquaintances but whom she never met. Hellman responded to charges of lying with characteristic anger. In 1980, when Mary McCarthy flippantly remarked on the *Dick Cavett Show* that she thought Hellman was "overrated" and "dishonest," Hellman responded with a $2.5 million lawsuit that was resolved only with her death in 1984.

From the beginning of her career, Hellman resisted being labeled a woman playwright, sensing that calling attention to her gender was a way to diminish her achievement. Later, when the publication of her memoirs and the subsequent film adaptation of "Julia" brought Hellman attention as an early feminist, she was equally reluctant to accept that label. Likewise, while four of Hellman's plays are distinctly southern in their subject matter, Hellman defies easy classification as a southern writer. Perpetually questioning her beliefs, reconsidering her past, and revising herself, Hellman is probably best understood by the title she chose to give herself—an unfinished woman.

Eudora Welty

Albert Devlin

Eudora Alice Welty was the eldest of three children born to Mary Chestina and Christian Welty in Jackson, Mississippi. Present-day Jackson is a metropolitan city of 300,000 whose explosive growth and sprawling commercial development Welty has deplored. In 1909, the year of her birth, it was a small provincial capital of 25,000, whose familiar, if no less harrowing, folkways would be absorbed into such stories of childhood as "A Memory," "A Visit of Charity," and "The Winds." After graduation from high school in 1925, Welty continued her education in the "flinty" North—principally at the University of Wisconsin, where she majored in English and from which she graduated in 1929—before returning to the family home after the untimely death of her father, a respected insurance executive. With the exception of sustained travel in the late 1940s and early 1950s, Welty remained in Jackson until her death in 2001, confirming in effect a basic tenet of her fiction, that "feelings are bound up in place." Her considerable distinction rests upon four collections of stories, two full-length novels, three novellas, a book of criticism, and a memoir. Her awards have mounted over the years to include two Guggenheim Fellowships, election to the American Academy of Arts and Letters, and a Pulitzer Prize for *The Optimist's Daughter* (1972). No one has spoken more astutely of her own unique work or the "business of writing" in general than Welty herself: "No art ever came out of not risking your neck. And risk—experiment—is a considerable part of the joy of doing, which is the lone, simple reason all writers of serious fiction are willing to work as hard as they do."

Shortly after Welty met her new agent in 1940, Diarmuid Russell wrote to say "how pleased" he was that this promising young writer had also "turned out to be a human being. I was scared," he said, "that you might have been otherwise." Russell was apprehensive, no doubt, of the usual gamut of authorial defects: vanity, jealousy, arrogance, and a rivalrous ambition to govern the world of letters. The rather shy and self-effacing woman from Mississippi, thirty-one years old and the author of several respected stories, was none of these; but Russell had been warned in earlier correspondence with Welty that she was steely and would follow her own artistic conscience. Irritated and perhaps dispirited by editors who had invoked the novel-first rule of commercial publishing, Welty firmly set the tone of her long and productive relation with Russell, and of her own "serious" endeavor in fiction: "Please do not tell me that I will have to write a novel. I do not see why if you enjoy writing short stories and cannot even think in the form of a novel you should be driven away from it and made to slave at something you do not like and do badly." Welty, of course, would come to terms with the novel—victim perhaps of her own penchant for "risk"—and make at least one important contribution to the form, *Delta Wedding* (1946), but in her own good time and, for good measure, "by accident."

Welty's early stories collected in *A Curtain of Green* (1941) show a range of mood and subject matter that marked the writer as far-ranging in vision and already superbly disciplined in her craft. Cleanth Brooks and Robert Penn Warren, editors of the *Southern Review,* became her first important advisors and selected two stories from *A Curtain of Green* for their influential anthology *Understanding Fiction* (1943). Their choices, "A Piece of News" and "Old Mr. Marblehall," probe the secret lives of characters who approach the "rare and wavering" moment of "possibility" evoked by Welty's pliant language. Reviewers were determined to make of Welty a social realist and especially a recorder of the southern grotesque, but they were anticipated by Katherine Anne Porter, whose introduction to *A Curtain of Green* locates this work not in any socioliterary cast, but in "that true and human world of which the artist is a living part."

If Welty has positioned a surrogate for the artist in the collection, it is the unnamed young man of "The Key." His humane instincts draw him to Albert and Ellie Morgan, "Deaf and dumb!" as the text puts it, who await the coming of a train in Yellow Leaf, Mississippi. His awareness of their isolation makes him vulnerable, as is any writer, Welty thinks, who exposes himself to the pathos of the world. "His look . . . was a hurried focusing of a very tender and explicit regard. . . . He was like a salamander in the fire. 'Take care,' you wanted to say to him." With this same "tender" regard, more patient than "hurried," Welty extracted the other buried lives of *A Curtain of Green*, immured as they were in the small Mississippi towns that she had toured in the 1930s as a "junior publicity agent" for the WPA. Their stories of grief ("A Curtain of Green"), guilt ("Keela, the Outcast Indian Maiden"), repression ("Clytie"), and longing ("Why I Live at the P.O.") culminate in the famous concluding story, "A Worn Path," in which old Phoenix Jackson casts a selfless benediction upon the "dark mysteries" (as the late critic Ruth Vande Kieft has put it) of *A Curtain of Green*.

In her three succeeding collections (*The Wide Net*, 1943; *The Golden Apples*, 1949; and *The Bride of the Innisfallen*, 1955), Welty continues to indulge her enjoyment and to expose herself to the dangers of her craft by writing ever more daringly "on the sharp edge of experiment." On the whole, the stories of *The Wide Net* are longer and more complex than those of the preceding collection, and they are also more closely related by virtue of their common setting along the legendary Natchez Trace. The challenge of such "out-reaching" is clear in Welty's description of drafting the opening story, "First Love": "Maybe that was the trouble with the story," she told Diarmuid Russell, "everything (for me) carried the burden of being so many things at once." Lurking within this excess (as Susan Donaldson has argued perceptively in an article for the *Mississippi Quarterly*, 1997) is a skeptical modernist, whose "desire for illumination, mastery, and unity" is subversively checked by her knowledge that "such moments are illusory, creations of the signs we see when we go looking for what is lost."

This tension is perhaps the most persistent feature of the collection, and as such it links the dramas of revelation that mark the territorial Mississippi of "First Love" and "A Still Moment" and the contemporary Trace of "The Winds." It is to the vaunting of Aaron Burr that the twelve-year-old Joel Mayes, an orphan without speech or hearing, looks for an inspiring gesture, and it is to the knowledge of the older girl Cornella that Josie mutely appeals as she approaches the mysteries of sexual encounter. In neither "First Love" nor "The Winds," however, does Welty's watching for the moment of revelation produce certitude so much as it does imagination, surprise, and lyricism. In "A Still Moment," the most intriguing story of *The Wide Net*, Welty channels her wide reading of the lore and legends of the Natchez Trace into a chance meeting of the evangelist Lorenzo Dow, the outlaw James Murrell, and the artist John J. Audubon. Reviewers who had come to expect from Welty a realistic casting of her fiction were especially perplexed by this story, whose form is a series of meditations upon a snowy heron that occasions for each traveler "the precipitous moment" of being. Earlier, in "The Key," Welty had likened the artist to "a salamander in the fire," asking implicitly if he could withstand the searing heat of his vocation. The danger is now revealed by Audubon to be self-inflicted, at least in part, for to paint the heron he must arrest its movement and possess its serene beauty. The shot that he fires is the artist's valediction to innocence, his tacit recognition, as Welty would observe many years later, that "order and form no more spring out of order and form than they come riding in to us upon seashells through the spray. In fiction they have to be made out of their very antithesis, life." It was this uneven struggle for mastery amid the unruly objects of perception that required the decentering narrative forms of *The Wide Net*.

Welty had a special regard for *The Golden Apples* (1949). Writing the stories of Morgana allowed her to explore her love both for mythology and for the poetry of William Butler Yeats. Welty was also surprised, and charmed, by the resilience of several characters who reappeared in stories as the collection gathered steam. One of them, Virgie Rainey, became the central figure in the "long, ruminative" stories "June Recital" and "The Wanderers"—ballast to the more chimerical "Shower of Gold" and "Sir Rabbit." "June Recital" reveals Virgie to be a pariah in the small Delta town of Morgana, marked as she is by a childhood excess of musical talent and passion that will soon break through artistic categories and evolve into "another way" of being. After a "fling in wicked Memphis," the seventeen-year-old Virgie returns to Morgana to begin a life of resistance to its stifling folkways. Not given to domestic pursuits, she nonetheless enjoys "struggling against a real hard plaid," a doubling image that subtly connects Virgie Rainey's stubborn sewing with Eudora Welty's own innate "love [of] hard things to write."

In the concluding story, "The Wanderers," Welty gathers Morgana for the funeral of Virgie's mother, Miss Kate Rainey. A comedy of grieving across social and familial lines is prominent in Welty's treatment of the wake, as is the death-defying stare of King MacLain, the roving patriarch (and perhaps Virgie's father) of *The Golden Apples* who has come home to die. Virgie's own imminent departure is an opportunity for Welty to deepen and complicate the base of meditation established in the earlier collections. As Virgie and an old black woman sit on the stile at MacLain, a nearby hamlet, they hear "through falling rain the running of the horse and bear, the stroke of the leopard, the dragon's crusty slither, and the glimmer and the trumpet of the swan." Welty's occult trajectory fulfills an earlier prophetic image of the moon as "a long silent horn" of "white light," a "connection" that now leads Virgie Rainey "far, far back." Only in "A Still Moment" had Welty approached the subjectivity that she now probed in "The Wanderers," but with a conspicuous difference. The longings of Dow, Murrell, and Audubon were inscribed within recognizable discourses—religious, pathological, or aesthetic—whose effect was to rationalize their inordinate desire. Virgie's moment of "dispersion" (as Ruth Weston has aptly termed it), far more unstable and mysterious than "the precipitous moment" of her antecedents, touches the same remote territory that Virginia Woolf once described as "a virgin forest . . . where even the print of birds' feet is unknown."

Welty's final collection, *The Bride of the Innisfallen* (1955), is notable for the several stories that reflect the writer's travel abroad from 1949 to 1950, when she held a second Guggenheim Fellowship, and 1951, when she toured Italy, France, England, and Ireland and met the writer Elizabeth Bowen, to whom the volume is dedicated. Reviewers were perplexed, if not bored, and made the familiar complaint that Welty was courting obscurity. Among the three "southern" stories in *The Bride of Innisfallen* is "The Burning," a long-delayed foray into Civil War writing whose value she greatly underestimated and indeed regretted having published. Of the four "travelogue stories" (as Suzanne Marrs termed them in an article for the *Mississippi Quarterly,* 1997) that take place outside the South, "No Place for You, My Love" is the one that carries the author's greatest self-awareness of having written "on the sharp edge of experiment"—a phrase that Welty used in the same essay that describes the composition of this curious ghost story ("Writing and Analyzing a Story").

"No Place for You, My Love" begins in the chatty social precincts of New Orleans but soon turns "south of South," as Welty reenacts a trip that she and a male acquaintance made to Venice, Louisiana, in 1951. The "amphibious" world they encounter quite literally dissolves the landscape and undermines narrative conventions as well, eventuating in a story whose focal point is that of a putative "third character," at once "more real, more essential," than the man and woman who have only recently met as strangers. This ghostly figure Welty invests with "the presence of a relationship" whose "being took shape as the strange, compulsive journey itself." At least superficially, Welty may seem to abjure character and seize upon abstraction, but her intention is to isolate the curious substrate of emotion that travels with the couple into a mythical land that is pure exposure. In each of Welty's earlier collections, place conferred identity and status by assigning social, sexual, and historical causality in what often resembled a comedy of southern manners. In "No Place for You, My Love," Welty was determined to avoid such a "conventionally tempting" psychology, and so she withdrew these familiar determinants of self. Place, or so the cryptic title would suggest, is no more substantial than identity itself, which is constantly being made and unmade by the "pervading and changing mystery" of relationship. The outbound stories of *The Bride of the Innisfallen*—the title story, "Circe," "Going to Naples," and "No Place for You, My Love"—are exquisite, challenging, and subversive experiments that are among the most personal stories Welty has written. By doubting the solidity of place and its power to name and identify, they set up a resistance, as it were, to the other stories of the collection and to the poetics of southern writing itself.

Welty's natural resistance to the novel was hardened no doubt by the way it often came recommended to her in the 1930s as the supreme test of artistic talent. In 1936 she was challenged by the New York editor Harold Strauss to "tackle a full-length novel," with masculine cant that her fine ear surely did not miss. Nonetheless, Welty has produced five extended narratives, only one of which, *Losing Battles* (1970), was a prolonged and difficult undertaking. The others—*The Robber Bridegroom* (1942), *Delta Wedding* (1946), *The Ponder Heart* (1954), and *The Optimist's Daughter* (1969/1972)—were written with evident zest and dispatch, and in each case began their unruly lives as stories. *The Robber Bridegroom*, a nineteenth-century fantasy of the Natchez country that Faulkner admired; *The Ponder Heart*, a comic monologue with verbal roots in Welty's famous story "Why I Live at the P.O."; and *The Optimist's Daughter*, a probing of family "trouble," were of novella length and thus not overly demanding of the dreaded monster, "plot." *Delta Wedding* and *The Optimist's Daughter*, one well-furnished even by the capacious standards of plantation romance, the other a sparse and tightly structured meditation, illustrate how teachable Welty was in the several ways of the novel.

Welty's long-awaited first novel takes place in 1923 in the Mississippi Delta and has for plot, if such it is, the equivocal marriage of a plantation belle and the local overseer. The whole tribe of Fairchilds, including aunts and great-aunts and myriad black retainers, regrets Dabney's "wildness" for Troy, the laconic overseer of Shellmound Plantation, but their dismay remains an undertone of gibe and jest rather than confrontation with the deliberate hill man from Tishomingo County. The novel takes little more than a week's time and ends with the return of the Flavins from their honeymoon in New Orleans. (Their sighting of a streetcar named Desire anticipates Tennessee Williams' famous title and perhaps is one of those serendipitous moments that make of writers a special company.) The wedding itself occurs in a wry Chekhovian aside and confirms the suspicion of one character that "nothing really so very much, happened," after all, at Shellmound. Welty has described *Delta Wedding* as "the most ill-planned or unplanned of books" and laughed to think that in writing it, she had done "something Diarmuid thought I could do."

The novel evolved from a still unpublished story entitled "The Delta Cousins" and was written against the background of World War II, a catastrophe that is present in subtle ways in the text, notwithstanding Welty's choice of the "uneventful" 1923 as neutral setting for the novel. Along with her daughters Shelley and Dabney and her niece Laura McRaven, Ellen Fairchild, the mistress of Shellmound, directs a narrative that taught Welty how to fill the far reaches of the novel with the same lyrical structures once reserved for her short fiction. In this regard, *Delta Wedding* reflects the practice of Virginia Woolf, whose posthumous collection of stories, *A Haunted House* (1943), Welty reviewed in 1944, as she oversaw the transformation of "The Delta Cousins" into a novel as loose and light as Woolf had required of her own experimental fiction. Perhaps the most impressive feature of Welty's first serious excursion into the novel is her grafting of poetic techniques derived from distant sources (principally Virginia Woolf and Katherine Mansfield) onto the native stock of the southern family romance. This may be the "risk" of the book, the "joy of doing" that helped Welty to overcome her antipathy to the novel and aligned her more closely with the techniques and thematics of literary modernism. At blithe Shellmound, Welty sorted out the rival claims of nostalgia for the old ways and her own modernist apprehension of fatality as the definitive plot of world history. The result is a brilliant shading of the Fairchild clan, as Welty chose a festive wedding to commemorate their dwindling way of life. Reviews of *Delta Wedding* were mixed, with the pointed exception of Elizabeth Bowen, who surmised that Welty's first full-length novel "may, in time, come to be recognized as a classic."

The appearance of *The Optimist's Daughter* in 1969 in the *New Yorker* broke a silence of nearly fifteen years in Welty's major publication. "Personal responsibilities" (as she put it) caused by family illness and death, primarily the ordeal of Welty's mother, may help to explain both the writer's relative silence and the exceedingly personal nature of *The Optimist's Daughter* itself. Into this slim volume, which claimed a Pulitzer Prize when it was issued as a book in 1972, Welty distilled her most intense feelings of "grief and loss." As an interior story that centers upon Laurel McKelva Hand, it is quite different from *Delta Wedding* and *Losing Battles,* far more encompassing tales of a wedding and a family reunion that were rendered by multiple points of view and steeped in dialogue and action. Considered as interrelated texts, *Delta Wedding, Losing Battles,* and *The Optimist's Daughter* mark a decisive shift in powerful southern mythologies—from collective family feeling and tireless talk to stark introspection and the silence that begins in loss and ends in the bittersweet possessions of memory. It is a shift that began earlier in Welty's short fiction, as travel beyond the South gradually undermined place and family as determinants of self. But in *The Optimist's Daughter* Welty approached this inevitable transformation with a conviction authorized by her own experience of love and its loss. It is the death of Laurel's father, the evasive "optimist" of the title, that leads her to reexamine both her own familial past and the changing patterns of civic life in Mount Salus. As she prepares to leave Mississippi for the North, Laurel affirms that "memory lived not in initial possession but . . . in the heart that can empty but fill again, in the patterns restored by dreams." There is finally a coolness at the core of Welty's fiction, a quietly held belief that "nothing gold can stay," but this was only provocation for her superbly conditioned literary mind. As Welty confirmed in her memoir, *One Writer's Beginnings* (1984), "I am a writer who came of a sheltered life. A sheltered life can be a daring life as well. For all serious daring starts from within."

Carson McCullers

Carlos L. Dews

In assessing Carson McCullers' literary reputation after fifty years of scholarship, Judith Giblin James, in her 1995 book, *Wunderkind: The Reputation of Carson McCullers, 1940–1990,* provides what might serve as an explanation of not only scholars' continued interest in the novelist, playwright, and short story writer's life and work but also what appears to be a recent reawakening of interest in her work vis-à-vis contemporary theoretical, critical, and political points of view: "She has been read as the last proletarian, a modernist, and a proto-postmodernist. And if the praise for her work has fallen somewhat from the pinnacle on which the wunderkind initially found herself, it is also true that the quality and variety of critical methods her work has invited have not diminished in recent decades and have, if anything, been beneficially expanded."

McCullers was born Lula Carson Smith, in Columbus, Georgia, in 1917, the daughter of Lamar Smith and Vera Marguerite Waters. Lula Carson, as she was called until age fourteen, attended public schools and graduated from Columbus High School at sixteen. An unremarkable student, she preferred the more solitary study of the piano. Encouraged by her mother, who was convinced that her daughter was destined for greatness, Carson began formal piano study at age nine but was forced to give up her dream of a career as a concert pianist after a childhood case of rheumatic fever left her without the physical stamina necessary for the rigors of practice and a concert career. While recuperating from this illness she began to read voraciously and to consider writing as a vocation.

In 1934 Carson sailed from Savannah to New York City, supposedly to study piano at the Juilliard School of Music but actually to pursue her secret ambition to write. Working various jobs to support herself, she studied creative writing at Columbia University and Washington Square College of New York University. Back in Columbus in the fall of 1936 to recover from a respiratory infection, Carson was bedridden for several months, during which time she began work on her first novel, *The Heart Is a Lonely Hunter.* Her first short story, "Wunderkind," was published in the December 1936 issue of *Story* magazine, edited by Whit Burnett, her former teacher at Columbia.

The Heart Is a Lonely Hunter, the story of a deaf mute to whom the lonely and isolated people of a southern town turn for silent solace, was published in June 1940, and it was an immediate and much-praised success. The novel includes the themes of loneliness and isolation that recur in much of McCullers' work. Rose Feld's New York *Times* review was typical of the positive response to the power of the young author's work: "No matter what the age of its author, *The Heart Is a Lonely Hunter* would be a remarkable book. When one reads that Carson McCullers is a girl of 22 it becomes more than that. Maturity does not cover the quality of her work. It is something beyond that, something more akin to the vocation of pain to which a great poet is born. Reading her, one feels this girl is wrapped in knowledge which has roots beyond the span of her life and her experience."

McCullers' second novel, *Reflections in a Golden Eye,* was published in 1941. Readers who expected a book like the author's first novel were shocked by the troubling story of voyeurism, obsession, repressed homosexuality, and infidelity set on a peacetime army base. *Reflections in a Golden Eye* received a mixed critical reception, and its author faced ridicule from the people of her hometown who saw negative reflections of themselves in the maladjusted characters of the novel.

The years 1943 to 1950 saw the publication of what many consider McCullers' finest creative work. *The Ballad of the Sad Café,* the lyrical story of jealousy and obsession in a triangular love relationship involving a bootlegging amazon, a hunchbacked midget, and an ex-convict, set in a small southern mill town, appeared in the August 1943 *Harper's Bazaar.* The work was later published by Houghton Mifflin in an omnibus edition of the author's work, *"The Ballad of the Sad Café": The Novels and Stories of Carson McCullers* (1951). March 1946 saw the publication of McCullers' fourth major work, *The Member of the Wedding,* the story of a lonely adolescent girl, Frankie Addams, who wants to find her "we of me" by joining with her older brother and his bride. McCullers' theatrical adaptation of the novel opened on Broadway in 1950 to near-unanimous acclaim and enjoyed a run of 501 performances. This adaptation proved to be her most commercially successful work.

The final fifteen years of McCullers' life saw a marked decline in the writer's health and in her creative output. Bedridden by paralysis from a series of debilitating strokes, McCullers was devastated by the failed production of her second play, *The Square Root of Wonderful,* which closed after only forty-five performances on Broadway in 1957, and the mixed reception of her final novel, *Clock without Hands* (1961). Her final book-length publication was a book of children's verse, *Sweet as a Pickle and Clean as a Pig* (1964). At the time of her death she was at work on an autobiography, *Illumination and Night Glare,* which was finally published in 1999.

In September 1937, Carson married James Reeves McCullers, Jr., a native of Wetumpka, Alabama, whom she met when he was in the army and stationed at Fort Benning, near Carson's hometown. The marriage was simultaneously the most supportive and destructive relationship in her life. From its beginning it was plagued by the partners' shared difficulty with alcoholism, their sexual ambivalence (both were bisexual), and the tension caused by Reeves's envy of Carson's literary successes. Moving to New York City in 1940 when *The Heart Is a Lonely Hunter* was published, Carson and Reeves divorced in 1941 but reconciled and remarried in 1945. While living near Paris in the early 1950s, Reeves tried to convince Carson to commit suicide with him. Fearing for her life, Carson fled to the United States. Remaining behind, Reeves took his life in a Paris hotel room in November 1953.

McCullers' life was blighted by a series of cerebral strokes caused by her childhood case of rheumatic fever. The first stroke in February 1941 temporarily impaired her vision and caused debilitating head pains. The second and third occurred in Paris in the fall of 1947. These strokes temporarily destroyed the lateral vision in her right eye and permanently paralyzed her left side. On August 15, 1967, McCullers suffered her final cerebral stroke. Comatose for forty-seven days, she died in the Nyack Hospital. McCullers was buried in Nyack's Oak Hill Cemetery on the banks of the Hudson River.

Assessing McCullers' stature in American arts and letters, Virginia Spencer Carr wrote in her biography of McCullers, *The Lonely Hunter* (1975), "Critics continue to compare and contrast McCullers with Eudora Welty, Flannery O'Connor, and Katherine Anne Porter, whom they generally consider to be better stylists in the short form than McCullers. They tend to rank McCullers above her female contemporaries as a novelist." In addition to New York Drama Critics Circle and Donaldson awards for her play *The Member of the Wedding* (1950), McCullers also received two Guggenheim fellowships (1942, 1946), an Arts and Letters Grant from the American Academy of Arts and Letters and the National Institute of Arts and Letters (1943), and various other awards and honors. McCullers was inducted into the National Institute of Arts and Letters in 1952.

Although all of her major works were set in the South and she considered herself a southern writer, McCullers' feelings about the South were ambivalent at best. McCullers did not live in the South after her departure for New York in 1940, when her first novel was published, and following her father's sudden death in August 1944, Carson with her mother and sister moved to Nyack, New York, where her mother purchased a house. McCullers spent most of the rest of her life in this house on the Hudson River. In an essay "How I Began to Write," McCullers described her feelings about her hometown and her desire to leave for New York as early as age 17: "By that winter [1934–35] the family rooms, the whole town, seemed to pinch and cramp my adolescent heart. I longed for wanderings. I longed especially for New York."

McCullers' negative response to the South was based on her Marxist views of the economic inequities of the South, the South's racism, and her own personal experience of the South's intolerance. Gender ambiguity (most significantly the negative reaction by those around her to her androgynous nature and masculine dress) was also a likely factor in her desire for escape from Columbus. McCullers experienced this intolerance first hand as an adolescent. In *The Lonely Hunter* Virginia Spencer Carr explains, "When Carson was younger, some of the girls gathered in little clumps of femininity and threw rocks at her when she walked nearby, snickering loud asides and tossing within hearing distance such descriptive labels as 'weird,' 'freakish-looking,' and 'queer.'"

An early McCullers short story, "Home Journey and the Green Arcade," written at the time she was studying in New York, includes an autobiographical character struggling with the ambivalent feelings associated with returning to the South after living in New York. Describing the character from this story, Carr writes, "For Carson's fictional youths, to live in the South was to rot in boredom, to stagnate; yet there was ever an ambivalent pull, for home was also a balm that soothed, healed, enveloped, protected." Carr also details the ambivalent pull McCullers felt about the South: "Her work demanded that she go back from time to time, just as she had told

Eleanor Clark . . . a few years earlier that she must periodically return to the South to renew her 'sense of horror.'"

Negative reaction to black and homosexual characters in her second novel, *Reflections in a Golden Eye,* confirmed McCullers' fears about the reception of her work in her native South. In her autobiography, *Illumination and Night Glare,* McCullers details the reaction she faced during a visit to her hometown after the publication of *Reflections in a Golden Eye* in 1940: "*Reflections In A Golden Eye* was just published, and this, with the attendant publicity made quite a stir in town and especially at Ft. Benning, the Army Post nearby. . . . The Ku Klux Klan even called me and said, 'We are the Klan and we don't like nigger lovers or fairies. Tonight will be your night.' I naturally called my Daddy and he quit work and came with a policeman to stand vigil over me." McCullers articulated her ideas about the racism and intolerance of the South and her lifelong ambivalence toward the region in her final novel, *Clock without Hands,* and she declined a request by the director of her hometown library for a donation of manuscripts because the public libraries in Columbus remained racially segregated.

In concluding her review of scholarship on McCullers, Judith Giblin James looks ahead to the future of criticism on McCullers' life and work: "[T]he territory ahead will be fascinating to explore. Throw away the old maps; find a scuppernong arbor and 'commence critic.' Read her as she was read in wartime. Read her for portents of what was to come. Read her as enmeshed in the private dramas of the gifted and the cursed. Read her against her favored Russian texts. Read her with your calculator handy, in respect for the affinity of mathematics and music." With the current renaissance of interest in her life and the seeming wealth of critical potential left untapped in her work, McCullers will continue to be among the first rank of southern women writers.

Flannery O'Connor

Sally Fitzgerald

In September of 1945 a shy young woman of extraordinary talent and hidden strength emerged from a small town in middle Georgia and turned northward to begin her graduate studies in preparation for a career in the arts. Her protective mother went along for the trip, to check out the living accommodations. By the time of her death less than twenty years later, Flannery O'Connor had become recognized, on the basis of a small body of work (two novels and two volumes of short stories, a handful of essays and a collection of her letters), as one of the preeminent American writers of this century, known and translated worldwide.

O'Connor was born in Savannah in 1925 and christened Mary Flannery. Both parents doted on her, and her interests and whims were usually indulged. She remained remarkably consistent in some of those, such as her lifelong delight in peacocks, her "chickens." Even in childhood she liked to write and kept journals and composed stories, poems, and essays for her parents' delectation. Her father, in particular, valued these and generally carried some about to show off to his friends. Most of those that survive show promise of the piercing clarity of eye and ear and the devastating humor of her later works.

This happy childhood ended all too early. Flannery's father had fallen ill with lupus erythematosus, the same disease that she herself would eventually develop. Flannery was twelve years old when the diagnosis was reached and the inevitable outcome became clear. Her early adolescence then was spent in the hush of the long, slow dying of her father, who had encouraged her hopes and plans to set out and make her mark as a writer rather than at the altar. She was fifteen years old when he died but was made older and wiser by this encounter with death, which became, in her own term, "brother to her imagination."

This is not to say that the loss induced morbidity in the artist. On the contrary, O'Connor was essentially a comic writer, but one deepened in mind by the sense that "all good comedy is about matters of life and death," and that matters of life and death are the purview of an ultimately loving deity. The startling violence to be found in her fiction was neither temperamental nor indicative of philosophical despair. She never discounted the evil in mankind or blinked at the horrors individuals could work on each other, and on themselves, but these were not subjects that interested her on their own account. Rather, her imaginative investigations into universal experience (only incidentally set in the South as the region she knew best and that served her as what John Crowe Ransom called "the world's body") were focused on what she described as "the action of grace in territory held largely by the devil." By this she meant not Georgia but the inscape of willful human souls everywhere and what she called "the lines of spiritual motion" to be discerned in their actions when they are singled out for corrective grace, as revealed in the course of her stories. However localized the settings and dialogue she handled so superbly, her characters are recognizable (not without some discomfiture to the reader) as universally true of human nature.

A melding of several vital factors occurred in this provincial southern girl to form the unique writer who emerged: her Celtic gift for language, at dead serious play in the rich vernacular of the American South; her deeply held and cultivated Roman Catholic Christianity, which provided her a firm intellectual structure and viewpoint from which to observe the mores and mind-set of the modern secularized world as she perceived them in the socially complex scene she called the Christ-haunted South; and her own personal history, which conferred not only propitious circumstances but particular gifts of hard-won understanding to accompany the difficulties and deprivation she would endure in the course of her writing life.

Although her writing was admired when she was in high school and college, most notably for its comic nature, it was as a graduate student at the University of Iowa that O'Connor first gained notable recognition. As soon as Paul Engle, the director of the prestigious Iowa Writers' Workshop, read samples of her work, he engineered her transfer from the school of journalism to the workshop. Meanwhile, O'Connor redirected her own efforts entirely to writing. She also dropped the "Mary" from her name, in favor of the more enigmatic "Flannery O'Connor" as signature. The first of her stories to be published, "The Geranium" appeared in *Accent* magazine in the summer of 1946, at the end of her first year. In it she introduced a subject to which she would return intermittently for the rest of her life: homesickness, literal and (especially) metaphorical.

During her second year in Iowa she began a novel she conceived when reading T. S. Eliot's *The Waste Land* (1922). The novel she would eventually complete and call *Wise Blood* (1952) bore only traces of this initial impulse and pattern. Two thousand discarded pages attest to the trials and errors of the early versions, but the bleak setting, "the Unreal City," was retained. Rather than Eliot's world-weary poet-pilgrim under the guidance of the mythical blind seer Tiresias, the protagonist who finally evolved in O'Connor's imagination was based on a figure more familiar and real to her: Saul of Tarsus, who after a blinding encounter on the road to Damascus had become Paul the Apostle. Here was a biblical history and a seer in whom she fully believed, whose words constituted an integral part of her intellectual and spiritual formation.

At the end of her second year in the workshop she received her M.F.A. and also the prize for a first novel, however far from completion it was. She was granted a third year at Iowa so that she could continue her struggle with that novel under the sometime tutelage of Andrew Lytle, the Tennessee novelist, who remained a lifelong friend. As the third summer approached, however, she accepted an invitation to Yaddo, the celebrated artists' working retreat near Saratoga Springs, New York. Here she would find an even better situation for developing her writing and new acquaintances who would figure largely in her ongoing personal and literary preparation. One of these was a quiet, scholarly poet friend, Robert Fitzgerald, also a Roman Catholic, who was about to move with his wife and children to a remote hillside house in Connecticut. The Fitzgeralds invited her to join them, and the rest of her short time away from the South was spent not only in compatible company but also in the relative isolation that permitted, not to say enforced, the intensive work she wanted to put into completing her novel. Fifteen months later, assisted by a donnée from Sophocles (when she read of the self-willed self-blinding of Oedipus), she had in hand a draft of her book.

At the same time, a heavy blow fell. In early 1951, she was diagnosed with a severe form of the lupus that would change her life completely. Vague symptoms had appeared in the preceding December, but by the time she reached home for Christmas at the family farm, Andalusia, the illness was dangerously advanced. She barely escaped death at this first attack, but spent the next eighteen months of what she thought was convalescence from a bout of acute arthritis readying her novel for submission to the publishers (now Harcourt, Brace, where Robert Giroux had become her editor after she declined to change her book in accordance with the objections of her previous editor at Holt, Rinehart). When she had finished it more or less to her satisfaction, she sent it to the Fitzgeralds in Connecticut. At Robert Fitzgerald's happy inspiration, she then allowed him to send it on to Caroline Gordon, who was not only a fine writer herself but also a celebrated teacher of the technicalities of the craft. Here began what might be called a master class, in which these two southern women were taught by and learned from each other for the remaining nine years O'Connor would live. Caroline Gordon's comments on *Wise Blood,* in the form of a nine-page letter pointing out certain weaknesses, took immediate effect in the author, who responded by composing some of the most memorable and important passages in the novel, greatly strengthening the whole. Everything she wrote was thereafter sent to Gordon before publication, even after the pupil's skills surpassed the teacher's.

In June of 1952 *Wise Blood* was published. Literary critics were puzzled but respectful of the strong talent behind the strange little work. Her fellow townspeople in Milledgeville were enraged, for the most part, holding the book to be derisive of the Protestant South, as well as immoral and salacious. O'Connor calmly accepted this misunderstanding and proceeded with what she considered her vocation, as she understood it. In personal journals dated 1946 and 1947, when she was still a student, she stated her firm intention to become—and remain—a religious writer (after her fashion), and she appears never to have wavered in this resolve.

Later in the summer of 1952, when she was told the real nature of her illness, her reaction was characteristic: supposing that she would live no longer than her father had, she made up her mind simply to write as much fiction as she could in whatever time remained to her and to indulge herself by ordering a pair of peacocks in the hope of breeding a flock. If possible, she meant to write another novel, and she soon began one, entitled, with a touch of gallows humor, "You Can't Be Any Poorer Than Dead." The intended first chapter, eventually published as a short story, grew by fits and starts over a period of years into her second novel, *The Violent Bear It Away* (1960). Meanwhile, she produced a series of arresting short stories, published in book form in 1955 as *A Good Man Is Hard to Find and Other Stories,* establishing her high reputation beyond any doubt. She had this book ready in exactly the three years she expected to live, but assiduous care of her health would give her nine more years and three additional books while her peacocks increased in number to forty.

Never a solitary by inclination, as she was sometimes thought to be, Flannery cultivated correspondence with a number of readers who sought her out and carefully sustained friendships from earlier years through memorable letters that, posthumously collected in *The Habit of Being* (1979), unexpectedly provided an autobiography and are now considered part of the canon of her works. In them she provided, as well, clarifying discussions of her fiction, furnishing the basis for the most insightful O'Connor criticism.

After the sacrosanct daily four morning hours of writing, visitors were welcome at Andalusia. Hospitality was liberally offered there, and callers grew in number. Further contacts were made, and friendships formed, in the course of occasional forays to literary conferences, where she read (with pleasure) and lectured (with considerably less). The talks she wrote for these occasions, along with two or three other essays prepared by her for publication, were gathered after her death into a small but durable volume under the title *Mystery and Manners* (1969). O'Connor disclaimed any expertise in literary criticism, but these unpretentious pieces reveal unexpected gifts in that realm, and her reputation as a critic has grown to the point that her pithily stated social and literary insights are almost as widely quoted as the pungent dialogue from her stories.

Friends abounded, but closer bonds were denied her. In 1955, one of her visitors, Erik Langkjaer, an attractive and cultivated young Dane representing her publisher, Harcourt, Brace, and later Caroline Gordon's editor at Scribner's, provided an important turning point in her understanding of what she came to realize was required of her. She fell seriously in love, and if her feelings had been returned, she no doubt would have faced a difficult decision. Her precarious health largely ruled out a strict Roman Catholic marriage such as she would have wished, and for O'Connor to have in effect set aside her most deeply held religious convictions in favor of temporal happiness would not only have impaired the steely integrity of character and intellect that made her the artist she was, but would most likely have diminished even the happiness marriage might otherwise have afforded her.

Nevertheless, it appears that such a defeat was at least a possibility, because in the end she was not put to a test she might have failed. A devoted friend who visited frequently and who delighted in her company, Langkjaer (admittedly a little intimidated by both her illness and her talent) did not fall romantically in love with her, and on a return visit to Denmark he married a young woman in Copenhagen. This anguishing disappointment brought O'Connor to the realization that her personal fulfillment would lie in other areas of achievement and that, moreover, her most important choices would to some extent be made *for* her. Thereafter she labored to perfect the graceful acceptance of her governing circumstances, as these changed or were revealed, as carefully as she perfected her art.

The Violent Bear It Away, the unsettling novel that finally emerged from the often discouraging struggle that had begun in 1953 with the seminal story, "You Can't Be Any Poorer Than Dead," appeared in 1958. Reviews were mixed. As had happened so often before, the work met with little understanding, and the author's aims and intentions were stood on their heads, though reviewers much admired the power of her storytelling. O'Connor herself, however, was satisfied that she had accomplished her purpose in this account of vocation willfully rejected and a latter-day Jonah brought to heel. No concessions were made to popular tastes or fashionable modes of explaining human behavior, and supernatural agency was affirmed in fully natural terms.

Honors accumulated both before and after her death. She was awarded honorary doctorates from the University of Notre Dame and Smith College, as well as numerous literary prizes and grants; invitations to speak and to read from her stories came from all sides. Her reputation grew throughout Europe and eventually in Asia, suggesting the basic unity of human nature and experience in whatever circumstances or settings. In 1971 a posthumous edition of *The Complete Stories* won the National Book Award, and her letters, collected in *The Habit of Being,* won a National Book Critics Circle award in 1979. In 1989 she became the first author born in the twentieth century to be published in the Library of America series.

O'Connor had undertaken a third novel, provisionally entitled "Why Do the Heathen Rage?" but as her energies diminished, it remained a short story, first published in *Esquire* in 1963. As in other instances, she meant to revise in that novel themes drawn from earlier works and to develop a character drawn from a preceding figure, this one first introduced in "The Enduring Chill," a whining "artist" condemned by his own folly to the prison of his mother's assertive care. As usual, she wished to tell the story of a change in a character, but now one not violently occasioned. A secondary theme was to be pursued in this new work: to probe the dangerous "innocence" of an inculpable moral moron, operating in a different field but akin to the girl who wreaks such havoc on "the comforts of home," in the story of that name.

She was not to complete this novel, however, but would expend her energies rather on the memorable stories published soon after her death, under the title *Everything That Rises Must Converge* (1965), a theological proposition drawn from Teilhard de Chardin. Only one of the nine, "The Partridge Festival," might be considered inferior to her earlier work, and one, "Greenleaf," was adjudged in 1999 to be among the fifty best short stories of the twentieth century, by a panel of judges led by John Updike.

In the title story of the collection O'Connor approached for the first time the social upheavals following in the wake of the civil rights movement. Here she deals out justice with an even hand. Only two of the characters—a six-year-old black child and a traditional-minded old white woman, politically incorrect in all her inherited views but like the child, sound of impulse in instinctive love—have their hearts in the right place. In the clash of simmering rage and misunderstanding, tragedy ensues, and a painful epiphany.

One of O'Connor's marked gifts was the ability to sum up in one compelling image a personage (or presence) and an ambience that together suggest an altered future as well as a past history with residual implications that starkly confront the present. It is ironic that this writer should now be judged quite harshly as a "racist" largely on the basis of her use of a now proscribed word occasionally (and never maliciously) in her correspondence and once (perfectly, from a literary standpoint) in the title of the story she considered to be the best she would ever write, "The Artificial Nigger." Drawn from a term she overheard by accident, this definitive example of southern speech—the Latinate elegance of "artificial" qualifying a crude colloquial noun—she used here to point to a telling admixture of historic evil and human suffering, and of sentimental self-deception with regard to both. The battered figure of a painted plaster lawn statuette—a blackamoor clutching a piece of brown watermelon and "meant to look happy but wearing instead a look of wild misery"—which the two protagonists term "an artificial nigger," served for O'Connor the purpose of suggesting to the reader what she calls "the redemptive power of Black suffering for us all." That is, it becomes a crucifix, suggesting the crucifixion of an entire people, whose sufferings may ultimately lead to the redemption of the society guilty of imposing them. For valid reasons (fragile health and family), O'Connor took no public part in integration activities, commenting simply that in this story she had said what she had to say on the subject in the way she could say it best.

In another story, "The Lame Shall Enter First," O'Connor made a more characteristic effort: to use not only materials contained in fragments discarded from preceding stories but also to improve her rendering of a character similar to one whose depiction in a previously published work she had

retrospectively found wanting. Here she redraws—much more successfully—a figure resembling Rayber, the obtuse academic sociologist in *The
Violent Bear It Away*, in the person of another self-appointed savior, the
"good Sheppard," who, in different but not altogether unrelated circumstances, suffers a loss and a lesson equal to or greater than his predecessor's.

O'Connor then made one more such effort to perfect in a newer version
a story embodying an old theme important to her. "Judgement Day" was a
greatly enriched *second* reworking of the subject of her first published story,
written while she was still a graduate student in Iowa. This time around, the
despairing gerontion of the earlier work evolved into a decisive octogenarian who not only suffers for his sins of pride, but also acts to reverse them
and find his way back to his true country and home dead or alive. This new
treatment, seamlessly conveying the simultaneous interaction of the temporal and the eternal in the lives of the simplest folk, the sparrows whose fall
was once described as always noted (and to this author is always important), measured O'Connor's growth as an artist.

"Parker's Back," penultimate of the three short masterpieces concluding
her final book, on the other hand introduced a wildly original new character
and a situation she had never before examined, recounting the progress of
an unwitting pilgrim, tattooed, for aesthetic reasons, over every inch of his
stocky body from the neck down and salutarily trapped in a marriage made
if not in hell, at least in purgatory. It is in the story "Revelation," however,
third from her last, that O'Connor summarizes her fiction as a whole in one
memorable image: a vision granted the pharisaical protagonist, a massive
country wife who, with her cowed husband, operates a model farm and
"pig-parlor." This social critic and confident judge of her fellows, individu-
ally and collectively, is stunned into awareness of the real goal of human
lives, and order of human precedence, by a fierce representative of the various lame, halt, and blind she has held in lofty contempt as she surveys those
assembled in the doctor's office where they are gathered in their need.

Written in the fall of 1963, less than a year before O'Connor's death, the
story was published first in the *Sewanee Review*, whose readers she thought
would best understand and appreciate it. It might have been chosen to close
her final volume, and life work. Both her pervasive themes and the prove-
nance of her characters, however numerous their variations, are memorably
summed up in the epiphany and ensuing vision that properly chasten the
self-satisfied heroine before she can begin to mount "the great swinging
bridge" envisioned by her author:

> At last she lifted her head. There was only a purple streak in the de-
> scending dusk. She raised her hands from the side of the pen in a ges-

ture hieratic and profound. A visionary light settled in her eyes. She saw the streak as a vast swinging bridge extending upward from the earth through a field of living fire. Upon it a vast horde of souls were rumbling toward heaven. There were whole companies of white-trash, clean for the first time in their lives, and bands of black niggers in white robes, and battalions of freaks and lunatics shouting and clapping and leaping like frogs. And bringing up the rear of the procession was a tribe of people whom she recognized at once as those who, like herself and Claud, had always had a little of everything and the God-given wit to use it right. She leaned forward to observe them closer. They were marching behind the others with great dignity, accountable as they always had been for good order and common sense and respectable behavior. They alone were on key. Yet she could see by their shocked and altered faces that even their virtues were being burned away.

Flannery O'Connor died on August 3, 1964, and is buried beside her father and mother in Milledgeville.

Harper Lee

Carolyn M. Jones

As Harper Lee struggled to rework the manuscript of *To Kill a Mocking-bird, Newsweek* reported in 1961, her supporters at Lippincott were "screaming and yelling, hollering, 'The book may not sell 2,000 copies, but we love Nelle.'" Their enthusiasm initiated that of a nation as Harper Lee burst onto the literary scene in 1960 with the publication of her first and only novel. *To Kill a Mockingbird* has never gone out of print, and its gentle but tough story of a small southern town, a racist act, a trial, an honorable man, and a lively young girl coming of age has influenced, now, nearly three generations of readers.

Nelle Harper Lee was born in Monroeville, Alabama, in 1926, a descendent of Robert E. Lee. Her father, Amasa Coleman Lee, on whom Atticus Finch, the major character in her novel is based, was a lawyer in the small town. He had been part owner and editor of the *Monroe Journal* and was in the state legislature from 1926 to 1938. He seems to have been a tough and principled person, defending blacks in the small town in various court cases—though not in one like the rape case in the novel. He died just after the film of *To Kill a Mockingbird* was completed in 1962. Michael Freedland, in *Gregory Peck: A Biography* (1980), says that Amasa Lee was immensely proud of his daughter because he believed she "had joined the ranks of [the] band of Southern writers . . . for telling *his* story."

Lee's mother, Frances, was from a Virginia family who moved to Alabama and founded the city of Finchburg. She is characterized by Gerald Clarke, in *Capote: A Biography* (1987), as a difficult and emotionally unstable woman who tried twice to drown Lee in the bathtub. Clarke writes that the child was saved each time by one of her older sisters. This story so infuriated Lee that she made, through her sister Alice, one of her few public statements. Lee had Alice tell the *Monroe Journal,* "I can't say that the story was a lie in enough ways to get the point across." Very little has been published on Frances Lee's life. She died on June 2, 1951, never seeing her daughter's success.

Lee was a tomboy who followed in her father's footsteps. She attended Huntingdon College from 1944 to 1945 and the University of Alabama law school from 1945 to 1949. Indeed, one of her few public appearances in recent years was at a graduation ceremony for the University of Alabama law school. She also studied one year at Oxford University. After completing her education, Lee moved to New York City, where she divided her time between writing—influenced by her literary heroes Jane Austen, Mark Twain, Nathaniel Hawthorne, and Eudora Welty—and working as a reservations clerk for Eastern Air Lines and British Overseas Airways. When her father became ill, Lee began to divide her time between New York and Monroeville. Given a present of time by a group of friends, she left the airlines to write full time.

Her only novel, *To Kill a Mockingbird,* was published first by Lippincott in 1960, intersecting with the important events of the then burgeoning civil rights movement. The novel was well received by the critical community. *Mockingbird* was called authentic and fresh, taking a common theme and making it work "forcefully," as Keith Waterhouse put it in the *New Statesman.* It offered, as Richard Sullivan observed in the Chicago *Tribune,* "a view of the American South, its attitudes, feelings, and traditions," without being a sociological novel. The novel was an immediate popular success, selling two and a half million copies in its first year and going through fourteen printings. It won the Pulitzer Prize for fiction in 1961, along with numerous other awards. It was Bestseller's paperback book of the year in 1962. And it became a Literary Guild selection, a Book-of-the-Month Club alternate, and a *Reader's Digest* condensed book. The novel continues to be widely read and has never been out of print. It has been translated into at least ten languages and has sold between twelve and fifteen million copies. On its strength, Lee was named, in 1966, to the National Council on the Arts.

The novel was made into an Academy Award–winning screenplay by Horton Foote. The course of the making of the film illustrates how potentially controversial Lee's novel was at the time of its publication. According to Michael Freedland, Rock Hudson originally brought the novel to Universal Studios. The major studios, however, were reluctant to consider the idea because of the political climate in the country. They did not want to make a "race picture" for fear of losing the whole southern audience. Hudson abandoned the project, and Alan Pakula and Robert Mulligan bought the rights; Pakula produced the film. Gregory Peck, who had filmed other "race pictures" (such as *Gentleman's Agreement,* a powerful and lyrical attack on anti-Semitism), made the film through his own production company. Peck recalls meeting Amasa Lee, who was frail, suffering with arthritis, but interested in all the proceedings. The film won Peck an Academy Award for best actor. Peck tells how Lee gave him her father's pocket watch: Amasa Lee had always toyed with the watch when in court, and Harper Lee schooled Peck in the use of the watch; when the filming was over, she gave it to him, and he carried it the night he won the Oscar. Freedland quotes Lee as saying that the film was her vision of the novel: "In that film the man and the part met. . . . I've had many, many offers to turn it into musicals, into TV or stage plays, but I've always refused. That film was a work of art." There is, however, a stage version of the novel by Christopher Sergel that is presented annually at the Old Courthouse in Monroeville.

Lee said she saw the novel as a simple love story—of Atticus Finch and justice. Lee clearly saw in her father someone who had always respected the rights of human beings, black or white, and who stood up for those rights. She demonstrates through the figure of Atticus Finch that the struggle for human dignity for African Americans had white supporters in the South long before the civil rights movement. The novel, however, is more than a novel of the South and its traditions and quirks and more than a novel of black-white relations and collisions. It is a portrait of the human heart of a just man, and how his principled life influences his children, his town, and, through Scout Finch's narration, a nation that, in 1960, was experiencing tension between itself and that for which it stands.

The novel concerns a period of about three years, 1933 to 1936, in the life of Jean Louise "Scout" Finch and her family in Maycomb, Alabama, and it describes two related events. The first is the trial of Tom Robinson for the rape of Mayella Ewell, a white woman. The trial and the tensions it reveals transform the sleepy town of Maycomb for Scout and her brother, Jem, as they are forced to interrogate the hierarchy of their society—to look through its surface manners and politeness and into the human heart and human mind, and to forge a new relationship to the world in which they live. The second is the children's investigation and the eventual emergence of Boo Radley, a "malevolent phantom," who ultimately saves Scout's and Jem's lives. Both Boo and Tom are "gray ghosts," with little role in Maycomb's society other than as phantoms or threats. For the children, however, they represent coming to terms with their heritage and their environment. Boo is, for the children, an exercise in coming to know the "other" within their own boundaries. Their wonder about Boo and their desire to know him is paralleled with the need for the adults in the town and on the jury to know Tom Robinson, that "other" who is familiar but also alien. Scout and Jem do what the adults of Maycomb and those of a modern America must do: learn to "read" their world (literacy is a major theme of the novel) and to make judgments based not on custom and prejudice but on character and truth.

Maycomb, a small southern town, is the scene of these complications of relationship and action. The Finch family, landholders and ex–slave owners, is one of its important families. The men in the family, Scout tells us early in the narrative, traditionally remain on the self-sufficient plantation, Finch's Landing, and "make their living from cotton." Atticus Finch and his brother leave Finch's Landing, while their sister Alexandra, who represents southern virtue, hierarchy, and prejudice, remains on the family land. Lee, without comment, shows us the interwoven lives that such a history creates. The Finch family housekeeper, Calpurnia, for example, is probably the descendant of one of the three slaves that Simon Finch brought to the landing. Such subtle clues about relationality and intimacy complicate the idea that the novel is simply young adult literature, the category in which it has been classified.

Atticus Finch's defense of Tom Robinson is his "moment of truth": he must stand up publicly for his private beliefs. This moment forces him to confront his own family's history as slaveholders, his choice to separate from that mode of being, and, at the same time, the truth that he cannot escape its legacy. This legacy of racism is present and embodied in his family and his neighbors. Finally, his act forces the reader to confront America's history as a slaveholding nation, the consequences of that legacy, and his or her own prejudices and fears. The novel utilizes symbols to remind us of the ambiguity of Atticus' situation and of the deep fears and desires the town, and by extension, the nation, faces in confronting the issues of race. For example, Mrs. Henry Lafayette Dubose's camellia is a symbol of her will and endurance and that of the antebellum South that she comes from and still loves, but it is also a symbol of the violence of the Ku Klux Klan. The mad dog that Atticus shoots and kills represents the mad dog of racism that must be dealt with, not violently, but through persuasion in a public structure of deliberation, the trial. Atticus bridges these antinomies. In the person of Atticus, we do not get the kind of existential angst that one often encounters in the modern hero. Rather, as he faces this trial, Atticus neither chooses detachment and exile nor does he try to make himself the center. He knows that he will lose, yet he gives his best. As the stoic Christian, Atticus chooses the path of duty, honesty, constancy, and compassion. Lee is asking through Atticus Finch, and through his children who carry forward his ethos, what of the past enables us to face the future? What lets us remain constant and yet acknowledge the need for and embrace change?

Although *To Kill a Mockingbird* is Lee's only novel, it is a masterpiece. When the novel was printed, Lee said that she was working on a second novel, but it has never appeared. Her other published work includes "Love—In Other Words," printed in *Vogue* (1961), and two articles for *Mc-Calls*, "Christmas to Me" (1961) and "When Children Discover America" (1965). A more recent essay, "Romance and High Adventure," Lee presented as a paper for the 1983 Alabama History and Heritage Festival. That gathering explored, as Jerry E. Brown explained in the editor's preface to *Clearings in the Thicket: An Alabama Humanities Reader* (1985), the thicket, the literal translation of the word "Alabama" and by extension, "human clearings, moments when minds and hearts catch up to experience and make something from it." Lee reinforced in her paper her insistence on the need for Americans to come to terms with history. She wrote: "We Americans like to put our culture in disposable containers. Nowhere is this more evident than in the way we treat our past. We discard villages, towns, even cities, when they grow old, and we are now in the process of discarding our recorded history, not in a shredder but by rewriting it as romance. . . . [We] want anything but the real thing." She then went on to discuss Albert James Pickett's *History of Alabama* (1851) in the same lively yet serious style that characterizes *Mockingbird*. It is unclear whether Lee plans to publish more; she told Claudia Durst Johnson in an unpublished interview that she has abandoned her second novel and is working on her memoirs.

Harper Lee need never write another word. Her only novel is one of the most popular and influential works of modern southern literature. It continues to be widely read and taught, and the public's fascination with the private Lee has led to an Internet site on Lee and the novel. The novel captures perfectly the South and the nation as they stand poised for change. The South and the nation are the same, in many ways, in 1936, 1960, and now: children still face rites of passage, lose their innocence, and decide what kinds of adults they will become. Racism still exists, and good people still fight it. The world, however, has changed: men and women like Atticus

Finch and his children and Tom Robinson's children have altered our relationships with one another. That it captures the perennially human and the challenge to change, as it offers the tools to face change—Scout Finch's curiosity and humor and Atticus Finch's courage, fortitude, and power—make this novel timeless.

Harper Lee leads an active but very private life. She continues to divide her time between New York and Monroeville. Kathy Kemp, in the Raleigh *News and Observer* (1997), tells the story of going to Lee's door and, when Lee answered, thrusting forward a copy of *Mockingbird*. Lee, noting that it was six in the evening, with "a look of disgust on her face," said, "Good gosh. It's a little late for this sort of thing, isn't it?" Nevertheless, she signed the book, and, when Kemp thanked her, she replied in "a voice full of warmth and good cheer, 'You're quite welcome.'" This lack of pretension points to a woman who is not reclusive but who seeks to lead a normal life despite her fame. In 1995, when HarperCollins issued an anniversary edition of her novel, the publisher asked Lee to write an introduction to the work. Lee wrote an introduction against introductions, stating that the book stands on its own. In the midst of this introduction, Kathy Kemp notes, Lee "offered a tiny personal note, which is more eloquent than any sentence about her by another writer": "I am still alive," she wrote, "although very quiet."

PART IV

The Contemporary South
(1960 to the Present)

Introduction to Part IV

Carolyn Perry

Although countless plantation columns still stand and the debutante ball remains the major social event for many southern families, images of the
South at the dawn of the new millennium point to the future more often
than to the past. Southern universities are known for their research in evolution and robotics as much as for histories of the Old South, or for embracing
postmodern theory at the expense of the New Critics. Atlanta, now the emblem of the New South, is known not only for Sherman's march and peach
trees, but also for hosting the 1996 Olympics and as the headquarters of
the Cable News Network. Even *Southern Living* has entered the twenty-first
century, having gone on-line to offer readers quick access to its world-
famous recipes, traveling tips for planning a southern vacation, or virtual
shopping at Piggly Wiggly. As the South today blends so effortlessly with
the rest of the nation, debate over its distinctiveness shapes discussion of
almost anything labeled "southern."

Although contemporary southern culture is in many ways American culture, the South is unable, and often unwilling, to sweep its distinct history
out the door. And while popular culture often capitalizes on the nation's
fascination with this distinctiveness—as sales of *Divine Secrets of the Ya-Ya
Sisterhood* (1996) or *The Southern Belle Primer* (1991) suggest—the haunting of the past points to deep social and psychological issues the South continues to confront. In many ways, the second half of the twentieth century

echoed the second half of the nineteenth: race relations, the "modern woman," and a changing landscape persisted as the most heartfelt concerns. Despite competition from country music and Hollywood, nowhere are these concerns more poignantly wrought than in the literature of the South—and perhaps most notably in works by southern women.

Images of the civil rights movement—the sit-ins, freedom rides, and dream speeches, the police dogs, fire hoses, and church bombings—raised questions for southern writers that have been explored in literature for almost half a century now. How can we understand the fierceness of prejudice? How does one live as the target of prejudice day after day? What drove black leaders to risk their lives repeatedly for the cause of equality? What brought white freedom fighters from the North to Mississippi that long, hot summer of 1964, and what did it feel like to face suspicion from blacks and violence from whites? How will this battle rage on in the minds and souls of Americans for years to come?

Although the South's identity extends far beyond questions of race, the civil rights movement has been as significant to contemporary southern writers as the Civil War was to its literary descendants. To date, Alice Walker's *Meridian* (1976) remains the most compelling work of literature focused on the movement. Its exploration of black identity and interracial relationships reaches issues well below the surface of racial tension, primarily to its psychological and even spiritual consequences. During the 1960s and 1970s, many other black voices made themselves heard as well. The work of Sonia Sanchez, for example, flourished in the 1960s, as she used experimental language and typography to challenge mainstream poetic form and lend power to the black arts movement. Sanchez was joined by Nikki Giovanni (b. 1943), who is known for her militant voice that consistently speaks out against racism and sexism. Toni Cade Bambara, although generally considered a northern writer, achieved her best work in *The Salt Eaters* (1980), a novel set in Claybourne, Georgia, that focuses on civil rights and racism as a psychological disease. Yet many African American women writers of the South have spent most of their lives in the North or West, as if they needed to establish some distance in order to write most profoundly about their experiences. Of the major African American women writing about the South today, only a handful have remained there. One of the most prominent, Margaret Walker, lived in the South until her death in 1998 and devoted her life to encouraging black southerners through her writing. By using Old Testament prophets as a backdrop against which to view civil rights leaders, for example, Walker's *Prophets for a New Day* (1970) gave new meaning to the "dreams and visions and prophecies" of Martin Luther King, Jr., and Malcolm X.

While white southern women do not often write about the civil rights movement directly, almost all who wrote in the 1960s and 1970s found themselves addressing race in some way. Harper Lee's *To Kill a Mockingbird* (1960) is perhaps the most widely known and widely taught of such novels, yet in the 1960s and 1970s writers such as Shirley Ann Grau and Doris Betts were also writing fiction focused on racial issues. Winner of the 1964 Pulitzer Prize for fiction, Grau's *The Keepers of the House* (1964) attacks the issue head on, openly demonstrating how racial conflict can draw out the worst in human nature. At the same time, Doris Betts uses the issue of race to come to an understanding of the complexities of human psychology in works such as *Beasts of the Southern Wild* (1973). Although Eudora Welty has generally addressed race subtly by poking fun at narrow-mindedness and stereotyping, when she wrote "Where Is the Voice Coming From?" (1963), based on the murder of Medgar Evers, she did not hold back, but blatantly attacked racist behavior. In her essay for this collection, Minrose Gwin finds in such works the need for both "remembrance and healing" as we continue to grapple with race in the twenty-first century.

While race continues to be a major issue in southern women's literature, during the 1970s and 1980s women's writing was shaped by the rise of feminism as much as by civil rights. Feminism after mid-century moved beyond the political and economic issues of the early twentieth-century women's movement—gaining the vote and political rights for women—to deeper social and personal issues, such as tearing down the hierarchical structure of gender roles and changing the way people view women, men, and gender. In an attempt to transform the view of literature as a masculine institution and therefore of woman as "other," feminist criticism seeks to uncover texts by women not previously considered part of the canon and to move them from their marginalized position to the center of literary study. At the same time, feminist criticism seeks to interpret or reinterpret the portrayal of women in texts by both men and women and to examine differences in the nature of "voice" in works by men and women. Such criticism, naturally, has a profound effect on the study of southern literature.

Given the recognition of the women's tradition in southern literature since mid-century, Fred Hobson's recent claim (in *The Southern Writer in the Postmodern World,* 1991) that southern writers since the 1970s are more likely to "operate not under the shadow of Faulkner but under that of O'Connor and Welty" comes as no surprise. Indeed, writers and scholars now acknowledge a female tradition that shapes the formation of characters, theme and style, and even sense of humor in women's writing. The female quest developed exquisitely in Zora Neale Hurston's *Their Eyes Were Watching God* (1937) weaves through works like Welty's *The Optimist's Daughter* (1972) to shape recent novels such as Kaye Gibbons' *Ellen Foster* (1987) or Anne Tyler's *Ladder of Years* (1995). The toll the fight for personhood takes on women, first explored in novels such as Glasgow's *Barren Ground* (1925), is also still felt in contemporary novels. In the 1980s and 1990s, women protagonists such as Ellen Gilchrist's Rhoda Manning or Anna Hand revealed both the hardships and triumphs of women acting out the feminist drama; in *In the Land of Dreamy Dreams* (1981) or *The Anna Papers* (1988), for example, Gilchrist's fiery women fight to become their own persons, yet personal flaws as well as the strength of a patriarchal South rarely allow them self-fulfillment. At the same time, the humor with which Welty or O'Connor approached their stories continues to influence southern women writers. In *Comic Visions, Female Voices* (1998), Barbara Bennett demonstrates how humor in works by writers such as Lee Smith, Jill McCorkle, or Josephine Humphreys—in the tradition of O'Connor or Welty—"attacks the order already in place, questioning its validity and control over society, and often suggesting new possibilities for a more positive social construct."

Perhaps because southern writers have often been scholars and critics as well as poets and novelists—Robert Penn Warren, Allen Tate, Doris Betts, and bell hooks (b. 1952) to name a few—criticism has made a place for itself within literary history. In the study of southern women's literature, gender studies and feminist criticism, in particular, have been significant. In addition to bringing to light writers previously ignored by scholars, most notably Kate Chopin and Zora Neale Hurston, critics of southern literature have broadened the scope of the canon as well as the scope of literary theory. During the past twenty years, countless books on southern women writers have been published, as well as several anthologies. Works such as Anne Goodwyn Jones's *Tomorrow Is Another Day: The Woman Writer in the South, 1859–1936* (1981) and Mary Louise Weaks and Carolyn Perry's *Southern Women's Writing, Colonial to Contemporary* (1995) seek to extend the female tradition back in time to include precursors from the antebellum and postbellum South. Yet critics are not solely responsible for bringing southern women's literature to the forefront. In her book *A Southern Weave of Women* (1994), Linda Tate links the resurgence of southern fiction to the rise of small, independent presses in the South. Whether presses such as Peachtree and Algonquin seek out southern writers, or others, such as Naiad, Banned Books, and Carolina Wren, promote political causes by the choices of books they publish, the tradition of southern women's literature has benefited from their support. Finally, conferences abound that are devoted to the study of southern literature, most notably the Southern Women Writers Conference held biennially at Berry College.

As racial and gender relationships have experienced significant changes in the second half of the twentieth century, so also has the landscape itself. The end of World War II brought economic expansion to the South, and increased mobility and the growing use of air conditioning made the South attractive to industry and migration of northerners to the region much more common. The Civil Rights Act of 1964, by putting an end to segregation, opened up more opportunities for southern cities. More recently, cities such as Charleston and Atlanta have become known for their convention centers and recreational sites, bringing in tourists and businesspeople from around the world. Urban growth in such cities has been phenomenal: Atlanta can boast a doubling in size from 1975 to the turn of the century. At the same time, since the 1960s and 1970s the South has seen drastic changes in agriculture: mass migration to urban centers means fewer small farms, yet mechanization and revolutionary farming techniques allow fewer farmers to produce more crops than ever before, and on smaller patches of land. While the agrarian life still dominates southern culture through its music, food, and family traditions, the image of the southern landscape is far more likely to be populated with fast-food chains, shopping malls, and suburbs than fields of tobacco or cotton.

Responses to the changing landscape in southern literature have become as diverse as the landscape itself. Certainly writers have felt the freedom to escape the southern setting entirely, and novels by southern women are often set in New York rather than Atlanta, or Rome, Italy, rather than Rome, Georgia. A few southern writers, such as Anne Tyler, immerse their characters in an urban setting, yet they are still a minority. Tyler, considered one of the few urban southern writers, presents a problem in that her most common setting is Baltimore, Maryland, and not all southerners claim cities so far north. Like Tyler's Baltimore, Jill McCorkle's settings are not always distinctly southern; she depicts small-town North Carolina with the soap-opera drama and gossip sessions that might be found in a small town in Kansas or Vermont. However, the North Carolina backdrop plays well off the specific locale of a novel like *Carolina Moon* (1995), in which the central setting, a homey rehab center for smokers, gently reminds us of the state's premiere cash crop. Lee Smith reveals her ties to the land most memorably in novels like *Fair and Tender Ladies* (1988) or *The Devil's Dream* (1992), which portray identities that cannot be known apart from Appalachia and its rural heritage, stifling though it may be. At the same time, writers like Alice Walker and Marilou Awiakta (b. 1936) take their love of the land in a more political direction, linking their commitment to environmentalism to their attachment to the southern land.

As the new century emerges, southern women's literature is perhaps most marked by its diversity, as Linda Tate demonstrates well in her essay for this volume. The space in the canon that feminism has created has allowed women with a wide range of experience to enter. Writers also seem more free to stress their differences, perhaps more now than ever before in the South. Lesbian writers have boldly attacked myths of southern womanhood and broadened the possibilities for writing about diverse relationships among women. Also, the Appalachian experience, too often associated with "white" experience, has been called into question as both African Americans and Native Americans are claiming their heritage there. As Tate explains, "For the black and white, poor and lesbian, Appalachian and urban southern writers of the second [southern] renaissance, the agenda is to insist on healing the pain of the past so that they and their characters may live more freely and joyously in the present."

Despite the radical changes in southern literature in the twentieth century, much remains that can be considered "traditional," and in many ways southern writers have resisted the pull of postmodernism. Thematically, the age-old list applied to southern literature dominates women's writing at the century's end. Most novels focus on family in some way, as well as on community, responses to the past, relationship to the land, and racial issues. In a recent review of novels by contemporary southern women (*Southern Review,* 1997), Dorothy Scura concludes that several of the major writers are dealing with old themes in powerful, but fairly conservative ways. Scura finds that they "have largely ignored the political issues of the day—violence, race relations, and so on—to focus on family." Family is certainly at the heart of literature by contemporary southern women, yet it is often by using this theme that writers work through other complex matters. Dorothy Allison's *Cavedweller* (1998), for example, deals with some very difficult issues—escaping physical abuse, abandoning one's children—yet it is finally about coming home to the South to pull family back together, about personal redemption and the power of forgiveness and love. Likewise, while Shay Youngblood's *Soul Kisses* (1997) is about a young girl's search for family, it also delves into tough questions of sexuality and racial identity.

Contemporary southern women writers may not be experimental in predictable ways, but they are experimenting with a wide range of forms. Their nonfiction prose and memoirs, for example, are steadily gaining recognition, so that when Welty wrote her recent autobiography, *One Writer's Beginnings* (1984), it was immediately accepted as part of the southern canon. Welty's autobiography is a natural outgrowth of her fiction and literary essays; similarly, lesbian writer Mab Segrest (b. 1949) uses the essay form to tell the stories of her childhood, but also, in collections such as *My Mama's Dead Squirrel* (1985), she attacks issues such as homophobia and racism. Recently, bell hooks has moved beyond her theoretical work into writing autobiography. *Bone Black* (1996), an imagistic exploration of her childhood memories through a series of short vignettes, was immediately followed by a second memoir, *Wounds of Passion: A Writing Life* (1997).

Although fiction still dominates southern women's literature, playwrights have also made names for themselves. In her best-known play, *Wedding Band* (1966), Alice Childress (1920–1994) explores an interracial relationship in South Carolina around the time of World War I. But she has also written about the Gullah-speaking people who lived on the Georgia Sea Islands in her plays *Sea Island Song* (1977) and *Gullah* (1984). More recently, Marsha Norman (b. 1947) has sparked considerable controversy with her plays, in particular *'night, Mother* (1983), which challenges traditional assumptions about suicide as a young woman calmly plans her own death. Beth Henley, likewise, has made a name for herself because of her dark humor and satirical portraits of southern society. Through such writers, we see how southern women are making an impact on Hollywood. Childress' story of a thirteen-year-old drug addict, *A Hero Ain't Nothin' but a Sandwich* (1973), was made into a film in 1977. Likewise, film versions of southern women's literature abound, from *I Know Why the Caged Bird Sings* (1970) to *The Color Purple* (1982) to *Crimes of the Heart* (1986) to *The Ballad of the Sad Café* (1990) to *Bastard out of Carolina* (1997).

As the new century dawns, southern literature remains an emblem of change in the midst of changelessness. Perhaps the image of the contemporary southern woman best symbolizes this state. In a recent issue of the *Oxford American* (1999), Donna Tartt concludes that the myth of the southern belle will not die because men and women alike sense in her "a bright old terrifying shard of her Goddess nature." In the same issue, Lee Smith and Branford Marsalis respond to the myth that southern women are frail and helpless: Smith claims that she never saw such women in the Appalachian South; in fact, she comments, "We were about as fragile as coal trucks." Likewise, Marsalis finds southern women "loyal, very sexy, polite to a fault, and, when necessary, razor-sharp in their wit," but he says that what is most important to know is that when pushed, a southern woman will—"in every possible meaning of the phrase—'Kick your ass!'" This portrait of the eternal and tough, spirited and feisty, likewise characterizes the literature of contemporary southern women, who, for all their differences, have created an enduring literary tradition not soon to be forgotten.

Myths of Southern Womanhood in Contemporary Literature

Kathryn Lee Seidel

In a number of genres that have appealed traditionally to women, recent critics have discovered subtexts that, rather than reinforcing traditional stereotypes, have affirmed women writers' subversive attempts to empower their heroines and readers alike. Janice A. Radway in *Reading the Romance: Women, Patriarchy and Popular Culture* (1984), Tania Modleski in *Old Wives' Tales, and Other Women's Stories* (1998), along with other scholars of popular culture, rehabilitated the romance, finding elements of protest against female subordination. In a similar manner, domestic novels of the nineteenth century have been reexamined by feminists and cultural critics— such as Jane Tompkins in *Sensational Designs: The Cultural Work of American Fiction* (1985)—for their presentation of the domestic realm as a place of sanctuary, a utopia for women in the midst of the predominant patriarchal culture.

In contemporary fiction in which the myth of southern womanhood persists, however, there is no similar subtext of empowerment. In fact, the myth of southern womanhood as it was first articulated in the early 1800s was almost immediately under intense scrutiny. Untangling the theses and antitheses that subsequent generations have taken toward this myth is an immense project whose skeins of interpretation have been the preoccupation of several of our best contemporary critics, including Anne Goodwyn Jones (*Tomorrow Is Another Day: The Woman Writer in the South, 1859–1936* [1981]), Anne Firor Scott (*The Southern Lady: From Pedestal to Politics, 1830–1930* [1970]), and Kathryn Lee Seidel (*The Southern Belle in the American Novel* [1985]). Southern womanhood as a concept is laden with symbolism, with iconic reference to the South as the Garden of Eden, both pre- and postlapsarian, and with the need of southern culture to justify its actions to itself and to the outside world. Contemporary writers inherit a tradition in literature that is over two hundred years old. Their verdict for southern womanhood in the literature of the 1980s and 1990s is in some ways more dismal than it was during the heyday of the Southern Renaissance. To understand contemporary uses of the myth of southern womanhood requires a brief background of this tradition.

In the southern domestic fiction of the late 1700s through the mid-nineteenth century, the myth of southern womanhood appeared. In John Pendleton Kennedy's *Swallow Barn* (1832), for example, most of the myth's defining elements are already intact: Bel Tracy is the "headstrong and thoughtless," lively, beautiful daughter of a rich plantation owner who seeks a husband for her. By mid-century these features were already recognized as stereotypical and soon blossomed into myth. First, this myth applied to the women in the privileged planter class only. Middle- and lower-class women and women of color were excluded from the myth because it was first articulated by male authors speaking for the planter class and realizing the connection of the myth of southern womanhood to the economy of the plantation South. In fact, the economic motive for this image was to present a perfected, if unrealistic, role model for the family drama of finding a suitable husband for the plantation owner's daughters. The economic motive of the father in these early novels taints the relationship of the young women heroines with others whom they may meet. The myth required that before marriage the young woman should be pure, but flirtatious, so as to attract a male. She practices these elements of flirtation with her father, who then is supposed to allow her to transfer these feelings to the suitable landed husband. In novels in this early period, the chief family relationship is between father and daughter, which novelists show as abnormally close.

The father-daughter tie is made even more intimate in these early novels by the fact that these young women have no mothers; the mother has died in childbirth or is incapacitated by some sort of illness. Historians such as Catherine Clinton, in *The Plantation Mistress: Woman's World in the Old South* (1982), point out the reality of the rigors of plantation life for the plantation mistress, whose illnesses and hard labor resulted in conditions in which women were indeed likely to die in their young womanhood and leave daughters for their husbands to rear. In these early novels the young women on the plantation are singularly isolated from others; they do not attend school, they associate with others only at parties and celebrations, and they have distant relationships with the African Americans on the plantations.

In the myth of southern womanhood, marriage having been successfully accomplished, the young woman is supposed to revert immediately to Victorian domesticity, which prizes purity, religion, and the domestic arts. In novels by E.D.E.N. Southworth (1819–1899) and Caroline Lee Hentz, heroines make this transition fairly well, with small, but significant protestations of disappointment in their new roles. After marriage, when the competition for men is left to the belles, women begin to form friendships with other women, who are of great significance in their lives, and who in many ways provide the solace and nurturing that their husbands do not. For example, in Kate Chopin's *The Awakening* (1899), the husbands are frequently away overseeing plantations in the countryside, or at their clubs in the city socializing, gambling, and drinking. The Victorian domestic ideal of the husband and father at home with his children was eroding in the domestic novel by the end of the nineteenth century.

In these early novels, women who embody the myth of southern womanhood increasingly represent the South's definition of itself. Indeed, novelists give their characters allegorical names such as Savannah, Virginia, and Carolina. After the Civil War, the symbolism of southern womanhood as the South increases. As W. J. Cash writes in *The Mind of the South* (1941), white male anxiety over the loss of the Civil War gave way to a new myth: black males were interested in wreaking revenge upon white southerners by raping white southern women. This myth mingled with the myth of southern womanhood in works such as Thomas Nelson Page's *Red Rock: A Chronicle of Reconstruction* (1898).

In the Southern Renaissance, writers such as William Faulkner, Ellen Glasgow, and Margaret Mitchell (1900–1949) inverted this and many other southern myths in reaction to the rose-colored reminiscences of their grandparents, who by then were presenting the South prior to the Civil War as an Edenic paradise lost. Southern Renaissance writers no longer blamed rapacious northerners and blacks for the fall. Instead, they pointed to the tragic implications of the myth of the Garden, that is, that the South fell not because of an external force, but because of its own tragic sins, the chief one of which was slavery, the second of which, according to many Southern Renaissance writers, was its treatment of women. In the Southern Renaissance, writers again veered toward the incest theme within the southern family; these writers show the father as ineffectual, no longer in possession of tracts of land, as, for example, Mr. Compson in Faulkner's *The Sound and the Fury* (1929). Mothers are repressed or ill but have tremendous influence over young southern women in urging repression of sexual desire and self-sacrifice as the prevailing virtues. Ellen Glasgow's *Virginia* (1913) and *The Sheltered Life* (1932) both show southern mothers whose belief in the myth of southern womanhood destroys their chance for happiness and prevents their daughters from forming normal relationships.

With this literary legacy, suspicion of the myth of southern womanhood remains high among contemporary southern women writers. The major components of the myth persist; women's roles before and during marriage, the influence of the mother and the father, and the influence of female friendships are major themes within contemporary southern fiction. Issues of social class differences take on less importance in contemporary literature than they did previously; many novels by southern women writers today show young southern women from the poorest socioeconomic backgrounds rising through the social caste system in spite of innumerable difficulties, most often within their own families. The women characters less frequently regard marriage as their opportunity for economic betterment, and when they do, authors quickly add to their misery until they are able to shed the offending husband.

In *Low Country* (1998), a novel by Anne Rivers Siddons (b. 1936), the middle-aged narrator, Caroline Venable, lives a privileged life with her developer husband on Peacock Island, a fictional island off the South Carolina coast. Caroline is a native of the country, and her love for the island and the feral ponies that live on it harkens back to the days of her childhood spent with her beloved grandfather. Courtship accomplished, Caroline marries Clay because of his wish to create houses that cherish the natural environment. The reader comes to find, however, that Clay has sold Caroline's birthright to developers who will raze the island and destroy the coastal habitat and the small Gullah community on it called Dayclear. Caroline's dilemma is whether to eject husband and marriage in order to preserve the land. The author appropriates the symbolism of southern novels; the island is an Eden, populated by a utopian community. As in earlier southern novels, Caroline is named allegorically for the region that she represents. She is another Scarlett O'Hara defending Tara against the Yankees in her midst, in this case, her own husband. She is assisted in this quixotic endeavor by two key friendships, one with Sophia, an African American anthropologist hired by the development company to study the small Gullah settlement and turn it into a theme park. Sophia joins with one of Alice Walker's characters, Dee/Wangero in "Everyday Use," an educated African American who regards her heritage as a trophy to be displayed on the wall, rather than as part of a living culture. The friendship between Caroline and Sophia is paralleled with Caroline's friendship with an Afro-Cuban man, who points out the vapidity of her life as a social hostess with her developer husband.

Caroline decides to oppose her husband and to save the island, which she calls, "not a peaceful Eden, not sweet, not idyllic, but . . . so ravenously alive and exuberant in its fecundity that I could almost feel the fabric of a still-wet new world forming itself around me." The idea that women are the landowners, the possessors and guardians of the land, has replaced the patriarchal notion of earlier southern fiction. Similarly, in Alice Walker's *The Color Purple* (1982), Celie moves from being a possession of her father to become a homeowner, a landowner, and an artist who creates new objects to be cherished and used. Walker's short story "Everyday Use" contrasts two sisters, one who cherishes African American traditions because they connect her with her female ancestors, and one who regards this birthright as an object to be valued in dollar amounts and displayed on museum walls. This story echoes Zora Neale Hurston's 1928 short story "Sweat," in which Delia sweeps the dirt around the porch in patterns and cherishes the cleanliness and beauty of her small house, calling it "lovely, lovely." Likewise, Ivy in Lee Smith's *Fair and Tender Ladies* (1988) establishes the homeplace that nurtures children and connects home to the most positive patterns of living of the rest of the family. In Smith's *Saving Grace* (1995), Florida Grace returns again and again to her family's home in Scrabble Creek, North Carolina. Eudora Welty's Laurel McKelva Hand in *The Optimist's Daughter* (1972) returns to her mother's house and garden to find reconciliation and peace. These authors are showing that women who own land and create beauty and harmony on it metaphorically own themselves, are not bound by their fathers and husbands, and reestablish ties with their mothers and women friends.

Writers of contemporary fiction regard the premarital period in the young southern woman's life not as a time of cotillions and parties but as a time in which young women are trapped by confused, dysfunctional families and their own misunderstood sexual desires in choosing a mate. Writers generally show that both conditions result in poor choices in marriage. In Lee Smith's *Saving Grace,* the heroine's father is a snake handler; his occupation disrupts family life and creates in young Grace a craving for stability in marriage that leads to unhealthy decisions. Her desire for self-fulfillment in passion leads to others. In Kaye Gibbons' *A Virtuous Woman* (1989),

Ruby marries a man "for his looks" but soon learns of his violence, indolence, and stupidity.

The issue of courtship as a path to economic security is found in the early fiction in the contemporary period. For example, in Elizabeth Spencer's *The Light in the Piazza* (1960), a young southern mother is in Italy with her mildly retarded adult daughter, Clara. She attracts the attention of the young son of an old and wealthy Italian family who want nothing more in a daughter-in-law than beauty and vivacity. Because Clara has these qualities in abundance, no one notices that she cannot do, as the novel says, long division. The mother's dilemma in this novel is whether to tell the Italian family of her daughter's disability. Thus, Margaret is in the position of marketing her daughter to the highest bidder, yet she knows that the commodity that she markets is flawed. A sophisticated comment on the earlier patriarchal difficulty of marrying the upper-class daughter to the right family, *The Light in the Piazza* takes on contemporary capitalism, critiques the South, and at the same time shows the triumph of Margaret as a southern matron whose ability to wield power in one of the world's great market places, Florence, exceeds even that of the Italians. In this novel, Spencer continues the theme of the southern woman representing the South, in that Clara is a flawed but beautiful object.

African American writers regard the issue of white southern women's clinging to the concept of southern womanhood as racist, cruel, and brutal. In *The Color Purple,* the laziness of Miss Millie, the wife of the mayor, leads her to exploit Sophie; her childish behavior indicates a woman who has not moved from the spoiled condition of adolescence into a responsible adulthood. In that Miss Millie is depicted as a slaveholder in her attitudes toward African Americans, she is a direct descendent of Marie St. Clare in *Uncle Tom's Cabin* (1852). In *Dessa Rose* (1986) by Sherley Anne Williams (1944–1999), Dessa's friendship with her former white mistress helps the selfish young woman grow in confidence, competence, and compassion.

In distinction from earlier writers, contemporary southern women writers show young southern women as sexually unrepressed, though they are often from families in which mothers urge that form of repression and self-sacrifice. Gail Godwin's young unmarried women have apparently satisfying sexual relationships with their boyfriends, but they perceive their mothers as bastions of southern refinement and hypocrisy. Some of these daughters cope with this tension by leaving their homes and sometimes the South, as does Cate in *A Mother and Two Daughters* (1982). In contrast, Godwin daughters who stay at home, as does Margaret in *Father Melancholy's Daughter* (1991), have a much more difficult time establishing a separate identity. Because her mother, Ruth, abandoned her and her father, and later died, Margaret feels responsible for her mother's departure; even from the grave her mother seems to be a critic. The ability of the young southern women to break free from the repressions of parents and family is the central issue for many contemporary writers. Similarly, in Anne Tyler's *The Accidental Tourist* (1985), Rose is able to marry, but she soon gravitates back to the familial home using the pretext that she must cook dinner for her eccentric brothers. Knowing that he cannot win against such odds, her husband joins the family and eventually moves in.

In several contemporary novels, the marriage ceremony is not the end of the novel but the beginning. Marriage brings a series of injunctions and difficulties that are more complex and challenging than in previous novels about the myth of southern womanhood. In a number of novels by major contemporary southern women writers, one sees the phenomenon that can be called the runaway wife. In Gail Godwin's *The Good Husband* (1994), the issue of marriage to a good but spiritually vacuous husband leads Alice to form a platonic relationship with Francis, whose wife, Magda, is dying. With the most spiritual of intentions, Alice moves away from her husband, first emotionally, and ultimately physically. Anne Tyler's novel *Ladder of Years* (1995) focuses on a runaway wife who finds herself walking one day to the beach, and rather than joining her family, she continues to walk—down the road on the eastern Maryland shore and out of their lives. Delia appears to be tired of the vacuum within her marriage; her husband is unaffectionate and distant and regards her as a convenient and high-ability servant. Delia, however, does not seem to learn much from her time away from her husband and family; she establishes a close family relationship with a man and his young son but abandons this family as well and returns to her husband on the occasion of her daughter's wedding. The blankness of this character and her insensitivity to the feelings of others is remarkable. Perhaps the novel is meant to represent independence from the myth of southern womanhood, but it is not a hopeful portrait.

The relationship of the protagonist with her mother persists as a major theme; contemporary protagonists have a mother, whereas in the earlier formulations of the myth of southern womanhood the mother is frequently absent. As has been mentioned, the mothers in contemporary literature are often troubled, remote, neglectful, and sexually repressed. When they are not repressed, often the sexual desires of the mothers so overwhelm them that they take up with men who are extremely destructive to their young daughters. The mother in Dorothy Allison's *Bastard out of Carolina* (1992), for example, is so overwhelmed by her sexual desire for her husband that she fails to protect her young daughter, Bone. The mother is as much a victim of her husband as Bone is, but as a result she cannot protect her daughter, rear her children, possess land, better herself economically, or find any autonomy or creativity within herself, all because of her relationship with her husband. Similarly, in Kaye Gibbons' *Ellen Foster* (1987), Ellen's mother fails to protect Ellen not only because she is ill, but also because she has endured abuse from her husband, has sunk into depression, commits suicide, and thus is no longer present in her daughter's life.

In novels in which the mother moves beyond sexual desire as her prime motivator, however, the mother is perceived as presenting a positive connection with female tradition. She is presented as a friend and role model who demonstrates the need to possess the land, to take pride in one's heritage, and to create beauty and harmony to the extent that one can. Dorothy Allison's *Cavedweller* (1998) opens with Delia attending the funeral of her rock star ex-husband in Los Angeles and then bringing her young daughter back to her home in rural Georgia. While Cissy resists her mother's attempts to refurbish the house and reclaim her heritage, the mother persists. In time, the transition into a female-centered society is complete, with mother, daughters, and female friends living harmoniously. These writers agree that southern women are complicit in perpetuating the male fantasy of the way women should be—docile, subservient, and powerless. Women who help preserve this myth feel "guilt, condemnation, and entrapment," as Anne Goodwyn Jones writes in her essay for *Women Writers of the Contemporary South* (1984). As Jones notes, Lee Smith's novels show that women who are protected from reality and defined by external standards become helpless, unprepared for modern life, and prone to consolation with soap operas and religiosity, but not spirituality and television. For example, Dori in Lee Smith's *Oral History* (1983) is unable to become the person she might otherwise be. Grace, in Smith's *Saving Grace,* partially throws off the notion that she must be subordinate to men, but she does not understand why her young daughters immediately reject the notion of southern womanhood.

The myth of southern womanhood has always included the situation of incest in cloaked form with the father, and sometimes with brothers or other close relatives. For example, Edgar Allan Poe's short story "The Fall of the House of Usher" (1839) contains the abnormal brother-sister relationship in a decaying southern family. Historians such as Bertram Wyatt-Brown in *Southern Honor* (1982) have noted that prior to the Civil War incest was indeed an inadvertent aspect of southern life, with one in eight southern couples likely to be related to one another. Contemporary writers move far beyond the historical, however, when they focus on the mother who is still caught in the myth of southern womanhood and its pejorative effects on her daughter in leaving her vulnerable to the sexual desires of the father. Having pursued their wives when their wives were teenagers themselves, the fathers and stepfathers of young women in contemporary novels turn to them when they become teenagers. These fathers are violent men, no longer owners of anything, impulsive and criminalistic. Autobiographical narratives, such as Maya Angelou's *I Know Why the Caged Bird Sings* (1970), and novels such as Walker's *The Color Purple* reveal the theme that Minrose Gwin, in her essay for *Haunted Bodies: Gender and Southern Texts* (1997), calls the narrative of the survivor of rape and incest. This reassertion of male dominance and privilege by force rather than patriarchal social order pervades contemporary fiction. In *Bastard out of Carolina,* Dorothy Allison shows the victimization and ultimate triumph of Bone against the violent assaults from her stepfather. Only through friendship with a single woman, and a lesbian at that, is Bone able to find within herself the resources to resist, first mentally, then emotionally, and then actually. In *Ellen Foster,* Ellen must fend off the drunken advances of her father after her mother dies. These men medicate their feelings of powerlessness with alcohol, thus continuing the traditional notion that southern men whose sense of honor and privilege is insulted will drink, become violent, and reassert their control over their family's women with rape and incest. To contemporary writers, men bring chaos and disorder into the southern family and cause its decay.

One antidote for contemporary southern writers to familial degeneration is female friendship, a theme developed by earlier writers, but which has flowered in recent fiction. The work of writers such as Rita Mae Brown, Margaret Walker, Toni Morrison, Gail Godwin, Kaye Gibbons, and many others, develops fully the solace, affirmation, empowerment, and release of creativity that strong female friendships can give. Some, such as Margaret Walker in *Jubilee* (1966), use the historical novel to show that black-white female friendships existed in spite of the social chaos of the Civil War and Reconstruction. Similarly, Toni Morrison's *Beloved* (1987) has but one positive white person in it, Amy, the young girl who helps Sethe give birth. Other authors, such as Gail Godwin in *A Mother and Two Daughters* (1982) and Anne Rivers Siddons in *Low Country,* are not able to create friendship born from shared experience between a white woman and a black woman. It appears that the friendships work best when the white woman is from the lower classes and closer in shared experience to the black woman. Since middle- to upper-class women continue to embody the myth of southern womanhood in contemporary fiction, their relationships with women of color remain remote, with much suspicion and tradition to over-come.

In this miasma of the southern family drama with its destructive fathers and absent mothers, there is a group of novelists who create heroines who not only survive but thrive because they endeavor to be free to pursue beauty, harmony, and creativity. Many writers select a protagonist who is or wants to be an artist. Eudora Welty's novel *The Optimist's Daughter* (1972) treats a woman artist who needs to come to terms with the repres-sions and constraints of her background in order to move forward as an artist. Alice Walker's work focuses not so much on the chaos of tradition as on the need to overcome and move through those forces that mutilate women both literally and figuratively, to become the powerful, artistic, and positive persons that all were meant to be. While most writers recognize the daunting consumerism of the New South with its Wal-Marts, Targets, inter-states, and body piercing, southern writers nonetheless appear to believe that far more influential than contemporary life is the mythology of the Old South. Reclaiming the South as a garden, a sanctuary for women and men, becomes their theme. In her book *In Search of Our Mothers' Gardens: Womanist Prose* (1983), Walker writes of the heritage of "beauty and re-spect for strength" from the mother who is not defined by the myth of southern womanhood. Southerners have always maintained that their home defines them. Contemporary women writers agree, but they exhort women to create that home in distinction from the myth of southern womanhood.

Southern Women Writers and the Women's Movement

Barbara Bennett

Most scholars of literature use 1945—or the end of World War II—as the dividing line between modern and postmodern literature; in southern literature, however, there is evidence to suggest another break around 1970, especially in southern women's literature. The women's movement is one of the major reasons for this break, a movement that gave birth to a literature with a distinct female voice. The 1970s brought new opportunities for women writers; for example, women writers no longer had to choose between writing and having a family—as many earlier novelists, such as Hurston, Welty, Glasgow, McCullers, and O'Connor, did—or to have someone else raise their children, as did Caroline Gordon and Zelda Fitzgerald. These new opportunities allowed for many new voices that would otherwise have been stifled through social constraints.

Beginning in the late 1960s and into the 1970s, there was strong resistance to feminism throughout the United States, but antifeminism was more powerful in the South than in any other region. Nine out of the fifteen states that refused to ratify the Equal Rights Amendment (ERA), for example, were southern states. Right-wing political groups like the Ku Klux Klan, the National States' Rights Party, the Conservative Caucus, and the National Conservative Political Action Committee denounced the ERA as a conspiracy to destroy the American home. The large rural population in the South—which was largely family-oriented and more religious and less well educated than other segments of society—was generally supportive of these right-wing groups. The women's movement gained strength in spite of this negative pressure, however, thanks to a few southern women who played prominent roles in feminist organizations and especially with the advocacy of Rosalynn Carter, who as First Lady spoke out in favor of the ERA.

Another significant threat to equality for women in the South was the large number of believers in fundamentalist religion, assemblies that saw women as traditionally—that is, biblically—subservient to men. Leaders of well-organized right-wing groups such as the John Birch Society, the Mormon Club, and various Protestant sects stressed to their followers that equality of men and women was against God's will. In addition, many southerners were misled to see feminism as antifemale, a frightening concept to citizens who believed the threats of unisex bathrooms and prisons as well as the visions of young mothers sent to fight on the front lines of combat. The South was still heavily entrenched in the ideas of chivalry and still fed its little girls on images of debutantes and beauty queens. (As one northern contestant in a national beauty queen pageant noted, southern girls should have their own category because "they've been doing this since they were born. They're professionals.") Therefore, the idea of a woman who was equal under the law—and also intelligent, self-sufficient, and strong enough to survive without a man—grated on many southern nerves, both male and female.

These long-propagated images of womanhood have been particularly resistant to change. The antifeminist stereotypes of the southern belle and the southern lady—women who are frail, virtuous, self-sacrificing, and helpless—were generated first by the southern man who long used the images as justification for racism—that is, subjugating and punishing African American men in the supposed pursuit of protecting the virtue of white women. Southern men are not the only culprits, however. The image of gracious southern living—which includes the romantic rural existence separate from the hectic charge of modern life, a place where men could be men and women were always ladies—has a firm hold on the minds of many Americans even today. Film, television, and advertising have all cashed in on the romantic ideal of the plantation myth, leading many nonsoutherners to imagine that the South has not changed since the days of *Gone with the Wind* (1936).

As Nina Baym has pointed out in her essay "The Myth of the Myth of Southern Womanhood" (1992), the fact that such a myth is a falsehood in no way means it lacks power, and so before a positive change could occur in the South, women writers have first had to acknowledge the stereotypes before reacting against them and replacing those stereotypes with more realistic and positive images of southern women. This put southern feminists in a precarious position—that is, they had to defend their region as unique, but also they needed to suggest that some things had to change for the betterment of all. In order for readers to be open to feminist ideas, a woman writer needed to offer those ideas in such a way as not to offend readers and turn them away.

Earlier male and female writers in the twentieth century—writers such as Ellen Glasgow, Frances Newman, Flannery O'Connor, Carson McCullers, and William Faulkner—had already begun using the belle in their literature to represent the darker side of the South, symbolizing the decaying traditions of the Old South crumbling in the face of modern life. Kathryn Lee Seidel explains in her book *The Southern Belle in the American Novel* (1985) that Faulkner, for example, uses pitiable Temple Drake in *Sanctuary* (1931) to show that the ideals of the Old South were impossible for a woman of the New South to exemplify, as well as to illustrate that adherence to such a belief could be destructive to self and society. Contemporary women writers, however, have had much less pity for characters like Temple Drake, finding their way of life not only destructive but also absurd and meaningless. The southern belle remains simply as a vestige of a life long outdated and impractical.

Betty Freidan published *The Feminine Mystique* in 1963, an act that historian Margaret Ripley Wolfe calls the "clarion call of the women's liberation movement," but in the South, more than one woman's portrayal of oppressed womanhood would be needed to change things. In fact, it would take the combination of black and white women protesting both sexual and racial inequality to improve life significantly for women of both colors. Like the female abolitionists of a century before, white women worked for racial equality, but this time they were rewarded with important gains in their own lives from legislation such as the Equal Pay Act of 1963 and the Civil Rights Act of 1964.

Some nonsouthern radicals like Bella Abzug and Gloria Steinem, however, still seemed too threatening in tone and behavior for most southerners of the 1960s and 1970s, with their talk of bra-burning, lesbianism, and military service. When the ERA was defeated and conservatism returned with the administrations of Ronald Reagan and George Bush, the women's movement in the country and especially in the South seemed to gasp its last breath. Instead, the movement metamorphosed to a much quieter but more effective "feminism." Changes continued to occur but on a different scale. Reproductive freedom, more leadership positions held by women, increased education opportunities, urban cohesiveness replacing rural isolation, and the movement toward economic equality have all contributed to an improving situation for women below the Mason-Dixon Line, as well as everywhere else in the country.

While the myths of southern womanhood still exist, fiction writers are helping to neutralize outdated images of women by attacking the myths with confidence, zeal, and a sense of humor. Rather than representing the weaknesses in such beliefs symbolically, these writers have turned to other approaches. Satire has played a major role in contemporary women writers' attacks on these images, becoming a strong weapon in the feminist position advocated in literature. In 1975, Florence King (b. 1936) published a satiric catalog of southern behavior called *Southern Ladies and Gentlemen* and ten years later published an equally facetious memoir entitled *Confessions of a Failed Southern Lady*. Both books take aim at the traditions and manners that can keep southern women—and men—from charting their own courses. By attacking the images that pigeonhole women, revealing those images to be absurd and impractical in today's world, King clears space for a woman to reevaluate her position in southern society and to take the role of feminist if she so chooses. King's satiric attack on the belle is continued by such writers as Marlyn Schwartz (b. 1947), whose book *A Southern Belle Primer, Or, Why Princess Margaret Will Never Be a Kappa Kappa Gamma* (1991) lampoons everything sacred to the belle, from silver patterns to sororities and chicken salad. Playwright Beth Henley also brutally satirizes such female southern traditions as beauty pageants, debutantes, and the Junior League in her plays *Crimes of the Heart* (1982) and *The Miss Firecracker Contest* (1985), exposing their lack of substance and worth for the woman of today's South.

Fiction writers have assumed the objective of diminishing the attraction of the belle and other restrictive images of women. Female protagonists now are virtually always strong in nature and independent in spirit, resisting all that is attached to bellehood. Writers such as Rita Mae Brown, Lee Smith, Gail Godwin, and many others present the debutante/social belle as not merely unattractive but detrimental to self and others. Such characters are portrayed as vacuous, vain, unrealistic, and useless. The young protagonist in *Daisy Fay and the Miracle Man* (1981) by Fannie Flagg (b. 1941) is told that the "only two books in the world that really mean anything are the Memphis Junior League Cookbook and the Holy Bible, in that order." Such blatant focus on social standing over everything else—including even God—

marks this writing as particularly feminist in the southern vein. It criticizes harshly such an elitist position, yet it does so in a subversive and nonthreatening style.

The most attractive—in every sense of the word—female protagonist of today's southern literature is no longer Margaret Mitchell's Scarlett or Melanie or Tennessee Williams' Blanche DuBois—a woman who attempts to maintain her beauty and delicacy in the face of terrible tragedy until a man shows up to help—but rather a woman who is an active agent in her own defense and welfare, able to take care of herself even if a man never arrives. Physical beauty and grace are no longer absolutely essential in the southern female hero. Southern women writers are reinventing southern womanhood one character at a time by replacing the stereotype with a strong, creative, and sexy woman who more often has a career than a beauty crown. Daphne Athas (b. 1923) describes her as a woman who "sees through things but also sees things through."

This female hero can escape from a kidnapper using her own wits—as Nancy does in Doris Betts's *Heading West* (1981). Betts's character at first waits to be rescued by policemen, waiters, campers, and tourists before finally realizing that she is in control of her own destiny, that she must rescue herself. Once she stops expecting external help and turns inside for strength, it is only a matter of time before she outmaneuvers her captor and becomes the vehicle for his destruction and her own freedom. This new hero can run away from a stifling marriage and start a new life—as Helen does in Josephine Humphreys' *Rich in Love* (1987). Faced with spending the next thirty years in an innocuous but stagnant marriage, Helen chooses to face the unknown and strike out to find a new life for herself, in spite of the fears and problems this change causes for herself and her confused family. Reminiscent of Edna in Kate Chopin's *The Awakening* (1899), Helen preserves her spirit at the expense of her family's, leaving them to learn the sometimes painful lessons of independence and self-reliance.

Another contemporary female hero consistently burns her abusive husband's dinner in passive-aggressive resistance. Mudear, in *Ugly Ways* (1993) by Tina McElroy Ansa (b. 1949), at first seems mentally ill. She turns away from her husband and three daughters and into herself—to save herself. Eventually, she stops performing the traditional maternal jobs—cooking, cleaning, and child rearing—and begins to live in a world of her own making. She gardens in the middle of the night by moonlight, she stays in bed and sleeps all day, and eventually she speaks from the grave to the reader, explaining but not excusing her choices in life. Perhaps her behavior could be seen as rather extreme, but as an African American woman in a male-dominated culture, resistance as subversive rebellion is her only weapon: it is her brand of feminism. And in the end, her three daughters are better women because they have been forced to stand alone and be strong.

One last example of effective feminism gone "underground" can be found in Fannie Flagg's *Fried Green Tomatoes at the Whistle Stop Cafe* (1987). In this novel, characters murder an abusive husband and serve him up as barbecue. The ones who commit this act are society's underlings: women and African Americans. When they realize that the reigning law in their small southern community will not protect or support them, they take steps to ensure their own safety by ridding the town of a man who seems to lack any positive qualities, who exists only to oppress those who have been powerless in southern society.

A Rita Mae Brown character in *Venus Envy* (1993) expresses her succinct—if not extreme—approach to modern southern life: "Why get married? It's easier to hang myself." This is not to say that feminist southern women generally see no need for men, but the relationships that fill the novels and short stories of contemporary southern women writers are based on equality if they work and inequality if they are dysfunctional, sending a clear message to men and women alike that feminism as a way of life is alive and well in the South, despite what some may call the demise of the women's movement. Jill McCorkle's collection of short stories called *Crash Diet* (1992) is representative of this new approach to love. The book offers eleven different women in struggles of independence versus dependence, femininity versus strength, preservation of self versus the family. During the course of each story, the protagonist becomes aware that her life is far from being the fairy tale that she was "promised" as a small southern girl, and therefore she realizes she must reinvent herself in order to survive and thrive. In contrast to traditional southern fiction, McCorkle's women and many of the female characters in today's fiction do not find solace in their families, churches, or communities; in fact, these are often the very things that fail them. Each woman must recreate her own space and identity, often but not always without a man.

In addition to presenting marriage and children as a choice for a woman rather than assuming that these roles are the only options, a number of contemporary women writers are exploring the place of the lesbian in the South. Unfortunately, some critics have misinterpreted the rise of lesbianism in literature as a rise in lesbianism itself and as a product of the women's movement, rather than as the women's movement acting as a freeing agent for lesbians finally to discuss and explore their lives in literature. Frederick Karl, in *American Fictions* (1983), for example, explains lesbianism as the

final stage of a pattern perpetuated by feminism—the need for independence, "defensiveness toward men," loyalty to the women's movement, and
ultimately "the movement toward lesbian relationships." Regardless of such
theories, novels such as Rita Mae Brown's *Rubyfruit Jungle* (1973), *Kin-
flicks* (1975) by Lisa Alther (b. 1944), and *The Revolution of Little Girls*
(1991) by Blanche McCrary Boyd (b. 1945) clearly indicate that the place
for lesbian women in southern society and society's acceptance of that new
place is expanding—and these protagonists will accept nothing less than exactly what they want. Molly Bolt in *Rubyfruit Jungle,* for example, locks
her mother in the basement until she promises not to make Molly learn traditional domestic skills like cooking, canning, and sewing. Such drastic mea-
sures seem called for in a society that values these skills above all others for
women.

When feminist theory first gained attention and momentum in the early
1970s, its goal included a reevaluation of women in texts as readers and as
authors—as well as an attempt to win respect from the community of scholars made up principally of white men who had long determined the canon.
The women's movement, with its increased opportunities for education,
brought more women into university communities both as students and professors, increasing the study of literature written by, for, and about women.
Scholars and students of women's literature began not only analyzing the
works of contemporary writers, but also reevaluating the literature of the
South written in previous decades and even centuries. In time, feminist theorists have expanded the canon to include "natural" writings of women—
such as diaries and letters—and studying these works in the classroom. In
southern studies, this change has led to debate about the definition of southern writing, a debate in which women have been pivotal, and scholars have
finally begun accepting as literature works like journals, autobiographies,
spirituals, oral storytelling, letters, essays, lectures, performance poetry, and
even cookbooks. What earlier male critics would have relegated to the subgenre of "local color" or "domestic fiction" in the nineteenth and early
twentieth centuries, feminist theorists now consider mainstream literature.

Expanding definitions also makes room for many different kinds of
southern female voices. The rise of "Grit Lit" by writers such as Bobbie Ann
Mason and Dorothy Allison signals a new kind of southern storytelling focusing on blue-collar characters, giving them a nobility rarely seen before in
literature. One of the reasons respect has been given to working-class deni-
zens of the South in stories where the hero no longer has to come from a
high social class is perhaps that so many new writers are from working-class

families—writers who before the women's movement would perhaps not have been given the opportunity to contribute to the canon.

By giving a voice to this new kind of southern woman, writers identify, empower, and legitimize all kinds of female lives that have been seen traditionally—in both a literary and a social sense—as marginal. The voices of contemporary southern women writers—writers such as Doris Betts, Florence King, Lee Smith, Alice Walker, and Rita Mae Brown, as well as southern female critics such as Anne Goodwyn Jones, Lucinda MacKethan, and Peggy Whitman Prenshaw—are strong, stubborn, powerful, and courageous. Their writing has become a vehicle for valuable change, re-visioning the past and present—and therefore the future—transforming the old, patriarchal, white South to a new South seen through the eyes of women of many colors.

These women have not turned their backs completely on the traditions of the pre-1970 South, however, nor have they altogether blurred the line between genders in life or literature. Generally, female fiction writers are more optimistic, more life-affirming, and more hopeful about the future of family and self than are male writers of the South. Even when they address serious and tragic subjects such as child abuse, dissolution of the family, death, rape, or mental illness, there is a sense of hope found in all their works, a hope based very often on the development of a strong and independent self, but a strength that is a building block for strong families and communities in which women are seen as valuable, contributing partners rather than as subservient, silent members. And while relationships of all kinds may traditionally be viewed as "female" topics, writers of today address them with force as well as compassion and the belief that positive change can be effected.

Contemporary Autobiography and Memoir

James H. Watkins

Over the last four decades, southern women from an increasingly diverse array of backgrounds have, like their southern predecessors and their counterparts outside the South, found autobiography and memoir to be an especially effective medium for articulating and affirming their own experiences of selfhood. Collectively, these women autobiographers and memoirists have used the special authority granted the autobiographical "I"—what Nancy K. Miller describes in "Facts, Pacts, Acts" (1992) in a more general context as the "truth effect" of autobiography—to reject restrictive models of female behavior and to resist monolithic constructions of "the South" and "the southerner," thus redefining the region in ways that more closely resemble its true heterogeneity. Whether through reminiscences by established literary figures or eyewitness testimonials by civil rights activists, trauma recovery narratives or multigenerational family memoirs, white racial conversion narratives or "redneck" autobiographies, contemporary southern women writers have established lines of affiliation and identification among and between women within the region and beyond its borders, in the present and of the past. As Eudora Welty observes at the conclusion of her luminous memoir, *One Writer's Beginnings* (1984), "The memory is a living thing—it too is in transit. But during its moment, all that is remembered joins and lives—the old and the young, the past and the present, the living and the dead."

In this so-called age of memoir, southern women engaging in self-representation play a significant role in perpetuating, in both the national and southern public imagination, perceptions of southern regional distinctiveness—this at a time when there is less empirical evidence than ever before to suggest its difference from the rest of the country. If Jefferson Humphries is correct in claiming that what is typically meant by the term "the South" is not so much a geographical entity as "an idea in narrative form, a discourse or rhetoric of narrative tropes," then the continued production of autobiographical narratives that recount characteristically southern experiences and affirm the ways in which those experiences shape the authors' sense of self should be seen as an important site for authorizing that rhetoric and anchoring it in the real. Bobbie Ann Mason's *Clear Springs: A Memoir* (1999) illustrates the point nicely. Known primarily for their "K-Mart realism," Mason's novels and stories typically feature strip-malled southern landscapes populated by characters whose lives are more connected to a homogenized national consumer culture than to any recognizable part of the southern past. Yet, in *Clear Springs,* Mason lays claim to her rural Kentucky background and its traditional way of life, especially as that way of life is exemplified by the generations of women who helped work that land. Admittedly, she takes care to show the extent to which mass media like radio, cinema, and later, television were deeply imbedded in that culture, but these superficially anomalous details only make her portrait of life in the rural South all the more convincing, as they highlight the continuity of traditional folkways amid the trappings of modernity. For Mason, then, as for many other contemporary southerners who make use of the autobiographical occasion, self-narration and self-location coalesce to participate in a uniquely authoritative discourse of southernness.

The proliferation of autobiographical writing during the period has been accompanied by a virtual explosion in theoretical and critical approaches to self-representation—with consequent implications for the ways in which life writing by southern women is produced and received. Beginning in the late seventies, developments in post-structuralist thought prompted theoreticians like Philippe Lejeune and Elizabeth Bruss, among others, to problematize the apparent immediacy and transparency of autobiographical discourse and to question the very possibility of defining autobiography as a genre. But it was not until feminist critics entered into the dialogue that the androcentric biases informing these initial studies were made evident. In "The Other Voice: Autobiographies of Women Writers" (1980), one of the first gender-centered critiques of autobiography studies, Mary G. Mason argues that women autobiographers have typically eschewed individualistic paradigms of selfhood, preferring instead to anchor their acts of self-narration to an identification with a chosen other. Drawing on the research of psychologists Sheila Rowbotham and Nancy Chodorow, Susan Stanford Friedman refines Mason's point by arguing that the privileging of individuation, separation, and autonomy as the distinguishing characteristics of "classic" autobiography has resulted in the canonical exclusion of virtually all women's life writing, since women's subjectivity is most often developed around and structured through "identification, interdependence, and community" ("Women's Autobiographical Selves: Theory and Practice," 1988). As a result of such critiques, more other-centered forms of self-representation such as the memoir are regularly included within the purview of autobiography studies. Recent feminist autobiography criticism has drawn on a wide range of disciplinary approaches, from Lacanian psychoanalytic theory and performativity studies to anthropology and queer theory. As editors Sidonie Smith and Julia Watson write in their introduction to the collection *Women, Autobiography, Theory: A Reader* (1998), where once it was all but ignored by the scholarly community, "[w]omen's autobiography is now a privileged site for thinking about issues of writing at the intersection of feminist, postcolonial, and postmodern critical theories."

Autobiography and memoir serve a crucial function as forums for bearing witness to lived historical experience, and the body of autobiographical writing generated by participants in the civil rights movement is arguably the most significant category of eyewitness testimonial produced in the United States in the latter half of the twentieth century. Perhaps the most widely read and frequently anthologized of these is *Coming of Age in Mississippi* (1968) by Anne Moody (b. 1940), though other accounts—including Maya Angelou's *The Heart of a Woman* (1981) and *Song in a Weary Throat* (1987) by Pauli Murray (1910–1985)—deserve mention. Moody's narrative recounts her impoverished childhood and her growing frustration with her family and community's accommodation to segregation and racism in rural and small-town Mississippi. In the last of the book's four sections, titled "The Movement," she describes her involvement in the NAACP during her senior year at Tougaloo College in Jackson, Mississippi, as well as the censure she faced from family members because of her activism. Despite repeated arrests and jailings for her work, which included registering voters and participating in sit-ins at the local Woolworth's lunch counter, her resolve is never shaken—not even when her mentor Medgar Evers is murdered. Unlike Moody, whose activities were largely confined to her home state of Mississippi, Angelou's work for the movement took place in the northeast, where she organized fund-raising activities for the Southern Christian Leadership Conference and worked as a liaison for Martin Luther King. While the section of *The Heart of a Woman* (the third installment in her serial autobiography) devoted to this part of Angelou's life may lack the drama of Moody's account, its perspective is more comprehensive, as Angelou ultimately links the struggle in the United States to global efforts to end exploitation of blacks. *Song in a Weary Throat* (published in 1987 and reprinted in 1989 as *Pauli Murray: Autobiography of a Black Activist, Feminist, Lawyer, Priest, and Poet*) is a sequel of sorts to her family memoir, *Proud Shoes: The Story of an American Family* (1956). In *Proud Shoes* the focus is on the earlier hardships faced by her mixed-race forebears in North Carolina during the post-Reconstruction period, as well as on her own childhood, while in *Song in a Weary Throat* she describes her own boundary-breaking career, which included student activism during the pre–*Brown v. Board of Education* era, her role in the formation of the National Organization for Women in 1966, and her ordination in 1977 as the first female African American Episcopal priest. Other notable narratives by women directly involved in the civil rights movement include Rosa Parks's *My Story* (with James Haskins, 1992), two memoirs by widows of slain leaders—Myrlie Evers' *For Us, the Living* (with William Peters, 1967) and Coretta Scott King's *My Life with Martin Luther King, Jr.* (1969)—and Charlayne Hunter-Gault's *In My Place* (1992), which tells of her experiences in 1961 as one of the first two African American students at the University of Georgia.

While southern whites' involvement in the civil rights movement was peripheral in comparison to that of southern African Americans and non-southerners, a number of white women from the South did participate in the struggle and write about their experiences. Their accounts are examples of what Fred Hobson calls the "white southern racial conversion narrative," which he describes as a category of "works in which the authors, all products of and willing participants in a harsh, segregated society, confess racial wrongdoings and are 'converted,' in varying degrees, from racism to something approaching racial enlightenment" (*But Now I See*, 1999). *The Desegregated Heart: A Virginian's Struggle in a Time of Transition* (1962) by Sarah Patton Boyle (b. 1906), centers on the author's efforts in Charlottesville, Virginia, and then on the state level, to end segregation. Given the real risks she took to act on her convictions and the consequences she faced in her personal life as a result, readers will probably forgive Boyle's occasional lapses into paternalistic thinking. *Outside the Magic Circle: The Autobiography of Virginia Foster Durr* (1987) shares some of Boyle's paternalism, but it too expresses a heartfelt commitment to racial justice while offering a more comprehensive retrospective of the author's life. Other examples of this kind of narrative include Florence Mars's *Witness in Philadelphia* (with Lynn Eden, 1977), Melanie Neilson's *Even in Mississippi* (1989), Mab Segrest's *Memoir of a Race Traitor* (1993), and Sara Mitchell Parson's *From Southern Wrongs to Civil Rights: The Memoir of a Civil Rights Activist* (2000).

The canonical preeminence once given to fiction, poetry, and, to a lesser extent, drama in the period of the Southern Renaissance has given way so that now such works as Maya Angelou's *I Know Why the Caged Bird Sings* (1970) and Welty's *One Writer's Beginnings* are recognized classics of late twentieth-century American literature. But the racial dichotomy suggested by these two widely anthologized works belies a process of democratization in southern letters that is especially pronounced in life writing from the region. Given the relatively egalitarian nature of the genre (which in the case of American women's narratives has featured the lives of social reformers, survivors of Indian captivity, and former slaves), it is not surprising that the pattern of greater inclusiveness Linda Tate describes in her essay "A Second Renaissance," included in this collection, is particularly evident in autobiography and memoir. The black-white racial dichotomy that remained intact at the beginning of the period has given way to include the voices of women from racial and ethnic groups that had, until recently, been consigned to the margins of southern literature. For instance, in *Selu: Seeking the Corn-Mother's Wisdom* (1993), Marilou Awiakta (b. 1936) includes numerous accounts of her childhood in East Tennessee that draw on the rich oral traditions of her Appalachian Cherokee background. For Cuban American essayist and children's book writer Carmen Agra Deedy (b. 1960), author of *Growing Up Cuban in Decatur, Georgia* (1995), suburban Atlanta provides the setting for her humorous reminiscences of bicultural childhood in the postsegregation South. And in *The Jew Store* (1998), Stella Suberman (b. 1922) recounts her Jewish father's journey from New York City to a small town in West Tennessee, where he ran a business, raised a family, and gradually earned the acceptance—albeit conditional—of his gentile neighbors.

In addition to the increased diversity along ethnic lines, southern life writing has become more class-inclusive as well. Where middle- and upper-class writers dominated southern literature prior to the mid-1970s, today we hear the autobiographical voices of women from poor and working-class backgrounds affirming their regionally specific class identity. Like the term *redneck* itself, which historically has had masculine connotations, the "redneck" autobiography has been the exclusive domain of male writers until fairly recently, but that situation is changing as more women from southern working-class backgrounds embrace that identity even as they describe the psychological and social problems resulting from their economic marginalization. For Dorothy Allison, author of two autobiographical nonfiction works, *Skin: Talking about Sex, Class, and Literature* (1994) and *Two or Three Things I Know for Sure* (1995), telling about the South necessarily involves telling about the spousal and child abuse she witnessed and experienced as a youth in Greenville, South Carolina, and the stigmatization she endured within that community because of her class status. While Linda Flowers' *Throwed Away: Failures of Progress in Eastern North Carolina* (1990) and Janisse Ray's *Ecology of a Cracker Childhood* (1999) present less graphic depictions of domestic life in the rural working-class South, they too examine the psychological damage arising from poverty and limited educational resources.

Although the changes in the contemporary South resulting from the women's movement may not be as immediately apparent as those resulting from the civil rights movement, progress is indisputable, as evidenced by the number of southern women's personal narratives that reflect feminist sensibilities and concerns. For many, those concerns are manifested in the author's open identification with her matrilineage and with a specifically female southern domestic tradition (rather than an ambivalent relationship to the southern patriarchal tradition). As may be expected, this approach is best represented in the family memoir, examples of which include Rosemary Daniell's *Fatal Flowers: Of Sin, Sex, and Suicide in the Deep South* (1980), Shirley Abbott's *Womenfolks: Growing Up Down South* (1983), Mary Lee Settle's *Addie: A Memoir* (1998), and Mason's *Clear Springs*. For others, the influence of feminism can be seen in their frank discussion of sexuality. Where that subject was rarely touched on in southern life writing prior to the 1970s, today more women writers than ever address their sexuality explicitly, often delineating the ways in which southern women's subjugation has been tied to the region's history of racial discrimination and to repressive religious attitudes concerning the female body and feminine desire. In Daniell's *Fatal Flowers,* the suicide of her mother prompts the author to explore the psychological consequences of sexual repression, which in turn leads her to understand the ways in which she too had been taught by the conventions of southern propriety to hate her body while, paradoxically, seeking self-worth primarily through her attractiveness to men. Like Daniell, bell hooks (b. 1955) uses the autobiographical occasion to describe the self-doubt and self-loathing that can result from a perceived failure to achieve culturally defined ideals of physical attractiveness. An African American academician who has written extensively on the intersections of gender and race, hooks uses her own childhood experiences to explore those connections in intensely subjective detail in *Bone Black: Memories of Girlhood* (1996). In *Confessions of a Failed Southern Lady* (1984) Florence King (b. 1936) treats the subject of southern women's sexuality with merciless humor as she lampoons her grandmother's Tidewater aristocratic pretensions and obsessions with bloodlines, polished silver, and gynecological pathology. The comic tone of King's *Confessions* is tempered, however, by the story of the author's emotionally devastating same-sex love affair—her first—with a fellow coed at the University of Mississippi who dies in an auto accident shortly after breaking off the relationship with King. Although in Mab Segrest's *Memoir of a Race Traitor* the author's sexual orientation is only vaguely alluded to, the topic assumes center stage in *My Mama's Dead Squirrel: Lesbian Essays on Southern Culture* (1985), which describes the ways in which the social conventions of the small-town South inhibited Segrest's struggle to come to terms with her own lesbianism. For Dorothy Allison, like Segrest another outspoken lesbian critic of southern homophobia, these difficulties in coming out are compounded by her lower-class socioeconomic status.

One especially recent development in southern life writing is the relatively sudden appearance of a number of autobiographies and memoirs by established women novelists. While the period has given rise to autobiography and memoir in general, between 1960 and 1998 only a handful of these—Welty's *One Writer's Beginnings* and playwright Lillian Hellman's four memoirs, *An Unfinished Woman: A Memoir* (1969), *Pentimento* (1973), *Scoundrel Time* (1976), and *Maybe* (1980)—were written by belletrists with a long record of literary achievement. Yet 1998 witnessed the publication of Elizabeth Spencer's *Landscapes of the Heart,* Ellen Douglas' *Truth: Four Stories I Am Finally Old Enough to Tell,* and Mary Lee Settle's *Addie: A Memoir.* These three works take different forms—*Landscapes of the Heart* is very much a writer's life and moves chronologically from childhood to the present, *Addie* is primarily a portrait of the author's maternal grandmother, and *Truth* is best described as a collection of autobiographical essays—but each reveals through finely crafted prose the author's struggle to come to terms with her family's past. The publication in the following year of Mason's *Clear Springs,* also very concerned with uncovering the mysteries of her family's past, and *Illumination and Night Glare: The Unfinished Autobiography of Carson McCullers* (though written in 1967) suggest that this development may indeed become a trend that remains vital in at least the immediate years to come.

At the beginning of the century, very few southern women had made use of the autobiographical occasion (especially when compared to the amount of life writing produced by southern men and by women living in the North), and only a handful had done so in ways that seriously questioned white patriarchal privilege and power. By the end of the century, however, with much of that privilege and power weakened, women had become the dominant voice in southern life writing, playing a more prominent public role than ever before in reassessing the region's past, making sense of its present, and giving shape to the ways in which the South and its inhabitants will be understood in the future.

Contemporary Writers and Race

Minrose C. Gwin

The act of writing, Eudora Welty observes in *One Writer's Beginnings* (1984), is a way of "discovering *sequence* in experience," of encountering connections and causal relationships as they slowly emerge like distant land-marks seen on a journey by train: "Experiences too indefinite of outline in themselves to be recognized for themselves connect and are identified as a larger shape. And suddenly a light is thrown back, as when your train makes a curve, showing that there has been a mountain of meaning rising behind you on the way you've come, is rising there still, proven now through retro-spect." The metaphor of the journey into the cultural as well as personal past is one that occupies contemporary women writers of the South whose travels through fiction, poetry, drama, and autobiography have engaged that fraught and often shifting "mountain of meaning": the subject of race.

This large body of southern women's literature bespeaks a shared cul-tural consciousness of a historical legacy that left deep and painful divisions in the South. Alice Walker describes these divisions as she relates a more literal journey in "Beyond the Peacock: The Reconstruction of Flannery O'Connor" (1975), when Walker and her mother return in 1974 to rural Georgia to view the land where their family lived in a four-room sharecrop-per's shack. Just down the road is the well-furbished farmhouse, Andalusia, where Flannery O'Connor lived until her premature death. In a conversa-tion with her mother, Walker says that she returns to the South to look for "a wholeness." As they eat lunch at a Holiday Inn, she reminds her mother that if the hotel and restaurant had existed during her girlhood in the 1950s, they would not have been open to African Americans: "[E]verything around me is split up, deliberately split up. History is split up, literature split up, and people are split up too. . . . I believe that the truth about any subject only comes when all the sides of the story are put together, and all their different meanings make one new one. Each writer writes the missing parts to the other writers' story. And the whole story is what I'm after."

For southern women writers that "whole story" is part of a much longer journey. From 1960 until the cusp of the twenty-first century, they, like many male authors, have traveled the long and rocky cultural terrain from past to present in exploring the multilayered narrative of southern racial relations and in bringing that "mountain of meaning" into sharper perspective. For these writers, race is a complex and preoccupying story—a journey burdened by the history of slavery and Jim Crow laws and complicated by the interconnected civil rights movement of the 1950s and 1960s, the black power movement of the 1960s and 1970s, and the black arts movement of the 1960s, as well as the women's movement of the same decades. Most recently, race also occupies the terrain of dramatic changes in contemporary life in a postmodern South of fast-food drive-throughs and Wal-Mart megastores, as well as the decay and impoverishment of urban environments and growing gang and drug cultures in northern and southern cities. In such a milieu, the topic of race is encumbered not only by the past but also by the present and future. Its "whole story" in the writings of southern women is often intertwined with matters of class, gender, and even sexuality, and perhaps has yet to emerge into full view.

Because almost every contemporary woman writer in the South has dealt in some way with race, even when race is not a primary focus, any summary of their endeavors will be partial. Some literature, such as the poems of Sonia Sanchez and Nikki Giovanni (b. 1943), has been associated with specific social and artistic movements. Many other writers have explored matters of race either peripherally or centrally in writings over a period of decades. The writings of Welty herself, who can be seen as a transitional figure in the history of southern literature between the first and second halves of the twentieth century, often engage matters of race, from subtle treatments of racial relations, as in "A Curtain of Green" (1941), "A Worn Path" (1941), and "The Demonstrators" (1966), to a searing analysis of the racist mind of the white assassin of a black civil rights leader in "Where Is the Voice Coming From?" (1963), a story with its origin in Byron De La Beckwith's slaying of Medgar Evers on June 12, 1963. Unlike those of writers such as Sanchez, Giovanni, and others, Welty's approach to questions of race is almost always indirect, subsumed by her remarkable range as a fiction writer but especially evident in her depictions of women and girls. Fiction should disclose the complex textures of life, not crusade for neat solutions, she writes in "Must the Writer Crusade?" (1965). Welty's own intensely vivid portraits of such characters as the indomitable Phoenix Jackson, the elderly African American grandmother on a quest for throat medicine for her grandson, or her chilling first-person narration of the white racist, for whom everything is "too hot," engage southern racial relations through the characters of southerners themselves.

Similarly, the fiction of Elizabeth Spencer of Carrollton, Mississippi, spans several decades, turning to race as subject matter in both peripheral and central ways during her writing career. Spencer's fiction has a broad geographic span and is often set outside the South, sometimes outside the United States. Her best known work, *The Light in the Piazza* (1960), for example, is set in Italy. Two works, *The Voice at the Back Door* (1956) and *Marilee: Three Stories* (1981), are especially notable in their treatments of race. Set in the mid-1950s in Mississippi hill country, *The Voice at the Back Door* narrates the ultimately futile attempts of a small-town sheriff to bring black and white to equality under the law. "Sharon," from the *Marilee* collection, is a story of the discovery by Marilee, a young white girl, of her uncle's relationship with Melissa, a black servant whose children, Marilee realizes, are her cousins: "That blood was ours, mingling and twining with the other. . . . It was there for good."

Josephine Haxton, whose books are written under the pseudonym Ellen Douglas, is another white Mississippian whose concerns with race span several decades, though those concerns are more central than either Welty's or Spencer's. A prolific writer of fiction and more recently, fictional autobiography, Douglas, over the course of her long and distinguished career, has consistently plumbed questions of racial guilt, cultural and personal, indicating the powerfully interlocking nature of the two. Douglas' most compelling narratives, fictive and autobiographical, focus directly on race and particularly on the difficulty of arriving at any approximation of truth concerning the southern racial past. Works such as *Black Cloud, White Cloud* (1963), *The Rock Cried Out* (1979), *Can't Quit You, Baby* (1988), and *Truth: Four Stories I Am Finally Old Enough to Tell* (1998), which are set specifically in Mississippi in places such as Homochitto, Chickasaw Ridge, and Philippi, evince a pattern of white individuals engaging questions of guilt and absolution for their own or their ancestors' racial misdeeds. Anna McGovern Glover, the white narrator of "Jesse" from *Black Cloud, White*

Cloud, struggles to ponder questions of white guilt and absolution: "There
are those of us who are willing to say, 'I am guilty,' but who is to absolve
us? And do we expect by our confession miraculously to relieve the suffering of the innocent?" Douglas figures these questions through arduous
journeys into the past and recurring symbols of water and drowning. Often
racial dynamics between black and white are played out in electrifying confrontations that bring history to bear on contemporary personal relationships, especially between women. In "Hold On," a novella also from *Black
Cloud, White Cloud,* the shorter version of which was selected for the
1961 O. Henry collection, Anna Glover wrestles with the guilt she feels at
having almost drowned her former housekeeper Estella, an African American, first by taking her out in a boat without a life jacket while knowing
she could not swim, and then after the boat capsized, violently kicking the
panic-stricken Estella away from her as they struggled together under
water.

In the novel *The Rock Cried Out* and the fictionalized autobiography
Truth, Douglas foregrounds the search for the truth of the past, knowing
always that, as the narrator of *Truth* (assumably Haxton herself) says in
attempting to get at the real "truth" of a violent local racial history in "On
Second Creek," "Something is always missing." In *The Rock Cried Out,*
Alan McLaurin, a self-described white hippie, returns to his family farm on
Chickasaw Ridge in 1971 in an attempt to confront the past: one day in
1964 in which the Ku Klux Klan burned a black church and his beloved
cousin Phoebe, then seventeen, was killed in an incident while riding in the
front seat of a car driven by Sam Daniels, an African American man. And
in *Can't Quit You, Baby,* perhaps Douglas' strongest psychological study of
race, two women, Tweet and Cornelia, black and white, the former working
for the latter, both evade and confront the deep tangle of their relationship.
The pervading symbol of this novel is of a water-skier skiing over a tangle
of water moccasins who wait to drag her under. Here Douglas takes the
southern racial story to another level by forcing the white narrator to admit
her own inability to acknowledge or express the complexity of her African
American character's life and to wonder, "What tangle of snakes have I been
skiing over?"

This tangle emerges as a family and community saga in the 1960s fiction
of Harper Lee, whose gripping *To Kill a Mockingbird* (1961) marks a transition to contemporary treatments of race; Margaret Walker, the author of
the historical novel *Jubilee* (1966), whose poetry is deeply connected to the
civil rights movement; and Shirley Ann Grau, whose novel *The Keepers of
the House* (1964) precedes Douglas' *Can't Quit You, Baby* in confronting

southern racial relations within the domestic sphere. All three of these novels focus on women characters and gender as well as racial issues. Writers whose aforementioned novels won Pulitzer Prizes, Lee and Grau link the maturation of white girls and women to their realization of the profound effects of racist violence within their own communities. Lee's still widely read novel is set in Maycomb County, Alabama, during the Depression and tells the story from the point of view of the child Scout, whose father Atticus Finch defends a black man, Tom Robinson, who has been accused, wrongfully, of raping a white woman. This novel, like Grau's, ends in senseless violence based on racist hatred, though the violence in *The Keepers of the House* is directed by whites toward whites when the Louisiana Gulf Coast community discovers that a secret biracial marriage has taken place in the past between the widowed white grandfather of the white protagonist, Abigail Howland, and a local African American woman who has borne his children. Having learned the family secret, which Abigail herself had not known, the bigoted white community wreaks vengeance on Abigail as a middle-aged woman who has been abandoned by her white supremacist politician husband years after her grandparents, Will and Margaret Howland, are dead. Abigail is the inheritor of the Howland wealth, which she uses to gain revenge against the community. Abigail's conflicted relations with her grandfather's biracial children and the fact that she resorts, at least in part, to violence in repaying violence leave her less than innocent.

In contrast to Lee's and Grau's more pessimistic treatments of the effects of racism, Margaret Walker's *Jubilee,* which originated in the stories of slavery about her great-grandmother told by her maternal grandmother, Elvira Ware Dozier, and was published in the turmoil of the mid-1960s, reenacts the historical past by celebrating African American vision and racial reconciliation. The indomitable Vyry Ware, the daughter of her master and his slave mistress, is a fictional version of Walker's great-grandmother. She is the moral center of *Jubilee* and the embodiment of what Walker has called in "The Humanistic Tradition of Afro-American Literature" (1970) a "new humanism" of "freedom, peace, and human dignity." From the death of Vyry's mother, Sis Hetta, in 1839, to news of the imminent death of her fourth child at the end of the saga, the novel depicts events of thirty years through the eyes of this larger-than-life biracial woman of the nineteenth-century South. Suffused throughout the novel are the folk beliefs, practices, and music that held enslaved people together. In Vyry's vehement rejection of racial bitterness and continuing connections with white women after severe mistreatment at the hand of her former mistress, *Jubilee* proffered, in a time of severe racial violence and civil unrest detailed in such autobiographical works of the civil rights movement as *Coming of Age in Mississippi* (1968) by Anne Moody (b. 1940), a regenerative and overwhelmingly optimistic response to a long history of racial oppression. Written both before and after *Jubilee,* Walker's poetry offers a powerful sense of vision in its heroic depictions of African American history and folk culture (in poems such as "For My People," 1942) and an equally strong sense of mourning for a South devastated by racist violence (in poems such as "October Journey," 1973).

It is as bold revolutionary poets of the black arts movement of the 1960s that both Sanchez and Giovanni came to public and critical attention. More on a national than regional level, both sharply confronted the issue of race, urging African Americans to embrace their black heritage and resist racist oppression. Although born in Birmingham, Alabama, Sanchez has spent most of her writing career in the North. Her poetry has evolved over the decades, from *We a BaddDDD People* (1970), for example, with its emphasis on black nationalism, but retains its gritty explorations of hard truths of life in the United States and its stylistic experimentation that characterized writings of the black arts movement. She has carried this experimental style into the 1990s (for example, in *Wounded in the House of a Friend,* 1995). Sanchez's and Giovanni's poems are strongly vernacular, and their readings and recordings of poetry have drawn large audiences throughout their careers. Also a poet whose writings have evolved over the years but whose poetry is more closely tied to region, Giovanni, born in Knoxville, Tennessee, became widely known for such poems as "Nikki-Rosa" (1968) and "The True Import of Present Dialogue, Black vs. Negro" (1968). Much of her early poetry was designed to shock readers and listeners into a reconsideration of racial relations. In "The True Import," for example, she asks,

> Nigger
> Can you kill
> Can you kill
> Can a nigger kill
> Can a nigger kill a honkie
>
> . . . .
> Can you kill the nigger
> in you

Although Giovanni has turned to many other topics in recent years, she has continued to write about issues of race in poems such as "Flying Underground" (1983) about the murder of Atlanta children in the early 1980s.

Another African American poet (and fiction writer) of the 1960s, Julia

Fields (b. 1938) of Alabama has often focused on class and color distinctions and issues of racial identity within the black community. Fields's ironic and often anthologized poem "High on the Hog" (1969), for example, features middle-class African Americans who reject their roots; her short story "Not Your Singing, Dancing Spade" (1967) describes the complicated relationship between a famous black entertainer and his black domestic servant.

Two other southern fiction writers whose works include racial material and who gained notice in the 1960s and early 1970s are Berry Morgan (b. 1919) of Port Gibson, Mississippi, and Doris Betts of Statesville, North Carolina. Morgan's collection of stories *The Mystic Adventures of Roxie Stoner* (1974), told from the point of view of a poor African American woman from a Mississippi plantation, attempts to move across those racial divisions between white author and black character that Ellen Douglas' narrator in *Can't Quit You, Baby* finds insurmountable. Race is not a central theme in Betts's fiction, but several stories figure race in very interesting contexts, including "The Ugliest Pilgrim" and "Beasts of the Southern Wild" in the early collection *Beasts of the Southern Wild and Other Stories* (1973). Like Douglas' fiction, these stories engage race and racism from the perspective of white women. In Betts's stories, however, the exploration of race is not so much an end unto itself ("The Sympathetic Visitor" in the 1954 collection *The Gentle Insurrection* is an exception) but a method of revealing the psychology of the main characters. "The Ugliest Pilgrim" is told by Violet Karl as she rides a bus from her home in Tennessee to Oklahoma, where she hopes to convince a televangelist to cure her face, which was badly scarred when an ax head struck her. Another passenger on the bus, Grady "Flick" Fliggins is black, and Violet's racist disgust for Flick seems layered with her own self-disgust at her disfigurement. In the second story, a white English teacher, Carol Walsh, slips in and out of elaborate sexual dreams about being enslaved by an African American man, who is far preferable to her boorish husband. *The River to Pickle Beach* (1972) also examines racism vis-à-vis sexual frustration.

The 1970s also ushered in the important literary treatments of race and gender in the autobiography and poetry of Maya Angelou, the disturbing fiction of Gayl Jones (b. 1949), and the widely read fiction, essays, and poetry of Alice Walker—all writers who link race and gender within African American communities and who are deeply concerned with the meaning of the past, personal and historical. Angelou's five sequenced autobiographies partake of the tradition of early African American autobiographical writings of the nineteenth century such as those of Harriet Jacobs and Frederick Douglass. Widely read by the public and often taught in classrooms, *I Know*

Why the Caged Bird Sings (1970), the first of these volumes, is the moving story of Angelou's life as a black girl growing up in the segregated small town of Stamps, Arkansas (and later in other places as a teenager). It is a narrative about boundaries set by race, class, and gender and a young black girl's dexterity within those boundaries. In Stamps, Angelou writes, "the segregation was so complete that most Black children didn't really, absolutely know what whites looked like." *I Know Why the Caged Bird Sings* also describes rituals of a southern black community and the care of a devoted yet stern grandmother, as well as young Maya's sexual abuse by her mother's boyfriend. Angelou's poetry from *Just Give Me a Cool Drink of Water 'fore I Diiie* (1970) to *Shaker, Why Don't You Sing?* (1983) often confronts issues of race in a variety of contexts. Her vision of the richness of American heritage through the many histories and cultures of all its peoples is expressed in her poem written for President Bill Clinton's inauguration, "On the Pulse of the Morning" (1993).

It is an understatement to say that the vision of Kentucky author Gayl Jones is less optimistic. Her novels *Corregidora* (1975) and *Eva's Man* (1976) are excruciating revelations of the cultural and personal histories of her African American characters, and link both kinds of history to a continual cycle of racial and sexual violence. The first book relates the history of slavery and incest in Brazil to the brutalization of black women in contemporary urban society. The fact that written records of Brazilian slavery were destroyed underscores the importance of an oral tradition through which black women can relate their history. Ursa Corregidora, a blues singer who bears the hated name of a Portuguese slave master who fathered both her grandmother and her mother, is charged by them with passing the story along so that it can never be forgotten. The complexity of racial identity is also an important theme in Jones's work. In the title piece of the collection *The White Rat: Short Stories* (1983), the racial identity of the protagonist, who identifies himself as black, is always questioned, both by blacks and whites; the fact of his racial ambiguity eventually plays havoc with his life. In general, Jones's fiction is deeply disturbing in its suggestions that the oppressed may come to love as well as hate the oppressor and that the difference between oppressor and oppressed is not as clear cut as one might think.

A contemporary writer whose work began to be published in the late 1960s and early 1970s, Alice Walker, a native of Eatonton, Georgia, is the best-known author among southern women writing today and one of the most widely read and anthologized American writers of the twentieth century. Strongly influenced by Zora Neale Hurston, whom she invokes in her important volume of essays *In Search of Our Mothers' Gardens* (1983),

Walker's self-described "womanist" writing throughout her distinguished career has turned upon the axis of black women's lives. Race, class, gender, and sexuality are so intertwined as to be inextricable in her fiction, poetry, and essays. A continuing theme in her writing, and one for which she has been criticized within the African American community, is the mistreatment of black women by the men in their lives and her insistence that black men, despite their own victimization, must take responsibility for their treatment of black women. *The Third Life of Grange Copeland* (1970), Walker's first novel, shows how the exploitation of African American men's labor can lead to their mistreatment of the women in their lives, just as Walker's best-known novel, the Pulitzer Prize–winning *The Color Purple* (1982), opens with the rape of the young Celie by the man she thinks is her father and revolves around Celie's attempts to find power within herself despite continued abuse by her stepfather and later her husband, Albert. Celie finds that power in a lesbian relationship with Albert's lover Shug, who unlocks Celie's own creative spirit. *Possessing the Secret of Joy* (1992) concerns the devastating effects of female circumcision. Several stories in the early volume *In Love and Trouble: Stories of Black Women* (1974) show both the effects upon black women and children of male violence within the family ("The Child Who Favored Daughter") and the institutionalized violence of racism on black children ("Strong Horse Tea"). One of the most widely anthologized stories in this volume, "Everyday Use," like the extremely important title essay of *In Search of Our Mothers' Gardens*, foregrounds the tradition of black women's creative heritage, forged under almost impossible circumstances, and the urgency of passing down that creative spirit, in whatever form it may take, from generation to generation.

Walker worked in the civil rights movement in Mississippi during the late 1960s. Evolving from that experience is the novel *Meridian* (1976), which shows the extreme stress attendant upon civil rights workers in the South and explores difficult questions of race relating to women's relationships through the fraught friendship of an African American woman and a Jewish woman working together during the movement and involved with the same man, an African American coworker. Likewise, some of the stories in *You Can't Keep a Good Woman Down* (1981) are about those who participated in the movement. For example, in "Petunias" an African American woman working in the movement finds her great-grandmother's bones dumped in her flower garden, and "Advancing Luna—And Ida B. Wells" relates the story of a young white woman's silence about her rape by an African American man for fear that revealing the crime would be detrimental to accomplishing the goals of civil rights. Several essays in *In Search of Our Mothers'*

Gardens deal specifically with the civil rights movement in the South and more generally with the history of dispossession of black southerners, who, Walker writes in "Choice: A Tribute to Martin Luther King, Jr.," "love the land and worked the land, but . . . never owned it." The fact that this essay was originally a speech given in 1972 at a Jackson, Mississippi, restaurant that refused to serve African Americans until forced to do so underscores how closely Walker's visionary activism in the arena of race and beyond has been tied to her role as a writer. Her large body of poetry, now collected in *Her Blue Body Everything We Know: Earthling Poems, 1965–1990* (1991), and the 1997 volume of essays, *Anything We Love Can Be Saved: A Writer's Activism,* reflect the breadth and depth of Walker's belief in both the power of language and the necessity of action in first imagining and then refashioning a split world into one that is whole. In the poem "We Have a Beautiful Mother" (1991), she imagines that world:

> We have a beautiful
> mother
> Her green lap
> immense
> Her brown embrace
> eternal
> Her blue body
> everything
> we know.

Other writers of the 1980s and 1990s have seen similar possibilities for racial healing; these possibilities, however, often emerge problematically in fiction about interracial relationships involving women whose attempts to confront the southern past and racist stereotypes are situated in a changed South and a changing world; their attempts meet with mixed results. As in Ellen Douglas' and Alice Walker's works of recent years, there seems to be an ongoing and more expansive conversation about race among contemporary southern women writers and a generally fuller sense that such conversations have become, like Walker's beautiful mother, as global as they are local. Gail Godwin's *A Mother and Two Daughters* (1982), for example, set in North Carolina more than a decade after the civil rights movement, presents an ambiguous description of the friendship between Lydia, a white woman who returns to college, and Renee, her African American professor. As an independent intellectual with a Harvard Ph.D., Dr. Renee Peverall-Watson is everything that Lydia wants to become; like Douglas' metaphoric water-skier, though, Lydia glides over the tangle of racial difference in her efforts to feel "closer to Renee than to her own sister." Yet Lydia is shocked when her son marries Renee's daughter, and the background of the novel is replete with Klan marches, racist comments in the grocery store about the biracial couple, and threats of violence. Lydia and Renee's generally positive, though limited, relationship is set in counterpoint with that of a well-to-do white friend, Theodora, with Azalea, her black maid, to whom she will give "anything but the minimum wage."

In *Playing in the Dark: Whiteness and the Literary Imagination* (1992), Toni Morrison suggests that Africanist personae often serve the purpose of white self-mediation in the texts of white writers. In the comic Pulitzer Prize–winning play *Crimes of the Heart* (1982) of Mississippi dramatist Beth Henley, a fifteen-year-old African American boy functions as a tabooed sexual object and thereby a means to personal freedom for Babe, one of the white MaGrath sisters of Hazelhurst, Mississippi. Babe shoots her abusive husband in a confrontation over a dog that the teenager Willie Jay, whom she has taken as a lover, has given her. The story of Willie Jay, whose character is never developed and who disappears from the story, also operates as an impetus for shared communication among the three sisters. On a more complicated level, *Ellen Foster* (1987) by North Carolina novelist Kaye Gibbons, connects the generosity of an almost always silent African American girl, Starletta, and her family toward young Ellen with the white girl's recognition of her own racism and privilege. Starletta's mother and father shelter Ellen for periods of time in their one-room house, often saving her from her father's drunken forays into her bedroom. Nevertheless, in a strange incident on New Year's Eve, Ellen's fear of her father's sexual abuse is described in terms of "a whole pack of colored men" her father brings home, one of whom seems to be encouraging him to abuse her. At the book's end, Ellen, whose young life has been a sequence of traumas, struggles to overcome her racism. She confesses to Starletta that "when I thought about you I always felt glad for myself" and recognizes that, as a white girl she did not have "the hardest row to hoe," despite her many struggles.

Two novels of the 1990s excavate the tensions of cross-racial relationships among female characters. It is notable that these female connections are forged in the absence of father figures. *Clover* (1990) by Dori Sanders (b. 1934) of York County, South Carolina, where Sanders grew up on one of the oldest black-owned peach farms, depicts the vexed relationship that develops between a ten-year-old black girl whose father dies and her newly married white stepmother from the city, who decides to stay and take care of her, despite protests from his African American family and from Clover herself. This book is similar to *Ellen Foster* in that it tells a story of racial reconciliation from the point of view of a child, this time a black child, who first adopts mores of racial division and then rejects them through the daily practice of a nurturing relationship. Like much of Douglas' fiction, *Night Talk* (1997) by Elizabeth Cox (b. 1942) of Chattanooga, Tennessee, presents a more disquieting view of southern racial relations, linking civil rights conflicts of the 1950s and 1960s with the present-day South. In the ironically named Mercy, Georgia, two generations of black and white females become close friends against all community standards when the black woman Volusia and her young daughter Janey Louise move into the home of Agnes, a white woman with two children whose husband has left her. Shifting back and forth from past to present, the novel follows Agnes' daughter Evie's slow and painful journey to understanding how blind she had been to the enormous differences between her life and that of her black friend Janey. Their closeness, she realizes as an adult, was "nothing but night talk," removed from the real world of daylight in which Janey's race made all the difference, from the racial prejudices that forced her to sit in the balcony of the movie house, to her rape by one of the town's leading white businessmen. What makes this novel so compelling is Cox's unwillingness to move to any easy reconciliation between the two when they return to Mercy as adults. Jane, who still suffers under southern injustice, does not forgive Evie's blindness, nor does Evie expect her to. Their friendship must encompass the fact of that blindness and Jane's refusal to overlook it. "Night talk"—personal closeness—does not alleviate history or white myopia.

At the turn of the millennium, ghosts of the racial past still roam the postmodern southern landscape. In *Baby of the Family* (1989) by Tina McElroy Ansa (b. 1949), the well-protected girl Lena McPherson from a prosperous African American family fails to understand the horrors of slavery until she encounters the ghost of a slave named Rachel, who walks the Georgia seashore and tells the story of having drowned herself to avoid capture. Another African American writer, the poet Brenda Marie Osbey (b. 1957), whose New Orleans heritage is rich in a mixture of histories, offers in her 1997 volume *All Saints* stirring meditations on history and memory. The poetry in this volume hovers around the history of slavery; the slave ancestors are everywhere, "beneath the swamps, inside / the bricks of which our / homes, our streets, our churches are made." Memory is a mist that cloaks the present. Osbey writes of living "among your dead, / whom you have every right / to love," an injunction for both remembrance and healing that may well point to the challenges of southern women's writing about race in the twenty-first century.

Contemporary Poetry

Carolyn Perry

Poetry by southern women has flourished over the past forty years, both within and outside of the South. Their poems have been found on the pages of *Poetry* and the *Kenyon Review* as well as in the *Southern Poetry Review* and *Shenandoah,* and publishers in New York and Boston have been taken by the work of southern women writers almost as often as editors in Baton Rouge. Likewise, although many southern women poets have remained in or returned to the South, many have lived in places as far away as California or New Hampshire. Despite their easy movement in and out of the South, southern women poets lay claim to a tradition all their own. They have stretched the boundaries of what it means to be southern, yet it is possible to find common threads that make their poetry distinctive. We find, for example, poets who devote at least a significant portion of their work to backward glances, taking hard looks at their personal histories within the region, if not the region's history more generally. At the same time, despite the cases made for universality in their work, the themes found in the poetry of southern women are in keeping with a long tradition of southern writing: a sense of the past informing the present, love of the land or specific southern places, and concerns of family and home. The important stylistic questions southern women poets have faced also stem directly from their tie to the region, such as whether to challenge or exploit the assumption that southerners love storytelling and therefore southern poets must write narrative poems. In addition to exploring the tension between lyric and narrative impulses, between the concrete and the abstract, and between traditional and experimental forms, southern poets wrestle with questions of poetic diction. If not hearkening back to Robert Penn Warren's notion of pure and impure poetry directly, then they are at least writing in the same vein, blending colloquial and formal speech, mixing harshly realistic detail with a romantic bent, and pushing the limits of what a "southern woman" would dare say in poetry.

During the 1960s and 1970s, the civil rights and feminist movements—two often complementary, sometimes competing forces—inspired the most fervent poetry by southern women, who generally responded to the social unrest from a distinctly southern perspective, coming of age, as they were, in the Mississippi or Georgia of the 1950s. Yet one of the most prominent poets of this time was a woman born a generation ahead of the others and who began publishing twenty years earlier: Margaret Walker, whose 1942 volume *For My People* was a definite precursor to civil rights poetry with its deliberately rebellious style. The main thrust of this collection is Walker's concern for the lack of progress African Americans faced in the 1930s. In poems such as "Molly Means," Walker challenges traditional form by using sounds that come closer to contemporary rap than iambic pentameter. She also experiments with line form, foregoing meter and rhyme for stanzas written as prose paragraphs. Walker reemerged as a poet in the 1970s with two collections, *Prophets for a New Day* (1970) and *October Journey* (1973), and she continued publishing until her death in 1998. Her poetry, which weaves in and out of poetic traditions, consistently portrays her passion for civil rights. A poem like "For Malcolm X," then, has the appearance of an Italian sonnet, yet includes shocking language we would not expect to find there; of Malcolm X she writes: "You have cut open our breasts and dug scalpels in our brains." Likewise, we can hear the celebratory sounds of both Walt Whitman and Langston Hughes in "I Want to Write," as she employs repetition and sharp imagery to explain her desire to "write the songs of [her] people": "I want to catch their sunshine laughter in a bowl; / fling dark hands to a darker sky / and fill them full of stars."

Younger poets shared Walker's insistence on civil rights, but they often took on a more strident tone. The turbulence of the 1960s inspired many poets to turn to the topic of race with a fervor never quite seen before in American poetry. While African American poets had long lamented the oppression of black America and expressed outrage at the slowness of change, poets of the first half of the century generally urged their white readers to join them in the fight for unity and equality. Now the poetry turned militant, refusing to wait for or join with anyone not passionate about the cause. At the forefront among southern women poets were Sonia Sanchez and Nikki Giovanni (b. 1943). Sanchez's early volumes, *Homecoming* (1969) and *We a BaddDDD People* (1970), were her most radical in both theme and style. By defying standard rules of grammar and punctuation, Sanchez brought out the richness of black language and the sounds of jazz. The poems are chants and songs that declare, as in "We a BaddDDD People,"

> our
> high must come from
> thinking working
> planning fighting loving
> our blk
> selves
> into nationhood.

In her later poetry, though still fighting for solidarity among African Americans, she does so with a tone that is more spiritual in nature, with a form that delves into haiku, the tanka, as well as the blues, and with subject matter that focuses on love and the importance of one's heritage. Likewise, Nikki Giovanni has written her share of militant poetry in such collections as *Black Feeling, Black Talk* (1968) and *Black Judgment* (1968). The most-often anthologized of these poems, "The True Import of Present Dialogue, Black vs. Negro," concludes by asking, "Can we learn to kill WHITE for BLACK / Learn to kill niggers / Learn to be Black men." Although Giovanni is as outspoken today as ever, her poetry over the years has softened, turning to more personal subjects and a broadening of her public concerns. Her recent style is difficult to characterize, for while she experiments with various forms of free verse, her poems range from playful children's verses to rap to prose poems. To date, her best-known poem is one of her earliest, "Nikki-Rosa" (1968), which describes how happy her childhood was in the midst of poverty, because "Black love is black wealth."

Although known primarily for their writing in other genres, Maya Angelou and Alice Walker are also key players in the development of African American poetry in the 1960s and 1970s. Maya Angelou, active in the civil rights movement early on, was appointed by Martin Luther King, Jr., as northern coordinator for the Southern Christian Leadership Conference (1959–60). Known primarily for her autobiographical prose, she has written five volumes of poetry, collected in 1994 as *Complete Collected Poems*. Perhaps one of the most stunning images in her poetry, as in her prose, is that of the caged bird. The poem "Caged Bird," from *Shaker, Why Don't*

You Sing? (1983), suggests that this bird sings because that is the one freedom left, and to sing is a declaration of an identity that cannot be silenced. Because Angelou's poetry is so fraught with hope, despite its harshly realistic detail, she challenges all Americans—black and white—to reach their potential. Likewise, Alice Walker explores the complexity of human relationships during the feverish years of the civil rights movement in *Meridian* (1976), arguably the most important novel written about this period. Also inspired by civil rights activism, however, the poems in *Once* (1968) describe the horrible conditions black people faced in both the South and in Africa in the 1960s. Walker has continued to write poetry as well as novels and nonfiction prose, and her most recent collection of poems, *Her Blue Body Everything We Know* (1991), continues to reflect the heartfelt concerns of her prose—healing and survival for all people and for the earth.

Although the poetry of these women has often been interpreted in light of civil rights issues, each poet has also been concerned with the development of a distinct female identity. With *And Still I Rise* (1978), for example, Angelou turns her focus to what it means to be a woman and looks at concerns of family and home. Likewise, during the 1970s and 1980s Giovanni became increasingly concerned with feminist issues, and Sanchez, with the publication of *Love Poems* (1973), branched out to include poems that were distinctive not only in their focus on relationships and female identity, but also in their increasingly spiritual explorations. In *Revolutionary Petunias* (1973) and *Good Night Willie Lee, I'll See You in the Morning* (1979), Walker moved more completely into feminist issues. In fact, because she so militantly focused on reclaiming the heritage of black mothers and building community among black women, her work was criticized by black male writers as working against unity for all African Americans. In her signature poem of the feminist movement, "On Stripping Bark from Myself" (1981), Walker claims she will not keep silent simply because she is a woman, and that she is "happy to fight / all murderers / as I see I must," in order to establish a rightful place for women in American society.

For southern women poets, fighting for "a rightful place" has been in part a battle against the land itself. These poets often embrace the southern landscape for its natural beauty or for the childhood memories associated with it, yet their relationship to the land is often problematic. In the rural South, many women's lives, even in the twentieth century, have been consumed by the domestic responsibilities of farming. As Ellen Bryant Voigt (b. 1943) suggests in "Farm Wife" (1976), a rural woman may have moments of transcendence (albeit imaginary) from her laborious life, but—in contrast to the soaring birds that suggest freedom in the poem—the woman's life is

characterized by working in the kitchen, producing children, and having little in her future but that time when

> the pulley cranks her down
> the dark shaft, and the church blesses
> her stone bed, and the earth seals its
> black mouth like a scar.

A further hindrance to women gaining their "rightful place" can be found
in southern literature itself, in the masculine pastoral, which traditionally
imbues the land with feminine qualities while objectifying women characters. Critics of southern fiction, Elizabeth Harrison in particular, have explored the way twentieth-century southern women have developed or
transformed the pastoral myth in their novels; similarly, in her essay "The
Pastoral in Southern Poetry" (1993), Laura Barge creates a definition of the
southern pastoral that can be applied to southern women's poetry. According to Barge, in addition to focusing on the rural landscape, contemporary
southern pastoral poetry wrestles with the religious dimension of the South
with a sharper edge than its precursors; blurs distinctions between human
beings and nature; and continues the quest for order that gives meaning to
human existence.

This rural vision is found in the poetry of women across the South. Betty
Adcock (b. 1938), for example, in writing of her childhood in east Texas,
blends the realistic not just with the romantic, but even the divine. "The
Case for Gravity" (in *Beholdings,* 1988), for example, initially describes a
child, falling into a bush, who "flopped hard, like a trout / on a world gone
bust"; by the end of the poem, however, Adcock has written a meditation
on the meaning of "falling," ultimately alluding to the concepts of original
sin and grace. The poem ends with a "bitten tongue" and a body "abloom
with bruises" in the midst of a religious moment: "say these are sheaves of
fishes in my hands." At the same time, Adcock often blurs the distinction
between the human and natural worlds, whether it be the blending of men
and mules or human mind and rhinoceros mind. Explaining her realistic
sensibility, Adcock claimed in an interview with Ernest Suarez (in *Southbound,* 1999) that "many of [her] poems attempt to confront, as directly as
possible, what human beings really are; it's not really pretty." In poems such
as "The Bird Woman" human beings may be earthy, but they are also beautiful. The woman who cares for birds may be confined to the ground, but
the way she gives flight to injured birds conjures up images of the woman
herself taking flight, "the way a saint / might travel. Or an angel." In addition, as Adcock wrestles with the theme of time in her poetry, she displays

characteristics of the pastoral. In the midst of a rapidly changing southern landscape, her poetry stands as a reminder that no matter how much the past slips from our grasp, we cannot quite lose it. In poems like "After Geology, after biology" or "Prophecy" (both in *The Difficult Wheel*, 1995) then, she describes a search, a longing for order, cosmic or otherwise, shared by poets and Baptists alike.

A strong sense of place is also found in works by Appalachian poets. In an article for *A Gift of Tongues: Critical Challenges in Contemporary American Poetry* (1987), George Ella Lyon acknowledges a tradition among mountain poets that dates back to the 1930s and 1940s and still exists today. The main thrust of Appalachian poetry, Lyon claims, is "to examine and most often to preserve the stories and values that have been islanded within the culture as a whole." Yet the changes in the land, as it has been damaged and modernized, have changed the Appalachian writer, making him or her less predictable and often more politically active. Marilou Awiakta (b. 1936) claims her goal in writing is to bring together what she calls her three heritages: mountain, Cherokee, and high tech. The result is that not only does she find a divine spirit in the Appalachian mountains, but she does so in the midst of technology. Awiakta grew up during World War II in Oak Ridge, Tennessee, where her father was part of the grand project to split the atom. Through this experience she learned to appreciate our potential as human beings to work with nature, but she warns of the danger of thinking we can control it—we should even consider the atom when we consider our connection to nature. The poem "Where Mountain and Atom Meet" compares the beauty of the Appalachian mountains to the beauty of the scientists' work at Oak Ridge, splitting the atom. For Awiakta, there is no issue of "getting back to nature" because there is no division between humanity and nature, and our role in this world is to integrate all parts of ourselves as human beings—which includes the elements of the natural world, of our everyday lives, and of the technological world we have created.

The blending of our lives with nature is possibly best represented in Awiakta's "Smoky Mountain-Woman" (in *Abiding Appalachia*, 1978), in which it is nearly impossible to tell whether the poet is describing a woman or the mountain itself; both (or the two together) represent powerful, life-giving forces. Equally able to depict strong mountain women is Kathryn Stripling Byer (b. 1944). The women who come to life in collections such as *Wildwood Flower* (1992) and *Black Shawl* (1998)—whether a tobacco-spitting grandmother (from "Tobacco") or a woman who hoes "thawed ground / with a vengeance" ("Wildwood Flower")—are tough women, able to take care of themselves as well as a host of others. One of the most stunning of Byer's depictions is found in "Ghost Story," which describes a phantom who "stalks these mountains / in high button shoes." The poem unravels the story of a brash, daring woman whose life away from the mountains was a difficult one and who had come home in death, as strong-willed as ever; in doing so, the poem recreates the sounds of the folk stories that are so much a part of Appalachian culture.

Similar to Awiakta's or Byer's love of Appalachia is Brenda Marie Osbey's attachment to New Orleans. Following Alice Dunbar-Nelson in blending African American, Creole, and Acadian cultures, Osbey (b. 1957) adds Native Americans and Haitians to give the full flavor of Louisiana over the past century. Osbey's four collections of poetry, *Ceremony for Minneconjoux* (1983), *In These Houses* (1988), *Desperate Circumstances, Dangerous Woman* (1991), and *All Saints* (1997), focus on New Orleans, and specifically on the women who live there, often in desperate or dangerous circumstances. For Osbey, New Orleans is the spiritual core of everything she does, and the city seems to take on a female persona as she writes of its people. But New Orleans functions as a specific place for Osbey in part because it is a place of death, its cemeteries one of its best-known features. Osbey explores New Orleans' obsession with death in *All Saints* as she delves into her own past: "i have never avoided / the tombed cities i was taught to tarry in. / and i have not let my dead lie," she writes. As she explained in an interview with John Lowe, one of our greatest sins is forgetting the past, forgetting to honor the dead and know our people.

Sometimes that strong sense of place can follow poets far from the South. Cleopatra Mathis' (b. 1947) Greek and Cherokee heritage is never far from her poetic eye, yet she seems most preoccupied with the way her southern roots have followed her to New Hampshire, where she has taught at Dartmouth University for the past twenty years. Her poems, recently collected in *Guardian* (1997) and *What to Tip the Boatman* (2000), tend to be filled with startling observations of family, almost always accompanied by some expression of loss or displacement. In a 1990 essay for the *Georgia Review*, Fred Chappell comments that while family is a common theme in most southern literature, "the female poet has found a sharper, pricklier way of handling it than the male poet, and she is edgier even than her sister in fiction." Mathis, in particular, writes about family with a sharpness that makes a lasting impression. Part of what makes Mathis' family poems so startling is that we no longer find the traditional southern motif of son or daughter struggling in relation to the dominating father, but instead, the troubled relationship is that caused by a lost child, and the suffering one is the sister or mother. In poems like "Elegy for the Other" or "Grace: Two

Versions" (*The Center for Cold Weather*, 1989) Mathis draws on her own experience of losing a younger brother. In "Figure of Formal Loss: Pearl," the speaker tries to get into the skin of the grieving mother, capturing an image of an old woman pausing at the grocery store, smelling a melon, and being taken back into all the joy and grief that was her life with her child, "passing through all suffering to the core." Yet even when not writing about the loss of a loved one, Mathis is a master of capturing brief moments of loss within a family setting. For example, in "The Good-bye," she describes an exquisite moment when a young boy, realizing that his family is permanently leaving his childhood home, goes back to kiss the house good-bye.

Theme and place are not the only concerns of contemporary southern women poets, however, for questions of form and language are always at the forefront of their work. Southern poets today have long stopped worrying about the formalities of poetic diction and instead embrace the sounds of the South. In an article for the *Georgia Review* (1997), Fred Chappell characterizes southern poetry by focusing on its relationship to modernism. Although he does not find many southern poets compelled to experiment with style, indicating a preference for form and order, he locates in southern poetry today the irony so common among modern poets; southern diction is "often a witty interplay of the intellectual and the homespun." The poetry of North Carolina's Eleanor Ross Taylor (b. 1928) exemplifies these traits. Similar to T. S. Eliot's describing the sunset as a "patient etherized upon a table," she reduces contemplation of the meaning of life to the "howling naked question" (in "Woman as Artist") or the burden of the passage of time to dusty goblets ("Dust"). In her most recent collection of poems, *Late Leisure* (1999), Taylor opens "Diary Entry, March 24" with the common sounds of a diary:

> Today
> walked home tho cold
> No coffee no Crackerjack no
> books $200 cash $3.50 taxi
> saved

By the end of the poem, however, the speaker has taken a sharp turn into the face of death, as a tossed hot dog container blown in the breeze becomes a coffin she must outpace. Likewise, when Taylor writes of coming to terms with the death of her husband, the novelist Peter Taylor, she does so through an extended metaphor of painting a picture ("Long-Dreaded Event Takes Place"), creating the sort of objectivity found in modern poetry.

One crucial question for the contemporary southern poet is that of how poetry can thrive in a land of story, in a place where storytelling is not only part of the culture, but assumed to be part of every southerner. Ellen Bryant Voigt challenges this notion in her essay "Narrative and Lyric: Structural Corruption" (1994), as well as in her own poetry. Although many of her poems contain elements of narrative, she fights for a place for lyric poetry among southerners. As she explained to Ernest Suarez in a 1997 interview (in *Southbound*, 1999), "[A] narrative manages events and actions that happen in time and have consequences. The lyric tries to do the opposite"—it "sings for the moment." Part of the reason this singing for the moment is so important to Voigt is that she was a musician before she became a poet; poetry, she says, is "truth set to music." She appreciates the lyric because it is "non-discursive and music-derived," suggesting how to feel about a situation rather than telling the story of how or why things came to be.

Voigt's own poetry moves effortlessly from lyric to narrative to somewhere in between. Blending elements of lyric and narrative, the poems in *The Lotus Flowers* (1987) together explore Voigt's sense of exile from the South once her parents no longer provided a direct connection there. For example, "The Visitor" opens with the elements of narrative: "Every summer, after the slender dogwood by the porch / has dropped its scalloped blossoms, my sister / moves back into the carcass of our house." Setting, character, even a sense of conflict and plot are all evident here. Yet the essence of the poem comes in a pause in the sister's voice, heard by the speaker across the telephone wire. The pause is enough to thrust the speaker into her own internal conflict, between desiring the southern home and feeling disconnected from it. It is this moment of intense feeling that makes the poem what it is. Likewise, Voigt's *Kyrie* (1995) consists of lyric sonnets in an overall narrative structure that tells the story of the 1918–19 flu epidemic in which nearly 25,000 people died.

Some southern poets embrace the narrative, such as Kate Daniels (b. 1953), who explains: "That my poems are narrative, tend toward colloquial language, and have strongly orchestrated closure all seem to me to be attributable to my origins and experience in the South." Kate Daniels sees the "need for story" as a natural part of southern poetry. In her essay "Porch-Sitting and Southern Poetry" (1996), Daniels describes poems that draw the reader in with the promise of a good story but then address critical issues often in shocking ways. Daniels herself writes just such poetry. In her collections *Niobe Poems* (1988) and *Four Testimonies* (1998), Daniels draws on stories from Greek mythology, recounts her own experience of a friend losing a child to drowning, recreates stories of the survivors of the collapse of the Nimitz Freeway in the 1989 San Francisco earthquake, and gets into the mind of religious philosopher Simone Weil, all the while weaving compelling stories into expressions of motherhood, loss, and grief.

As we look to the future of southern poetry by women, we see a rich collection of work that constantly challenges definitions of a southern tradition. Susan Ludvigson (b. 1942) for example, writes more passionately about land far from the South—Wisconsin, Spain, France—than within it, and she frequently uses her poetry to retell history in poetic form. Her poems, such as those collected in *Trinity* (1996), are daring portrayals of women's lives that compel re-vision: the Gospel according to Mary Magdalene, who in French legend and Ludvigson's poetry, marries Jesus and bears his children; the secret life of Emily Dickinson, as portrayed through letters to her from God; a portrait of a woman as artist, who travels to Rennes-le-Château, a village in the French Pyrenees that holds dear the legend of Mary Magdalene. Ludvigson rarely writes about the South specifically, yet, as David Kirby argues in his review article "Is There a *Southern* Poetry?" (1994), the speakers in her poetry are often surprised by their own southernness. Even when in France, the speaker in "October in the Aude" is drawn back home as "sun spills / into [her] eyes, a blinding that makes pines / disappear in a golden blaze" and she floats "on the quick heat that could be / midsummer" as hawks circle overhead. As nature and humankind become one, Ludvigson's poem harks back to her southern landscape.

Although few critical studies of southern poetry exist, numerous anthologies have collected the work of southern women writers throughout the past forty years, including *White Trash: An Anthology of Contemporary Southern Poets* (1976, reissued in 1984), *Contemporary Southern Poetry* (1979), and *The Made Thing: An Anthology of Contemporary Southern Poetry* (1987, reissued in 1999). In addition, Ernest Suarez and Amy Verner recently published a collection of interviews with southern poets, *Southbound: Interviews with Southern Poets*. However, a volume that most clearly defines the state of southern poetry today is *Buck and Wing: Southern Poetry at 2000*, a special edition published by *Shenandoah* in the spring of 2000. Almost thirty women are represented in this collection, and together they demonstrate the vast range of women writing in and of the South today, suggesting mythical proportions within a homespun frame.

Found in this collection is "Blues in the Blue Ridge" by Elizabeth Seydel Morgan (b. 1939) in which Euripides and Electra fit naturally beside images of sunflowers and goldfinches on a Virginia mountainside or a trumpet dirge in New Orleans. Likewise, Cathy Smith Bowers' "The Flower We Could Not Name" points out that southerners can *always* name a tree, a flower, or a bulb, and as she lists "Desert-Candle, / Tiger-Flower, / Star-of-Bethlehem," "Narcissus," and "Hyacinth," we begin to hear echoes of Homeric catalogs, though stuff of the earth has replaced the gods. Such classical musings take on special resonance within the framework of southern womanhood in a poem like "The Gold Bird" by Diann Blakley (b. 1957) which tells the story of Yeats's golden bird in "Sailing to Byzantium" from the bird's perspective. Within southern culture, the poem not only plays off Angelou's caged bird, but it also suggests the trappings of the beauty myth still alive in the South. Because the emperor loves the bird, and because she no longer has to worry about growing gray and fat like her friends, she enjoys the cold, lifeless perfection of her golden body and song. Likewise, Heather Ross Miller (b. 1939) tells the story of Leda and the Swan once again, but in "Leda Talks," she defiantly states, "I will get you back." Many of the poems paint a picture of the South with the kind of romantic realism that marks poetry by southern women today. In the succulent lines of "Earth Elegy" by Margaret Gibson (b. 1944) the beauty of the South cannot be suppressed:

> Rain on the shingles, on the maples—
> this evening,
> ground fog and cloud
> mingled in the hollow between the ridges,
> and a sorrow so gentle it could be
> the mud I took this morning into my hands.

Yet there's more: Gibson's poem blends imagery of divine creation and recreation ("another [world] made real only by dying, or by / living in the holy world of worlds") with earthy creation and re-creation (the new bloom from the buried root) and with her own ability to create and re-create with words ("I am, crown to bole, just this sun / so recklessly arising."), rendering the poet godlike through her attachment to the natural world.

In the preface to *Buck and Wing,* Robert Wrigley describes southern poetry as "that insistence on speaking to and of the margins . . . the willingness to look at the thin veil that separates the dead from the living, the present from the past, the oppressed from the oppressor." Wrigley asserts that this "willingness, this insistence is part of the Southern poet's character . . . to observe and to deny nothing but the boundaries themselves; to cross over to the other side, to the shark's parlor, to the other blood." Southern women poets have had the courage to enter the shark's parlor and to settle in, to tell their stories, even to sing. We cannot help but listen.

Southern Women Writers in a Changing Landscape

Connie R. Schomburg

In *Southern Women's Writing* (1995), Mary Louise Weaks and Carolyn Perry identify three characteristics that make contemporary southern women writers' works distinctly southern: the "stabilizing image" of home that permeates their work, the "extension of southern traditions beyond the region," and "the continuity of the writers themselves." Yet another defining characteristic of contemporary southern women's writing may be one that has made the literature of this region distinct from the very beginning: an exploration of the importance of the land. Indeed, as Perry and Weaks note, "this youngest generation of southern writers may be the last to claim a distinct tie to the region, perhaps the last to remember a distinctly 'southern landscape' that is now rapidly becoming part of the larger American past." Though perhaps harder to discern precisely because, as Elizabeth Harrison notes in *Female Pastoral* (1991), "the country's transition from a rural to an urban society is almost complete," this focus on the land can nevertheless be found in the works of southern women writers generally and in that of three specifically: Bobbie Ann Mason, Alice Walker, and Marilou Awiakta.

Born within a decade of each other—in 1940, 1944, and 1936, respectively—Mason, Walker, and Awiakta are important writers to consider with regard to a changing southern landscape for a number of reasons. First, and most obviously, the three represent the diverse racial, cultural, and historical backgrounds the contemporary South comprises. All three writers are also concerned with change and in their works present a wide variety of responses to the late twentieth century's rapidly changing landscape. Finally, Mason, Walker, and Awiakta offer surprising answers to the question of whether a distinct southern literature exists, and will continue to exist—answers that demand careful attention. Deeply and personally affected by the changes to the land wrought by technology and urbanization, these three writers respond to the changes in ways that sometimes intersect, sometimes collide. For Mason, for example, the results of urbanization and the technology revolution are a chaos that, for the most part, she finds exciting, while for Walker these same phenomena more often elicit horror and dismay. Acknowledging the dangers of technology like Walker yet also understanding its necessity and permanence like Mason, Awiakta seeks to bring into harmony these disparate responses and to build a bridge between the old and the new by which respect for the land and for the awesome power of the atom may both be affirmed.

In his book *Bobbie Ann Mason: A Study of the Short Fiction* (1998), Albert Wilhelm argues that "Mason's works develop contrapuntal patterns by playing the old pastoral ideal against antipastoral skepticism about the continued feasibility of that ideal." These polyphonic patterns may be seen both in Mason's fiction and her nonfiction writing, which present a progression in her characters' relationship to the land. For example, in her interviews, essays, and, most recently, in her family memoir *Clear Springs* (1999), Mason makes clear her own understanding of and attitude toward the land of western Kentucky where she was born and raised, and which she later left and then returned to. Perhaps the most telling passage is in *Spence + Lila* (1988), when Spence looks at his fields and thinks, "This is it. This is all there is in the world—it contains everything there is to know or possess, yet everywhere people are knocking their brains out trying to find something different, something better. . . . Everyone always wants a way out of something like this, but what he has here is the main thing there is."

In a 1991 interview with Bonnie Lyons and Bill Oliver, Mason claimed that Spence's view is her own: "I think Spence is very wise and what he says is absolutely true." Similarly, in her 1995 essay "The Chicken Tower," Mason writes that she thinks "about what a farmer knows up there on his tractor or walking behind his mules—the slow, enduring pace of regular toil and the habit of mind that goes with it, the habit of knowing what is lasting and of noting every nuance of soil and water and season. What my father and my ancestors knew has gone, and their language lingers like relics. Soon my memories will be loosened from any tangible connection to this land."

Even as she respects her ancestors' toil on the land and their close connection to it—and acknowledges her own tenuous one—Mason makes no apologies for her desire, as a child and young adult, to move beyond the land. Elsewhere in the same essay she both questions and explains her own position: "What happened to me and my generation? What made us leave home and abandon the old ways? Why did we lose our knowledge of nature? Why wasn't it satisfying? . . . We didn't want to be slaves to nature. Maintaining the Garden of Eden was too much work—endless hoeing, fences to fix, hay to bale, and cows to milk, come rain or come shine." As she puts it in another essay from 1995, "The Burden of the Feast": "Granny didn't question her duties, but I did. I didn't want to be hulling beans in a hot kitchen when I was fifty years old." Further, Mason concludes that it was because of her parents' desire for "better lives for their children" that she and her siblings "have been free to roam, because we always knew where home is."

Yet, if Mason has a clear familiarity with her past and a sure sense of her own rootedness to the land of her birth, the characters in her short fiction rarely have this understanding or this connection. Often described as "numb," "anxious"—even "grotesque"—the majority of Mason's characters tend to move through their lives much like Leroy in "Shiloh," who in all his years as a truck driver "never took time to examine anything. He was always flying by scenery." As Mason told Albert Wilhelm in a 1995 interview, "What I write about essentially is culture shock—the bewildering experience of moving from the land into modern urban life. Culture shock has been my experience, in moving from the South to the North, and I see versions of it in everybody at home as they deal with change." One manifestation of this culture shock is a distance from or indifference to the land, a symptom clearly seen in many of Mason's short story characters. Georgeann, in "The Retreat," though presented with the opportunity to enjoy and connect with nature at a lodge at Kentucky Lake, instead spends the majority of her weekend in the basement of the lodge, playing video games. Neither Liz in "Sorghum," Sabrina in "A New-Wave Format," nor Waldeen in "Graveyard Day" has any seeming connection to the land, only unsatisfying relationships and uncertain futures. Certainly, there are characters who are trying to heal wounds and draw sustenance from the land—Ruth and Barbara in "Bumblebees" and Sandra in "Offerings" come immediately to mind—but these women's efforts are for the most part ineffectual. Sandra seems to derive little comfort from her retreat to the country, and Barbara and Ruth's experiment seems likewise doomed: they plant trees in the wrong place and later lose their garden to rain. Although they're dedicated to carefully tending the land and reclaiming the house that stands on it, the farm for Barbara "sometimes . . . suddenly seems strange, like something she has never seen before."

With her three novels, Mason presents a different set of possibilities for her characters in terms of their relationship to the land. Unlike her short stories, which are almost always set in the present and involve characters in their mid-twenties to early forties, Mason's novels present a wider scope in terms of time period and characters' ages, and the degree to which her characters are able to establish a sustaining connection with their homeland is dependent on the generation to which they are born. For example, Sam Hughes, the seventeen-year-old protagonist of Mason's first novel, *In Country* (1985), is very similar to the aforementioned short story characters in her lack of a close tie to the land. Although critics such as Linda Tate have argued for Sam's success in finding a connection to the land and, along with it, to her past, there is strong evidence to suggest that no such connection is achieved. At a number of key moments when opportunities for enlightenment present themselves—in the scene when a frightened Emmett finds her at Cawood's Pond, for example, or in the final scene when she finds her father's name as well as her own on the Vietnam Veterans Memorial—Sam responds not with new understanding or genuine recognition but with the same tired clichés and irrelevant references to pop culture that have marked her speech throughout the novel.

Based on Mason's own parents and their generation, the title characters in Mason's *Spence + Lila* have a tie to the land and to each other that it is doubtful Sam will ever achieve. As noted earlier, Spence knows that the life on the farm that he has carved for himself and his family "is the main thing there is," and his wife Lila clearly shares his view. During her stay in the hospital Lila has time to reflect not only on her love for Spence and their children, but on her deep satisfaction with her life's work on the farm, with its opportunity to "be outdoors": "Playing in her uncle's creek when she was little . . . meeting Spence down in that creek . . . years later when his tractor got stuck in their own creek, hauling him out with the truck. . . . She and Spence have spent a lifetime growing things together." Not only does this couple find fulfillment and identity in their tie to the land, but they also respond to each other with imagery taken from nature. When Lila returns home after her successful surgery at the book's end, for example, Spence observes her joy in being able to inspect her garden once again: "Her face is rosy, all the furrows and marks thrusting upward with her smile the way the okra on the stalk reach upward to the sun. Her face is as pretty as freshly plowed ground, and the scar on her neck is like a gully washed out but filling in now. . . . And then he imagines the look on Lila's face when she catches one of those oversized catfish he has slipped into the pond."

Like Spence and Lila, Christie and James Wheeler of Mason's *Feather Crowns* (1993) derive a deep sense of fulfillment and identity from their tie to the land. Set at the turn of the century, the earliest time period Mason has yet depicted in her work, this novel also presents Mason's clearest vision of a woman who is empowered by her nurturing relationship to the land. When James first brings her to his people's eastern Kentucky homestead to begin a new life on their own farm, Christie

> set the baby in her husband's arms and ran out across the open field. She tried to see everything: the railroad tracks, the cows in the pasture, a flock of blackbirds taking off from an isolated dead tree. . . . This was her new home, the fields where her children would play and work, where she'd raise her chickens and work her garden. . . . She imagined the sunrises and sunsets from this spot. The exhilarating freedom that ran through her now was like the stir she used to feel when she watched James on his horse, in her front yard, talking to her father while she hid inside. She ran through the stubby, dead cornstalks in the field, with her arms spread open to the sky. Now, she thought.

Although her life on the farm will hold backbreaking work and heartbreaking loss, Christie's view of the land at the end of her long life remains much the same as when she was a young bride. As she tells her granddaughter at the novel's end:

> When you're old, you feel so wise sometimes, it seems like you've learnt everything you need to know before you die. But it don't stop you from wanting to repeat ever day, from here to eternity. Just the simple pleasures—coffee and bacon-and-eggs in the morning; the sunrise, which I NEVER miss; finding a bird feather on the porch step; or hearing a bull bawling to his cows; seeing a pair of kittens tangled up a-playing; seeing roses bloom on the trellis once again, from the same rosebush I started in 1897. . . . But I don't aim to live out my days all hunched over my memories. I want to watch the sun come up and hear a hen cackle over a new-laid egg and feel a kitten purr. And I want to see a flock of blackbirds whirl over the field, making music. Things like that are absolutely new ever time they happen.

For Mason, then, those works set in earlier times depict women who are involved with and strongly identified with the land, while for her more contemporary characters such bonds are rarely, if ever, established; instead, these women more often experience alienation from or failed attempts to connect with the land. Like Mason herself, these contemporary characters may express an appreciation for the old ways, but are for the most part uninterested in "maintaining the Garden." Although Mason acknowledges in her doctoral study of Nabokov (1974) that a garden is "a microcosm, a miniature realm in which ideally all is ordered, fruitful, and beautiful," only those of her parents' generation and those who came before are able to create and maintain such gardens.

But if there are limits on who can attempt—and succeed in—creating gardens in Mason's work, such is not the case for Alice Walker or for the myriad women who inhabit her poems, short stories, novels, and essays. Through her numerous works in these many genres, Walker presents a multilayered exploration of her connection to "the earth and Nature and the Universe, my own Trinity" generally, and to her southern homeland in particular (*The Same River Twice*, 1996). As with Mason, gardens for Walker represent an individual's attempt to bring order to chaos, but they also embody much more: they serve as a statement not only about the resilience of southern black women, but about their often overlooked but nonetheless magnificent artistry.

In perhaps her best-known essay, "In Search of Our Mother's Gardens" (1974), Walker says: "Like Mem, a character in *The Third Life of Grange Copeland,* my mother adorned with flowers whatever shabby house we were forced to live in. And not just your typical straggly country stand of zinnias, either. She planted ambitious gardens—and still does—with over fifty different varieties of plants that bloom profusely from early March until late November." Walker notes further that "it is only when my mother is working in her flowers that she is radiant, almost to the point of being invisible—except as Creator: hand and eye. She is involved in work her soul must have. Ordering the universe in the image of her personal conception of Beauty." For Walker, her mother's face, "as she prepares the Art that is her gift, is a legacy of respect she leaves to me, for all that illuminates and cherishes life." Significantly, when Walker's mother died some ten years after this essay was written, she was "given a splendid farewell ceremony to which hundreds of people came. . . . There was an endless cortege, pickup trucks filled with the flowers she loved" (1996). In death as in life, Minnie Tallulah Grant Walker was known for the abundant beauty borne of her respect and tender care of the earth.

Though none of the characters in Walker's early fiction or poetry arrive at the level of satisfaction or artistry in their gardens that her own mother did, many nevertheless take pride and find identity in their work on the land, primarily with flowers. In the title poem from *Once* (1968), for example, it is flowers—not the brutality of the police or of the system that has brought them to jail—that the speaker's friend notices first. And in "South: The Name of Home," the speaker asks "what secrets will not / the ravished land / reveal / of its abuse" but also prays that God will "give us trees to plant / and hands and eyes to / love them." Though the South for most of Walker's characters represents overwhelming racism and oppression, it also holds much beauty. Of her second book of poetry, *Revolutionary Petunias* (1970), Walker has said, "These poems reflect my delight at being once again in a Southern African-American environment, and also my growing realization that the sincerest struggle to change the world must start within. I was saved from despair countless times by the flowers and the trees I planted" (*Her Blue Body Everything We Know*, 1991). The importance of this connection to the land is evident in Sammy Lou of this collection's title poem, who as she is led to the electric chair reminds her listeners, "Don't yall forgit to water / my purple petunias." The hope that the southern homeland inspires is also voiced by the speaker in "View from Rosehill Cemetery: Vicksburg":

> Here we are not quick to disavow
> the pull of field and wood
> and stream;
> we are not quick to turn
> upon our dreams.

Similar connections to the southern landscape may be seen in Walker's first two collections of short stories, *In Love and Trouble* (1973) and *You Can't Keep a Good Woman Down* (1981). Although recognized primarily as portraits of black women struggling to survive and searching for wholeness, these stories also suggest that a tie to the land can help the women achieve both. A recognition of her tie to her Georgia home gives Sarah in "A Sudden Trip Home in the Spring" a new understanding of and confidence in her art, and it is the daughter who has maintained a close connection to her southern roots whose gifts and choices are affirmed by her mother in "Everyday Use."

While evidence of the importance of a connection to the land can be found in Walker's stories and poems, this theme is given even fuller expression in her first three novels. In fact, in *The Third Life of Grange Copeland*

(1970), *Meridian* (1976), and *The Color Purple* (1982) there is a progression in the heroines' relationship to the land, one that leads to a turning point in both the subjects and settings of Walker's later works. As noted earlier, Mem of *The Third Life of Grange Copeland,* like Walker's own mother, finds solace and stability in the gardens she plants. Though her husband's self-hatred and violence ultimately destroy her, she nevertheless derives some sense of decency and wholeness from the flowers she plants and tends right up until her death.

Though a woman of different times and circumstances, the title character of *Meridian* is similar to Mem in her awareness of the comfort that a tie to the land can bring. As a young girl, she is both frightened and intrigued by her father's compassionate tears for the Indians whose land he has come to own. And later, before that same land is stolen by the federal government, she comes to love it, like her father, for the bounty it produces and the opportunity it provides to experience the spiritual ecstasy of their ancestors. Meridian carries this early reverence for the land with her to college, where she plants a "wild sweet shrub bush" when Medgar Evers is assassinated, and adorns her room with "large photographs of trees and rocks and tall hills and floating clouds, which she claimed she *knew."* Her tie to the land is still later manifested in her life's work, in her tie to the people of her southern homeland, a people whose culture she values and whose lives she never ceases to try to improve.

Although not aware as a young girl, like Meridian, of the benefits of a close connection to the land, Celie in *The Color Purple* does learn that lesson by novel's end. Though perhaps not as pronounced as the lessons in self-love, esteem, and wholeness that she also learns, it is a recognition of her tie to nature that, it could be argued, makes her other learning—and thus her transformation—possible. While initially viewing the natural world as an inanimate object to imitate—as when she wishes herself a tree in order to insulate herself against her husband's abuse—Celie eventually learns to appreciate it as Shug does. Warning Celie that "it pisses God off if you walk by the color purple in a field somewhere and don't notice it," Shug also helps Celie revise her own notions of God and in so doing accept and respect herself as a part of nature. As Celie writes to Nettie after a conversation with Shug, "I never truly notice nothing God make. Not a blade of corn (how it do that?) not the color purple (where it come from?). Not the little wildflowers. Nothing. Now that my eyes opening, I feels like a fool. Next to any little scrub of bush in my yard, Mr. ———'s evil sort of shrink." Finally, as Elizabeth Harrison notes in *The Female Pastoral* (1991), "Celie's cottage industry of creating folkspants . . . results not only from Shug's encouragement but from her own developing awareness of herself as an individual empowered by her connection to nature."

In these three novels, then, there is a progression in the female characters' awareness of the importance of a tie to the land. Significantly, while Walker was exploring her characters' connection to the land in these three novels set in the South, she was also exploring the personal meanings of her southern homeland in numerous essays of the period. Published in 1974 as *In Search of Our Mothers' Gardens,* Walker's first collection of essays reveals a woman whose quest for wholeness necessarily involves an examination of her tie to the southern landscape. Not surprisingly, given the number of essays devoted to her experiences as a civil rights activist, her essays dealing with the impact of Martin Luther King, Jr., present most clearly her understanding of her relationship to the land. As she writes in "Choice: A Tribute to Dr. Martin Luther King, Jr." (1973): "[King] gave us back our heritage. He gave us back our homeland; the bones and dust of our ancestors, who may now sleep within our caring and our hearing. He gave us the blueness of the Georgia sky in autumn as in summer; the colors of the Southern winter as well as glimpses of the green of vacation-time spring. Those of our relatives we used to invite for a visit we now can ask to stay. . . . He gave us continuity of place, without which community is ephemeral. He gave us home." Having been restored to the land of her birth by King and other activists—and by her own sheer will—Walker comes to another realization in the essay "Choosing to Stay at Home" (1973): "And if I leave Mississippi—as I will one of these days—it will not be for the reasons of the other sons and daughters of my parents. Fear will have no part in my decision, nor will lack of freedom to express my womanly thoughts . . . it will be because I have freed myself to go; and it will be My Choice."

This declaration of freedom marks a turning point for Walker personally and for the fiction and essays that would follow. After *The Color Purple,* Walker's novels—including *The Temple of My Familiar* (1989), *Possessing the Secret of Joy* (1992), and *By the Light of My Father's Smile* (1998)—no longer focus solely, if at all, on the land of the South. In these novels and in her most recent collections of essays her canvas has expanded, and so too has her discussion of the importance of the land, wherever that land may be. As indicated by the title of the essay collection *Anything We Love Can Be Saved* (1997) and by individual titles such as "Everything Is a Human Being" and "The Universe Responds" in *Living by the Word* (1988), Walker continues to argue for the necessity of acknowledging the interrelatedness of all living things; she continues to explore the possibilities for wholeness inherent in a close connection to the land. This argument receives its fullest fictional treatment in *By the Light of My Father's Smile*. Here, Walker presents an imaginary tribe in Mexico, the Mundo, whose elders teach the young from birth about the sacredness of the earth and their place within it. What the Mundo have—equality of the sexes, healthy and wholesome sexual expression, abiding respect for all of the natural world—is shown to be even more desirable when Walker reveals the devastating effects on her character Magdalena of having intimately known that world only to have it taken away.

From her earliest work to her most recent, then, Walker's exploration of the connection to the land is a rich, multilayered one. Unlike Mason, who presents clear limits on the possibility of maintaining close ties to the land, Walker seems to acknowledge no such restrictions. In the face of the continued assaults on the earth that she addresses throughout her work, though, one could argue that Walker must resort to an imaginary people to embody her ideal relationship to the earth and to each other. Such is not the case for Marilou Awiakta, who instead turns to her Cherokee and Appalachian past for models of the ideal connection to the land. In her work, which includes numerous essays and poems, a children's story, and her multigenre book *Selu: Seeking the Corn-Mother's Wisdom* (1993), Awiakta insists that "nature is the human heart made tangible." As such, it must be honored and respected not just for its own sake, but for the sake of our very survival. Like Walker's, Awiakta's work presents an in-depth study of the search for wholeness and balance. Awiakta argues that this wholeness can be achieved by listening to and learning from the wisdom of the ancestors, who urge a building of bridges to reconcile the disparate forces in one's personal life and to resolve the tensions of the larger world.

Although, like Mason and Walker, Awiakta presents tensions that involve the conflict between the old and the new and between love of the land of her birth and despair for her ancestors' dispossession of it, they also consist of something more. When Awiakta was nine years old, she and her family moved to Oak Ridge, Tennessee, site of the headquarters of the Manhattan Project. As Vicki Johns notes in "Of Atoms and Appalachia" (1997), this change "made a profound impression on the budding writer. Through stories told by family, Awiakta had already become steeped in Appalachian and Cherokee culture. But 'growing up in Oak Ridge gave [her] yet another culture, because the scientific and high-tech world had its own value system, its own world view, and its own language.'" In *Abiding Appalachia: Where Mountain and Atom Meet* (1978), Awiakta attempts to fuse her three heritages—Cherokee, Appalachian, and scientific—through poems that reflect on how seeking balance between seemingly opposing forces can result in harmony within the individual and in her relationship to the land.

In the opening poem of that collection, "An Indian Walks in Me," Awiakta declares that "no more / will I follow any rule / that splits my soul." As she traces in the poems that follow those forces responsible for the split—the tragic history of her Cherokee ancestors' "removal" from their homeland as well as the advent of the nuclear age literally in her own backyard—she also employs metaphor to signal the wholeness possible in viewing the land and its human inhabitants as one and the same. In "Smoky Mountain-Woman," for example, Awiakta simultaneously describes both a woman and a mountain, and in "Where Mountain and Atom Meet" she joins these apparently irreconcilable forces through her reference to the "great I am" that also claims humans as its own. As Johns notes in her essay and as the writer herself describes at length in *Selu,* Awiakta was not to be content to end her attempt at fusion with the reconciliation of personal tensions in *Abiding Appalachia.* Deeply disturbed by her ineffectual efforts to prevent the flooding of ancestral Cherokee burial grounds by the Tellico Dam project in East Tennessee in 1979—and encouraged by a personal visit with Alice Walker in 1982—Awiakta turns her attention in her third book, *Selu,* to the problem of nuclear energy. Fusing her personal history as a child of Oak Ridge and the questions arising from that experience with her new ones about the uses of technology, she sets out to answer the question, "Do we have enough reverence for life to cope with the atom?"

What she hints at in her earlier book—that the atom's power is to be respected as one of nature's many benevolent forces—is presented in *Selu* in the form of an entirely new metaphor. In the best-known essay of the collection, "Baring the Atom's Mother Heart," Awiakta discusses nuclear energy from "a Cherokee and female point of view," envisioning the atom as a fierce yet nurturing feminine power. As she explained in a 1990 interview with Thomas Rain Crowe, "My thinking about the atom deepened and expanded. It struck me that the atom is really the 'mother heart' of nature, the generator of life—circular in motion, always moving, always fusing into new forms." Because this is so, as Awiakta repeatedly warns, "to separate the gender that bears life from the power to sustain it is as destructive as to tempt nature herself."

Awiakta announces another connection in "Baring the Atom's Mother Heart," one that she first recognized while visiting the American Museum of Science and Energy in Oak Ridge in 1977. As she explained in the Crowe interview,

I was looking at an immense translucent blue model of the atom. Inside it, tiny lights, representing electrons, whirl in orbit. As I watched this, my state of consciousness slowly altered, and suddenly I saw Little Deer leaping in the heart of the atom. (In Cherokee, *Awiakta* means 'eye of the deer.') At this moment the words of Neils Bohr . . . came to me. . . . 'When it comes to atoms, language can only be used as in poetry. The poet, too, is not nearly so concerned with describing facts as with creating images and mental connections.' This was my spontaneous understanding of how the world of traditional Native American thought and the world of scientific thought meet deep in the mystery.

For that reason, Awiakta took Little Deer, "a Cherokee spirit of reverence, and placed him in the center of the atom to be the logo for [her] life and [her] work. If we have reverence for nature, humanity, and the Creator, we can live in harmony. Otherwise, we will destroy all that lives."

Having found a personal connection in her Little Deer name and logo to the mysterious tie between traditional Cherokee thought and scientific thought, Awiakta offers her readers yet another metaphor for this tie: the image of Selu, "corn-mother of us all." As she explained to Crowe, "Even if we destroy this earth and ourselves, the atom's mother heart—the regenerative core of nature—will keep creating life. I connected this idea with the traditional before-white-contact Cherokee concept of woman, which links her to the sacred regenerative power of Mother Earth." Her book *Selu*, then, is Awiakta's gift to her readers, a gift of wisdom for understanding the vital, time-immemorial connection between humans and every other life form. Appropriately, Awiakta identifies the nature of this gift in a poem appearing early in the book, "I Offer You a Gift":

> Awake in the dark
> you know
> I know
> We may not make it.
> Mother Earth may not make it.
> We teeter
> on the turning point.
> Against the downward pull,
> against the falter
> of your heart and mine,
> I offer you a gift
> a seed to greet the sunrise—

>Ginitsi Selu
>
>Corn, Mother of Us All.
>
>Her story.

And as each new page in *Selu* reveals, the corn-mother's story is one of hope in the face of overwhelming obstacles. As Awiakta explains in the "fax" that opens the book, the content of the book is Selu's "survival wisdoms (time tested)"; the organization is a "doublewoven basket" that allows author and reader to "walk the path together, gather thoughts, then contemplate Selu's wisdoms as presented by Native Americans who have preserved them"; and the "Reason for Making Our Journey" is "So we won't die. Neither will Mother Earth."

To the question of whether a distinct southern literature exists and will continue, then, these three women writers suggest some surprising responses. If a tie to the land continues to distinguish this literature, then for Bobbie Ann Mason the answer appears to be "probably not," for though she appreciates the former agrarian way of life, she and her contemporary female characters have seemingly already begun the loosening "from any tangible connection to this land." For Alice Walker, a tie to the land is vital, although her ever-widening canvases indicate that such a tie may be made anywhere, and that out of necessity or choice or both the tie won't be made to the South. Finally, Marilou Awiakta's answer is an earnest "yes," and even though like Walker her concern is for a connectedness to the land wherever one is, she also makes it clear that the respect and balance she advocates must be achieved in the South—for the survival of the land itself and for its people.

A Second Southern Renaissance

Linda Tate

Since Walter Sullivan declared, in his 1976 assessment of southern literature entitled *A Requiem for the Renaissance,* that the Renaissance ended with World War II, many critics have joined in chanting the requiem. Yet in many respects the Renaissance has never truly died. Indeed, the last two decades have seen a remarkable outpouring of literature by southerners, and in many ways, this second southern renaissance is far more robust and diverse than the first heralded watershed period in southern literary history. Scores of writers are bringing the stories of ordinary southerners to life through their writing. This, it would seem, is the true renaissance: the outpouring of literature by writers from all walks of life—writers of color, writers from poor and working-class backgrounds, gay and lesbian writers, writers from the mountains and from the cities. If the first renaissance represented the unleashing of the creative juices of the well-to-do and gave wealthier southerners, mostly men, the opportunity to come to terms with the legacy of the past in the present, this second southern renaissance marks the liberation of all southerners. It is very much a postsegregation literature, and while many writers seek to come to terms with the past, the emphasis is much less on apology and the purging of guilt and much more on the reclaiming of one's voice, one's own citizenship in the South. For the white men of the first southern renaissance, the concern was to make sense of the burden of its slaveholding past; for the black and white, poor and lesbian, Appalachian —

and urban southern writers of the second renaissance, the agenda is to insist on healing the pain of the past so that they and their characters may live more freely and joyously in the present. Quentin Compson has met his match in Alice Walker's Celie, who, transformed as she is from brutalized oppression to joyful love, stands as an emblem of the new era.

In "The Real Beginning of the Southern Renaissance" (1993), Carol S. Manning claims that "significant literary movements are most likely to develop in times of tension," and she goes on to say that traditional scholars of the first southern renaissance used that conventional wisdom to mark the beginning of that post–World War I movement when, in Allen Tate's classic statement, "the South reentered the world—but gave a backward glance as it slipped over the border." For her own purposes, Manning looks back to another time of tension, the turn-of-the-century women's movement, to identify the roots of the first renaissance. When considering the continued outpouring of southern literature, however, Fred Hobson's insights about the 1960s are also pertinent. In *The Southern Writer in the Postmodern World* (1991), he defines this period, the time of the civil rights movement and the women's movement, as "a watershed in southern thought." If it is true that "significant literary movements are most likely to develop in times of tension," then it is no surprise to discover that women and blacks have come to the foreground of southern literature with increasing visibility since the 1960s. Certainly, many men have contributed to this lively period in southern literature, Larry Brown, Charles Frazier, Ernest Gaines, Clyde Edgerton, and Reynolds Price among them. But in large part this second southern renaissance is a movement of women's voices, and finally, after far too many years, we are hearing from many African American writers and a handful of Native American writers.

The issue of race has dominated southern writing for so long that it is difficult to imagine this literature without the vexing issue of relationships between blacks and whites. Although William Faulkner, Eudora Welty, and Flannery O'Connor, among many others, have given us fascinating depictions of black-white relations in the South, it is only very recently that white writers have looked so self-consciously and so unflinchingly at connections between blacks and whites. Ellen Douglas returns to this theme again and again in her work, most fully in her landmark novel *Can't Quit You, Baby* (1988), and Nanci Kincaid (b. 1952) considers the traditionally taboo topic of black-white sexual relationships in the aptly titled *Crossing Blood* (1992). In these novels, we hear the echoes of Lillian Smith, who, alone of her generation, looked at the South's enduring racial legacy in such a penetrating and insightful manner.

Despite these courageous novels by white women, black southern women lead the vanguard of current writing about race in the South. Kentucky-born-and-bred bell hooks (b. 1952) provides the theoretical lens through which to view racial tensions in the South and throughout the United States. Alice Walker has had an immeasurable impact on southern literature, though since the publication of *The Color Purple* (1982), she has regrettably left the South behind, focusing most of her attention instead on themes related to Africa. Maya Angelou has been a lively force in American culture, and her autobiography *I Know Why the Caged Bird Sings* (1970) has become as well known to today's American schoolchildren as a classic novel of 1961, Harper Lee's *To Kill a Mockingbird,* was to students of earlier generations. Toni Cade Bambara (1939–1995), Gayl Jones (b. 1949), Dori Sanders (b. 1934), and Shay Youngblood (b. 1959) have broadened the numbers of African American women contributing to southern literature. And the Affrilachian poets—poets who are wedding their dual heritages as African Americans and as Appalachians—have brought a new energy to southern poetry. A movement begun by Frank X. Walker, the group in large part consists of women: Kelly Ellis; honorary member Nikki Giovanni (b. 1943); and the extraordinary Nikky Finney (b. 1957), whose 1995 volume of poems, *Rice,* merits much greater critical attention.

Perhaps the matriarch of the southern black women writers of the last three decades was Margaret Walker, whose powerful 1966 novel *Jubilee* did so much to reconstruct black women's roots in the South. More recently, filmmaker Julie Dash gave us a lush visual and literary journey into the cultural and regional past in *Daughters of the Dust* (1991), and Toni Morrison, one of only a few American women to win the Nobel Prize, sets her work primarily in the Midwest but reminds us in novel after novel how inextricably tied she and her African American characters are to their knotty roots in the South. Dash, Morrison, and both Alice Walker and Margaret Walker have been part of a larger African American countermigration, a return—either literally or imaginatively—to the South, now understood, as Farah Jasmine Griffin argues in *Who Set You Flowin'?* (1995), as a place of "ancestral wisdom and spirituality," a region full of "possibilities for black redemption." In this vein, Linda Beatrice Brown (b. 1939) tries to make sense of the South's history, the legacy its black sons and daughters have inherited. In *Crossing over Jordan* (1995), she chronicles the past of one African American family as it beats down, denies, and ultimately comes to term with the legacy of slavery. Hermine, the lone survivor of the family and the unacknowledged daughter of the aptly named Story, is left alone at the end of the novel to sort through all that she has discovered about her ancestors.

She pieces together her mother's journals and her grandmother's scraps of paper, recipes inscribed with her despair. Overwhelmed for a long time by the family "garbage" she feels she must carry, Hermine does not discover until the end of the novel that reconstructing the past and telling that family story will ultimately set her free:

> She could talk to the living now. She could tell her story. She could talk it or tell it or write it, so it wouldn't have to be stuck away in boxes and on little pieces of paper. And even if I can't get there all the way, I can try, I can reach, and that's what makes us holy, Mama, that's all we have. That's what gives a bottom to the river and a refuge in the storm. That's what brings us to the journey's end, Mama, and that's what lets us cross over Jordan.

This passage, so rich in its significance, speaks to the very need for Brown and writers like her to tell the story of the invisible southern past, to give voice to what was silenced before.

Also contributing to the multiple-voiced South of this second renaissance are a handful of Native American writers. Because members of the five southeastern tribes (Cherokee, Chickasaw, Creek, Choctaw, and Seminole) were forcibly removed to the Indian Territory in 1838, most writers of these originally southern nations are now based in Oklahoma. In *Faces in the Moon* (1994), Betty Louise Bell (b. 1949) writes about a part-Cherokee woman whose family wishes to deny its Indian ties, while Linda Hogan (b. 1947) is without a doubt the most important of the Oklahoma-based Native American writers (although she now resides in Colorado). Closer to home, only Marilou Awiakta (b. 1936) stands out as an Indian-identified writer of the South. Her 1993 book, *Selu: Seeking the Corn-Mother's Wisdom,* weaves together poetry, fiction, and essays. Increasingly, a few southern writers who are identified primarily as black or white are beginning to ac-knowledge their Native American ancestry. Barbara Kingsolver (b. 1955), a southerner by birth and world citizen by choice, downplays the significance of her Cherokee lineage, but other writers such as Alice Walker and Shay Youngblood have sometimes referred in their work to their biracialism. *River of Hidden Dreams* (1994) by Floridian Connie May Fowler (b. 1959) takes as one of its major topics the hidden and nearly lost Indian ancestry of many southern whites. In an epilogue to this novel, entitled "No Snap-shots in the Attic: A Granddaughter's Search for a Cherokee Past," Fowler challenges traditional history that obscures the reality of Indian-white mar-riages and their many offspring who now populate the South:

These distinctions between European facts and Indian facts are not trivial. The manipulation of our past is an attempt, unconscious or not, to stomp out evidence of the success and value of other cultures. My grandmother's decision to deny her heritage was fueled by the fear of what would happen to her if she admitted to being an Indian and by the belief that there was something inherently inferior about her people. And the falsehoods and omissions she lived by affected not just her; her descendants face a personal and historical incompleteness.

It is this "personal and historical incompleteness" that drives Fowler and other southern writers of Native American descent to explore their own connection to the past and to use that exploration as the basis of their fiction, poetry, and memoirs.

The outpouring of multiple voices has not been confined to southern women writers of color. Women from poor and working-class backgrounds have also made their voices heard in the last two decades. Bobbie Ann Mason ushered in the southern literary movement known as "Grit Lit," but she has since deepened her work. Her 1999 memoir, *Clear Springs,* is an insightful and personal account of growing up in Mayfield, Kentucky, and as with so much of her fiction, it brings to the page the lives of ordinary, hardworking southerners. Kaye Gibbons has turned attention to the plight of poor and brutalized white women and girls, particularly in *Ellen Foster* (1987) and *A Virtuous Woman* (1989). Without a doubt, however, the writer who stands out as a voice for the poor and disenfranchised in the South is Dorothy Allison. From her early collection of short stories *Trash* (1988) to her most recent novel, *Cavedweller* (1998), Allison writes unflinchingly and unromantically about taboo topics such as gut-wrenching poverty, violence in families, incest and emotional abuse, lesbianism, and sexual diversity. Allison has spoken on a number of occasions to her palpable need to make people like herself and her family visible to the American reader. In "A Question of Class" (1994), she states:

> I have never been able to make clear . . . the extent to which I feel myself denied: not only that I am queer in a world that hates queers, but that I was born poor into a world that despises the poor. The need to make my world believable to people who have never experienced it is part of why I write fiction. . . . [I]f I can write a story that so draws the reader in that she imagines herself like my characters, feels their sense of fear and uncertainty, their hopes and terrors, then I have

come closer to knowing myself as real, important as the very people I have always watched with awe.

And in the preface to *Trash,* Allison recounts her early experiences of writing, when she would lock herself in her room every night after work and write the story of her life on one yellow legal-size pad after another. "Writing it all down was purging," she says. "I put on the page a third look at what I've seen in life—the condensed and reinvented experience of a cross-eyed working-class lesbian . . . on the page and on the street, for me and mine."

A final group of women writers who stand in sharp contrast to the dominant voices of the first southern renaissance are the writers who have emerged since the 1970s as part of the Appalachian Renaissance. Novelists, poets, dramatists, and short story writers are springing up in other far-flung outposts of the South—most notably Florida—but it is in Appalachia where we find the liveliest community of southern women writers. Joyce Dyer's 1998 volume, *Bloodroot: Reflections on Place by Appalachian Women Writers,* provides an excellent introduction to a wide range of women writing in the mountains. Poets Rita Quillen (b. 1954) and Kathryn Stripling Byer (b. 1944) join company with children's book authors George Ella Lyon (b. 1949) and Cynthia Rylant (b. 1954), who find ways to speak to adult readers as well. Playwrights and short story writers from Appalachia— women such as Jo Carson (b. 1946), Sheila Kay Adams (b. 1953), and Meredith Sue Willis (b. 1946)—bring oral tales to the written page. Novelists writing about the mountains and their history abound, Sharyn McCrumb (b. 1948), Denise Giardina (b. 1951), Mary Lee Settle among them. And the region even lays claim to those farther-flung Kentuckians Barbara Kingsolver and Bobbie Ann Mason. Without question, Lee Smith leads this movement of mountain women writing the stories of their region, but in characteristic southern fashion, she is known in this circle of writers as much for her nurturing of new talent as she is for her own powerful writing. As Nancy C. Parrish shows in *Lee Smith, Annie Dillard, and the Hollins Group: A Genesis of Writers* (1998), Smith's own formative years at Hollins College, years she spent with such future literary luminaries as Annie Dillard, Anne Goodwyn Jones, and Lucinda MacKethan, were vital not just in her own development but also in the creation of a lively and new community of southern women writers.

In her memorable essay on Flannery O'Connor, Alice Walker—one of the early leading voices of this second southern renaissance—writes, "I believe that the truth about any subject only comes when all the sides of the story are put together, and all their different meanings make one new one. Each writer writes the missing parts to the other writer's story. And the whole story is what I'm after." This second southern renaissance is not that constructed by the Agrarians so long ago, a movement of the wealthy, landed aristocratic South who looked—even if sometimes lovingly—at the poor and the "other." Rather, this renaissance is the full and unfettered outpouring of multiple voices in the region: African Americans, Native Americans, poor whites, lesbians, mountain folk, the invisible and disenfranchised claiming their own rightful space in the region, the silenced telling their own stories.

Margaret Walker

Joyce Pettis

Margaret Walker's heritage as a black daughter of the South is arguably her major asset in her vision and craft as a writer. In her poetry, for example, she reveals an ear for the nuances of rhythm, meaning, and music in black vernacular language. In *Jubilee* (1966), her only novel, Walker elevates southern folk culture to literary prominence. As important, she conveys the indomitable will of black people who survived slavery, Reconstruction, and Jim Crow. In a fictional recreation of her maternal great-grandmother, Vyry, Walker offers a woman subjected to the physical and psychological cruelties of her era, but one who emerges without bitterness. Thus, Walker captures the struggles of the nineteenth-century slave community and simultaneously communicates a humanist vision as the heritage of future generations.

Born in 1915 in Birmingham, Alabama, Walker began writing poetry as a child. After being educated at Northwestern University and the University of Iowa, she earned her reputation as a significant poet with her first volume of poetry, *For My People* (1942), which won the Yale Younger Poets award. In this early work, Walker signals her ability to balance her southern heritage against the tenor of contemporary time. Divided into three sections, *For My People* condemns an inertia that seems evident in the political and economic life of black America in the 1930s and criticizes conditions in the South. However, one group, including "Southern Song," "Sorrow Home," and "Delta," consists of lyrical poems acknowledging psychological ties between the speaker and the physical beauty of the southern landscape, but also recognizing the dangers for black people in the region. In several poems Walker refers to the African past of black Americans and brings attention to historical lineage and ancestral homelands. The middle section of ten poems celebrates the folk of the South. As many of her literary predecessors, such as James Weldon Johnson and Zora Neale Hurston, had recognized, the folk tradition represents a vital and creative culture of sustaining power. Walker's acclaimed folk poems include "Molly Means," about a "hag and a witch" who uses her root-working ability for evil purposes until someone reverses her spell so that she dies "at the hand of her evil deed," and "Poppa Chicken," about Poppa, a "sugah daddy" who keeps his charms until he is old, "Walking round . . . with his gals / Pimping every day."

Walker asserts that her signature poem, "For My People," was typewritten in only fifteen minutes. Structurally, its nine stanzas of free verse are dependent upon the assertive sentences of the tenth stanza for their completion and meaning. Stylistically, the cadence of black southern pulpit rhetoric informs the tight parallel structure and controlled repetitive phrases. Meaning and form blend imaginatively to convey a panoramic history of black America. The speaker in each stanza identifies scenes from the rural and urban black experience so that the prominent images suggest an intricately patterned mosaic. In a rushing tumble of verbs and gerunds, but using almost no internal punctuation within stanzas, Walker conveys an urgency in the black community. Nevertheless, the people remain "lost disinherited dispossessed and happy / people filling the cabarets and taverns and other / people's pockets." They are still "blundering and groping and floundering in / the dark of churches and schools and clubs . . . / deceived and devoured by money-hungry glory-craving leeches." To end the stasis, in the last stanza the speaker demands that a "new earth," "another world," and a "bloody peace" come to fruition through a new race of men. The passion of "For My People" engages readers as no other Walker poem has done.

Meeting the conflicting demands that still face many women writers, Walker balanced her writing with marriage and a family, university teaching, course work and examinations for a Ph.D. degree from the University of Iowa, and the research for her novel, *Jubilee*. In an essay published in *The Writer on Her Work* (1980), Walker admits to the complications of gender in her writing career: "Sometimes the only quiet and private place where I could write a sonnet was in the bathroom, because that was the only room where the door could be locked and no one would intrude. I have written mostly at night in my adult life and especially since I have been married, because I was determined not to neglect any member of my family; so

I cooked every meal daily, washed dishes and dirty clothes, and nursed sick babies."

Walker, nevertheless, produced a second volume of poetry, *Prophets for a New Day* (1970), that grew mostly out of the civil rights decade. Only "Elegy" and "Ballad of the Hoppy-Toad" are not indebted to the movement. Drawing on her knowledge of biblical prophecy, Walker uses analogy to bring together biblical sages with contemporary, sacrificing leaders of the 1960s. Not surprisingly, the southern preacher's diction, familiar to her from childhood, and reprised in the rhetorical flourishes of orators like Martin Luther King, Jr., Jesse Jackson, and Malcolm X, informs these poems. Through inclusive vision Walker pays homage to historic predecessors such as Nat Turner, Gabriel Prosser, Denmark Vesey, and countless others whose names history has not retained, but who established the traditions of protest and self-sacrifice in antebellum America. In "At the Lincoln Monument in Washington, August 28, 1963," the legendary Moses leading his people to the Promised Land is certainly Reverend Martin Luther King, Jr., unidentified by name. Andrew Goodman, Michael Schwerner, and James Chaney, the three young civil rights workers murdered in Mississippi, are identified in a poem named for them. Other leaders named or obliquely referenced in poems include Malcolm X, Medgar Evers, Rev. Ralph Abernathy, and Dr. Benjamin Mays. Jackson, Mississippi, home to Margaret Walker for fourteen years by 1963, was nonetheless a site of intense racist hate during the 1960s. But it is also home to black people who have invested their labor and energy, "have planted . . . seeds of dreams and visions and prophecies." Recognizing the antithesis of hating and loving, Walker ends the poem titled for her city with these ambivalent lines: "I give you my brimming heart, Southern City / for my eyes are full and no tears cry / And my throat is dusty and dry."

October Journey (1973), a brief collection of thirty-eight pages of mostly previously published poems, maintains links with Walker's other volumes. For example, its title poem is thematically connected to the contradictions of earlier poems extolling the beautiful southern landscape but denouncing racial injustice. Stanzas two and three of "October Journey" contain some of Walker's most extravagant images of physical southern beauty:

> woods are like a smoldering plain—
> a glowing caldron full of jewelled fire;
> the emerald earth a dragon's eye
> the poplars drenched with yellow light

and dogwoods blazing bloody red.
Travelling southward earth changes from gray rock to green velvet.

This volume also contains poems celebrating writers Gwendolyn Brooks, Paul Laurence Dunbar, Robert Hayden, and Owen Dobson and historical figures Harriet Tubman, Mary McLeod Bethune, and Phillis Wheatley. *This Is My Century: New and Collected Poems* (1989) contains her previously published volumes, including *Farish Street* (1986), and thirty new poems under the title "This Is My Century." Thematically, structurally, and rhythmically, these poems resonate with the poems of the other volumes.

Walker's novel *Jubilee* was also her dissertation for the Ph.D. degree she earned in 1965 from the University of Iowa. Conceived when Walker was an undergraduate in the early 1930s, its starts and stops, extensive research about slave life, and its revisions took thirty years, a saga Walker tells in *How I Wrote "Jubilee"* (1972). Like much early black historical fiction, Vyry's story in *Jubilee* is inspired by stories of Walker's maternal ancestor who came of age during slavery in Georgia. Vyry's story and the life of her community are situated against the institution as it is experienced on the Dutton plantation. The daily lives of the slaves, their music, food, and religion, are given emphasis. As protagonist, Vyry emerges without personal rancor and without spiritual defeat. Her survivalist spirit constitutes Walker's significant legacy to black women writers who would take center stage in literary production in the 1970s.

The detailed folk culture of *Jubilee* marks a distinctive component of the novel. Each of the fifty-eight chapters is prefaced by folk proverbs or lines from spirituals. Characters sing folk songs, a sermon is included, children's rhymes and games are part of the narrative, incidents of conjuring occur, and herbs for folk healing are described. This expressive culture communicates the rich creativeness of slave life.

Walker's retirement as professor of English at Jackson State University in 1979 did not mean she retired from writing. Although working through several illnesses over the years, she published *Richard Wright, Daemonic Genius* (1988); an essay collection titled *How I Wrote "Jubilee" and Other Essays on Life and Literature* (1990); and a collection of essays written from 1932 to 1992, titled *On Being Female, Black, and Free* (1997). Walker's creativity was stilled by her death in November 1998. Her continuation of academic and creative activity throughout retirement and the many artists who paid her homage elevated her to the realms of literary legend prior to her death. The College Language Association, for example, one among many organizations that honored her, named its annual undergraduate creative writing award for Walker. A videotape, *The Life and Writing of Margaret Walker,* completed a few months before her death, preserves her intellectual vitality, love of literature, and the value she placed on the South as her home and literary inspiration. The emphasis on humanism and place in her work, among other qualities, places her solidly within the tradition of southern literature.

Mary Lee Settle

Loretta Martin Murrey

Mary Lee Settle has proven to be a writer of significance in twentieth-century American literature. She has written many highly respected works in a variety of genres, particularly the novel but also including nonfiction, autobiography, and juvenile works, as well as some early poetry and drama. Her Beulah Quintet enlarged the concept of American identity and expanded the form of the historical novel by using the genre in nontraditional ways, and her novel set in Turkey, *Blood Tie* (1977), won the 1978 National Book Award.

Mary Lee Settle was born in Charleston, West Virginia, on July 29, 1918, the daughter of Joseph Edward Settle and Rachel Tompkins Settle, both of English and Scottish descent. After a childhood in West Virginia, Kentucky, and Florida, she graduated from Charleston High School in 1936, attended Sweet Briar College from 1936 to 1938, and modeled for Powers and Harry Conover in the late 1930s. Settle's early life in England, Canada, and the United States was turbulent, both personally and professionally. She first married Englishman Rodney Weathersbee in 1939, and they moved to Canada, where son Christopher Weathersbee was born. She moved with her son to England in 1942 and began her military service career, first in the Women's Auxiliary Air Force from 1942 to 1944 and then at the Office of War Information in England from 1944 to 1945. When she returned to New York in 1945, she began work as an assistant editor of *Harper's Bazaar*.

After her divorce and her move back to England, she married Douglas Newton and worked for *Woman's Day* and *Flair* magazines. In 1956, after her divorce from Newton, she returned to West Virginia. She later married William Littleton Tazewell, a retired newspaper editor and teacher. Settle was a visiting lecturer at the University of Iowa in 1976 and at the University of Virginia in 1978. Her political affiliation is Democrat, and she considers herself a liberal; her recent *Choices: A Novel* (1995) is dedicated to "Southern liberals, past and present wherever they may be." Earlier in life, she listed her religion as Episcopalian, but in 1987 she was confirmed in the Roman Catholic Church. After living in London, Paris, Rome, and Turkey, she now resides in Charlottesville, Virginia.

When she was at Sweet Briar College, her teacher Joseph Dexter Bennett steered her toward a career in writing. Although she experimented with poetry and drama—her *Juana La Loca* was produced at the American Place Theatre in New York City in 1965—Settle has written mostly fiction and nonfiction, having felt almost compelled to do so. "The fictional process," Settle wrote in the *New York Times Book Review* (1948), "is a mixture of nonchalance, memory, chaos, subjective and sensuous vision, formed in the unconscious and raised into reality." And at a Kentucky Writers' Conference in 1982, Settle gave this advice to aspiring writers: "If you're a writer, you'll know it—inside. . . . [The idea for a novel] has to get you by the hair so you can't get loose. . . . I've got a hundred ideas in my head, but only the one that really grabs me is the one I work with. . . . And you can't impose form on a book—it has its own form and you have to find it." Settle believes writing serves an important function, but she does not particularly enjoy writing—calling it the hardest job she's ever had—or the role of a writer.

A significant amount of the Settle canon deals with southern Appalachia, and her ability to depict accurately the complexity and diversity of the region has earned her a respected position in the field of Appalachian literature. *The Kiss of Kin* was the first book Settle wrote, and *The Love Eaters* was the first book she published. *The Love Eaters*, which deals with a theatrical group in a mountain coal town, was rejected in the United States and then published in England by Harper in 1954. *The Kiss of Kin*, published also by Harper the following year, details the Passmore family struggling with the death of the family matriarch.

Her best-known southern Appalachian work is the Beulah Trilogy, which later became the Beulah Quintet. The title is based on an album of revivalist hymns by Burl Ives. The Beulah Trilogy includes *O Beulah Land* (1956), *Know Nothing* (1960, published as *Pride's Promise* in 1976), and *Fight Night on a Sweet Saturday* (1964). Settle conceived the trilogy as one work unified by geography and family that would answer the question of who came to Appalachia and why. The trilogy answers this question by describing a rootless generation. In a *Contemporary Authors* interview, Settle noted that four-fifths of Virginia settlers from 1675 to 1775 were felons, but no modern Virginians seem to have descended from them.

However, Settle was not satisfied with the trilogy. She became more interested in the seed of the generation of settlers and its progeny, particularly as they were involved in the conflicts of the English Civil War, the American Revolution, the American Civil War, World War I, and the Vietnam War. Because the revolutionary sense was missing from the trilogy, Settle added *Prisons* (1973, published in England as *The Long Road to Paradise* in 1974), which tells the story of a volunteer in Oliver Cromwell's army, and because she felt a need to portray the parents of characters in *Fight Night on a Sweet Saturday*, she added *The Scapegoat* (1980). She also revised *Fight Night on a Sweet Saturday* into *The Killing Ground* (1982). The resulting Beulah Quintet includes *Prisons* (set in England from 1642 to 1649, with a flashback to Christmas, 1634), *O Beulah Land* (set in Virginia, 1754–1774), *Know Nothing* (Virginia, 1837–1861), *The Scapegoat* (Virginia, June 7–8, 1912), and *The Killing Ground* (West Virginia, 1960–1980).

Written over a twenty-eight-year period and published over twenty-six years, the Beulah Quintet develops the journey concept of historical fiction, examining the American experience and identity from familial roots in England through the end of the twentieth century, and in the process illuminating what it means to be an American. Chronologically, the Beulah Quintet begins with the metaphor of *Prisons*, suggesting the importance of freedom that underlies the entire quintet, and in *The Killing Ground* she points out that there is always a "price of freedom," whether it be breaking the law, disinheritance, or death. Settle also makes clear that freedom from various types of subjugation must be won over and over again. She sees the roots of democracy in the healthy oscillation of the American system of checks and balances. Some of the many dichotomies in the Beulah Quintet are dream and reality, anarchy and dictatorship, fathers and sons, rebels and slave owners, wanderers and settlers, mine operators and workers, freedom and responsibility, Antigone and Creon, and the American metaphors of Brother Johnny and Uncle Sam. In an interview with John Crane in the *Paris Review*, Settle said, "What I tried to do was become contemporary with the time so that I was empathetic with what people thought was happening, and who they thought they were, rather than using the knowledge that we have as hindsight" (1990). To learn the correct language for *Prisons*, Settle did not read anything written after 1774 while working on that book. Before writing *O Beulah Land,* she read for ten months without taking notes until finally one night she dreamed she had forty acres in Virginia with a landlord in England and had to build a house to vote. Then she knew she was ready to write. Settle experimented with time by employing the flash-forward technique in *Scapegoat* and *The Killing Ground.* The most difficult part of the Beulah Quintet, she says, was sustaining the patterns and details of characters and their families over a period of many generations.

The partially autobiographical *The Clam Shell* (1971), which examines college class hostility; *Charley Bland* (1989), which tells the story of a woman, widowed and in her thirties, who returns home to West Virginia and falls in love with the town rogue; and Settle's more recent *Choices: A Novel,* which tells of coal wars and civil rights, all share some names, characters, places, and themes with the Beulah Quintet. Settle says the apparent joy in *Celebration* (1986), her next novel after the Beulah Quintet, reflects her joy at having finished the Beulah Quintet. *Celebration* tells the story of expatriates in London building a community and learning to live responsibly without cynicism.

Settle writes about new lands, like the American frontier, and old worlds, like Turkey. Both the Beulah Quintet and her books set in Turkey, *Blood Tie* and *Turkish Reflections: A Biography of a Place* (1991), deal with individuals seeking their identity. Settle first went to Turkey in 1972 and stayed three years. *Blood Tie,* dealing with expatriates in Turkey, was the result. She went back in 1989 to know all of Turkey, not just the coast, and *Turkish Reflections,* part travelogue and part history, was the result.

Settle has said a writer should end her career, not start it, with autobiography: "So many young writers start out by writing thinly disguised autobiography. I think you should end up with it, not begin with it. A writer should start out by discovering what he *doesn't* know rather than depend so heavily on what he does—that's too easy" (1980). Settle has written autobiography intermittently throughout her career. *All the Brave Promises: Memories of Aircraft Woman 2nd Class 2146391* (1966) recounts, some twenty years later, Settle's experience in England in the Women's Auxiliary Air Force during World War II, and the partly autobiographical *The Clam Shell* (1971) was written some thirty-five years after her time at Sweet Briar College. Settle has said her own autobiography can be found in the character of Johnny Church in *Prisons.* Her more recent *Addie: A Memoir* (1998) is Settle's biography of her grandmother Addie.

Besides her novels, Settle has frequently contributed short stories and articles to *Harper's, Paris Review, Argosy,* and other publications. Her children's books include *Story of Flight* (1967), *The Scopes Trial: The State of Tennessee v. John Thomas Scopes* (1972), and *Water World* (1984). Settle has also encouraged other writers by establishing the PEN/Faulkner Award in 1980 at the branch headquarters of PEN-South at the University of Virginia in Charlottesville, where Faulkner was once writer-in-residence. This annual $15,000 award to help new southern writers goes to the writer of the most distinguished work of fiction. The breadth and depth of Settle's career establishes her as a major southern writer. As critic George Garrett claims in his *Understanding Mary Lee Settle* (1978), Settle "may well be remembered as the 20th-century American novelist who most splendidly recorded the passion and ideals of our history."

Elizabeth Spencer

Peggy Whitman Prenshaw

In her life and in her fiction Elizabeth Spencer mirrors much of the twenti-eth-century transformation of the American South from agrarian, small town enclaves to urban, cosmopolitan aggregations of people on the move. Her early work was set in her native Mississippi, portraying characters closely attached to family and place and depicting situations that grew from land disputes, clan loyalties, and family honor. A crucial turning point seemed to come for Spencer with her third novel, *The Voice at the Back Door* (1956), in which she dealt explicitly with the complex intermingling of racial injustice and local political power in a fictional Mississippi county, one that resembled her home in north central Mississippi. After the publica-tion of that novel, her life and imaginative vision turned expansively out-ward, to Europe, and then to Canada, where she resided for many years with her English husband John Rusher, and eventually to Chapel Hill, North Carolina, a southern town, to be sure, but one hardly comparable to the Carrollton, Mississippi, of her birth in 1921. In her later novels and short fiction, Spencer has created a vivid array of twentieth-century figures, many of whom live scattered, fragmented, rootless lives, but who nonethe-less seek spiritual and societal moorings.

Elizabeth Spencer grew up in a time and place where family connections largely defined one's identity and future prospects. Her mother's extended family furnished her with a model of readers who enjoyed talking about books and writers they admired. They also gave her a connection with the land in the family plantation, Teoc, located at the border of the hill country and the Delta. Both of Spencer's staunch Presbyterian parents valued education highly and encouraged her to excel in school and attend college. She graduated in 1942 with a degree in English from Belhaven College in Jackson, Mississippi, and completed a master's degree at Vanderbilt University the following year. She worked for a time as a reporter for the Nashville *Tennessean* but quit the job in order to complete *Fire in the Morning* (1948), a novel set in the Mississippi hill country that she knew well. The protagonist Kinloch Armstrong moves through a dense web of family ties, ethical intentions gone awry, and old animosities involving a shameless clan of land grabbers and liars. The moral progress and self-discovery of the hero are somewhat reminiscent of nineteenth-century fiction, but as a stylist, Spencer, who was an avid reader of Faulkner, Warren, and other modern writers, incorporates many of the techniques of modern fiction in this and subsequent work.

In *This Crooked Way* (1952) Spencer employs both omniscient and first-person multiple narrators to portray the memorable Amos Dudley, a God-obsessed American Adam whose drive for material success and status almost brings him down, blighting the family and friends who surround him. The novel, which in the conclusion turns unexpectedly toward comedy, explores not only the ethical themes implicit in such a drive for power but, interestingly, the psychological consequences for a power seeker who has been reared in a tradition of religious mysticism and judgmentalism.

In *The Voice at the Back Door* Spencer continues her concerns with ethical conflicts played out against family complications and community expectations. As mentioned, the novel's exploration of injustice focuses upon race, but it also probes sexual hypocrisies, familial betrayals, political lies, and above all, the ethical difficulty of assessing and acting upon wrongs that are inextricably bound up with virtues. Duncan Harper, the town sheriff, emerges as one of Spencer's most affecting characters, and the novel, an extraordinarily astute portrait of southern county politics in the first half of the twentieth century, warrants contemporary rereadings and historicist attention.

Spencer completed her third novel while living in Italy, assisted by a Guggenheim Fellowship. As she has noted in commentary about the book, she began the novel with the hopeful view that, after World War II, the South might move progressively toward a more racially just society. But, seeing the region's reaction to the *Brown v. Board of Education* decision, she felt the prospects for such change disappearing, even as she was composing the novel. Married in 1956, she moved to Montreal in 1958 and began to publish fiction about Americans abroad. Her novella *The Light in the Piazza* (1960), perhaps her best-known work, winner of the McGraw-Hill Fiction Award (and made into a Metro-Goldwyn-Mayer film), portrays a situation reminiscent of Henry James, but with a decided difference. During a visit to Italy, a beautiful American girl meets and weds an Italian suitor, aided by the promotion of her mother and the connivance of the young man's father. The bride, victim of brain damage from a childhood accident, has the mental ability—and vivacity—of a ten year old, but her incapacity ironically poses little problem for her marital prospect—that is, her role as an obedient wife and protected mother in a traditional Italian marriage. Spencer's compression of plot and lucid prose style uniquely mark this work, which includes not only interesting feminist ironies but complex ethical conundrums that haunt the simplicity of the surface story.

A subsequent novel, *Knights and Dragons* (1965), continues Spencer's exploration of female protagonists and settings outside the South. Martha Ingram, beset by conflicts with a demonic former husband and fearful inner compulsions, gives evidence of Spencer's interest in connections between psychic vitality and a willingness to acknowledge and confront mysterious, threatening undertows in oneself and others. In this work and in the following long novel, *No Place for an Angel* (1967), Spencer creates characters who push toward the edge of convention and personal security, even sanity. For Catherine Sasser, a southern exile, the world presses the individual with unrelenting evils that are played out in family and marital betrayals and dishonor, feckless friendships, and world affairs constantly threatening doom. Set in Europe and the United States in the 1950s and 1960s, the plot follows a group of restless characters whose spiritual emptiness lies heavy upon them, though Catherine does discover something of a haven at the end of her journey. In both novels Spencer employs shifting chronological sequences and heightened, even hallucinatory interior perspectives to depict characters' psychic stress and suffering.

In many ways the 1970 novel *The Snare* stands as a culmination of Spencer's effort to plumb the ambiguities of evil. At its center is Julia Garrett, a well-to-do, respectable young woman who is seduced and then mesmerized by a handsome musician connected with New Orleans underworld characters trafficking in drugs. Spencer explores Julia's fascination with "the human swamp" as a component of her vitality and intelligence, her sexuality, and her determination to live her life beyond the bounds of genteel respectability. Arguably Spencer's most powerful work, *The Snare* incorporates characters and themes portrayed in many guises and perspectives in earlier work—a vivid setting (in this instance, New Orleans) richly tied by nuance and suggestive symbol to personal relationships, characters who variously represent the occupations and psychic preoccupations of contemporary Americans, and complex themes that grow from the country's multiethnic mix of people and from the tensions arising from a traditional society giving way to a modernist and exploitative commercialism.

Two later novels, *The Salt Line* (1984) and *The Night Travellers* (1991), portray the individual and societal traumas left in the wake of the cultural transformations of the 1960s. Spencer employs the setting of the Mississippi Gulf Coast after the devastating 1969 Hurricane Camille and a protagonist seeking refuge from the university upheavals of the decade to explore the destructive and yet cathartic effects of dramatic change. In *The Night Travellers,* which moves from North Carolina to Canada and elsewhere, Spencer portrays even more threatened and threatening characters whose lives are interwoven with the secrecy and lies of the Vietnam era. Mary Kerr Harbison, suggestive of Julia Garrett and Catherine Sasser, contends with unstable and destabilizing figures on all sides, but she is inextricably tied to them by relationships of kin, intimacy, acquaintance, and her own impulses of attraction to and need for human connection, even in malignant circumstances. In both works Spencer offers an astute understanding of contemporary American social history and its effects upon individual men and women.

Spencer's notable achievement in the novel is matched by her publication of nearly fifty short stories, most of which are to be found in *The Stories of Elizabeth Spencer* (1981) and *Jack of Diamonds and Other Stories* (1988). Her characters, themes, and narrative techniques give evidence of an extraordinary range and skill. Fiction like "The Girl Who Loved Horses," "I, Maureen," the Marilee stories, "A Business Venture" and "The Cousins" make major—and lasting—contributions to American literature. And in her most recent book, the memoir *Landscapes of the Heart* (1998), Spencer's candor and gift for telling detail—expressive, memorable anecdote and dialogue and descriptive phrase—as well as her drive to understand herself within her time and place, have contributed significantly to the growing genre of contemporary autobiography. Indeed, in a writing career stretching over a half century, Elizabeth Spencer has produced an estimable body of work few contemporaries have matched.

Ellen Douglas

Mary Louise Weaks

"If you're the kind of child I was—," Ellen Douglas once said in an interview, "the kind who sits behind the sofa and eavesdrops on the grown people and then turns out to be a writer—you've absorbed a great deal of complex material that comes out of family life, out of people's conflicts with each other and their loves and hates." That "great deal of complex material" became the core of Douglas' literary achievement: six novels, two collections of short fiction, and a memoir. Although she prefers not to refer to herself with labels such as "southern writer" or "woman writer," Douglas' work has been greatly influenced by the southernness and the femaleness of her extended family. In an interview published in the *Mississippi Quarterly,* she describes the South of her childhood as "still isolated by poverty and still feeling the effects of the end of the Civil War and of Reconstruction, and not really having a very large slice of the American cake." Growing up in a South that defined women's roles as wife, homemaker, and mother, Douglas, looking back now, seems thankful for the role models who gave her the courage to move beyond such engrained traditions. Her mother, Douglas says, was pleased that her father was willing to move away from their hometown of Natchez, Mississippi, because it was "a world in which women's roles were defined in a way that didn't suit her." Her mother "wanted to get away from that post–Civil War world." Two of her aunts also offered models of women not confined to traditional roles; they were not southern belles, but poor women who had to support themselves and did so successfully. Widowed early, her grandmothers both "defined their households" and made them "whatever they wanted them to be."

Partially out of concern for these women, and also to acknowledge one grandmother's influence on her writing career, Douglas for many years went solely by her pen name, although more recently she has become almost as well known by the name Josephine Haxton. Named Josephine Ayres at birth, Douglas has given several reasons for renaming herself "Ellen Douglas." "Maybe I wanted to separate my private life and my family from my public life. Maybe I was shy," she said in an interview with Sylvia Campbell. She has also noted more specifically that because her first published novel, *A Family's Affairs* (1962), made particular use of material from her own family, two of her aunts asked her to write under a pseudonym to preserve their privacy and the privacy of the family. Douglas has said that she chose the name Ellen—her grandmother's name—because her grandmother wrote stories, stories in which her own children and grandchildren were the heroines. Douglas saw that writing could be something she also could do.

Born in Natchez, Mississippi, on July 12, 1921, Josephine, with her parents and three siblings, also lived in Hope, Arkansas, and Alexandria, Louisiana, while she was growing up. The family returned each summer to Natchez to visit the relatives, whom Douglas describes as "old Mississippi." She began her undergraduate education with two years at Randolph-Macon Woman's College in Virginia and then finished her degree at the University of Mississippi in 1942 with majors in English and sociology.

While Douglas was studying at Ole Miss, she met Kenneth Haxton, whom she married in 1944. In 1945, the couple moved to Greenville, Mississippi, where Kenneth Haxton worked in his family's clothing business and she raised their family of three sons. Douglas also explained in the *Mississippi Quarterly* interview that she was particularly mindful in choosing a husband, noting that she was "consciously aware of how dangerous it would be to marry a man who wanted me to fulfill his idea of the role of a Southern woman." She was also "very careful to marry a man who was interested in the arts and intellectual matters and bought books and listened to music. I wanted that just as much as I wanted children." The Haxtons' marriage, however, ultimately ended in divorce in 1983, and Douglas left Greenville to move to Jackson, Mississippi.

As a writer, Douglas started late in life. Although as a child she had such aspirations, she did not take up writing seriously until she was in her mid-thirties, and she was forty when her first book was published. Settling into life as a homemaker and mother after her marriage, she was able to devote time to her work only after her youngest son went to nursery school. Douglas says that her writing apprenticeship was probably the time she spent typing and revising a novel her husband was writing, "And then," she says, "I got so interested in it that I started doing it myself."

Her first novel, *A Family's Affairs,* which took six years to write, has been noted by scholars as highly autobiographical. A collection of stories that Douglas worked together into novel form, *A Family's Affairs* revolves around a Mississippi grandmother, Kate Anderson, and her children and grandchildren. Douglas herself is probably represented in the character of Anna McGovern, one of the granddaughters. The novel encompasses a family's bonds, as characters move in and out of the family circle and meddle in each other's problems but always return to the old truths of the hymn "Blest Be the Tie that Binds."

The publication history of *A Family's Affairs* perhaps suggests Douglas' desire to protect her own family ties. Unbeknown to Douglas, a friend of hers had passed along a copy of her manuscript to an editor at Houghton Mifflin. When the editor called Douglas asking her to submit the manuscript to a Houghton Mifflin competition, Douglas at first declined, saying that she did not believe the book was polished enough for publication. The editor explained to her that if she agreed to enter the manuscript in the competition, then he would be able to tell her that she had already won the prize. Douglas did, and the book won the Houghton Mifflin Fellowship for 1961.

While Douglas' first novel and her second book, *Black Cloud, White Cloud: Two Novellas and Two Stories* (1963), both include autobiographical elements, *Black Cloud, White Cloud* deals more specifically with racial issues. As Douglas says in her afterword to the 1989 edition of this short-fiction collection, the book focuses on "the moral dilemmas posed for the child and young woman [Anna] living among black people in the South." The book, as Carol Manning has written in an essay included in *Contemporary Fiction Writers of the South* (1993), also deals with responsibility, another frequent topic of Douglas' work. "How could I," Douglas asks in the afterword, "living in this time and place, fail to write about these lives— about the corrosive hatreds, the crippled loves, the confusions, the flashes of nobility and heroism, the ways of making do, making room?" Both *A Family's Affairs* and *Black Cloud, White Cloud* were named best works of fiction for the years of their publication.

In her next three works of fiction—her novels *Where the Dreams Cross* (1968), *Apostles of Light* (1973), and *The Rock Cried Out* (1979)— Douglas moves away from the autobiographical elements of her first two books. With *The Rock Cried Out,* she once again takes up the issue of race, which is a prominent interest in her writings, but she focuses on the civil rights movement of the 1960s and early 1970s and white guilt over inaction during the movement. *Apostles of Light* examines the treatment of the elderly in nursing homes and thus takes up characters who have been of increasing interest to Douglas, the elderly and the middle-aged. These three novels garnered Douglas more awards, including two nominations for the National Book Award and a grant from the National Endowment for the Arts.

A Lifetime Burning (1982), Douglas' fifth novel, is structured in the form of a diary rather than as a traditional narrative. Told from the point of view of a sixty-two-year-old English professor named Corinne, the book is about Corinne's own attempts to deal with the truths and pain of her own past, including her discovery of her husband's affair with another woman. Although she says that she writes her diary for her grown children, she in fact seems to have a greater need for the diary as a tool for self-examination and dealing with her own emotions. Nevertheless, because the book deals with an individual's inner reflections and human frailties, readers are left wondering about the real "truth" of Corinne's story. Jonathan Yardley perhaps best summed up the book in a review for the *Washington Post Book World* when he wrote that "Lies, distortions, deceptions, evasions—these are essential to the maintenance of the delicate fabric of which family and society are made."

Douglas' most recent novel, *Can't Quit You, Baby* (1988), which is set in Mississippi during the 1960s, portrays the friendship of a black woman named Julia and the white woman who employs her, Cornelia. The narrator of the novel tells the stories of Cornelia's past, while Julia, who is much more forthcoming in their conversations, tells her own story in her own words. It is, in fact, what confines these women in southern society to their races and genders that actually brings them together: the domestic world, and specifically, the kitchen. Their friendship grows because Julia has been hired to cook for Cornelia and Cornelia has a love for cooking, but that friendship is continually marred by the abstract parameters of southern racial inequalities. Cornelia, for example, cannot bear to cross the line of familiarity by calling Julia by her nickname, "Tweet." Nevertheless, their friendship grows. Linda Tate explains in *A Southern Weave of Women: Fiction of the Contemporary South* (1994) that "Douglas's novel marks an important step in the developing relationship between black and white communities in the South. . . . Douglas suggests that with determination and love, black and white women can shape new patterns of relating to one another if they wish."

Because of Douglas' skill and brilliance as a writer, she has held several prominent teaching posts and has been awarded a number of prizes for her work. Douglas has taught at various schools including the University of Mississippi, Northeast Louisiana University, the University of Virginia, Hollins College, and Millsaps College, where she held the Eudora Welty Chair of Southern Studies. She has also served on the faculty of the Sewanee Writers' Conference. Awards for her work include the Hillsdale Award for Fiction from the Fellowship of Southern Writers and two awards from the Mississippi Institute of Arts and Letters. Her work has also been the focus of a special issue of the *Southern Quarterly*.

Douglas' most recent book, *Truth: Four Stories I Am Finally Old Enough to Tell* (1998), is based on stories from her own family's past and, as Douglas says, is about "remembering and forgetting, seeing and ignoring, lying and truthtelling. . . . It's about truth in fiction and the fiction in truth." After she finished a draft of the first story in the book, entitled "Grant," she says that she read Winthrop Jordan's *Tumult and Silence at Second Creek* (1993). The book recounts the story of an 1861 slave uprising in Adams County, Mississippi, which Douglas calls "a terrible event—a horrible event." Reading the book, Douglas explained in an interview with *Fore-Word Online*, started her thinking that perhaps "Grant" was about a similar theme: "[I]t was about things that are suppressed and forgotten, only on a society-wide scale instead of just on a personal scale. And I began to think I might have a book." The result was *Truth*.

Perhaps Douglas' most telling statement about the book is her comment that *Truth* is "not exactly a memoir. It's not really about me. It's about the world that I've lived in." In her work in its entirety, through her explorations of southern culture and particularly the strong women that shaped it, Douglas reflects upon the trials and tribulations of women and men, blacks and whites—humanity as a whole.

Maya Angelou

Wallis Tinnie

Maya Angelou, internationally recognized author, poet, actress, singer, dancer, stage and screen director and producer, scriptwriter, playwright, historian, civil rights activist, and humanities lecturer, is one of America's best-known and most beloved public figures. Much of the popularity of her work lies in her emphasis on the dignity, beauty, and potential of every individual human being. Drawing inspiration from her own adventurous life, from her deeply felt southern roots, African and African American heritage, and extensive readings and travels, Angelou has emerged as a quintessential voice of America and of the human spirit. Angelou's literary oeuvre is most recognized for the series of autobiographical works depicting, with disarming honesty, the trials and triumphs of her early life, adolescence, and maturity. As if in a rhythmic counterpoint to these narratives, Angelou has published several collections of poetry, essays, and children's stories.

Born Marguerite, daughter of Bailey Johnson and Vivian (Baxter) Johnson in St. Louis, Missouri, in 1928, Angelou would grow up in humble but profoundly nurturing circumstances in the rural town of Stamps, Arkansas. There, as a sensitive and observant child, Angelou would experience first-hand not only the resilience and strength of the African American community, but also America's troubled legacy of racism, intolerance, and violence. Angelou's literary South, rooted in the vernacular of the small community of Stamps, can be traced to her upbringing in the Johnson family's general store, where young Maya was privy to stories and tales told by her grand-mother Annie Henderson's quilting circle. She also learned of the gothic horror of the menacing racial climate and the fragility of her family's free-dom, especially through the experiences of her crippled Uncle Willie. Ange-lou's southern roots can be traced also to her family's devout membership in the Christian Methodist Episcopal Church, which Angelou attended "Sunday, all day, and every evening of the week" for ten years. Angelou's romance with words points back to the tutoring by a family friend who en-couraged Angelou's love of reading and performance. From the church and the store, emblems of the sacred and the commercial, emerge the sermons, spirituals, gospel, folktales, tall tales, cultural and historical narratives, and the rhythms of the South. These experiences are recounted with a decep-tively easy eloquence in Angelou's best-known work, *I Know Why the Caged Bird Sings* (1970), which takes its title from the poignant words of the poem "Sympathy" by the acclaimed African American poet Paul Lau-rence Dunbar.

Caged Bird would become the first in an autobiographical series in which many challenges of life are seen through the lens of Angelou's full gamut of experiences and structured in a storytelling style that has won her interna-tional acclaim. This celebrated text records the three-year-old Maya's ar-rival in Stamps, Arkansas, accompanied by her four-year-old brother, Bailey Johnson, Jr. The children have been sent alone from Long Beach, California, following their parents' divorce, to live with their paternal grandmother, Annie Henderson, already caretaker of her own crippled son, whom the children call "Uncle Willie." Young Maya, whose name is derived from her brother's affectionate epithet for her, "Mya sister," and Bailey spend the next five years of their lives learning the rituals of communal living along-side the dark pantomimes of racial hysteria informing the lives of blacks living in this Deep South community where "the impudent child was de-tested by God," where neighbors were "obliged by custom to stop and speak to every person," and where "World War II was well along before there was a noticeable change in the [Depression] economy." It is a commu-nity in which Annie Henderson, who has been a black entrepreneur for twenty-five years when Maya and Bailey arrive, is both respected and envied in the social system divided hierarchically by custom and law: whites on top and blacks on the bottom, just beneath the "po' white trash." For young Maya, Grandmother Henderson's store, which doubles as a community gathering spot for the town's black citizens and is officially called "Wm. Johnson General Merchandise Store," is a magical place. After five years, the tough love Maya receives in Stamps is replaced by the warmly detached love of her mother, uncles, and grandparents in St. Louis. It is here that the eight-year-old Maya undergoes the trauma of rape. The outcome of this abuse is a return to Stamps and a retreat by the young victim to a world of silence that lasts for almost five years. With the nurturing provided by a family friend in Stamps, Maya learns to love books and to speak again. After she graduates from Lafayette County Training School, thirteen-year-old Maya and brother Bailey are taken to California, where they begin their lives with their mother, Vivian Baxter Jackson, and stepfather, Daddy Clidell Jackson. Maya discovers her independence through a series of both planned and unplanned events: she finds herself in a school where she is one of only four black students; she is accepted in a school where she enrolls in dance and drama; she is forced to drive a car fifty miles down a rough Mexican mountain; she lives on the streets of Southern California for one month and learns to appreciate the diversity that characterizes America; finally, she becomes pregnant and gives birth to her only child, Guy Johnson.

In addition to the powerful literary achievement realized in *I Know Why the Caged Bird Sings*, Angelou has published four additional volumes of her life story in which, Sondra O'Neale in *Black Women Writers (1950–1980): A Critical Evaluation* (1983) claims, "No Black women . . . are losers": *Gather Together in My Name* (1974); *Singin' and Swingin' and Gettin' Merry like Christmas* (1976); *The Heart of a Woman* (1981); and *All God's Children Need Traveling Shoes* (1986). Evaluated against a long tradition of slave narratives and modern "success" stories, these autobiographies represent what has been called the cornerstone of African American literary traditions. However, Angelou's literary universe encompasses an even larger canvas and speaks to a broader vision. The story of author James Baldwin's urging her to accept a publisher's challenge to write a literary autobiography has become part of the Angelou folklore. It was a dare she says she could not refuse. Its success, five literary volumes later, is still to be fully acknowledged and documented. Angelou's incredible contributions to the genre, as she probes the broad deep canon of Western literature and American vernacular culture to render her life as art, clearly reveal her not only as a powerful writer who loves a mental challenge, but also as one who uses the opportunity to critique the genre and provide a gifted contribution, employing her genius to weave the primordial purity of black sacred music in a finely crafted carnival discursivity in which, as one critic comments, her "prose sings."

While *Caged Bird* has received a fair amount of critical acclaim, praised both for its carnivalesque stylistics and its presentation of the self as representative of collective black wisdom and struggles, the entire autobiographical series has not been as fortunate. The second work in the series, *Gather Together in My Name,* finds Angelou as the young mother with infant Guy living at home where she is weighing her options, subsequently choosing a rather shaky independence. Angelou presents the world through the consciousness of this young girl going through the excesses and lack of centeredness that characterize youth. Understandably, *Gather Together* has been regarded as without a moral center. However, Dolly McPherson, in *Order Out of Chaos: The Autobiographical Works of Maya Angelou* (1990), observes that, in *Gather Together,* Angelou "explores . . . the state of the relation between the romantic imagination—innocence—and the objective reality to which it ultimately must be reconciled." Surely this is the intention of the autobiographer who has made a deliberate attempt to speak in the narrative voice of a teenager being initiated into adulthood: Angelou encounters her "first love," her first experiences with smoking marijuana, her humiliating return to Stamps and her classmates' scorn and derision, her beginnings in the performing arts and her bungling and naïve attempts as madam, prostitute, and fencer. The adolescent Maya finally understands that there is only the knowledge of the ceremony of innocence and the possibility of beginning anew again and again and again. A somewhat wiser Maya concludes: "I had no idea what I was going to make of my life, but I had . . . found my innocence."

As a chronicle of youthful Maya's growth from adolescence to adulthood, *Gather Together* announces its redemptive strategy within the story's title. The safety net always within reach for the young heroine is Jesus' promise in the book of Matthew that "where two or three are gathered together in my name, there am I in the midst of them." Yet, the chaos of World War II, forgotten in the aftermath described in the opening scene of the book, in many ways parallels the chaos felt by young Maya in the church scene in *I Know Why the Caged Bird Sings.* In both instances, there is no one on whom to blame the chaos: in *Gather Together,* the war happened; in *I Know Why the Caged Bird Sings,* white supremacy, a legacy of the Civil War, happened. And like the forgotten devastation of war in its festival aftermath in San Francisco, white supremacy in Stamps has its gothic horrors: little powhitetrash girls who turn up their bare behinds to their elders; young black boys forced to witness and participate in the discovery and retrieval of a now-bloated black murder victim; a licensed dentist who refuses to practice medicine on a small child; a law enforcement officer whose idea of justice is to have a crippled, seriously disabled man spend several hours in a wooden box hiding under the weight of white potatoes to evade the rampaging insanity of white men covered in white sheets, terrorizing and murdering for often invisible wrongs. These are the gothic elements that pervade Angelou's special little plot of southern soil in Stamps.

The third book of the autobiographical series, *Singin' and Swingin' and Gettin' Merry like Christmas,* spans the years 1949 to 1955 and begins the unraveling of suppressed, unremembered beauty and pain in a forgotten African American discourse. As a cachet of the Angelou of world renown, the title itself serves as a paean to the triumph of both spirit and talent that it conveys. Angelou is finally hired to do that for which she was anointed— perform for people. She is discovered dancing in a strip club where she is not required to strip. The luminous quality of her dancing, however, creates a following and the reward of her first big break, the opportunity to perform at San Francisco's famous Purple Onion. With this, Angelou's life takes on the quality of sacred oracular rhythms. Marguerite Johnson Angelos becomes Maya Angelou, accepts the friendship of white supporters and black opera singers, and is later invited to tour Canada, Europe, and Africa as a member of the cast of the internationally acclaimed opera *Porgy and Bess.* Still, the miracle of success in the world of show business is mitigated by Angelou's ongoing challenge to reconcile her career and a need for income with her role as mother to Guy Johnson.

Illusive transcendence defines the struggles of Angelou's fourth autobiography, *The Heart of a Woman* (1981). The text offers pivotal scenes between mother and son and details Angelou's moves from a California suburb to New York's Harlem Writers Guild; from the theatrical revue, *Cabaret to Freedom,* a successful benefit for the civil rights struggle produced with Godfrey Cambridge in New York's Village Gate, to her position as Dr. Martin Luther King, Jr.'s, northern coordinator of the Southern Christian Leadership Conference; and then from a powerful New York run of Genet's *The Blacks* to a brief period of domesticity in Cairo, Egypt, as wife of South African freedom fighter Vusumzi Make. The imagery suggested by the volume's title, taken from a poem by Georgia Douglas Johnson, a black poet of the Harlem Renaissance, points to an anguished heart in an "alien cage" with "sheltering bars," words clearly exposing a spiritual plight similar to that expressed in *Caged Bird.* As the text concludes, the reader finds Angelou living in a small cottage in Ghana, West Africa, having just spent three months in the agony of Guy's recuperation from a serious neck injury, and now sending Guy off to enter his first year of study at the University of Ghana. This Ghanaian tableau is clearly, notwithstanding the lonely aching suggested by the eponymous poem of the book's title, a scene of hope and completion.

Angelou's fifth and last-published autobiographical volume, *All God's*

Children Need Traveling Shoes (1986), covers Angelou's three-year stay in the newly liberated Republic of Ghana, which had been, originally, a stopover during which a critical injury to Guy turned into a healing lovefest for both Angelou and her son. Both are welcomed by the University of Ghana, she as an administrative assistant; he as a student. These critical years include the death of W. E. B. Du Bois, a visit by Malcolm X, and a confrontation with the reality that although the very soul of African American (and American?) vernacular culture is African, Africans and their descendants in the United States are treated in Ghana as Americans, foreigners. Still, Angelou is able to offer the reader valuable insights into Africa. The communal esteem for children is evidenced when a local family travels by lorry from deep inland to honor Angelou and her housemates for tutoring their son in the Brioni (white man's) education. The elders, after presenting the household a bountiful harvest, an indication of familial wealth, inform Angelou: "Kojo did not come from the ground like grass. He has risen like a banyan tree. He has roots. And we, his roots, thank you."

These deeply anchored roots suggest the one gift Angelou craves from Mother Africa: understanding of the nearly five hundred years of spiritual exile in America. The answer comes toward the end of her journey when she must face Africa's memory of the injury, ruin, and pain of the slave trade legacies. She finds herself the emblem of an unspeakable loss when the people in the small village of Keta, near Accra, descendants of children orphaned by slave hunters, recognize her, they think, as the daughter "descended from those stolen mothers and fathers." It is a moment of both extreme sadness and great ecstasy for Angelou who is now ready to go home secure in the knowledge that her link to Africa is the gift of life, the opportunity to begin again on "brand new streets," with a strong ancestral memory. It is that story that Angelou would tell over and over in her public performances. Repeatedly, she reminds her audiences that African Americans are still quite African: "We [have] sung it in our blues, shouted it in our gospel and danced the continent in our breakdowns. . . . [I]t was Africa which rode in the bulges of our high calves, shook in our protruding behinds and crackled in our wide open laughter." Upon her return to America, Angelou would recount her epiphany at Keta as she would share her extensive knowledge in the classroom, in documentaries for television, on the lecture circuit, and in her writings.

Angelou's poetry, especially, documents this journey of transcendence. Each of Angelou's five major volumes of poetry acts as a rhythmic bridge between each autobiography; the luminous quality of the word play—of southern tall tales and "funky" blues, of Old World cadences and urban rap—segues to the next installment. In each volume, Angelou appropriates a deceptively guileless rhetoric to mask the syncopated rhythms of Europe, the American South, and Africa, stylistics germinating during quiet years of hearing and reading and internalizing the singsong melodies of Victorian couplets, the iambic pentameter of Shakespeare's sonnets, the biblical cadences and blues lyrics of African American poetry, the agony and transcendence of spirituals and gospel, and the coded, hieroglyphic messages of communal black southern language. Angelou's literary genius is firmly rooted in her southern heritage and crisscrosses several genres as she champions peace, redemption, and the sanctity of each human being. Angelou's first volume of poems, *Just Give Me a Cool Drink of Water 'fore I Diiie* (1971), situated to link *Caged Bird* and *Gather Together,* was nominated for a Pulitzer Prize. Subsequent volumes appear at appropriate intervals: *Oh Pray My Wings Are Gonna Fit Me Well* (1975), *And Still I Rise* (1978), *Shaker, Why Don't You Sing?* (1983), and *I Shall Not Be Moved* (1990). A Random House edition containing a complete set of all five books was issued in 1994.

Through a mesmerizing public persona, Angelou has become the people's poet and world cultural griot (keeper of the story to be passed on) at the birth of the new millennium, a position that allows her to appropriate oracular sustenance from a bottomless cultural well. For in addition to a sterling reputation for *Caged Bird,* Angelou has achieved international prominence through the riveting, genuinely moving television delivery of three separate poems during the last decade of the 1900s: "On the Pulse of Morning," created especially for the January 1993 inauguration of fellow Arkansan William Jefferson Clinton as United States President; "A Brave and Startling Truth," composed for the fiftieth anniversary celebration of the United Nations in San Francisco in June 1995; and "Paeans," heard by millions the world over and rendered only moments before the year 2000 dawned in the eastern United States. The inaugural poem, for example, in which the poet personifies the natural emblems of a rock, a tree, and a river, is framed by references to black sacred music. Angelou uses three familiar hymns to solidify her message: "No Hiding Place Down Here," "I Shall Not Be Moved," and "I Will Study War No More." This sacred music of black Americans, which served both spiritual and political ends in the antebellum South, becomes a source of transcendence as the poet intones the sacred lines. Angelou converts this music into a wellspring from which all people can drink and be fulfilled. This is what the cultural griot/shaman does; she turns the violence and mayhem into healing medicine through the power of natural rhythms and word magic.

In 1970, Angelou was writer-in-residence at the University of Kansas and distinguished fellow at Yale University. Before her 1975 appointment as a Rockefeller Foundation scholar in Italy, Angelou was distinguished professor at Wichita State University, California State University in Sacramento, and Wake Forest University. Holding a lifetime appointment as the first Reynolds Professor of American Studies at Wake Forest University, Angelou has honorary degrees from several colleges and is fluent in several languages including West African Fanti, Spanish, French, and Italian. This academic emphasis does not diminish the humor and compassion for which Angelou is known. Her essays *Wouldn't Take Nothing for My Journey Now* (1993) and *Even the Stars Look Lonesome* (1997) offer refreshing, often very playful, insights into aging, fame, humility. Moreover, Angelou has created several volumes just for children. These are always illustrated by recognized artists, such as *Kofi and His Magic* (1996) with photos by Margaret Courtney-Clarke and *Life Doesn't Frighten Me* (1993) with illustrations by Sara Boyers and Jean-Michel Basquiat.

Maya Angelou emerges in her mature years not only with a solid reputation in poetry, prose, and a host of other expressive forms, but as a national matriarch who speaks to the world with a depth of wisdom that could only have been forged in the crucible of the American South. This renaissance woman, whose remarkable life of traumas and triumphs has made her the very emblem of America's tortuous conflict with its own soul, brings forth in the easy, sometimes oblique and artful indirection of incisive southern discourse, typified by William Faulkner, Mark Twain, and most notably Zora Neale Hurston, a maternal voice that quells fear and celebrates every human being's legacy of high achievements. Angelou transcends the binary divisions and oppositions that have become so characteristic of Western ideology: white/black, male/female, north/south, good/bad, us/them. For Angelou, everyone is "we," and the only question worth pondering is what "we" make of our gift of shared life. This vision will surely frame the forthcoming, and final, volume of autobiography she has promised. It is this vision in the new millennium that will finally allow critics to appreciate fully the true place of this southern genius in the shaping of literary creativity.

Shirley Ann Grau

Linda Wagner-Martin

Shirley Ann Grau (b. 1929) continues to publish fiction that stretches the parameters of conventional southern writing as it was conceptualized during the 1960s and the 1970s. Her most recent novel, *Roadwalkers* (1994), narrates the story of two black women who had, as children, been abandoned during the Depression. Treated like "frog spawn" and "dropped off . . . like extra unwanted baggage," the girls had little choice but to survive the hostility of the rural South of which they were a part. The slighter of the two, Baby, is the hero, even though she is so small "she could wriggle through the least crack in a fence or window." In Grau's impressionistic format, the stories of the two—stoically recounted in part by Nanda Woods, Baby's only child, who is now thirty-six—take on the aspects of heroic performance.

Grau's fiction has usually belied her thoroughly genteel and traditional background. In this her seventh novel, she once again creates a form germane to the narrative and its characters: fragmentary, elusive, and in some ways allusive, *Roadwalkers* draws on the memories of lonely childhood to vivify the stories of the two black women. In its use of apt organic structure, scenes appearing and fusing with others as if caught in the wash of memory, this novel is reminiscent of Grau's first, *The Hard Blue Sky* (1958), and her second, *The House on Coliseum Street* (1961). These two novels, published as she was turning thirty only a few years after her first collection of stories,

The Black Prince and Other Stories (1955), explore the psychological state of Annie, a woman searching for love, and of Joan, a woman facing abortion. Both books could well be described as women's fictions. Yet each of the two was considered something better than that phrase suggests; that is, they were seen as "serious" fiction, worth being reviewed. Realistic, almost existential, *The Hard Blue Sky* treats poor characters caught in bayou life. Plagued with remorseless deaths, the warring families of the novel accept loss of life as a given, and Annie's attempt to escape with Inky is her effort to leave behind the pattern of grief that marks the other characters' lives.

The House on Coliseum Street is even more blatantly a woman's story and, in its intricate structural arrangement, makes the reader deal with the unforgettable effects of abortion—both its contemplation and its aftermath—on the necessarily secretive Joan. As in *The Hard Blue Sky,* Grau here employs a bevy of modernist techniques. Perhaps her readers were so impressed with the way the story was told that they could accept the dissonance between Joan and her often-married mother as just another part of the younger woman's isolation. The narrative of the book itself keeps Joan isolated from everyone who might help, including the father of the foetus. While *The House on Coliseum Street* does not employ the cast of characters that prefaces *The Hard Blue Sky,* alerting the reader that the quasi-naturalistic book is a recorded, not a lived, fiction, it does disrupt the reader's expectations about time sequences and about what the author—or the fictional character—might reveal about the trauma of abortion.

Still, it was 1958 and 1961 when these novels were published, and no matter what the social circumstances of poverty, lack of education, and abortion were, writing about those matters in women's lives should have placed Grau in the political camp of such emergent women as Joyce Carol Oates, Marge Piercy, and Margaret Atwood a decade later. Perhaps the import of her first two novels' themes attracted less attention than did their milieu and general cast of characters; perhaps Grau was ahead of the tendency to devalue women's writing because of its ostensible politics. Just as the stories in *The Black Prince* had been praised as psychological explorations of the characters' states of mind and heart, so these novels came to be read as interesting character studies.

One of the reasons these early fictions could be separated from the identity of Shirley Ann Grau as author was her personal history. Possibly relieved that Grau was not jumping on the "confessional" bandwagon, reviewers tended to read her work strictly in terms of her southern origins. Born in New Orleans in 1929, Grau was reared between that city, her mother's choice of location, and Montgomery, Alabama, her father's preference.

Educated at the Booth School and Ursuline Academy, she received much training in languages. Aiming to attend Tulane University, she instead was accepted to Sophie Newcomb College, the appropriate place for women. While there, she grew to love the courses in its creative writing program and became one of its strong students. She graduated from Newcomb in 1950 with a B.A. degree. As John Husband, her teacher there, noted, Grau was not his most gifted writer, but she worked hard to become much more than proficient. Writing steadily to prove to her critical father that writing was a profession, Grau had by 1967 married and given birth to four children. Her life in a New Orleans suburb and, during the summers, on Martha's Vineyard, has never been structured to promote her writing—but she has managed to find ways to do the work she has come to love.

The impetus for that continuance was, in part, the fact that she received the Pulitzer Prize for fiction in 1965. Her prize-winning novel, *The Keepers of the House* (1964), brought together the earlier strands of Grau's technical brilliance and her theme of southern lives caught in the social matrix of history, convention, and religion. *The Keepers of the House* is Grau's most traditionally southern novel. Fascinated with the image of the house as a trope for the standing or the place of the southern family and its lineage, many writers of the South have shaped narratives around this image. From Edgar Allan Poe's "The Fall of the House of Usher" (1839) through William Faulkner's Sutpen's Hundred in *Absalom, Absalom!* (1936) to Richard Ford's suitably ironic plethora of houses in *Independence Day* (1995), the equation between character and house has become predictable in southern fiction. Grau's use of the trope is different, however, because she focuses on Abigail Howland, one of the "keepers" of this house, the person who— amid a confusion of ownership issues and racially complicated lineage— tries to maintain the values of the past rather than simply to extend the pride and privilege of white southern history. That Abigail must, at the novel's complicated ending, defeat her own relative in order to maintain those values is a part of Grau's contemporary scrutiny of her South.

Replete with "shadow" families, with contradictions between family beliefs and social roles, *The Keepers of the House* manages to tell a purposefully ornate southern story while doing so in a lyric mode more like Grau's stories than her novels. Again, it might be that reviewers were so interested in the way this narrative was being told that they overlooked some of its more dangerously political areas, for Grau is surely questioning the price of maintaining family history against human odds, the role women play within a stable patriarchy, the fate of generations of lies when confronted with honest people who demand answers. Grau is, in short, voicing the 1960s condemnation of hypocrisy. She is a part of that questioning voice. And yet she is an important southern novelist.

The Keepers of the House seems to fit into the tradition of southern narrative. Given in sections of discourse, it traces the patriarchal lines, the development of the house and lands; much of its bulk is so occupied, in fact. But the four-page preface, which is Abigail speaking after "history" has played itself out, embodies the ameliorating tone—life goes on, after Grau's sound and fury, after the demise of southern ideals, after women have taken over. Much of the novel's attention to ceremony and ritual, the pivotal scenes of housekeeping, is a means of reinforcing the significance of women's roles within southern history. Such attention is also typical of Grau's fiction, in which a great many key scenes are devoted to family interaction, meals, birthdays, holidays, and bedtimes. Most admirable is the way Grau orchestrates the narrative voices to provide both the quantity of information and the basic tone for the novel, and in this regard, her novel resembles Kaye Gibbons' 1998 novel, *On the Occasion of My Last Afternoon,* another tour de force of a woman's speaking voice.

Grau's next two novels, *The Condor Passes* (1971) and *Evidence of Love* (1977), also probe the theme of a decaying southern society, again using "the old gentleman" as a central character. Her success with the William Howland figure from *The Keepers of the House* and the patriarch in "One Summer," a major early story, led her to use the character of the rich, powerful, but aging white southern male as the focus for the narratives. In *The Condor Passes,* the antagonism of race holds center stage, and the imaginative equation of the black bird of the aging Mr. Oliver with his black valet, Stanley, is a pervasive trope. So too is the composition of the character of Oliver's son-in-law, the Cajun Robert Caillet: men's judgments are shown to be in error, as Caillet spins the evils that injure not only Oliver's wealth but also his daughter. *Evidence of Love* shares the theme of men searching for appropriate inheritors, defining those people as male and overlooking the women in their lineage who would have been more apt and more responsible caretakers.

Although Grau's later writings have received less attention than her earlier work, probably because the current southern renaissance has provided numerous books by southern women writers deserving of reviews and essays, it seems clear that her last two books continue the themes of these mentioned above. Her 1985 story collection, *Nine Women,* tells stories of women who could well be the inheritors of their families' history, wealth, and honor—or dishonor. Moving from this book to her 1994 novel, *Roadwalkers,* shows how steadfast Grau has become in her newly conceived project of telling women's stories. The elaborate envelope structures, the layering of men's narratives upon and within those of women, have been replaced with a much more straightforward telling: it is as if women's stories have legitimated their place in southern history and life. Perhaps readers can expect even more effective fiction from Shirley Ann Grau in the future.

Doris Betts

Mary Anne Heyward Ferguson

Doris Betts is a southerner by any definition. Born in North Carolina in 1932, she has spent her entire life there except for brief trips, most notably to the Grand Canyon beginning in 1971. Her three volumes of short stories and six novels are all set in the South; most of her characters are southern-ers, though some move away. She has devoted her life to promoting the welfare of her native state. As a journalist from the age of fourteen, she has been concerned about issues of education, work, and justice in North Carolina. Though she married in 1952 without finishing her undergraduate degree—but not before being elected to Phi Beta Kappa—Betts has had a phenome-nally successful academic career. She has taught at the University of North Carolina in Chapel Hill, first from 1966 to 1974 as a lecturer in the English department, teaching writing; she wrote a text on creative writing for the extension division there. In 1974 she was made associate professor—the first tenured woman in the English department—was promoted to full pro-fessor in 1978, and served as assistant dean of the honors program from 1978 until 1981. Her service to the university was recognized when she was named a distinguished professor in 1980; her teaching has been recognized with several awards, including a national award from the Modern Language Association in 1986. She has been awarded six honorary degrees. Betts has managed this extremely full professional life while married to Lawry Betts, a lawyer who became a judge, and having three children.

Betts's success as a writer began in 1953 with a prize for a short story from *Mademoiselle;* her first collection, *The Gentle Insurrection* (1954), won the University of North Carolina–Putnam award in 1954; and her third, *Beasts of the Southern Wild and Other Stories* (1973), was a finalist for the National Book Award in 1973. A story from that collection, "The Ugliest Pilgrim," was made into a short film, *Violet,* which won an award for the best short feature in 1981. Made into a musical in 1996, *Violet* moved to Broadway, had a very successful three-month run, was named the best musical of 1997 by the New York Drama Critics Circle, and received the Richard Rodgers Award. She has another collection in preparation. It is no wonder that Betts said in an interview in 1981 that she preferred writing short stories to writing novels, which she produced in response to publisher's demands.

Given all her other activities, it is not surprising that there have been long intervals between the six novels. Her first, *Tall Houses in Winter* (1957), focuses on the unhappy family life of three siblings, seen from the perspective of a brother who returns home, mortally ill with cancer, after an absence of ten years. Though viewed by critic Dorothy Scura as "an apprentice work," the novel won the Sir Walter Raleigh Award, as did her second, *The Scarlet Thread* (1964), a historical novel about effects of the Ku Klux Klan after the Civil War. These two novels, as well as most of the short stories, portray the lives of ordinary people in a small town in the Piedmont, Betts's native environment. In *The River to Pickle Beach* (1972) the characters move to the coast, and Betts moves to contemporary times, showing that the assassinations of Martin Luther King, Jr., and Robert Kennedy in 1968 had roots in the violence of everyday life. Jonathan Yardley, writing for the *New York Times Book Review* (1972), stated that with this novel Betts moved into the mainstream of American literature and deserved national recognition.

In all these works, spread over twenty years, Betts portrays lower-middle-class characters caught in dilemmas to which there is usually no good solution. She uses children, women, blacks, and males as central consciousnesses, and in the novels she usually shows the same events from different perspectives. She unflinchingly portrays disappointment, loneliness, poverty, racism, old age, rape, murder, a chain gang, dysfunctional families in which fathers are ruthlessly patriarchal or absent and mothers reject their children. Yet the characters face their fates with dignity; often their interior monologues show self-irony. Betts manages to keep her characters real primarily through her matter-of-fact but subtle prose; her use of dialogue gives even the most sensational twists of plot verisimilitude, and her quiet humor makes the characters' reactions and decisions believable. In one of her earliest stories, "The Gentle Insurrection," for instance, a brother reprimands his sister for insisting that their mother's assertion that their sharecropper father had died was a denial of his desertion; the mother reprimands her for her frequent use of swear words. They both apologize to the mother, who persists in believing the three of them will eventually own their own land. They concur with her delusion, but the brother goes on to wash dirt that he says will never come off, knowing that his sister is planning to leave with a man. From the beginning we have thought that the sister is about to escape, for she sees all of her actions as for the last time and hence endurable. The title implies that she does escape, but at the end of the story that seems problematical. Treating these characters as complex and aware of their own delusions, Betts affirms their dignity; the value of life is in the process of living, not in success or rewards.

Betts's humor is frequently in evidence, sometimes in grotesque situations but more often as ironical self-revelation and irony of plot. One character addresses his daughter as a widow, in the presence of her husband, whom he hates. Another learns to read by stealing a hymnal and deducing the words from his knowledge of the hymns; he files the words but since he does not know the alphabet, they have no order. "Benson Watts Is Dead and in Virginia" begins, "After I died, I woke up here. Or so it seems"; in it a pregnant woman ghost finds that the advantage of being dead is not to have to plan or save money. In "Beasts of the Southern Wild" five scenes of imagined miscegenation are made believable by a white woman's musings about the brutality of her beast of a husband. It is ironic that the Ugliest Pilgrim's external scars do not prevent the perception of her inner beauty by a stunningly beautiful man who falls in love with her; the reader is always aware of the pathos of her belief in a faith healer, but in finding love she never needs to test that faith. Betts's humor serves to make the unbelievable seem normally possible: her fiction is as strange as truth.

Betts's humorous devices help to affirm life in spite of the tragedies she describes, but it is her use of many literary, religious, and artistic allusions and symbols of nature and animals that underlies her theme that omnipresent evil is not the whole story of life. As Elizabeth Evans points out in *Doris Betts* (1997), deep religious meanings underlie Betts's happy endings. Both in *The River to Pickle Beach* and in her fourth novel, *Heading West* (1981), for example, heroines escape the pursuit of psychopaths and find happiness in heterosexual love. *Heading West* is about the journey of a thirty-year-old librarian who is kidnapped and forced to head for the Grand Canyon, a symbol of freedom and self-discovery Betts uses as Melville used the ocean.

Though facing possible rape and murder, Nancy is ironically happy to be leaving her dead-end job, her dependent mother, and disabled brother; the journey becomes a quest for meaning. Her ultimate rescue affirms that life has meaning; but the fact that a sketchily characterized male is her means of rescue seems a weakness in the novel. Betts has more than made up for this flaw in her sixth novel, *The Sharp Teeth of Love* (1997), where through his many internal dialogues the male hero is convincingly shown to be a suitable mate, though it is his fiercely independent mother who is the couple's actual liberator. The novel focuses on the consciousness of Luna (short for her middle name Lunatsky but used by her fiancé as short for "Mad Lunatic"), a successful illustrator of medical books who goes with him from Chapel Hill toward Reno, where she intends to marry him. Though not a kidnapping victim, Luna is caught by her own image of herself as married to the handsome Steven, who—in love with himself—is using her for his own purposes. The journey becomes Luna's quest for self-knowledge and ironically ends like a fairy tale in her discovery of a man she can truly love. The novel has many supernatural aspects, chiefly Luna's obsession with the ghost of Tamsen Donner of the notorious nineteenth-century Donner party, which reportedly resorted to cannibalism. Betts manages to make Luna's belief in ghosts as well as her fantastic rescue of an abused boy credible; unlike Nancy in *Heading West,* who flees from responsibility, Luna assumes it when she and Paul adopt Sam. Because of the richness of this book, the *Women's Review of Books* included it in its list of one hundred best books by women writers in the November 1998 issue.

In Betts's fifth novel *Souls Raised from the Dead* (1994), there is no spatial journey but one through time. The style is close to stream of consciousness, without any chapter breaks, as a father and his daughter, Mary Grace, in a small North Carolina town move from her mother's desertion of them when Mary Grace is ten years old to Mary Grace's death at age thirteen. Betts is especially skillful in moving seamlessly from the father's to the child's perspective. Frank Thompson assumes full responsibility for raising his daughter as if he were her mother. As a highway patrolman, he is convincingly present at disasters, but it is his innocent daughter who discovers the body of an elderly neighbor, murdered because of her association with Al Capone. To all who knew her, the death of Mary Grace from kidney failure requires spiritual journeys from despair to affirmation. This novel is the strongest evidence for Elizabeth Evans' contention, borne out by interviews with Betts, that deeply felt religious belief underlies all of her writing. Francis Thompson's poem "The Hound of Heaven," in which Christ relentlessly pursues mankind, gives *Souls Raised from the Dead* a solid grounding in optimism. It is Frank's soul that is raised from the dead through a discovery of faith in the universe.

In this fifth novel Betts focuses entirely on the North Carolina Piedmont; her next novel, which she has been working on for some time, may be one that traces a family there from the 1890s into the 1970s. Betts has recently decided to retire and will do only part-time teaching for a few years; perhaps retirement will enable her to complete this ambitious project, which may well combine her many strengths as a writer who does not need to leave home.

Sonia Sanchez

Joanne V. Gabbin

Sonia Sanchez, poet, playwright, essayist, and educator, carries her south-ernness in the rhythms of her song. The spoken word, the singing/chanting voice are her quintessential features. The cultural rhythms that pulse through her poetry result from a confluence of qualities rooted in her southern imagination. Though she spent only a short time in the South, her way of looking at the world reflects values she learned during her childhood in Birmingham, Alabama. A deep and abiding humanism, the importance of family and love relationships, a fascination with the past and ancestry, a search for roots and identity, an exploration and appreciation of the folk culture, an evangelical religious experience, and a militancy that slices like a blade of sugarcane shape her personality and her poetry. Hers is a voice that invents, attacks, and resuscitates the past. Even the silences in her poetry are often as telling as the words, for she is a master of understate-ment, nuance, and ellipsis. Her poems witness an exorcism of pain and rage done within the province of love.

Few poets have sustained the intensity that Sonia Sanchez has over three decades of literary outpouring. In her poetic retrospective, *Shake Loose My Skin* (1999), Sanchez speaks about her beginnings, locating herself in a world of contrasts and contradictions. In the poem "Aaaayeee Babo (Praise God)," she provides some major clues to her life and purpose:

I came to this life with serious hands
I came observing the terrorist eyes moving in and out of
Southern corners
I wanted to be the color of bells
I wanted to surround trees and spill autumn from my fingers
I came to this life with serious feet—heard other footsteps
gathering around me
Women whose bodies exploded with flowers.

As a writer and activist "with serious hands," Sanchez, through the publication of fourteen books, from *Homecoming* (1969) to *Shake Loose My Skin,* continues to trust in the power of the written word to capture her community's most sacred meaning. In an essay in Mari Evans' *Black Women Writers (1950–1980): A Critical Evaluation* (1984), Sanchez says that the poet has the power "to create, preserve, or destroy social values, to manipulate the symbols, language, images which have been planted by experience in our collective subconscious, and ultimately to bring forth the truth about the world as she sees it." In keeping faith with this philosophy, Sanchez has been an activist for a long time. Even before she joined ranks with Amiri Baraka, Larry Neal, and Askia Touré in the political and cultural activism of the black arts movement in the mid-1960s, even before she fought from 1967 to 1969 to get the first black studies program at San Francisco State University, she "came to this life with serious feet." The South had already rooted her in a history of black struggle, with its lessons of fear, segregation, and rebellion, and in an awareness of her place. It was the specter of an enforced place, the demanded silences, and the marauding fear that the young girl absorbed in her consciousness and later spat out in stutters.

In 1934, Sonia Sanchez was born in Birmingham to Wilson L. Driver and Lena Jones Driver. Given the communal name Wilsonia Benita, she was only one year old when her mother died in childbirth, and she and her sister were left to the care of their father's mother, Elizabeth "Mama" Driver. Mama Driver, whom Sanchez describes as a "heavy-set, dark complected woman," was the head deaconess in their African Methodist Episcopal church and became the foundation upon which the child built her understanding of the struggle between sin and salvation and the attendant hypocrisies. She symbolized Wilsonia's sense of the community in which family constituted continuity and well-being. In *Under a Soprano Sky* (1987) Sanchez expresses the legacy of love from which she sprang:

My life flows from you Mama. My style comes from a long line of
Louises who picked me up in the nite to keep me from wetting the

bed. A long line of Sarahs who fed me and my sister and fourteen other children from watery soups and beans and a lot of imagination. A long line of Lizzies who made me understand love. Sharing. Holding a child up to the stars. Holding your tribe in a grip of love. A long line of Black people holding each other up against silence.

When her grandmother died, Wilsonia was a frail child of five. As a way of managing her loss, she withdrew behind a veil of stuttering that remained with her for the next twelve years.

Moving to Harlem at the age of nine, she attended the public schools, began writing poetry, and earned a B.A. in political science at Hunter College. She also attended New York University, where she took a course from poet Louise Bogan, a prolific writer and teacher who inspired Sanchez's serious interest in writing. She later organized a writers' workshop that met every Wednesday night in Greenwich Village. It was there that she met Amiri Baraka and Larry Neal and began to read with them in the jazz nightspots. These experiences provided Sanchez with the foundation to launch her developing consciousness, one that began to reject the Western aesthetic tradition and embraced an aesthetic of black liberation. As Joyce A. Joyce writes in *Ijala: Sonia Sanchez and the African Poetic Tradition* (1996), "The content and physical form of the Black poetry of the 1960s are outward and visible signs of a new consciousness. . . . The Black Power Movement, Stokely Carmichael's speeches, Malcolm X's speeches, John Coltrane's music, and the new Black poets repudiated this imitative relationship, emphasized the uniqueness of Black history and stressed the Black community's need to withdraw from the malign influence of the Euro-American political, social, and aesthetic entrapments."

The career of Sonia Sanchez stretches over three decades, and she remains a consistently strong and relevant voice. In her first books of poems, *Homecoming, It's a New Day* (1971), *Love Poems* (1973), *A Blues Book for Blue Black Magical Women* (1974), and *I've Been a Woman: New and Selected Poems* (1978), her voice is experimental, radical, sometimes scatological, and often saturated with the sounds and rhythms of black speech and black music. Her tone ranges from gentle to derisive as she unveils public and private hurts, celebrates her heroes, and analyzes the political and social upheavals that dramatically changed American society. The complexity of her full-voiced lyricism is readily seen in *A Blues Book*. In *Southern Women Writers* (1990), edited by Tonette Bond Inge, this writer suggests that *A Blues Book* signaled a turning point in her writing: "The scope here is large and sweeping. The language is no longer the raw vernacular of

Homecoming, though, as in *We a BaddDDD People* (1970), it is possessed by rhythms of the chants and rituals. At its most prosaic, it is laden with the doctrine of the Nation of Islam and ideologically correct images. At its best, it is intimate, luminous, and apocalyptic. Tucked inside *A Blues Book* is a striking spiritual odyssey that reveals the poet's growing awareness of the psychological and spiritual features of her face."

During the 1980s Sanchez showed the further deepening of her consciousness. In *Homegirls and Handgrenades* (1984), she goes inside herself to explore her residual memory. From the past, she draws images that explode the autobiographical into universal truths. Here she introduces her prose poem, a genre Joyce A. Joyce says "captures the most dynamic and dramatic dimensions of her craft." Bubba, the Black Panther of Harlem, lost in a sea of drugs and unfulfilled dreams; Norma, black genius that lay unmined; Sandy, in "After Saturday Night Comes Sunday," valiant in her love and sacrifice for a drug addicted husband; or the old "bamboo-creased" woman in the prose poem "Just Don't Never Give Up on Love" show Sanchez distilling "sweet/astringent memories" from her own experience. In two of the most important poems in the volume, Sanchez moves the urgency of her message to global relationships. She concludes the volume with "A Letter to Dr. Martin Luther King" and "MIA's." Though very different in form, they are companion pieces that articulate her impatience with the democratic evils (racism, apartheid, imperialism) that stunt the physical and spiritual growth of black youth, corrupt hope through gradualism, and stall freedom. In "MIA's (missing in action and other atlantas)," the datelines— Atlanta, Johannesburg, El Salvador—serve to show the world of oppression in microcosm, and the machinations that promote death.

Under a Soprano Sky (1987) features the mature, lyrical voice of the poet expressing the source of her spiritual strength, establishing and reestablishing connections that recognize the community of humankind, and singing of society's strange fruit sacrificed on the altars of political megalomania, economic greed, and social misunderstanding. The poem "Elegy (For MOVE and Philadelphia)" is emblematic of the steady and searing scream the poet reserves for institutions and principalities that desecrate life: "How does one scream in thunder?"

In the 1990s Sanchez shows in her poetry the intensity with which she began her career. However, it is different, more directed, more moving. She continues to blast racism, sexism, intolerance, classism, and violence perpetrated on innocents. In *Wounded in the House of a Friend* (1995), the speaker in the title poem has been rejected in love and is psychologically and spiritually wounded. In a dramatic dialogue, the two estranged lovers operate at different points on the continuum called relationship, one using every ruse to destroy the relationship and the other using every trick to preserve it. Using the biblical scripture Zechariah 13:6 as the leitmotif, Sanchez speaks of hurt and ultimate wholeness that comes with the realization, "I SHALL BECOME A COLLECTOR OF ME . . . AND PUT MEAT ON MY SOUL." Emerging from her own "grave" experience, the new woman ascends to a higher level of self-actualization and redemption.

Sanchez in *Does Your House Have Lions?* (1997) fingers the tender chord of grief at her brother's death from AIDS. Dying in 1981 before a name was attached to the disease, her brother is portrayed in compassionate strokes as he confronts his father, rejects his sister's overtures of love and reconciliation, and weaves around his mother a necessary web of fantasy and myth. Writing in the elaborate complexity of rhyme royal stanzas, Sanchez makes uncommonly beautiful and poignant the epic migration of a family through estrangement, terror, reconciliation, forgiveness, and love:

> brother. let our mouths speak without harangue
> let my journey sing a path they sang
> O i will purchase my brother's whisper.
> O i will reward my brother's tongue.

In *Like the Singing Coming off the Drums* (1998), Sanchez trains her own tongue to curl around the many sounds of love. Whether they are elegiac, bluesy, romantic, sisterly, or sensual, the notes she strikes vibrate with her essence—compassion, concern, humanity, hunger for justice, vulnerability, and strength. In this volume she returns to the haiku and the tanka, which appeared earlier in *Love Poems* and *I've Been a Woman: New and Selected Poems,* and adds the blues haiku, and the sonku, an invented form. She writes:

> love between us is
> speech and breath. loving you is
> a long river running.

Almost twenty years later Sonia Sanchez more than ever deserves the incisive critique of Margaret Walker Alexander in a 1980 review in *Black Scholar* that her poetry is "consistently high artistry that reflects her womanliness—her passion, power, perfume, and prescience."

Aware of her own indebtedness to generations of women who shaped her poetic vision, Sanchez makes the final poem in *Shake Loose My Skin,* "Aaaayeee Babo (Praise God)," a fitting praise song to "women whose bodies exploded with flowers." From Mama Driver, from Shirley Graham Du

Bois, from eighty-four-year-old Mrs. Rosalie Johnson, from the not so small voices of LaTanya, Kadesha, Shanique, from Mrs. Benita Jones, an angry black woman in Philadelphia, hounded by racism out of her home, Sonia Sanchez has extracted the sweet nectar of their lives and has it nourish and sustain her. For it is these women, and many more like them, who in "recapturing the memory of our most sacred sounds" remind Sanchez of the humanity, the peace, the community, and the purpose that she learned while encircled by the big Charles White arms of her southern upbringing.

Ellen Gilchrist

Margaret D. Bauer

At the center of Ellen Gilchrist's fiction is the upper-middle-class South from the 1940s to the present. Gilchrist examines class, race, and gender issues, but her central concern is with the southern woman who tries to escape her dominating family. Opportunities for women may be broadening beyond marriage and motherhood, but the southern family Gilchrist writes about still tries to raise debutantes rather than ambitious daughters.

Ellen Gilchrist was born on February 20, 1935, in Vicksburg, Mississippi. Her father moved his family around during her childhood, so she lived for a time outside of the South (in Indiana and Illinois), but she returned regularly to the Mississippi Delta for summer visits with her mother's family, and her family moved back to the South, to Franklin, Kentucky, when she was in high school. There she began her writing career as a columnist for the Franklin *Favorite,* the local newspaper, when she was only fifteen. She had to give up her column, "Chit and Chat about This and That," when her father again moved the family. It was a foreshadowing event, for Gilchrist would eventually put aside her writing for her own family obligations. She wrote in college but not professionally until two of her three sons were grown and the third a teenager.

Gilchrist enrolled in Vanderbilt University in 1953 for her freshman year and in the University of Alabama at Auburn in 1954 for her sophomore year. In 1955, she married Marshall Walker, who would be the father of her children: Marshall Peteet Walker, Jr., born in 1956; Garth Gilchrist Walker, born in 1957; and Pierre Gautier Walker, III, born in 1961. In between the births of her second and third sons, Gilchrist divorced their father and married James Nelson Bloodworth, then divorced him and remarried Walker. She divorced Walker again in 1963 and went back to school to finish her bachelor's degree at Millsaps College in Mississippi. She then married Frederick Sidney Kullman in 1968.

Gilchrist and Kullman lived in New Orleans, which would be the setting of many of her works, including several stories in her first collection of short stories, which satirize New Orleans aristocracy. During her residence in New Orleans, Gilchrist resumed her writing and took another position with a newspaper: from 1975 to 1978, she was a contributing editor of the *Vieux Carré Courier*. According to Mary A. McCay, in her book *Ellen Gilchrist* (1997), Gilchrist considers 1975 "the beginning of her professional poetry career." In 1976, she enrolled in the creative writing M.F.A. program at the University of Arkansas, commuting between Fayetteville and New Orleans until her divorce from Kullman in 1981, after which she took up permanent residence in Fayetteville.

Although Gilchrist did not complete the M.F.A. program, during her tenure at the University of Arkansas, Fayetteville's Lost Roads Press published her first book, a collection of poems entitled *The Land Surveyor's Daughter* (1979), and the university press published her first book of fiction, *In the Land of Dreamy Dreams* (1981). This short story collection attracted the attention of Little, Brown and Company, which republished it in 1985, after having published her first novel, *The Annunciation* (1983), and a second short story collection, *Victory over Japan* (1984), the latter of which won the American Book Award for fiction. Little, Brown has since published all of her books except for her second collection of poetry, *Riding Out the Tropical Depression* (1986), and a historical novel set in ancient Greece called *Anabasis* (1994).

In the Land of Dreamy Dreams introduces Rhoda Manning, a character who would become Gilchrist's most popular recurrent character. Rhoda is the protagonist of four stories in that first book, stories in Gilchrist's other short fiction collections, and the novel *Net of Jewels* (1992). Most of the Rhoda stories and excerpts from the novel are collected in a volume called *Rhoda, A Life in Stories* (1995). The precocious, spoiled, strong-willed, rebellious Rhoda is the prototype for the protagonists of most of Gilchrist's fiction, including the other recurrent characters, Nora Jane Whittington, also introduced in *In the Land of Dreamy Dreams* and central to stories in

Gilchrist's other collections, and Crystal Manning Mallison Weiss, a central character of several works and a minor character in others.

The Gilchrist prototype also evolves with the author's development of Anna Hand in *The Anna Papers* (1988). In this novel, Gilchrist's characterization of Anna fulfills the promise of her original prototype, Rhoda, who was not able to overcome her conflict with her dominating father and brother or her consequential belief that her value as a woman depends on the opinions of the men in her life. Though a talented writer with the promise of a career ahead of her, Rhoda drops out of college after eloping, then has several children right away. She divorces her husband but continues to focus most of her energy on finding a mate rather than on the writing she still longs to do. In contrast, by the time in Anna's life covered by *The Anna Papers*, Anna has put behind her the experience of several miscarriages and disappointing marriages and has focused her attention on her career. Her success as a writer seems connected to her ability to follow her own rules of living: shirking familial obligations if need be and choosing her lovers according to her own whims without regard for whether society or her family would approve of them (one of her current lovers is married, the other a college student about twenty years younger than she). Then, when she discovers that she has cancer, Anna takes her own life rather than have it limited even by illness.

Following the creation of Anna Hand, Gilchrist's protagonists are divided between manifestations of the original Rhoda prototype and those whose characters reflect the evolution of the prototype, Anna Hand. By continuing to create characters with Rhoda's weaknesses, Gilchrist reminds her readers that overcoming gender strictures is not so easy, even for women growing up since "women's liberation." Whereas Rhoda, Crystal, Anna, and most of Gilchrist's other early protagonists are members of the author's own generation—children during World War II, teenagers and young brides in the 1950s—many of the protagonists of her post–*Anna Papers* works are girls and young women of the next generation who are reaching maturity in the 1980s. Sadly, Gilchrist's plots suggest that not much is changing for these young women from old southern families still hanging on to their inherited value system, which prizes compliant daughters who find fine husbands and provide heirs. Having a career may be more accessible to these women and more socially acceptable in the world at large, but they are still fed the fairy-tale code of conduct: "Be a good girl, and you'll meet your handsome prince and live happily ever after."

In one of the first Rhoda stories, "1957, a Romance," Rhoda is trying to get an abortion. At only nineteen, she has already had two children and is unhappily married. After prostituting herself to one doctor to get the name of another who will give her a safe abortion, she must rely on her father's money to pay for the procedure. Such were the times; it was before *Roe v. Wade*. (Luckily for Rhoda, her father is wealthy, had not approved of her choice of husband, and sees this as a way to bring Rhoda back under his control.) In one of Gilchrist's novellas in *I Cannot Get You Close Enough* (1990), Anna Hand's niece Jesse finds herself, a generation later, pregnant at about the same age. Legally, Jesse has more of a choice regarding what to do about this child, conceived out of wedlock with a man who is still struggling with a drug problem, but Jesse does not consider options. She gets as caught up in the romance of the situation as Rhoda did when she eloped from college. Though a generation apart, both women are influenced by lingering social expectations that, as women, their primary goals are marriage and motherhood rather than a career.

Gilchrist's belief in her prototype's potential to overcome the oppression of women, reflected in humor found in her early fiction, seems to have waned by the time this novella was written, perhaps a result of recognizing that the world is not yet ready for an Anna Hand. Certainly the reviewers' reaction to the character—finding fault with her libido and her positive self-image, perceiving her decision to die as a cowardly escape from pain rather than a courageous refusal to compromise her life—suggests as much. Gilchrist seems to have summoned up her hopefulness again for the development of, for example, Anna's other niece Olivia in the novel *Starcarbon* (1994), stories of an older Rhoda in *The Age of Miracles* (1995), the continuation of Nora Jane's adventures in the first section of *The Courts of Love* (1996), and the creation of a new Anna-like protagonist for the novel *Sarah Conley* (1997), but the optimism seems forced. Victoria Jenkins suggests in her review of *Starcarbon* for the Chicago *Tribune* that Gilchrist is being a "fairy godmother" to her characters, "an overly fond *deus ex machina* who lets her charges teeter on the brink of disaster but can't bear to see anyone topple" (1994).

Besides the titles already mentioned, Gilchrist has published four other collections of short fiction, *Drunk with Love* (1986), *Light Can Be Both Wave and Particle* (1989), *Flights of Angels* (1999), and *The Cabal and Other Stories* (2000), as well as journal entries and National Public Radio commentaries collected under the title *Falling through Space* (1987).

Gail Godwin

Lihong Xie

Gail Godwin was born in Birmingham, Alabama, in June 1937 and grew up in Asheville, North Carolina. After receiving her master's degree in 1968 and her doctorate in 1971 from the University of Iowa Writers' Workshop, she lectured intermittently at the University of Illinois at Urbana-Champaign, Vassar College, and Columbia University. She now lives in Woodstock, New York, and devotes her time entirely to writing. She has published ten novels, two collections of short stories, four librettos, and numerous essays. She contributes essays and short stories to *Atlantic, Antaeus, Ms., Harper's, Writer, McCall's, Cosmopolitan, North American Review, Paris Review,* and *Esquire* and reviews contemporary fiction for the *New York Times Book Review* and other publications.

Godwin is one of the most articulate contemporary writers to pursue the idea of the self, a major theme of nearly all her writing. Her heroines, most of them southern women caught between the ideal of southern womanhood and contemporary feminism, struggle to form a personal identity that is strong, complex, dynamic, and continuously evolving. Godwin's vision of the female self has changed significantly over the course of her writing career. Her earliest novels, *The Perfectionists* (1970) and *Glass People* (1972), emphasize themes of female victimization, with the protagonist seeking an independent identity outside of marriage but ultimately failing to create the plots of her own life. Her more mature work dramatizes the ambiguities of female identity and explores the ways in which modern women seek to develop strong, evolving identities from fragmented experiences. Central to her heroine's growth is memory, a backward and inward journey of painful but liberating encounters with sundry versions of herself. The act of remembering, narrating, and interpreting the stories of her life allows the heroine to grow in self-understanding and enables her to affirm both female sexual identity and autonomous self-definition. A trip home to bury her beloved grandmother, for example, sets Jane Clifford, the protagonist in *The Odd Woman* (1974), on an intensely psychological journey of self-scrutiny. She recollects versions of the "love story" in her own family as well as in literature and life, particularly the story of her great-aunt's tragic elopement and of her own stalemated love relation with a married man. With memory's aid, Jane gradually comes to a penetrating self-understanding: despite her feminist determination, she is still deeply entrapped in the plot of the love story, playing the role of a patiently waiting mistress. Violet Clay, the title character of Godwin's fourth novel (1978), narrates her story of artistic self-definition in the first person, using memory to reassess her past selves, to contest and reject various self-conceptions: Violet as orphan, victim, gothic heroine, and artist-near-success. From such anguished internal dialogue comes Violet's insight—her self-deceptive use of a failed novelist as a symbol of promised success.

In *The Finishing School* (1984), Justin Stokes, an established actress, revisits her turbulent adolescence in an IBM-dominated suburb of upstate New York, narrating—again in the first person—her painful struggles to find her selfhood by intensely identifying, almost psychologically merging with and yet ultimately rejecting a charismatic older woman. In remembering and narrating her past, Justin reclaims her mentor, muse, and spiritual mother, making the memory journey part of her own continuing growth, at a point when she, as her older friend used to warn her, is in the greatest danger of congealing into a final, complacent self.

Speaking musically about her fiction, Godwin describes some of her novels as written in a "minor" key and others as in a "major" key. Private and psychologically intense, minor-key novels, most notably *The Finishing School,* are characterized by the single point of view. They explore the ways in which complex interpersonal relationships structure women's search for a centered identity, often through the prism of memory. Major-key novels, such as *A Mother and Two Daughters* (1982) and *A Southern Family* (1987), are characterized by a formal expansiveness and a broad social spectrum. In these novels Godwin constructs multiple characters and points of view interacting with one another in the rich fabric of society. In *A Mother and Two Daughters,* for example, three heroines experience the generational and familial conflicts that have shaped their individual identities and their relationships. Memory, internal dialogue, and solitary quest are still important to each heroine's growth, but the interplay of diverse voices—of three very different women pursuing their separate journeys of self-discovery and of a multitude of characters in their discrete social worlds—places individual consciousness in the larger phenomenon of human interconnectedness.

Taking multiple points of view a step further, Godwin in *A Southern Family* dispenses entirely with main characters and creates a cacophony of vastly different voices, languages, and consciousnesses vying for recognition and significance. Nearly every chapter of the novel is assigned to a single character—the center of consciousness in that chapter—providing his or her unique version of the deeply entangled life of an extended southern family where no one knows the whole truth, where familial strife is embedded in class conflict and in a war of languages. In this "hybrid" novel, Godwin's southern family assumes the character of a little southern society, one of great diversity that crosses borders of class, gender, region, race, and generation, one that juxtaposes aspiring middle-class professionals with poor mountain hillbillies, compromised mothers with questing daughters, the fleeing heroine with the returning one, tragic failure with hard-won success, all at the meeting place of Old and New South.

Godwin's recent novels continue to explore the idea of the female self in intimate relationships with God, father, and husband. *Father Melancholy's Daughter* (1991) extends the search for selfhood into the spiritual realm of the Episcopal Church, bringing a theological dimension to the concept of self-becoming. Unfolding within the liturgical year, Margaret Gower's story—of understanding the meaning of her mother's life and death and the nurturing role she takes up in looking after her melancholy father—links the intensely personal search characteristic of Godwin's fiction and the highly spiritual quest first developed in *Father Melancholy's Daughter.* Focusing on love and marital relations, *The Good Husband* (1994) traces the emotional journeys of two married couples and depicts how they struggle, each in a unique way, to work out the meaning of their life stories, both as individuals and as partners—"matches" or "mates"—in an intimate relationship. *Evensong* (1999), a sequel to *Father Melancholy's Daughter,* weaves together themes of faith and intimacy. While striving to make more of herself in her service to God and her parishioners, Margaret Gower, now an Episcopal priest, must struggle to sustain the emotional center within her marriage and to achieve greater intimacy and oneness with her husband, a union of body and soul that makes more of them both.

Throughout her novels, Godwin is preoccupied with the construction of a self that will adequately express the complexity of contemporary reality and embrace the possibilities of continuous growth and fulfillment. She situates her questing heroines in a world quivering with change, fraught with confusion and fracture, and increasingly rich in multiple voices—individual aspiration, feminist consciousness, cultural imperatives, family, region, class, and spirituality. She portrays their complex responses to social, psychological, and spiritual challenges and dramatizes their struggle to achieve coherent identities. With each succeeding novel, Godwin's concept of the self becomes increasingly multiple; her thematic emphasis shifts from female victimization, through the psychological space of reconstructing past selves, to the broad social context in which diverse voices interact with one another, with emphasis, in her most recent novels, on spiritual quest and fulfillment of love in marriage. Constantly contesting and reshaping her concept of the self, Godwin sees growth as continuous and dynamic, encompassing the interpersonal and social process of interaction, the internal process of memory, as well as the spiritual dimension of self-identity.

Most of Godwin's fiction takes place in the South, usually in the mountains around Asheville, North Carolina. Often, the action of the novel is set in contemporary time but is shaped by an emotional tone of the earlier South of Godwin's childhood memories. Her most revealing use of the South is in her portrayal of southern daughters' complex, ambivalent feelings toward their birthplace, a region where, in Godwin's own words, "a girl growing up has an image of womanhood already cut out for her, stitched securely by the practiced hands of tradition, available for her to slip into, ready-made" ("Southern Belle," *Ms.,* 1975). Nearly every southern daughter has an image of a "perfect lady" who embodies the essence of traditional southern womanhood—duty, grace, tact, self-effacement—rejected by the questing heroine as an inadequate role model yet sometimes resurrected to provide a nostalgic haven. Their complex but vital relationships with their mothers and grandmothers both separate them from and bind them to the South, propelling them to flee the region only to return in memory as well as in person. Ultimately, the rebellious southern daughters must go beyond their adolescent rejection of the South; they must acknowledge its cultural legacies and confront, even embrace, the region as part of their personal history and identity.

Godwin has peopled her fiction with vibrant women seeking to take charge of their lives, growing into heroines with strong and evolving personal identities—a name, an occupation, a future. Her focus upon various dimensions of individual development—memory, personal history as identity, place, family, love, friendship, and spirituality—links her work to a specific genre, the *Bildungsroman*, a long-established literary tradition that was male-centered (about male protagonists, written by male authors, and studied by male literary critics) until very recently. In her ten novels, Godwin concentrates on female experiences over the life cycle, from childhood to old age; embeds her characters in family, region, culture, and class; and explores in depth the relationship between social and familial constraints on the development of an individual and her/his struggle to resist and transcend these constraints.

With desire and passion, Godwin's spirited heroines take us beyond the ending of their own stories to the larger, open-ended stage of humanity's becoming, with each person, as Godwin exquisitely puts it in her autobiographical essay "How to Be the Heroine of Your Own Life" (*Cosmopolitan*, 1988), "cutting her unique swath through the landscape of her times, adding her particular style and contribution to the great myth of humanity."

Bobbie Ann Mason

Joseph M. Flora

Among southern women writers living at the end of the twentieth century, apart from Eudora Welty, few have more national visibility than Bobbie Ann Mason. Following the appearance in 1982 of Mason's first book of fiction, *Shiloh and Other Stories,* Mason's ascendance was dramatic. That first collection earned the Ernest Hemingway Award, and "Shiloh," the lead story—Mason's most famous—may be regarded as her signature story. It has taken its place as one of the defining minimalist works in contemporary literature, making Mason something of a female counterpart to Raymond Carver. The story resonates with the gender issues to the fore at the end of the century, memorably caught in its opening image: "Leroy Moffit's wife, Norma Jean, is working on her pectorals."

Mason's career as a writer mirrored that of Norma Jean. Although she had been putting words to paper for a long time, Mason was forty-two years old when her first book of fiction appeared. She had first applied her energies to journalism and writing for such magazines as *Movie Stars, Movie Life,* and *T.V. Star Parade* and then turned to graduate study in English at the University of Connecticut, earned a Ph.D., and began college teaching in Pennsylvania. Her first books—*The Girl Sleuth: A Feminist Guide to the Bobbsey Twins, Nancy Drew, and Their Sisters* (1974) and *Nabokov's Garden: A Guide to "Ada"* (1974)—grew out of her academic training and might have been steps toward traditional academic ascension, but like

Norma Jean, Mason was restless and unsatisfied, and kept lifting those weights.

As an undergraduate at the University of Kentucky, Mason took courses in creative writing, but she found no significant encouragement there. As she later reported, no one ever told her she was good. Mason would find the encouragement and counsel she needed only after she had received her Ph.D. and returned to writing stories. The needed mentor was Roger Angell, a fiction editor for the *New Yorker.* Mason marked the importance of Angell to her emergence by dedicating her second collection of stories, *Love Life* (1989), to him. (The dedication of *Shiloh and Other Stories* to "Roger" may apply in spirit to Angell as well as to Mason's writer-editor husband, Roger Rawlings.) With "Shiloh" leading the way in 1980, Mason's stories began to appear in the *New Yorker* and *Atlantic Monthly* with some frequency. Titling her first collection as she did, Mason identified not only a signature story but the pioneering place of "Shiloh" in her career as a writer.

Born in Mayfield, Kentucky, on May 1, 1940, to farming parents Wilburn A. and Christie Lee Mason, Bobbie Ann Mason grew up familiar with the demands of farming. The rural school she attended was not very challenging. She was a shy child who read a lot—but nothing very good. As she grew older, Nancy Drew and the Bobbsey twins, as she would later testify, provided important foci of a dream life, a life that was intensified by much listening to the radio as she discovered all kinds of popular music. Singers, not movie stars, became primary in her imagination. No group was more important to her than the Hilltoppers, a male quartet named for the college mascot at Western Kentucky State College. Not only did Mason like such songs as "Till Then" and other Hilltoppers hits, but she also exulted in the discovery that someone from Kentucky could find great fame. Mason started a Hilltoppers fan club, devoting much energy to it throughout her high school years, earning the gratitude of the Hilltoppers, and making with her mother numerous forays out of the pocket of Kentucky she found stifling to be with the Hilltoppers. (It was an extraordinary honor for her to be national president of the Hilltoppers fan clubs.) The impulse to escape would later become a major theme of Mason's work, which often contrasts characters who are "residents" with those who are transients. Her parents were rooted in the Kentucky land; they were residents.

With more options than Norma Jean Moffit, Mason not only bypassed junior college and the alma mater of the Hilltoppers, but she also made the step so rare in her own fiction—she entered the University of Kentucky, an experience that broadened her world and sent her to New York City following graduation. Like many other rural southerners who leave for the Northeast, Mason experienced negative judgments on her origins, her accent, her culture, and she labored to fit in—all the way to the Ph.D. and a dissertation on the sophisticated Nabokov.

Later, however, settled in her rural Pennsylvania home with her husband and beginning to take up the craft of fiction rather than writing criticism of it, Mason discovered her fictional country in the western Kentucky country of her youth. The characters who kindled her imagination invariably live in and around Hopewell (a fictionalized Mayfield, another name carrying possibility in its first syllable), and for them Paducah is the usual center of progress and vitality. Using the icons and metaphors of American culture, she made her Kentuckians resonate with a life that also transcends Kentucky. Less a transient than she had seemed, Mason became a "resident." In 1990 Mason decided that the time had come to move closer to the land that had been nourishing her fiction. But rather than returning to Mayfield, she settled on a small farm near Lexington, knowing that she would have to be close to an airport.

Mason's strength as a writer comes from her strong sense of a place and the people who live in that place. Her primary instinct is not confessional. She is southern in her attention to family and family connections, and her own family is reflected in some of her work, though one finds a degree of reticence as well. Her emphasis is usually on the fictive rather than on the autobiographical. For Ernest Hemingway, the recurring Nick Adams in many short stories reminds readers of biographical connections. For Katherine Anne Porter, Miranda keeps reappearing in stories—a Miranda who seems to be part of Porter's re-creation of a usable past for herself. So far, Mason has not been much drawn to reappearing characters in her stories or in depicting family sagas, as Faulkner was. Two stories placed near the end of *Shiloh and Other Stories* deal with the same characters, and one does bear important similarities to Bobbie Ann Mason, the Nancy Culpepper who appears in the story of that name and in "Lying Daggo." In the first story, Nancy has returned to Kentucky from a country home in Pennsylvania because her parents are moving her grandmother into a nursing home. Transient Nancy, vaguely yearning to return to Kentucky, senses the momentousness of the event and wishes to save Granny's photographs, to reclaim some of her heritage, to understand herself better. "Lying Daggo" is the collection's single story not set in Kentucky; it portrays Nancy, her husband Jack, and their son Robert (Mason has no children) as they deal with the impending death of their aging dog. Much of the story is given to describing the fifteen-year marriage of Nancy (who makes frequent trips to her family in Kentucky) and Jack (a transient by instinct), a union that reflects the restlessness and freedoms of young rebels and intellectuals of the 1970s—a counterpoint to the prevailing patterns in Hopewell, Kentucky. Nancy Culpepper does not return to Mason's fiction until the publication of the short novel *Spence + Lila* (1988), the most autobiographical of Mason's works. It is dedicated to her parents and to "Janice, LaNelle, Don, and Roger," Mason's two sisters, brother, and husband. Sister LaNelle provided illustrations for this family-centered book, which is a realistic, humorous, and loving tribute to the solidity of her parents' lives and their love. The family has gathered because Lila must have a mastectomy and then a second surgery for a clogged artery. Nancy is the only offspring who no longer lives in Kentucky, the intellectual daughter who embarrasses Lila by questioning the doctor somewhat aggressively. Nancy and her family do not appear in any of the stories of Mason's second collection, *Love Life* (1989).

Because Mason has been so focused on ordinary lives and because she writes in a style appropriate to those lives, her stories have been described not only as minimalist (the least offensive of the labels), but also K-Mart Chic, Mall Fiction, Grit Lit. Writers usually protest such labels—including the label "southern"—and the labels surely have their limits in describing the worth and skill of a writer. What critics who use these labels mean to describe is a writer's focus on middle-class, usually lower-middle-class, characters whose primary concern is the immediate. In technique, less is usually more. The stories tend to be open ended. The writer is removed, nonjudgmental. The mall is indeed an important destination for characters in Mason's short stories, depicting the mobility of even rural populations in late-twentieth-century America and the increasing sameness: malls are everywhere and nowhere. Like a large percentage of the national population, Mason's characters watch a lot of television. Television has caused the people of what used to be isolated pockets to become familiar with national heroes and stars—icons; fictional characters of television become their points of reference. Concurrently, the dominance of evangelical religion has lessened in Mason's Hopewell. It is still a force, held onto more by her older women characters; generally, her men keep their distance—conversions are treated with skepticism.

Because popular culture greatly impacts the lives of Mason's characters, references to it abound in her stories, influencing structure and theme. Indeed, the label *telefiction* might be used to describe Mason's stories; they are stories segmented, and readers move quickly from one scene to another, as movies and television carry viewers. The single-scene story (Hemingway's "Hills like White Elephants" or John Updike's "A & P") is not her métier. From "Shiloh" onward, Mason relies on montage-like effect. Mason often heightens the television-like sense of speed and immediacy by using present tense, as do other women writers who are counted in the minimalist camp. The very content of her stories often duplicates situations found in television dramas. Although educators, intellectuals, and ministers often lament the importance of television in modern culture, Mason never does. The effect of television on her characters is very different from the effect of it in, say, a Raymond Carver story. In "Shiloh," Leroy Moffit understands his wife better because talk shows have helped clue him in to what women want in a man, in a marriage. In "Love Life," the lead story of Mason's second story collection, there is something wonderfully affirmative about the addiction of retired math teacher Opal to MTV.

Mason's stories differ from most TV fare, however, in being more thoughtful, more subtle, more varied. Mason's enduring topic in stories and novels is change—hence, the tendency of her stories—again beginning with "Shiloh"—to be open ended. The reader cannot be certain what action the characters will take next. Is Norma Jean beckoning Leroy? Or is she exercising those pectorals—on the way to ending her marriage? Mason leaves the reader to weigh possibilities, signaling the end of the story (as she later ends so many stories) with an image: "The sky is unusually pale—the color of the dust ruffle Mabel [Leroy's mother-in-law] made for their bed."

But even if the Moffits divorce, "Shiloh" is not chilling or somber. Mason chose to tell the Moffits' story by focusing on the male perspective, and the reader sees Leroy changing as he deals with his own history and his wife's transformation. Mason's title at once suggests the battle between the sexes and a decisive moment in the history of the South and the nation, reminding readers how much Mason's South has changed. Living in a century when cultural change has accelerated exponentially, Mason sees the change bringing more freedom to her characters. If her stories sometimes seem the stuff of soap operas (the divorce rate of Hopewell and the incidents of infidelity are surely keeping up with national statistics), her characters control their destinies more than their parents did and infinitely more than their grandparents could.

Mason has been charged with dipping too often into the same ink in writing her stories, but she keeps experimenting. She must be credited for covering a range of characters at various stages of life. She has been as successful at telling stories from the male point of view as the female. As she had in portraying Spence and Lila, in *Love Life* Mason sometimes pairs points of view in a story. In the lead story, she uses third-person narration to pair the perspective of a retired teacher with that of her much younger niece; in "Marita," using interior monologues for Marita and third-person narration for her mother, she pairs the widowed Sue Ellen and her college-age daughter.

Love Life is experimental in several ways. It reaches a broader range of contemporary issues (abortion, the effects of the Vietnam War, adjustments to divorce and death) than did *Shiloh,* and the rural past is more distant. While the title *Shiloh and Other Stories* emphasizes the separateness of the stories, the title *Love Life* appropriately titles a collection of stories that emphasizes a thematic totality. *Love Life* has much of the collective force of a composite novel. Although there are no recurring characters in the stories, they are unified by time, place, and theme. Readers know Hopewell and vicinity as definitely as they might know Winesburg, Ohio, in Sherwood Anderson's prototypical composite novel of 1919. Mason's arrangement of the stories suggests a larger intention; she sandwiches the many stories of sexual and romantic love in a variety of contexts with stories dealing with older characters who look back at their love lives. Poignantly, the last story is titled "Wish," and that title reverberates with virtually every story.

Mason's first—and surely lasting—fame came with her short stories. Her importance to the genre is emphasized with the publication in 1998 of *Midnight Magic,* which selects stories from her first two collections. Success in the short story earned, Mason followed her first collection with *In Country* (1985), a novel with the Vietnam War at its center by a woman who had not been in that combat. But Mason recognized that Vietnam had been pivotal for her generation and the contemporary South, as the Civil War had been the looming reality for Faulkner's generation. It is in part a coming-of-age novel, the story of Samantha Hughes ("Sam," she calls hers herself, as do her friends, reflecting Mason's depiction of changing gender expectations). Sam has just graduated from Hopewell High and is searching for the father she never knew, who was killed in Vietnam before she was born. Sam embodies the need of a nation to understand a war that, like the Civil War, divided it. Although *In Country* teems with images of popular culture, Sam's search challenges easy notions about Mason and "Grit Lit." As Fred Hobson has pointed out in *The Southern Writer in the Postmodern World* (1991), Sam bears resemblance to Faulkner's tormented Quentin Compson and his obsession with personal and cultural history. Sam's search is enhanced early in the novel through her reading of letters from her father to her mother and late in the novel through reading a journal her father kept. As a consequence of that reading, she takes her own imaginative journey "in country" when she spends a night alone at dangerous Cawood's Pond. The impact of Vietnam is also made real through the portrayal of several Vietnam veterans. Sam is as comfortable with and understanding of them as

Mason is in her many portrayals of male experience. Most important of these veterans, and the most haunted, is her uncle Emmett, with whom she has been living in the strange world that the Vietnam War helped bring about.

In Country is framed by the journey Sam takes with Emmett and Grandma Hughes to the Vietnam Veterans Memorial in Washington, and it ends with a closure not found in the stories. Although the ending, with Sam and her grandmother finding Dwayne's name, has been criticized as falsely affirmative, the ending at the wall can be defended on several grounds, not the least of which is the validation of the search to reclaim a past. The wall is also appropriate to the basic assumptions of Mason's fiction with its emphasis on ordinary men and women. Vietnam was an equalizer. The war gave the nation no Eisenhower or MacArthur, no Iwo Jima heroes on whom to focus. The wall, reflecting those who inspect it, is an appropriate symbol for the meaning of Vietnam, as it lists the names—all equally important—in an order that is not alphabetical, an order that demands search. A novel that takes many risks, *In Country* was filmed in 1989; the movie followed the novel in demanding reflection on the part of Americans.

Mason's concern with understanding the past is at the core of her second and most recent full-length novel, *Feather Crowns* (1993). Written at the end of the twentieth century, the novel takes readers to its beginning. Many people in western Kentucky viewed the arrival of the new century with alarm, expecting (as many evangelical preachers led them to expect) great destructions—the end times. In place of the abundance of references to popular music and television that mark her other work, Mason provides references to numerous folk beliefs earlier people devised to explain their world; the feather crown image is one of these. With *Feather Crowns,* Mason marks a century of rapid change; the characters who are best able to survive recognize what changes are positive, what changes destructive. Although most of the action takes place in the early years of the century, the heroine, Christie Wilburn Wheeler (her maiden name is that of Mason's mother), has lived to an old age and takes a long glance at the changes of her lifetime, giving the resolution that characterizes older family saga novels.

In *Feather Crowns* Mason studies the often repressive force of family structures, particularly on women, in the early years of the century. The novel portrays the fierce demands of physical labor on farms and the difficulties involved in finding personal (often sexual) fulfillment in such a context. Usually a woman had to find it or not find it in marriage. Christie and James Wheeler have made a good start on such fulfillment, complicated by her having to fit into the Wheeler family structure, when Christie surprises herself and eventually the country by giving birth to quintuplets—an unheard-of occurrence then, and surely some supernatural sign, probably punishment, she thinks, for enjoying sexual passion. A taste of the exploitation that would become increasingly common later in the century takes place as the multitudes flock to see this wonder. The babies are, of course, too frail to live long, the science of the day too primitive to nurse them to full size. But the technology is there to preserve their bodies, and Christie and James are cajoled into taking the preserved bodies on tour into distant towns. For Christie the tour provides revenge against the mobs, who surely hastened the deaths, and she replaces James as the stronger force in the family. Eventually, she realizes what has happened to them, and they are able to reclaim their love and in unity escape the grotesque circumstances to which they have been led. Like *In Country,* the novel ends in new understanding. Perhaps the greatest strength of *Feather Crowns* is its skill in depicting the ambience of the mind-set at the beginning of the century: family structures, folk beliefs, religious experience, sexual attitudes, and racial attitudes. Mason's upland South not having been a region of the plantation, blacks are not visible in her stories; Mason depicts them here for the first time.

Panoramic rather than intensive like *In Country, Feather Crowns* affirms Mason's tendency to take new approaches as she explores the South that produced her and the South that now is. In this work, as through her rich and varied career, Mason has secured an important place among the fiction writers of the South—in novel as well as in short story.

In 1999, Mason also took her place among the major writers of autobiography in the modern South. Although Faulkner and most white writers from the first half of the twentieth century (in contrast to African American writers) eschewed autobiography, in the second half of the century the trend was reversed and produced such memorable works as Willie Morris' *North toward Home* (1967), Harry Crews's *A Childhood: The Biography of a Place* (1978), Tim McLaurin's *Keeper of the Moon* (1981), and Reynolds Price's *Clear Pictures: First Loves, First Guides* (1990). Even Eudora Welty made a foray into the genre with *One Writer's Beginnings* (1983). In several works, most notably *I Know Why the Caged Bird Sings* (1970), Maya Angelou made clear that the genre would continue to be important to African American writers.

Mason's *Clear Springs: A Memoir* brings to the fore the autobiographical impulse that Mason had revealed in the Nancy Culpepper stories and in *Spence + Lila.* She dedicated the book to her mother and the memory of her father and grandparents. Nancy Drew–like as well as Nancy Culpepper–like, Mason researched the family lines of both sides of her family; she shares with the reader a chart of the family tree as well as a map of their Kentucky geography. Portraying three generations, the book is intimately concerned with place, farm life, and the pressures that bring change. Describing rural family dynamics and Wilburn Mason's intense commitment to his land, the memoir strikes numerous southern chords. Chief among them is the issue of class—and how tenuous the demarcation between the classes can be. Especially for Wilburn, Mason's father, it is important that the family not be considered "trash." He is overly scrupulous in keeping his grass trimmed, his yard neat.

The memoir also explores the gender issues that arise from Wilburn's commitment to family. He promises his father that his mother will never be left alone, and after her father dies, his mother moves into Wilburn's house. But she misses her own place so much and complains so relentlessly that six months later the family moves into Granny's house—where Mason's mother had begun her married life. When Mason's brother Don and sister LaNelle (the two children still dependent) revolt and move back to their own house, their mother decides to move also. In a compromise, Wilburn takes his meals with the family, but repairs to his mother's house after supper, where he sleeps. As Mason notes, "Duty to elders was primary; a wife's wishes were secondary."

The reader learns not only about Bobbie Ann Mason's growing up, but also about her path to becoming a writer. Absent from that presentation is the streak of self-pity that sometimes accompanies the strengths as well as the drawbacks of that heritage. She both understands and celebrates those "clear springs." But the real heroine of the memoir is her mother, a woman of strength who, realizing that she lives in a culture where men make the final choices about most important matters, makes the necessary adjustments. If, as we sometimes hear, the best preparation for a writer is an unhappy childhood, Mason makes it clear that such is not what she experienced.

Clear Springs is compelling not only for what it reveals about a writer's life, but for its vivid portrayal of rural culture from 1880 through most of the twentieth century. It is a moving salvaging of an era that has mainly disappeared. Having first made her mark creating stories set in the contemporary world, Bobbie Ann Mason is deeply committed to understanding the past—a step necessary for dealing wisely with the present.

Anne Tyler

Susan Elizabeth Sweeney

To consider Anne Tyler's position in the tradition of southern women's writing means, ironically, to underscore her own attentiveness to the very notion of place. Tyler's characters regard their physical and psychological placement with the same ambivalence that Faulkner's Quentin Compson displays when, having been asked in *Absalom, Absalom!* (1936) why he hates the South, he replies: "I dont! I dont hate it! I dont hate it!" Her first novel, *If Morning Ever Comes* (1964), features a similar exchange in which Ben Joe Hawkes keeps insisting to a telephone operator that he *does not* have a southern accent, despite evidence to the contrary. Tyler's fiction, like Faulkner's, demonstrates that you cannot help being shaped by the place you came from, no matter how much you wish you had come from somewhere else. Such emphasis on regional identity may, indeed, be characteristically southern. However, instead of Faulkner's moody, grandiose gothicism—or, for that matter, the sad grotesqueries of Carson McCullers, Flannery O'Connor, and Eudora Welty—Tyler assesses the painful effort involved in navigating such aspects of everyday domestic geography as placing a telephone call, mailing a package, or doing laundry. In her fourteen novels to date, she investigates home as a physical and psychological space that is both prison and refuge.

Most of Tyler's novels take place in or around Baltimore, Maryland, a setting that further complicates her identification as a southern writer. Tyler was born on October 25, 1941, in Minneapolis, and raised first in midwestern and southern Quaker communes and then in the North Carolina mountains. Her family eventually moved to Raleigh, where she attended high school and then, at age sixteen, entered nearby Duke University. After graduating with a Russian major, Tyler studied at Columbia University and worked briefly as a Russian bibliographer at Duke and at McGill University, but by 1967 she and her husband, Taghi Modarressi, had settled for good in Baltimore. That she immediately began writing about Baltimore indicates how important local color is to her work. Tyler's application of southern regionalism to a large East Coast city is particularly interesting; Reynolds Price, who taught her at Duke, calls her "the nearest thing we have to an urban Southern novelist." As a setting for southern fiction, moreover, Baltimore displays the in-betweenness that characterizes Tyler's fiction in other ways. She illustrates Baltimore's borderline position in *Dinner at the Homesick Restaurant* (1982), for example, when Cody Tull and his mother dispute whether it is better to live in the North or the South—until "it emerged that Pearl was assuming Baltimore was North and Cody was assuming it was South."

Tyler's imaginary Baltimore, like that of filmmakers Barry Levinson and John Waters, whose narratives are also haunted by this city, is a place of many contradictions. Characters are marked by their origins—privileged Roland Park, suburban Timonium, rural Garrett County—even as they strive to leave them behind. Tyler's novels are striking, moreover, for her detailed descriptions of these characters' dwellings, from Rose Leary's kitchen shelves, "so completely alphabetized, you'd find the allspice next to the ant poison," to Morgan Gower's bedroom closet, crowded with the colorful costumes he wears for his daily impersonations. She explores homes that manifest the differing personalities of multiple occupants (like Morgan's); that belie traditional domestic space (Ezra Tull's Homesick Restaurant, for example); or that combine private living areas with public businesses (the photography studio in *Earthly Possessions* [1977], the craft store in *Morgan's Passing* [1980], the frame shop in *Breathing Lessons* [1988]). Her characters have occupations, too, that dramatize the interdependence of domesticity and alienation: a restaurateur for nostalgic diners, an author of travel guides for reluctant travelers, an attendant in a nursing home, a specialist in ridding homes of clutter, and in her latest novel, *A Patchwork Planet* (1998), an employee at "Rent-A-Back" whose job consists mostly of making others feel less lonely. (The notion of "borrowing" or "renting" family members appears in several Tyler novels.)

Tyler's characters confront this distinction between "inside" and "outside" in various forms: as introversion and extroversion, closeness and distance, familiarity and foreignness. As Mary F. Robertson shows in her essay "Medusa Points and Contact Points" (1985), Tyler's novels alternate moments of paralyzing closeness within the family with instances of meaningful connection outside it. Even Tyler's paradoxical titles express this tension between remaining at home and running away: *Dinner at the Homesick Restaurant, The Accidental Tourist* (1985), *A Patchwork Planet*. Her plots usually celebrate a protagonist's feeling of connectedness to complete strangers, despite—or rather because of—their difference. Tyler often describes it as a transcendent sense of one's spiritual and geographical place: for example, Pearl Tull, weeding the garden, realizes that she is "kneeling on such a beautiful green little planet," and Macon Leary, looking out an airplane window, suddenly understands "that every little roof contained actual lives."

In tracing these themes, Tyler's fiction has grown steadily more powerful. Her first four novels—*If Morning Ever Comes, The Tin Can Tree* (1965), *A Slipping-Down Life* (1970), and *The Clock Winder* (1972)—indicate her intent, from the very beginning, to tell deceptively simple stories about everyday lives. The early novels are somewhat sentimental and feature less fully developed characters than her later work. With *The Clock Winder*, however, she began to experiment with point of view and temporal progression. The novel alternates several perspectives (one chapter consists solely of correspondence, for example), and its action stretches over a decade. This structure—a series of intense, exquisitely observed moments in one place, usually a home, over several years and across several generations—recurs throughout Tyler's subsequent fiction.

Her next novel, *Celestial Navigation* (1974), catapulted her to higher levels of artistry and critical success. This novel concerns a helplessly reclusive artist, Jeremy Pauling, as observed by various perspectives over a thirteen-year period. Tyler's next three novels—*Searching for Caleb* (1976), *Earthly Possessions*, and *Morgan's Passing*—conduct further experiments in narrative structure. *Searching for Caleb* is especially impressive in its attempt to recapture the Baltimore of seventy years earlier and its emphasis on patterns of conformity and rebellion that repeat from generation to generation. *Morgan's Passing*, although less successful, also innovates in following the repercussions of one character's actions.

Dinner at the Homesick Restaurant, Tyler's ninth novel, demonstrates new depth, maturity, and confidence. Many critics consider this novel—which is noticeably darker than her earlier work—to be her best. However, the novels that followed *Dinner* are also splendid, each in its own way. *The Accidental Tourist* traces Macon Leary's efforts to resist a family history of insularity by marrying vulgar, tempestuous Muriel. *Breathing Lessons* is a tour de force: surpassing Tyler's previous experiments with narrative time, it concentrates on an eighteen-hour period that evokes the Morans' entire past and future. *Saint Maybe* (1991) is an experiment of a different kind; whereas earlier novels paid little heed to spirituality, or characterized clergy (like Elizabeth's father in *The Clock Winder*) as hypocritical or controlling, *Saint Maybe* depicts a familiar Tyler theme—the slow working out of guilt in response to a family crisis—in spiritual terms.

Ladder of Years (1995) is also a departure, in more ways than one. It is one of the few novels in which Tyler focuses not on the family members who stay behind—Jeremy in *Celestial Navigation,* the Learys in *The Accidental Tourist,* Ian in *Saint Maybe*—but on those who leave. Middle-aged Delia walks away from her husband and family on their summer vacation and invents a new life for herself in another town. Like Elizabeth in *The Clock Winder,* she then becomes ensnared in someone else's family; unlike Elizabeth, however, Delia returns home—but on her own terms. Tyler's most recent novel, *A Patchwork Planet,* repeats the redemptive theme of *Saint Maybe.* Although Barnaby Gaitlin does not blame himself for his brother's death, as Ian did, he has been a misfit in his wealthy family ever since his arrest for stealing other people's keepsakes (much as Slevin, Jenny Tull's stepson in *Dinner,* gets into trouble for taking items that remind him of his mother). Barnaby wishes that his guardian angel would appear to set him on the right path, as his great-grandfather's guardian angel supposedly did. That is exactly what happens—or seems to—in the ensuing novel, and by the end, even Barnaby recognizes that he is trustworthy. *A Patchwork Planet* is especially interesting, in contrast to Tyler's previous work, because Barnaby narrates it himself. While Tyler's novels often feature male protagonists, she has never before used a first-person male narrator—not even to convey Jeremy's perspective in *Celestial Navigation.*

Anne Tyler has established a permanent place for herself in southern writing and in American literature. She received the 1989 Pulitzer Prize (for *Breathing Lessons*); she is consistently nominated for other prizes, such as the National Book Award; and she is a member of the American Academy of Arts and Letters. She is also an extremely popular writer, whose books have never gone out of print and whose recent best sellers have been adapted for cinema (*Earthly Possessions, The Accidental Tourist*) or television (*Breathing Lessons, Saint Maybe*). Although she receives relatively little attention from literary scholars, studies of her fiction now include numerous essays, a published dissertation, an edited volume, and a handful of monographs on her work. Meanwhile, Tyler is, as she has said, "still writing," steadily adding to an oeuvre of increasing richness and complexity.

Alice Walker

Barbara T. Christian

> all that night
> I prayed for eyes to see again
> whose last sight
> had been
> a broken bottle
> held negligently
> in a racist
> fist
> God give us trees to plant
> and hands and eyes to
> love them.
>
> —*Alice Walker, "South: The Name of Home"*

Alice Walker is internationally recognized as a writer of the American South and activist in the world. Her first three collections of poems, *Once: Poems* (1968), *Revolutionary Petunias and Other Poems* (1973), and *Good Night Willie Lee, I'll See You in the Morning* (1979); her first collection of short stories, *In Love and Trouble: Stories of Black Women* (1973); her first three novels, *The Third Life of Grange Copeland* (1970), *Meridian* (1976), and *The Color Purple* (1982); and many of the essays of *In Search of Our Moth-*

ers' Gardens: Womanist Prose (1983) are rooted in the history and values of the South and are primarily set in that region. Her writings about the South have won her many literary awards including the Pulitzer Prize for fiction for *The Color Purple* in 1983, the first time this prize was awarded to an African American woman fiction writer. Not only was this novel about a southern woman a best seller, but it was also made into a film that became popular throughout the world.

Nevertheless, Walker's early works do incorporate geographical settings beyond the South—the North, for example, in *The Third Life of Grange Copeland* and Africa in *The Color Purple*. Her more recent works—including her last three essay collections, *Living By the Word* (1988), *The Same River Twice: Honoring the Difficult* (1996), and *Anything We Love Can Be Saved* (1997); and her last three novels, *The Temple of My Familiar* (1989), *Possessing the Secret of Joy* (1992), and *By the Light of My Father's Smile* (1998)—transverse continents. But while settings vary in Walker's voluminous opus and while she continues to evolve in her writings, she is still very much a southern writer. Her poetry, fiction, and essays are indelibly marked by her roots in the American South, the ancestral site where African Americans are becoming a free people and are retaining their cultural uniqueness. Her work is characteristically southern in its immersion in nature, its engagement with family and ancestors, its celebration of black southern folk traditions (particularly those nurtured by black women), its language, its intense spirituality, and its unflagging commitment to social justice. Like Zora Neale Hurston, a sister-elder whose writings Walker helped to resurrect from the oblivion black women writers had been assigned to in the first half of the twentieth century, she is both a southerner and a world traveler, both a compassionate observer and a critical insider. Not only actively involved in the southern revolution of the 1960s, Walker has also been an international activist for social change in the post-1960s era.

Alice Walker was born on February 9, 1944, near the town of Eatonton, Georgia, during segregation that she calls our American apartheid. Her parents, Minnie Lou Grant and Willie Lee Walker, were sharecroppers whose work in the fields barely brought them enough income to survive. Their eighth and last child, Alice grew up in the post–World War II era as the civil rights movement was emerging, a modern movement that affected even Eatonton, Georgia, and enlarged the opportunities available to her.

A traumatic childhood experience marked her for life. At eight she lost the sight of one eye when an older brother accidentally shot her with a BB gun and when no one with a car—meaning a white person—would stop to take her to a hospital. Her eye was covered by a scar until she was fourteen, when a relatively simple operation corrected the disfigurement. She tells us in *Warrior Marks* (1993), the companion book to the videotape protesting female genital mutilation that she produced with Pratibha Parmar, that because she was blamed for her own injury, she felt devalued and thoughts of suicide dominated her early life. But because she learned how to transform her wound into a "warrior mark," she could "see" other warrior marks, such as the effects of racist violence on southern black folk and the cultural practice of female genital mutilation, which she would glimpse on her first trip to Africa.

Walker was able to transform her wound by writing poems in the fields. Early in her life, nature became Alice Walker's solace and teacher. Nature is a visceral element in all of Walker's writing from the Sojourner tree in *Meridian* to animal familiars in her last three novels. The emphasis on Mother Earth as the ground of spirituality has deepened in her most recent work. In her essay about the origin of *The Temple of My Familiar*, "Anything We Love Can Be Saved" (1997), she tells us how language for her is in nature: "A year or so after being there [outside San Francisco] I reconnected with the world of animals and spirits—in trees, old abandoned orchards, undisturbed riverbanks—I had known and loved as a child. I became aware that there is a very thin membrane, human-adult-made, that separates us from this seemingly vanished world, where plants and animals still speak a language we humans understand, and I began to write about the exhilarating experience of regaining my child empathy." She knew from her southern world that our ancestors are nature and are always there for us.

In 1970, the South was seen by those in northern black movements of the late 1960s as backward. Walker insisted in the essay "The Black Writer and the Southern Experience" (1970), "No one could wish for a more advantageous heritage than that bequeathed to the black writer in the South: a compassion for the earth, a trust in humanity beyond our knowledge of evil, and an abiding love of justice." Black southerners have a functional community of struggle that Walker names "One Life" in her novel of struggle *Meridian*, comprising both the "living" and their ancestors. Aware of that community, she retained her maiden name Walker in memory of her great-great-great-grandmother May Poole, who lived to be one hundred and twenty-five, who walked from Virginia to Georgia in the post-emancipation era, and who embodied that spirit of activism about which Walker persistently writes. In the midst of segregation, Walker's father, despite the threat of death, was the first black to vote in their county. Her teachers, against great odds, insisted on high expectations for their students, and the men of Eatonton supported those expectations by building schools. When Walker graduated as valedictorian of her senior class and was awarded "a rehabilitation scholarship" from the state of Georgia, which had systemically oppressed blacks, her black southern community contributed funds to help her to go to Spelman College.

Walker was fortunate in that her mother was a walking history and the church mother of her community. That southern matrilineal history is woven throughout all of her work. In "In Search of Our Mothers' Gardens" (1983), Walker lyrically analyzes how her mother passed on the legacy of creativity that is the spiritual basis of art. Treated by society like "mules of the world," black women used what was available to them—cooking, storytelling, gardening, quilting—to create functional works of art and established artistic models for later generations of African American women. The quilt, a beautiful composition made out of throwaways for everyday use, is capable of infinite patterns and a wide range of expressiveness. Black women of the South kept alive and developed this folk art that came with them from Africa, as so many recent books of scholarship have now demonstrated. Because of the literary activism of writers like Alice Walker, the quilt is now seen as an artistic medium, one that is used by contemporary black women visual artists like Faith Ringgold, who created an art piece based on Alice Walker's novel/quilt, *The Color Purple*. Still, in her southern way, Walker cautions us in her story "Everyday Use" (1973) that the quilt is not a priceless artifact. Rather, the process of quilting is a living representation of the history of the people put to use. So art is a process that illuminates and cherishes all life rather than one that is primarily technique.

Early on, Walker did question her southern heritage. Perhaps because she did leave the South when she was a junior in college to go to Sarah Lawrence College in New York City, perhaps because as a college student she traveled to Europe and Africa, she had to explore the meaning of "home." In the short story "A Sudden Trip Home in the Spring" (1993), Sarah, a college student who is studying painting in the North, returns home to bury her father. While her family may not altogether understand what she is doing, Sarah discovers that her folk "are a very old people in a very young place." When Walker was born in 1944, her family on both sides had already been very much a part of the land. In the BBC documentary "Alice Walker and *The Color Purple*" (1985), she comments that if it is true that the land belongs to those who have buried many ancestors in it, then the land on which she grew up is truly hers.

Walker's love for the earth that she inherited from her ancestors is organically intertwined with an intense spirituality and with a constant, energetic love of justice. The young Walker could not help but be affected by the violent racist system of the South. In *The Third Life of Grange Copeland,* when it was certainly not "politically correct" to do so, she wondered whether the violence in her black community, often within black families, was caused by outside social forces. That insistence on telling the truth the young Walker attributes to "the people involved in the liberation of black people in the South [who] never spoke of expediency, but always of justice, of telling the truth, of standing up and being counted, of fighting for one's rights, of not letting nobody turn you around."

In that tradition Walker has, when it was extremely dangerous to do so, championed local, national, and international movements for justice and has written about how American black women's rights to social, sexual, and spiritual fulfillment are related. She has publicized the unjust treatment of political prisoners in the United States, such as Dessie Woods and Mumia Abu Jamal; she has on the international scene protested female genital mutilation in her novel *Possessing the Secret of Joy;* she has exposed the neocapitalist formation of contemporary African leaders in *The Temple of My Familiar;* she has critiqued fathers' abusive control of their daughters' sexuality in *By the Light of My Father's Smile;* she has protested the destruction of indigenous peoples, whether they be in El Salvador or in California. In a recent interview, Walker enunciated that courage, integrity, and practicality she gleaned from her southern tradition: "I can't imagine anybody whispering in my ear to tell me to write anything that I don't feel like writing. And I don't take advances. When my publisher knows that I have a book coming, it is already on his or her desk. I'm the daughter of sharecroppers and I know if you become indebted to people, often you can never pay them back."

What is specifically southern about Walker's manner of protesting is that it always takes place within the possibilities of healing. So she has supported those movements that she finds to be supportive of fulfillment and happiness: Cuba as a society in pursuit of health and well-being, the anti-apartheid movement in South Africa, animal rights and environmental justice, the movement of indigenous peoples wherever they might be on this planet. As she says in *Anything We Love Can Be Saved,* her willingness to use all that she is flows from her deep awareness that "to be such a person or to witness anyone at this moment of transcendent presence is to know that what is human is linked, by a daring compassion, to what is divine."

This arc toward healing is also characteristic of Walker's writing: in each of her novels, major characters who are wounded in some way go through a process of healing. Sometimes these major characters, as in the case of Celie, whose character is based on Walker's step-grandmother Rachel, are related to Walker's own ancestors. Although some might vilify the ancestors' language, as in the controversy around the black folk English in *The Color Purple,* Walker points to how it is through their language—which is the sound of their world view—that we can still know them. The ancestors and their language are always there for Walker, and she is always there for them. As she stated in an interview for *Black Issues* (1999), "Part of what we do is heal the ancestors. If you can heal the ancestors, you bring peace to the present. This thought has kept me going through a lot of the turmoil that has accompanied my life as a writer. I feel like I know what my job is, even if nobody else has a clue."

This perspective is especially apparent in Walker's most recent novel, *By the Light of My Father's Smile,* where a father who has died must come back to witness how he has negatively affected the sexuality of his grown daughters. In the process he learns to support his daughters completely, including and especially their sexuality. Walker's concern with female sexuality is not new. In *The Third Life, In Love and Trouble,* and *Meridian* in the 1970s, Walker explored the ways in which woman is punished for her sexuality. She noted in an early interview with John O'Brien that she had become pregnant when she was in college, and because she knew how ashamed her parents would be, she decided to commit suicide. Convinced that she would die, Walker wrote the poems that would become her first volume, *Once.* Thus, her writing career is connected to her awareness of herself as having a female body.

Partially because of her own literary and social activism in feminist movements, a multitude of American women in the 1970s began to insist on their own autonomy, which fueled Walker's optimism in the early 1980s. In *You Can't Keep a Good Woman Down* and *In Search of Our Mothers' Gardens,* she articulated the concept of Womanism. As is so often true with Walker, the folk tradition of black women was her guide, in this case the expression "You acting womanish"—denoting willfulness as woman's source of autonomy. Walker's last three novels, with their emphasis on female sexuality, and her last book of essays, *Anything We Love Can Be Saved,* provide a collection of earth-maps demonstrating how spirituality, the pursuit of justice, and female sexuality are central to the universe renewing itself.

In her most recent publications, Walker continues to delve into her southern heritage, especially as it relates to women and poor people, particularly blacks, who are often maligned in the Christian religion. Walker's essay "The Only Reason You Want to Go to Heaven Is That You Have Been Driven out of Your Mind" (1997) both celebrates her mother's dedication to the church and questions the ways in which that church violates women and poor people. The essay concludes with an affirmation and rejuvenation of the lessons Alice Walker has learned from her parents and black southern communities: "All people deserve to worship a God who also worships them. A God that made them, and likes them. That is why Nature, Mother Earth, is such a good choice."

Rita Mae Brown

Harold Woodell

An outspoken lesbian artist, Rita Mae Brown is quite possibly the most controversial southern writer of the last half of the twentieth century. She has developed personas in both her literature and private life that have raised the eyebrows of the literary establishment and disturbed mainstream readers with their dramatic and at times sensational challenges to orthodox beliefs in race, politics, and sexuality. Novelist, poet, political essayist, scriptwriter, feminist, and farmer, she has throughout her varied career remained a constant champion of justice for minorities, equality for all people, and respect for the working underclass. From first to last, her enemies have been what William Blake called the "mind-forged manacles" of humankind: prejudice, bigotry, hypocrisy, and artificial class distinction.

Born November 28, 1944, in Hanover, Pennsylvania, to an unwed mother, Brown was adopted by Ralph and Julia Brown, a working-class couple who lived in Hanover until she was eleven years old, when the family moved to Florida. The location of Hanover, a few miles from the Mason-Dixon Line, has had an enduring impact on Brown's life and writings. In Florida, Brown proved to be an outstanding student-athlete and won a scholarship to the University of Florida; however, she was asked to leave the university in 1964 for her active support of the civil rights movement and for lesbian activities. She went on to receive an A.A. degree (1965) from Broward Junior College, a B.A. in English and classics (1968) from New

York University, a cinematography degree (1968) from the School of the Visual Arts, and finally a Ph.D. in English and political science (1976) from the Institute for Policy Studies in Washington, D.C., making her one of a small handful of important literary artists with an earned doctorate.

An avid feminist during the late 1960s and early 1970s, Brown organized and supported various causes in the second wave of the women's movement. However, her strong sense of independence and her firm defense of lesbians as normal people who should be taken seriously led her into conflict with several leaders for women's rights, and she subsequently broke her affiliations with groups like the Radicalesbians, the Furies Collective, and the National Organization for Women, after concluding that they were counterproductive in the struggle for complete equality. Brown then turned to literature as her primary interest, writing first poetry and fiction, and later teleplays and film scripts. After a lengthy series of successes and failures, she returned to the South in the 1990s and purchased a farm near Charlottesville, Virginia, where she now lives with her friends, cats, dogs, and horses.

Even a brief sketch of Brown's life reveals important themes that thread their way through all of her work. First and foremost are the facts that she was adopted, that she lived her childhood on the borderline between the North and the South, that she was well aware of the class distinctions between the blue-collar workers and the wealthy, and, above all, that she grew up accepting her sexuality as normal to her but different from that of her contemporaries. Thus, from early on, she saw her lot in life as that of an outsider, as one who did not fit the preconceived notions of what constituted a proper southern girl.

Brown's outsider status is identical to that of a major component of the literature of the South. In story after story, from George Washington Harris' Sut Lovingood (a "Nat'ral Born Durn'd Fool") in the humor of the Old Southwest to William Faulkner's Quentin Compson in *Absalom, Absalom!* (1936) and Flannery O'Connor's Misfit in "A Good Man Is Hard to Find," southern authors have portrayed characters outside the boundaries of normal life and on the periphery of society as pariahs—flawed, eccentric, and atypical—yet human beings whose experiences with life's lesions help bridge the gap between inhumanity and compassion.

So it is with Brown's literary creations. After a shaky start with poetry, a genre for which her talents were not suited, she hit her stride with the remarkable first novel *Rubyfruit Jungle* (1973), the first lesbian work written in America that did not portray homosexual women as perverse, mentally disturbed, or emotionally troubled. Quite the contrary, Molly Bolt, the heroine of the novel and a thinly disguised version of Brown herself, is convinced she is better-adjusted than the orthodox heterosexuals who surround and isolate her from a "normal" existence. As can well be imagined, a novel like *Rubyfruit Jungle,* the title of which refers to female genitalia, did not find a ready publisher even as late as 1968. After rejections by every major publishing house in the East, Brown submitted the manuscript to Daughters, Inc., where it became a cult classic before being sold to Bantam Books. Considered one of America's "permanent" books, the novel has now sold over a million copies worldwide.

Often compared to Huckleberry Finn, Molly Bolt resembles Mark Twain's creation in her courage and strength of will to think for herself. However, a more apt parallel to Molly is found in an even earlier picaresque novel, with a character who shares her first name—*The Fortunes and Misfortunes of Moll Flanders* (1722). Both Daniel Defoe's Moll and Brown's Molly are exuberant characters filled with high humor and a lust for living life on the margins of danger and convention. And, curiously enough, Moll Flanders finds herself at the end of Defoe's narrative a wealthy planter in Virginia, not too unlike the actual rags-to-riches career of Rita Mae Brown.

By 1973, Brown had published a volume of translated plays, *Hrotsvitha: Six Medieval Latin Plays* (1971), and two volumes of poetry, *The Hand That Cradles the Rock* (1971) and *Songs to a Handsome Woman* (1973). On occasion she has branched out from fiction into other fields as well: *A Plain Brown Rapper* (1976), a series of political essays; *Starting from Scratch: A Different Kind of Writers' Manual* (1988), an unconventional writer's guide; and several scripts, the most notable being the teleplays "I Love Liberty" (1982) and "The Long Hot Summer" (1985). Nevertheless, the success of *Rubyfruit Jungle* determined that Brown's major career as a writer would be in the realm of fiction, a career that to date has produced a total of seventeen novels. In general, the development of her fiction shows a steady progression in both an increased mastery of style and structure and in a change of subject matter from the personal concerns of the self to the more universal experiences of all women who have had to struggle to maintain their self-worth in a male-dominated culture.

Brown's second novel, *In Her Day* (1976), is a sequel to *Rubyfruit Jungle.* Here, the Molly Bolt character is named Carole Hanratty, and she lives through the radical 1960s and 1970s in Greenwich Village. Carole's involvement with feminist and lesbian groups parallels Brown's own tribulations during those heady days. In her next two novels, *Six of One* (1978) and *Southern Discomfort* (1982), Brown moves from a strictly first-person autobiographical narrative to third-person treatments of women in order to examine relationships in both the past and the present. Like William Faulkner, Brown came to believe that the individual in the present is a product of people's actions in the past. Only through an understanding of the moral and cultural imperatives of the past can a person living in the present understand and accept the flawed human condition.

Six of One begins in the present of 1980 but quickly moves to a third-person omniscient account that delineates the relationship between two sisters, Julia Ellen and Louise. Moving back and forth in the lives of these two women from the present to 1909, the story focuses on the artificial barriers that divide working-class people from the aristocrats who reside in the small town of Runnymede, Maryland. The Mason-Dixon Line, which runs through the center of the town, becomes an apt emblem of the divisions that limit human interaction, whether they be the North versus the South, the New South versus the Old South, or the masculine world view versus the feminine.

Brown's fourth novel, *Southern Discomfort* (1982), is her fullest exploration of the borders and barriers that human beings construct for themselves to the detriment of love and understanding. The narrative explores the separation theme through the social strata that divided the haves from the have-nots in Montgomery, Alabama, in 1918 and 1928. The time span is especially relevant because the South finally began to industrialize and re-enter the American mainstream after World War I only to have its dream of success shattered by the arrival of the Depression. After *Southern Discomfort,* Brown published six more novels centered on strong women and feminist issues. *Sudden Death* (1983), a novel about the professional women's tennis circuit, was inspired in part by the author's relationship with Martina Navratilova, a world-class tennis champion who was one of the loves of her life. The subsequent feminist novels include *High Hearts* (1986), in which a woman joins her husband as a combatant during the American Civil War; *Bingo* (1988), a sequel to *Six of One*; *Venus Envy* (1993), about the need for gays to accept themselves; *Dolley: A Novel of Dolley Madison in Love and War* (1994), which focuses on the wife of President James Madison; and *Riding Shotgun* (1996), a time-travel novel that sends a woman from a fox hunt in Virginia in the present to one in 1699.

In 1990 Brown's career took an unexpected but profitable turn with the publication of *Wish You Were Here,* the first of a series of murder mysteries she pretends to have coauthored with her cat Sneaky Pie Brown. To date this duo has penned seven narratives that involve a postmistress, Mary (Harry) Hariteen, in the small town of Crozet, Virginia, her two house pets, a cat named Mrs. Murphy and a dog, Tucker Tee. Written in the style of the detective story known as a "cozy," these stories portray the recently divorced

Harry as the center of a village that sees an unusual number of murders—mysteries she solves along with the help of Mrs. Murphy and Tucker Tee. These mysteries have delighted and dismayed many of Brown's fans, but have also won her a large mainstream audience who love a well-told thriller. One of these was televised under the title "Murder, She Purred" in the fall of 1998 on *The Wonderful World of Disney.*

All in all, Brown's career has shown a remarkable development from its origins in the social upheavals of the 1960s to the farm life of rural Virginia in the 1990s. Her most enduring work, *Rubyfruit Jungle,* was published over a quarter of a century ago, and the fact that it is still in publication is a tribute not only to its artistry and lasting power as a novel about lesbianism but also to its enduring portrait of the struggle for self-identity that everyone must undergo. While Rita Mae Brown is often considered the foremost lesbian author America has yet produced, she herself rejects all such labels that suggest political bias. Instead, she would prefer to explain her career in more universal terms, as she did in an interview in *Publisher's Weekly* in October of 1978: "I'm a writer and I'm a woman and I'm from the South and I'm alive, and that is that."

Lee Smith

Nancy Parrish

Lee Smith's 1992 novel, *The Devil's Dream,* recounts the rise to prominence of a family nearly legendary in the Nashville country and western recording industry. In reflecting upon the source of her personal achievement and that of her family, the family's twentieth-century descendent, Katie Cocker, concludes, "I know where we're from. I know who we are." No theme could be more quintessentially southern; yet in her short stories and novels Lee Smith adapts the traditional southern story to a more human scale, one more closely tied to historical fact and cultural verisimilitude. As her career has progressed, Smith increasingly infuses her stories and characters with research, exploring subjects and populations—housewives, beauticians, mountain folk, and others—that have, traditionally, been marginalized by mainstream cultures. A hallmark of her writing has been this deeply held respect in portraying the extraordinary drama that exists in the lives of ordinary people. In pursuing these subjects, Smith contributes not only to the new southern regionalist movement, which includes Kaye Gibbons, Anne Tyler, and Jill McCorkle, but also to the wider conversation about how self-knowledge is gained in a postmodern South. Smith's witty prose, exceptional ear for voice, and humane portraits of the domestic and social rituals amount to an almost missionary advocacy of the value of the ordinary life.

Lee Smith was born in Grundy, Virginia, a small town tucked away in the Appalachian mountains, in 1944. Her earliest "novel," written at age eight, was "Jane Russell and Adlai Stevenson Go West in a Covered Wagon," a twelve-page story constructed around the two celebrities she admired most at that time. In a sense, Smith's writing interests have always sprung from people and places she has loved. Her Appalachian roots, however, took some time and distance for her to appreciate. Her parents sent her to St. Catherine's girls' school in Richmond, Virginia, in order to help her escape the educational and cultural limitations of Appalachia. From there she attended Hollins College where, guided by Louis D. Rubin, Jr., and influenced by peer writers Annie Dillard, Lucinda MacKethan, and Anne Goodwyn Jones, Smith gained crucial ground in her development as a writer in that she began to experiment with intimate, conversational prose styles and began to see Appalachia as a potential wellspring for subject matter. Her forthcoming book, *The Last Girls,* is based upon some of her experiences at Hollins. By the end of her senior year in college, Smith had won a $3,000 Book-of-the-Month Club Writing Fellowship prize for *The Last Day the Dogbushes Bloomed* (1968). She married poet James Seay in 1967 and, with him, had two sons before they divorced in 1982. In 1989 she married syndicated columnist Hal Crowther, with whom she now resides in Hillsborough, North Carolina.

From 1969 until 1970 Smith worked as a feature writer and editor for the Tuscaloosa *News* Sunday magazine. This writing experience formed the basis for her novel *Fancy Strut* (1973), a series of stories loosely based upon local news and individuals. The flaws in the structure of the novel reflect the difficulty Smith had in her early career in attempting to sandwich her writing career between her job and family responsibilities. Still, Smith was already mastering the techniques of capturing a particular voice and developing fully realized characters. She persisted in writing even while teaching in Nashville's Harpeth Hall School (1971–74) and at the Carolina Friends School in Durham, North Carolina (1974–77). As she achieved more success with her writing, Smith began to teach in college settings: a semester as writer-in-residence at Hollins College; instructor of creative writing in the Continuing Education School of Duke University (1977); and lecturer in fiction writing at the University of North Carolina at Chapel Hill (1978–81). From 1981 to 1989 she served as assistant and then associate professor of English at North Carolina State University; in 1989 she became a full professor.

Smith's early professional writing interests initiated an increasingly open consideration of the victimization of women in American society and the ways women have learned to overcome that condition. Her early stories describe girls and young women who have been literally or figuratively silenced, limited, or raped. Her later novels, by contrast, reveal women who resist cultural restraints, find their own voices, and succeed at unique life goals that oppose conventional expectations. Her first novel, *The Last Day the Dogbushes Bloomed,* is a story concerning loss of innocence, a child's account of the evil or strangeness she sees entering her life. Nine-year-old Susan works to decipher the family codes that leave her isolated, even within her own house, but she never finds the precise words to name these interlopers, which are, in fact, sex and death.

Something in the Wind (1971) continues this examination of lost innocence. The novel is, in part, based upon the culture shock she felt as an Appalachian teenager suddenly enrolled in an exclusive eastern girls' school. Brooke Kincaid is cast as a protagonist in danger of losing her identity by measuring herself against the social definitions of what a southern lady should be. In challenging that definition, Brooke loses not simply her virginity but her belief in the clichés that have guided her life to that point. *Black Mountain Breakdown* (1980) reflects an intensification of Smith's interest in cultural restrictions. The focus of this novel, originally explored by Smith's short story "Paralyzed," is, in a sense, the point toward which Smith had been heading in her first two novels: a woman so completely defined by social roles and male expectations that she literally paralyzes herself. Smith's divorce followed soon after the publication of this novel, and with it came a turning toward Appalachian subject matter, the material that would signal a transformation of her female protagonists from victims to women who could determine their own destinies.

Although as a teenager she wanted to escape from the circumscribed life of Appalachia, by the time Smith was an adult, she had virtually reversed that position and, as the author of books such as *Oral History* (1983), *Fair and Tender Ladies* (1988), and *The Devil's Dream* (1992), has made Appalachia both substance and metaphor for her explorations of self and other in American society. Her poignant portraits of mountain hollows stricken with poverty and young women burdened by cultural expectations echo the artistic interests of Eudora Welty and Flannery O'Connor. Her structural devices, however, owe more to Virginia Woolf and William Faulkner, though her humor allows a much wider range in style than that achieved by any of her models. In these Appalachian novels Smith exhibits an adroit control of voice, a skilled handling of point of view, and an almost scholarly attention to historical accuracy.

Oral History was the first novel Smith conceived of as a novel rather than as an elongation of a short story and was the story that brought Smith's writing to national prominence. The story employs multiple first-person narrators and in doing so combines the rich oral heritage of storytelling in the South and the significance of geographical place with a postmodernist perception of truth as being mere subjectivity. It is a frame tale chronicling the history of the Cantrell family, a poor Appalachian family whose story of exploitation, poverty, and persistence is a metaphor for the history of Appalachia itself. Smith's next novel, *Family Linen* (1985), based upon a newspaper story of a woman who suffers from headaches because she has repressed the memory of her father's murder. Again in this novel Smith exhibits her fine ear for gossipy southern personae and an attentiveness to the complexities that characterize family relationships. Smith made another significant advance in *Fair and Tender Ladies*, an epistolary novel recording the historical dramas of Appalachia from 1900 to the 1970s through the eyes of narrator Ivy Rowe. Rowe is perhaps Smith's strongest protagonist, a woman who weathers every physical obstacle, successfully resists social censure, and ends life happily because she learns that she has the right to determine her own life. *The Devil's Dream* is a natural successor to *Fair and Tender Ladies*. Rather than a series of letters narrating a life, Smith structures her novel as a "record album" of "songs" linking an Appalachian family's growth to the development of the country-and-western music industry. Eschewing any single first-person narrator in this later novel, Smith implicitly asserts that all voices must be heard in a society. Protagonist Katie Cocker, like Ivy Rowe, learns from the school of hard knocks that knowing "where we are from" and "who we are" is, in essence, the foundation for self-determination in life. Smith's recent novel *Saving Grace* (1995) returns to some of her earlier themes in that it records the struggle of a young Appalachian woman trying to escape the violence and exploitation of fundamentalist religion to find a sign that will reveal some meaning in her life. The multiple meanings of the title suggest Smith's vital concern that women explore possibilities for their lives.

Smith's writing has been a shaping force in the development of contemporary southern literature. Her humor and historical research deconstruct traditional southern myths surrounding gender and social class while, concurrently, reflecting an almost familial care for the lives of ordinary people. This perceptive, edgy tension among multiple perspectives, historical accuracy, and humor establishes Smith as perhaps the most intellectually independent of the postmodern southern writers.

Josephine Humphreys

Elinor Ann Walker

Although she has published only three novels, Josephine Humphreys and her work have received thoughtful attention from scholars and readers who find her lyrical, allusive prose and her deftness at manipulating narrative voice compelling reasons for closer study. Preoccupied by place, family, and history, Humphreys perpetuates the southern writer's abiding obsession with these themes. However, her texts are populated not only by the familiar and angst-ridden voices of musing white males who lament the changing landscape and lost ideals of the South, but also by incisive female voices that question accepted versions of history. Furthermore, Humphreys readily grants characters marginalized by class or race significant roles in her fiction. Imaginative possibilities abound for Humphreys' characters as they create and revise the public and private versions of their identities.

Humphreys was born on February 2, 1945, in Charleston, South Carolina, attended Duke University, where she received her A.B. degree in 1967, and went on to graduate school at Yale University, earning her master's degree in English there in 1968. Humphreys then enrolled in a Ph.D. program at the University of Texas in Austin, where she studied from 1968 to 1971, completing her course work and all other requirements except the dissertation. In 1971, she returned to Charleston and began teaching at Baptist College (now called Charleston Southern University), where she was an assistant professor of English until 1978. Married and with two children,

Humphreys did not begin writing her first novel until she was thirty-three years old, even then taking five more years to complete the book, seeking to balance motherhood and authorship.

This novel, *Dreams of Sleep* (1984), met with critical praise upon its publication, winning the Ernest Hemingway Award for the best first novel in 1985. Set in Charleston, South Carolina, the novel focuses on three characters, Will and Alice Reese, a well-educated, upper-middle-class white couple, and Iris Moon, their babysitter, who is also white but whose socio-economic status differentiates her sharply from the Reeses. Iris is in love with an African American man, the son of a woman who works for Will's mother. Alternating among Will's, Alice's, and Iris' points of view, the novel assesses familial collapse and its tentative reconstruction as Will and Alice struggle with their marital bonds in the wake of Will's affair with his secretary while Iris seeks independence from her drunken and irresponsible mother. Their stories cross the boundaries imposed by gender, class, and race; Humphreys suggests that the fragmentation of society necessitates a renegotiation of both self and other.

Will Reese, particularly, is obsessed with society's deconstruction, on both literal and figurative levels. He bemoans that historical statues are losing their noses, that houses are being divided into apartments, and that he can no longer remember significant lines of poems. Professing stoicism, Will neglects his relationships with his wife and his best friend, Danny, and in his characterization Humphreys parodies the character type of the paralyzed but thoughtful white male that so often appears in southern and, indeed, in western literature. (One thinks of Faulkner's Quentin Compson, Wolfe's Eugene Gant, Warren's Jack Burden, and Percy's Will Barrett but also of Shakespeare's Hamlet, Eliot's Prufrock, Updike's Harry Angstrom.) It is Iris, rather than Will, who salvages the Reese family by inspiring Alice to emerge from her depression. A Phi Beta Kappa and an erstwhile mathematician, Alice has succumbed to her own paralysis, but unlike Will she transcends this state imaginatively, remembering a dream that allows her to nurture not just one self but many: wife, mother, creative person. Energized by Iris' literal touch—the simple gesture of a hand on her arm—Alice assumes responsibility for her world and for herself. Although the novel ends happily, with Alice and Will's reconciliation, Humphreys asserts that love requires a kind of diligence that surpasses the superficial profession of fidelity in words. Enrapt by language, particularly that which extols the past, Will Reese often forgets the present and the reality that the word "love" is supposed to signify.

Rich in Love (1987) also documents familial disintegration. Told in the first person by the adolescent narrator Lucille Odom, the novel recounts the sudden departure of Lucille's mother, her father's subsequent breakdown, her sister's return home with her new husband and unplanned pregnancy, and Lucille's own uncharacteristic affair with her sister's husband, who is, not coincidentally, a historian. Fascinated by history and what Lucille calls its "insides," that which resists accurate telling, Lucille exposes the rift between the visible and invisible parts of the self as she struggles to reconcile her own behavior with prior assumptions she has made about her life. In the process, she also observes that words such as "family" are prey to changing definitions, continuing to manifest Humphreys' own preoccupation with language's instability. Finally, it is Rhody, an African American friend of Lucille's mother, who identifies Lucille's emotional fragility and who pronounces that, in order to see and interpret events correctly, one must recognize the narrow parameters of one's own vision. As Lucille struggles to make sense of her own history and the more abstract southern history of her hometown in South Carolina, she discovers that all events are told from someone's particular point of view, a perspective that may be clouded by personal bias or need. Acknowledging that things are not always what they seem, Lucille permits the visible and the invisible to coexist; in so doing, she, like Alice Reese, finds that many selves inhabit her and that there is room for them all.

Also set in South Carolina, in this case again in Charleston, *The Fireman's Fair* (1991) centers on Rob Wyatt, a white upper-middle-class attorney from whose perspective the story is told. Humphreys juxtaposes Rob's bumbling attempts to salvage his life from the ordinary and his best friend Albert's meaningful and understated existence. Inspiring comparisons to many a Walker Percy character, particularly Will Barrett, Rob Wyatt quits his lucrative job and moves out of his house into a much simpler and barren beach bungalow, where he gives voice to his malaise as a hurricane barrels toward the coast. Enthralled by both his long-lost love, Louise, who has married his former law partner because Rob never thought to propose, and the much younger and waiflike Billie (cf. Percy's Allie), Rob bungles relationship after relationship, usually because his words and promises prove hollow and unreliable. By contrast, Albert, an African American bartender and former church sexton, uses language responsibly, continually reminding Rob of Rob's own failure to do so. In Rob, Humphreys pushes the parodic envelope. Rather than afflicting him with some outward sign of his absurdity, like the dizzy spells or amnesia that Percy's characters often suffer, Humphreys creates a white male who lacks the expected trappings of stoicism to redeem him from his solipsism. Eternally passive, Rob waits for whatever comes without trying to effect change in himself. Albert, on the other hand, provides the gloss on Humphreys' parody, at once pointing out Rob's shortcomings and exemplifying more mature behavior. Because he insists upon the responsible use of language, Albert emerges as the novel's reliable voice, even as he remains silenced by the world that Humphreys describes.

Humphreys' work manifests her fascination with family, community, history, race, and all of the complexities pertaining thereto. However, she differs from her southern literary foremothers, such as Ellen Glasgow, Eudora Welty, Carson McCullers, and Flannery O'Connor, in that Humphreys' characters are concerned mostly with fashioning some space for themselves that does not depend upon anything else in their worlds. This space is figurative, not literal, provides self-restorative energy, and depends solely on the individual, not another person or abstractions such as religion or history, for its construction. In other words, Humphreys' characters dwell much more often in interior landscapes of thought than those of Glasgow, Welty, McCullers, or O'Connor, whose female characters, particularly, navigate their lives very much in relation to the concrete pull of their environments. Since community, family, and place are all subjects whose influences are not unconditionally positive, none of these entities guarantees a character's successful cultivation of his or her identity. Especially in the case of female characters such as Alice Reese, Iris Moon, or Lucille Odom, Humphreys in fact emphasizes that their dreams and stories of self-realization bear but a tenuous connection to their environments. Certainly she shares these concerns with other contemporary southern women writers such as Kaye Gibbons, Jill McCorkle, Anne Tyler, and Bobbie Ann Mason, among others.

Triumph over circumstance inspires Humphreys in real life, as well. She facilitated the publication of and wrote the introduction for *Gal: A True Life* (1994), the memoir of a young black woman who came to Humphreys seeking help with the transcription of her manuscript. Published under the pseudonym Ruthie Bolton to preserve its author's anonymity, the book recounts its teller's childhood experience of abuse at her grandfather's hands and documents the courage and determination that led her to pursue her education despite the overwhelming odds against her.

A surprising number of critical articles have been written about Josephine Humphreys' work, suggesting that she is a contemporary writer of some significance despite the relative smallness of her canon. Interviews with Humphreys appear in journals such as the *South Carolina Review,* the *Southern Review,* and the *Southern Quarterly.* Generally, her fiction has met with positive reviews. Upon publication, all three of her novels were reviewed in the New York *Times,* where fellow southern writers such as Ellen Douglas, Fred Chappell, and Pat Conroy routinely found not only promise in her fiction but also true talent. In fact, Ellen Douglas wrote that *Dreams of Sleep* was "the best first novel I've read in years." Humphreys' most recent novel, *Nowhere Else on Earth* (2000), which takes place in North Carolina during the Civil War, has been compared to Charles Frazier's *Cold Mountain.*

In addition to her fiction, Humphreys has authored several essays that attest to her interest in southern life and culture, especially as those subjects pertain to her family and to her native state of South Carolina. She has written about southern cuisine, architecture, and land development, among other topics. One memoir entitled "My Real Invisible Self" documents her indebtedness to her grandmother for encouraging the young Humphreys to nurture her creative self and write. Humphreys also credits Reynolds Price as one of her mentors, and like Price she sometimes labors beneath the shadows of their southern literary predecessors. But Humphreys' fiction departs in many ways from this legacy, at once paying homage to and deconstructing previous southern literary paradigms.

Dorothy Allison

Carolyn E. Megan

In her 1993 collection of essays entitled *Skin: Talking about Sex, Class, and Literature,* Dorothy Allison writes, "I have known I was a lesbian since I was a teenager, and I have spent a good twenty years making peace with the effects of incest and physical abuse. But what may be the central fact of my life is that I was born in Greenville, South Carolina, the bastard daughter of a white woman from a desperately poor family." In this collection, Allison addresses the roles that class, sexuality, and poverty play in forming a person's world view. Indeed, these are the themes that underscore all of Allison's fiction and nonfiction writing: narratives that look unflinchingly at what Allison refers to as the "harder truths." The success of these narratives draws upon Allison's own struggle to identify, name, understand, and move beyond the poverty she experienced as a child.

Born in 1949, Dorothy Allison was raised by her mother and an abusive stepfather in Greenville. The family was appallingly poor, with both parents working several jobs yet continuously struggling to get out of debt. Born out of wedlock and into a society that held impoverished people in contempt, Allison learned what it was to be marginalized and to live on the periphery. It was through reading the works of writers such as James Baldwin, Flannery O'Connor, John Steinbeck, and Carson McCullers that Allison learned how to survive.

When she was a teenager, Allison's family moved to Florida so that her stepfather could escape debt. In Florida, free from the perceptions held about her back in Greenville, Allison developed as a student and as a writer. She was the first in her family to graduate from high school and then to go on to college. While in her early twenties, Allison became involved in the feminist movement and began for the first time to understand the importance of giving voice to her stories. Through naming her experience, Allison was no longer compartmentalizing her different roles as an illegitimate child, incest survivor, daughter, sister, student, lover, lesbian, poor person.

This process of storytelling, of naming the hard truths, is the focus of Allison's work. Her discussions of poverty are not a vehicle for looking at the middle class, nor are they tales of morality featuring the ennobled poor white southerner. Instead, these are the voices of people who are in difficult circumstances, struggling to move through and beyond their problems. The stories look at the positive and negative choices that people make. By only seeing one perspective, Allison's work suggests, people become debilitated and destroy any possibility of growth. Allison's goal is not to judge but rather to understand the tensions and desires behind people's choices and the true and false stories people create in order to survive. For Allison's characters, it is the recognition of these choices that allows them the opportunity to flourish.

All of Allison's writing begins with the development of voice. In her earliest work, *The Women Who Hate Me* (1983), the voices take the form of narrative poems. Within this raw collection, Allison describes the brutality of poverty as witnessed through her narrator. In the poem "Upcountry" for example, Allison writes:

> When the uncles came to visit
> pickups parked aslant the yard
> bottles that rocked from board to rim
> shotguns point down beside the gears
> a leather holster or canvas sling
> I watched the neighbors squint their eyes
> "no-count, low down, disgusting,"
> I put my nails to the bones of my neck
> squeezed, trying to understand.

Allison's narrator begins the process of finding herself through naming and identifying the subject matter. The narrator not only describes in great detail her uncles' visits but also registers her neighbors' reactions.

In her collection of short stories entitled *Trash* (1988), Allison pushes these narrative poems into new territory by exploring the relationship between storytelling and survival. In the story "Preface: Deciding to Live," the narrator says, "Writing it all down was purging. Putting those stories on paper took them out of the nightmare realm and made me almost love myself for being able to finally face them. More subtly, it gave me a way to love the people I wrote about—even the ones I had fought with or hated." In these stories, Allison establishes the themes for all her work to follow: the driving force of hunger, the desire to change, and the importance of storytelling in creating change.

In her first novel, *Bastard out of Carolina* (1992), which was nominated for the National Book Award, Allison successfully weaves together the strands from her previous work. The novel tells the story of Bone, a young girl who searches for her own identity in response to the abuse she has suffered at the hands of her stepfather. Bone seeks identity through the stories her mother, aunts, and uncles tell her, and then later in the gospel revival shows that come through town. Ultimately, by listening to her own voice and through naming the true horrors of her life, Bone sets in place the possibility of moving beyond her family's history.

Underlying this plot line are the deeper themes of poverty and choice. In hopes of escaping a life of poverty and providing a better upbringing for her daughter, Bone's mother, Annie, decides to stay with an abusive man. This decision, however, prevents Annie from fulfilling her hopes, as she is forced to flee with her husband after he rapes Bone. Allison uses Annie's actions to delve into the deeper idea of the novel. The theme of choice is addressed by Bone's aunt when she attempts to explain Annie's actions:

> "We do terrible things to the ones we love sometimes," she said. "We can't explain it. We can't excuse it. It eats us up, but we do them just the same. You want to know about your mama, I know. But I can't tell you anything. None of us can. No one knows where she's gone. I can't explain that to you, Bone. I just can't, but I know your mama loves you. Don't doubt that. She loves you more than her life, and she ain't never gonna forgive herself for what she's done to you, what she allowed to happen."

In *Bastard out of Carolina,* Allison treads the fragile ground between judgment and understanding, violence and redemption. In the end, Allison suggests, people will suffer the ramifications of their choices by the very lives they lead.

Cavedweller (1998), Allison's second novel, explores the relationship between identity and place. In this novel, Delia Byrd returns from her ten-year exile in California to her hometown in Cayro, Georgia. Several years earlier,

Delia had abandoned her two daughters in Cayro, and this trip home is her attempt to reacquaint herself with them. Delia's journey is developed physically and psychologically through the metaphor of several caves near Cayro, where Delia goes spelunking. Literally, Delia's spelunking reflects the darkness she must embrace in order to understand why she left Cayro, why she returns, and how land and place inform a person even from a great distance. In essence, Delia is returning to embrace all of the stories of her life.

Allison's nonfiction work includes *Skin: Talking about Sex, Class, and Literature* and the autobiography *Two or Three Things I Know for Sure* (1995). In these two books, Allison restates her theme of storytelling as a means of survival and understanding. In *Two or Three Things I Know for Sure*, Allison writes, "Two or three things I know, two or three things I know for sure, and one of them is that to go on living I have to tell stories, that stories are the one sure way I know to touch the heart and change the world. . . . Two or three things I know for sure and one of them is that telling the story all the way through is an act of love." Allison's work speaks to a number of people, including lesbians, abuse survivors, feminists, southerners, displaced southerners, and the impoverished. What all these voices share in common is Allison's belief that it isn't enough to live in a place of injustice and outrage alone. The writer's job, each person's job, is to delve further, to question, to hold the ambiguous difficult middle ground, to record, to be attentive, to name, to speak, to write.

Beth Henley

Karen L. Laughlin

Crimes of the Heart (1982), Beth Henley's first professionally produced play, was a phenomenal hit, winning the 1981 Pulitzer Prize for drama even before its impressive 535-performance run on Broadway. While her Pulitzer was the first awarded to a woman playwright in twenty-three years, theater critics focused less on the potential feminism of her work than on her place within a southern dramatic and literary tradition. *Newsweek*'s Jack Kroll, for example, described *Crimes* as "a tangy variation on the grits-and-Gothic South of Tennessee Williams, Eudora Welty, and Flannery O'Connor" (1981). It was not long, however, before feminist scholars began debating the significance of Henley's achievement. Suspicious of plays that achieved such popular success, some faulted Henley for locating her women characters within the home—a place that has both defined and confined them in negative ways—without offering avenues for either re-visioning or escape. While Henley's brand of feminism may not please those who favor more revolutionary modes, much of her work presents an intriguing blend of social critique and awareness of the constraints of the commercial stage, filtered through a clearly southern lens.

Born on May 8, 1952, in Eudora Welty's hometown of Jackson, Mississippi, Elizabeth Becker Henley shares with Welty and many other southern writers a strong sense of place and of the powerful impact of both region and community values. Henley's first six plays are all set in the Deep South, two in Louisiana (*Am I Blue* [1982] and *The Lucky Spot* [1987]), and four in small Mississippi towns to which Henley has personal connections. Hazlehurst, home to her father's family, is the setting for *Crimes of the Heart*. Her second professionally produced play, *The Miss Firecracker Contest* (1985), takes place in her mother's hometown of Brookhaven. Henley went to camp in Canton, the setting for *The Wake of Jamey Foster* (1983), and Hattiesburg, the setting for *The Debutante Ball* (1991), is home to an aunt and uncle. As these links suggest, family ties also provide a focal point for these plays, often expressed in terms of what Billy J. Harbin calls "a typically southern sense of family duty." But Henley clearly genders this depiction of place and familial duty, revealing how the domestic realm, and the slightly wider arena of the small southern town and its values, define and confine her female characters.

The entire action of *Crimes of the Heart* takes place in the kitchen of Old Granddaddy's Hazlehurst home. The choice of this single setting, as well as of a limited cast, was governed in part by Henley's practical awareness of production costs, and it certainly partakes of the tradition of stage realism. But Henley is also quick to point out the role of the kitchen as a place of confinement, tying women to the domestic sphere and to their roles as caregivers. The oldest MaGrath sister, Lenny, has actually taken to sleeping there in order to be better able to attend to her grandfather's needs during the night. Here Lenny also experiences the pressures of community standards for female behavior, particularly as embodied in the sisters' judgmental cousin Chick. Claiming to be sick "of you trashy MaGraths and your trashy ways: hanging yourselves in cellars; carrying on with married men; shooting your own husbands," Chick bemoans the fact that such behavior jeopardized her own acceptance into the Hazlehurst Ladies Social League.

While critical of Chick's self-serving social ambitions, Henley does not condone the actions Chick mentions but rather makes it clear that such acts of rebellion against community values carry a high personal cost for those who perform them. Babe (who has shot her husband) is twice driven to contemplate repeating her mother's act of suicide; the wild sister, Meg, seems to have cut herself off from her emotions; and the virtuous Lenny has apparently resigned herself to a spinster's life as "Old Granddaddy's nursemaid." In probing some of the causes of these rebellious acts—the father's desertion, Meg's deep-seated desire "to please Old Granddaddy," Babe's history of domestic abuse at the hands of her lawyer husband—Henley also politicizes the sisters' domestic space. As Minrose C. Gwin suggests, Henley conflates the personal and the political in order to begin demolishing "the father's house whose foundation has been, and still is, their division." Both the sisters' strangely appropriate laughter at the news of their grandfather's impending death and Lenny's banishment of Chick from what she now claims as her own home (using that most domestic of weapons, a broom) signal at least a temporary dismantling of the patriarchal power both Chick and Old Granddaddy represent.

In several plays, Henley ties the pressures of small-town values specifically to female identity and its rootedness in beauty, the body, and the social position these can bring. The two cousins in *The Miss Firecracker Contest,* Elain and Carnelle, play out opposite but equally destructive social roles. Elain, a former winner of the town's annual beauty contest who returns home at the start of the play, declares dramatically, "It's such a burden trying to live up to a beautiful face." As the play develops, we begin to see the truth of what she says. For Elain, winning beauty contests became her only means of securing her mother's approval and of subsequently finding the "rich husband" her mother saw as her ultimate goal. Though she returns to Brookhaven recognizing the emptiness of this life, the community admiration Elain experiences later in the play merely renews her faith in beauty as her true identity. Elain returns to her children and husband not out of love or even duty but because, as she says, "I'm used to better things now . . . my face cream . . . my clocks. . . . And he adores me. I need someone who adores me." Perhaps the closest Henley comes to creating a southern belle, Elain suggests the rootedness of that feminine stereotype in an unfulfilling materialism and bodily ideal.

Both Carnelle, the protagonist of *Miss Firecracker,* and Teddy, the heroine of *The Debutante Ball,* likewise seek community approval through a social ritual based on the display of female beauty and the body. Both plays open with a performance that underlines the inherent theatricality of these rituals. We first see Carnelle practicing her "talent routine that requires tap dancing, marching and baton twirling, none of which she is extremely adept at." At twenty-four, Carnelle (known in the community as "Miss Hot Tamale" in honor of her sexual exploits) is making a last-ditch and ultimately unsuccessful effort to reproduce her cousin's victory in the Fourth of July pageant. *The Debutante Ball* begins with Teddy receiving instructions for her formal presentation as her mother reminds her, "You are one hundred times more beautiful and alive than any of the jackasses sitting out in that banquet hall." Whereas Carnelle suffers a verbal assault from pageant spectators taunting her because of her promiscuity, Teddy's preparations for what is, not surprisingly, a disastrous debut include increasingly brutal assaults on her own body, ranging from the application of "corrective makeup" and a fierce plucking of eyebrows to violent scratches to her face. Both the onstage performances of Carnelle and Teddy and the fateful, off-stage public events reflect on the nature of femininity *as* performance and the difficulty of living up to society's standards, especially through the flawed female bodies these characters feel that they possess.

A further, striking dimension of the southern spaces Henley's women inhabit is that, most often, these spaces do not actually belong to them. The "dreary and suffocating and frightening" southern living room of Aunt Ronelle's house in *Miss Firecracker* is but one of several spaces in which Henley's heroines find more of a shelter than a home. In *The Wake of Jamey Foster,* the unfaithful title character lays claim to his wife's family home even in death when his corpse is laid out in the parlor, much against her wishes. But just as Lenny's banishment of Chick reasserts the MaGrath sisters' claim to their own space in *Crimes,* Marshael finally reclaims her home; as the play ends, we see her refusing to play the expected role of grieving widow at Jamey's burial service and instead drifting off to sleep in what is now her own room once again.

Living in spaces that are often not their own, many of Henley's heroines also live out dreams and desires that are scripted for them by others, as seen, for example, in Meg's pursuit of a Hollywood career in order "to please Old Granddaddy." This interplay of socially constructed desires takes its most interesting turn in *Abundance* (1990). With this play, Henley leaves the contemporary southern small town behind and begins to head westward, choosing the Wyoming Territory in the late 1860s as her setting. Taking a more experimental turn than her previous plays, *Abundance* covers a twenty-five-year time span and uses nineteen short scenes to tell the story of two mail-order brides making their way in the "wild West."

Perhaps reflecting Henley's own move west (since 1976 Henley has lived in California, where she has written several successful screenplays), *Abundance* shows us a feminine version of "western fever." Initially, at least, the two women's dreams are the stuff of fiction—more precisely of dime novels, in the case of the adventurous Macon, and fairy tales, in the case of the romantic Bess. But in one of Henley's most intriguing plot twists, the women each come to live a more pragmatic side of the other's dream, taking on aspects of the other's already-scripted identity. Though not in love with her one-eyed husband, Macon becomes attached to the material comforts of the cozy home of Bess's dreams while Bess lives a harshly beautiful side of Macon's imagined adventures when she is captured by Indians. By the play's end, both women have in a sense prostituted themselves as well as their dreams. We see this literally in the syphilitic sores on Macon's face and figuratively in Bess's agreement to "demand the immediate extermination of all Indian tribes" when she takes her captivity story on the lecture circuit. But both women also recognize the hollowness of these constructed and commercialized desires and, like Carnelle from *Miss Firecracker,* come to ask themselves "what you can, well, reasonably hope for in life."

In Henley's world, the answer to this question seems, on one level, to be just what Carnelle's friend Mac Sam tells her: "Not much, Baby, not too damn much," though Mac Sam adds a hint of Flannery O'Connor's religious questioning when he rather cynically continues, "There's always eternal grace." While "eternal grace" eludes them, there is still a degree of hope in many of Henley's conclusions, as her characters find moments of bonding or companionship that provide comfort if not resolution. Though unable to transcend them fully, many of her characters also come to recognize the limits of their socially mediated desires and actions, just as Henley herself has perhaps come to recognize the challenges and compromises involved in marketing her plays and screenplays.

Two more recent plays have continued Henley's exploration of the American West and the entrepreneurial spirit already evident in the pioneer characters of *Abundance. Control Freaks* (2000), a one-act that marked Henley's debut as a director in 1992, shows a much darker side of this disposition. Set in a family home in contemporary Los Angeles, the play locks four characters in a violent battle for control of their own and each others' passions as Carl and his fourth wife, Betty, scheme to buy a furniture emporium by cheating Carl's sister out of her inheritance. *Signature* (2000), produced in 1990, takes place in the year 2052 in what New York *Times* critic Alvin Klein describes as "a futuristic Hollywood . . . a land without mind or heart, ruled by 'celebrity swine' and agents whose religion is ambition." Reflecting Henley's familiarity with the realm of film and television, and the violence and sexuality that permeate this realm, these plays provide further commentary on the emptiness and destructive potential of the public images she had already begun to explore in plays like *The Miss Firecracker Contest* and *The Debutante Ball.* As in *Abundance,* identity is shifting and fragile (underscored by the multiple personalities of Sister in *Control Freaks* and the madness of the lovesick graphologist of *Signature*), and materialism appears to have won out over romance.

In some ways more traditional than their immediate predecessors, two of Henley's latest offerings are woman-centered family dramas that nonetheless break with stage realism. *Family Week* (produced in 2000 and not yet published) uses quasi-Brechtian supertitles to mark off a relentless series of vignettes documenting a weeklong visit to an Arizona treatment center by the mother, sister, and daughter of a middle-aged woman. Her most recent play, *Impossible Marriage* (1999), returns to a distinctively southern locale for its story of a society matriarch and her two daughters. But Bess's dreams of a fairy-tale romance in *Abundance* now take a more whimsical and mythic turn, as a childlike heroine named Pandora dons blue wings for her wedding to a "hairy old goat" of a novelist in the mysterious garden of her mother's Savannah estate. The move out of the father's house and into the mother's garden does not prove entirely liberating. Fear of scandal and other social pressures conspire against the marriage of Pandora and her groom, as they do against the two other May-December romances of Pandora's mother and her pregnant sister. Like many of Henley's earlier plays, this one ends on a note of hope as the two daughters leave the garden with the men they purport to love. Just before leaving, however, Henley's artist figure asks whether the hope released from the mythical Pandora's box might itself be "the final pestilence." The closing image of the ailing matriarch and the groom's son eating raspberries seems marked as much by an almost Beckettian inertia as it is by a more fulfilling companionship.

Critical reception of these and other recent Henley offerings has been mixed, and several have closed after relatively short runs. Nevertheless, Henley continues to find both new and familiar venues for her darkly comic dramatic works. The publication of a volume containing four of her plays by Heinemann/Methuen (1992) as well as of the recent Smith and Kraus edition of her *Collected Plays* (2000) signals a growing recognition of Henley's achievements after *Crimes of the Heart*. In displaying the ever-broadening range of Henley's work, these volumes should encourage a deeper appreciation of her quirky but compassionate worlds and the characters and compromises that shape them.

Jayne Anne Phillips

Suzanne Disheroon-Green

Jayne Anne Phillips is considered one of the finest southern writers to emerge in recent years. The author of several collections of short stories and novels, Phillips began winning awards with her earliest work of short fiction, *Sweethearts* (1976), which received the Pushcart Prize and the Fels Award for fiction. Also to her credit are the short story collections *Black Tickets* (1979) and *Fast Lanes* (1984). Her novels include the critically acclaimed *Machine Dreams* (1984), which was honored by a New York *Times* best book citation, a National Book Critics Circle award nomination, and a citation as a Notable Book by the American Library Association. Her second novel, *Shelter* (1994), received high praise for its lush use of language and its adept shifting of narrative perspectives. Most recently, Phillips has published another major novel, *MotherKind* (2000), which examines the strength of the bond between mother and daughter, demonstrating that this bond often grows stronger as the parent approaches the end of her life. Phillips' fiction has received international critical acclaim, which is demonstrated in part by the translation of her work into fourteen languages.

Phillips hails from Buckhanon, West Virginia, where she was born in 1952, and much of her fiction reflects her southern roots, most especially her focus on family relationships, alienation from the larger community, and issues arising from sexuality and violence. Phillips received her B.A. from West Virginia University in 1974, finding success in writing and publishing her work before she completed her degree. Phillips received the M.F.A. from the University of Iowa in 1978 and has held teaching positions at the University of Iowa, Humbolt State University, Radcliffe College, Boston University, and Harvard University. In 1996, she was named writer-in-residence at Brandeis University, where she currently serves. Phillips has been the recipient of numerous prestigious awards as well, including two National Endowment for the Arts fellowships, the Guggenheim Fellowship, the Sue Kaufman Prize for First Fiction in 1980, and the Academy Award in Literature in 1997.

Like the work of many southern writers, much of Phillips' fiction examines familial and domestic issues. Phillips frequently writes about the ways families establish a collective identity, and then accept or reject that identity, as well as the ways in which individual family members come to terms with their own experiences outside of the family. For example, in *MotherKind,* Kate tries to create a second home for her stepsons, despite the fact that the boys' mother intentionally sabotages Kate's attempts. Kate's desire to build a family with her husband, her baby, and her stepsons demonstrates Phillips' interest in what she described in a 1998 interview in *Passion and Craft* as "what home now consists of." According to Phillips, "Because we move around so much, families are forced to be immediate; they must stand on their relationships rather than on stereotypes or assumptions or a common history." Rather than drawing strength from a community that understands her struggles or shares a part of her familial history, Kate must build a life for her family away from the support system that is commonly seen in the fiction of earlier southern writers. Kate's struggle to form a cohesive family unit—one whose members self-identify as a family—meets with resistance from within the family unit as well. Her husband, despite his outward support of Kate's mother, tells her shortly before Kathcrine's death, "sometimes I wonder what we'll have left when this is over." Despite the profound emphasis on family in southern culture, the modern era has led to the dissolution of the traditional family unit. Writers such as Phillips are no longer in the position of being able to presume the existence of a familial unit; instead, one must often be created in unconventional ways. However, the birth family defines much of an individual's identity, and by extension, one's ability to create a cohesive family of his or her own, and this idea is seen repeatedly in Phillips' fiction.

Even though she deals with domestic issues in much of her writing, Phillips' fiction does not generally demonstrate a cohesive family group, even in the stereotypical, dysfunctional Faulknerian sense of the Snopeses, Compsons, or Bundrens. Rather, Phillips' families tend to be alienated both from each other and from the larger community. Mitch, in *Machine Dreams,* lives much of his life in his own world of vivid memories of days in the Philippines during World War II, chafing under the familial responsibilities that descend upon him when he returns from the war. Upon his return, his Uncle Clayton, the family patriarch, crawls into a bottle of liquor, willingly relinquishing his position of head of the family. Much of the frustration and alienation that Mitch experiences is communicated through the same internal monologue technique that Faulkner perfected in *As I Lay Dying* (1930). This sense of alienation is further seen through the fact that many of the women in Phillips' fiction have ended their relationships with their husbands, choosing to spend the remainder of their days alone. According to Danner in "Blue Moon" (from *Fast Lanes*), women such as her mother, who never recovered from an early disappointment, were "supremely confident, unfulfilled wom[e]n, vigilant and damaged." Despite the ability of Phillips' women to function effectively—to care for children, support them financially, guilt them onto the right path—they generally do not enter into romantic relationships because of the unhealed wounds inflicted by earlier relationships. Even in the case of women such as Jean—the mother who appears in both "Blue Moon" as the strong-willed woman who would assure her son's future and *Machine Dreams* as the bedridden woman whose imminent demise drives her daughter into a loveless marriage—marriage does not constitute romance. Instead, Phillips' women live the long-standing southern stereotype of the strong woman, the woman who, by all outward appearances, can care for others while caring nothing for herself.

Despite their flaws, however, these dysfunctional families possess the strength to intervene to protect their children from the threat of unworthy interlopers; often, the children in question realize that their dalliances with the lower classes cannot, and should not, lead to more permanent alliances. The long-standing southern tradition of protecting one's sons from trashy, social-climbing young girls is often evident in Phillips' fiction. Reb Jonas in *Machine Dreams* is amused by the antics of Marthella Barnett, which include jumping off a cliff into the water below and begging him to engage in sexual acts with her; even though he willingly gives in, everyone, including Reb, "knew Reb Jonas wasn't about to marry a Barnett." Similarly, Billy in "Blue Moon" becomes intimate with Kato, a "trashy" girl who is madly in love with him, but his parents send him away when the relationship shows signs of becoming too serious. Even in the most alienated of families, southern mores concerning social class are firmly in place in Phillips' fiction.

Closely intertwined with the husband-wife relationships that Phillips most often dismisses with disdain are the mother-daughter relationships that she explores, and these relationships quite often involve the death of the mother. As we often see in the writing of southern authors, Phillips' fiction contains elements of the autobiographical, especially as reflected by the recurring deaths of mothers. In several of Phillips' stories, the mothers linger, then die of cancer, and with each such narrative, we are exposed to detail that seemingly can only be so realistic because it has been lived by the author. In *Machine Dreams,* Jean's daughter speaks of her mother's impending death predominantly in generalities, focusing most pointedly on her fear of losing a beloved parent, rather than on the progression of the disease itself. In the more recent and more mature *MotherKind,* Phillips illustrates the day-by-day progression of Katherine's terminal cancer, sparing us few of the details of Katherine's growing weakness, her rapid decline, and her excruciating death. Phillips generally portrays relationships between female parent and child as loving friendships, albeit unequal relationships because the mothers rarely relinquish their position of authority over their daughters until shortly before their deaths.

Phillips' fiction also looks at the experiences of individuals, particularly individuals who are in some way disenfranchised or alienated from society. A particularly compelling example is found in "How Mickey Made It," which appears in *Fast Lanes.* Told through the colloquial, urban voice of a young hustler, the story is a stream-of-consciousness narrative that relates wild tales of Mickey's sexual exploits and his attempts to make it in the music business, of his outward unwillingness to become involved with anyone beyond the level of casual sex. However, Mickey's descriptions make it apparent that he is in fact desperately lonely, and that he is using sex as a means of temporarily acquiring the closeness to another human being that is lacking in his life. Reminiscent of the ungrounded seeker who fills his time with casual affairs and movies in Walker Percy's *The Moviegoer* (1961), Mickey grandiosely offers his friendship to the women with whom he has affairs because it gives him a feeling of power in the relationship and obscures the fact that he is completely alone. A similar sense of alienation is present in the story "Rayme" (in *Fast Lanes*), a narrative that demonstrates the effects of a "communal life [that] seemed a continual dance in which everyone changed partners, a patient attempt at domesticity by children taking turns being parents. We were adrift but we were together." Absent a strong family to rely on, this group of students attempts unsuccessfully to build a family among themselves, in part because they constantly switch roles, in one instance, filling the position of sexual partner, in another acting as a parent or confessor. The title character offers an extreme example of what may become of the disenfranchised, of the utter disregard for one's fellow beings that often overtakes those who are not connected to others in any meaningful way. Just as Annie in Dorothy Allison's *Bastard out of Carolina* (1992) leaves her broken daughter behind so that she can be with the man who tormented and raped the child, Rayme makes choices that please herself, demonstrating blatant disregard for the effects her decisions have on others.

Much of the best southern fiction is influenced by the religious tenets that frame much of southern rhetoric and mores. Phillips' *Shelter* demonstrates the effects religious fervor, especially when combined with disenfranchisement from a supportive community, may have on social behavior. In the novel, Parson, a vagrant who hangs around Camp Shelter, is obsessed with the abusive sociopath Carmody, whom he views as the devil incarnate. Parsons had become acquainted with Carmody in prison, and after seeing his behavior in prison and the sexual abuse of his child, follows him home to the area surrounding Camp Shelter and makes it his mission in life to rid the world of Carmody's evil. Yet the narrative focuses predominantly on two young sisters, Lenny and Alma, who spend their summer vacation at Camp Shelter. Setting her story against a backdrop of sexual abuse, Phillips draws upon the gothic tradition—its dark settings, menacing characters, and evil intentions—to show the coming-of-age of these two girls separated from their family at a critical juncture in their lives.

Phillips' body of work is indeed representative of the southern tradition. Her grapplings with family, alienation and the self-centered narcissism that may result from it, death, and the exploration of sexuality and religious ideologies draw upon the same pervasive themes that influenced the writers of the Southern Renaissance. Yet Phillips does not represent these themes in a worn-out fashion, but, influenced by the tide of postmodernism and late twentieth-century American culture, she creates scenes that are believable and characters who are humanized by their very imperfections. Jayne Anne Phillips is one of a new generation of southern women writers who are examining and rediscovering what it means to be a woman in the South in a new century.

Jill McCorkle

Jenifer B. Elmore

Jill McCorkle was only twenty-five years old when she made her national literary debut in 1984 with the simultaneous publication of her first two novels. Three additional novels and two short story collections have since placed her among the most prolific and versatile of contemporary fiction writers. Southern in setting and dialect, her five novels and two collections of short stories give voice to characters of all ages and classes—old-money grandmothers and tacky bank tellers, lonely-heart handymen and careworn cleaning ladies, bourgeois cheerleaders and melancholy trailer dwellers. With humor to help them cope with their disillusionment and insecurity, these characters experience family and community life in its tenderness, tediousness, absurdity, and intensity. McCorkle gracefully and profoundly explores traditional themes—coming of age, marriage, parenthood, intrigue, disillusionment, forgiveness, and healing—through markedly contemporary tales of divorce, single parenthood, abuse, addiction, abortion, eating disorders, and mental breakdowns.

The daughter of medical secretary Melba Collins McCorkle and postal worker John Wesley McCorkle, Jr., Jill Collins McCorkle was born on July 7, 1958 (the date that she later turned into the title of her second novel), in the town of Lumberton, North Carolina, which provides the setting for much of her fiction. She was a cheerleader at the local high school, as was the protagonist of her first novel, *The Cheer Leader* (1984). These close correspondences between her life and her art do not mean that her fiction should be read autobiographically, but they do confirm that McCorkle knows her setting intimately. As she explains in her essay "What to Wear on the First Day at Lumberton High," her hometown as she remembers it from her adolescence is the "setting that always comes first" to her mind when she begins to construct a story—a basic clay that she alters and molds into numerous and distinct fictional scenes.

One of the most refreshing and impressive aspects of McCorkle's work, however, is the fact that her perfectly pitched dialogue, small-town tragedies, and complex intergenerational relationships neither stretch into belabored southern epic or devolve into stereotypical southern nostalgia. McCorkle chronicles changes in the South in the second half of the twentieth century without lamenting or romanticizing old ways. In *Ferris Beach* (1990), for example, the young heroine Kate Burns remembers that the leader of the local historical society had desperately announced, "The split-levels are coming! The split-levels are coming!" in an effort to block the development of an old rural neighborhood, while she herself had "rejoiced in finally having someone my own age close by." This kind of opposition reflects the larger ambivalence of McCorkle's South. Her most recent novel, *Carolina Moon* (1996), shares one of its settings with *Ferris Beach*. In both novels, Ferris Beach is a real place with mythical significance for certain characters; their memories and desires endow the place with the power either to anchor or to unhinge their lives. The feelings and immediate experiences of the individual characters—not an overarching southern agenda or theory of southern culture—drive the action and set the tone of the fiction. McCorkle's South is no more and no less than *all* of the people who happen to live there.

McCorkle graduated from the University of North Carolina at Chapel Hill in 1980 with highest honors in creative writing. At Chapel Hill, Lee Smith, Louis Rubin, and Max Steele were among her teachers. With their advice and encouragement, she earned an M.A. in 1981 from Smith's alma mater, Hollins College in Virginia, where Madison Smartt Bell was her classmate and friend. After graduate school she worked sundry jobs to support her writing, including clerical and teaching positions. A short-lived first marriage ended in divorce in 1984, the same year that Rubin and his newly established Algonquin Books of Chapel Hill displayed enormous confidence in the young author by publishing her first two novels simultaneously. Encouraging reviews prepared the way for her next novel, *Tending to Virginia* (1987), which attracted wider and more influential critical notice and was generally regarded as more mature and ambitious than her first two books.

With the overwhelmingly positive reception of *Ferris Beach* in 1990, McCorkle's status as a serious writer with a national audience was secure. She has since published two collections of short stories, *Crash Diet* (1992) and *Final Vinyl Days* (1998), as well as *Carolina Moon*. From 1984 to 1989, she taught creative writing part-time at the University of North Carolina at Chapel Hill, Duke University, and Tufts University. She married physician Daniel Shapiro in 1987; their daughter was born in 1989 and their son in 1991. They have lived in Boston since 1992, where McCorkle writes and teaches creative writing at Harvard University. She also teaches at Bennington College in Vermont.

Sometimes cited as a warm-up *Bildungsroman* for the more mature *Ferris Beach*, McCorkle's first novel, *The Cheer Leader*, is the story of the emotional breakdown of the most popular girl in a small southern town. With an intact and exceptionally functional family to love and support her, Jo Spencer, head cheerleader and honor student, lives in a world of girlfriends and boyfriends, ball games and dances, and a seemingly endless future of giddy moments and cute outfits. A relationship with a boy from the wrong crowd challenges her assumptions, however, and by the time her tragically dowdy almost-friend Beatrice attempts suicide, the perky high-schooler has become a disturbed college freshman whose adolescent sensibility rivals that of J. D. Salinger's Holden Caulfield and recalls Sylvia Plath's *The Bell Jar* (1963).

Jo is the first in a long line of heroines who have made McCorkle as much a writer of contemporary women's experience as she is of southern life. So many young white women populate her tales, however, that her not infrequent departures from them are sometimes overlooked. *July 7th* features young male protagonist Sam Swett, as well as a fully developed octogenarian matriarch and a particularly well-crafted wise black woman whom McCorkle allows to do housework for a suburban white family without lapsing into predictability. The understanding between young Corky Revels and her grandmother in *July 7th* anticipates the richer and more fully developed relationships that bind three generations of female kinfolk in McCorkle's third novel. In an interview accompanying a review of *Tending to Virginia* in the *New York Times Book Review*, McCorkle reminisces about spending time with her grandmother and absorbing her family lore: "As a child, I was fascinated by my grandmother and hung out with her all the time. She lived across town in an old house, and going there was like going back in time."

McCorkle is clearly a writer of the present, but it is often her insight into the past that gives her contemporary narratives their psychological depth. Her fictional shopping malls, condos, and convenience stores resonate with meanings and potential histories as complex as those of the farm, the church, and the grand old house. This ability to render the quotidian with novelty and the common with dignity is most apparent in her short fiction, which has been published in her two collections, in addition to appearing in periodicals such as the *New Yorker,* the *Atlantic Monthly,* and the *Oxford American* and in such annuals as *New Stories from the South.* The title story of *Crash Diet* features a chronic dieter who loses weight and finds an identity only after her husband abandons her. The voice of the protagonist-narrator in this story sets the tone for most of the volume—a kind of flat, self-deprecating humor that emphasizes the characters' ordinariness and their pathos at the same time. The story begins: "Kenneth left me on a Monday morning before I'd even had the chance to mousse my hair, and I just stood there at the picture window with the drapes swung back and watched him get into that flashy red Mazda, which I didn't want him to get anyway, and drive away down Marnier Street, and make a right onto Seagrams. That's another thing I didn't want, to live in a subdivision where all the streets are named after some kind of liquor."

Several of the eleven *Crash Diet* stories, notably "First Union Blues" and "Waiting for Hard Times to End," follow a similar pattern of blissful naïveté disillusioned by a sudden betrayal or chance discovery that sets in motion a slow and painful but ultimately rewarding process of rebuilding. Taken together, however, the lesson put forth in these tales is that change and growth never really end. As the narrator of "Man Watcher" explains, just when she thought she had learned all there was to know and married her perfect life partner, she actually had a long way to go: "My snapping to was like a dream inside of a dream, a hallway of doors where with every slam I woke up all over again. I had barely begun to snap to." This theme of open-ended personal development extends even to old age; two *Crash Diet* stories, "Departures" and "Migration of the Love Bugs," explore the later-life turning points of widowhood and retirement.

While McCorkle will probably always be discussed as a southern woman writer, what makes her best work great may have more to do with issues of class than with either region or gender. Her blue-collar workers and suburban housewives alike consistently overturn expectations, confound stereotypes, and expose biases. Mary, the middle-aged narrator of "Words Gone Bad" (in *Crash Diet*), is a black woman with little schooling who works as a janitor on a university campus. Far from simply envying, resenting, or admiring the young black college students she observes each day, she sees the compromises they make in exchange for membership in a middle-class world still dominated by whites. Her best friend and coworker Bennie is far more optimistic than she; Mary is a defeatist version of Malcolm X to his Martin Luther King, Jr. Without deflecting the real racial issues that drive the ongoing debate between these two friends, McCorkle uncovers the personal experiences that have enabled Bennie to maintain his idealism and those that continue to deny Mary the luxury of believing that peace can ever be achieved in this world.

McCorkle's fiction often creates the illusion that she has rescued valuable individuals from oblivions of stereotype, prejudice, and misinterpretation, just as her protagonists rescue themselves from destructive patterns and relationships. In the process of discovering the hidden value of characters who may at first annoy or inspire ridicule, the reader feels challenged and perhaps chastised, but eventually grateful for the enlightenment. In what is arguably the best story in *Final Vinyl Days*, "It's a Funeral! RSVP," the title invokes extreme tackiness and the ultragauche, and the opening sentence inevitably conjures an image of the looniest lady in town: "I have spent my life looking for the right occupation and have finally found it: I throw funerals." Who would be so undignified as to lower the solemn rites of the dead to the level of balloons and paper streamers? The reader starts out expecting to get a good laugh out of this crazy woman and ends up believing instead that the miracles she performs in reconciling dying people to their pasts and to their deaths qualify her for saintly canonization.

McCorkle's characters—women, certainly, but also men such as Tom Lowe of *Carolina Moon*—typically accomplish such miracles of self-definition through personal mythmaking. Recalling her one act of adultery, the protagonist of "It's a Funeral! RSVP" explains that though she still feels a little guilty "for loving every minute of it and the way it took years off my heart," the experience never threatened her marriage: "In my mind it brought my two halves together and linked them up like two full and heavy train cars getting ready for the long haul." Here, as elsewhere in McCorkle's fiction, actions—often rebellious, daring, or otherwise unconventional— lead to insights that alter characters' interpretations of their own histories, allowing them to take control of their own lives and connect with the lives of others simultaneously.

Kaye Gibbons

Veronica Makowsky

Although not autobiographical in the sense of a mechanical one-to-one correspondence between art and life, Kaye Gibbons' six novels thematically reflect the paradise lost of her early childhood. Born in North Carolina in 1960, Gibbons was aware that her lower-middle-class origins, signaled by her house's tin roof, placed her below those who lived in brick houses. Her early consciousness of class differences, however, did not spoil her pleasure in a tight community focused around church, the store, and school. The epicenter of Gibbons' childhood and her fiction, though, is her close bond with her mother, which unraveled with her mother's mental health until her suicide when Gibbons was ten, followed by her father's gradual death from alcoholism. After a peripatetic few years living with various relations, Gibbons found relative stability in the home of an older brother.

The themes of Gibbons' fiction emerge from the trials and triumphs of her life and the need to provide similarly spunky examples for her readers. First, the development of self-reliance allows her protagonists to join a community and contribute to and to receive its benefits. This self-reliance interwoven with community is marked by the protagonist's achievement of a distinctively individual yet empathetic voice in Gibbons' characteristic first-person narratives. Such a bond between self and others is also part of another of her most powerful themes: the mother-daughter relationship. A girl suffers from a vanished or ineffectual mother, but a strong mother can overwhelm her developing voice. This absent or overly symbiotic relationship is often transcended through the presence of an African American woman who teaches the protagonist how to be her own mother so that she can nurture others and receive their nurturing. As this paradigm suggests, men in Gibbons' novels tend to be portrayed as peripheral yet constant problems because they are childish, often to the point of selfish monstrosity. In her later novels, however, Gibbons depicts more sympathetic men or delineates the causes of masculine cruelty as she delves further into the roots of southern culture.

As all these paradigms suggest, Gibbons' basic theme is the search for order in an unstable universe. In her fiction, women seek order through their domestic arts, particularly the mutual nurturing of feeding and clothing. They also provide meaning for life's chaos through their talk, as Gibbons herself does in her highly oral art. Gibbons and her female protagonists follow this essential maxim from "Joyner's Store" (1997): "In this world there are plenty of good things that you can have for cheap" if you learn how to find them and develop a voice to share them.

The appreciation of everyday pleasures, the "good" and "cheap," is found in one of Gibbons' early influences, the African American poet James Weldon Johnson, who, Gibbons writes, could "make art out of everyday language. Inspired by him, I wanted to see if I could have a child use her voice to talk about life, death, art, eternity—big things from a little person." In a world of seemingly inexplicable chaos and vicious and indifferent adults, the young title character of *Ellen Foster* (1987) is confronted with a choice between two modes of survival. The first is the traditionally masculinist challenge of the novel's epigraph, which is the epigraph to Ralph Waldo Emerson's "Self-Reliance" (1841), "Cast the bantling on the rocks," the mode of child rearing of Ellen's abusive and negligent father. The second is "just work . . . in the trail my mama left," the mode of traditional female passivity that leads to her mother's suicide. Ultimately, the orphaned Ellen rejects both parents' modes and their name when she chooses to live in a foster family and take "Foster" as her surname. The foster family is a woman-centered community in which independence is balanced with concern for the welfare of others. Ellen achieves such equilibrium when she overcomes her prejudice against her African American friend Starletta and uses her hard-earned voice to tell her that she values her for what she is.

In early interviews, Gibbons attributed her mother's death to natural causes, not suicide, for fear that the autobiographical subtext of her fiction would dominate its reception, but she continued to probe women like her mother in her fiction. *A Virtuous Woman* (1989) explores the plight of an upper-middle-class woman, like Ellen Foster's mother or Gibbons' own mother, who marries "white trash." As Ellen's mother kills herself with the medication that she needs to live with her abusive spouse, so Ruby Pitts, in her marriage to the adulterous John Woodrow, becomes addicted to the cigarettes that will ultimately kill her. After a childhood under the passive supervision of a mother who allowed her father and brothers to so overprotect Ruby that she barely learned to cut the meat on her plate, Ruby learns self-reliance the hard way. She recognizes her family's reliance on the African American woman who presided over her childhood home when she states that "somebody like Sudie Bee covers for people." After John Woodrow's death, Ruby has no one to cover for her, so she tries again with a marriage to another lower-class man, the childish but decent Jack Stokes. She takes pride in her housekeeping and cooking and in her ability to nurture Jack and her foster daughter June. June grows up into a strong yet caring woman. Ruby's nurturing of Jack, however, seems to have made him more dependent, and he transfers that dependence to June after Ruby's death. Gibbons' technique of counterpointing Ruby and Jack's narratives throughout the novel emphasizes the fine line between mutual support and immature dependency in a heterosexual marriage.

Ruby Pitts Woodrow Stokes is a woman of the generation of Ellen Foster's or Kaye Gibbons' mother, and Gibbons continues to delve further into the southern and maternal past in her next two novels, *A Cure for Dreams* (1991) and *Charms for the Easy Life* (1993), in which her protagonists' formative years take place during the Depression and World War II. Both Betty and Margaret, respectively, are educated by the words and examples of strong matriarchs in troubling times: Betty's mother, Lottie, and Margaret's grandmother, the healer Charlie Kate. Both young women learn from these matriarchs that many men suffer from "a condition caused by ingrown selfishness," but that some men can be decent and untroubling nonentities, such as Betty's husband Herbert, or even fine human beings, like Margaret's intended, Tom Hawkings. Both Betty and Margaret must also learn that they cannot always depend on their strong mother figures. Margaret discovers that Charlie Kate is not omnipotent when their former servant, African American Maveen, dies a torturous death from a white doctor's malpractice while Charlie Kate was first ignorant of, then powerless before, her plight. Upon the imminent birth of her first child, Betty takes the advice of African American midwife Polly that "you as much as anybody needs to do this one thing this time without Miss Lottie," and Betty does not summon her mother to attend the birth. *A Cure for Dreams* and *Charms for the Easy Life* foreground the pedagogical potential of women's talk over the generations as women use conversation to achieve individual voices while maintaining community

In contrast, young Hattie Barnes of *Sights Unseen* (1995) must reestablish a connection with her mother when, after many years, Maggie receives successful treatment for manic-depressive disorder. The household chaos that Hattie must confront during Maggie's illness is much like that facing Ellen Foster, and, like Ellen, Hattie initially must learn self-reliance at the cost of having her need for maternal intimacy met. "I knew better than to need anything," Hattie comments, but she also acknowledges that "Pearl was my salvation." Pearl Wiggins, the Barnes's African American housekeeper, saves Hattie in the sense of supplying a reliable maternal presence. Pearl is also Hattie's savior when she inadvertently lets Maggie out of the house during a manic episode. When Maggie intentionally injures a woman with her car, the Barnes family is forced to stop covering up for her and get her the treatment that returns her to stability in time for the onset of Hattie's puberty. As Hattie remembers her mother's life, she recovers her own life and voice: "Both forgiving and healing are true arts, and in telling my mother's story I have been able to forgive the past without reservation and heal myself without concern over a lapse into acute sorrow over her death."

Emma Garnet Tate Lowell of *On the Occasion of My Last Afternoon* (1998) cannot so readily forgive herself after her mother's death, and she needs to reexamine her past in her own voice to do so. She believes that "simply and regrettably, my mother was the price I paid for finally being able to lie down in peace" when she escaped her home through marriage. Essentially, the novel begins as a retelling of *Ellen Foster* set in antebellum tidewater Virginia, with a self-made man, Emma's father, abusing her genteel and passively suffering mother. The difference in setting, however, is crucial because Gibbons is probing the cultural mores that produce men and women like the Tates. Mrs. Tate has been trained for a southern lady's pedestal and is consequently unable to ameliorate or curb her husband Samuel's cruelty, including killing one of his slaves and driving their eldest child to his death. Samuel's behavior, while not excused, is traced to the horrors of his "white trash" childhood and his constant struggle to prove himself in a society that values birth and breeding over achievement. Gibbons indicts southern culture because the ineffectuality of its aristocrats and the cruelty of its parvenus lead not only to misery in households, white and black, but also to the horrors of the Civil War and Reconstruction.

When Emma finds salvation in marriage to a Yankee, Quincy Lowell, Gibbons is praising a northern society that she perceives as valuing women more, as in the couple's endless mutually supportive conversations. She also advocates a northern work ethic, with Emma's assistance at Quincy's war hospital and her charity work after the war. Gibbons also criticizes southern society's failure to value African Americans as once more a black woman acts as deus ex machina. The Tates' servant, free woman Clarice, rescues Emma by leaving the Tates to assist the young Lowells, thereby keeping them away from the Tates' madness. Clarice also absolves Emma of her guilt about leaving her mother at the mercy of her father by pointing out the excellent relationship that Emma has consequently achieved with her own three strong and capable daughters. Clarice's presence and her words "Happy mother, happy children" could serve as the emblem and motto for Gibbons' body of fiction as well as her admonition against a patriarchal and racist southern culture that leaves the building of subcultures of community to women and children.

As an undergraduate at the University of North Carolina at Chapel Hill, Gibbons took a graduate fiction seminar with distinguished scholar of southern literature Louis D. Rubin, Jr. This seminar was the genesis for *Ellen Foster,* an imaginative transformation of Gibbons' childhood, which Rubin's Algonquin Press published in 1987. The acclaim that greeted her first novel presaged Gibbons' steady production of high quality fiction despite her treatment for manic-depressive disorder, a divorce, a sojourn in New York City, a return to North Carolina, and a marriage that gave her a household in Raleigh of five children—her three daughters and a stepdaughter and stepson. In the midst of these vicissitudes, her work has won her much critical acclaim and many awards, including the Sue Kaufman Prize for First Fiction from the American Academy and Institute of Arts and Letters, and a National Endowment for the Arts fellowship.

In her ambivalence toward southern culture, Gibbons is clearly descended from the writers of the Southern Renaissance, particularly William Faulkner, whom she further resembles, as critics have noted, for her strong and complex use of first-person narrators. Gibbons, however, is also heir to the southern female tradition of storytelling as a domestic art, manifested in works by nineteenth-century southern women writers such as Grace King; in *Balcony Stories* (1893), for example, women tell their tales in a liminal space on the balcony, separate from the street and men, but also temporarily removed from domestic responsibilities within. Similarly, twentieth-century writers manifest this tradition, found in works like Eudora Welty's "Petrified Man" (1939), in which women tell their stories in the female space of the beauty parlor, or in novels and stories by Gibbons' contemporaries such as Lee Smith and Jill McCorkle, which also privilege women's spaces and voices. In contrast to these writers, though, Gibbons gives voice to lower-class women, as does her contemporary Dorothy Allison. Yet, unlike Allison with her confrontational presentation of "white trash" life, Gibbons attempts to mediate between her literate and middle-class audience and her characters through her heroines' aspirations to rise from their origins through their own efforts. Although some critics fault Gibbons for her protagonists' idealized strength and success, one must remember that before her literary talent was recognized, Gibbons had planned to be a teacher and has channeled this vocation into providing women with powerful and magnetic role models.

Afterword: The Future of Southern Women's Writing

Mary Louise Weaks and Carolyn Perry

Not long ago, an unreconstructed southerner living in the North sent his oldest child—then in junior high—to the language lab at the local college to listen not to foreign language tapes, but to tape recordings of southern voices. Now that the family was living far removed from the South, the father hoped to preserve at least some measure of the child's southernness in his speech patterns. The tapes probably had little effect on the child's speech, but the father's efforts to teach his child about their southernness and his determination that his child feel a connection to their southern roots must have made quite an impression. Simple acts such as talking about family connections in the South, telling stories of a southern past, and, most importantly, reminding a child of his southernness shape the way he sees himself. By envisioning himself as southern, the child *is* southern.

For southerners like this child, the complexities of a modern world where job opportunities take a southern family "into exile" are not the only issue. In fact, the fate of the South, in general, is now being called into question. Frequently debated subjects nowadays are whether the South still exists as a distinct region and whether that region is a reality or an imaginative construct. In the history of the United States, the South evolved in opposition to an Other—the North. But as the country expanded westward, that otherness became represented in the separation of the country into four distinct regions: North, Midwest, West, and South. Although regional association was, and still is, in the past strongly identified with concrete geographical borders, the lines between regions are—not surprisingly—blurred. Antebellum Missouri, Kentucky, Maryland, and Delaware, were slave states, for example, but none of these states officially seceded from the Union during the Civil War. What, then, defines *southernness?* The political designations are not fully accurate, for many present-day citizens of Missouri, Kentucky, Maryland, and Delaware identify themselves as "southern" although their states were not part of the original Confederacy. In this respect, southernness is more of an abstract construct than a concrete reality. In addition, the concept of southernness has evolved as people—not just southerners—have spoken and written of the region as the South. "Southern is not a consistent identity," explains Michael Kreyling, "but an idea invented by our written and spoken discussions of it."

This concept of the South reflects the larger scope of contemporary thought. In a time when recorded history, the nature of "truth," and even the essence of human nature are being called into question, it is only fitting that critics of southern literature and culture would question the existence of southernness. Jefferson Humphries, standing in agreement with Kreyling, states that "we are southerners because we, and our ancestors, and the rest of the nation, have felt a compelling need to make up stories about southerners and because we then chose to act as though those stories were as true or truer than fact itself."

While it may seem that the notion of an invented South is a relatively new one, it really is not. Historically, southerners have written themselves into being because they have been forced to confront issues of identity that are inextricably bound to the nature and the durability of southernness. One particularly revealing example is the model of the southern lady. In *The Plantation Mistress: Woman's World in the Old South* (1982), Catherine Clinton describes the visit of a gentleman to an antebellum plantation where he met a beautiful plantation mistress—a charming, graceful woman who played the role of the perfect hostess. However, the gentleman faced a quandary one day when he came across his hostess hard at work, with her hoop removed, her appearance unkempt, and her arms deep inside a salting barrel. The gentleman visitor knew not whether to speak to her or to walk on and pretend he had not come across his hostess "behind the scenes." He walked on, preferring to maintain the illusion of the southern lady. By refusing the reality of the woman's life and preferring to accept only the image that society had created for her, the gentleman enacted the process of making a story "truer than fact."

Southern literature also shapes and perpetuates this process. The division between North and South, for example, became increasingly apparent in literature as sectional divisions increased and as the South set itself apart from the rest of the United States. In *The Planter's Northern Bride* (1854), for instance, Caroline Lee Hentz represents the Other—the northerner—as overtly materialistic, self-absorbed, and overbearing in his attempt to sway the South to the northern point of view. Written for political reasons, as a reaction to Harriet Beecher Stowe's *Uncle Tom's Cabin* (1851), the book describes southerners as caretakers who provide for their slaves because they feel they have a "duty to deliver them from the horrors and miseries of want." Northerners, according to Hentz, may "rave of the condition of slaves in the South, but they hold out no hand to redress them" when freed or escaped slaves find their way north. In writing such a novel, Hentz was creating a version of the South that made slavery acceptable. A more realistic picture of the Old South is found in Harriet Jacobs' slave narrative, in which she emphasizes the horrors of a slave society that treated her as if she were not human. Yet through writing *Incidents in the Life of a Slave Girl* (1861), Jacobs likewise created a powerful version of the southern story, one which claimed for black southerners their very humanity.

The years following the Civil War led to intense questioning of regional and personal identities. How do white southerners retain their southernness when they have lost a war to their Other? Very often, white writers of the postbellum period responded with nostalgia to recreate the southern past as a lost idyllic place, the best examples being the stories of Katherine McDowell (1849–1883) and Thomas Nelson Page. More and more, women writers questioned how women could return to their previous roles when the war brought poverty and deprivation to many white southerners. Southern women writers increasingly responded with new versions of southern womanhood and in some cases created shocking heroines, like Chopin's Edna Pontellier, who refused to be bound by traditional values of home and family. Whether intentionally or unintentionally, in creating a heroine like Edna, Chopin also reinforced the ideals of the early women's movement in the South. The association between fiction and reality was complex. For while Chopin had herself been caught smoking (a practice typically associated with the New Woman), Chopin at times chastises the New Woman in her fiction. Correspondingly, African American women such as Anna Julia Cooper recognized at once their attachment to the South and their inability to identify with it. For Cooper, Du Bois's notion of "double-consciousness" was for her a consciousness divided in at least three ways—being black, a woman, and a southerner. While Cooper called herself a southerner, Roberta Maguire explains, she also presented herself as an "outsider to southern womanhood" when she said that she had "tried to understand the southern woman's difficulties; to put herself in her place." Cooper's experiences as a black woman bore little resemblance to the lives of white southern women, who may have suffered extreme loss of family and property, but never had to question their humanity.

In the twentieth century, the Renaissance is clearly framed by these same questions of identity, especially as the first woman's movement in the South took root and came in conflict with the traditional image of southern womanhood. The conflict between the old and the new—in this case between traditional female identity and the New Woman—is the hallmark of Ellen Glasgow's early novels, including *The Descendent* (1897), *Phases of an Inferior Planet* (1898), and *Virginia* (1913), works that mark the dawning of the Renaissance. While women writers confronted the evolving image of southern woman, southern men were brought into a new world as they fought alongside northerners for the first time in two world wars. In William Faulkner's *Absalom, Absalom!* (1936), Shreve the northerner asks Quentin to explain himself and his region, urging him to *"Tell about the South. What's it like there. What do they do there. Why do they live there. Why do they live at all."* Shreve's questions have special resonance for the literature of the Southern Renaissance. For in the years after World War I and continuing through the 1950s, southerners experienced a clash between the southern past and the realities of their present lives—the move from an agricultural to an industrial society, the growth of southern cities, the flight of some of the best southern writers from the South—that was in some ways more intense than the earlier periods of transition experienced by southerners.

Perhaps the greatest test of southernness is that experienced by contemporary southerners, who face lingering racial conflicts that question regional identity, changing gender roles that put old stereotypes to rest, and increasing urbanization and commercialization. At the same time, as Fred Hobson explains in *The Southern Writer in the Postmodern World* (1991), contemporary southern writers must deal with the implications of an "unfallen South": they have lived not with the memory of defeat but through a period of increasing prosperity as more and more corporations and businesses have relocated to the South. Commercialization has become a two-edged sword for the South and for southern literature. On one hand, it has caused the region to blend more naturally with the rest of the country: the urban experience has become almost as common as the rural; the Egg McMuffin has replaced grits and bacon for breakfast; and country music is now as much a part of American culture as southern. On the other hand, however, media hype promotes southern writers as never before, and the southern label often brings increased attention to a writer's work.

To speak of the future of southern women's writing thus entails an understanding of the permanence of southernness, for southern regional identity will continue to influence this literature as long as women write consciously of the South. At the same time, however, the notion of southernness also remains intact when writers speak of its loss, for even as contemporary critics bemoan the loss of southernness, they are helping to ensure the South's endurance. Likewise, Bobbie Ann Mason says that when she was living in New York City, she would find herself "walking down Park Avenue, but . . . also thinking back to my earlier self, the cow pastures. All the juxtapositions are jarring; that's the exile mentality." By identifying herself as an exile, Mason at once sees herself as placeless and linked to a place through a subconscious attachment that recreates in her mind images from childhood. The cow pasture becomes an enduring image for Mason, who often writes of a South homogenized by television, pop culture, and shopping malls. Given this tension in her relationship to the South, it is fitting that Mason's most recent book is a memoir entitled *Clear Springs* (1999). In the book Mason reflects, as she begins a new garden, "When I plunged my hands into the black New England soil, I felt I was touching a rich nourishment that I hadn't had since I was a small child. It had been years since I helped Mama in the garden. Yet the feel of dirt seemed so familiar. This was real. It was true. I wheeled around and faced home." In turning toward home, Mason faces the South—her past—and through her creative journey she recovers some sense of the permanence of her southernness through memory.

Perhaps one of the greatest influences on the body of southern literature as a whole in recent years has been a broadening of the scope of the term "southern." Specifically, gender and racial lines have been reevaluated, and literature of this second renaissance has been profoundly shaped by a changing societal structure in the South following the civil rights and women's movements of the 1960s and 1970s. Clear examples of this distinct shift within southern literature are changes within the scholarly publications on the literature, including critical analyses and anthologies. One specific example is *The History of Southern Literature,* published in 1985. Even though the book includes more women and minority writers than any previous study of southern literature, the collection focuses by and large on the white male writers of the South, and it includes little or no information on many of the southern women writers discussed in *The History of Southern Women's Literature,* Caroline Gilman, for example, receives only a passing reference in *The History of Southern Literature,* even though Gilman called for a distinctly southern literature before William Gilmore Simms did. Her *Southern Rose,* which published writers such as Simms, Nathaniel Hawthorne, and Harriet Beecher Stowe, was one of the first southern magazines to gain recognition on a national level. Since the publication of *The History of Southern Literature,* scholarship on the writings of southern women has increased tremendously. A number of anthologies have been published, among them *New Stories by Southern Women* (1989), *Downhome: An Anthology of Southern Women Writers* (1995), and *Southern Women's Writing: Colonial to Contemporary* (1995). The list of scholarly books and articles on southern women writers is particularly extensive, including books like MacKethan's *Daughters of Time: Creating Woman's Voice in Southern Story* (1992), Manning's *The Female Tradition in Southern Literature* (1993), and Tate's *A Southern Weave of Women: Fiction of the Contemporary South* (1994). Such works as these have done much to establish the literary history of southern women. At the same time, the work of many southern women is being reevaluated within the contexts of gender and race, and as a result, gender and race lines have become less apparent in general scholarship on the literature of the South.

An additional equation in the construction of contemporary southern literature is the influence of literary theory. Before the 1970s, southern literature was, with few exceptions, analyzed within a New Critical context. Given that most of the New Critics, including Robert Penn Warren, Allen Tate, Caroline Gordon, and John Crowe Ransom, were southerners with both creative and critical acclaim, their influence was felt in southern criticism long after the movement was nationally surpassed. Recent southern scholarship increasingly reflects the influence of contemporary literary theory. For example, the essays in Jones and Donaldson's *Haunted Bodies* (1997) explore gender construction in southern literature, while the essays in Humphries' *Southern Literature and Literary Theory* (1990) demonstrate the influence of cultural criticism on ways of reading. Such works represent the profound importance of judging southern literature—both recent and remote—within new contexts. Literary publishers have also been influenced by recent moves within American society toward inclusion, whether that be race, gender, or sexuality. For example, Daughters, Inc., one of the first lesbian presses, was responsible for publishing Rita Mae Brown's *Rubyfruit Jungle* (1973) and for supporting many southern women writers; Peachtree Publishers recently produced an audio tape of Carmen Agra Deedy's *Grow-*

ing Up Cuban in Decatur, Georgia, and in 1999, Scholarly Books published the journal of an early-twentieth-century woman who revealed what it was like being southern and Jewish, *Heart of a Wife,* by Helen Jacobus Apte. The list of authors covered in *The History of Southern Women's Literature* was also greatly influenced by the broadening scope of scholarship. Recent work by Richard Lounsbury, for example, drew our attention to the writings of Louisa McCord, who is rarely mentioned in critical studies. Likewise, although she fell into obscurity despite winning a Pulitzer Prize for her portrayal of rural African American life in *Scarlet Sister Mary* (1928), Julia Peterkin has recently reclaimed critical attention because of Susan Millar Williams' study of her work, *A Devil and a Good Woman, Too: The Lives of Julia Peterkin* (1998).

Within these new contexts for reading southern literature, the central question that contemporary writers seem to confront is "How do we retain our southernness in an increasingly homogenized world?" Others ask, "Why should we try?" Has the distinctiveness of the southern voice been reduced to the occasional twang and a request for a Coca-Cola rather than a soda? Despite the changes in the South and in ways of approaching literary texts, some traits of southern culture seem determined to follow southern literature into the new millennium.

One characteristic of southern literature that seems destined to endure in writing by women is the importance of concreteness. Whether writing novels or stories, southern women take great care in recreating the sights, sounds, and even smells of the places they describe. The prevalence of food is perhaps the best example, figuring prominently in the literature as a connection to earlier generations who raised their families on homemade dishes. Renaissance writers used references to food as a means of preserving southern culture, in particular, Marjorie Kinnan Rawlings (1896–1953), who published an entire cookbook on Cross Creek cookery and filled *The Yearling* (1937) with images of food. This tradition is just as popular in contemporary literature, with *Dori Sanders' Country Cooking* (1995) selling thousands of copies. By century's end, the grocery store and the mini-mart may have made their appearance in women's literature, but homemade food still brings people together. In the case of Fannie Flagg's *Fried Green Tomatoes at the Whistle Stop Cafe* (1987), the contemporary world of 1986 is a world of Piggly Wiggly supermarkets that sell Corn Curls, Cokes, candy bars, and Fig Newtons. The past is a time of familial ties and friendships, a place where a café like the Whistle Stop served iced tea and fried green tomatoes. When Evelyn wants to prepare her friend Mrs. Threadgoode a treat, she fixes "a plate of perfectly fried green tomatoes and fresh cream-white corn, six slices of bacon, with a bowl of baby lima beans on the side, and four huge light and fluffy buttermilk biscuits." Likewise, in Beth Henley's *Crimes of the Heart* (1982) food is at the center of all that happens. All the action takes place in the kitchen, and this setting and the constant attention to food ultimately suggest ties of love and compassion that sustain the family. Meg's entrance at the end of the play with Lenny's bakery birthday cake saves Babe from sticking her head into the gas oven, and although it is breakfast time, the sisters join together to eat the cake ravenously in celebration of Lenny's "being born." Although murder charges, shriveled ovaries, and a faltering career still loom in their future, for the moment they find comfort in their communion.

An image almost as vital to the South today as the ruined mansion is the cemetery. At the turn of the century, no picture of New Orleans is complete without its massive tombstones, and in Memphis, Elvis fans visit Meditation Garden daily to view the graves of the Presley family. Southern literature is filled with such images of cemeteries: from Katherine Anne Porter's Miranda standing over the graves of her ancestors in "The Grave" and Alice Walker tramping through cemeteries in search of Zora, to the Civil War tombstones that loom over Bobbie Ann Mason's "Shiloh." Like writers of the Renaissance, contemporary writers use the family cemetery as a physical remainder and reminder of a southern past that still survives. In Lee Smith's *Oral History* (1983) the final gathering place is the Cantrell family plot on top of Hoot Owl Mountain. At the end of the novel, a theme park takes over the homeplace, but the house—though "vines grow up through the porch where the rocking chair sits, and the south wall of the house has fallen in"—still stands, "smack in the middle of Ghostland." Despite the fact that the cafeteria has taken over the burial ground, through images of the grave, Smith clearly suggests the permanence of the past.

A likely theme of southern writers in the new millennium is the importance of looking back while at the same time moving ahead; another Mason story, "Graveyard Day" (1982), illustrates this theme well. In the story, Waldeen, a divorced mother, has trouble letting go of the past when thoughts of her ex-husband keep her from making a commitment to Joe Murdock. The central action stems from Joe's asking Waldeen and her ten-year-old daughter, Holly, to go with him to clean his family graveyard. The fact that Joe accepts his turn at clearing off the graves suggests his connections to both living and dead relations. Perhaps because she does not accept Joe's explanation that such caretaking is "a family thing"—to be taken seriously—Waldeen suggests they have a picnic at the graveyard. Their picnic is not a traditional homemade meal, but instead a bucket of fried chicken, store-bought slaw, and beer. Yet as she watches Joe and his friend C. W.

rake leaves into a huge pile, she comes to recognize the importance of simple actions and family, and the importance of not only remembering the past but also taking a chance on the future. After a "long, running start," Waldeen "takes a flying leap" and "lands in the immense pile of leaves, up to her elbows." The cemetery here is not a place of endings as in Mason's "Shiloh," but of possibilities and renewal of family.

At the same time, when contemporary writers look to the past, they more often do so with a revisionist's eye. For writers like Rita Mae Brown, Sherley Anne Williams, and Kaye Gibbons, in particular, the antebellum and bellum South is the impetus for novels focusing on women who step beyond the boundaries of traditional southern femininity. In Kaye Gibbons' *On the Occasion of My Last Afternoon* (1998), the heroine of the novel, Emma, in effect serves as surgeon during the Civil War. In a more extreme version of gender "confusion," Rita Mae Brown's heroine Geneva in *High Hearts* (1996) assumes the role of a Confederate soldier. Geneva marries Nash Hart on April 12, 1861, the day the guns were first fired at Fort Sumter, South Carolina. When Nash joins the Confederate Army five days later, Geneva follows him, cutting her hair and enlisting under the name "Jimmy." Yet in battle their gender roles are reversed: Nash shrinks back from the violence of battle, while Geneva is energized by the fighting. Presenting a revisionist view of both gender and race in the Old South in *Dessa Rose* (1986), Williams explores the many complications of racial and sexual relationships by creating an alternative world: a plantation owned by a white woman who takes in and protects runaway slaves. Through the friendship between this woman, Miss Rufel, and Dessa Rose, leader of a slave rebellion, Rufel comes to realize that she is in no way superior. According to Elizabeth Harrison, who discusses *Dessa Rose* in her book *Female Pastoral* (1991), the novel is based only loosely on historical accounts and is more utopian than realistic, yet it allows readers to imagine interracial relationships marked by healing.

Finally, the future of southern women's literature rests secure on the power of the southern storytelling tradition, which seems in no danger of waning. In addition to a continual outpouring of fiction, southern women writers are telling their own stories. Bobbie Ann Mason's memoir *Clear Springs* recounts her life—as well as that of her parents and grand-parents—in rural Kentucky; likewise, Mary Lee Settle's 1998 memoir, *Addie,* has at its center not Settle's own life, but that of her West Virginian grandmother. Similarly, Sonia Sanchez's *Does Your House Have Lions?* (1998) is a book-length poem recounting her brother's struggle with AIDS and the intensity of her family's involvement in the tragedy. Yet contemporary southern women writers seem committed not only to creating stories and to telling their own, but also to bringing to life the stories of unknown southern women. Having collected her writing in a trunk until she was well past seventy, Lou Crabtree enrolled in an adult education course taught by Lee Smith. Smith was so taken with Crabtree's tales of her life in the mountains—teaching in a one-room schoolhouse, suffering through thirteen miscarriages (yet naming every child)—that she helped Crabtree edit a selection of them; Louisiana State University Press published *Sweet Hollow: Stories* in 1984. Similarly, Josephine Humphreys recently recorded and transcribed the story of Ruthie Bolton (a pseudonym), who described to Humphreys her triumph over poverty and abuse. Although Bolton had already produced a manuscript, Humphreys preferred that she tell her story in a more southern way—orally—and the written record is found in *Gal* (1994).

Linda Tate could have been speaking of all these stories when she described Kaye Gibbons' *A Cure for Dreams* (1991) as a "verbal quilt," "weaving together . . . women's stories" while suggesting "the organic matrix of female empowerment." Women's literature in the South will endure because women writers insist on looking back to a distinctly southern past while embracing the future with a sense of determination and hope. Like the storytellers of the South, anthologies and histories of southern literature also do more than record the past or comment on the present. They invent the future. Studies such as *The History of Southern Women's Literature* make new connections among writers of different eras, bring writers on the margin to the center of literary study, invite explorations of old texts from new theoretical perspectives, and look forward to those contemporary writers who will lead us into the twenty-first century. In doing so, the scholars' voices that have come together in this volume join with the voices of countless southern women to perpetuate a richly varied and enduring literary tradition.

Appendix: The Study of Southern Women's Literature

Anne E. Rowe

Several definitive statements may be made about the study of southern women's literature. Although the formal study of southern women writers is less than three decades old, it has increased rapidly in volume and scope. A survey of critical writing about southern women's literature reveals that it is characterized by repeated and related themes, most notably those of marginality and community. This essay makes no attempt to be inclusive of all major works but through representative examples will give an overview of the development of critical study in this field.

There was evidence of interest in the work of southern women writers as early as the mid-nineteenth century. Julia Freeman's *Women of the South Distinguished in Literature* (1861), Mary Tardy's *Living Female Writers of the South* (1872), and *Southland Writers: Biographical and Critical Sketches of the Living Female Writers of the South* (1870) are examples. Louise Manly's *Southern Literature from 1579–1895* (1895) is a textbook described by Thomas Inge in *The History of Southern Literature* (1985) as including "a conscientious and thorough selection" of southern women writers. It should also be noted that Caroline Gilman called for a southern literature (although not specifically a female southern literature) before William Gilmore Simms did.

The beginnings of the study of southern women's literature are often traced to Anne Firor Scott's *The Southern Lady: From Pedestal to Politics* (1970). In her preface Scott writes: "I came to understand that southern women in the years before 1860 had been the subjects—perhaps the victims—of an image of women which was at odds with the reality of their lives. This image was weakened but not destroyed by the experiences of the Civil War and Reconstruction. It continued to shape the behavior of southern women for many years and has never entirely disappeared." Scott's groundbreaking study of the image of the lady and its effect upon southern women brought critical attention to the history of southern women and to the discrepancy between the myth perpetuated in southern writing and the reality.

Books and articles on major individual women writers such as Ellen Glasgow, Eudora Welty, and Flannery O'Connor had appeared, of course, before the 1970s, but generally women writers were treated as *southern* writers with little emphasis on their gender. By the end of the 1970s and the beginning of the 1980s, the number of books on southern women writers was increasing. In 1982, for example, William J. Stuckey in *Modern Fiction Studies* reviewed thirteen recently published studies of Glasgow, Welty, McCullers, and O'Connor. The articles in this issue were also devoted to southern women writers. Stuckey comments that in the 1959–60 issue of *Modern Fiction Studies* devoted to southern writers, "it would have seemed absurd to single out women writers for special notice or even to have suggested that they might be read in ways significantly different from the ways in which men writers are read. None of the textbooks, commentaries, critical books, or articles made any such distinctions."

The pivotal work of the opening of the 1980s and one that is frequently referred to by more recent critical studies is Anne Goodwyn Jones's *Tomorrow Is Another Day: The Woman Writer in the South, 1859–1936* (1981). In the book, Jones analyzes the writings of seven women, Augusta Jane Evans Wilson, Grace King, Kate Chopin, Mary Johnston, Ellen Glasgow, Frances Newman, and Margaret Mitchell, who "were raised to be southern ladies, physically pure, fragile, and beautiful, socially dignified, cultured, and gracious, within the family sacrificial and submissive, yet, if the occasion required, intelligent and brave." For these women, Jones says, "the very act of writing itself evoked . . . a sense of self-contradiction, for southern ladies were expected to defer to men's opinions, yet writing required an independent mind." Of these writers, Jones concludes, "all criticize the ideal of southern womanhood point by point in similar ways." In contrast to Scott's work, Jones's emphasis is less on the image of southern womanhood and more on the "literary manifestations" of this concept. Jones concludes that the code of honor remains generally constant from *Beulah* (1859) to *Gone with the Wind* (1936); however, "in each novel and story, the models and injunctions for southern ladyhood have been directly or indirectly challenged." Noting the ambivalence of some of the writers in their fiction, Jones concludes that it "should be forgiven; it is quite a magician's trick, after all, to make a marble statue live and move, and then to make it speak."

A related subject is treated by Kathryn Lee Seidel in *The Southern Belle in the American Novel* (1985)—the myth of the belle and its effect on southern women. Seidel credits Jones with beginning "to analyze the tension created within the southern woman trying to conform to psychologically contradictory ideals. . . . Jones's purpose, however, was not to describe or analyze the belle figure created by male and female authors; hence the diverse manifestations of the belle remain to be reconciled." In a study of writers including Glasgow, Newman, and Faulkner, Seidel traces the history of the belle figure in American literature with special emphasis on its mythic significance.

Other book-length studies of the 1980s develop and expand upon themes appearing in the earlier works, most notably to include treatments of the work of minority and contemporary writers. For example, *Women Writers of the Contemporary South* (1984), edited by Peggy Prenshaw, is a collection of essays treating writers whose work appears after 1945. Prenshaw finds that these younger writers "differ perhaps most noticeably from earlier twentieth-century writers in their depiction of a Southern region more typically urban than rural and in their portrayal of characters more mobile and transient than rooted in the Southern past." The essays in this collection provide descriptions of plots and discussions of major themes and concerns of individual writers. For example, an excellent essay by Anne Jones on Lee Smith concludes that "the meaning of her stories challenges . . . *critical discourse* itself. . . . Her tendency to prefer traditionally female immanent art to traditionally male transcendent art parallels her preference for the spoken to the written word." Jones concludes, "To call a *written fiction Oral History* is Lee Smith's latest, best joke."

In *Gender, Race, and Region in the Writings of Grace King, Ruth McEnery Stuart, and Kate Chopin* (1989), Helen Taylor notes the influence of feminist criticism on her work, which she describes as "an attempt to extend [Anne] Jones's project by examining selected women writers working in a single southern state over a period of roughly twenty years." Stating that her "choice of women writing about Louisiana after the Civil War is intended to suggest new links between regionalism and feminism," Taylor focuses on "analyzing the specific ways women related to the Local Color movement and explored the meanings of Louisiana's historical, cultural, and mythic heritage and problems," noting that despite the fact that King, Stuart, and Chopin all achieved popularity, their lasting critical reputations have differed. In spite of these differences, however, Taylor concludes, "It now seems clear that white women's writing about the Civil War and its aftermath follows a different trajectory from men's, in ways that are linked inextricably to women's specific experiences and relationships in the South, and to the ideological constructions of the defeated South and its white and black population around gender and race images and stereotypes."

In the 1990s there has been a dramatic increase in books dedicated to the study of southern women's literature, and the influence of feminist criticism has become more pronounced. Lucinda MacKethan in *Daughters of Time: Creating Woman's Voice in Southern Story* (1990) comments on the growth in scholarship since the publication of Scott's seminal work and states that, "In large part through my reading of southern women writers, the word 'voice' has come to have for me, as it has for many women, a metaphorical dimension, encompassing all that goes into the expression of unique selfhood." Although southern women writers depict "a culture that remained patriarchal even longer than other regions of America," MacKethan's study treats "the possibilities for reversal, for empowerment, that southern women seized upon when they moved beyond the role of daughter and into the role of story teller." MacKethan first looks at letters of a plantation wife (Catherine Hammond) and the autobiography of a female slave (Harriet Jacobs), noting in each "her revisions of the standard portrait of the white patriarch." She then turns to a consideration of Glasgow, Zora Hurston, and Eudora Welty: "They began their quests clearly defined as daughters, yet in their journeys from and returns to southern homeplaces, they became creators, developing a tradition of strong woman's voice in southern writing." In a postscript treating Alice Walker and Lee Smith, MacKethan shows how a contemporary writer can take the process of finding a voice even further. In *The Color Purple* (1982) and *Fair and Tender Ladies* (1988), "the characters quite literally write themselves into being through letters that celebrate motherhood and daughterhood but, most importantly, sisterhood as the defining connection for women's experience within southern families." MacKethan notes that her "emphasis falls on the points where the gender interests of white and black women intersect to create similar expressions of growth into voice." Glasgow, Hurston, and Welty, she concludes, were all successful in writing "their way out of the cage of southern patriarchy."

Also using a revisionist approach, Elizabeth Jane Harrison in *Female Pastoral: Women Writers Re-Visioning the American South* (1991) analyzes the work of a group of southern women writers who she argues are creating a "celebratory pastoral" that no longer depends upon the courtship plot: "Romance is no longer the main focus of fiction in this new tradition; instead the reactive heroine becomes active hero—she begins her own quest." Stating that her study takes up where the work of Annette Kolodny ends, Harrison traces the development of the pastoral tradition, documented by W. J. Cash, and notes three versions of the southern male pastoral: antebellum, postbellum, and Southern Renaissance. In contrast to the male pastorals depicting the passive southern lady, "For twentieth-century women writers . . . all these representations of female characters are problematic. None allows for full psychological development of a woman protagonist." For Harrison the female pastoral "envisions new class relationships and stresses not individual but cooperative action." Glasgow, Willa Cather, Harriette Arnow, Alice Walker, and Sherley Anne Williams "subvert [the plantation romance and local color] by rescuing the female protagonist from her role as plantation mistress or mammy in antiplantation romances or, alternately, by re-imagining the poor tenant farmer as an independent land owner." Using such works as Glasgow's *Barren Ground* (1925) and Walker's *The Color Purple*, Harrison argues that "both black and white versions of the southern garden challenge a reductive view of women characters and both use land or nature as a means of liberation from an oppressive society. By disassociating the woman protagonist from her representation *as* landscape, the female pastoral first allows her to develop autonomy."

Will Brantley also explores connections among southern women writers in *Feminine Sense in Southern Memoir: Smith, Glasgow, Welty, Hellman, Porter, and Hurston* (1993). In his introduction Brantley quotes Welty's response to a question about whether she was part of a literary community: "I'm not sure there's any dotted line connecting us up," Welty said, "though all of us knew about each other and all of us, I think, respected and read each other's work and understood it." Brantley's purpose, he says, "is to connect some of the more significant 'dots' . . . through an intertextual examination of selected nonfiction prose that acknowledges each writer's distinctiveness and changing perspectives over a lifetime." Brantley's examination of these self-portraits leads him to conclude, "If any one thread is central to an understanding of the self-writing [of these women] it is their shared independence, their need to define themselves as intense individualists." Brantley also notes, however, that "The all too frequent omission of women writers from the intellectual history of the Southern Renaissance suggests . . . the inability of masculinist critics to accommodate women's texts to paradigms derived almost solely from the texts of men."

Linda Tate in *A Southern Weave of Women: Fiction of the Contemporary South* (1994) has a dual focus—that of the state of scholarship by southern critics as well as perceptions of southern institutions from outside the South. Tate finds that "The frustration of trying to understand the complexity and multiplicity of the 'southern woman' results not only from male- and white-dominated scholarship but also from the popular myths of the South and of southern women that continue to thrive—especially outside the South." Additionally, "southern women often define themselves too narrowly and fail to see beyond the confines of race, ethnicity, and class." Tate urges inclusiveness in what is called southern, and in her study "seeks to articulate those cultural characteristics that concern all southern women writers—black and white, the upper middle class as well as the lower classes, deep South and Appalachian." In addition to finding the common themes that run through the works of a diversity of southern women writers, Tate also is concerned with "the forces that keep contemporary southern women's writing on the margins of literary discourse." The six chapters in Tate's book deal with the relations of black and white writers, re-visioning the South's past, the "erasure" of the South through films that rely on southern stereotypes, and the marginality of southern writing.

Among important collections of essays appearing in the first half of the 1990s, Tonette Bond Inge's *Southern Women Writers: The New Generation* (1990) is a collection of fifteen essays about women writers working in the second half of the twentieth century, including Maya Angelou, Sonia Sanchez, Lee Smith, and Nikki Giovanni. Inge's book also has a useful bibliography including many articles on southern women writers. Doris Betts in the introduction sets the tone of this collection by paraphrasing Frederick Karl's criticism that "women novelists do not seem especially modern or postmodern." She responds, "Like immigrants pushing wide-eyed off Ellis Island, some are still hollering, 'Hey! We just got here!' . . . If we are not as Whitmanesque as some prefer, neither are we as restricted as clichés would have it."

Friendship and Sympathy: Communities of Southern Women Writers (1992), edited by Rosemary M. Magee, also treats the marginal status of women writers in the South. Noting how women have often had to write at the kitchen table and have not been a part of "societies, clubs, universities, and bars" where men meet, she says they "have had to create alternate forms of communities. . . . Southern women writers of the past and present in offering 'friendship and sympathy' to one another transcend the boundaries of time and space, of rigid definitions of literature and life, and they bear witness to a vibrant literary unfolding." Magee notes the friendship between Glasgow and Marjorie Rawlings as an example of this kind of support. The essays that follow are a wonderful cross collection of writers writing about the distinguishing qualities of one another's works. For example, Porter says of Welty, "she need not follow a war and smell death to feel herself alive." Anne Tyler writes of Welty, "She does not admit to belonging to a literary community, but what she means is that she was never part of a formal circle of writers." Alice Walker says of O'Connor, "Being white she would automatically have been eligible for ladyhood, but I cannot believe she would ever really have joined." Doris Betts says of Tyler's work, "home is central to many Tyler openings—and so is somebody's itch to get away from it." Magee concludes that women writers have "discovered new forms of community. . . . The importance of place—of shared idiom, locale, and experience, however separated by physical space—lingers with contemporary writers even as the very concept of the South undergoes revision and expansion." Linda Wagner-Martin makes a similar point. In "'Just the Doing of It': Southern Women Writers and the Idea of Community" (*Southern Literary Journal*, 1990), she argues that "For southern women writers of recent times, the idea of community has gotten more and more specific, and more and more matriarchal."

Much of the writing about southern women's literature discussed thus far has been concerned with making sure that women writers have their place in the literary canon, including the recovery of forgotten women writers of the nineteenth century. Carol S. Manning, editor of *The Female Tradition in Southern Literature* (1993), raises even more questions about the state of southern literary scholarship. In her introduction, "On Defining Themes and (Mis) Placing Women Writers," she states that now that the study of southern literature has been established for several decades, "The time has come for an assessment of the critical literature and a reconsideration of terms, themes, and canons." Noting that the essays in this edited volume have "implications [that] are revisionist and feminist," Manning makes the point that in spite of the increasing amount of scholarship in southern literature, it was only in the 1980s "that feminist murmurs about Southern literature began to be heard." Manning argues that with the professionalization of literary study begun in the 1920s and the canonization process that followed, nineteenth-century women writers were excluded and the result was "a literary map that privileges certain texts and themes and undervalues the contributions of minority and women writers." Critics who defined "the Southern family romance through the figures of the father and grandfather only" fail to include the role of the southern woman.

In a chapter entitled "The Real Beginning of the Southern Renaissance," Manning also asserts that the definition of the Southern Renaissance of the 1930s "as bounded by two wars, quarterbacked by the Fugitives/Agrarians at Nashville, and inspired by the South's attempt to move forward while looking backward—is neat and convenient, but it is hardly realistic." Noting that this definition excludes Ellen Glasgow and Kate Chopin, she concludes, "To mark the boundaries of this literary phenomenon by two wars is a characteristic historical, and masculine, conceit that ill fits the territory. . . . [W]hile the women writing in the late nineteenth and early twentieth centuries were lone and isolated voices in that South described by H. L. Mencken as 'the Sahara of the Bozart,' the Fugitives and after them the Agrarians at Nashville were voices speaking in unison and consciously proclaiming a new day for Southern letters."

Manning's collection includes essays on Hurston, Welty, O'Connor, Alice Walker, and Zelda Fitzgerald and provides excellent revisionist criticism. The concluding essay by Doris Betts eloquently speaks to gender differences: "For certain Southern writers, the mystery lay in Vicksburg, Chicamaugua; the mystery lay in owning slaves, or being them. Women growing up in the same latitude heard in the kitchen less of battles or emancipation, more of fevers and bastard babies and deathbed sayings." Betts also looks forward to contemporary southern writing: "Since Appomattox . . . the age of puberty has dropped from seventeen to thirteen. Near-babies know where babies come from now, and their older sisters are off the pedestal and on the pill."

In the latter half of the 1990s the study of southern women's literature continued to flourish and expand. The publication in 1995 of a new anthology, *Southern Women's Writing: Colonial to Contemporary*, edited by Mary Louise Weaks and Carolyn Perry, redresses the relatively small number of women included in earlier anthologies. The editors note that "The major texts for the study of southern literature . . . all give a slim overview of the women's tradition in the South. The larger body of specialized anthologies of southern literature tend to be period or genre studies." Although that problem has been somewhat corrected with the appearance of later works like the Norton anthology *The Literature of the American South* (1998), which includes many more women and minority writers than earlier anthologies, *Southern Women's Writing*'s special focus on the relationships among women writers is especially important; as the editors note: "Perhaps our greatest challenge as anthologers lay not just in reshaping the southern literary canon but in making sense of the impassioned voices of women who have struggled with and against each other because of class divisions and gender or racial inequality."

Scholarship on southern literature by African Americans has grown dramatically in the last three decades. An excellent example of this growth is the increase in scholarship on Zora Hurston. In her foreword to Hurston's *Their Eyes Were Watching God,* Mary Washington recounts the discovery of this novel and finds, at least symbolically, that Alice Walker's search for Hurston's grave represents a reclaiming of Hurston critically. In MLA First Search, there are nine references to Hurston from 1963 to 1975. For 1976 there are six, and from 1977 to the present over 375. The date of Walker's article on Hurston is 1975, and it seems clear that this work marks the resurgence of interest in Hurston that has been followed by an outpouring of work on earlier writers such as Harriet Jacobs as well as later writers including Maya Angelou, Nikki Giovanni, and Sonia Sanchez. Some representative scholarly works include Karla Holloway's *The Character of the Word: The Texts of Zora Neale Hurston* (1987) and *Moorings and Metaphors: Figures of Culture and Gender in Black Women's Literature* (1992); Elizabeth Brown-Guillory's *Their Place on the Stage: Black Women Playwrights in America* (1988); Frances Smith Foster's *Written by Herself: Literary Production by African American Women, 1746–1892* (1993); Deborah E. McDowell's *"The Changing Same": Black Women's Literature, Criticism, and Theory* (1995); and Brenda Scott Wilkinson's *African American Women Writers* (2000).

Studies of southern women's writing are also appearing that focus on previously undertreated aspects of women's culture. For example, Danny L. Miller's *Wingless Flights: Appalachian Women in Fiction* (1996) is concerned with the exploration of the roles of Appalachian mountain women in fiction. In a study of such writers as Mary Murfree, Jesse Stuart, and Harriette Arnow, Miller finds that in the fictional portrayal of Appalachian women, wives are often called the "'silent, wingless mate[s]' of their husbands," whose lives are overshadowed by their victimization. Miller argues, however, that "the qualities which most consistently define them are admirable and positive ones. Though 'wingless,' the Appalachian mountain woman often flies to heights of courage, endurance and heroism."

Another new approach to southern women's writing is taken by Barbara Bennett in *Comic Visions, Female Voices: Contemporary Women Novelists and Southern Humor* (1998). Bennett's major premise is that "Humor is an intricate part of many southern women writers' works, helping to define voice, communicate theme, and establish new definitions of southern literature. . . . [M]ost female humor has a distinct voice and vision; iconoclastic, yet ultimately unifying; challenging traditional relationships, yet affirming the self and family." Noting that before the twentieth century, southern women's voices were often silenced, Bennett traces the emergence of women's humor in the twentieth century, focusing on the work of Zora Neale Hurston, Anne Tyler, Jill McCorkle, Rita Mae Brown, Lee Smith, Josephine Humphreys, Bobbie Ann Mason, Tina Ansa, Alice Walker, Dori Sanders, and Lisa Alther. She concludes, "Whereas male writers may attack the institutions of church and marriage, female writers attack not only the institutions but also the male figures behind those institutions." She also notes the increasingly important role of comedy and satire in women's writing: "In the past, according to Anne Jones, women writers have criticized the Ideal Southern Woman through 'imagery, plotting, characterization, and narrative point of view,' but with new writers, satire has become a much stronger weapon."

Expansions of the canon and the importance of women writers' finding a community in which to flourish are likely to continue to be major issues in the study of southern women's literature. For example, Nancy Parrish's *Lee Smith, Annie Dillard, and the Hollins Group: A Genesis of Writers* (1998) examines the supportive environment created at Hollins College in the 1960s that benefited writers Lee Smith and Annie Dillard as well as literary critics Lucinda MacKethan and Anne Goodwyn Jones. Although Parrish notes the institutional support given by such professors as Louis D. Rubin, Jr., and the writing skills the four women developed there, she cites as equally important their shared sense of community: "by their own judgement, their association with each other at Hollins was the most significant influence on their progress as writers." Manning notes in her book that during the Southern Literary Renaissance male literary critics were becoming as central to southern literature as the writers they treated; in Parrish's book Jones and MacKethan are also accorded a role equal to the creative writers.

The study of southern women's literature has also benefited from the significant work of scholars of southern history. Anne Scott's groundbreaking work has been mentioned. Other important historians following her include Elizabeth Fox-Genovese (*Within the Plantation Household: Black and White Women of the Old South,* 1988) and Catherine Clinton (*The Plantation Mistress: Women's World in the Old South,* 1982).

One of the best examples of a recent book that continues to expand the breadth of critical study in southern women's writing is *Haunted Bodies: Gender and Southern Texts* (1997), edited by Anne Goodwyn Jones and Susan V. Donaldson. The editors describe the essays in their collection as having "to use Michel Foucault's phrase, 'a multiplicity of discourses' about manhood and womanhood in the South, discourses that may have little to do with overtly prescribed gender. We discover a central preoccupation with gender in fields ranging from law to music. We also learn in careful detail how practices and narratives of southern masculinity and femininity have in fact been plural, unstable, and subject to bewildering shifts ever since the eighteenth century." The essays in this collection range from treatments of the colonial period to the present and are far more inclusive in term of texts considered than many earlier critical studies, ranging from diaries to court records, short stories to architectural plans. For example, Anne Goodwyn Jones's "Engendered in the South: Blood and Irony in Douglass and Jacobs" explores the reasons that "Douglass had become a heroic figure in the public, predominantly male world, while Jacobs, despite an equally dramatic escape from slavery . . . remained in the female world of domesticity." "The Dining Room Door Swings Both Ways: Food, Race, and Domestic Space in the Nineteenth-Century South" by Mary Titus explores how "we can read conflicting postbellum representations of antebellum plantation life from the perspective of the dining room." Titus argues convincingly that "The threshold between kitchen and dining room represents a crucial margin across which food passes; we could name this threshold the locus of the second most intimate possible relation between blacks and whites." Elizabeth Fox Genovese in "Slavery, Race, and the Figure of the Tragic Mulatta: or, The Ghost of Southern History in the Writing of African-American Women" writes that "Like the Russian peasants' proverbial rat, southern history has stuck in the throat of African-American women writers, who can neither swallow it nor spit it out."

In the concluding essay of *Haunted Bodies,* entitled "Gender, Race, and Allen Tate's Profession of Letters in the South," Susan Donaldson writes of Tate's "grumpily" noting in a letter to John Peale Bishop in 1935 that he had just written an essay on a topic "not of his own choosing"—an essay in which he concluded "that the Southern tradition has left no cultural landmark so conspicuous that the people may be reminded by it constantly of what they are. We lack a tradition in the arts; more to the point, we lack a literary tradition." Donaldson notes that while in this essay and other places "Tate . . . yearned to find an image of what he thought of as the ideal southern tradition *and* writer—white, male, conservative, rooted to time and place, and unified in sensibility—he nonetheless had the integrity to acknowledge, albeit with very bad grace, the possibility that such an image would always prove chimerical or, at the very least, radically unstable." The study of southern women's literature, particularly as it has culminated in the work of such critics as Manning in *The South and the Female Tradition* and Jones and Donaldson in *Haunted Bodies, has* contributed to destabilizing the canon. It has brought into focus many of the marginal and silenced voices. Most importantly, it has explored the possibilities of new kinds of communities, places where diverse voices and experiences can have a place in southern writing.

Bibliography of General Secondary Sources on Southern Women's Literature

Alderman, Edwin Anderson, and Joel Chandler Harris, eds. *Library of Southern Literature.* 15 vols. New Orleans: Martin and Hoyt, 1907.

Ammons, Elizabeth. *Conflicting Stories: American Women Writers at the Turn into the Twentieth Century.* New York: Oxford University Press, 1991.

Andrews, William L. *To Tell a Free Story: The First Century of Afro-American Autobiography, 1760–1865.* Urbana: University of Illinois Press, 1986.

Andrews, William L., et al., eds. *The Literature of the American South: A Norton Anthology.* New York: Norton, 1998.

Andrews, William L., et al. *Oxford Companion to African American Literature.* New York: Oxford University Press, 1997.

Awkward, Michael. *Inspiriting Influences: Tradition, Revision, and Afro-American Women's Novels.* New York: Columbia University Press, 1989.

Ayers, Edward L. *The Promise of the New South: Life after Reconstruction.* New York: Oxford University Press, 1992.

Baym, Nina. *Feminism and American Literary History: Essays.* New Brunswick: Rutgers University Press, 1992.

———. *Woman's Fiction: A Guide to Novels by and about Women in America, 1820–1870.* Ithaca: Cornell University Press, 1978.

Beatty, Richmond Croom, Floyd C. Watkins, and Thomas Daniel Young, eds. *The Literature of the South.* 1952. Reprint, Chicago: Scott, Foresman, 1968.

Bell, Bernard W. *The Afro-American Novel and Its Tradition.* Amherst: University of Massachusetts Press, 1987.

Bell, Roseann R., Bettye J. Parker, and Beverly Guy-Sheftall, eds. *Sturdy Black Brid-*

ges: Visions of Black Women in Literature. Garden City, N.Y.: Anchor/Doubleday, 1979.

Bennett, Barbara. *Comic Visions, Female Voices: Contemporary Women Novelists and Southern Humor.* Baton Rouge: Louisiana State University Press, 1998.

Bernhard, Virginia, et al., eds. *Southern Women: Histories and Identities.* Columbia: University of Missouri Press, 1992.

Brantley, Will. *Feminine Sense in Southern Memoir: Smith, Glasgow, Welty, Hellman, Porter, and Hurston.* Jackson: University Press of Mississippi, 1993.

Braxton, Joan M. *Black Women Writing Autobiography: A Tradition within a Tradition.* Philadelphia: Temple University Press, 1989.

Brown, Dorothy H., and Barbara C. Ewell, eds. *Louisiana Women Writers: New Essays and a Comprehensive Bibliography.* Baton Rouge: Louisiana State University Press, 1992.

Brown-Guillory, Elizabeth. *Their Place on the Stage: Black Women Playwrights in America.* New York: Greenwood, 1988.

Bryan, Violet Harrington. *The Myth of New Orleans in Literature: Dialogues of Race and Gender.* Knoxville: University of Tennessee Press, 1993.

Bryant, Joseph Allen. *Twentieth-Century Southern Literature.* Lexington: University Press of Kentucky, 1997.

Carby, Hazel V. *Reconstructing Womanhood: The Emergence of the Afro-American Woman Novelist.* New York: Oxford University Press, 1987.

Cash, W. J. *The Mind of the South.* New York: Vintage, 1941.

Castille, Philip, and William Osborne, eds. *Southern Literature in Transition.* Memphis: Memphis State University Press, 1983.

Clinton, Catherine. *The Plantation Mistress: Women's World in the Old South.* New York: Pantheon, 1982.

———. *Tara Revisited: Women, War, and the Plantation Legend.* New York: Abbeville, 1995.

Core, George, ed. *Southern Fiction Today: Renascence and Beyond.* Athens: University of Georgia Press, 1969.

Coulter, E. Merton. *The South during Reconstruction, 1865–1877.* Vol. 8 of *The History of the South,* ed. Wendell Holmes Stephenson and E. Merton Coulter. Baton Rouge: Louisiana State University Press, 1947.

Davidson, James Wood. *The Living Writers of the South.* New York: Carleton, 1869.

Davis, Richard Beale, C. Hugh Holman, and Louis D. Rubin, Jr., eds. *Southern Writing, 1585–1920.* New York: Odyssey, 1970.

Dillman, Caroline Matheny. *Southern Women.* New York: Hemisphere, 1988.

Dixon, Melvin. *Ride out of the Wilderness: Geography and Identity in Afro-American Literature.* Urbana: University of Illinois Press, 1987.

Douglas, Ann. *The Feminization of American Culture.* New York: Doubleday, 1988.

Dyer, Joyce. *Bloodroot: Reflections on Place by Appalachian Women Writers.* Lexington: University Press of Kentucky, 1998.

Evans, Mari, ed. *Black Women Writers (1950–1980): A Critical Evaluation*, Garden City, N.Y.: Anchor/Doubleday, 1984.

Fani, Sidney Saylor. *Appalachian Women: An Annotated Bibliography*. Lexington: University Press of Kentucky, 1981.

Faust, Drew Gilpin. *Mothers of Invention: Women of the Slaveholding South in the American Civil War*. Chapel Hill: University of North Carolina Press, 1996.

Fetterly, Judith, and Marjorie Pryse, eds. *American Women Regionalists, 1850–1910*. New York: Norton, 1992.

Fitzhugh, George. *Sociology for the South*. Richmond: Morris, 1854.

Forrest, Mary (Julia Deane Freeman). *Women of the South Distinguished in Literature*. New York: Derby and Jackson, 1860.

Foster, Frances Smith. *Written by Herself: Literary Production by African American Women, 1746–1892*. Bloomington: Indiana University Press, 1993.

Fox-Genovese, Elizabeth. *Within the Plantation Household: Black and White Women of the Old South*. Chapel Hill: University of North Carolina Press, 1988.

Gibson, Mary Ellis. *New Stories by Southern Women*. Columbia: University of South Carolina Press, 1989.

Gossett, Thomas F. *"Uncle Tom's Cabin" and American Culture*. Dallas: Southern Methodist University Press, 1985.

Griffin, Farah Jasmine. *Who Set You Flowin'?: The African American Migration Narrative*. New York: Oxford University Press, 1995.

Gwin, Minrose. *Black and White Women of the Old South: The Peculiar Sisterhood in American Literature*. Knoxville: University of Tennessee Press, 1985.

Hall, Wade. *The Smiling Phoenix: Southern Humor from 1865 to 1914*. Gainesville: University Press of Florida, 1965.

Harrison, Elizabeth Jane. *Female Pastoral: Women Writers Re-Visioning the American South*. Knoxville: University of Tennessee Press, 1991.

Hawks, Joanne V., and Sheila L. Skemp, eds. *Sex, Race, and the Role of Women in the South*. Jackson: University Press of Mississippi, 1983.

Hayes, Kevin J. *A Colonial Woman's Bookshelf*. Knoxville: University of Tennessee Press, 1996.

Henry, Robert Hiram. *Editors I Have Known since the Civil War*. Jackson, Mississippi: n.p., 1922.

Higgs, Robert A., Ambrose N. Manning, and Jim Wayne Miller, eds. *Appalachia Inside Out*. Knoxville: University of Tennessee Press, 1995.

Hobson, Fred. *But Now I See: The White Southern Racial Conversion Narrative*. Baton Rouge: Louisiana State University Press, 1999.

———. *The Southern Writer in the Postmodern World*. Athens: University of Georgia Press, 1991.

———. *Tell about the South: The Southern Rage to Explain*. Baton Rouge: Louisiana State University Press, 1983.

Holloway, Karla F. C. *Moorings and Metaphors: Figures of Culture and Gender in Black Women's Literature*. New Brunswick: Rutgers University Press, 1992.

Honey, Maureen, ed. *Shadowed Dreams: Women's Poetry of the Harlem Renaissance*. New Brunswick: Rutgers University Press, 1989.

hooks, bell. *"Ain't I a Woman?": Black Women and Feminism*. Boston: South End, 1981.

Hubbell, Jay B. *The South in American Literature, 1607–1900*. 1954. Reprint, Durham: Duke University Press, 1973.

Huggins, Nathan Irvin, ed. *Voices from the Harlem Renaissance*. New York: Oxford University Press, 1976.

Hull, Gloria T. *Color, Sex, and Poetry: Three Women Writers of the Harlem Renaissance*. Bloomington: Indiana University Press, 1987.

Humphries, Jefferson, ed. *Southern Literature and Literary Theory*. Athens: University of Georgia Press, 1990.

Humphries, Jefferson, and John Lowe, eds. *The Future of Southern Letters*. New York: Oxford University Press, 1996.

Inge, Tonnette Bond, ed. *Southern Women Writers: The New Generation*. Tuscaloosa: University of Alabama Press, 1990.

Jones, Anne Goodwyn. *Tomorrow Is Another Day: The Woman Writer in the South, 1859–1936*. Baton Rouge: Louisiana State University Press, 1981.

Jones, Anne Goodwyn, and Susan V. Donaldson, eds. *Haunted Bodies: Gender and Southern Texts*. Charlottesville: University Press of Virginia, 1997.

Jones, Jacqueline. *Labor of Love, Labor of Sorrow: Black Women, Work, and the Family from Slavery to the Present*. New York: Basic, 1985.

Kelley, Mary. *Private Woman, Public Stage: Literary Domesticity in Nineteenth-Century America*. New York: Oxford University Press, 1984.

Kennedy, Richard S., ed. *Literary New Orleans: Essays and Meditations*. Baton Rouge: Louisiana State University Press, 1992.

Kierner, Cynthia A. *Beyond the Household: Women's Place in the Early South, 1700–1835*. Ithaca: Cornell University Press, 1998.

———. *Southern Women in Revolution, 1776–1800: Personal and Political Narratives*. Columbia: University of South Carolina Press, 1998.

King, Richard H. *A Southern Renaissance: The Cultural Awakening of the American South, 1930–1955*. New York: Oxford University Press, 1980.

Kirby, Jack Temple. *Rural Worlds Lost: The American South, 1920–1960*. Baton Rouge: Louisiana State University Press, 1987.

Kolodny, Annette. *The Lay of the Land: Metaphor as Experience and History in American Life and Letters*. Chapel Hill: University of North Carolina Press, 1975.

Kreyling, Michael. *Inventing Southern Literature*. Jackson: University Press of Mississippi, 1998.

Ledger, Sally. *The New Woman: Fiction and Feminism at the Fin de Siècle*. New York: Manchester University Press, 1997.

Lerner, Gerda. *Creation of Feminist Consciousness: From the Middle Ages to Eighteen-Seventy*. New York: Oxford University Press, 1993.

MacKethan, Lucinda H. *Daughters of Time: Creating Woman's Voice in Southern Story.* Athens: University of Georgia Press, 1990.

Magee, Rosemary M., ed. *Friendship and Sympathy: Communities of Southern Women Writers.* Jackson: University Press of Mississippi, 1992.

Manning, Carol S., ed. *The Female Tradition in Southern Literature.* Urbana and Chicago: University of Illinois Press, 1993.

Marzolf, Marion. *Up from the Footnote: A History of Women Journalists.* New York: Hastings, 1977.

Massey, Mary Elizabeth. *Bonnet Brigades.* New York: Knopf, 1966.

May, Caroline. *The American Female Poets with Bibliographical and Critical Notices.* Philadelphia: Lindsay & Blakiston, 1846.

McDowell, Deborah E. *"The Changing Same": Black Women's Literature, Criticism, and Theory.* Bloomington: Indiana University Press, 1995.

McWhiney, Grady. *Cracker Culture: Celtic Ways of the Old South.* University, Ala.: University of Alabama Press, 1988.

Mee, Susie. *Downhome: An Anthology of Southern Women Writers.* San Diego: Harcourt, Brace, 1995.

Miller, Danny L. *Wingless Flights: Appalachian Women in Fiction.* Bowling Green: Bowling Green State University Press, 1996.

Morgan, Robin. *The Word of a Woman: Feminist Dispatches 1968–1992.* New York: Norton, 1992.

Moss, Elizabeth. *Domestic Novelists in the Old South: Defenders of Southern Culture.* Baton Rouge: Louisiana State University Press, 1992.

Nelson, Dana D. *The Word in Black and White: Reading "Race" in American Literature, 1638–1867.* New York: Oxford University Press, 1992.

Parrish, Nancy C. *Lee Smith, Annie Dillard, and the Hollins Group: A Genesis of Writers.* Baton Rouge: Louisiana State University Press, 1998.

Pattee, Fred Lewis. *A History of American Literature since 1870.* New York: Cooper Square, 1968.

Patterson, Orlando. *Slavery and Social Death: A Comparative Study.* Cambridge: Harvard University Press, 1982.

Pickett, Albert James. *History of Alabama and Incidentally of Georgia and Mississippi, from the Earliest Period.* 2nd ed. Charleston: Walker and James, 1851.

Prenshaw, Peggy Whitman, ed. *Women Writers of the Contemporary South.* Jackson: University Press of Mississippi, 1984.

Pryse, Marjorie, and Hortense J. Spillers, eds. *Conjuring: Black Women, Fiction, and Literary Tradition.* Bloomington: Indiana University Press, 1985.

Rable, George C. *Civil Wars: Women and the Crisis of Southern Nationalism.* Urbana: University of Illinois Press, 1989.

Radway, Janice A. *Reading the Romance: Women, Patriarchy, and Popular Culture.* Chapel Hill: University of North Carolina Press, 1984.

Reed, John Shelton. *Southern Folk, Plain and Fancy: Native White Social Types.* Athens: University of Georgia Press, 1988.

Ridgely, J. V. *Nineteenth-Century Southern Literature*. Lexington: University Press of Kentucky, 1980.

Roses, Lorraine Elena, and Ruth Elizabeth Randolph, eds. *The Harlem Renaissance and Beyond: Literary Biographies of 100 Black Women Writers, 1900–1945*. Cambridge: Harvard University Press, 1990.

Rubin, Louis D., Jr. *The American South: Portrait of a Culture*. Baton Rouge: Louisiana State University Press, 1980.

———. *The Writer in the South: Studies in Literary Community*. Athens: University of Georgia Press, 1972.

———, ed. *The Literary South*. New York: Wiley, 1979.

Rubin, Louis D., Jr., et al., eds. *The History of Southern Literature*. Baton Rouge: Louisiana State University Press, 1985.

Rubin, Louis D., Jr., and Robert D. Jacobs, eds. *South: Modern Southern Literature in Its Cultural Setting*. Garden City, N.Y.: Doubleday, 1961.

Rutherford, Mildred Lewis. *The South in History and Literature; A Hand-book of Southern Authors, from the Settlement of Jamestown, 1607, to Living Writers*. Cleveland: Arthur H. Clarke, 1906.

Scott, Anne Firor. *Making the Invisible Woman Visible*. Urbana: University of Illinois Press, 1984.

———. *The Southern Lady: From Pedestal to Politics, 1830–1930*. Chicago: University of Chicago Press, 1970.

———, ed. *Unheard Voices: The First Historians of Southern Women*. Charlottesville: University Press of Virginia, 1993.

Seidel, Kathryn Lee. *The Southern Belle in the American Novel*. Tampa: University of South Florida Press, 1985.

Sherman, Joan. *Invisible Poets: Afro-Americans of the Nineteenth Century*. Urbana: University of Illinois Press, 1974.

Showalter, Elaine, ed. *Daughters of Decadence: Women Writers of the Fin de Siècle*. New Brunswick: Rutgers University Press, 1993.

Simkins, Francis Butler, and James Welch Patton. *The Women of the Confederacy*. Richmond: Garrett and Massie, 1936.

Simpson, Lewis P. *The Dispossessed Garden*. Athens: University of Georgia Press, 1975.

Singal, Daniel Joseph. *The War Within: From Victorian to Modernist Thought in the South, 1919–1945*. Chapel Hill: University of North Carolina Press, 1982.

Spruill, Julia Cherry. *Women's Life and Work in the Southern Colonies*. 1938. Reprint, New York: Norton, 1972.

Sterling, Dorothy. *We Are Your Sisters: Black Women in the Nineteenth Century*. New York: Norton, 1984.

Sternberg, Janet, ed. *The Writer on Her Work*. New York: Norton, 1980.

Sullivan, Walter, ed. *The War the Women Lived: Female Voices from the Confederate South*. Nashville: J. S. Sanders, 1995.

Sweeney, Patricia. *Women in Southern Literature: An Index*. New York: Greenwood, 1986.

Tardy, Mary. *Living Female Writers of the South*. Philadelphia: Claxton, Remsen, and Haffelfinger, 1872.

———. *Southland Writers: Biographical and Critical Sketches of the Living Female Writers of the South*. Philadelphia: Claxton, Remsen, and Haffelfinger, 1870.

Tate, Claudia. *Domestic Allegories of Political Desire: The Black Heroine's Text at the Turn of the Century*. New York: Oxford University Press, 1992.

Tate, Linda. *A Southern Weave of Women: Fiction of the Contemporary South*. Athens: University of Georgia Press, 1994.

Taylor, Helen. *Gender, Race, and Region in the Writings of Grace King, Ruth McEnery Stuart, and Kate Chopin*. Baton Rouge: Louisiana State University Press, 1989.

Taylor, William R. *Cavalier and Yankee*. New York: Harper, 1961.

Tompkins, Jane. *Sensational Designs: The Cultural Work of American Fiction*. New York: Oxford University Press, 1985.

Underwood, John Levi. *The Women of the Confederacy*. New York: Neale, 1906.

Walker, Nancy A. *A Very Serious Thing: Women's Humor and American Culture*. Minneapolis: University of Minnesota Press, 1988.

Walker, Nancy A., and Zita Dresner, eds. *Redressing the Balance: American Women's Literary Humor from Colonial Times to the 1980s*. Jackson: University Press of Mississippi, 1988.

Wall, Cheryl A. *Women of the Harlem Renaissance*. Bloomington: Indiana University Press, 1995.

Weaks, Mary Louise, and Carolyn Perry, eds. *Southern Women's Writing: Colonial to Contemporary*. Gainesville: University Press of Florida, 1995.

Welter, Barbara. *Dimity Convictions: The American Woman in the Nineteenth Century*. Athens: Ohio University Press, 1976.

Westling, Louise H. *Sacred Groves and Ravaged Gardens: The Fiction of Eudora Welty, Carson McCullers, and Flannery O'Connor*. Athens: University of Georgia Press, 1985.

Whites, LeeAnn. *The Civil War as a Crisis in Gender: Augusta, Georgia, 1860–1890*. Athens: University of Georgia Press, 1995.

Wiley, Bell Irvin. *Confederate Women*. Westport, Conn.: Greenwood, 1975.

———. *The Plain People of the Confederacy*. Baton Rouge: Louisiana State University Press, 1943.

Wilkinson, Brenda Scott. *African American Women Writers*. New York: J. Wiley, 2000.

Willis, Susan. *Specifying: Black Women Writing the American Experience*. Madison: University of Wisconsin Press, 1986.

Wilson, Charles Reagan, and William Ferris, eds. *Encyclopedia of Southern Culture*. Chapel Hill: University of North Carolina Press, 1989.

Wilson, Edmund. *Patriotic Gore: Studies in the Literature of the American Civil War*. 1962. Reprint, New York: Norton, 1994.

Woodward, C. Vann. *Origins of the New South, 1877–1913*. Vol. 9 of *A History of the South,* ed. Wendell Holmes Stephenson and E. Merton Coulter. Baton Rouge: Louisiana State University Press, 1951.

Wyatt-Brown, Bertram. *Southern Honor: Ethics and Behavior in the Old South.* New York: Oxford University Press, 1982.

Yellin, Jean Fagan, and Cynthia D. Bond, comps. *The Pen Is Ours: A Listing of Writings by and about African American Women before 1910.* New York: Oxford University Press, 1988.

Young, Thomas D. *The Past in the Present: A Thematic Study of Modern Southern Fiction.* Baton Rouge: Louisiana State University Press, 1981.

Contributors

WILLIAM L. ANDREWS is E. Maynard Adams Professor of English at the University of North Carolina at Chapel Hill. He is the author of *To Tell a Free Story: The First Century of Afro-American Autobiography* (1986), coeditor of *The Norton Anthology of African American Literature* (1997) and *The Oxford Companion to African American Literature* (1997), and general editor of *The Literature of the American South: A Norton Anthology* (1998).

MARGARET D. BAUER is Associate Professor of English at East Carolina University and editor of the *North Carolina Literary Review*. She is also the author of *The Fiction of Ellen Gilchrist* (1999).

MAURINE H. BEASLEY is Professor of Journalism at the University of Maryland and coeditor of *The Eleanor Roosevelt Encyclopedia* (2001). She has written, coauthored, or edited seven books, mainly concerned with the history of women journalists.

BARBARA BENNETT is Assistant Professor of English at Wake Forest University in Winston-Salem, North Carolina. She is the author of *Comic Visions, Female Voices: Contemporary Women Novelists and Southern Humor* (1998) and of *Understanding Jill McCorkle* (2000).

DORIS BETTS, who retired in 2001 as Alumni Distinguished Professor of English at the University of North Carolina at Chapel Hill, is the author of nine books of fiction, most recently *The Sharp Teeth of Love* (1997).

WILL BRANTLEY is Associate Professor of English at Middle Tennessee State University, where he teaches southern literature, film studies, and professional writing. His book *Feminine Sense in Southern Memoir: Smith, Glasgow, Welty, Hellman, Porter, and Hurston* (1993) received the Eudora Welty Award for a distinguished work of interpretive scholarship in southern studies.

GEORGE BROSI teaches Appalachian studies, humanities, and English at Somerset Community College, Eastern Kentucky University, and the University of Kentucky. He is the author of *The Literature of the Appalachian South* (1992).

BARBARA T. CHRISTIAN was Professor of African American studies at the University of California at Berkeley until her death in 2000. Christian is the author of *Black Women Novelists: The Development of a Tradition, 1892–1978* (1980), *Black Feminist Criticism: Perspectives on Black Women Writers* (1985), and *Alice Walker's "The Color Purple"* (1987). In addition, she edited a casebook, *Alice Walker's "Everyday Use"* (1994).

ALBERT DEVLIN is Professor of English at the University of Missouri. He has authored *Eudora Welty's Chronicle* (1983) and *Welty: A Life in Literature* (1987) and edited *Conversations with Tennessee Williams* (1986). He serves on the editorial board of the *Mississippi Quarterly* and has prepared, with coeditor Nancy Tischler, Volume 1 of *The Selected Letters of Tennessee Williams* (2000).

CARLOS L. DEWS is Associate Professor of English at the University of West Florida. He is the editor of *"Illumination and Night Glare": The Unfinished Autobiography of Carson McCullers* (1999) and the founding president of the Carson McCullers Society.

SUSANNE B. DIETZEL is a feminist scholar who lives in New Orleans. Her research focuses on southern women and discourses of landscape. Her work has been published in *Southern Quarterly* and *Feminist Teacher*. She is affiliated with the Newcomb College for Research on Women at Tulane University.

SUZANNE DISHEROON-GREEN is Assistant Professor of American literature at Northwestern State University in Natchitoches, Louisiana. She is coauthor of *Kate Chopin: An Annotated Bibliography of Critical Works* (1999) and coeditor of Chopin's *"At Fault"*: *A Scholarly Edition with Background Readings* (2001) with David J. Caudle, and of *Songs of the New South: Writing Contemporary Louisiana* with Lisa Abney (2001).

ANNA SHANNON ELFENBEIN is Associate Professor of English at West Virginia University. Author of *Women on the Color Line* (1989) and coeditor of *Engendering the Word* (1989) and of *From My Highest Hill* by Olive Tilford Dargan (1998), Elfenbein has focused on recovering and reevaluating the works of radical southern women authors.

JENIFER B. ELMORE is a Ph.D. candidate at Florida State University. She is an assistant book review editor for the American Society for Eighteenth-Century Studies Book Reviews Online project.

BARBARA C. EWELL is Professor of English at City College of Loyola University of New Orleans and a native Louisianian. Her work on southern women writers includes *Kate Chopin* (1986) and *Louisiana Women Writers* (1992). With Pamela Menke, she is coeditor of *Southern Local Color: Stories of Region, Race, and Gender* and a new edition of *The Awakening*.

MARY ANNE HEYWARD FERGUSON earned two degrees from Duke University and a Ph.D. from Ohio State University. She was chair of the English Department and Founding Mother of Women's Studies at the University of Massachusetts, Boston, and edited five editions of *Images of Women in Literature*.

BENJAMIN F. FISHER is Professor of English at the University of Mississippi. Fisher specializes in American and Victorian literature, particularly Edgar Allan Poe, A. E. Housman, and American and British women writers at the turn of the nineteenth into the twentieth centuries. He is currently editing Ella D'Arcy's letters for book publication.

SALLY FITZGERALD graduated from Stephens College and received an A.B. from the University of Southern California in 1937. She began work on Flannery O'Connor's papers in the mid-1960s, publishing with her husband Robert Fitzgerald *Mystery and Manners* in 1969, then, singly, *The Habit of Being* in 1979 and, for the Library of America, *O'Connor: Collected Works*, in 1988. Fitzgerald has held the position of research scholar at Emory University and is working on a biography of Flannery O'Connor, *The Mansions of the South*.

JOSEPH M. FLORA is Professor of English at the University of North Carolina at Chapel Hill. Flora is author of many works, including *Vardis Fisher* (1965), *Frederick Manfred* (1974), and *Ernest Hemingway: The Art of the Short Fiction* (1989), and coedited *The Companion to Southern Literature* (2001) with Lucinda MacKethan.

FRANCES SMITH FOSTER is Charles Howard Candler Professor of English and Women's Studies at Emory University. She has written and edited many books on African American literature, including *Written by Herself: Literary Production by African American Women, 1746–1892* (1993), and is a coeditor of *The Norton Anthology of African American Literature* (1997) and *The Oxford Companion to African American Literature* (1997).

ELIZABETH FOX-GENOVESE is Eléonore Professor of the Humanities and Professor of History at Emory University, where she is also the founding director of the Institute for Women's Studies. She is the author of *Feminism Is Not the Story of My Life* (1996), *Feminism without Illusions* (1991), and *Within the Plantation Household* (1988). She is coeditor of *Reconstructing History* (1999) and is completing with Eugene Genovese a study of the intellectual and cultural life of the slaveholders of the Old South.

JOANNE V. GABBIN is Professor of English at James Madison University, where she directs the university's honors program. She is the author of *Sterling A. Brown* (1985) and editor of the essay collection *The Furious Flowering of African American Poetry* (1999). Her articles have appeared in *Wild Women in the Whirlwind, Southern Women Writers: The New Generation, The Oxford Companion to Women's Writing in the United States,* and *The Oxford Companion to African American Literature.*

LINDA M. GARNER is Associate Professor of English and Assistant Athletic Director for Academics at David Lipscomb University in Nashville, Tennessee. She published "Mark McQueen: The Tall Man of Wilma Dykeman's *The Tall Woman*" in the 1995 *Tennessee Philological Bulletin.*

ANNE RAZEY GOWDY is Associate Professor of English and teaches American literature at Tennessee Wesleyan College in Athens, Tennessee. She is the editor of *A Sherwood Bonner Sampler, 1869–1884* (2000).

MINROSE C. GWIN is Professor of English at the University of New Mexico and the author or editor of four books in southern literature and/or feminist studies, including *Black and White Women of the Old South: The Peculiar Sisterhood in American Literature* (1985) and *The Feminine and Faulkner: Reading (Beyond) Sexual Difference* (1990).

JOAN WYLIE HALL teaches at the University of Mississippi and has published essays on William Faulkner, Tennessee Williams, Willa Cather, Ruth McEnery Stuart, and other American writers. She is author of *Shirley Jackson: A Study of the Short Fiction* (1993) and is currently writing a book about Stuart and 1890s southern regionalism.

ELIZABETH JANE HARRISON is author of *Female Pastoral: Women Writers Re-Visioning the American South* (1991) and coeditor of *Unmanning Modernism: Gendered Re-Readings* (1997). Currently, she is an independent scholar living in the United Kingdom.

SUSAN MORRISON HEBBLE is an independent scholar living in the Chicago area. She specializes in twentieth-century American literature.

FRED HOBSON is Lineberger Professor of the Humanities at the University of North Carolina at Chapel Hill and coeditor of the *Southern Literary Journal*. He is the author of several books on southern literature, including *The Southern Writer in the Postmodern World* (1991), *Tell About the South: The Southern Rage to Explain* (1983), and most recently, *But Now I See: The White Southern Racial Conversion Narrative* (1999).

JANELL HOBSON received her M.A. from Teachers College, Columbia University, and is completing her Ph.D. in Women's Studies at Emory University. She has contributed to the *Historical Encyclopedia of Black Feminism* and has presented papers at national conferences on women's studies and on African American and Caribbean literatures.

W. KENNETH HOLDITCH is Research Professor Emeritus at the University of New Orleans and a free-lance writer. Additionally, he is editor of the *Tennessee Williams Journal* and coeditor of the Tennessee Williams volumes for the Library of America. His publications include essays on William Faulkner, Lillian Hellman, and Richard Ford. He also gives literary walking tours of the French Quarter in New Orleans.

ANNE GOODWYN JONES is Professor of English at the University of Florida, where she specializes in southern literature and women's studies. She is the author of *Tomorrow Is Another Day: The Woman Writer in the South, 1859–1936* (1981) and coeditor of *Haunted Bodies: Gender and Southern Texts* (1997), as well as author of numerous articles on southern women's literature.

CAROLYN M. JONES is Associate Professor of Religious Studies and English at Louisiana State University. She has written articles on the work of Toni Morrison, Albert Murray, Harper Lee, and others. She is currently finishing a book on Toni Morrison, tentatively titled "The Fiction and Criticism of Toni Morrison." Her interests include African American and southern literature, postcolonial and postmodern theory, women's spirituality, and ancient and modern intersections in fiction.

NANCYLEE NOVELL JONZA is the author of *The Underground Stream: The Life and Art of Caroline Gordon* (1995). A full-length narrative and critical biography, *The Underground Stream* won the 1995 Violet Crown Book Award for nonfiction.

CLARA JUNCKER is Associate Professor at Odense University, Denmark, where she directs the Center for American Studies. She has published widely within the fields of nineteenth- and twentieth-century American literature, including *Black Roses: Afro-American Women Writers* (1986) and *Through Random Doors We Wandered: Women Writing the South* (forthcoming).

PARKS LANIER, JR., is Professor of English at Radford University. He specializes in British Romanticism and Appalachian studies, and he has edited the *Journal of the Appalachian Studies Association* (1989) and *The Poetics of Appalachian Space* (1991). Recently he was honored by the Appalachian Writers' Association for his contributions to Appalachian literature.

KAREN L. LAUGHLIN is Associate Professor of English at Florida State University. She specializes in modern and American drama, critical theory, women's studies, and film. She is coeditor of *Theatre and Feminist Aesthetics* (1995) and has published numerous articles and book chapters on modern playwrights, including Samuel Beckett, Susan Glaspell, and Beth Henley.

RICHARD C. LOUNSBURY is Professor of Classics and Comparative Literature at Brigham Young University. He has edited the writings of Louisa S. McCord for the Southern Texts Society Series and is now at work on a study of the reception of classical antiquity in the antebellum South.

JOHN LOWE, Professor of English at Louisiana State University, is author of *Jump at the Sun: Zora Neale Hurston's Cosmic Comedy* (1994), editor of *Conversations with Ernest Gaines* (1995), and coeditor of *The Future of Southern Letters* (1996). He is currently completing *The Americanization of Ethnic Humor* and editing a collection of essays on southern culture.

LUCINDA H. MACKETHAN is Alumni Distinguished Professor at North Carolina State University, where she teaches southern and African American literature. She is author of a Mercer Lecture Series book, *Daughters of Time: Creating Woman's Voice in Southern Story* (1990), and she has recently edited two Civil War memoirs, *Lyddy* (1998) and *Recollections of a Southern Daughter* (1998). She is coeditor of *The Companion to Southern Literature* with Joseph Flora (2001).

ROSEMARY M. MAGEE is Associate Vice President for Arts and Sciences and Senior Associate Dean at Emory University. As an adjunct professor she has taught courses on southern women writers and other topics. In addition to reviews and essays, she has published *Conversations with Flannery O'Connor* (1987) and *Friendship and Sympathy: Communities of Southern Women Writers* (1992).

ROBERTA S. MAGUIRE is Assistant Professor of English at the University of Wisconsin, Oshkosh, where she teaches African American and southern literature and culture. She is the editor of *Conversations with Albert Murray* (1997) and has also published work on Alice Childress and Walker Percy.

VERONICA MAKOWSKY is Associate Dean of the College of Liberal Arts and Sciences at the University of Connecticut and is the editor of *MELUS*. She has published books and articles on southern women writers, including *Caroline Gordon: A Biography* (1989) and *Susan Glaspell's Century of American Women* (1993).

CAROL S. MANNING is Professor of English at Mary Washington College and the author of *With Ears Opening like Morning Glories: Eudora Welty and the Love of Storytelling* (1985) and editor of *The Female Tradition in Southern Literature* (1993). She has published articles on several southern authors, including Eudora Welty, Ellen Glasgow, Ellen Douglas, and Anne Tyler.

AMY THOMPSON MCCANDLESS is Professor of History at the College of Charleston, where she teaches classes on women and gender in the United

States and Europe. Her book *The Past in the Present: Women's Higher Education in the Twentieth-Century American South* was published by the University of Alabama Press in 1999.

KATHRYN MCKEE is McMullan Assistant Professor of Southern Studies and Assistant Professor of English at the University of Mississippi. She has published articles on William Faulkner, Josephine Humphreys, Kaye Gibbons, and Bobbie Ann Mason.

CAROLYN E. MEGAN teaches English and fiction writing at Babson College in Wellesley, Massachusetts. Her interview with Dorothy Allison appeared in the fall 1994 issue of the *Kenyon Review*.

ELISABETH MUHLENFELD is President of Sweet Briar College in Sweet Briar, Virginia. She is the author of four books, including a biography of Mary Boykin Chesnut, a forthcoming work on Chesnut's novels from University of Virginia Press in the Southern Texts Society series, and an edition of Chesnut's original diaries, coedited with historian C. Vann Woodward. *Mary Boykin Chesnut: A Biography* (1981) was nominated for various prizes, including a Pulitzer.

LORETTA MARTIN MURREY is Associate Professor of English at Western Kentucky University's Glasgow campus, where she teaches courses in literature, language, and communication. She has primarily published articles about southern women writers, including Eudora Welty, Barbara Kingsolver, and Mary Lee Settle. Currently Murrey is working on a book-length oral history of Kentucky Poet Laureate Joy Bale Boone.

NANCY PARRISH received her Ph.D. in American Studies from the College of William and Mary. Her book *Lee Smith, Annie Dillard, and The Hollins Group* (1998) was nominated for the Merle Curti Award in American Intellectual History and in American Social History. Parrish is currently writing a book about the teaching profession.

CAROLYN PERRY is Associate Professor of English at Westminster College in Missouri, where she teaches courses on southern women's literature. She is coeditor of *The Dolphin Reader* (1999) and, with Mary Louise Weaks, coedited *Southern Women's Writing: Colonial to Contemporary* (1995).

JOYCE PETTIS teaches black literature in the English department at North Carolina State University. In addition to essays on Margaret Walker and

Charles Chesnutt, she has authored *Toward Wholeness in Paule Marshall's Fiction* (1995). She is currently working on a book about black American poets.

KATHERINE POWELL is a lecturer in English at Berry College and has served as codirector of Berry's Southern Women Writers Conference.

PEGGY WHITMAN PRENSHAW, Fred C. Frey chair of southern studies in the English department at Louisiana State University, is author of *Elizabeth Spencer* (1985). She has edited books on Spencer, Welty, and other southern women writers. She also serves as the general editor of the University Press of Mississippi's Literary Conversations series.

MARY D. ROBERTSON is Adjunct Professor of History at Armstrong Atlantic State University in Savannah, Georgia. She is the editor of *Lucy Breckinridge of Grove Hill: Journal of a Virginia Girl, 1862–1864* (1979) and *A Confederate Lady Comes of Age: The Journal of Pauline DeCaradeuc Heyward, 1863–1888* (1992).

ANNE E. ROWE is Professor of English and Associate Dean of the College of Arts and Sciences at Florida State University. She is the author of two books, *The Enchanted Country: Northern Writers in the South, 1865–1910* (1978) and *The Idea of Florida in the American Literary Imagination* (1986). She is currently at work on a book treating the use of domestic imagery by southern women writers.

KATHRYN LEE SEIDEL is Professor of English at the University of Central Florida–Orlando. She is the author of several books on southern literature, including *The Southern Belle in the American Novel* (1985), and coauthor of *Zora in Florida* (1991). Her published articles include work on Kate Chopin, Alice Walker, and Gail Godwin.

CONNIE R. SCHOMBURG is a teacher and scholar living in Fremont, Nebraska, who specializes in ethnic literature and literature of the Great Plains. She has published and presented articles on Toni Morrison, Sherley Anne Williams, Wilma Mankiller, and Langston Hughes.

MIRIAM J. SHILLINGSBURG is Professor of English and Dean of Liberal Arts and Sciences at Indiana University at South Bend. She is the author of numerous articles on southern literature, including southern women writers.

She is also the editor of two scholarly editions and the author of *At Home Abroad: Mark Twain in Australasia* (1988).

MERRILL MAGUIRE SKAGGS is Baldwin Professor of the Humanities at Drew University. She is the author of *The Folk of Southern Fiction* (1972), *After the World Broke in Two: The Later Novels of Willa Cather* (1990), coauthor of *The Mother Person* (1975), and editor of *Willa Cather's New York: New Essays on Cather in the City* (2000).

KAREN MANNERS SMITH teaches women's history at Emporia State University in Kansas. She is the author of *New Paths to Power: American Women 1890-1920* (a volume in the Young Oxford History of Women in the United States series that was published in 1994) and is currently completing a biography of Mary Virginia Terhune.

CINDY A. STILES received her Ph.D. in American and southern literature from the University of South Carolina in 1994. She is currently an independent scholar living in Atlanta, Georgia.

JANIS P. STOUT is Professor of English, Dean of Faculties, and Associate Provost at Texas A&M University. She is the author most recently of *Katherine Anne Porter: A Sense of the Times* (1995) and *Through the Window, Out the Door: Women's Narratives of Departure, from Austin and Cather to Tyler, Morrison, and Didion* (1998).

WALTER SULLIVAN is Professor of English Emeritus at Vanderbilt University. He is the author of three novels, three volumes of criticism, and *Allen Tate: A Recollection* (1988). Among books he has edited is *The War the Women Lived: Female Voices from the Confederate South* (1995). He is a founding member of the Fellowship of Southern Writers.

SUSAN ELIZABETH SWEENEY is Associate Professor of English at Holy Cross College. She has published numerous articles on Anne Tyler, Edith Wharton, and Vladimir Nabokov.

LINDA TATE is Associate Professor of English at Shepherd College, Shepherdstown, West Virginia. The author of *A Southern Weave of Women: Fiction of the Contemporary South* (1994), she is currently working on a nonfiction novel, *Power in the Blood,* which reconstructs the story of her Cherokee-Appalachian family over the last 150 years.

HELEN TAYLOR is Professor of English at the University of Exeter, England. A southern specialist, she has published widely on Kate Chopin and other Louisiana writers. She is the author of *Scarlett's Women: "Gone with the Wind" and Its Female Fans* (1989) and of *Circling Dixie: Circum-Atlantic Contemporary Southern Culture* (2001).

WALLIS TINNIE is Professor Emerita of English at Miami-Dade Community College and Adjunct Professor of American Literature at Florida International University in Miami. Tinnie's research has focused on the institutionalized use of masked racial codes in the literature, criticism, and legal language of the American South and the Caribbean, specifically in the literature of William Faulkner, Jean Rhys, and Jean Toomer.

ELLEN H. TODRAS has worked in educational publishing as a writer and editor for many years. *Angelina Grimké: Voice of Abolition* (1999) is her first book. She received a B.A. in English from Goucher College and an M.Ed. from Central Washington University. She lives in Oregon with her family.

LINDA WAGNER-MARTIN is Hanes Professor of English at the University of North Carolina at Chapel Hill. Wager-Martin is author of many studies of American modernists and the biographer of both Sylvia Plath and Gertrude Stein. In addition to several recent publications, she has coedited *The Oxford Companion to Women's Writing in the United States* (1995).

ELINOR ANN WALKER received her Ph.D. from the University of North Carolina at Chapel Hill and has taught at Rockford College and the University of the South. She has published essays on Walker Percy, Josephine Humphreys, and Jill McCorkle and a book on Richard Ford for the Twayne U.S. Authors Series (2000).

JAMES H. WATKINS is Assistant Professor of English at Berry College in Rome, Georgia, where he teaches southern literature, autobiographical studies, and other courses in American literature and film. He is the editor of *Southern Selves: A Collection of Autobiographical Writing* (1998) and has written extensively on southern autobiography.

MARY LOUISE WEAKS is Hazel Koch Professor of English and chair of the English Department at Rockford College in Illinois. She is coeditor of *Talking with Robert Penn Warren* (1990) and, with Carolyn Perry, of *Southern Women's Writing: Colonial to Contemporary* (1995).

KAREN A. WEYLER teaches American literature at the University of North Carolina at Greensboro. She has published essays and reviews in *Early American Literature, Legacy, American Literature, Studies in Short Fiction, Southern Quarterly,* and the *Companion to Southern Literature.* She recently completed a book on early American fiction, tentatively titled "Intricate Relations."

MARY WHEELING is Assistant Professor of English at Methodist College in Fayetteville, North Carolina, where she also directs the Southern Writers Symposium. As Mary Wheeling White she published *Fighting the Current: The Life and Work of Evelyn Scott* (1998) and is currently editing Scott's collected short fiction.

SUSAN MILLAR WILLIAMS is the author of *A Devil and a Good Woman, Too: The Lives of Julia Peterkin* (1997), winner of the 1998 Julia Cherry Spruill Award given by the Southern Association of Women Historians. She teaches at Trident Technical College in Charleston, South Carolina, and has written for the *Nation* and the *Southern Review.*

HAROLD WOODELL is Professor of English at Clemson University, where he teaches southern literature. His publications include *The Shattered Dream: A Southern Bride at the Turn of the Century: The Daybook of Margaret Sloan* (1991) and *"All the King's Men": The Search for a Usable Past* (1993).

EMILY POWERS WRIGHT is Assistant Professor of English at Berry College in Rome, Georgia, where she helped create the Southern Women Writers Conference. Her forthcoming essay "The 'Other South' of Caroline Miller" examines the impact of class and gender on the formation of the southern literary canon.

LIHONG XIE is Associate Editor of *The Writings of Henry D. Thoreau* at Northern Illinois University. She has published several articles on Gail Godwin and is the author of *The Evolving Self in the Novels of Gail Godwin* (1995).

Index